CUBA

CUBA
The International Dimension

Edited by

Georges Fauriol
and
Eva Loser

With a Foreword by

Irving Louis Horowitz

Transaction Publishers
New Brunswick (U.S.A.) and London (U.K.)

Library of Congress Catalog Number: 89-27883
ISBN: 0-88738-324-6
Printed in the United States of America

Library of Congress Cataloging-in-Publication Data

Cuba : the international dimension / edited by Georges Fauriol and
    Eva Loser.
        p.   cm.
    ISBN 0-88738-324-6
    1. Cuba—Foreign relations—1979– I. Fauriol, Georges A.
II. Loser, Eva, 1962–   .
    F1788.C8245   1990
327.7291—dc20   89-27883
                                                        CIP

Contents

Foreword
CUBA: The International Dimension
Fidel Castro Redux

Castro was reported to have recently said to a group of astonished diplomats in Havana: "If these changes go on in the U.S.S.R., they will soon be describing us as those madmen in the Albania of the Caribbean." Whether this is a piece of apocrypha or an actual interview, the fact is that Albania and Cuba remain, albeit for quite different reasons, holdouts in the revolutions that have swept communist regimes from power in Eastern Europe, and have roiled the political process within the Soviet Union proper. It is entirely appropriate therefore for Georges Fauriol and Eva Loser to have explored the reasons for this apparent anomaly, in short, to locate the changing perceptions of Cuba throughout its thirty-one-year-old history. They have assembled a group of high-quality specialists to review the international dimensions of Cuba's hardened political arteries. This comes at a significant historical juncture, since Cuba as a "strategic outpost" and proxy for global power struggles explains much of what would otherwise appear as sheer aberrant political behavior.

The volume is graced not only by serious studies of the sort of bilateral relations one might well expect in a Fauriol project, but by a final section on functional policy areas that constitutes six of the fourteen chapters. This is fit, proper, and innovative. For, in a series of excellent papers by Michael J. Mazarr, Constantine Menges, Jorge Pérez-Lopez, Jorge Sanguinetty, Paula J. Pettavino and Juan M. del Aguila, we are moved beyond conventional versions of Latin American militarism and policy into the complex sources and mixed games of Cuban foreign policy; a policy now in a state of atrophy at best and shambles at worst.

One comes away from this text with an appreciation of the fact that Cuba is neither socialist nor Third World in the classical sense. Caudillismo is more prevalent in Cuba than in most Latin American societies; indeed, the caudillo image is probably truer for Cuba now then it has been in its past (pre-Castro) epoch. The armed forces (whether in the form of the internal ministry or the armed forces directly) have occupied a most favored status from the outset of the Castro regime some thirty-one years ago. This has been muted because the extreme Left was able to define the situation, insisting upon casual designations of Cuba as socialist or communist. There was a presumption, entirely false with respect to Cuba at least, that radical regimes tend to undercut long-standing Latin traditions of the miliary figure on horseback. But the military man *cum* guerrilla is much the same thing. The key is not the horse nor the back pack, but the militarized character of the society—the carrier of Cuba's international dimension. The military is the only social force that has been institutionalized in contemporary Cuba. The analysis of Cuba's security apparatus by Michael Mazarr, herein contained, is perhaps the best single paper available on the neo-Stalinist characteristics of Castro-style militarism.

A special part of Castro's "foreign policy" is the elimination of rivals through heavy outward migration. It cannot be overlooked that unlike East Europe, there is no "wall" or border, but an ocean between Cuba and the United States. Travel was difficult after the Cuban Revolution, but for the impatient and insistent, entrepreneurs and convicts alike, it was continuous. As a result, the most discontented and determined ended up in exile and not in armed insurrection against the regime. Castro in this sense learned well the lessons of sociology: permitting emigration is the functional equivalent of tranquilizing a discontented people. Such a policy also tranquilized would-be critics of the regime; at least until events in Eastern Europe reminded scholars of the "Albanianization" of Cuba.

A key element permitting Castro a free hand in forging foreign adventures no less than foreign policies is the remoteness of Cuba from the dorsal spine that links North and South America. External ideas and influences filter in only with difficulty, unlike, for example from Poland to Hungary or Hungary to Rumania. Cuba is an island society par excellence. As a result, Castro is capable of shutting down information, even from the U.S.S.R., at the whim of the leader. Insularity is built into the structure of Cuban geography no less than into its society. Local issues become global in perceived importance. Irritations, major and minor, that occur in nations sharing common borders and uncommon social systems did not affect

Castro's Cuba; at least not to any serious extent as a threat to regime stability or as a modifier of its foreign policy.

Despite all the signs of a coming crisis, the economic collapse of Castro's Cuba is prevented by continuing Soviet support. The papers by Jiri Valenta and Jaime Suchlicki make the character of such "core relationships" painfully evident. Unlike Poland and other nations of Eastern Europe that paid the U.S.S.R. reparations and provided goods, the situation is reversed: the U.S.S.R. pays Cuba roughly six billion dollars annually, or one fourth of its foreign aid, to remain in the communist fold. This is starting to change—but its full impact had not yet hit home at the time of the completion of this volume. While Soviet supplies to Cuba have slowed, and in reprisal, exports of Cuban foodstuffs to the U.S.S.R. have also slowed, the reasons are still described in technical terms, i.e., a breakdown in shipping capacities, rather than a profound change in policies. There remains only limited evidence of a new policy as such over the long haul. But several papers in this volume make it clear that Cuba is at a critical juncture in its foreign policy; especially as it affects its relations with the Soviet Union and the Eastern Bloc.

The character of what Jiri Valenta calls the Leninization of Cuba, or what I still prefer to view as neo-Stalinism, as an independent element in the survival of Cuban communism, cannot be overlooked. There are solid grounds for describing Castro as a Leninist, since unlike the Stalin dictatorship, the genocidal potential of the Castro regime has only sporadically been brought to bear on the Cuban citizenry. But the elements of continuity from Lenin to Stalin were brought into play: they include lawlessness of the system, lack of accountability (both to its own people and to outside powers), and secrecy in decision-making. In the absence of public accountability, actual foreign policy decisions often came as surprises to the outside world. The idea that Leninism is simply bare-boned repression misses the point. For as Valenta correctly notes, the foreign policy adventures serve in the short run to ease internal mechanisms of repression. Symbolic terror, and the everyday social force of the Committee for the Defense of the Revolution, are adequate to the task. It might be added that the existence of such quasimilitary cadres makes likely a bitter civil struggle, as in Rumania, perhaps more likely than the benign transition to a mellow socialism that a few of the participants in this volume envision, or at least hope for. It might be that the gradual transformation of Cuba from a totalitarian to an authoritarian state envisioned by Juan del Aguila will still take place, much in the fashion of the U.S.S.R. under Gorbachev. But it seems less likely—in an environment in which Cuba is the sole surviving communist state in the hemisphere, with a leader who has absorbed the pathology, but not the power of early communism—that

Cuba will become an island of communist probity in a sea of capitalist vice.

Dynastic communism as such enters the Cuban equation. While it shares many of the properties of neo-Stalinism, the familial features of the Castro regime have long been recognized as factors in its policy making. As Douglas Payne recently pointed out, capriciousness plays a role. "Castro's career has been marked by numerous sharp turns in both domestic and foreign policy. The possibility cannot be excluded that he might suddenly declare himself a champion of *perestroika* and swear, in typically egoistical fashion, his *perestroika* is the best. He would then demand immediate concessions from the United States, including an end to economic embargo, and would have the full support of Moscow." This is, of course, a possible (not inevitable) scenario; one anticipated by several contributors to this volume. Nonetheless, it indicates the hazards of even informed guesses about Castro's foreign policy directions in a political environment of near-total political illegitimacy. Perhaps a new law of political science or better, an equation, is that levels of predictability are a function of democracy. This is so because the caprice of a single individual is at least checked by the caprices of others. But in the absence of checks there are no balances, and without the latter, prediction becomes plausible in therapeutic rather than analytic terms. It is to the credit of the tone set by the editors of this volume that such intellectual risks are fully appreciated.

What then pushes the Cuban political process to the breaking point? Primarily the foreign, overseas conditions in which Cuba finds itself. This begins with a profound and growing isolation of Cuba from the rest of Latin America, Castro's crusades to muster support from Puerto Rico to Porto Alegre notwithstanding. William Ratliff and Ernest Evans clearly give expression in their respective contributions to this strange symbiosis between isolation at home and adventure abroad.

Then there is the dependence upon Soviet economic support, if not agreement with Soviet political policies, that fuels Cuban foreign policy; well noted in several papers. The complex relations of Cuba with Europe and Canada, coupled with a declining interest on the part of former Eastern European allies like Czechoslovakia, is well documented by Scott B. MacDonald. The question for now is whether the European "door" will in fact remain "half-open" or increasingly shut.

Then there is the willingness of the United States to let Castro simply continue to twist in the wind, coupled with a near breakdown in Cuba's ability to meet its own basic trade and sales obligations, even at the bartering levels. There is an increasing urgency in forcing the United States to say "what if . . ." with respect to a post-Castro Cuba. But thus far, this impulse to announce scenarios in advance of actions has been resisted, and the laisser faire approach described by Fauriol, and dominant since the parallel crisis of the Bay of Pigs misadventure and the Missile Base confrontation remains intact.

A new, potentially explosive factor, one that unfolded substantially after this volume was assembled, but which nonetheless is critical to the conduct of Cuban foreign policy, is the emergence in Nicaragua of the Sandinistas as leaders of a Gorbachev type of state, which, now forced into opposition, functions in bold relief to the Leninist or Stalinist (take your pick) system to be found in Cuba. Daniel Ortega and the Sandinista National Liberation Front took their appeals to the people, and lost decisively to the broad democratic coalition headed by Violeta Barrios de Chammoro, leader of the National Opposition Union. The Nicaraguan election campaign was conducted on broad multiparty terms. The electoral process, which is a harbinger of things to come throughout Eastern Europe no less than Latin America, served to institutionalize political legitimacy. The regime and opposition alike in Nicaragua can now chart a democratic path, in a way that communism in Cuba has never been able to achieve, or even to imagine. Beyond the political, Nicaragua never did completely destroy the private sector; hence it was, and remains, in a position to change the economic "mix" without a sense of severe rupture. These developments in Nicaragua have taken place to the bitter chagrin of Fidel Castro. The impact of events in Nicaragua will certainly exacerbate Castro's growing sense of hemispheric isolation, and more dangerously, sense of desperation.

What these developments indicate is a continuing round of instabilities in Cuba until some form of opposition can crystallize. And that some opposition is now fusing becomes evident when reports indicate that Cuban youth are talking of political change openly and defiantly for the first time since the 1959 revolution. This is after all a situation best described in processual terms of when and not structural terms of whether. It takes little to recollect that the late Premier of Rumania, Nocolae Ceaucescu, mustered a massive if sullen public rally only one week before his demise. He had to face that same crowd in total opposition one week later. And one week later still he was tried, convicted and executed for crimes against the people. This volume was assembled prior to the shattering events of 1989 in most parts of Eastern Europe. Hence, its prognoses are for more benign (and slower) forms of change than seem to be taking place in the communist world of which Cuba is very much a part.

Still, we must remember the dangers in the Cuban situation. In Spain, Francisco Franco endured long after any utility, but there was a monarchist tradition that provided a key element in the transition to Spanish democracy in the 1970s. Such an element does not exist within Cuba proper. It is, however possible that the exile community may function in such a restorative capacity, at least to cushion the shock of transition during the early stages of a return to democratic norms.

That many of the contributions to *Cuba: The International Dimension* conclude in admittedly speculative terms indicates that some form of closure to the Cuban dictatorship is at hand—if not in 1990, then assuredly in the decade of the nineties, and probably in the early years. Castro is down to the bare bones of the family. The costs of his foreign policies are too high and the results too limited to enlist continuing Soviet support. The administrative infrasturcture is demoralized, the earlier passion among the military cadres for international adventure has, as Juan Benemelis and Gillian Gunn point out, been sapped by battles in Africa and trials in Cuba, and the energy of the best and the brightest has long ago migrated to points North and West.

In any post-Castro context, it might well turn out that the most serious problems of reconstruction will be political rather than economic. The forces of a new turn in international affairs, whether administrative or military, have not yet emerged in identifiable form. Under such circumstances, what we have is best described as a continuing political tragedy, especially for the internal victims of Castro's foreign policy adventures. Rejoicing over any perceived foreign policy setbacks should be muted in the face of the calamitous oucome of this revolution; one begun in high expectations and concluding with the near-total paralysis of a major Caribbean nation. The great length of time under which Cuban people have suffered tyranny will make the task of democracy harder and the potential for disillusion greater. Fortunately, the quality of Cuba's people, their endurance, diligence and patience should serve to cut down the retooling time of the society in its effort to return to the family of democratic nations. Still, we would be well advised to reflect carefully on the heavy price paid by blind passions and a revanchist spirit in past efforts to impove the lot of the Cuban people and system. In so doing, we must start with curbing our own euphoria while passing along our current wisdom (without laundering past follies) to the next generation. The contributors to *Cuba: The International Dimension* help us walk out from under the shadows of the past in an appropriately modest way. If the lessons of this collective portrait are properly understood, we can then hold open the prospects for a future in which Cuba will play a constructive, and much needed, foreign policy role in hemispheric affairs.

IRVING LOUIS HOROWITZ
Rutgers University

Introduction

If, in language attributed to José Martí, the Caribbean is the "pivot" of the Americas, then Cuba has become the axis upon which much of recent U.S./Latin American policy frustration has been based. Fidel Castro's revolution and its foreign policy extensions have, perhaps unwittingly, consumed more U.S. resources and political capital than any other contemporary hemispheric concern. The reason for this lies not only in the ideological tug-of-war with the United States but also in the extraordinary and almost global sweep of Cuba's national pretensions.

Thirty years after the Cuban revolution, there may be no more compelling example of the costs of U.S. foreign policy complacency than Castro's aging revolutionary government. The 1960s were marked by a deep concern over how a radical regime—a "Soviet strategic outpost" in the Caribbean Basin—would impinge upon the successful pursuit of broader U.S. foreign policy goals. Washington and Havana shadow-boxed through a number of confrontations in the Americas, and, in the 1970s, even in Africa—and the Castro regime survived. Cuba's eccentric relationship with the Soviet Union has provided the Soviet Bloc with a strategic asset from which to test the United States. But by the late 1980s, the Cuban revolutionary mystique has tired. Castro's regime is viewed as an expensive failure by Moscow's "reformers," as a weakened if implacable foe by Washington, and as an interesting relic of the turbulent 1960s by the world's intellectual community. Where, then, lies the real global symbolism of the Cuban revolution?

This symbolism can be found in three events of recent Caribbean history. It was over Cuba that the two superpowers clashed, coming to within a few degrees of a nuclear exchange—a unique event in the post–World War II era. Likewise, it was ultimately against Cuba that this country's most lopsided but psychologically rewarding recent military engagement was won in Grenada. And finally, it is because of Cuba's cooperation with the Sandinista movement that a second Marxist, Soviet-allied state is being implanted in the Western Hemisphere. No other nation in the world has engaged both superpowers in the manner that Cuba has over the past three decades.

Cuba, unlike any other nation except perhaps Israel, has acquired a stature, authority, and perceived level of achievement that far exceeds what could be predicted or justified by its territorial and population size. Fidel Castro has leveraged his island country's limited conventional capabilities through his ability to win what, overall, has been unflagging support from a distant superpower. This has been based in part on a convergence of interests that the two involved parties recognize, appreciate, and exploit. In the past, a bemused tolerance in the Kremlin of Castro's radicalism gave Cuba a certain stardom among Third World leftists and progressive intellectuals of the First World. Thus, by Castro being alternatively the loyal orthodox communist or an incalculable nuisance, his international pursuits have generated a cacophony of impressions rather than real evaluations.

More than thirty years have passed since Fidel Castro's triumphant entry into Havana. From the outset, the Cuban revolution reached out for a wide constituency and has left little doubt as to its sense of activism. Cuban foreign policy behavior has since then evidently become institutionalized. The frustration of dealing with Cuba thus hangs over every U.S. action in the Caribbean Basin, and even elsewhere in the world. Deriving from the regime's ideology, the promotion of armed struggle and the compulsion for revolutionary action have become prominent Cuban foreign policy features. Cuba's ability in skillful diplomatic maneuvering, the addition of theatrical touches to international politics, and the blending of ideological injunctions for communist unity with sustained expressions of hatred or peaceful appeals to successive American governments have propelled a small island nation to the forefront of global intrigue and crisis. These features will likely continue—but along which lines?

Cuba's internationalism is now at a crossroads. Future choices derive from possible shifts in African policy, the residual political impact of the Grenadian debacle within Cuba's leadership, developments in Central America, potential fallout in the aftermath of the Ochoa narcotics episode, and, perhaps most significantly, the degree of tension with both Moscow and Washington. A further element in this puzzle also relates to a Cuban leadership succession beyond Castro. This poses critical choices for the United States. Although considerable attention is presently focused on Central American issues and southern Africa, the future characteristics of

U.S./Cuban policy must inevitably be raised. Precisely how this environ-ment will be managed in the 1990s is a matter of considerable debate.

A primary issue is the Cuban regime's relative, if perhaps temporary, isolation within the Soviet bloc. Mikhail Gorbachev's arrival on the world stage in the mid-1980s has posed a unique challenge for Castro—ideologi-cally, economically, and generationally. Soviet dissatisfaction with both the returns on, as well as the continued need to supply, a $5 billion annual aid package to Cuba has been a serious technocratic management problem. Ultimately, issues of ideology are more profound, to the extent that the adoption of Soviet-style "glasnost" policies in Cuba are perceived as a mortal threat to the very character of the regime. Obviously, Soviet tinkering with Marxist orthodoxy does provide Cuba with at least tempo-rary refuge as a defender of the "true cause."

However, resurrecting the failed 1960s moral incentives policy to infuse vitality into Cuban life or joining North Korea to boycott the 1988 Olympic games has limitations that the Castro government most certainly appreci-ates. By its adherence to strict Marxist-Leninist doctrine, Cuba runs the risk of becoming an irrelevant anachronism (the "Albania of the Carib-bean") in the groundswell of change surging throughout the communist world. Moreover, Castro's supporters in Latin America and elsewhere have faded from the political scene. In intellectual circles, the Cuban "model" is being replaced as an era of "human rights" and "democracy" are now the battle cries from Beijing to Warsaw as well as Santiago, Chile. Is Fidel Castro facing a two-edged ideological and generational challenge? Indeed.

It would likewise appear that the regime is confronting not only external challenges, but internal ones as well. The 1989 show trials and subsequent execution of four high-ranking Cuban officials, including General Arnaldo Ochoa, on charges of narcotics trafficking conducted outside of the re-gime's purview, ring somewhat hollow. Instead, there is evidence to suggest that the basis for this action was a preemptive move by the Castro brothers against younger, charismatic contenders for power.

What are the foreign policy implications of these developments? The Ochoa affair reinvigorated the debate regarding the character of U.S./ Cuban ties. Narcotics trafficking and attendant cooperative interdiction efforts with Washington emerged as the key issues. But clearly, narcotics is not the preeminent issue in U.S./Cuban relations—rather, drugs are a symptom of the kind of external interactions which the Cuban regime has developed. On the other hand, Cuba retains pivotal strategic investments made in the 1970s: southern Africa and Nicaragua. Furthermore, as several chapters in this study suggest, Cuban linkage with radical elements around the world remains firm. Ultimately, Castro retains an immeasurable opportunistic capability and incalculable nuisance value. With the long-term verdict of political and economic liberalization within the communist world still undecided, one of these opportunities could involve a turnaround—some would suggest a setback—in Soviet glasnost/perestroika policies.

Reviewing a 30-year track record of Cuban foreign affairs is the topic of this CSIS-sponsored volume. It follows an earlier effort that assessed Castro's Cuba in its domestic context.[1] In the present study the analysis shifts to Cuba's international dimensions, its geographical and functional policy activities and objectives. However, it also goes beyond these normal conceptual distinctions and addresses broader dimensions: Cuba as a "model"; Cuba's image-building diplomacy; and the perceptions or even fascination with Cuba held by the international community.

A project of this kind is a team effort. Fourteen of this nation's established or up-and-coming specialists on Cuba's international behavior contributed many months—some would correctly argue, years—of work and rework. Like its predecessor, *The Cuban Revolution,* this study is not encyclopedic in character. Its objective has been to provide a cross section of a major subject in contemporary international politics. In this context, this volume has not sought to include a homogenous group of authors, but instead a collection of experts covering a multiplicity of disciplines as well as political viewpoints. The stable of project participants, along with some preliminary conclusions, includes:

- *Strategic Relationships*: Jaime Suchlicki, and Jiri Valenta (University of Miami).

  Cuba and the Soviet Union have arrived at a joint strategy of cooperative interventions and military aid designed to promote Marxist-Leninist-oriented, anti-Western regimes and movements in the Third World. This joint strategy does not imply Cuban acquiescence, but instead provides Havana with considerable room for autonomy in pursuing its strategic goals. The degree of Cuban autonomy varies from case to case; thus, Cuba is neither a subservient nor compliant ally.

  In its strategic setting, Cuban foreign policy is guided by a desire to foster Cuban and Soviet strategic objectives and undermine U.S. security interests. As such, any accommodation with the U.S. would not only go against Cuban foreign policy tenets, but would be fraught with uncertainties and dangers for the Castro leadership. Instead, Castro perceives the required conditions for normalization as an attempt by the U.S. to deny its claim to a great power role, to isolate the revolution, and to strengthen anti-Castro forces within the island, thus posing a threat to the stability of the regime.
- *Regional Policies*: Juan Benemelis (former Cuban diplomat); Ernest Evans (Christendom College); Gillian Gunn (Carnegie Endowment for

International Peace); Scott MacDonald (Office of the Comptroller of the Currency); and William Ratliff (Hoover Institution).

In structuring Cuban regional relations, a combination of Marxist-Leninist orthodoxy, solidarity with the Soviet bloc activism, and anti-Americanism form the cornerstones of foreign policy. Translated into practice, this blending of features has revealed a high degree of opportunism. For example, relations have been maintained with Western Europe and Canada to create a third pole of influence beyond those of the United States and the Soviet Union. Relations with the West have also been maintained to insure access to goods and resources not readily available from the U.S.S.R.—commercial credits and manufactured and high-technology products. Opportunism was also evident in the deterioration of Cuban relations with China: Cuban global strategy with the Soviet Union clearly took precedence over ideological kinship with Mao Tse-tung during the years of the Sino/Soviet split.

The predominance of Cuban external involvement has revolved around relations with the Third World. In tabulating a balance-sheet assessment of the history of Cuban support of Third World revolutionary movements, a mixed scorecard of results is produced. While benefits have evidently been gained, the costs have likewise been high—in both economic and politicodiplomatic terms—at home and abroad. In an era of declining global resources, it is therefore possible that full-scale Cuban involvement overseas may likewise decline, but also that pragmatism and opportunism will continue to be the hallmarks of Cuban strategy.

- *Functional Considerations*: Michael Mazarr (Center for Strategic and International Studies (CSIS)/Political-Military Studies Program); Constantine Menges (American Enterprise Institute); and Jorge Pérez-López (U.S. Dept. of Labor).

The psyche of the Castro leadership has developed in a manner such that defense of the revolution at home is to be guaranteed by the nation's external behavior—or in other words, foreign policy is a derivative of the domestic course of the revolution. Given the island nation's inherent economic limitations, this has meant that 30 years of socialism has changed neither the basic openness of the economy nor the need for capital inflow from abroad to finance development. The only major change has been the economy's turn away from the West and integration into COMECON. More than ever, the Cuban economy remains highly vulnerable to international economic trends.

In the politico-security realm, the day-to-day execution of policy is largely carried out by the Ministries of the Revolutionary Armed Forces and of the Interior (MINFAR and MININT). The development and evolution of these two critical institutions has closely paralleled the internal course of the revolution.

- *Comparative Analyses*: Juan del Aguila (Emory University); Paula Pettavino (Analytic Sciences Corp.); and Jorge Sanguinetty (Development Technologies, Inc.).

In attempting to create both "the good society" and "the new socialist man," the actions of the Cuban revolution mesmerized the international community. Certainly, the Castro regime's skillful use of both conventional and non-conventional forms of diplomacy (media, communications, tourism, health programs, cultural activities, and physical culture/athletic competitions) focused attention on the developing revolutionary culture. As a result, Cuba has earned a level of prestige on a global scale that would have been impossible through conventional diplomatic means.

However, in the intervening 30 years external perceptions of Cuba have been altered but have not been fully absorbed. In this context, the nation's abysmal failure to promote either aggregate or per capita prosperity has not been lost on Latin America's political leadership. Clearly, the lessons learned have yet to be put into application by the rest of the region: namely, reliance on public-sector in lieu of private-sector development remains the norm. In the realm of foreign policy, the paradox lies in the fact that despite knowledge of the nation's menacing posture, claims of non-intervention in the affairs of other sovereign nations are oftentimes believed. Perhaps the only community which has irrevocably rejected the "fruits" of the Cuban revolution—which, ironically, began as its biggest supporter—is the intellectual community.

This effort has also benefited from many reviews and critiques in Washington and from elsewhere around the country. Several at CSIS have devoted long hours; the assistance of Pat Pickerall in the early phases and Carmen Pinelli at the end stand out. CSIS also acknowledges the support provided by the project donors, in particular the Cuban American National Foundation and its staff, and the Carthage Foundation and its appreciative ear, Dan McMichael. And finally, we wish to express our thanks to the contributing authors for their dedication to this project.

GEORGES FAURIOL
Senior Fellow and Director
Latin American Studies, CSIS
and
EVA LOSER
Fellow
Latin American Studies, CSIS

Note

1. *The Cuban Revolution: 25 Years Later,* by Hugh S. Thomas, Georges A. Fauriol, and Juan Carlos Weiss (Boulder, Colo.: Westview Press, 1984).

I
THE CORE RELATIONSHIPS

1

Cuba in the Soviet Alliance System

Jiri Valenta

Introduction

The political and military implications of Cuba's key position in the Caribbean Basin have traditionally been recognized by all American policymakers since the time of Thomas Jefferson. Writing in 1823, Jefferson pointed out that United States domination of Cuba would give the United States "control over the Gulf of Mexico, and the countries and isthmus bordering on it, as well as all those whose waters flow into it. . . ." Natural conditions being relentless, Cuba continues to command the Florida Straits, the entrance to the Gulf of Mexico, and the water passages to Central and South America. In this context, due to geographic destiny, ideology, advancing militarization, and proximity to the United States, contemporary Cuba—despite limitations of size and underdevelopment— poses an ongoing, ever-present threat to the stable world order that the United States seeks to maintain and, potentially, to U.S. national security.

Instead of being dominated by the United States, as American forefathers dreamed, Cuba enjoys close military ties with the Soviet Union. At times this has aroused strong emotion among the American people and suspicion and controversy among policymakers who question the eventual objectives of a hostile power in the waters bathing the southern U.S. periphery. Their sense of alarm quickly found factual form during the October 1962 missile crisis, when the Soviet deployment of medium-range ballistic missiles in Cuba brought the superpowers the closest they had ever come to the threshold of nuclear war. The Cuban threat was subsequently manifested several times: in 1970, when the Soviets were attempt-

3

ing to construct nuclear submarine facilities at Cienfuegos Bay; during the 1978 deployment of Soviet MIG-23 fighter bombers in Cuba; and in 1979, during revelations about the existence in Cuba of a "Soviet brigade."

Notwithstanding the strategic and national security implications of previous unsuccessful Soviet attempts to deploy offensive weapons in Cuba, the American consensus regarding Soviet/Cuban military ties is that the latter are primarily aimed at fortifying Cuba with sufficient defensive potential to deter any invasion by superior U.S. forces. Deterrence against a direct U.S. attack is supposedly strengthened by the maintenance of a trip-wire Soviet brigade—having much the same function as U.S. forces stationed in West Berlin. Granted the defensive purposes of these measures, it is sometimes difficult to distinguish defensive from offensive capabilities. The fine line separating the two has become blurred with increasing Soviet military aid and its extension to other countries in the area. In essence, Cuba has become a medium-strength military power with the capability of projecting overwhelming force, in comparison to its smaller, less well-armed Caribbean neighbors. And although not directly threatening to the United States, Cuban military capabilities could have a measurable effect on U.S. activity during any protracted conventional conflict between the superpowers, posing significant military constraints on U.S. operations in likely European or Middle Eastern theaters.

Cuba's threat to Western security, of which the United States is the major guardian, is somewhat easier to analyze, but more insidious; it is the concern of this essay. The argument proposed here is that in the early 1970s Cuba and the U.S.S.R. arrived at a joint strategy of coopeative interventions and military aid designed to promote Leninist-oriented, anti-Western regimes and movements in the Third World. During this period, the Soviets gradually became convinced that the Cuban trajectory—from revolutionary through vanguard-party to proper Leninist regime—had demonstrated the validity of the Leninist process for a whole host of Third World revolutionaries. Subsequently, over the past decade, Soviet-backed Cuban military interventions and assistance have helped to insure the victory and/or survival of six Third World client regimes in Angola, Ethiopia, Nicaragua, Mozambique, South Yemen, and, until October 1983, Grenada. With Soviet support, the Cubans also continue to assist and train a number of Leninist revolutionary groups, including the Farabundo Martí de Liberación Nacional (FMLN) in El Salvador and the South-West African People's Organization (SWAPO) in Namibia.

The defeat of Leninist forces in Grenada by forces of the United States and the Organization of Eastern Caribbean States (OECS) in October 1983 is viewed in retrospect as only a temporary setback in the overall highly successful Soviet/Cuban stragegy. This conclusion has been reached since it did not set in motion the trend toward "rolling back" Third World Leninist regimes implied in the "Reagan Doctrine." This has become apparent at the close of President Ronald Reagan's eight-year tenure. Although some of these regimes have been seriously challenged by indigenous resistance movements (particularly in Angola, but also in Nicaragua and Mozambique), they nonetheless survive, and, in spite of the best efforts of the Reagan administration, strategically important Nicaragua has been able to evolve into a Central American hybrid of Leninist Cuba.

One key to the U.S. failure to grapple with the Cuban threat to world stability is a misunderstanding of Cuba's and Castro's complex role-playing in the Soviet alliance system. U.S. policymakers have been, and some remain primarily, concerned with the Cuban threat to U.S. physical security, demonstrated in 1962 during the Soviet missile deployment and in 1970 during the Soviet attempt to build a submarine base at Cienfuegos. After these crises receded, the second, less clearly defined threat to more broadly defined U.S. security interests—as a global power, the guardian of Western security—has tended to be regarded as less important or viewed simply as part of the overall Soviet threat in which Cuban activities are perceived as an extension of Soviet power.

The main point—often misunderstood on all sides of the U.S. political spectrum—is that while Cuba must agree with the Soviets on major foreign policy issues, it has considerable room for autonomy in pursuing its own strategic goals, particularly in Africa and the Caribbean Basin. Thus, the degree of Cuban autonomy differs from case to case. In light of this, the United States should avoid the old mistake of trying to deal primarily and directly with the U.S.S.R. regarding Cuban international conduct, except in instances that impinge directly on U.S./Soviet security relations, such as the deployment of missiles or submarines in Cuba. The unique, complex arrangement between the U.S.S.R. and Cuba is quite unlike any of the other Soviet alliances with junior partners in Europe and Asia, with the possible exception of Vietnam. Cuba is neither an unrestrained, independent actor nor a completely subservient Soviet surrogate. In fact, as this discussion shows, Cuba has never been a subservient and easily compliant Soviet ally, particularly not in the 1960s. Although it has become a Leninist regime and a Soviet dependency, it has managed to preserve domestic autonomy and, in some instances, foreign policy-making autonomy as well.

For purposes of clarification, as used here, a Soviet ally is not a state controlled by the U.S.S.R. but rather one which, by using Soviet military and economic aid, pursues policies that ultimately benefit Soviet strategic objectives. In addition, while the U.S.S.R. holds preponderant military and economic power, its Cuban ally maintains and commands such assets as an independent interventionist military force.

In order to accurately assess the nature of the Soviet/Cuban alliance, one must understand the roles that Cuba plays. For a long period Cuba acted as an unruly junior ally. Later, as Soviet/Cuban relations began to improve, Cuba tended to play the role of broker between the Soviet Union and radical Third World regimes, and, under some circumstances, the role of proxy or joint interventionist.

The various roles that Cuba has played in the alliance—from unruly ally to privileged ally (and now again, perhaps, unruly ally)—have been characterized by contention and suspicion on the one hand, and closeness and mutual confidence on the other. At the present time, the alliance is entering a new, unpredictable era. The nearing end of Fidel Castro's rule and the new dynamism of Mikhail Gorbachev's leadership—defined internally as *perestroika* (restructuring, radical reform) and *glasnost* (openness), and in foreign policy as *novoe myshlenie* (new thinking)—could give some new twists to the Soviet/Cuban alliance. For the moment, Gorbachev's reforms, flexibility, and bold experimentation appear hardly compatible with the immobilism of *fidelismo* and Castro's megalomaniacal leadership style.

Understanding and anticipating the complex, multiple role-playing of Cuba within the Soviet alliance system is essential to devising a coherent U.S. strategy to cope with modes of behavior that appear the same, but have different motivations and values. Whether future presidents and their administrations will deal effectively with the Cuban issue remains dependent on their ability to grapple with the intricacies of this alliance. Its dynamics—though hard to foresee—are ripe with challenge and opportunity.

Cuba's Multiple Roles

There are two extreme views regarding the Soviet/Cuban alliance. The first portrays Cuba as a surrogate of the U.S.S.R., simply implementing Soviet orders, whereas the second view depicts Cuba as an unconstrained, totally autonomous actor. However, both schools ignore the mutual constraints and leverages in the Soviet/Cuban alliance. The U.S.S.R., primarily because of its superior military and economic might, plays the dominant role in the alliance. In this context, the Soviets exercise great influence on Cuban foreign policy in general and Cuban policy in the Third World in particular, with Cuba enjoying only a small degree of relative autonomy in both areas. But Cuba does provide limited inputs into Soviet foreign policy, most especially regarding Third World issues.

Cuba has never been simply subservient or compliant, least of all in the

1960s when unruliness and unpredictability were very marked in the Cuban behavior. In the 1970s, however, one could say that the Cuban status changed to that of a cooperative and privileged junior partner. In this period, Cuba acquired two new roles: that of broker between the U.S.S.R. and new Leninist forces and regimes in the Third World, and that of cooperative interventionist, poised to undertake joint military ventures with the U.S.S.R. as a junior ally or surrogate military force.

With its special status in the Soviet alliance system, Cuba can play different roles at different times but also simultaneously. This multiple function, marked by elements of both autonomy and dependency, is what has made the complex Soviet/Cuban alliance so valuable to the U.S.S.R., in spite of all the difficulties and disagreements that may arise.

Unruly Junior Ally of the 1960s

When U.S./Cuban differences became unbridgeable and the United States withdrew from Cuba in 1959, the Soviets, after a period of hesitation, tried to fill the resulting political and economic vacuum. Their opportunity came with the failed Bay of Pigs invasion attempt in 1961, after which Nikita Khrushchev and his colleagues started to forge a major alliance with Castro. Initially the Soviets were exuberant about the success of the Cuban revolution, appearing to believe that the Cuban example could be exported, with Soviet backing, to other countries in Latin America. The outcome of the Cuban missile crisis of 1962, however, which the Chinese described as the "Caribbean Munich," contained an admission by the Soviets of their limited power in the area.

In Castro's view, Khrushchev mishandled the crisis with serious repercussions on the Soviet/Cuban relationship. The newly available evidence suggests that during the crisis the Soviets were unable to fully control the irate Castro. Reportedly, at the peak of the turmoil, a key Soviet surface-to-air base was attacked by Cuban troops. In the fray, the Soviets apparently suffered some casualties; furthermore, it is conceivable that they may have lost control over the SA-2 batteries that shot down the U.S. U-2 spy plane on October 27 that year. That event prompted the U.S. ultimatum that the U.S.S.R. withdraw its missiles. Khrushchev complied, almost instantaneously, but without consulting Castro. After this slight, the Soviet leaders had to exert considerable pressure on Castro to convince him to give up the Soviet IL-28 bombers. However, on the issue of external inspection and verification measures, Castro refused to acquiesce.

Castro's general reaction to the missile affair was to seriously question, for a long time to come, the degree of the Soviet commitment to protect Cuba against U.S. intervention. At the time, he, like many others, did not realize what would become clear only in the 1970s. As humiliated as he was, Khrushchev had won his main objective. In exchange for agreeing to remove the missiles from Cuba, he extracted an informal, ambiguous American pledge not to try to topple the Cuban regime. The United States never formalized the tacit understanding of 1962 or its reaffirmation by both superpowers after the 1970 Cienfuegos crisis. As Castro explained in 1979, however, both the Soviets and the Cubans interpreted the understanding as "a guarantee from the United States not to invade Cuba."

In good Leninist fashion, Khrushchev was prepared to move back a step so that later on he could move forward two steps. On the other hand, the rather nearsighted United States did not exact the severance of Soviet/Cuban military ties or the cessation of Soviet support for revolution in the Third World that it had been seeking. And Cuba, doubly favored—albeit without the missiles and the bombers—evolved into a Soviet military outpost in Latin America and a key Soviet ally in the support of Leninist-type revolution. Considering the success of joint Soviet/Cuban conventional military operations in the Third World in the 1970s, it appears that Khrushchev indeed scored a victory over President Kennedy in the famous missile showdown.

In the immediate aftermath of the missile crisis, the formulation of Soviet Third World policy was complicated by profound Soviet/Cuban doctrinal disagreements and differences concerning a strategy for Latin America. As a result, Soviet/Cuban relations in the late 1960s were strained almost to the breaking point.

The Soviets were pessimistic regarding the "revolutionary potential" of the area and realistically wary of becoming actively involved given the forceful U.S. response to the Soviet/Cuban-supported guerrilla revolutions in Venezuela and other Latin American countries up to that point. Other internal and external factors compounded their cautious assessment. Preoccupied with a domestic power struggle after Khrushchev's dismissal in 1964, the course of the Vietnam War, and the deepening Sino/Soviet dispute, the Soviets in the late 1960s were unwilling and unable to sponsor Castro's call to create "two or three Vietnams" for the United States in Latin America.

Castro's strategy, on the other hand, which adhered to Che Guevara's and Regis Debray's concept of guerrilla-peasant insurgency, contradicted and even challenged the Soviet doctrine allowing for diversified roads to socialism, including the electoral path. Castro favored the use of revolutionary violence and criticized the U.S.S.R. for dealing with capitalist governments in Latin America. Young, pro-Castro elements present in some other Latin American communist parties, particularly those of

Guatemala and Venezuela, also resisted the Soviet advice to proceed gradually and with caution.

Regis Debray, who has defined a Leninist as "an opportunist with principles," has stated that Castro is an excellent example of a Leninist. In this vein, despite foreign policy disagreements with the Soviets, Castro did gradually embrace their Leninist organizational model for the vanguard party. (Castro's communist party was officially established in 1965.) This model was promoted because he wanted to perpetuate his rule, and Leninism's iron-disciplined, centralized, and elitist organizational model has proved to be an effective means for keeping power. Thus, as Carlos Franqui, a former Castro associate, said, Castro's power "became linked to the Soviet structure."

Castro also needed a new source of military and economic aid after his break-up with the United States. His embrace of the Leninist organizational principles and structures and his strategic alliance with the U.S.S.R.—to practice Leninist proletarian internationalism—meant that the U.S.S.R. would accept and support his regime more readily. However, the fusion of the Leninist model with militant, Castroist *caudillismo* has resulted in a political system that some would quip is more *machista-leninista* than traditional.

For the Soviets, Castro's gradual conversion to Leninism, fully accomplished in 1975 when the Cuban Communist Party held their first party congress, demonstrated the validity of the Leninist recipe for other radical Third World regimes. The successful Cuban experiment proved that a vanguard, socialist-oriented regime built around the principle of democratic centralism can evolve into a proper Leninist regime. And this powerfully motivated the Soviets, with Cuban aid, to try to reenact that metamorphosis—under varying national, regional, and global circumstances—elsewhere in Latin America, the Caribbean, and Africa.

By 1974, the Soviets and Cubans had arrived at a mutually concessionary strategy whereby the Soviets approved support for guerrilla activities in some African and Latin American countries with extremely pro-American, anti-Communist regimes and the Cubans gave their blessing to the Soviet pursuit of diplomacy with other friendlier nations. The death of Ché Guevara and the general defeat of his revolutionary concept in Latin America in the late 1960s impressed the Cubans with the need to overcome their differences and coordinate their policies with Moscow. As Castro perceived it, there were no immediate revolutionary opportunities in Latin America in the 1970s, although the case was otherwise in Africa. Thus, he grudgingly approved the Soviet policy of employing diplomatic, commercial, and cultural channels—in addition to revolutionary tactics, where feasible—in order to expand relations with "progressive forces" on the

Latin American continent. The merger of the Soviet and Cuban strategic visions, resulting in basic agreement on the dialectics of revolutionary strategy in the Third World in general and in Africa and the Caribbean in particular, was much facilitated by the growing dependence and Leninization of Cuba.

Soviet diplomatic initiatives in Latin America in the 1970s yielded some political and economic payoffs, among other things helping to invalidate the political and economic blockade of Cuba. Subsequently, Cuba was able to normalize relations with many Latin American countries. However, the U.S.S.R. and Cuba had not given up the notion of supporting revolutionary movements in the Third World—the militant track. The Soviet/ Cuban posture was a temporary concession to real circumstances, not acquiescence. Neither the Soviets nor the Cubans renounced the efficacy of violent revolution as a means for overthrowing unfriendly, anticommunist governments. The fact that revolutionary means proved temporarily inefficacious in the unripened medium of Latin America in the mid-1970s only led them to direct their attention elsewhere, particularly Africa— Angola in 1975–76 and Ethiopia in 1977–78. The Latin American situation changed dramatically, however, with the successful Sandinista revolution in Nicaragua in 1979, the New Jewel Movement (NJM) coup in Grenada the same year, and the upswing in guerrilla warfare in El Salvador in 1980– 1981.

Junior Ally of the 1970s—Cooperation and Privilege

The signing of the Havana Declaration in 1974 was proof that the majority of differences between Cuba and the U.S.S.R. had been overcome by that time. The Cubans described the declaration as an "historic" document marking "a new stage" in the ever-closer cooperation between strategic allies pursuing "common goals" within the parameters established by the Leninist principle of proletarian internationalism. In the late 1970s, as the Soviet/Cuban alliance was being further cemented, a key strategic objective was to selectively build "socialist-oriented" or Leninist-oriented regimes that would eventually serve as bridges to other revolutionary forces. The most advanced of these regimes were to be those with evolving "vanguard" parties or elitist Leninist organizations modeled on the principle of "democratic centralism"—in other words, iron discipline reinforced by the top party leadership—and guided by cadres either trained in the U.S.S.R. and other communist countries or, at a minimum, having good connections with the Soviet and Cuban bureaucracies. The regimes in Afghanistan, Ethiopia, Angola, Mozambique, South Yemen,

Nicaragua, and (prior to October 1983) Grenada had these characteristic qualities.

In pursuing these goals, Cuba acted neither independently nor even semi-independently. Cuba's emergence as an interventionist power in Africa and the Caribbean in the mid-1970s became possible mainly because of growing Soviet military and economic power and the Soviet exploitation of changes in the international system. Cuba's dependence was suggested at the time by the growing Cuban integration in the Soviet alliance system.

The Leninization of Cuba, which has been supported and actively encouraged by the Soviet Union and its allies in the Warsaw Pact, has been accompanied by a corresponding process of political-ideological, military-security and economic integration within the Soviet alliance system. The political-ideological integration was directly spearheaded by the Soviet and East European advisors who trained Cuban cadres in the East and assisted in their training in Cuba. Hundreds of high- and middle-level Cuban Central Committee officials and Cuban Communist Party instructors have graduated from party schools in the U.S.S.R. and Eastern Europe (primarily East Germany, Czechoslovakia and Bulgaria). Party-to-party ties were further encouraged by dozens of party officials of both sides during working visits between Cuba and the Soviet Bloc. Extensive ties also were established among auxiliary political mass organizations in Cuba and in the Warsaw Pact countries.

The process of security-military integration among Cuba, the U.S.S.R., and the Warsaw Pact member countries has proceeded along as well. The Cuban intelligence service, the General Directorate of Intelligence (DGI), became integrated with and was basically controlled by the KGB as of early 1970. The DGI has developed close cooperation with the Soviet and East European security services abroad, primarily in Third World countries, and has helped to build a network of guerrilla training camps in Cuba. Third World revolutionaries are trained primarily in Cuba, but some Soviet and East European counterparts lend a hand as well.

Soviet/Cuban military ties have also been enhanced by the gradual return to Cuba of hundreds of Cuban military officers upon graduation from military schools in the Warsaw Pact countries, particularly the M.V. Frunze Academy in the Soviet Union. The graduates of this school hold the most important posts in the Cuban armed forces. The closely knit network of Soviet military school graduates—both fluent in Russian and having excellent ties with their Warsaw Pact counterparts—appears to have formed the most influential pro-Soviet lobby in Cuba. In fact, by the 1970s, Soviet/Cuban military integration had advanced to the point that Soviet pilots would refer to Cuba as their aircraft carrier in the Caribbean.

The Cuban military elite have strong ties with Soviet military and security representatives in Cuba, whose numbers have increased through-out the 1970s and 1980s. At present, there are approximately 2,800 Soviet military advisors and technicians in Cuba, a 2,600-man army brigade including a motorized infantry regiment, 2,000 security personnel serving in a Soviet-operated signal intelligence facility (the largest outside the U.S.S.R.) which monitors U.S. military and civilian communications, and numerous others engaged in training Cuban forces for joint (Soviet/Cuban) military operations. Since 1975, Soviet and Cuban naval units have regularly exercised together and Soviet reconnaissance aircraft (TU-95 Bear) as well as antisubmarine warfare aircraft (TU-142 Bear F) have utilized Cuban military airfields in conducting their missions.

The political-ideological and military-security integration of Cuba within the Soviet alliance system has likewise been accompanied by Cuba's integration within the Soviet-dominated Council for Mutual Economic Assistance (CMEA). Cuba became a full-fledged member of the CMEA in 1972. Since then, Cuban five-year economic plans have been coordinated with those of the U.S.S.R. and other members of CMEA—the Eastern European countries, Mongolia, and Vietnam. Key Cuban economic activities are also integrated with long-term CMEA cooperative programs supervised by joint advisory commissions, and monitored by dozens of Soviet and East European advisors and thousands of Cuban economic personnel and technicians educated in the Soviet Bloc. Surveying statistics alone, the upshot of economic integration with CMEA for Cuba has been the creation of a dependency relationship. In the mid-1970s, Cuban trade dependency vis-à-vis COMECON surpassed the 80 percent mark.

In addition to its close ties with the U.S.S.R., the Castro regime has developed special ties with the East European countries—above all, East Germany and Vietnam. The close alliance with East Germany was motivated by that nation's activist policies in the Third World and by its special geopolitical location at the borders of NATO, directly facing the "enemy," in a position similar to the one in which Cuba sees itself. Cuba's special comradeship with Vietnam stems from the former's perception that between 1965 and 1975 Vietnam was a victim of direct U.S. aggression, as Cuba was in the early 1960s. Another contributing factor is that the Cuban leadership admires the Vietnamese political will in actively supporting anti-U.S. and anti-Chinese Leninist forces in Southeast Asia—much as Cuba supports anti-U.S. forces in the Caribbean and Central America.

In the 1970s and early 1980s, the Soviet/Cuban military activism in the Third World was also enhanced by the Soviet assumption of a new global role. From a Khrushchevian, and basically regional and premature global power, the U.S.S.R. gradually emerged under Leonid Brezhnev's leadership into a fully developed, globally oriented superpower. The acquisition of strategic parity with the United States in the early 1970s, as well as the immeasurably improved conventional capabilities marking this transformation, helped to facilitate Soviet/Cuban ventures in Africa.

In the Angolan and Ethiopian episodes, it was clear that the Soviets had learned from their experience in 1960 in the Congo (now Zaire) how poor coordination, inexperienced personnel and a lack of air- and sea-lift capabilities had led to serious difficulties and ultimately the failure of the Soviet operation. In later years, a rectification of these drawbacks greatly enhanced the Cuban role not only in Africa but in the Caribbean Basin as well. As important as the upgrading of Soviet weaponry, coordination, and military-strategic cover has been, the Soviet underwriting of the Cuban economy, estimated at over $4.9 billion per year, has been of equal significance. Conditions and attitudes in the United States also contributed to the success of Soviet/Cuban strategy in the 1970s. Public and congressional fears of a new Vietnam nightmare, the weakening of the American presidency following the Watergate affair, and the unwillingness of U.S. policymakers to use military power in the Third World in the customarily assertive manner—demonstrated only a decade or two before in Lebanon (1957), Zaire (1960), and the Dominican Republic (1965)—all paved the way for Soviet and Cuban activism. Other congruent opportunities, such as the disintegration of the Portuguese colonial empire in 1974–75, made it even easier for the U.S.S.R. and Cuba to vigorously exploit ensuing local conflicts in Angola and elsewhere.

In the final analysis, Cuba and the Soviet Union not only share the same strategic vision but also basically agree on how to coordinate and implement policies to meet such objectives. Cuban strategic priorities, however, are not necessarily identical to those of the Soviets. The U.S.S.R. is a superpower with global interests, responsibilities, and capabilities; Cuba, notwithstanding the abundant rhetoric of Castro, is basically a regional power, culturally and historically a part of the Latin American and, specifically, Caribbean communities. As a result, subtle and not so subtle differences tend to distinguish the Soviet and Cuban policies. The differences are perhaps the most apparent with regard to policies concerning the Caribbean Basin, which, while of marginal geopolitical importance to the U.S.S.R., are of paramount importance to Cuba. Nevertheless, Cuba's strategic vision extends beyond the surrounding regions to other Third World areas, with special emphasis on the kindred countries of Africa.

Broker and Cooperative Interventionist

One of the most important roles of Cuba in the Soviet alliance system is that of broker. Castro's influence in the alliance has been both direct, in consultations with Soviet leaders, and indirect, in brokering between Soviet and Third World leaders. Brokerage, in this context, refers to the active participation of the Cuban leadership, and in particular Fidel Castro, in arranging political marriages or alliances with other revolutionary regimes (in Angola, Ethiopia, Mozambique, South Yemen, Nicaragua, and Grenada) and with revolutionary guerrilla forces (in El Salvador, Guatemala, and Namibia). These and other similar alliances have been extremely valuable to the Soviets.

The Soviet Union rarely gives explicit instructions or assigns tactical missions to Leninist or socialist-oriented revolutionary regimes (and military forces) in Third World arenas in which they themselves lack experience and knowledge, or which are strategically less important and, at the same time, geographically very distant. (The explicitness of the Soviet directives to junior allies in Afghanistan has been due to Afghanistan's geographical location and the direct engagement of Soviet armed forces there.) Instead, aspiring Leninist leaders in the Third World are usually at liberty to use their imagination—with Cuba or Vietnam often acting as broker—to cultivate ties with the Soviets and explore basic Soviet strategic objectives and limits of tolerance. Thus, since the late 1970s, the primary task of Angolan, Ethiopian, Nicaraguan, Grenadian and other aspiring Leninist leaders has been to demonstrate their usefulness to a skeptical Soviet leadership, much as Castro had to do after 1959. As revolutionary leaders consolidate power and in other ways "prove" themselves, the Soviets gradually become interested in strengthening more direct ties with them. In this context it should be recalled it took fifteen years for Cuba to cultivate a close relationship with the Soviet Politburo, as frankly admitted by Cuban leader Rafael Rodriguez to Grenada's ambassador to Moscow in the early 1980s.

The newly available documents from Grenada, El Salvador, Nicaragua, and Mozambique support this conclusion. As they demonstrate, there exists a certain degree of tentativeness and ambiguity in Soviet policies toward Third World nations—and the commitment to help establish Leninist regimes is not made without regard to cost. In many instances the Soviet Union prefers that its allies (Cuba in Africa and Latin America, Vietnam in Southeast Asia) "micromanage," or act as brokers, in arranging their relationships with aspiring Leninist forces and in carrying out the initial stages of Leninization.

As the leaders of Leninist-oriented regimes succeed in consolidating power, the Soviets try to reduce the Cuban brokerage and develop their own direct relations with these regimes. This is sometimes attempted in an abrupt fashion, as well as by encouraging violence to favor the more pro-Soviet factions. This strategy became apparent in Angola in 1977 when the

Soviets appeared to encourage the building of the pro-Soviet faction that organized an unsuccessful coup against the Angolan president and Cuban friend Agostinho Neto. It may also have been a factor in the internal leadership conflict in Grenada in October 1983 between the Leninist Deputy Prime Minister Bernard Coard and the less orthodox Prime Minister Maurice Bishop. As for the Sandinistas in Nicaragua, the outcome of the leadership struggle in Grenada may have strongly influenced their seeming intention to present at least a facade of unity for the sake of a revolution they all support.

The Cuban brokerage between the U.S.S.R. and various Third World revolutionary leaders has been possible primarily because of Fidel Castro's unique personality. Castro can play several roles at one time: that of an "internationalist" while trying to reschedule the Cuban debt with the U.S.S.R.; that of a "new Bolivar" while debating anti-U.S. strategy with Latin American revolutionaries such as Eden Pastora; and that of "Soviet victim" while explaining Soviet/Cuban relations to Latin American "bourgeois" leaders such as the Venezuelan Carlos Andres Perez. Because many Third World leaders see Castro as erratic yet intelligent, brave, courageous, and charming, he serves as a highly effective intermediary. As a former member of the Nicaraguan junta under the Sandinistas, Arturo Cruz Sr., frankly revealed when describing his impressions of an encounter with Fidel Castro, "He was very charming and his long nose, so pitiful, that he made me feel sorry for him. While talking to this man, who played so beautifully the charming role of a Leninist Bolivar, I had to remind myself that this is a dictator, this is a bloody dictator."

Cuba's Payoffs

What ideological, political, security, and economic payoffs does Cuba expect for helping to promote Soviet strategy? Ideological satisfaction is intrinsic to Cuban activity in the Third World. Although Castro has never been renowned for his theoretical conceptualization of Leninism, the Cuban revolution is relatively young and Castro's ideological commitment to the revolutionaries in Africa and Central America would seem to be more genuine than that of the Soviet leadership. Contemporary Soviet strategic priorities were forged under the close scrutiny of plodding Central Committee bureaucrats, whereas Cuban strategic priorities were formed by those who vividly remember the revolution against Fulgencio Batista.

Furthermore, Cuba maintains a strong ideological affinity with revolutionary Third World nations that is strengthened by common Latin and African ancestries, colonial legacies, and exploitation by outside powers. Castro, himself a sort of "Red Robin Hood," has been a vehement and long-standing supporter of various revolutionary movements and a close friend of their leaders. Cuban support of revolutionary groups in Africa and Latin America has, in most cases, been consistent since 1960, without the ups and downs characteristic of Soviet support for some of these same organizations. This consistency of commitment was seen in the Cuban handling of the Popular Movement for the Liberation of Angola (MPLA) guerrillas who began to train secretly on Cuba's Isle of Youth—along with other revolutionary groups from Nicaragua, Mozambique, and else-where—even in the early 1960s.

Although more ideologically motivated than the Soviet Union, Cuba has also witnessed the passing of its initial revolutionary exuberance and élan. Today, in addition to ideological concerns, Castro has strong security, political, and economic interests in pursuing a joint strategy with the Soviets. His security objective is to ensure the survival of the Cuban revolution and obtain further guarantees for his state in the face of continuing U.S. hostility. In political and economic terms, Castro's regime hopes to rebuild the bridges to all the Latin American countries that supported the expulsion of Cuba from the Organization of American States (OAS) in 1962.

Over the last decade, Castro has tried to increase the prestige and influence of his regime among members of the Nonaligned Movement. Since the unpopular Soviet invasion of Afghanistan, however, Third World leaders have become less willing to accept Castro as Nonaligned leader and defender of progressive Third World regimes. They realize that a "natural alliance" with the U.S.S.R., as advocated by Castro at the Havana conference of the Nonaligned Movement in 1979, can lead to an "unnatural death," as befell Afghanistan's President Hafizullah Amin only several months following the conference. The Soviet war in Afghanistan in the 1980s has had a detrimental effect on Cuba's political standing in the Third World. It has likewise affected not only Castro's ambition to refur-bish the prestige of his regime but his personal image as the recognized leader of the Nonaligned Movement as well.

Soviet/Cuban economic and political relations have been greatly en-hanced by Cuba's willingness to deploy regular troops and furnish military support and assistance on behalf of vanguard-party regimes in Africa and the Caribbean Basin. As these activities were indispensable to Soviet policies toward Africa and the Caribbean Basin, Havana gradually gained the status of a privileged junior partner, and was able to insist on adjust-ments in the Soviet/Cuban relationship. (In Castro's words, Cuba has enjoyed "every privilege" in its economic association with the U.S.S.R.) The Cuban contribution of combatants, in particular, has provided Castro with some measure of leverage while bargaining with the Soviets regarding levels of military and economic aid.

In the aftermath of Cuba's participation in the invasion of Angola in 1975, the intervention in Ethiopia in 1978, and the victories of the Frente Sandinista de Liberación Nacional (FSLN) in Nicaragua and the NJM in Grenada in 1979, the Cubans were able to negotiate a continuation of the Soviet subsidies of Cuban sugar and nickel production and petroleum prices into the 1980s, greater economic aid, new credits, a further increase in commerce, and a postponement in repaying the cumulative Cuban debt, with a suspension of interest payments. In addition, the U.S.S.R. has continued to provide a stable market for a great many Cuban products and manufactured goods. As a result, as long as Cuban interventionist activity contributes to the multiplication and fortification of Leninist-oriented regimes in the Third World, the Soviets are apparently quite willing to continue their underwriting of the Cuban economy. As indicated by a former senior official of the Cuban government, until now Cuban officials have received most of what they wanted, eventually, finding their way to senior leaders such as Leonid Brezhnev, when initial demands for increased assistance were frustrated by Soviet middle-rank officials.

The principal military-security payoff has been the Soviet modernization of Cuba's armed forces. The Cuban force (225,000 active-duty troops, 190,000 trained reservists, and over 1 million Territorial Troop Militia) is the best-equipped in the region and outflanks all others in the Caribbean Basin, including that of the much larger Mexico. In Latin America it is second in size only to the armed forces of Brazil. Of the U.S.S.R.'s Warsaw Pact allies, only Poland, which is four times the size of Cuba, is more formidably represented. The Soviets have also helped Cuba to build a small, but modern and efficient, coastal navy and merchant fleet. In the overall context of Soviet arms assistance programs, Soviet arms transfers to Cuba are quite advanced.

Africa and the Middle East: Broker/Interventionist in Angola, Proxy in Angola and South Yemen

Soviet policy toward Africa has been particularly dependent—and remains dependent to some extent—on the willingness of Fidel Castro and his colleagues to provide ground forces for joint Soviet/Cuban adventures. In Angola and Ethiopia (unlike in Afghanistan), the Soviets were cautious about committing their own troops in a direct fashion for several reasons. First, the use of Soviet combat troops might have elicited a firmer response from the United States. Second, two factors favored the use of Cuban troops: the presence of a substantial number of blacks and mulattos in the

Cuban forces (40 to 50 percent in Angola, although this percentage is higher than in the Cuban armed forces as a whole), and the Cubans' relative linguistic affinity with the Portuguese-speaking MPLA soldiers.

Angola

Contrary to widespread belief, it was originally Castro's idea, not the Soviets', to intervene militarily on behalf of the embattled MPLA in Angola. The involvement of Cuban military personnel in Africa goes back to 1964 and 1965 when the Cubans began assisting Guinea and fought briefly in the former Belgian Congo (now Zaire) against the incumbent government supported by the United States. Prior to the Cuban involvement in Angola, Castro had been a long-standing supporter of the MPLA and was a close friend of MPLA leader Agostinho Neto. In the spring and summer of 1975—and even in the initial stage of the intervention in the fall—the growing force of Cuban military personnel in Angola appeared to have been more eager than the Soviets to become vigorously involved on behalf of the MPLA. (Ironically, this coincided with American apparent readiness to normalize relations with Cuba.) Thus, in the Angolan cases it would be misleading to view Cuban policy as subservient to Soviet policy—quite simply, the Cubans were not ordered into war by the Soviets.

In part relating to initial uncertainties as to the American response, the Soviets were cautious about committing themselves in a direct military fashion in Angola. Nevertheless, in late 1975 and early 1976, they took over the Cuban air- and sea-lift, transforming the Angolan campaign into a massive operation in which both the Soviet air force and navy were operationally active. A small, yet effective, Soviet naval task force provided physical and psychological support to the Cuban combat troops, protected the Cuban staging areas against local threats, served as a strategic cover for established sea and air communications, and worked as a deterrent against possible U.S. naval deployment. It is clear that the hurried air- and sea-lift of Cuban reinforcements saved the MPLA, as well as the advanced Cuban units around the capital of Luanda, from almost certain defeat. Furthermore, it is quite possible that if Moscow had not become involved in Angola and if the South Africans had been actively encouraged by the United States to continue their blitz campaigns, the Cubans would have been defeated.

Ethiopia

In comparison to the Angolan operation, coordination was even tighter in the case of the Soviet/Cuban intervention in the Ogaden (Ethiopia) in

1977–78. In cooperation with Soviet officials, in the spring of 1977 Castro acted as mediator between Somalia and Ethiopia, attempting to negotiate a "socialist federation" of the two countries, along with Djibouti and South Yemen. But this brokerage did not work. As in Angola, the fear of the collapse of an important client regime in a strategically important region, and the subsequent weakening of the credibility of the U.S.S.R. as a global superpower and reliable protector of revolutionary regimes, played an important role in the Soviet/Cuban shift of support from Somalia to Ethiopia in the fall of 1977. After the break with Somalia, a defeat in Ethiopia would have meant a definitive liquidation of the Soviet investment in the Horn of Africa. On an operational level, there appeared to have been a more careful coordination of Soviet and Cuban activity than in Angola, attributable in part to the supervision of the entire Ethiopian campaign by four Soviet generals. Also, in the Ethiopian case, the Soviets became vigorously involved from the very beginning. In this context, during the initial stage of the operation in Angola, Cuba had temporarily functioned as an autonomous actor. In contrast, during the Ogaden conflict, Cuba generally assumed a more subordinate role—if not, indeed, the role of a Soviet proxy.

South Yemen

Soviet/Cuban military cooperation in South Yemen in January 1986 was also very close, with the Soviets acting in a clearly supervisory position. As was the case in Grenada in October 1983, the South Yemenese Leninist-oriented government had collapsed amid violent factional infighting. However, unlike in Grenada, the Soviets and Cubans were obviously united in their joint intervention on behalf of the rebel faction seeking to overthrow President Ali Nasir Muhammed. Soviet and Cuban officers reportedly directed the fire of the rebel units while the Soviet navy and air force bombarded the airfields and directly supplied the rebel forces with ammunition.

Overall, the interventions in Africa and the Middle East demonstrated the Soviet ability to sustain, with allied support from a subordinate Cuba, a major military operation or "surgical" strike in the Third World in order to effect political change in the Soviet favor. At the same time, these actions also demonstrated the very large degree of Cuban dependence. Without substantial military and economic support from the U.S.S.R., Cuba could not have engendered or sustained the specific military commitments it made to Angola, Ethiopia, and South Yemen.

Latin America and the Caribbean: Broker in Grenada and Nicaragua

Grenada

The Grenada Documents provide many new insights about the role of Cuba as broker. To begin with, Cuba, not the Soviet Union, trained the NJM militants who took power in Grenada in 1979; and thereafter, Cuba played the more active role in helping the NJM to Leninize Grenada. (Whereas the Cubans in the 1960s had studied primarily the Soviet and East European institutions as possible models for their Leninist evolution, the Grenadians, in the early stage of their revolution, studied primarily the second-hand Cuban model.) In terms of Moscow's reaction, the Soviets were cautious. First, as reported by the Grenadian embassy in Moscow, the Soviets saw Grenada as "very distant" and not located in one of their designated strategic "priority areas." This led the Grenadian ambassador to explain to the NJM leadership, "We have to work on the Soviets for some considerable time before we reach the stage of relationship that, for example, we have had with the Cubans."

The Cuban brokerage was very valuable in advancing Grenada's international contacts—particularly with the U.S.S.R. As such, Cuba became the foremost advocate of the Grenadians in Moscow, as they have also been for the Angolans. This was recognized by the Grenadian diplomats, one of whom frankly conceded, "Cuba has strongly championed our case." The Grenada Documents leave no doubt that Cuba was the most important source of guidance and confidential assessment in Grenada's dealings with the U.S.S.R. and other Leninist regimes. Because of the Soviet's perception of the stability and durability of the NJM's Leninist orientation, the Soviets, after a year or so of Cuban prodding, began to make a significant, though guarded, commitment to Grenada. The character of the commitment was determined by three factors: the special vanguard-party ideological status assigned to the NJM party by the Soviets; the radical political, social, and economic reforms being undertaken by the party; and the NJM's ardently espoused anti-Americanism. Advanced ideological ranking, in particular, presupposed considerable weapons commitments to strengthen NJM defenses against internal and external enemies of Leninism.

The Soviet and Cuban involvement in Grenada did not represent an immediate security threat to the United States. The Soviet-supplied arsenal, however, did make the Grenadian armed forces a factor to be reckoned with in the immediate West Indian environment. Even though the Soviets were supposedly interested in "reducing the areas of conflict with the USA" in the Caribbean, as explained by the Grenadian ambassador to

Moscow, there was a possibility that (barring the U.S./OECS intervention) Grenada might have become a component in Soviet military planning, serving as a bridge to revolutionary forces elsewhere in the region—as Cuba has been for the last quarter-century.

Nicaragua

The Cuban brokerage was essential in helping the Soviets forge a strategic alliance with the Sandinista leadership in Nicaragua. Years earlier, the Soviets had courted the founding father of the FSLN, Carlos Fonseca, who had spent some time in Moscow in 1957. In addition, it is likely that the KGB assisted in the training and financing of the FSLN in the 1970s. The major part of military aid to the Sandinistas, however, was provided by and funneled through Cuban intermediaries. The available evidence suggests that the Cubans—and particularly Fidel Castro—were the primary external force supporting the anti-Somoza insurgency in Nicaragua. Since 1959, Cuban advisors had been helping to organize the armed struggle in Nicaragua and a number of senior FSLN leaders and militants were trained in Cuba, although a few were also trained in Moscow. Cuban military aid, guidance, and moral support were even more essential in the final stage of the Sandinista struggle between 1977 and 1979, as acknowledged by the Sandinista leaders. No less important than the actual materiel assistance was Castro's demand for unification of the Sandinista guerrilla factions under a single command and control as a condition for continued Cuban assistance. In retrospect, the Sandinista victory would have been impossible without Cuban aid and the Castro-sponsored unification measures.

As in the case of Grenada, Cuba helped the Soviets "discover" the vanguard-party-led revolutionary force in Nicaragua. And, likewise as in the Grenada case, the Soviets kept a low profile vis-à-vis the FSLN insurgents in the initial stage. On the diplomatic level, however, the Soviets recognized the FSLN regime precisely one day after the fall of Somoza. In the case of the FSLN (as opposed to the NJM in Grenada) Moscow was confident of dealing with a relatively small, elitist "known quantity" that had come to power on the wings of a legitimate popular revolution.

In both Nicaragua and Grenada, the Soviets were more cautious than in Angola and Ethiopia. They committed themselves only gradually, pending additional, conclusive evidence about the stability of the leadership, the consistency and durability of their professed "socialist orientation," and the level of American response their contemplated actions might elicit. After a probation period of one year (which was shorter than in Grenada), the Soviets decided to establish a broad framework for party-to-party relations, significant military assistance, and some economic aid to the Sandinistas. As envisioned by the Soviets, the long-term role of the FSLN was that of a revolutionary bridge to leftist forces in Central America and the Spanish-speaking Caribbean. As the Grenada Documents illustrate, the necessary contacts for doing this work were already established in a secret regional caucus of Caribbean Basin leftist parties, in which both the FSLN and NJM participated.

As in Grenada, the Cubans, with Soviet backing, were engaged in assisting two general military tasks: building a large armed force sufficient to deter any U.S. intervention in Nicaragua, and helping with construction projects having immediate or potential military and intelligence applications beyond Nicaragua. As in Angola, Ethiopia, and Grenada, the Cuban advisory role in Nicaragua has been much stronger than the Soviet. In this context, it is thus significant that between 1983 and 1986, the group of Cuban military advisors in Nicaragua was headed by the Cuban Deputy Minister of Defense General Arnaldo Ochoa, who played a prominent role in the Cuban military operations of the 1970s in Africa. Nicaragua's military build-up during this time and thereafter considerably altered the immediate Central American military equation, with the Nicaraguan armed forces becoming the dominant factor in the regional balance of forces.

In Nicaragua the Cubans have perpetuated the pattern of brokerage/advocacy first established on behalf of Angola and Grenada. As skilled lobbyists by now, their intercessions have helped to insure a continuation of the Soviet commitment to Nicaragua. Although we do not have the parallel "Nicaragua Documents" to demonstrate this, the hints of Cuban leaders suggest that they have consistently advocated and lobbied for appropriate economic and military aid from the U.S.S.R. and other CMEA nations to what they perceive as "embattled" Nicaragua. In response, Moscow has made a guarded commitment to Nicaragua, as it did to Cuba almost 30 years ago. As the outcome in Grenada and various Soviet signals between 1984 and 1988 have begun to suggest, however, the FSLN cannot count on anything more than materiel aid and political and economic support from the U.S.S.R. in the event of a direct confrontation with the United States.

Within the complex Soviet alliance phenomenon, it is clear that the U.S.S.R. does not actually direct the foreign policies of allied or friendly nations. In some instances, the contrary might appear to be true, with the Soviet Union acting as a proxy for quasi-independent Cuba both in Africa (Angola) and in the Caribbean Basin (Nicaragua and Grenada). Soviet policy decisions regarding revolutionary regimes in Africa and Central America reflect, at least marginally, Cuba's conviction about the necessity of actively supporting these regimes, particularly since these policies became possible only because of Cuban willingness to provide forces and/ or large contingents of military and civilian advisors. As the actor having the greatest interest in, and knowledge of, the Caribbean Basin region, Cuba surely "discovered" the revolutionary opportunities in both Nicaragua and Grenada. And it could be argued that Cuba drew the Soviet Union into the region, much as Vietnam helped to encourage deeper Soviet involvement in Southeast Asia.

At the same time, the Soviet leadership determines the limits of Cuban options in the Third World. Although Cuba could refuse to become involved in a large-scale military operation with the U.S.S.R. (as in the war in Eritrea in 1978), it could not initiate a substantial military operation (as in Angola or Ethiopia) without Soviet approval. In addition, Cuba is highly vulnerable to Soviet politicoeconomic coercion. It should be recalled that Soviet leaders have used this tool to their advantage in the late 1960s when they slowed down the supply of oil and arms to Cuba in order to encourage Castro to appreciate the subtleties of Soviet "antiimperialist" strategy. The Soviets are likely to use this leverage again should the need arise.

The tactics of junior Soviet allies such as Cuba may be formulated independently, but they must win the approval of the Soviets who provide the needed military and economic assistance. In spite of occasional Soviet/ Cuban tactical disagreements—such as those witnessed in Angola in 1977 and Grenada in October 1983—the division of labor between the Soviet Union and its allies ultimately favors Soviet global interests. Thus, the Soviets exercise leverage, if not control, over the key decisions of Cuba and other allies. Soviet preponderance, however, does not preclude autonomous Cuban or Vietnamese ventures in strategic areas of the Third World from which the Soviets may benefit and gain advantage with little risk, as they cannot be held responsible for such operations if they fail.

Gorbachev and the Soviet Union Alliance

Gorbachev's structural reforms and openness at home and "new thinking" in foreign affairs, if allowed to flourish, can have a serious impact on the state of the Soviet/Cuban alliance. The structural reforms (perestroika), in particular, with their emphasis on radical economic change and decentralization as well as incorporation of market incentives, run contrary to Castro's emphasis on implacable moral incentives and his erratic, dictatorial management of the Cuban economy. Furthermore, Castro is apprehensive that the "opening up" of Soviet society can have undesirable consequences for the closed and tightly controlled Leninist societies that have developed in countries like Cuba. In foreign affairs, the new Soviet thinking *(novoe myshlenie)*, particularly as it affects U.S./Soviet diplomacy, is perceived as tactically useful, but in substance it suggests the potential for the Soviet sacrifice of Cuban interests on the altar of arms control.

Perestroika in the Economy

Castro's erratic, impulsive management of the economy and his emphasis on ideologically-based socialist ethics to motivate the worker have helped to build an economy that cannot be easily reformed along the more practical principles of *perestroika*. Furthermore, Castro does not have much penchant for toiling at such domestic issues as economic reform. Rather, it is more interesting and exciting for him to play the role of powerful political and military broker between the U.S.S.R. and aspiring Third World revolutionaries than to tackle the bold yet time-consuming and very risky business of radically restructuring the domestic economy. Conducting international relations is Castro's forte and it is difficult to teach an old Leninist "new tricks." But even if Castro had dedicated years of effort to running a viable economy, he would not relish the prospect of resolving an economic crisis of the disastrous proportions now existing in Cuba, and less so through the radical innovations being advocated by Gorbachev.

If Castro could serve a little apprenticeship in South Florida, where Cuban exiles function as both the vanguard of the great Third World immigration northward as well as the leading force in an impressive economic boom, he might find remedies for the ills afflicting his own political and economic vanguard. Rumor has it that he is somewhat mystified by the growing economic success of the Cubans just across the Florida Straits—a success that is rather dramatic against the backdrop of a Cuban national economy that has continued to stagnate since the Mariel boat lift of 1980, and now appears to be entering a critical stage.

In spite of some undeniable social achievements, persistent structural problems in the Cuban economy are now compounded by sharply reduced imports and very high unemployment. These indicators are reflected in the 1986–1990 Five-Year Plan—whose guidelines were revised when it became clear that the original goals could not be met. The economic crisis is further aggravated by the recently publicized personal corruption of a number of Cuban officials and an increasing number of defections by senior Cuban officials like Brigadier General Rafael del Pino, deputy commander of the Cuban Air Force and a hero in the war against Batista. General del Pino has reported a growing popular as well as elitist perception that Angola is becoming Cuba's Vietnam and that the role of Cuban troops in Angola are to keep the unpopular MPLA ruling elite in power.

Castro's belief that the economic market mechanism is not a substitute for working class consciousness undercuts the very premises of *perestroika*. In place of *perestroika,* Castro, in the last several years, has introduced restrictive policies, including austerity, discipline and the rectification of errors, closing of the peasant markets, elimination of all small producers, and the demotion of those from his leadership who support Soviet kinds of economic reformism. Not surprisingly, Soviet officials are displeased with Castro's economic policies—they contradict the very essence of *perestroika*. Other Soviet allies have either inspired (as Hungary has) or fallen into line with the demands of *perestroika* (as have Bulgaria, Czechoslovakia, and even Vietnam).

Perestroika dictates that moral incentives alone cannot adequately stimulate economic growth; thus, Leninist regimes must use market incentives and economic decentralization to help restructure their economies and insure economic growth. Soviet and Cuban views have clashed in the open press, where Soviet writers have begun to criticize the poor state of the Cuban economy, the "rectification" campaign, and even the Cuban defense expenditures as a burden on the Cuban population. In response to one of the sharpest critiques, published in the Soviet journal *Novoe vremiia,* Cuban Vice President Carlos Rafael Rodriguez has accused the Soviets of not understanding the Cuban situation and presenting a "one-sided" negative view. Brigadier General Rafael del Pino, who visited the U.S.S.R. shortly before his defection to the United States in April 1987, reported that Gorbachev's *perestroika* is taboo in Cuba where it is sowing confusion among the elite. Thus, the Cuban leadership censors Cuban press references to *perestroika* and *glasnost* in the U.S.S.R. As del Pino explained:

> Gorbachev has started to undertake a process of adjustment, but in a direction totally contrary to that of Fidel Castro with his tropical socialism. Gorbachev has legalized a variety of highly important economic reforms which in Cuba are taboo. . . . What is being done in the Soviet Union right now is not understood. There is great confusion among . . . our students there. They see the Soviet government, after seventy years of socialism, reverse itself and adopt a variety of reforms . . . in contrast to what is happening in Cuba. . . . And finally and forcefully, in a speech given in July 1988, Castro himself publicly rejected the applicability of *perestroika* to conditions within Cuba.

Glasnost in Politics and Society

Equally discordant to Castro's ears is the concept of *glasnost*. Everything that is known about him, in fact, suggests a consistent opposition to the flourishing of more open forms of communism.

Castro grudgingly approved the Soviet invasion of Czechoslovakia as a necessary evil and later advocated an intervention against the Polish Solidarity movement on the grounds that it was necessary to save Leninism from "subversive imperialist activities." Traditionally, Castro has always had better relations with the pro-Soviet regimes—Bulgaria, post-Dubcek Czechoslovakia, and East Germany which, as noted, Castro admires most of all—rather than with the independent China and Yugoslavia, liberal Hungary, unstable Poland, or maverick Rumania. No doubt, some aspects of *glasnost* must be distasteful reminders of the heresies of Dubcek's Prague Spring and the Solidarity of Polish workers. The fact that the Cuban people are anxiously following Gorbachev's reforms—witnessed by an increased sale of Soviet publications in Cuba—is a warning that the spirit of *glasnost* can swiftly traverse the Atlantic.

But information also flows in the opposite direction, and Castro must be furious that *glasnost* makes it possible for the Soviet press to report on the poor condition of the Cuban economy. However, an even more alarming prospect for Castro—who witnessed the historic openings in Prague in 1968–69 and in Warsaw in 1980–81—must be the potential impact of *perestroika* and *glasnost* on the cohesion of the Soviet Union and the Soviet alliance in Eastern Europe. The demonstrations in Armenia and the unrest in Estonia and Hungary in the spring of 1988 are indicators that the Soviet reformation could destabilize the commonwealth and thereby impact on Soviet economic and political commitments to Cuba and other revolutionary dependencies.

"Novoe Myshlenie" and Soviet Foreign Policy Commitments

Gorbachev's new approach toward international relations encompasses some bold diplomatic initiatives, such as nuclear arms control with the United States and the resolution of (non-nuclear) armed struggle in critical Third World regions. These initiatives supplement, but do not replace, traditional Leninist foreign policy and tactics. By promoting new thinking about regional conflicts (national reconciliation through negotiation among warring parties in Nicaragua, Afghanistan, Angola, and Cambodia), the Soviet leadership has not discarded traditionally Leninist tactics, such as counterinsurgency operations against anti-Leninist guerrillas that have sprung up in these countries. By supplementing military offensives and counteroffensives with bold diplomatic onslaughts, Gorbachev hopes to achieve objectives which thus far have been elusive on the battlefield. (There is nothing novel about such Soviet tactical thinking.)

Such diplomacy is also motivated, however, by the need to reduce the economic aid and political costs of running the Soviet empire. As reported by former Cuban Vice Minister Manuel Sanchez Perez, Cuban officials in Havana interpreted Gorbachev's rise to power between 1983 and 1985 as signaling new obstacles for Castro in his dealings with the Soviets—in the future he may not be as successful in lobbying for Soviet economic and military aid either for Cuba or for other Third World revolutionary regimes. The Brezhnev era of selective, yet vigorous, foreign policy activism and new commitments to revolutionary forces in the Third World appears to have been replaced; instead, the Gorbachev era is likely to involve a concentration of Soviet efforts on the consolidation of existing Leninist regimes and the reduction of existing commitments—and certainly not the taking on of new commitments.

Castro is rumored to be skeptical about Gorbachev's new thinking— above all his commitment to revolutionary regimes such as Angola and Nicaragua—and fearful that superpower negotiations about the fate of these countries may exclude him. Whereas he believes that the U.S.S.R., as Cuba, should be willing to sacrifice the needs of its people in order to meet "the internationalist duty," the pragmatic Gorbachev is determined to compromise, at least for the moment, and reduce the Soviet commitment to a manageable level.

Castro, nonetheless, is determined to preserve Cuba's position as a privileged Soviet ally. He may ultimately be successful, although he will certainly encounter difficulties in terms of economic aid. In this regard, the Soviets have already taken some initial steps to reduce the cost of their economic support of Cuba. Gorbachev is said to have told Castro that Moscow cannot continue to increase indefinitely its current level of economic aid to Cuba, and thus one can expect to see a reduction in Soviet subsidies in the coming years.

These reductions clearly reflect a perceived need to cut expenditures throughout the Soviet empire, but they probably also intend to relay a specific message to Castro—namely, there are limits to Cuba's autonomy in domestic affairs, especially if the domestic course contradicts *perestroika*. Gorbachev probably believes that *perestroika,* if implemented in Cuba, will make the country economically more self-sufficient and less of a burden to the U.S.S.R. In 1968, the Soviet "oil stick" was used to exert leverage on Cuba, at that time an unruly junior partner; the result was oil rationing and an overall economic slowdown in Cuba. In the 1970s, when Cuba became a more cooperative ally, the Soviets made the oil more available on better terms and on schedule. In terms of being in the Soviet favor, Castro was at his pinnacle under the Khrushchev and Brezhnev leadership. At present, with Gorbachev at the helm, his position appears shakier. (Castro got a much cooler reception on his recent, much-postponed visit to Moscow in 1986 than on previous visits. Likewise, some foreign visitors to Cuba, such as Argentine journalist Jacobo Timerman, report that the Cuban leaders lack enthusiasm for Gorbachev because he has never experienced combat, and they tend to ridicule his reforms.) Still a privileged ally, whose revolutionary courage and enthusiasm are much admired, Castro has, nonetheless, annoyed the Soviet leaders. Their reaction is similar to that of a Soviet researcher who complained to this author about Castro's presumption of knowing "everything better." On the other hand, Vietnam, which has embraced elements of *perestroika,* has received substantial increases in Soviet economic assistance in the last few years.

Castro now is probably more concerned than ever about the degree of the Soviet commitment to Cuba, which appears rather nebulous in light of the Soviet inaction in the defense of Grenada in October 1983 and the well-publicized "political" (not military) commitment to Nicaragua. Apparently, Soviet leaders are still unwilling to intervene militarily on behalf of Leninist regimes flaunting their flags in the American backyard, particularly when Washington *is* willing to intervene on behalf of its perceived self-interest. The greatest risk the Soviets see in their relationship with Cuba remains a possible confrontation with the United States. As we saw, the Soviets have tried to reduce that risk by avoiding a contractual military alliance with Cuba and by repeatedly refusing to give their support during confrontations with the United States (in 1961, 1962, and 1983). Not surprisingly, Castro tried to elicit and even guarantee against a Soviet backing-off during various U.S./Cuban confrontations. During the 1962 missile crisis, for example, the Cubans were said to have attacked a Soviet anti-aircraft missile site. More recently, as reported by Brigadier General del Pino, the Cuban Air Force was practicing retaliatory strikes on the U.S. Air Force base at Homestead, south of Miami, Florida, to be implemented if ever the United States would launch a strike against Cuba. Unsure of Soviet support in the event of a U.S. intervention, the Cubans felt this capability would give them the means to escalate the conflict and thereby force the Soviet hand.

It is unlikely that Gorbachev will turn his back on Cuba. Moscow has made enormous ideological, political, security, and economic investments in Cuba. In addition, Cuba remains essential to Soviet strategies in Africa and Central America. The ties are equally strong at the Cuban end. Soviet strategic, economic, and political support are essential to Cuba, and Cuba is not only too dependent on the U.S.S.R., but also too committed to revolutionary change to try to alter the relationship. In contrast, while the Soviets are committed to supporting Cuba's Leninist regime and institutions, they are not committed to perpetuating Castro's rule. Assuming Gorbachev remains in power, there exist several bones of contention between the two men, although both leaders will try to avoid an open rift. A potential conflict could arise, however, as Castro's succession draws near. In this context, the series of past successions in Eastern Europe have illustrated that the Soviet commitment to Leninist regimes and institutions tends to be much more enduring than to Leninist leaders. Thus, the Soviets can be expected to try to preserve and strengthen their alliance with Cuba—but not necessarily and unconditionally with Fidel Castro.

Lessons for the U.S. Policymaking Community

As the past seven U.S. administrations have had to confront the Cuban issue, future administrations must likewise have to confront the volatile issue of Cuba under Castro. In this context, the key to a sound U.S. policy on Cuba will be an understanding of the unique, complex role that Cuba plays within the Soviet alliance system. As this preceding discussion has illustrated, Cuba is neither an unrestrained, independent actor—nor a completely subservient Soviet surrogate. It is a privileged junior ally whose degree of foreign policy autonomy differs from issue to issue.

Cuba's alliance with the Soviet Union threatens U.S. national security in two manners. One potential threat stems from Cuba's position as a Western Hemisphere outpost of Soviet military power. A less direct, but more immediate danger comes from the continuous support that Cuba and the U.S.S.R. give to various vanguard-party movements and regimes— Leninist hybrids like the FSLN in Nicaragua and the MPLA in Angola— that are not only anti-U.S. and antidemocratic but strategically allied with the U.S.S.R. as well. The mushrooming of these regimes in the last two decades has continuously challenged the broadly defined U.S. security interest in maintaining a just and stable world order.

In dealing with Cuba, U.S. policymakers should keep in mind several guiding principles. The nature of the issues (Soviet/Cuban support for revolutionaries abroad, actions that threaten U.S. physical security, or other actions) should determine whether U.S. policymaking is directed primarily toward Havana or primarily toward Moscow, or, in degrees, toward both. U.S. decisionmakers should recognize and learn from the mistakes of their predecessors—above all, Kennedy's understanding with Khrushchev in 1962. If Soviet-backed Cuban interventionism continues, this informal agreement should be revoked. In general, U.S. policies should accentuate the risks of, and thereby help to deter, Soviet and Cuban activism in the Third World. To succeed, there must be policy continuity from administration to administration. Such a posture naturally presupposes a degree of bipartisanship on foreign policy. New U.S. policy initiatives vis-à-vis Cuba should be undertaken at times when the United States is perceived as having strong bargaining leverage.

On a more specific level, in addressing Cuban interventionism in Angola, U.S. policymakers should heed the lesson of Afghanistan where a political settlement became acceptable to the Soviets only after the cumulative political, economic, and security costs of the war became unacceptable; thus, costs became prerequisites to a political settlement. U.S./Cuban negotiations—like U.S./Soviet negotiations on Afghanistan, which were once considered illusory—need not be excluded as a policy option, as long as they take place within acceptable parameters (and not, for example, during times when the United States is perceived as having weak bargaining leverage or being constrained by the politics of presidential campaigning). In general, U.S. policy toward Cuba should be designed to actively contain Cuba, to promote *glasnost* (openness) through Radio and TV Martí, and to prepare to meet the challenges and opportunities of the coming Cuban succession.

The Issues Should Determine U.S. Policy Direction

When there is a direct threat to U.S. security—for example, deployment of Soviet offensive weapons in Cuba or Nicaragua—the United States must deal primarily with the Soviet Union. Such were the circumstances during the missile crisis of 1962; a potential danger of this kind also provoked the Cienfuegos "mini-crisis" of 1970. The United States has also had to deal with Cuba as broker and joint Soviet interventionist in Africa, the Middle East, Latin America, and the Caribbean. This threat to more broadly defined U.S. security interests requires that the United States adopt a flexible strategy to deal with both actors (the Soviet Union and Cuba)— according to the role of each. Obviously, on issues such as Cuban immigration the United States must deal primarily with Cuba, keeping in mind, however, that such bilateral issues also impact upon the Soviet/Cuban alliance.

Drawing Lessons from Past Mistakes

In dealing with the Soviet/Cuban alliance, the United States should be careful not to repeat the errors of the past. The informal understanding between Kennedy and Khrushchev in 1962, reaffirmed by Nixon and Brezhnev in 1970, has conditioned Soviet/Cuban relations ever since. The understanding also provided Castro with the rationale for blocking an American intervention in Cuba—but did not block Cuba from becoming a revolutionary interventionist and a broker between the Soviets and other aspiring Leninist regimes. Looking back to 1962, long-term U.S. interests probably would have been better served either by a military intervention in Cuba or, better yet, an acceptance of the Brazilian proposal assuring U.S. nonintervention in exchange for a complete removal of the Soviet and U.S. military presences and, just as crucial, de facto Cuban nonalignment. Such an understanding, if it had been accepted by Fidel Castro, could have made Cuba's interventionist role in the Third World more difficult, if not impossible.

If Cuba continues to act as a junior interventionist Soviet ally, deploying combat troops in yet other Third World locales, U.S. administrations should be prepared to revoke the 1962 Kennedy/Khrushchev understanding about U.S. nonintervention in Cuba. The historical evidence suggests that both the Soviets and the Cubans would seriously heed a reassessment of this type, especially if made explicit. Such was the case in 1981 when Secretary of State Alexander Haig warned that the United States would not tolerate Cuban support for the guerrillas in El Salvador. Haig was explicit, noting that the United States was reviewing the 1962 Kennedy/ Khrushchev agreement and, if necessary, would go to the source of the problem (meaning Cuba), using a naval blockade or other military measures if Cuban military aid continued, through Nicaragua, to the Salvadoran guerrillas. In response, the Cubans and Nicaraguans scaled down considerably their commitment to revolutionary allies in El Salvador. Furthermore, the Cubans launched a large mobilization of their national defenses—which appeared to have some serious effects on the Cuban economy and to have significantly increased the overall cost of the Soviet military and economic commitment to Cuba.

Accentuating Perceived Risks

Moscow and Havana continuously calculate the risks involved in joint ventures. When the risks have seemed minimal—because of U.S. inaction, retreat, or vacillation—Soviet/Cuban assertiveness in response to Third World opportunities has risen. This was convincingly demonstrated in 1975–79, in the wake of the Vietnam debacle. Twice during this period Republican and Democratic administrations alike tried to break the bilateral deadlock and improve relations with Cuba—and twice these diplomatic initiatives were followed by Soviet/Cuban interventions in Africa.

The first attempted normalization occurred despite the escalation of Soviet arms shipments and Cuba's infiltration of military advisors into Angola in 1975. Assuming therefore that the United States was acting from a position of weakness, the Soviets and Cubans accelerated their activism on behalf of the Angolan MPLA in the spring and summer of that year. It is evident that the U.S. government made two general mistakes during the Angolan crisis. First, in 1975 the Ford administration intelligence experts and policymakers both misperceived and underestimated the Cuban and Soviet commitment to an MPLA victory in Angola. As a result, Washington did not react to the initial build-up of the Soviet/Cuban military presence, which was accomplished gradually, in increments—as if to test the limits of U.S. tolerance. Second, the Ford administration, which was interested in normalizing relations with Cuba, decided to signal at this very inopportune time (Spring 1975) that it was considering lifting the sanctions against Cuba and suspending the reconnaissance flights over the island.

Instead of accentuating the perceived risks of the creeping escalation in Angola, the Ford administration extended still other olive branches. This included limiting support provided to the anti-MPLA (anti-Leninist) rebels like Jonas Savimbi's UNITA, and forswearing any plan to become directly involved on their behalf in the Angolan conflict. However, at a later stage of the crisis (in the fall of 1986), the United States gave public warning that Soviet activism in Angola would threaten U.S./Soviet relations. Momentarily reevaluating their policies in light of U.S. warnings, the Soviets briefly halted the deployment of Cuban troops. The Tunney Amendment, however, passed by the Senate on December 19, cut off covert aid to the anti-Leninist forces and presumably convinced the Soviet leaders that domestic constraints on U.S. policymakers were too strong to allow them any real options. In compounding previous mistakes of the executive branch, the U.S. Congress gave a green light to the Soviets and Cubans to escalate the conflict in Angola. This enabled the MPLA to score a decisive victory in the Spring of 1976.

Policy Continuity

Future U.S. administrations should likewise consider new diplomatic initiatives vis-à-vis Cuba—but only after careful consideration and after making clear to Havana that they will strive foremost for policy continuity. The need for policy consistency is suggested by the unfortunate outcome of the Carter administration policies, which inadvertently helped to compel, rather than impede, the 1977–78 Soviet/Cuban intervention in Ethiopia. As in the intervention in Angola in 1976, the Ethiopian intervention followed a U.S. initiative toward normalizing U.S./Cuban relations. The first attempted normalization in Spring 1975—interrupted by the Ford administration because of the Soviet/Cuban intervention in Angola—was resumed with vigor by President Carter after January 1977. Seemingly oblivious to Castro's burlesque of President Ford's efforts, President

Carter lifted the ban on U.S. tourism to Cuba, halted intelligence over-flights of the island, and agreed to an exchange of diplomatic interest sections between the two nations. These overtures paralleled the U.S./Soviet arms control negotiations, culminating in the signing of the SALT II agreement by President Carter and Leonid Brezhnev in the Summer of 1979.

The deleterious effects of incontinuity in U.S. policy vis-à-vis Cuba cannot be overly stressed. In 1976, Henry Kissinger—representing the Ford administration—had warned that the United States would not tolerate a second Cuban intervention in Africa (Kissinger was referring to and anticipating an intervention in Namibia, Angola's southern neighbor), and in the case of an intervention, would abrogate the 1962 Khrushchev/Kennedy understanding and consider direct military action. However, only a year later in 1977, the conciliatory stance of the newly-installed Carter administration was interpreted by the Cubans and the Soviets as a break with the original Kissinger line. It was further interpreted as a signal that they could proceed with the interventionist policy begun two years before in Angola.

Thus, the Soviet/Cuban intervention in Ethiopia not only reversed the process of U.S./Cuban normalization but almost led to a breaking off of the SALT negotiating process. One year later, in December 1979, the Soviet invasion of Afghanistan delivered the coup de grace to SALT II, which the U.S. Senate simply refused to ratify.

Bipartisan Approach and a Strong Bargaining Position

The Soviets and Cubans can demonstrate remarkable restraint in crisis management when the U.S. government enacts a bipartisan policy and approaches a crisis (alone or with its allies) from a perceived position of strength that communicates to the Soviets a willingness to escalate a crisis—militarily, if necessary. Such was the case during the missile crisis of 1962, during the Grenada crisis of 1983, and even during the less well-known 1978 Shaba province crisis (Shaba II) in Zaire. With regard to the latter, instead of helping the Congolese National Liberation Front (a Leninist-oriented MPLA ally) to escalate the invasion of Shaba, the Soviets and Cubans reacted with restraint in light of the U.S. support of the French and Belgian counter-intervention.

In spite of campaign rhetoric, some bipartisanship and continuity of policy vis-à-vis Cuba were present during the transition from the Carter to the Reagan administration. In 1979, President Carter made serious efforts to curb Soviet-backed Cuban interventionism in the Third World by reinstating an intensive intelligence surveillance of Cuba and by establishing a permanent Caribbean Contingency Joint Task Force (CCJTF) with headquarters in Key West, Florida. And in 1980, before leaving office, Carter authorized U.S. military assistance to the legitimate government of El Salvador in its fight against the Soviet- and Cuban-supported FMLN guerrillas.

In taking office in 1981, President Reagan continued and intensified the Carter administration's efforts to curb the activities of Leninist forces in Central America and the Caribbean Basin. This trend reached a high point in October 1983 as the United States and the OECS intervened in Grenada. The intervention (which had the bipartisan endorsement of Walter Mondale, the Democratic presidential candidate in 1984) was seen as a sign that the United States might be recovering from the "Vietnam syndrome." For Castro, moreover, it was a reminder, like the Cuban missile crisis 20 years earlier, of the fragility and ambiguity of the Soviet commitment to revolutionary regimes in the Caribbean Basin.

After the events in Grenada, the Soviets and Cubans ceased to theorize optimistically about long-term positive changes favoring the Soviets in the worldwide correlation of forces. At that moment, the United States was perceived as having regained the will to use force in furthering its interests in Third World areas. With this bargaining leverage, it is possible that Washington could have engaged in far-reaching negotiations with Havana and Moscow at that time. However, in the aftermath, the U.S. inability to cope with the consolidation of the Nicaraguan revolution, compounded by the subsequent Iran/Contra affair, began to erode the perception that a new moment was generated by Operation "Urgent Fury" (code name for the Grenada operation).

The Afghanistan Lesson: Make Protracted Soviet Military Engagements Prohibitively Costly

Simply stated, as political and economic costs of Soviet and Cuba involvement in Third World conflicts become unacceptable, negotiated settlements become possible. At the time of this writing, this appears to be the case in Afghanistan. Overall, the combined U.S. pressures, especially military and economic aid to the anti-Leninist insurgencies—initiated by President Carter in Afghanistan and carried on by President Reagan not only in that country but also in Angola, Nicaragua, and, with China, in Cambodia—significantly increased the costs of Soviet, Cuban, and Vietnamese activism between 1981 and 1988, and contributed very directly to Gorbachev's new way of thinking about the resolution of various regional conflicts. The U.S. Senate's decision to repeal the Clark Amendment in 1985—thereby preparing the way for the government to renew military support for anti-MPLA UNITA forces in Angola—and the decision to dramatically upgrade support for the mujahedeen in Afghanistan in 1986 were crucial. The sophisticated Stinger missiles that began to arrive thereafter were instrumental in changing the course of both wars. The costs of the war in Angola are reflected by the growing Cuban resentment over the dead, wounded, and missing in action—which have been estimated at 10,000, according to Cuban defector Brigadier General del Pino.

Acceptable Parameters for U.S./Cuban Negotiations

In terms of negotiations with Cuba, the lessons for future U.S. administrations are evident from the Ford and Carter experiences. As long as the large Cuban military presence in Angola and Ethiopia continues, the United States should not reinstate the process of normalization. Instead, the U.S. should continue with various pressures and increase the costs of the Cuban involvement, much as U.S. pressure has increased Soviet costs in the war in Afghanistan. Thus, for example, the U.S. government should pressure for a rapid Cuban withdrawal from Angola. The latter is not too much to expect and the time is indeed propitious, particularly if the Soviet withdrawal from Afghanistan proceeds as anticipated.

Although previous, limited agreements with the Castro regime did not advance the U.S. national interest, future American administrations should nonetheless still be open to future negotiations if the circumstances are right. In the past, some of the partial agreements concluded unilaterally with Castro appeared to be primarily escape valves for internal Cuban pressures. The chaotic Mariel boat lift of 1980, which brought 125,000 Cubans to Florida's shores, served two and perhaps three purposes. First, it humiliated the United States; but it also helped to diffuse discontent in Cuba, transferring some of it to Florida. Similarly, the renewal of the immigration agreement with Cuba in the fall of 1987, which normalized emigration from Cuba by allowing more than 20,000 Cubans to enter the United States every year, was aimed at releasing internal pressure. It also preempted the U.S. drive for a resolution condemning Cuba before the U.N. Human Rights Commission in Geneva in March of 1988. The same accord provided for Cuba to take back about 2,500 Mariel refugees (criminals and the mentally ill). One can only speculate whether the cunning Castro anticipated the negative impact of this agreement in the United States, namely, the prison riots.

The timing—the spring of 1988—of the most recent U.S. initiatives (the decision, for example, to allow two Cuban nuclear experts to tour a U.S. nuclear power plant) may suggest that the Reagan administration is again striving to improve relations with Cuba. However, this initiative, like some limited agreements with Cuba in the past, has not been well integrated, as it should be, with an overall U.S. strategy for lessening Soviet/Cuban activism in the Third World.

The Perils of Negotiating with Cuba during Presidential Election Year Transitions

A sense of Cuban foreign policy presupposes an understanding of Cuba's role in the Soviet alliance system, and, no less important, an understanding of the personality and motives of Fidel Castro, for now the prime mover of Cuban politics. Castro is a cunning and brilliant politician who has always known how to manipulate the crowds in Cuba, the U.S. media, and even some prominent U.S. personalities—the latest being John O'Connor, Archbishop of New York. Castro has likewise attempted to manipulate the U.S. presidential process. Cognizant of the political weight of public opinion in the United States, Castro, like his colleagues in Vietnam and now in Nicaragua, has developed an ambitious program for receiving foreign visitors from the United States.

At the present time, it appears that he is trying to influence the U.S. electoral process in much the same manner as in 1980 when Castro released Americans who had been serving prison terms in Cuban jails, returned to the U.S. the Cuban refugees who had hijacked U.S. jets to Cuba, and ended the Mariel boat lift of Cuban refugees. Perhaps he sought to placate President Carter, whom he considered less dangerous than the Republican presidential hopeful Ronald Reagan. Furthermore, one cannot exclude the possibility that Castro will, in future years, once again attempt to make his own imprint on the U.S. presidential race. Judging by past and present initiatives, the timing of this new trend alone suggests that Castro still believes that the dynamics of U.S. domestic politics tend to overwhelm U.S. foreign policymaking during election years.

Exploiting Cuba's Vulnerabilities (Promoting ''Glasnost,'' Preparing for Succession)

Cuban behavior during the Ford and Carter administrations, the pathological anti-Americanism of Castro, and his refusal to allow even a modicum of *perestroika* and *glasnost* are all good indications that there will be no meaningful rapprochement of Cuba with the United States as long as Castro remains in power. In this climate, the current efforts of the Reagan administration to ease tensions with Cuba are, at best, not well-timed. As suggested earlier, a better schedule for negotiations with both Cuba and the U.S.S.R. would have been right after the Grenada intervention, in the 1983–84 period, perceived as a time of the resuscitation of American national resolve. At the present time Castro may suspect that any U.S. effort to improve bilateral relations is motivated by the weakness of the Reagan administration following the Iran/Contra scandal and by the politics of the presidential election.

It is unlikely that Castro will rethink his overall political strategy, either at home or abroad. Although the Soviets balk at Castro's cult of personality and his rejection of *perestroika* and *glasnost,* the alliance is stronger than ever. Furthermore, Castro has no intention of trading in the alliance with the Soviet Union for a good-neighbor relationship with the United States. Under Gorbachev, he will surely have a much more difficult time maintaining Cuba's status as a privileged ally, but the Soviet payoffs so far have been very good, and the prospects for a comparable U.S. "carrot" are too uncertain. The United States can never outperform the Soviets as a major supplier of economic aid, military clout, and political prestige to Cuba.

Future U.S. administrations should likewise not rush into a process of normalization with a Cuban regime that rejects even modest reform at home, and is not prepared to seriously compromise abroad. Instead, the United States should continue to explore the internal contradictions of the Cuban regime and its economic, political, and psychological vulnerabilities. In this regard, the United States Information Agency's (USIA) Radio Martí program and the evolving plan for a TV Martí are powerful instruments capable of breaking Castro's monopoly of the news. This is particularly the case with regard to such taboo subjects as the cost of the Cuban intervention in Angola—where the extent of Cuban casualties is unknown even to most of Castro's supporters. (A survey by Radio Martí indicates that most of the Cuban populace listen to its programs.)

Ultimately, however, the United States will perhaps have to wait for Castro's succession to reach any meaningful rapprochement with Cuba. Judging from the various successions in other Leninist regimes—primarily in Eastern Europe—the eventual Cuban succession might uncover some unexpected opportunities for the United States. Surely there is no one in the Cuban leadership who can replace Fidel Castro in his unique role of Third World broker. In this context, if Raul Castro takes the place of his brother, it is more than likely that Cuba will become just another Soviet proxy. Thus, future U.S. administrations should attempt to anticipate the changes in Cuba—and be ready to respond. In the interim, Washington should capitalize as much as possible on the present opportunities provided by the Gorbachev-inspired reforms in the Soviet Union and other communist countries, and Gorbachev's stated commitment to diplomacy in resolving regional conflicts.

Sources

This essay is based upon my own research and writing on the Soviet and Cuban alliance in the Third World during the last fifteen years. Although not footnoted, every opinion advanced here is supported by careful analysis of Soviet, Cuban, East European, and Third World sources, including the invaluable "Grenada Documents" and documents from Central America, Namibia, and Mozambique. I have also utilized material from extensive personal interviews with former high officials of the Cuban government such as José Luis Llorio-Menendez, and from lengthy published accounts of interviews with Brigadier General Rafael del Pino and others. I have carried on extensive discussions, furthermore, with various former officials of the Nicaraguan government, including former head of the Nicaraguan National Bank Alfredo Cesar and my colleagues at the University of Miami, former member of the Sandinista revolutionary junta Arturo Cruz, Sr., and former FSLN ambassador to Ecuador, Alvaro Taboada. My lengthy discussions with numerous former members of the revolutionary government of Grenada and with present and former members of various revolutionary movements in Latin America, the Caribbean, Africa, and Asia have also been invaluable, as were informal discussions with various Soviet officials visiting the United States. The reader seeking detailed documentation should consult my numerous academic contributions on the Soviet/Cuban alliance.

Books
Jiri Valenta and Herbert Ellison (eds.), *Grenada and Soviet/Cuban Policy: Internal Crisis and U.S./OECS Intervention* (Boulder, Col.: Westview Press, 1986)
Jiri Valenta and Esperanza Duran (eds.), *Conflict in Nicaragua: National, Regional and International Dimensions* (Boston: Allen and Unwin, 1986)
Howard Wiarda and Mark Falcoff, with Ernest Evans and Jiri and Virginia Valenta, *The Communist Challenge in the Caribbean and Central America* (Washington, D.C.: American Enterprise Institute for Public Policy Research, 1987)

Articles
"Soviet/Cuban Intervention in Angola, 1975," *Studies in Comparative Communism,* Vol. XI, nos. 1 & 2 (Spring/Summer 1978), pp. 11–33.
"Soviet/Cuban Intervention in Ethiopia, 1978: Impact and Lessons," *Journal of International Affairs,* Vol. 34, no. 2 (Fall/Winter 1980/1981), pp. 369–94.
"Soviet/Cuban Intervention in Angola," *Proceedings,* U.S. Naval Institute (April 1980), pp. 51–57.
"Comment: The Soviet/Cuban Alliance in Africa and Future Prospects in the Third World," *Cuban Studies/Estudios Cubanos,* Vol. 10, no. 2 (July 1980), pp. 36–43.
"The USSR, Cuba and the Crisis in Central America," *Orbis,* Vol. 25, no. 3 (Fall 1981), pp. 715–46.
"Soviet Policy in Central America" (includes text of Valenta's testimony before

the Kissinger Bipartisan Commission on Central America), *Survey,* Vol. 27, nos. 118–19 (Autumn/Winter 1983), pp. 787–803.

"Leninism in Grenada," *Problems of Communism* (July–August 1984), pp. 1–23 (also printed in Spanish, *Problemas Internacionales*). With V. Valenta.

"Nicaragua: Soviet Pawn or Nonaligned Country?" *Journal of Inter-American Studies,* Vol. 27, no. 3 (Fall 1985), pp. 163–75.

"On Nicaragua" (an exchange of views between Lord Wayland Kennet, MP, Social Democratic Party, London, and Jiri and Virginia Valenta), *Problems of Communism,* (May–June 1986), pp. 90–92.

Book Chapters

"Soviet and Cuban Response to New Opportunities in Central America," in Richard Feinberg, ed., *The International Aspects of the Crisis in Central America* (New York: Holmes and Meier, 1982), pp. 127–59.

"Soviet/Cuban Intervention in Angola: Politics, Naval Power, Strategic Implications," in Steven Rosefielde, ed., *World Communism at the Crossroads: Military Ascendancy, Political Economy and Human Welfare* (Boston: Martinus Nijhoff, 1980), pp. 89–105.

"Soviet Decisionmaking on the Intervention in Angola," in David Albright, ed., *Communism in Africa* (Bloomington: Indiana University Press, 1980), pp. 93–117.

"Soviet Policy and the Crisis in the Caribbean," in H. M. Erisman and John Martz, eds., *Colossus Challenged: The Struggle for Caribbean Influence* (Boulder, Col.: Westview Press, 1983), pp. 47–82.

"The USSR and Cuba in Africa," in Carmelo Mesa-Lago, ed., *Cuba in Africa* (Pittsburgh, Pa.: University of Pittsburgh Press, 1982), pp. 141–48. (Also printed in Spanish, Ediciónes Tres Tiempos, Buenos Aires, Argentina, 1984.)

Conference Reports

Jiri Valenta and Esperanza Duran, *Conflict in Nicaragua: National, Regional, and International Dimensions* (Coral Gables, Fla.: Institute for Soviet and East European Studies, University of Miami, 1986).

Jiri Valenta and Herbert Ellison, *Soviet/Cuban Strategy in the Third World after Grenada: Toward Prevention of Future Grenadas* (Washington, D.C.: Kennan Institute for Advanced Russian Studies, Woodrow Wilson International Center for Scholars, 1985).

Newspaper Articles

"A debate on the U.S. and the 'Contras': Keep Pressing Managua," *New York Times,* 10 February 1985.

"Grenada: A Friend the Russians Couldn't Protect," *Boston Globe,* 14 November 1983.

"On the Falklands Crisis, Moscow and Havana," *New York Times,* 23 June 1982.

2

Cuba and the United States

Jaime Suchlicki

In the 1980s, Cuba remains a troublesome spot for U.S. interests. Castro's military involvement in Africa and elsewhere in the Third World, growing Soviet and Cuban military capabilities in the Caribbean, and instability in Central America—exacerbated by Cuba's support for guerrilla and terrorist groups—clearly undermine American foreign policy interests and goals. Other problems such as Castro's involvement in narcotics trafficking, the unpaid nationalized U.S. properties in Cuba, and the return of the undesirable Mariel refugees continue as important irritants in U.S./Cuban relations. Yet the Soviet/Cuban connection and Castro's insistence on promoting violent anti-American revolutions throughout the world remain as the most damaging and dangerous aspects of Cuba's foreign policy and the most threatening to the security of the United States.

The longstanding intimate relationship between Cuba and the Soviet Union remains as one of the cornerstones of Cuba's foreign policy. Yet divergent postures on recent international developments, as well as Cuba's unfulfilled expectations of increased Soviet aid have caused some friction. Concurrently, Cuba's leaders have adopted a dual attitude toward the United States, characterized by both hostility and overtures of rapprochement. In this context, Castro seems willing to offer minor concessions to the United States without renouncing his relationship with the Soviets, his commitment to revolutionary violence, or his insistence on playing a major role on the international stage.

The Historical Setting

Castro's rise to power in 1959 ushered in a period of hostility between Cuba and the United States. In the early months following the revolution,

41

Castro reasserted his independence from the United States, but maintained normal relations. During his visit to the United States in April 1959 he turned down offers of aid, but insisted that Cuba stood with the West in the Cold War. He also met with several U.S. government officials, including then Vice President Richard Nixon. Yet as time went on, Castro increased his inflammatory denunciations of the United States, accusing the northern neighbor of launching every exile raid perpetrated against his country, as well as blaming the United States for Cuba's economic and political ills.

Ideologically, Castro was far from being a Marxist; instead, he belonged to Cuba's vague populist political tradition. José Martí and Eduardo Chibas—the forerunners of this tradition—had called for an end to political corruption, the destruction of Cuba's dependence on monoculture and one foreign buyer, and the development of a unique and nationalistic identity. Although strongly influenced by Falangist and Fascist ideas while a high school student, and Marxist ideas while at the University of Havana, Castro did not embrace these ideologies in their totality. He was instead a product of the Martí–Chibas tradition, although he broke with it in several fundamental aspects. While Martí and Chibas had envisioned a framework of democratic reforms in a nation politically and economically independent from the United States, they both advocated friendly relations with the "northern colossus." Castro opposed such a vision; he was anti-American since his student days when he distributed anti-U.S. propaganda in Bogotá. As Castro and part of the Cuban revolutionary leadership perceived it, the possibility of a repetition of earlier U.S. interventionist policies in Cuba was a major deterrent to achieving profound socioeconomic changes on the island and to the consolidation of Castro's personal rule—and Castro was committed to both of these goals. Perhaps because of his anti-Americanism, and particularly because of his conviction that a major revolution with himself in absolute control could not be undertaken within Cuba's political framework or with a harmonious relationship with the United States, he broke with the Martí–Chibas tradition and opted for a totalitarian and anti-American revolution.

Initially, the United States followed a "wait and see" policy. The Eisenhower administration seemed to have been caught by surprise over events in Cuba, and failed to grasp the magnitude either of the changes transpiring or the nature of the leader sponsoring those changes. Differences arose between those who believed Castro was a Marxist—thus advocating a hard line toward Cuba—and those who counseled patience with the bearded leader.

Although tensions arose in connection with the public trials and execution of Batista supporters, serious differences grew after the promulgation of the 1959 Agrarian Reform Law. To no avail, the United States protested the expropriations initiated under the law. Agricultural expropriations were followed by further attacks on foreign investments, notably in the mining and petroleum industries. Further complicating relations between the two nations were arrests of U.S. citizens, Castro's refusal to meet with U.S. Ambassador Philip W. Bonsal in late 1959, and the sabotage and raids carried out by the Cuban exiles from U.S. territory.

Castro's militant Caribbean activities also fueled Washington's apprehensions. During the first year of the revolution, Cuban filibusters, joined by exiles from various Caribbean nations, launched a series of abortive expeditions in an attempt to raise the standard of revolt in several neighboring countries. Many of these exiles had contributed to Castro's victory and now saw an opportunity to develop an international movement to dislodge dictators from the region. However, Castro's relationship to these expeditions has never been clearly defined. On several occasions, Castro openly condemned some of the attempts and halted vessels loaded with weapons and men. But, although it appears likely that Castro was unconnected with these attempts, the fact remains that expeditions at this early period were launched from Cuba against Panama, the Dominican Republic, and Haiti.

Whether or not the Cuban regime supported these attempts, Fidel Castro, Che Guevara, and Raul Castro believed that the political, social, and economic conditions which had produced the Cuban revolution existed in other parts of Latin America. In this context, they believed revolutions would occur throughout the continent. From 1960 onward, Cuban agents and diplomatic representatives established contact with revolutionary groups in the region and began distributing propaganda and aid. In the interim, several Cuban diplomats were expelled for interfering in the internal affairs of these countries. As tensions mounted with the United States, Castro's assertion of the international character of his revolution increased, as did his involvement in promoting violence in Latin America. By July 1960, Castro boasted he would convert "the Cordillera of the Andes into the Sierra Maestra of Latin America," as money, propaganda, men, and weapons began to flow in increasing quantities from Havana to foment "anti-imperialist" revolutions.

The radicalization of the revolution and the deterioration of relations with the United States grew apace with Cuban/Soviet rapprochement. In February 1960, following the visit to Havana of Soviet Deputy Premier Anastas Mikoyan, Cuba signed a major trade agreement with the Soviet Union. The agreement provided for Cuba to receive Soviet oil in exchange for sugar, among other products. But in June, the United States and English-owned refineries in Cuba refused to process Soviet oil. In addition, the U.S. House of Representatives approved a bill granting presidential authority to cut foreign sugar quotas at his discretion. Castro retaliated, and on June 28 nationalized the oil companies. In July, the United States eliminated the remaining tonnage of that year's Cuban sugar quota. In the following months, Castro nationalized the remaining U.S. properties in addition to most major Cuban-owned businesses. In October, the United States announced an embargo on most exports to Cuba, and when Castro restricted the staff of the U.S. embassy to eleven persons, the United States severed diplomatic relations and withdrew its ambassador with the following statement: "There is a limit to what the U.S. in self-respect can endure. That limit has now been reached."[1]

By that point, the United States had embarked on a more aggressive policy toward the Castro regime: groups of Cuban exiles were being trained under the supervision of U.S. officials in Central American camps for an attack on Cuba. The internal situation on the island then seemed propitious for an attempt to overthrow the Cuban regime. Although Castro still counted on significant popular support, the amount of it had progressively decreased. At the same time, his 26th of July Movement was hopelessly split on the issue of communism. Likewise, a substantial urban guerrilla movement existed throughout the island, composed of former Castro allies, Batista supporters, Catholic groups, and other elements that had been affected by the revolution. Finally, significant unrest was evident within the armed forces.

The urban underground saw the landing of the U.S.-sponsored invasion force as the culminating event in a series of uprisings and acts of sabotage which they hoped would fragment Castro's army throughout the island and thus weaken the regime's hold over the people. This event was to coincide with Castro's assassination and a coordinated sabotage plan. In the weeks prior to the invasion, violence increased, bombs exploded, and shops were burned.

Yet the planners in exile were not counting on the forces inside Cuba. Anti-Castro elements within and outside of Cuba did not coordinate their activities. The latter group placed an unjustified faith in the invasion's success, and feared that the underground might have been infiltrated by the regime. Arms that were to be shipped to Cuba never arrived, and communications between the exiles and underground forces remained sporadic and confused. The underground was not alerted to the date of the invasion until April 17—the day of the landing—when it could only watch the Bay of Pigs disaster in confusion and frustration.

In retrospect, the whole affair was a tragedy of errors. Although the Cuban government was unaware of the date or exact place where exile forces would land, it was widely known, both in and outside of Cuba, that an invasion was in the offing. The weapons and ammunition that were to be used by the invading force were all placed in one ship, which was sunk the first day of the invasion. The site for the invasion was sparsely populated, surrounded by swamps, and offered little access to nearby mountains where guerrilla operations could be carried out if the invasion failed. The invading forces could, therefore, all but discount any help from the nearby population.

Some of the air raids by Cuban exiles that were intended to cripple Castro's air force were cancelled at the last minute by a confused and indecisive President, John F. Kennedy. Perhaps either trying to reassert his authority over the CIA-sponsored invasion, to stymie possible world reaction, or to appease the Soviets, Kennedy ceased further American involvement. In tandem, Castro's Sea Furys and T33s had the capability to shoot down the exiles' B26s and maintain control of the air. While the invasion was in progress, Khrushchev threatened Kennedy: "The government of the U.S. can still prevent the flames of war from spreading into a conflagration which it will be impossible to cope with. . . . The world political situation now is such that any so-called 'small war' can produce a chain reaction in all parts of the world."[2]

The failure of the invasion and the brutal repression that followed smashed the entire Cuban underground. On the first day of the invasion, the regime arrested thousands of real and suspected opponents; the resistance never recovered from the blow. With a strengthened and con-solidated regime, Castro emerged victorious and boasted of having de-feated a "Yankee-sponsored invasion." The disillusionment and frustra-tion caused by the Bay of Pigs fiasco among anti-Castro forces, both within and outside of Cuba, prevented the growth of significant organized oppo-sition. Meanwhile, American prestige in Latin America and throughout the world sank to a low point.

Following the Bay of Pigs debacle, the United States turned to other methods of dealing with Castro. It pursued a vigorous, although only partially successful, policy to isolate the Cuban regime and strangle it on an economic level. It pressured its allies throughout the world to reduce their commerce with Cuba. In the Organization of American States (OAS), the United States forced the suspension of Cuba by a slim majority in January 1962, and several countries broke diplomatic relations with the Castro regime at that time. In 1964, after Castro had increased Cuba's level of subversive activities in Latin America and had moved fully into the communist camp, the OAS voted to suspend trade and diplomatic relations with Cuba. Furthermore, all countries that had not already done so severed relations—except Mexico, which strongly supported the prin-ciple of self-determination and refused to bow to U.S. pressures.

As Cuban/U.S. relations deteriorated, closer ties with the Soviet Union developed. Initially, Moscow maintained a cautious stance toward Castro. In its view, the Cuban "petit bourgeois" leader seemed impotent to defy the "northern colossus," and the ability of an anti-American regime to survive so close to the U.S.' shores seemed remote, particularly in light of the 1954 Guatemalan experience. Furthermore, the Soviets were not greatly interested in distant, raw material-producing Latin America—an area which they considered to be the backyard of the United States. Likewise, Khrushchev's attempts at detente with the United States, and his desire to extract concessions from Washington over Berlin, were important considerations in limiting Soviet involvement in Cuba lest the latter provoke a strain in U.S./Soviet relations. Finally, the Soviets recognized that Castro's attempts to identify himself with the Soviet camp (such as his April 1, 1961 speech declaring the Cuban revolution to be socialist, or his December 1961 speech in which he declared himself a Marxist-Leninist) were designed to involve the Soviet Union in Cuba's defense against possible hostile actions by the United States.

In spite of these difficulties and apprehensions, over time, the Soviets gradually came to accept the bearded leader. The growing nationalism of Latin America and the enormous popularity of the Cuban revolution in the region were factors which limited the ability of the United States to implement hostile actions against Castro during the first two years of his regime, and encouraged the Soviets' hopes for the survival of the revolution. Castro's radicalization and his expanding conflict with the United States also increased Moscow's interest. The Soviets saw in Cuban/U.S. tensions an opportunity to offset their failures to obtain U.S. concessions over the Berlin issue. The embarrassment that the "loss" of Cuba could mean for the United States served as an added incentive for the Soviets, who were still suffering from the scars left by the rebellion of its own Eastern European satellites. The growing Sino/Soviet dispute was also an important factor pressuring the Soviets into a more militant policy in support of anti-imperialist revolutions in developing countries.

The single most important event that encouraged and accelerated Soviet involvement in Cuba was the Bay of Pigs fiasco. The failure of the United States to act decisively against Castro gave the Soviets some illusions regarding American determination and interest in the island. The Kremlin leaders now perceived that further economic, and even military, involvement in Cuba would not entail any danger to the Soviet Union itself and, furthermore, would not seriously jeopardize U.S./Soviet relations. This view was further reinforced by President Kennedy's apologetic attitude concerning the Bay of Pigs invasion, and his weak performance during his June 1961 summit meeting with Khrushchev in Vienna.

The Soviets moved swiftly. New trade and cultural agreements were signed and increased economic and technical aid was sent to Cuba. By mid–1962, the Soviets embarked on a dangerous gamble by surreptitiously introducing missiles and bombers onto the island. Although Khrushchev's precise motives remain a mystery, it is generally believed that through these actions both he and the Kremlin leadership hoped to alter the balance of power and force the United States to accept a settlement of the German issue. A secondary, and perhaps less important, motivation was to extend to Cuba the Soviet nuclear umbrella and thus protect Castro from any further hostile actions by the United States. On October 22, President Kennedy publicly reacted to the Soviet challenge, instituting a blockade of the island and demanding the withdrawal of all offensive weapons from Cuba. For the next several days the world teetered on the brink of nuclear holocaust.

Finally, after an exchange of hectic correspondence, Premier Khrushchev agreed to remove the missiles and bombers, and to allow United Nations-supervised inspection of the removal in exchange for the United States' pledge not to invade Cuba. Although Castro refused to allow a UN inspection, the missiles and bombers were removed under U.S. aerial surveillance and the crisis ended. The United States has never publicly acknowledged that it pledged not to invade Cuba, but subsequent U.S. policies indicate that a U.S./Soviet understanding was reached over Cuba, which included a "hands-off" U.S. policy toward the island.

The missile crisis had a significant impact on the countries involved. While it led to a thaw in U.S./Soviet relations, it significantly strained Cuban/Soviet relations. Castro was not consulted throughout the Kennedy–Khrushchev negotiations, and the unilateral Soviet withdrawal of the missiles and bombers wounded Castro's pride and prestige. All in all, it was a humiliating experience for the Cuban leader, who was relegated throughout the crisis to a mere pawn on the chessboard of international politics. Castro defiantly rejected the U.S./Soviet understanding, and publicly questioned Soviet willingness and determination to defend his revolution.

It is ironic that the crisis—hailed at the time as a U.S. victory—was nothing more than an ephemeral victory. In return for the removal of offensive weapons from the island, the United States was satisfied to accept a Communist regime only a few miles from its shores. Even the withdrawal of nuclear weapons proved to be only temporary. As recent events have shown, the Soviets have brought more sophisticated weapons to Cuba, but in a different form, using the island as a strategically important base for its nuclear submarines.

In spite of the humiliation he suffered, the real victor was Castro.

Enjoying a consolidated regime with its survival guaranteed, Castro embarked on an aggressive policy to export violence throughout Latin America. The island's leader proclaimed that the duty of every revolutionary was to foment revolution and the tenet in Communist doctrine which stipulated that the Communist Party should play the "leading role" in the national liberation struggle was to be rejected. In a small book entitled *Revolution within the Revolution?* by Regis Debray, a young French Marxist, Castro's new line was elaborated. Not only are Communist theory and leadership—which insist on the guiding role of the party and diminish the possibility of struggle in the countryside—a hindrance to the liberation movement, but parties and ideology are unnecessary in the initial stages of the struggle. Debray explains that the decisive contribution of Castroism to the international revolutionary experience is that "under certain conditions the political and the military are not separate but form one organic whole, consisting of the people's army, where the nucleus is the guerrilla army. The vanguard party can exist in the form of the guerrilla *foco* itself. The guerrilla force is the party in embryo." At the Tricontinental Conference in Havana (1966), attended by revolutionary leaders throughout the world, Castro insisted on his independent line, seeking to gain the undisputed leadership of a continent-wide guerrilla struggle and offering to provide the institutional means to promote his methodology.

However, his attempts at revolution all ended in disaster. The Venezuelan adventure turned into a fiasco, with the majority of the Venezuelan people rejecting Cuba's interference in their internal affairs. Led by Che Guevara, the other major effort to open a guerrilla front, in Bolivia, ended in his capture and death in 1967. Neither another Cuba nor "many Vietnams," as Castro had prophesied earlier, erupted in Latin America.

In the early 1970s, Castro's speeches downplayed the concept of Latin American revolutions; attention instead was focused on domestic, political, and economic issues. As such, the official Cuban media routinely called for revolutionary action, but without declaring, as was customary, that armed struggle is the only road to power. An August 1972 publication of the Cuban-engineered Continental Organization of Latin American Students (OCLAE) urged Latin American students to devote themselves to the struggle's "final consequences." It proposed "new forms of organization to confront imperialist violence," but strikingly omitted any reference to the once-standard demands for guerrilla warfare. Hence, Castro came to recognize that there were "different roads to power." While not completely renouncing his original goal of exporting his own brand of communism, he certainly became more selective in furnishing Cuban support.

The electoral failure of the Popular Front in Uruguay and more importantly, the 1973 overthrow of the Allende regime in Chile marked a turning point for the Cuban-inspired revolutionary struggle in Latin America. The Cuban leadership examined its strategy and tactics in the region and concluded that the way to obtain power in Latin America was not through ballots, but through bullets. Beginning in the mid–1970s, Castro increased his support to select groups (particularly in Central America), providing them with propaganda material, training, advisers, financial help, and ultimately, weapons. An acceleration of revolutionary armed struggle in the region followed.

This change in strategy coincided with the U.S. debacle in Vietnam and the Watergate scandal. The inability of American administrations to respond swiftly and decisively to conditions in Central America, as well as in other parts of the world, and to the Soviet/Cuban challenge in Africa, emboldened the Cuban leader. It should be recalled that over 40,000 Cuban troops, supported by Soviet equipment, were transferred to Africa in order to bring communist regimes to power in Angola and Ethiopia.

Cuba's commitment to revolution in Africa dated back to the mid–1960s when Che Guevara visited the area to promote violent anticolonialist resistance. In particular, the Popular Movement for the Liberation of Angola (MPLA) and its Marxist leader Aghostino Neto were supported by Castro, the Portuguese Communists, and the Soviets. The possible defeat of Neto's group—one of the three major contenders and perhaps the weakest of those fighting for power—produced a convergence of Soviet and Cuban policies in Angola in the mid–1970s. Cuban involvement enhanced Castro's international prestige and influence, encouraged the creation of Marxist regimes friendly to Cuba, showed Cuban solidarity with Moscow's interests in the area, and also tested the combat readiness of Cuban troops.

Emboldened by Cuban/Soviet victories in Angola and Ethiopia, the Castro regime focused its attention on the rapidly deteriorating conditions in Nicaragua. There, archaic and unjust social, political, and economic structures dominated by an oppressive, corrupt, and inefficient dynasty, began to crumble in the face of increasing popular discontent. Cuba, jointly with Panama and Venezuela, increased support to the Frente Sandinista de Liberación Nacional (FSLN), the principal guerrilla group opposing the Somoza regime and led by, among others, Castro's long-time friend, Marxist leader Tomás Borge. In July 1979, Somoza fled to the United States and the FSLN rode victorious into Managua.

The Sandinista victory in Nicaragua stands as an imposing monument to Cuban strategy and ambitions in the hemisphere. The overthrow of Somoza gave the "Castro line" its most important boost in two decades. It vindicated, although belatedly, Castro's ideological insistence on the value of violence and guerrilla warfare as the correct strategy to attain power in Latin America. Castro's two long-held beliefs that the political, social, and economic conditions which had produced his revolution in Cuba either existed or could be created in other parts of Latin America, and that the concept that revolution would occur throughout the continent, seemed at last justified. Jesús Montane Oropesa, member of the Cuban Communist Party Central Committee, emphasized that the revolutionary victories in Nicaragua and Grenada were the most important events in Latin America since 1959. "The triumph in Nicaragua," explained Montane, "verified the effectiveness of armed struggle as a decisive means of taking power."[3]

From that time on, the tempo of Cuban-supported violence accelerated in Central America. Aided by an extensive network of intelligence and military forces, and a sophisticated propaganda machinery, the Cuban government increased its support to various groups in the area. In cooperation with Sandinista leaders, Cuba aided insurgent groups in El Salvador, Guatemala, and Colombia. Castro's commitment to revolutionary violence was reinforced by the Sandinista victory showing convincingly that the Cuban leadership was, and is, willing to seize opportunities and take risks to expand its influence and power.

Cuban Internationalism

It seems unlikely that in the near future Cuba will reduce its commitment to violent revolution and its support for anti-American groups throughout the Third World. Indeed, fraternal aid to revolutionary groups in Latin America and in the Third World has been one of the cornerstones of Castro's foreign policy. Efforts to improve relations with Castro under Presidents Ford and Carter did not prevent massive Cuban interventions in Angola and Ethiopia. While these actions have generally been carried out with Soviet support and acquiescence and, in the case of Africa, with direct Soviet military involvement, it should be emphasized that commitment to revolutionary adventures has been an integral component of Cuban foreign policy since the beginning of the revolution. This is part of Castro's mystique, his desire to weaken U.S. influence worldwide, and to safeguard the Cuban revolution. Fidel sees this commitment to revolution as his most significant contribution to modern revolutionary theory, and as the policy that will provide both himself and his revolution a place in history.

To pursue this strategy, the Soviets provide Cuba with the protective umbrella that allows Castro's adventurism in the world. Fidel is a willing surrogate/ally of the Soviets. While not providing the principal motivation for Castro's policies, the protection and aid of the Soviet Union enhances Cuba's policies and actions. Thus, it is important to emphasize that Soviet willingness to restrain Castro, even if achieved as a result of a U.S./Soviet understanding, may not be sufficient to prevent Cuba's involvement with revolutionary groups. After all, in the 1960s, Castro engaged in revolutionary exploits throughout the world—many times to the chagrin and dismay of the Soviets.

American analysts generally neglect the personality factor as a key to the behavior of a revolutionary society dominated by the charisma and philosophy of a single individual. Notwithstanding the prominent attention that has been given to Castro the leader, there is still inadequate appreciation of Castro the man, and of the integral roles that violent revolution and "internationalism" exert in his personal makeup.

Thus, we tend to forget that revolutionary violence has been Castro's preoccupation ever since, as a 22-year-old university student, he received military training and enrolled in a subsequently aborted expedition against Dominican dictator Rafael L. Trujillo. One year later, in 1948, he participated in the "Bogotazo"—a series of riots in Bogotá, Colombia following the assassination of Liberal Party leader Jorge E. Gaitan. Attending an anti-American student meeting in Bogotá, Castro was caught up in the violence that rocked Colombian society: he joined the mobs and roamed the streets distributing anti-U.S. propaganda and inciting the populace to revolt.

For Castro, violence represented the only available path to oppose Batista's 1952 military coup. By then a seasoned revolutionary, Castro organized a group of followers and on 26 July 1953, attacked the Moncada Barracks in western Cuba. He was captured, tried, and sentenced to several years in prison. While in jail he wrote to friends, urging them to create a movement "where ideology, discipline and leadership would be indispensable, especially the latter." "Be friendly to everyone," he emphasized, "there will be time enough later to crush all the roaches together."[4]

After being released during an amnesty in 1955, Castro traveled to Mexico to organize an expedition against Batista. In 1956, he and 81 followers landed in Oriente province. This group formed the nucleus of the guerrilla operation which seized power after the crumbling of the Batista regime and the collapse of the Cuban Armed Forces on 1 January 1959. "Guerrilla war," emphasized Castro, "came to be fundamental in the armed struggle."[5]

In turn, armed struggle has remained fundamental to Castro's mystique, as well as to the image that he has projected onto the larger world stage—on which he is determined to play a leading role. While over time other revolutionary leaders may shed their doctrinaire excesses in favor of the pragmatic pursuit of comfortable rule, there is truly nothing evident in Castro's personal makeup to suggest that he could forsake the global floodlights and resign himself to the role of just another authoritarian-paternalistic *caudillo* on an insignificant tropical island.

Activism and Anti-Americanism in Cuban Foreign Policy

There can be little doubt that since its inception, the Cuban revolution has been committed to international activism. For Castro and the Cuban leadership, an anti-American posture and support of revolutionary groups fighting "American imperialism" were paramount to protect the revolution as well as to expand Castro's influence and prestige in Latin America and throughout the world. Since attaining power, Castro has never appeared content to be solely the leader of a tropical island—his ambitions and objectives transcended the warm waters of the Caribbean.

The tenets of Cuba's international relations have developed into seven main themes:

• survival of the Castro revolution;
• internationalization of Castro's personal prestige and charisma and the resulting power and influence the former convey;
• maintenance of a close alliance with the Soviet Union and its interests throughout the world;
• preservation of an anti-American posture in an attempt to weaken American power and influence worldwide;
• acquisition of influence and supportive allies in Third World states;
• development of a "new international economic order"; and
• continued support of "movements of national liberation" in Asia, Africa, the Middle East, and Latin America.

The Cuban government offers one primary rationale for its activist foreign policy and its strong commitment to foreign countries and groups: proletarian internationalism. In practice, this has meant assistance to a broad range of "progressive forces," terrorist groups, and religious fanatics opposing the United States. However, in spite of its Marxist rhetoric, since the 1970s the regime has been increasingly willing to establish ties with conservative Latin American states. It thus seems clear that ideology is not the sole factor shaping Cuba's external behavior. Cuban interest in developing such relations has been motivated by a desire to foster Cuban, and at times Soviet, objectives and to undermine U.S. interests in the region. For example, in the Malvinas/Falklands War, Cuba supported the reactionary Argentine military junta (not democratically elected, but trading increasingly with the Soviet Bloc) and opposed England, a close ally of the United States.

Another interesting characteristic of Cuba's foreign policy is its attempt to achieve goals with low risks. Failures abroad would hurt Castro's prestige and weaken his leverage. Successes, on the other hand, feed the leader's ego and result in tangible rewards: worldwide influence, leverage vis-à-vis the Kremlin, and domestic support for these initiatives. These rewards likewise compensate for the continuous economic failures and hardships endured by the Cuban people. In other words, successes abroad justify sacrifices at home.

In spite of the expansive role of Cuba, and the daring successes of certain Cuban initiatives (especially in Africa), Cuban foreign policy has had its share of failures and has recently shown signs of possible entrapments. The U.S. invasion of Grenada is a clear case of a forced Cuban reversal. The difficult situation of the Sandinista government in Nicaragua, as well as that of the insurgents in El Salvador, show the limits of Cuba's internationalism. Similarly, the costs of Cuban involvement in Angola and Ethiopia may rise, particularly if Cuban troops begin to suffer increasing casualties. A withdrawal from Angola, or a bloody stay, may further weaken Castro's prestige and lead to increasing internal pressure not to engage in similar adventures elsewhere in the Third World.

The image of a nonaligned Cuba has been repeatedly tarnished due to Castro's close partnership with the Soviets. His failure to condemn the 1979 Soviet invasion of Afghanistan cost him dearly. It is difficult for Castro, the "champion" of nonintervention and a constant critic of past U.S. interventions, to justify the brutal Soviet intervention in Afghanistan. Likewise, it is difficult for honest and responsible leaders of the Third World to accept this dual standard. Castro's recent attempt to rally Latin American leaders to repudiate their foreign debt contrasts sharply with Cuba's continuous commitment to pay its own debt to the Soviet Union as well as to Western countries. The preaching of morality at home and the practice of cynicism abroad are indeed difficult to reconcile.

The Soviet Connection

Cuba's foreign policy—in particular, its commitment to revolutionary anti-American violence—remains as one of the most troublesome areas in U.S./Cuban relations. However, placed in a geostrategic context, it is the Soviet military presence which is ultimately the most damaging to U.S. interests. While Cuba, despite its large military establishment, does not by itself pose a serious military threat to the United States, the growing Soviet military presence in Cuba, the Caribbean, and along the shores of the United States raises some important security and political problems for the United States and for Soviet/U.S. relations.

The significance of these developments extends beyond their specific effects on the U.S./Soviet strategic military balance or their impact on Latin America. They also have an impact on the respective global prestige and power image of the United States and the Soviet Union, thereby influencing Moscow's policies and risk calculations in other areas of the world.

It is important to remember several elements of Moscow's perception of the U.S./Soviet relationship. In the general power competition, the Soviet Union has been coming from behind; one of its objectives, therefore, has been to achieve, and subsequently maintain, parity with the United States. This required not only Soviet acquisition of the necessary quantity and quality of strategic weapons, but also demonstrations of growing Soviet power. The Soviets have sought to prove their ability to project a presence in sensitive areas, thus eliciting from the United States either tacit or overt acknowledgement of this power. The unwillingness or inability of the United States to exclude a significant Soviet military presence from sensitive areas of major interest to the United States would, in Moscow's view, constitute an acknowledgement by the United States of Soviet power. This fact, in turn, accrues to Soviet global prestige and influence.

The Soviet Union has suffered for decades from an inability to engage in, and support, its political activities in areas remote from Europe. The lack of a military "reach" has made it difficult to uphold or defend Soviet interests in distant areas and to secure advanced positions in such distant countries as Cuba. The sole manner in which the Soviet Union could defend such areas was to threaten nuclear war, an action which in turn raised questions concerning the credibility of such a Soviet posture. In the past the Soviet Union has been essentially a land-based, landlocked power forced to limit its expansion to areas contiguous to its historical borders. However, since the mid-1950s Moscow has become increasingly committed to the support of national liberation movements and revolutionary "anti-imperialist" wars in the Third World. Soviet leaders have been well aware that U.S. naval and air mobility and the availability to the United States of friendly bases around the globe allowed the United States to intervene in distant revolutionary wars and to deter similar interventions by Soviet forces. The Soviet Union has also been quite sensitive to America's ability to deploy strategic weapons along the periphery of the Soviet Bloc.

The augmentation of Soviet naval power has helped the Soviet Union to escape from its geographic limitations and to begin to play the role of a global power—capable of both projecting and supporting its interests in distant areas. As a result of its growing military "reach," Moscow has been able to expand its defense commitments from those limited to the Soviet Union and its European allies to "friends" in other areas. The Soviets assert that they are now able to increasingly restrain the "imperialists" from intervening in national liberation struggles.

Although the Soviet Union is achieving a growing capability to engage in its own brand of "gunboat diplomacy" and to display its military power in distant areas, the flexibility of Soviet naval power is limited by the lack of bases to support its deployments. Therefore, it is in the Soviet interest to acquire a network of friendly bases that its navy and long-range air force can use in various parts of the world. In view of its campaign for the abolition of U.S. overseas bases, Moscow will be careful to avoid identifying any of its bases as being under Soviet control. Instead, the host countries will retain formal jurisdiction while the Soviet Union, Cuba, Nicaragua, or other allies build facilities which Soviet ships and aircraft will find useful during "visits" to those countries.

The Soviet Union perceives Latin America as the "strategic rear" of the United States. It is the region in which the United States exercises its influence and control to the fullest with the least interference from powers outside the Western Hemisphere. Consequently, there is a certain parallel between Latin America's relationship to the United States and Eastern Europe's to the Soviet Union. While Moscow recognizes the sensitivity of the United States to Soviet penetration of and any reduction of U.S. influence in the region, these facts also tend to make successful penetration of, and challenges to, the dominant U.S. position appear all the more significant. At a minimum, they are perceived as public confirmation of changes in the U.S./Soviet balance of power, of growing constraints on U.S. freedom of action, of Moscow's widening policy options, and of the increasing independence of Latin America.

In the case of Cuba, Nicaragua, and the Caribbean, it is likely that due to the sensitivity of this area and the uncertainties of U.S. reactions, the Soviet leadership has no single objective in mind in exercising a regional Soviet naval presence. Instead, the Soviets perceive a range of military and political benefits which may accrue, depending on how far the United States permits such activities to develop. There can be little doubt that Soviet strategists would like to acquire additional naval facilities in the Western Atlantic and on the Pacific coast of Nicaragua. To date, the Soviet Union has been testing U.S. reactions to Soviet activities while trying to stake out a claim for maintaining a naval presence in the area.

It is possible to postulate the various potential gains which the Soviet Union may derive from maintaining a military presence in the Caribbean and Nicaragua, and from the use of Cuban bases, but it is not possible to determine Moscow's priorities. Furthermore, no observer can accurately assess the impact which such a deployment might eventually have on Latin America and U.S. interests in the region, or on the East/West balance of power and Moscow's political and military risk calculations in general. It should be pointed out, however, that an increased Soviet military presence in the Caribbean may frighten some Latin American nations and thus have the effect of weakening rather than strengthening any possible Soviet appeal and influence among Latin American nations. As the 1962 missile crisis showed, most Latin American nations perceived Soviet actions in Cuba as a threat to hemispheric security and rallied behind the United States.

It is evident the Soviet Union currently prefers to avoid a confrontation with the United States over their military use of Cuba. Likewise, it is clear the Soviets are willing to deal with such questions on a bilateral basis with the United States. However, it is also evident that Moscow is prepared to continue to test the limits of U.S. tolerance and that it may perceive political and prestige benefits in U.S. public recognition of the Soviet Union as a contestant in the Western Hemisphere. Therefore, it is reasonable to expect that Soviet naval and air activities in Cuba, Nicaragua, and the Caribbean will continue. Furthermore, through a desensitization process, this may lead to a familiarization of the United States with Soviet military presence which, in time, will progressively become a fait accompli.

How far the Soviet Union may be able to move in this direction will depend above all on U.S. responses, both locally and in the broader arena of U.S./Soviet relations, as well as on the receptivity of these actions among Latin American nations. Whether the United States can, in fact, set specific limits on Soviet activities remains to be seen. Such limits are likely to be effective only if the United States can convince Moscow of the fact that it is prepared to enforce them at all costs. Otherwise, the Soviet Union will seek to violate the limits and by doing so will expect to gain political and prestige advantages, while the United States in turn will appear to be weak and suffer political defeats. Since the U.S./Soviet global competition involves a large degree of image-building by both players, American policies must be careful to avoid actions which may help to magnify the significance of Soviet successes or to establish positions which may merely challenge Moscow to violate them.

In the 1980s, Cuba is firmly entrenched in the Soviet camp. Since the late 1960s, relations between Havana and Moscow have taken the form of a progressively closer alliance. The incorporation of Cuba into the Soviet orbit has been evident not only in economic terms (Cuba is a member of the Council for Mutual Economic Assistance (COMECON) and is heavily dependent on Soviet economic and military aid and trade), but is clearly manifested in its model of governance and its international behavior. The nature of this alliance is more complex than the theories that describe Cuba as a simple satellite, or the Soviets as the center of an empire with a series of allies on its periphery. Undoubtedly, in most cases, Cuba is subservient to Soviet interests, but Havana has considerable leverage with Moscow as well as some freedom to act and react in external affairs (especially in the Caribbean, Central, and South America). Instead, what best defines the relationship is a commonality of interests and a mutuality of gains.

In spite of this intimacy, the Soviet/Cuban relationship has encountered difficulties, temporarily souring the partnership. The early years of the 1980s were marked by minor, but revealing, tensions. In 1984 bilateral relations reached their lowest point since 1968, when the Soviets quarrelled with Castro over several issues including his attempt to promote violent revolution in Latin America, his somewhat independent ideological maneuverings, and his failure to put order into Cuba's faltering economy.

It is of more than passing interest to note that while differences in the 1980s originated primarily in the foreign policy sphere, in the economic arena the Cuban government continued to emphasize the importance of Soviet assistance to the island's economy. Castro attempted to underscore his limited independence in international policies vis-à-vis the Kremlin, but mitigated possible negative repercussions by praising the Soviets' vital economic lifeline to his regime.

Recent tensions between Cuba and the Soviet Union can be traced to the Grenada invasion; clearly the U.S. invasion represented a setback for Cuban influence in the region. Wishfully expecting a stronger Soviet reaction, the Cubans were disappointed by the Kremlin's lack of support. Concurrently, several regional leftist organizations, such as the Workers' Party of Jamaica, criticized Cuba for not providing military assistance to the Coard group during the Grenada crisis. In turn, Castro blamed his military commanders in Grenada for having failed to resist the U.S. intervention, and subsequently demoted several officers whose performance was deemed unacceptable. Castro also showed impatience with the Soviet level of support for Nicaragua and with the Kremlin's unwillingness to challenge the United States in defense of the Sandinista revolution. Finally, Castro's failure to attend the COMECON meeting in 1984 and the absence of a high-level Soviet delegation at the anniversary celebration of the Cuban revolution that same year were additional signs of strains in the relations.

By early 1985, an ironing out of differences between Havana and

Moscow was on the way. Raul Castro and a top-level Cuban delegation attended Chernenko's funeral in Moscow. In 1986, Fidel attended the anniversary celebration of the Bolshevik Revolution in Moscow and insisted that there was no friction with the Soviets, claiming that relations were better than ever. To an American journalist who visited the island and questioned Cuba's loyalty to the Soviets, Castro replied: ''I am no Sadat.'' For the foreseeable future Cuba's policies and actions in the international arena will continue to operate in the larger framework of Soviet objectives. And naturally, Castro will continue to pursue his own policies as long as they do not clash with those of the Soviets.

The U.S. Card

To be sure, the rocky past of Cuban/Soviet relations might logically tempt the Castro regime to reduce its reliance on the Soviet Union and find some sort of accommodation with the United States. Rapprochement with the United States could lead to a loosening of the embargo and even provide access to an important and proximate market for Cuba's goods. It could likewise bolster Cuba's immediate security position and provide Castro with greater leverage in his dealings with the Soviet Union. Recognition by the United States might also translate into an important psychological victory for Castro. In Latin America, it would be interpreted as a defeat for ''Yankee imperialism'' and as an enforced acceptance of the Castro regime as a permanent, albeit irritating, neighbor in the Caribbean.

In the 1980s, Castro has pursued a dual strategy to deal with the United States. On the one hand, Havana has made verbal overtures seeking a reduction of tensions. These pronouncements have taken concrete form in the migration treaty signed in December 1984 (in which Cuba agreed to accept undesirable *Marielitos* in exchange for U.S. acceptance of a number of Cuban political prisoners),[6] and the visit of U.S. political and religious leaders to the island. On the other hand, Castro continues to attack the Reagan administration while stepping up the militarization of the island and reaffirming Cuba's support for revolutionary movements worldwide.

Once again, Castro seems willling to negotiate with the U.S. as he has in the past. The question for the United States is not over whether to enter negotiations, but rather, over Castro's willingness to make meaningful concessions to the United States. Such concessions would relate to Cuba's relationship with the Soviet Union, the Soviet military arsenals and attendant presence on the island, Cuba's fomenting of revolutionary and terrorist insurgencies in the Western Hemisphere, and the direct involvement of Cuba's military forces in Africa and elsewhere. Castro is neither ready nor willing to make these concessions. It is interesting to note that Castro's overtures to the United States are usually followed by the now-standard qualifier: "Since certain things are sacred—independence, the country's sovereignty, its revolutionary principles—its political and social systems cannot be renounced. Whoever seeks to destroy them will have to fight us."[7]

Yet recurrently, U.S. administrations have hoped for an accommodation with Castro. Castro has periodically extended ostensible olive branches to the United States—but only to retract them. However, the expectation remains that somehow a negotiated settlement can be found in order to contain Castro's internationalism and the accelerating currents of instability and conflict in Central America, and to make less difficult the choices that the United States confronts in responding to these developments. Clearly, Cuba would have to be a party to such a settlement. Optimistic appraisals of the possibility of a "deal" with Castro have also been encouraged to a large extent by the spectacle of Cuba's deepening economic problems.

The Economic Mirage

Prior to the revolution most of Cuba's foreign trade was with Western nations, almost 70 percent with the United States. Since Castro's takeover, Cuba's trade has been reoriented primarily toward socialist countries. Today, 80 percent of Cuba's trade is with the Soviet Union and Eastern Europe, and only about 20 percent with Western nations. To many American businesses the possibility of reopening this market to American products seems natural, given the prerevolutionary tradition, the geographical proximity of the island, and the needs of the Cuban economy for American "know-how" and technology. The notion of trade with Cuba is also surrounded by a certain mysticism that attaches gargantuan proportions to the Cuban market enhanced by the vision of selling to a state-controlled economy with its massive purchasing power.

There is little question about Cuba's chronic need for U.S. technology, products, and services. Yet need alone does not determine the size or viability of a market. Cuba's large foreign debt, owed to both Western and socialist countries, the abysmal performance of its economy, and the low prices for its major exports make the "bountiful market" perception a perilous mirage.

The Cuban revolution has reached a critical stage in its development. Persistent structural and managerial problems in the economy, low prices for Cuba's export products, and the inability to break away from economic dependence on the Soviet Bloc are forcing Havana to reexamine its basic goals. Since production in most key sectors has fallen short of expected targets, emphasis is being placed on increased planning with more modest goals. The regime has opted for a more rigid economic model (as practiced by some Eastern European countries), relying on regimentation and strict discipline to increase productivity. For the foreseeable future the Cuban people can expect more austerity, a greater rationing of food and consumer goods, and therefore harder times. The third revolutionary decade is proving to be as harsh as the preceding two, and probably harsher.

The establishment of a Soviet-type centrally planned economy has burdened Cuba with a vast and cumbersome bureaucracy that stifles innovation, productivity, and efficiency. Popular expectations for rapid economic improvement have been replaced by pessimism. There is dwindling enthusiasm among Cuba's labor force and increasing signs of weariness with the constant revolutionary exhortations. Underemployment is rampant, and labor productivity is at a low point.

Given this dismal economic picture, Cuba's ability to use its scant foreign exchange to buy U.S. and Western products will remain quite limited for the foreseeable future. The island's economy has fallen from a position of regional economic leadership to a level below the median Caribbean per capita income. In the process, Cuba has amassed a foreign debt in excess of $10 billion, of which an estimated $3.5 billion is owed to Western countries, and the balance to the Soviet Union. The servicing of this debt has created an added burden to the economy. Yet this debt does not take into consideration the more than $14 billion in aid the U.S.S.R. has granted Cuba between 1961 and 1985, including commodity subsidies, absorption of balance of trade deficits, and a current annual level of aid in excess of $3.6 billion. Cuba's indebtedness to the Soviet Union and the high level of economic assistance it receives from Moscow are illustrative of its dependency, its subordination to decision-making mechanisms other than its own, and its inability to divert significant resources to purchase Western goods.

Obviously, Cuba's dependency on foreign powers has greatly increased relative to the prerevolutionary era. This exacerbation of dependency must be judged in terms of Cuba's loss of economic flexibility and alternatives as a result of the politico-ideological commitments of the revolution. Likewise, commitment has exacted a high economic price not only through heightened international dependency, but also through a massive concentration on sugar that has weakened Cuba's possibilities to diversify its exports, as well as its choice of trading partners.[8]

If a resumption of U.S./Cuban economic relations were to take place, the United States would have to be prepared to barter its products for Cuban sugar. Given Cuba's chronic shortage of hard currency, bartering is the only mechanism available to the Castro regime to acquire U.S.

goods. But Cuba's gain of any share of the U.S. sugar market implies it must come at the expense of other sugar producers in the Caribbean as well as sugar producers in the United States itself. This arrangement would deal a considerable blow to the American sugar industry, and would be particularly devastating to the economies of a score of friendly nations structurally dependent on sugar exports to the United States. These nations, such as the Dominican Republic, Costa Rica, Guatemala, and El Salvador would face additional hardships, stifled growth, and enlarged debt burdens that could threaten their political stability as well as U.S. security interests in the region.

It is also important to point out that domestic protectionism in the United States has already resulted in reduced sugar quotas for most regional producers. Furthermore, given Cuba's political and ideological values, sugar exports would not be constrained by economic rationality. A specific danger is that Cuba, with its Soviet ties, could subsidize sugar exports. In other words, Cuba could employ predatory pricing tactics and "dump" sugar exports at prices below marginal cost. For the Caribbean states dependent upon the export of sugar for economic survival, this would represent an economic dislocation of the first magnitude. The same argument holds, in varying degrees, for other potential Cuban exports such as nickel, tobacco, and rum.

Ultimately, Cuba's products are neither economically nor strategically important to the United States. In the short term, with a worldwide sugar supply far in excess of demand, sugar prices are likely to remain depressed. In the long term, the availability and desirability of low-calorie sugar substitutes point to further decreases in U.S. per capita sugar consumption.

Perhaps the most damaging indictment of the "bonanza market" perception has been provided by the international business community. In 1982, Cuba reversed its long-standing policy of prohibiting foreign investment. With the enactment of a new joint venture law, Cuba opened the door to Western companies and actively promoted the investment opportunities created by the law. Cuban officials have reportedly held discussions with potential joint venture partners from the United Kingdom, Brazil, Canada, France, Spain, and Mexico. However, the Cuban market has yet to attract a single investor.[9]

From the U.S. point of view, therefore, the reestablishment of commercial ties with Cuba would be at best problematic. It would create severe market distortions for an already precarious regional economy. It would provide the U.S. market with products that are of little value and in abundant supply. And, while some U.S. firms could benefit from a resumed trade relationship, it would not in any significant way help the U.S. economy.

Prospects

Uncomfortable as he may feel in the embrace of the Russian bear, Castro's options are limited. Although relations with China have improved from their nadir in 1967, the Chinese seem unable or unwilling to take on Cuba as an expensive client. Castro's support of Moscow's policies are decried by Beijing as "revisionist," and his denunciations of Mao in the late 1960s are still remembered with bitterness by the Chinese.

Strengthened commercial ties with Western Europe and Japan may beckon as a healthy development from Cuba's standpoint. Nevertheless, the ability of these countries to absorb the island's sugar exports is limited, and Havana has scant cash reserves with which to purchase European and Japanese goods. Cuba's heavy economic commitment to the Soviet Union and the East European countries is an additional deterrent to a broadening of trading partners, while U.S. pressures on Western allies tend to limit their willingness to trade with Cuba.

From Cuba's standpoint, accommodation with the United States would be fraught with uncertainties and danger for the Castro leadership. It would entail a loosening of Cuba's military ties with the Soviet Union, the curtailment of support for violent revolutions in Latin America and elsewhere, and the withdrawal of Cuban troops from Africa and other parts of the world. These are conditions that Castro is not willing to accept: he perceives such conditions as an attempt by the United States to deny Cuba its claim to a great power role, to isolate the revolution, and to strengthen anti-Castro forces within the island, thus posing a threat to the stability of the regime. The close ties of the Cuban economy to the Soviet Union would prevent a rapid reorientation toward the United States, even if this were politically feasible.

There is nothing in Castro's rhetoric or actions that would suggest a Cuban willingness to trade its commitment to revolutionary violence or its alliance with the Soviet Union for an improvement in U.S./Cuban relations. American economic inducements will do little to change Castro's policies. Indeed, it is a measure of the strange and pervasive economic determinism in the American outlook that the U.S. still tends to assign priority to economics in trying to understand the motivations of revolutionary Marxist regimes, such as the Castroite model. The history of the past two and a half decades offers clear proof that economic considerations have never dominated Castro's policies. On the contrary, many of the initiatives and actions that the Cuban leadership has undertaken abroad (such as involvement in Angola, Ethiopia, Grenada, and Nicaragua), as well as constant mass mobilizations at home, have been costly, disruptive, and detrimental to orderly economic development. If the economic welfare of the Cuban people had been the *leitmotif* of Castro's policies, we would be confronting a totally different Cuba today.

Notwithstanding Castro's periodic and tactically motivated statements regarding rapprochement with the United States, he appears neither willing nor really able to offer those meaningful concessions which would be indispensable to a U.S./Cuban accommodation. Castro's political style and ideology and his apprehensiveness regarding U.S. motivations make him more prone to deviate to the left than to the right of the Soviet line. His awareness of his regime's vulnerability is reinforced by the increasing influence of Cuban-Americans in U.S. politics. Commitment to violent revolution and solidarity with the Soviet Bloc remain the cornerstones of his foreign policy. He cannot modify, let alone abandon, these cornerstones without risking his power and obscuring his personal place in history, a consideration that is perhaps uppermost in Castro's outlook.

Notes

The author wishes to acknowledge the editorial help of Dr. Alexander H. McIntire, Director of Publications at the Graduate School of International Studies and the research assistance of José Azel, doctoral candidate at the University of Miami's Institute of Interamerican Studies.

1. *State Department Bulletin*, January 23, 1961.
2. *The Current Digest of the Soviet Press*, 18 April 1961.
3. *Radio Havana*, 21 October 1980.
4. Luis Conte Aguero, *Cartas del Presidio* (La Habana: Editorial Lex, 1959).
5. Fidel Castro, *La Experiencia Cubana* (Barcelona: Editorial Blina, 1976).
6. The abrogation of this agreement by Castro in retaliation for Radio Martí is further evidence of the unreliability of the Cuban leader.
7. Foreign Broadcast Information Service, 30 July 1984.
8. See Antonio Jorge and Jaime Suchlicki, "Cuba: The Failure of Socialism," in Jaime Suchlicki, ed., *Cuba: Continuity and Change* (Coral Gables, Fla.: Cuban Studies Project, University of Miami, 1985).
9. See Jorge F. Pérez-López, *The 1982 Cuban Joint Venture Law Context, Assessment and Prospects* (Miami, Fla.: University of Miami Press, 1985).

II
CUBA AND LATIN AMERICA

3

Fidel Castro's Crusade in the Caribbean Basin

William Ratliff

Introduction

Imagine millions of people living for centuries in small countries in and around a broad sea. And imagine that over many generations a dark, oppressive cloud has engulfed the sea and that the millions wear chains of servitude. And now imagine that a bright light has recently come to the sea to challenge the darkness. Suppose that the light breaks through to a few of the prisoners who shake off their chains and depart the darkness, as through a curtain, learning for the first time of their true conditions and a way to change them. Finally, in time, the few perceive that they have been brought into this new existence for their comrades' sake, not only for their own; that it is now up to them, by persuasion or by force, to unite and enlighten the other prisoners who can then share the benefits and contribute to the common good in all of the small lands and beyond.[1]

Fidel Castro and his supporters believe the victory of the Cuban Revolution in 1959 marked a turning point in the history of the Caribbean Basin and beyond. Their critics agree with them. The differences between them relate to the precise nature of the change and its repercussions.

One typical Cuban friend of the revolution, using much the same imagery earlier introduced, wrote that the significance of Fidel Castro's victory:

extended beyond the island's border to affect the very development of the anti-imperialist struggle, strengthening existing revolutionary movements and intensifying the mass movement throughout the continent. The Cuban revolutionary victory stood as a beacon to the Latin American people's aspirations and goals. . . . [It] broke through U.S. geographical dominance, sparking shifts formerly believed dogmas, and exposing the modis operandi [sic] of imperialist neocolonial domination. The revolution began a new chapter in the history of the Western Hemisphere, as shown by the Second Declaration of Havana, approved in the Cuban People's General Assembly on February 4, 1962: "What is Cuban history but the history of Latin America? What is Latin American history but the history of Asia, Africa, and Oceania? What is the history of these peoples, but the history of imperialism's most merciless and cruel exploitation of the whole world?"[2]

Cuba's interest in Central America, and the similarities between Cuba's revolutionary struggle and the struggles of other people in the region, flow from striving to overcome what they perceive as similar imperialist oppression. As Castro acknowledged in January 1984, Cuba has supported armed struggles in Nicaragua and other nations; the impetus to undertake such policies is arrived at when Cuban leaders conclude that other roads to change are closed. Beginning in the early 1970s, but in practice, primarily in the mid-1980s, Castro has indicated a preference for change through negotiation—but charged that the United States and its allies, particularly in Central America, often insist upon military oppression and conflict instead.[3]

The majority of analysts outside of Cuba agree that two of Fidel Castro's main objectives have always been, in a sense, traditional enough: the survival of his regime, and its domestic growth and well-being. But that is only the beginning in understanding Cuban foreign policy (and domestic policy as well). Cuba is not just one among many nations in the Caribbean Basin or the Third World, with typical, if individual, domestic and international policies and interests. Cuba has been ruled for almost three decades by Fidel Castro—which makes all the difference.

The essence of Fidel Castro's world view is contained in two convictions: first, that only his own domestic programs can bring true independence, development, and justice to the Cuban people; and second, that the United States will forever seek to overthrow his government, reverse his domestic programs, and thwart the international policies he represents and undertakes on behalf of Cubans and the oppressed people of the world. Cuban domestic and foreign policies reflect these convictions and, for obvious geostrategic reasons, are most consistently reflected in Cuba's policies toward countries in the Caribbean Basin.[4]

Following the advent of the Cuban Revolution, Castro moved into the Soviet orbit for the obvious reason that only with such a powerful ally could he stand up to, and challenge, the American superpower and its allies, particularly in Latin America and the Caribbean Basin. An alliance with the Soviet Union provided a shield behind which he could pursue his anti-American vendetta, even as he satisfied his extraordinary and otherwise totally unrealistic ambition to become a leading actor on the world stage. Despite this background, relations between Castro and Soviet leaders have fluctuated over the years. However, beginning in the late 1970s, trends suggest that in the Caribbean Basin Moscow wishes and even expects Castro to take the initiative, test and support potential Soviet Bloc allies—within the parameters of basic Soviet objectives. And indeed, this is what Castro has done.[5]

Nuts and Bolts of Cuban Policy in the Basin

After Cuban leaders set the direction of Cuban foreign policies, a number of individuals and organizations are charged with promoting them and carrying them out. What follows is a brief survey of this process.

On the most obvious level, Cuban leaders propound their aims at domestic and international conferences, where the objective may be simply stoking the anti-imperialist flames or promoting a specific campaign, group, or profession. Sometimes policies are developed at meetings in Cuba, whether of the Communist Party or of the country's mass organizations. Often, they are presented and/or developed at international conferences convened in Cuba or abroad. Some of the most prominent international conferences in Cuba include the Tricontinental Congress in 1966; the Cultural Congress of Havana and Organization of Latin American Solidarity (OLAS) conferences in 1968; the Conference of 24 Latin American and Caribbean Communist Parties in 1975; the First Consultative Meeting of Anti-imperialist Organizations of the Caribbean and Central America in 1984; and conferences on the Latin American and Caribbean foreign debt in 1985. These events may be either openly sponsored by the Cuban government, or by one of its international front organizations, such as the Continental Organization of Latin American Students (OCLAE, a particularly active group with a widely circulating monthly journal).

The dissemination of propaganda abroad is carried out at all meetings of the Nonaligned Nations and United Nations. It is likewise done at such gatherings as the European and Latin American Parliaments in Brazil in 1985, the First Latin American Congress on Anti-Imperialist Thought in Managua in 1985, and sessions of such Soviet front organizations as the World Federation of Trade Unions.

Cuban interests are sometimes promoted indirectly by cultivating the good-will of opinionmakers in Basin countries. Intellectuals—from poets and professors to political leaders—more than any other ground, crave recognition, and the Cubans have zeroed in on this craving. Even if Castro's repression of artists and thinkers at home does occasionally tarnish Cuba's image and repel intellectually honest individuals such as Peruvian writer Mario Vargas Llosa, many foreign intellectuals are downright solicitous of the international recognition Cuba can provide. The attention comes through interviews—Grenadan Prime Minister Maurice Bishop, for example, and Nicaraguan Defense Minister Humberto Ortega—in the Cuban electronic and printed media; articles and literary works by and about such varied authors as Sandinista Minister of Culture (and poet) Ernest Cardenal and Haitian writer Martha Jean Claude, which are printed in a variety of Cuban publications, from *Casa de las Américas y Revolución y Cultura*. *Casa de las Américas* has for years given literary prizes to many Basin (and other) writers. Cuba also cultivates the present generation of intellectuals by publishing generally anti-U.S. works of the famous deceased, from Guatemalan Nobel Prize-winning novelist Miguel Asturias to the main founder of the Sandinista movement, Carlos Fonseca Amador.

Many activities are conducted partly or wholly undercover. In some cases, the agents (or part-time agents) are teachers or technicians working in foreign countries, especially during some periods in Nicaragua, Grenada, and Jamaica; in other cases, they are "refugees" living in foreign communities. Among the organizations sometimes (or always) acting as front groups promoting Cuban interests are: Cubana Airlines; the Institute for Friendship With the Peoples (ICAP); and the news agency, Prensa Latina. The latter organization, with offices in at least eleven Basin and South American countries, combines intelligence work, disinformation, and "dirty tricks" with news-gathering and dissemination.[6] It is interesting to note that in 1986, Prensa Latina was appointed chair of the Non-Aligned News Agencies Pool which pledged to give special attention to developments in Central America.[7]

A large number of Cuban-controlled businesses abroad indirectly, but actively, promote Cuban policies. The U.S. government's "List of Specially Designated Nationals," for example, identifies some of the individuals and organizations considered "agents or front organizations" of the Cuban and other governments. Of 166 designated nationals noted at the end of 1986, some 101 were Cuban fronts located in Panama.[8] These fronts operate in other countries as well—including the United States, particularly in Miami.

Most agents—some of whom pass themselves off as teachers or businessmen or whatever—are members of one of several Cuban intelligence organizations, all of which have been strongly influenced by the Soviet Union and its interests since at least the early 1970s. These include three agents within the Ministry of the Interior, among them the General Directorate of Intelligence (DGI), and two within the Communist Party's Central Committee, including the Americas Department (DA). Cuban Interior Minister Ramiro Valdés once said that "there is hardly a single international mission'' in which his ministry's special operations personnel ''have not played an impressive part.''⁹ The U.S. government reports that DA officials are found in every Cuban diplomatic mission in the Basin and that they have held ambassadorships in special target countries, including Barbados, Dominca, St. Lucia, Jamaica, Suriname, and Nicaragua. The quality of Cuban intelligence is suggested by a high-ranking Cuban intelligence officer who defected in 1987, and reported that for many years more than 90 percent of U.S. CIA covert operations in Cuba have been controlled by the DGI.¹⁰

Themes of Cuban Policy

Throughout his decades in power, Fidel Castro has promoted a variety of themes in the Basin and beyond—issues that transcend the confines of individual countries. In Castro's view, all have focused on the objective underlying Cuban foreign policy: "liberating" the region from exploitation by "Yankee imperialism." Two of the main themes that have touched on the Basin have been guerrilla warfare and the foreign debt.

Guerrilla Warfare

Particularly during the 1966–68 period, Cuba advocated continental war against the United States. This translated into Cuban moral and ideological support, supplemented by varying levels of training and materiel support, including at times even Cuban commanders and troops. This line was promoted in particular at two conferences held in Havana during this period: the Tricontinental (January 1966), which drew at least 118 delegates from nineteen Caribbean Basin countries and territories, and the OLAS Conference (July–August 1967), which attracted 107 people from nineteen Caribbean Basin countries and territories; three of the four vice presidents of OLAS were from the Basin.¹¹ This theme was also played out around the continent, from the perpetual conflict in Guatemala, to, most dramatically, Che Guevara's misadventure in Bolivia.

Latin Americans did not rise to the occasion, however, and Cuba's indiscriminate promotion of guerrilla warfare declined after 1968. From the late 1970s, nonetheless, Castro continued to support the path of armed struggle to attain power in some countries, stressing—and helping to bring about—unity among revolutionaries within countries and with like-minded groups abroad, as demonstrated most impressively in the cases of Nicaragua and El Salvador. As Castro indicated in his speech at the meeting of Anti-Imperialist Organizations in 1984, he continues to support guerrillas seeking change when, in his judgement, "Yankee imperialism" will not permit change to come by peaceful means. At times, he says, he favors negotiations—for example, those proposed in the 1980s by the Contadora countries and Costa Rica President Oscar Arias—between what he considers good guerrillas (e.g., Farabundo Martí de Liberación Nacional [FMLN] in El Salvador) and bad governments (the Duarte government). The expectation is that the latter will make major concessions, though not between bad guerrillas (the Nicaraguan resistance) and good governments (the Sandinistas).

The Foreign Debt

Castro claims correctly that he was one of the first leaders to warn about the danger of massive borrowing by Latin America and other Third World countries. At least as early as November 1971, he asserted that the debts of the "relatively least developed countries" prevented development and should be canceled.[12]

Periodic references to the matter turned into a campaign at the end of 1984 and an obsession during 1985, when a rash of continental conferences focusing on the debt were convened in Havana and elsewhere. Each conference brought together from hundreds to thousands of women, journalists, labor leaders, youth, political leaders, and others from the Basin, often loosely coordinated with Soviet-Bloc international fronts. They called for renunciation of the debt, for "capitalist" countries to pay their banks off with money taken from 10 to 12 percent reductions in expenditures for armaments, and concluded with demands for a new international economic order which would be more just and help the development of the Third World.[13] While there was no tidal wave of support from political leaders in the Basin and beyond, Castro's influence was significant on many lesser opinionmakers.[14]

When Brazil announced its decision to suspend payment on its debt in February 1987, Castro said "the day of the world's poor people has arrived," and added that "whether there are negotiations or not it will be the debtors who will have the last word from now on." His campaign became more subtle after 1985, for two reasons: First, no Latin American political leader would endorse it, while some openly denounced it; and second, Castro's apparent hypocrisy in calling for others to renounce their obligations, while he worked overtime to renegotiate his own very large debt.[15]

An Overview of Cuban Policy in the Caribbean Basin

During the 1960s, Castro's name and Cuba's policies were associated almost entirely with support for guerrillas seeking to overthrow seated governments. Immediately after taking power, in what Tad Szulc has called his "first Bolivarian gesture," Castro announced that Cuba would help Latin Americans who wanted to overthrow dictatorships in their countries. During his first year, expeditions were launched from Cuba (or involving Cubans) against the governments of Panama, Nicaragua, Haiti, and the Dominican Republic.[16] The reaction of the Basin countries was immediate, and by 1962 Cuban diplomats had been expelled from many nations of the Western Hemisphere, including Panama, Nicaragua, Guatemala, El Salvador, and Honduras. In July 1964, documented Cuban support for guerrillas trying to oust the democratically elected government of Venezuela prompted the Organization of American States (OAS) to impose diplomatic sanctions on Cuba. This translated into a break in formal relations between Havana and all of the region's governments except Mexico and Jamaica (while not a member of the OAS, Jamaica maintained consular relations).[17] A motion in 1972 to lift the sanctions was defeated, though four of seven countries supporting it—Mexico, Panama, Jamaica, and Trinidad and Tobago—were from the Basin. However, during that year, four Basin countries (Barbados, Guyana, Jamaica, and Trinidad and Tobago) as a group recognized Castro's government.

OAS sanctions were lifted officially in 1975, though even by 1987 formal relations between Cuba and Basin countries, by and large, remained on a low level. The sanctions were lifted for a variety of reasons, including domestic pressures within individual Basin countries and the declining authority of the United States in the region. More importantly, after 1968 Castro became much more discriminating in his policies toward Basin countries: that is, he stopped promoting guerrillas everywhere and welcomed relations with governments that did not criticize him, despite their treatment of local communist and revolutionary groups. As an editorial in the Cuban Communist Party organ *Granma* put it on 12 June 1972: "Our country is willing to establish relations with those governments that are independent and are willing to express and to show their conduct in real steps of sovereignty and national independence." Thus Cuba did not condemn Mexico, which had refused to follow the OAS sanctions in 1964— even when the government in Mexico City harshly repressed student demonstrations in 1968 and then crushed a spate of guerrilla groups in the years following. And during the 1970s, relations generally were good with Jamaica under the leadership of Michael Manley, Panama under General

Omar Torrijos, and Guyana under Forbes Burnham, even when those leaders were in varying degrees at odds with Castro's revolutionary friends in their countries.[18]

Central America and Panama

Castro has had few friends among the governments of Central America since taking power; even in 1987, Cuba had normal diplomatic relations only with Nicaragua and Panama, both of which will be covered in the next section of this chapter. Cuban leaders rarely paid any attention to Honduras until the 1980s, when they started condemning it as a base for "U.S. imperialism" in the region.[19]

During the 1960s, Cuba supported guerrilla movements in several countries, particularly in Guatemala, where leftist Jacobo Arbenz had been overthrown with CIA assistance in 1954.[20] Tensions eased somewhat in the early and mid-1970s, when Cuban aid to guerrillas generally had declined, though Cuba supported Belize in its endeavor to remain independent of Guatemala. Then in 1982, Cuba played a role in uniting the Guatemalan guerrillas in the Guatemalan National Revolutionary Unity (URNG), a largely inoperative grouping that nonetheless draws Castro's praise. Cuba has had a few good words for Guatemala's newly elected civilian President Vinicio Cerezo. Immediately after Cerezo's inauguration in 1985, he tried to maintain a policy of "active neutrality"—in practice a worried neutrality—in relations with Cuba, and in the Central American conflict. However, there was little Cuban thought that he would bring significant domestic change; for Havana, the URNG is the group dedicated to securing democracy and peace.[21]

El Salvador did not become a primary interest for the Cubans until after the Sandinista victory in Nicaragua. In October 1979, a group of young military, political, and other civilian leaders launched a coup in El Salvador and installed a government with broad leftist participation. But even before that government fell in December, Castro called the Salvadoran guerrilla factions (who already were attacking the new government from the left) to Havana, to unify them for an expanded struggle for power. This unification resulted in the May 1980 formation of the FMLN. The new entity launched its abortive "final offensive" against the Salvadoran government (and indirectly against the United States) with strong Cuban and Nicaraguan support, as both governments admitted long after the fact.[22] In February 1982, Cuba endorsed a cooling-off initiative toward the FMLN by Mexican President José López Portillo, without terminating assistance altogether. Cuban/Nicaraguan support for the FMLN declined as the Nicaraguan civil war expanded, but as of December 1987 the support had not ended. Cuban leaders are consistently critical of Salvadoran President Duarte while the latter points to Cuba as a source of support for the guerrillas.[23]

Castro did not support a military invasion of Costa Rica in 1959, although he attacked that country's popular president, José Figueres, when the latter visited Havana and advised the new Cuban government to maintain good relations with the United States. Economic, and then diplomatic, ties were established in the 1970s, in part through the activities of the pro-Soviet Costa Rican communists. However, at the beginning of the next decade they were broken following disputes over the treatment of dissidents in Cuba, as well as Cuban policy in Central America. Since that time, Cuba officially supported Sandinista participation in the peace talks initiated in early 1987 by Costa Rican President Oscar Arias.

The Caribbean

Relations with the Dominican Republic, the major Spanish-speaking nation aside from Cuba in the Caribbean Sea, were poor from the beginning. Cuba had been involved in the 1959 "invasion" of the island, and in 1965 the United States led forces from several OAS countries in preventing what some believed to be a Cuban-sponsored takeover of the nation. Although Dominican democracy has functioned with some distinction since the 1960s, Cuba has considered the successive governments as minions of Washington. In the mid1980s, pressures increased on the Dominican president to establish diplomatic relations with Havana, although ties had not been formed by late 1987.

In the case of Haiti, unbroken bilateral hostility has existed between Castro and the Duvalier governments since 1959. Cuba was not impressed when the United States eased "Baby Doc" Duvalier out in early 1986, and does not expect significant changes under the new government.

In the English-speaking Caribbean, which Anthony Maingot has called "politically radical but sociologically conservative," the Cubans encountered savvy political leaders who "all face one dilemma: how to retain power in societies that are politically complex, restless and eager for better days, yet hardly revolutionary." After a slow start in the 1960s, by the 1970s "the Cubans were clearly on the move. . . ."[24] Contrary to popular belief, Cuba never offered these countries a viable economic or social model. During much of the 1970s, the region's leaders could be divided into three camps: (1) those who were openly pro-Cuban (Jamaica, Guyana, and Grenada); (2) those who had diplomatic relations but were privately critical (Trinidad and Tobago and Barbados); and (3) those who were openly hostile (among them St. Vincent and Antigua). But whatever category a Caribbean leader fell into, relations with Cuba had a critical political component and the "Cuba card" was used "as political leverage in some instances, as a protective shield in others, and in more and more cases as a straw man." For some governments, relations with Cuba gave a veneer of "revolutionary legitimacy while at the same time providing the arms, intelligence, and training essential for grabbing power and keeping it."[25]

Guyana set the region's pace in bilateral relations in the early 1970s. The path promoted by the Conference of 24 Communist Parties of Latin America and the Caribbean—the largest meeting up to that time of Western Hemisphere communist groups—served as an inspiration to many of the Basin's radical leaders. In fact, in 1977, the prominent Guyanese Marxist Clive Thomas indicated at a conference in Trinidad that the Havana declaration "virtually underwrites all the major propositions of the theory of noncapitalist development" and marks "a definite shift in emphasis in the struggle for decolonization of socialism in the Third World."[26]

Special Cuban Interests in the Basin

After scattershot support for guerrillas during the 1960s, Castro began focusing his attention with more discrimination and impact on specific countries in the Basin. This included a particular emphasis on Puerto Rico, Jamaica, and Grenada in the Caribbean, and Nicaragua and Panama on the Central America mainland. In Puerto Rico, Cuba supported those who actively sought independence from the United States. In Jamaica and Panama, Cuban support was thrown to noncommunist governments which for various reasons wanted friendly relations with Havana. In Grenada and Nicaragua, support was thrown behind revolutionaries who overthrew seated governments allied to the United States, and set up anti-U.S. regimes allied to Cuba.

Puerto Rico

Puerto Rico is one of the most obvious foreign policy interests for Castro in light of the fact that it is a small, Spanish-speaking island near Cuba that is a commonwealth of the United States—for him, almost a Guantanamo writ large. In this context, the Cuban position has been that Puerto Rico should be independent. Since the early 1960s, Castro has promoted such as position at the United Nations—in the General Assembly and the Decolonization Committee—as well as in the Nonaligned Movement and other organizations. According to the leader of the main pro-Cuban independence group in Puerto Rico, Castro's support has been indispensable.[27]

This issue was particularly hot during the mid-1970s, even as the prospects for improved U.S./Cuban relations seemed to be at their highest since the Bay of Pigs. In March 1975 the Coordinating Bureau of the Non-Aligned Nations met in Havana and issued a General Declaration condemning U.S. "colonial domination" on the island and in August of that year, Cuba introduced a resolution in the U.N. Decolonization Committee based on the Coordinating Bureau document.[28] In September 1975, Castro hosted an International Conference of Solidarity with the Independence of Puerto Rico sponsored by the Soviet-front World Peace Council. The intensity of the Cuban campaign toward Puerto Rico in the mid-1970s, together with the deployment of thousands of Cuban troops to Africa, led to a reversal of apparently improving U.S./Cuban relations under the Carter administration.

In tandem, Cuba has often been accused of supporting Puerto Rican terrorists active in New York and other U.S. cities. In 1985 a number of Puerto Rican Marxist-Leninists were indicted by a federal grand jury in Connecticut stemming from an armed robbery in 1983. According to the U.S. Federal Bureau of Investigation, there was a direct tie to Cuba.[29]

Despite Cuba's policy vis-à-vis Puerto Rico, the main stumbling block is that it is rejected by the Puerto Rican people. Support for independence, as demonstrated in elections, fell from 19.6 percent in 1952 to 3.5 percent in 1984 while support for statehood parties rose from 13.3 percent to 48.6 percent during the same period; support for improved commonwealth status declined from 67.1 percent in 1952 to a still very strong 47.8 percent in 1984. However, the urge for some improvement in Puerto Rico's status is almost unanimous on the island and unless constructive changes are made, the Puerto Rican issue will retain its explosive potential.[30]

Grenada

Grenada is a small, extraordinarily beautiful island strategically located just off the coast of northeastern Venezuela. In March 1979, several dozen New Jewel Movement (NJM) revolutionaries led by Maurice Bishop overthrew the government of the eccentric authoritarian Eric Gairy. Most Grenadians were glad to be rid of Gairy, and thus paid little attention to the fact that Bishop had long been a friend of Fidel Castro, and that Cubans may have trained the NJM revolutionaries or even participated in the coup itself.[31] Whatever the Cuban role may have been in the coup, NJM leaders were from the beginning hostile to the United States and received aid and support from Cuba. As Bishop remarked during a May Day rally in Havana in 1980 thanking Cuba for its military aid immediately after the revolution, "without the Cuban revolution of 1959 there could have been no Grenadian revolution. . . . We look to the people of Cuba, we look to your revolution and your leadership to ensure that the revolutionary process in the Caribbean and Central American region continues to go forward with strength."[32]

Cuban ports and airfields handled heavy traffic in supplies and personnel from the Soviet Bloc to Grenada, and Cuba played an active role providing guidance on domestic affairs and training and development assistance for the NJM. Examples of assistance included: organizing and training the People's Revolutionary Army and People's Militia; constructing the international airport at Port Salines, which one NJM Central Committee member wrote would be "used for Cuban and Soviet military;" and the activities of the Americas Department of the Cuban Communist Party evaluating the Grenadian church.[33] Of particular importance to the NJM was the Cuban role in three major areas: orienting the NJM leaders to the complex world of international politics, promoting NJM interests to Soviet leaders, and pushing secret aid agreements contracted between Grenada and Soviet Bloc and other revolutionary governments. As early as July 1979, with the Declaration of St. Georges (named after the capital of Grenada) signed by the prime ministers of Grenada, St. Lucia, and Dominica, the NJM sought to play a leading role in the reorientation of Eastern Caribbean politics; documents captured in 1983 revealed Grenada's determination to "serve as a bridge between the CPSU and the left parties of the English-speaking Caribbean."[34] As Soviet/Cuban influence grew, ties were reported between the island's Marxist-Leninist government and revolutionaries in many of the region's nations.[35]

By 19 October 1983, NJM infighting culminated in the murder of Bishop and ten supporters, as well as the imposition of a militantly Stalinist regime under the control of former Deputy Prime Minister Bernard Coard and former Chairman of the Revolutionary Military Council Hudson Austin. This subsequent regime terrorized the country and helped provoke what the vast majority of Grenadians call the "rescue mission" by the United States on 25 October. Events leading up to and including the overthrow of the Grenadian revolutionary government demonstrated, among other things, that despite close ties, Castro was not as well informed as he believed regarding factional rivalries and fighting within the NJM.

In December 1984, the vast majority of Grenadians elected Herbert Blaize as prime minister; the Maurice Bishop Patriotic Movement (MBPM), which effectively replaced the NJM as the country's official communist party, garnered only 5 percent of the vote. While the MBPM keeps a lower profile than the NJM did, it maintains ties to Cuba and the Soviet Bloc. In December 1986, more than a dozen former members of the NJM, including Coard and Austin, were convicted of murdering Bishop, though all immediately appealed the convictions. By the end of 1987, the once wrecked national economy had improved markedly—up 5 percent in 1986—with the help of $90 million in U.S. aid, although unemployment remained high.[36]

Nicaragua

Castro's formal relations with Nicaragua have fallen into two contrasting periods. For the first 20 years of Castro's rule, the Somoza dynasty ruled Nicaragua; hence, there were no diplomatic ties between the two countries. Instead, there was continuous hostility, initiated by reports in early 1959 that Cuba had sponsored a military landing in Nicaragua, and magnified by Cuban exile use of Nicaragua as a staging area for the Bay of Pigs invasion in 1961. By way of contrast, since the inception of the Sandinista government in July 1979, relations were those of strong revolutionary allies.

The Sandinista National Liberation Front (FSLN), founded by three disgruntled ex-members of the Nicaraguan Socialist Party (PSN, the country's Moscow-oriented communist party) grew out of the experience of the Cuban war against Batista. Sandinista founder Carlos Fonseca Amador traced the influence of Castro and Guevara back to 1958. "With the victory of the Cuban Revolution," he said, "Nicaraguan spirit of rebellion recovered its resplendence [lost with the death of Sandino and his followers in the 1930s]." The FSLN was conceived in 1960, formulated in 1961, and "born" at the beginning of 1962. The new movement "seized the Marxism of Lenin, Fidel, Che, Ho Chi Minh" and resumed the essential guerrilla road to power. In the words of Tomas Borge, the only surviving FSLN founder:

> Fidel was for us the resurrection of Sandino, the answer to our reservations, the justification of the dreams of heresies of a few hours before. The victory of the armed struggle in Cuba stirred the enthusiasm of the Nicaraguan people and stimulated the struggle against the tyranny.[37]

The original motivation of the three to join the PSN, and then to break with that organization and form the FSLN, derived primarily from one central conviction, which they share with Castro: that Nicaragua (or Cuba) cannot be secure in its independence—as they define independence—as long as "Yankee imperialism" has influence in the region, whether on its own or though its "surrogates." An FSLN statement released in September 1971 by Fonseca in Havana pictured the United States and its threat as follows: "Nicaragua was among the first victims of Yankee power, which in time became the major threat to humanity, particularly to the peoples of Asia, Africa and Latin America."[38]

Nicaraguan President Daniel Ortega has said that the "peoples" of Central America will combine their "rifles and blood" in defense of the Sandinista revolution, should an attack come from the United States. Cuba has suggested much the same thing, although polls in neighboring countries show that large majorities of the population would like to have seen the Sandinistas overthrown. A top-level defector from the Nicaraguan Defense Ministry has said the Sandinistas truly expect a U.S. attack, as they have been asserting for years in public statements. However, Castro and other Cuban leaders have stated, since the U.S. action in Grenada, that Cuba will not provide military defense for Nicaragua in the event of a North American attack, although Castro has implied that Cubans already in the country will fight alongside Sandinista forces.[39]

As Defense Minister Humberto Ortega has said, from the early years of the FSLN Castro's moral support and assistance sustained the movement, providing safe haven and training for many of its leaders and putting them in touch—years before they took power in Managua—with other revolutionary organizations around the world. The latter ranged from Colonel Muammar Qadhafi and the Palestine Liberation Organization to some of the major communist powers, who have become even closer allies since July 1979.[40]

The Sandinistas split into three feuding factions during the 1970s; it was Castro, above all, who pulled them back together in the beginning of 1979 when Cuba became their primary source of military assistance. By mid-1981 the Sandinistas, with strong Cuban support, had built the largest army in the history of Central America, although even the FSLN admits that the United States did not begin arming what were to become known as the Contras until the end of that year.[41]

In 1985, Daniel Ortega admitted having almost 800 Cuban military advisers in Nicaragua; U.S. government estimates were about 2,500 to 3,000 military advisers and about 4,000 teachers, construction workers, and others.[42] Soviet Bloc economic assistance to Nicaragua rose from $35 million in 1981 to more than $500 million in 1986. Military assistance increased from $35 million in 1981 to $600 million in 1986. Cuba's $50 million economic assistance in the mid-1980s was in addition to other Soviet Bloc aid; Cuban gave Nicaragua 100 tons of oil between January and August 1987 alone. Cuban pilots fly Soviet helicopters in battle against the U.S.-supported resistance. Sandinista leaders have repeatedly and openly consulted Castro since taking power on many important foreign policy issues.[43]

Cuban influence also has been felt in other ways. For example, Castro promoted Nicaragua as the site for the Ninth Non-Aligned Nations meeting scheduled for 1989; Cuba's Committees for the Defense of the Revolution were the model for the Sandinista Defense Committees; and in 1987 the two countries renewed a maritime agreement originally signed in 1982 and announced that total sea freight over the five years had been nearly 220,000 tons.

Jamaica

The first government in the English-speaking Caribbean to make a prolonged play toward Cuba was Jamaica during the two presidential terms of Michael Manley (1972–80). Manley has had several distinct political incarnations over the decades, but the one he chose to live as president was as a socialist. Domestically, he juggled relationships between moderates and leftists in his own People's National Party (PNP) and beyond, playing the Cuban card often and with much flair—always asserting that his transformation of society were based on principle. This flirting with Cuba meant, among other things, playing politics with economics, and covering over many incompetently managed, wasteful policies.[44]

In foreign affairs, as noted earlier, Jamaica had never actually broken relations with Cuba since it was not a member of the OAS when sanctions were imposed. Nonetheless, it joined three other Caribbean governments in establishing full diplomatic relations with Havana in December 1972—a move which triggered the end of OAS sanctions in 1974. Manley attended the Algiers summit of the Non-Aligned Nations in 1973, traveling with Guyanese leader Forbes Burnham and Fidel Castro in Castro's personal jet. In February 1974, Jamaican Foreign Minister Dudley Thompson said, "Cuba is very close to Jamaica and it is impossible for me to plan Jamaica's foreign policy without keeping that country in mind. . . ." Manley made an official visit to Cuba in 1975, during which he was lavishly praised by the Cuban leader, and signed technical and other agreements with Havana.[45]

As two terms of the (post-Manley) Seaga government wound down in 1987, and opposition prospects seemed good for the forthcoming election, Manley met with Castro and pledged to reestablish diplomatic relations which were severed in 1981. However, the PNP leader added that ties to Cuba would not be as extensive in a new Manley administration as before.[46]

Panama

Castro's relations with Panama got off to a bad start in 1959, when Cuba was accused of being involved in an effort to overthrow the government.

But ties improved rapidly after General Omar Torrijos took power in a coup in 1968; eight years later, the Panamanian leader was given the José Martí National Order, the highest award the Cuban government gives to foreigners. But this can easily suggest a higher degree of friendship than actually existed. Relations with Panama seem to reflect, once again, two governments using such ties both for their own interests and in order to meet common goals, albeit for their own reasons.

Torrijos noted Castro's impact on Panama in an interview with Georgie Anne Geyer published in 1970: "It started with Fidel Castro. . . . Suddenly there was a new orientation. We had more contact with the people. In all the military schools the orientation changed immediately. After Cuba there was a preoccupation with social forces in the course. We studied the case of Cuba . . . philosophy . . . social justice. We came to the conclusion that there was a direct relationship between social justice and explosive violence."[47] During his years in power, the Panamanian general put through some domestic urban and rural reforms, reflecting the social consciousness mentioned above, that in certain respects took on the "structural and ideological trappings of the Cuban Revolution."[48]

But the main tie that developed between Castro and Torrijos flowed from overlapping national and personal interests—in the Panama Canal and Nicaragua—and not from a common Marxist-Leninist ideology.[49] On the one hand, Torrijos wished to secure ownership and control of the Canal for Panama and sought support from the region's democracies, as well as the Third World generally—where Castro was a prominent actor. On the other hand, the Cuban leader wanted to use the Canal issue as a prime feature in his ongoing and many-sided campaign against "U.S. imperialism." In addition, both leaders actively supported the overthrow of the Somoza government, although Torrijos did not favor a communist regime in Managua and, before his death in 1981, had become critical of excessive Cuban involvement in the country.

During the mid-1980s Cuban relations with Panama became still closer. Cuba accused the United States of trying to deprive Panama of its national identity for two reasons. Washington: (1) resented Panama's participation in the Contadora peace process; and (2) was trying to renege on the 1978 Canal treaties which will turn the Canal over to Panama in the year 2000.

In exchange for this and more material support for Panama, Cuba benefited in even more tangible ways from the ties established with Torrijos and increased later under Manuel Antonio Noriega, who became chief of the Panama Defense Force (PDF) in 1983 after a decade as head of intelligence. Though many of the actual contacts with Castro came through Roberto Díaz Herrera, second-in-command of the PDF until his forced retirement in 1987, Noriega was primarily responsible for passing intelligence on the U.S. Southern Command and other matters to the Cuban DGI and Soviet KGB. The closed fishing village of Vacamonte, just southwest of Panama City, became a haven for Soviet intelligence-gathering ships and is a major source of Soviet intelligence on U.S. operations in Panama and beyond. Other Cuban benefits from the Panama connection include the "designated nationals" noted above—agents and/or front organizations that facilitate the transfer of U.S. technology to Cuba through the Panama free port.[50]

As the confrontation between Noriega and the United States worsened in 1987 and early 1988, the Panamanian government became even more hostile to the United States and friendlier to the Soviet Bloc (including Sandinista Nicaragua). It allowed the Soviet airline Aeroflot to begin landing in Panama, and signed a service contract to provide drydock and other shore facilities for the Soviet fishing fleet—the Vacamonte connection. By early 1988, U.S. intelligence had confirmed the arrival in Panama from Cuba of three planeloads of Soviet military equipment.

The Trade Component

The overwhelming preponderance of Cuban trade (export and import) has been with the Soviet Union and the Soviet Bloc. The OAS resolution prohibiting economic and other relations with Cuba, in force from 1964 to 1975, meant in practice that in all of Latin America, only Mexico (which did not go along with the prohibition) had any open trade with Cuba prior to the 1970s. Ever since the formal ban was lifted, Cuba's trade with most of the countries covered in this chapter has been nonexistent or insignificant. However, during certain periods, trade with a few nations—principally Nicaragua, Grenada, and Jamaica—has been marginal from the Cuban perspective, if somewhat more important to the other party. Between 1972 and 1980, exports or imports with the region did not total as much as 0.1 percent of Cuba's total for a year, and the amount was usually far lower.[51]

Listed in Tables 3.1 and 3.2 are official figures from the Cuban government on trade with the Central American Common Market (CACM) and Caribbean Community (CARICOM) countries, given only by region, not individual country. According to United Nations calculations for the years 1975–84, imports from the Caribbean have never totalled more than 0.1 percent (in 1975) of Cuba's total imports; imports from Central America have also never totalled more than 0.2 percent (1983, 1984) of Cuba's total imports. Exports to Central America have been a maximum of 0.7 percent (1983) of Cuba's total, and exports to the Caribbean have been too small to register.[52]

TABLE 3.1
Cuban Trade Figures to and from Central American Common Market
(CACM) Countries, 1958–1985
(in thousands of Cuban pesos)

Year	Exports to CACM	Imports from CACM
1958	1,431	1,764
1965	—	—
1970	1	—
1975	2	—
1980	5,620	3
1981	2,258	9,691
1982	8,216	1,036
1983	41,074	13,284
1984	31,236	10,852
1985	19,756	8,572

Source: Comité Estatal de Estadisticas, Anuario Estadistica de Cuba: 1985, Havana, pp. 386–87.

TABLE 3.2
Cuban Trade Figures to and from Caribbean Community (CARICOM)
Countries, 1958–1985
(in thousands of Cuban pesos)

Year	Exports to CARICOM	Imports from CARICOM
1958	1,535	228
1965	4	—
1970	—	—
1975	4,358	3,529
1980	5,687	302
1981	6,144	79
1982	1,455	2
1983	690	197
1984	2,035	1,370
1985	3,789	1,461

Source: Ibid., pp. 390–91.

Conclusions

The real tragedy of Fidel Castro is that in an important sense he did bring a sort of light into some portions of the Western Hemisphere. However, because of his uncompromising hatred of the United States, the glow blinded rather than enlightened, and increased rather than lessened, the hardships and insecurities of the Cuban and the region's peoples. In foreign policy terms, the three critical elements have been Castro's defiance of the United States, his alliance with the Soviet Union, and the impact of these two elements on his relations with, and influence on, the U.S. and other countries.

In 1959, the levels of poverty, inequality, and exploitation in much of the Caribbean Basin ranged from serious to appalling; many political systems had been unresponsive, or only marginally responsive, to the population's basic needs. Some enlightened Cubans, as well as individuals and groups in other nations, saw that changes were needed and realized that despite a checkered history of relations with the United States, the northern giant was necessarily the major partner in bringing these changes about.

But Fidel Castro and a minority of other Cuban leaders, heavily influenced by an anti-American Leninism, thought otherwise. Over the decades, the United States had been preoccupied with crises in other parts of the world and largely indifferent to events in the Caribbean Basin. However, this indifference was maintained only as long as there appeared to be no strategic threat to the Panama Canal or other lines of transportation through the region. But to Castro and his emerging anti-American, Leninist allies (prominent among them the young Sandinistas) Washington's lack of long-term interest in reform and its periodic interventions demonstrated that the U.S. was inherently predatory. Thus, it posed an ongoing threat to the very existence of the Cuban—or any similarly constituted and motivated—government. In time, Castro's hatred of the United States took on a life of its own.[53]

Working from this perspective, which he sought to propagate throughout the Basin and Third World, Castro launched a partially defensive, but in reality offensive, war against the United States. These battles were fought mainly in other people's countries in the name of their liberation. Castro's defiance of the United States appealed to some in Basin countries who in varying degrees resented the power and policies of the U.S. Some were receptive to Castro's example, and his direct or indirect leadership, because of the international allies he developed; others were receptive in spite of them. Furthermore, other leaders—in Jamaica, Guyana, and Panama, for example—played the "Cuba card" in a game of pressures with the United States.

Castro knew he could tap a reservoir of anti-American feeling in the Basin, but he also knew that in order to wage the long war he had in mind against the United States—his "true destiny," as he once described it to Celia Sanchez—required an ally that could shield him from a fatal U.S. retaliation. Only the Soviet Union could offer such a shield, and with the formation of this alliance, the East/West conflict was dragged into the heart of the Caribbean. The injection of that rivalry, in large part, shaped

Cuban policies toward Basin countries and their reactions to Cuba, and fixed the American position.

In important respects, Castro's vendetta against the United States has led him to strive for goals that defy common sense and Cuban tradition—not to mention the histories and needs of other countries in the Basin he supposedly wished to help "liberate." For example, his policies have cut him off from the natural and massive U.S. market, and from much of the world's convertible currencies and advanced technologies. This clearly has salient implications for a Cuba, Grenada, or Nicaragua seeking development. Furthermore, by introducing the East/West rivalry into the Western Hemisphere, Castro assured conflict with the United States, and greatly increased the prospects for small- and even large-scale violence in the region.

But Castro's battle in the Basin has continued to confront difficulties. Cuba's increasing dependence upon the Soviet Union for economic support, and the deepening militarization of the island, have generated regional apprehensions. These concerns assured broad support in 1983 among Eastern Caribbean States for the U.S. intervention against the NJM (and Cuba) in Grenada.

At the same time, U.S. acquiescence to the massive Soviet presence in Cuba, and to Cuba's subversive policies in other nations, also has had, in varying degrees, an intimidating effect on nearby nations. As Jamaican Foreign Minister Thompson said, he *had* to keep Cuba in mind when planning Jamaican policies. This became increasingly the case while U.S. activity and authority in the region were declining during the 1970s under Presidents Nixon, Ford, and Carter. It is also the case in the 1980s because of the perception that Americans are so divided among themselves vis-à-vis regional policy, that Washington can no longer act decisively even in an emergency. For example, the 13 March 1987 vote against the United States, and for Cuba, in the United Nations Commission on Human Rights may to some degree show, as Venezuelan Carlos Rangel has argued, that many in Latin America (including Venezuela and Colombia, in the broader definition of the Basin) increasingly view the United States as an "incompetent imperial power" on the short end of history.[54]

The influence of the Cuban/Soviet alliance has spread considerably since 1979. While the Soviet Union refused to openly support most revolutionary movements in the Basin during the 1960s (except to some degree in Guatemala), by the end of the 1970s, indirect and, occasionally, direct Soviet support for military movements increased around the Basin, usually introduced through Cuban efforts. This change occurred for many reasons, including the pattern of Cuban/Soviet cooperation in Africa during the mid-1970s, and Castro's ability to convince Soviet leaders that these movements are worth some investment in training and materiel.

Indeed, in 1979 Castro was on a foreign policy "high," just as he had been at the OLAS Conference in 1967 only weeks before Che Guevara was killed. In surveying the landscape in 1979, revolutions had put Castro's Marxist-Leninist followers in power in Grenada and Nicaragua, friendly governments held office in Jamaica, Panama, and Guyana, prospects for a revolutionary victory seemed excellent in El Salvador, and Castro took over as president of the Non-Aligned Movement at a fiery session in Havana.

But almost immediately it began to unravel. The Soviet invasion of Afghanistan left Castro, as the Third World's chief apologist for the U.S.S.R., trying to defend what most nonaligned countries considered indefensible. Michael Manley was defeated by a pro-American candidate in the 1980 Jamaican elections; some 125,000 Cubans fled abroad in the Mariel exodus, causing Castro great domestic and international humiliation; Cuban jets recklessly sank a Bahamas Defense Force patrol boat and killed several Bahamians; the Salvadoran guerrillas' "final offensive" fizzled; and Ronald Reagan was elected President of the United States. In the years that followed, Bishop was murdered by his erstwhile NJM colleagues and the United States rescued Grenada from its revolution; the Sandinistas came under increasing, if irregular, pressure; Castro's foreign debt renunciation schemes drew no support from the hemisphere's leaders; and the new chief in the Soviet Union was decidedly unenthusiastic about Castro's increasingly ineffective domestic policies and counterproductive reform measures.

There are many ironies in all this: successes that lead to setbacks and threats that lead, for a time, at least, to security. Cuban support for the Grenadian and Nicaraguan revolutions had a fortifying impact on those countries, at least in the short and medium term. But almost immediately after the NJM took power in Grenada, there was an open swing against leftist revolutionary forces elsewhere in the English-speaking Caribbean, with many Barbadians and others wondering why it took the United States so long to throw the NJM out. During the mid-1980s, support for the Sandinista regime declined at home and abroad, despite setbacks also for the United States.[55] And just as Castro's triumph in 1959 had inspired President John Kennedy to launch his Alliance for Progress and counterinsurgency training, the successes in Grenada and Nicaragua precipitated the Caribbean Basin Initiative, the Kissinger Report, and expanded U.S. involvement in the region—from U.S. military buildups in Key West and Honduras to support for resistance fighters in Nicaragua.

What more have Castro's policies wrought? Domestically, a country that in 1959 was among the most equitable and developed in the Third World, and thus in an usually good position to accomplish more of the same, has become a repressive economic basket case that is dependent on massive Soviet Bloc aid amounting to a quarter of its annual GNP. Thus, few in the Basin aside from dogmatic Marxist-Leninists find much of value to imitate in the Cuban intellectual or economic experience.[56] In any event, as Jorge Dominguez has noted, "there does not appear to be any systematic relationship between internal conditions in Cuba and the trends in Cuban foreign policy."[57]

But only a fool would pronounce Castro an anachronism. For nearly three decades, he has waged a remarkably effective and protracted struggle against an often flustered and indecisive United States. Furthermore, he has turned Cuba into the most highly armed military and intelligence station in Latin America, with facilities that can (and do) support Soviet Bloc interests thousands of miles from Cuban and Soviet shores. Many in the region, however, are concerned about Cuba's inordinate Soviet-backed military strength and Castro's role in training guerrillas and other vanguard groups. These groups, although small in number, can have a decisive impact in countries with ineffective defenses against professional subversion. And, according to a high-ranking Cuban defector, Cuban and Soviet agents have made monkeys of U.S. intelligence in Cuba and perhaps beyond.

In the broadest sense, Cuba may have significantly improved its position within the Basin in the mid-1980s. Contributing to this assessment are Cuba's increasing bilateral diplomatic contacts and the possibility that Havana will soon be readmitted to inter-American organizations, or become a member of new organizations that do not even include the United States. In part, this change stems from the perceptions of Cuba "behaving itself" in the international community, but perhaps more importantly it may be traced to Cuba's filling a vacuum left by an indecisive United States. Indeed, some analysts who oppose the Soviet Bloc have, in effect, agreed with Soviet analysts that a shift in the correlation of forces is underway and that Cuba is a beneficiary as well as contributor to that much larger realignment.

Notes

1. "The Allegory of the Cloud and the Light," attributed to Fidel Castro. Tomás Borge, a founder of the Frente Sandinista de Liberación Nacional (FSLN) movement in Nicaragua, may have had this in mind when he wrote that the victory of the armed struggle in Cuba was "the drawing back of innumerable curtains, a flash of light. . . ." See Borge, "Carlos, El Amanecer Ya No Es una Tentacion," *Casa de las Américas* (Havana), No. 114 (May–June 1979), p. 107.

In this chapter, Caribbean Basin will mean the countries and territories of the Caribbean Sea and Central America, including Panama. Mexico and the nations on the northern rim of South America, geographically part of the Basin, are covered in other chapters.

2. Rene Anillo Capote, "About the 20th Anniversary of the First Conference of Solidarity of the Peoples of Africa, Asia and Latin America," *Tricontinental* (Havana), (January–February 1986), pp. 29–30. The author is secretary general of the Cuba-based organization set up at that conference, called the Tricontinental.

3. See Francisco López Segrera, *Cuba y Centro América* (Mexico City: Claves Latinoamericanas, 1986), pp. 49–51. This book, by a member of the Instituto Superior de Relaciones Internacionales de Cuba, is misnamed: it is more an attack on U.S. policies in Central America than a study of Cuba and Central America.

4. For a study of Cuban relations in the region emphasizing the traditional objectives, but with information on secondary objectives as well, see Jorge I. Dominguez, "Cuba's Relations with Caribbean and Central American Countries," in Alan Adelman and Reid Reading, eds., *Confrontation in the Caribbean Basin* (Pittsburgh, Pa.: University of Pittsburgh Center for Latin American Studies, 1984), pp. 167–68. For an examination of Castro's non-traditional personal motivations and style, see Edward Gonzalez, and David Ronfeldt, *Castro, Cuba and the World* (Santa Monica, Ca.: The RAND Corporation, 1986). A recent U.G. Government survey is U.S. Department of State, *Soviet Influence Activities* (Washington: U.S. Government Printing Office, 1987), pp. 66–67.

5. Cuban Professor Miguel A. D'Estefano Pisani recounts the long list of "charges the peoples of Our America have against Yankee imperialism" in "An Essential Dossier," *Tricontinental*, No. 92 (1984), pp. 10–19. The director of the Cuban Center for American Studies wrote in the mid-1980s that the history of Cuban policy toward Latin America has fallen into four stages, each identified according to Cuban relations with the United States and the region's governments: (1) 1959–62, when Cuba "reentered the Latin American and Caribbean scene" and opposed the U.S. hegemonic system, but still was prepared to negotiate differences with Washington; (2) 1962–69, the period of isolation, when U.S. support for dictators and military coups was on the rise, and mass mobilizations and guerrilla war were promoted as the best way to restrain Washington; (3) 1970–79, the "erosion of the blockade and rupture of official isolation" as a result of rising Latin American opposition to the United States; and (4) 1979–present, which brought revolutions in Grenada and Nicaragua, greater unity among Latin Americans against the U.S., and a "consolidation of ties" between Cuba and the region's governments. Cuba has been so persistent in its international policies, he concludes, "it has beyond doubt contributed to the erosion and virtual defeat of the diplomatic, economic, and political blockade set up by the United States against our tiny island." See Luis Suárez Salazar, "La política cubana hacia América Latina," *América Latina* (Moscow), No. 8 (1987), pp. 6–9, 12.

6. See Timothy Ashby, *The Bear in the Backyard: Moscow's Caribbean Strategy* (Lexington, Mass.: Lexington Books, 1987), pp. 60–61 and notes.

7. See Prensa Latina, 27 March 1986, cited in Radio Martí, *Quarterly Situation Report,* Washington (April–June 1986), p. II/16.

8. See *Federal Register,* Washington, D.C. Vol. 51, No. 237 (10 December 1986), pp. 44459–62; also, Jay Mallin, *The Washington Times,* 22 August 1983.
9. Valdés quoted in Dominguez, p. 177. Also see Jeffrey Richelson, *Sword and Shield: The Soviet Intelligence and Security Apparatus* (Cambridge, Mass.: Ballinger Publishing Co., 1986), pp. 210–12, 215–16; Ashby, pp. 57–61, passim; Jay Mallin, *The Washington Times,* 22, 23, 24, 25, and 26 August 1983; R. A. Hudson, "Castro's America Department: Systemizing Insurgencies in Latin America," in *Terrorism: An International Journal,* No. 2 (1987), pp. 125–67.
10. Hudson, p. 129; *Wall Street Journal* (27 November 1987).
11. See William Ratliff, *Castroism and Communism in Latin America* (Washington: American Enterprise Institute/Hoover, 1976), pp. 199–208. "Olas" means "waves" in Spanish; Castro told the delegates, "OLAS is the wave of the future, symbol of the revolutionary waves sweeping a continent." *Granma* (Havana), 20 August 1967.
12. See "Palabras del Primer Ministro de Cuba, Comandante Fidel Castro Ruz, e la CEPA," In *Fidel en Chile* (Santiago: Editorial Quimantu, 1972), p. 238.
13. See Wallace Spaulding, "International Communist Organizations," *1986 Yearbook,* pp. 399–401. For typical presentations of the issue, see Castro's speech at the Meeting on the Latin American and Caribbean Foreign Debt in Havana on 3 August 1985, in *Tricontinental,* No. 103 (1985), pp. 4–25; and the article by Silvio Baro Herrera, "Crisis y deuda externa en américa latina y el caribe," in *OCLAE,* No. 7 (1985), pp. 4–13.
14. For example, when the popular and prolific Mexican cartoonist Rius published his *LA DEUDA (y como NO pagarla)* [The Debt (and how NOT to pay it)] (Mexico City: Editorial Grijalbo, 1985), a number of pages were textual quotes from Castro; two of the six sources in his bibliography are Castro and one is the Cuban Communist Party daily *Granma.*
15. Interview by EFE, Madrid, 24 February, in *Foreign Broadcast Information Service,* Latin America. Also see William Ratliff, "Castro's Debt Crusade," in a forthcoming volume, *The Latin American Debt: Problems and Policies,* edited by Robert Wesson. Cuba's debt to the Soviet Union in late 1987 was estimated at more than $22 billion; Cuba owed Western banks and governments about $3.42 billion in hard currency and $85 million in commercial credits; see Department of State, *Soviet Influence Activities,* p. 66.
16. In Tad Szulc, *Fidel: A Critical Portrait* (New York: William Morrow, 1986), p. 491, the author argues that Castro was embarrassed by these early landings and reports suspicions at the time that the attacks had been authorized by Raul Castro. According to Pamela Falk, *Cuban Foreign Policy* (Lexington, Mass.: Lexington Books, 1986), p. 25, Castro has admitted giving assistance only to the invasion of the Dominican Republic, though she herself believes (p. 156) that as early as 1959 Cuba began to aid small revolutionary brigades in Venezuela, the Dominican Republic, Panama, and Haiti. Ernesto Betancourt, who was in the Cuban government at the time, sees Cuban involvement in all four; see Betancourt, "Exporting the Revolution to Latin America," in Carmelo Mesa-Lago, ed., *Revolutionary Change in Cuba* (Pittsburgh, Pa.: University of Pittsburgh Press, 1971), p. 114.
17. Suárez Salazar, p. 6.
18. See Henry Gill, "Cuba and Mexico: A Special Relationship?" in Barry Levine, ed., *The New Cuban Presence in the Caribbean* (Boulder, Colo.: Westview Press, 1983), p. 78; and Anthony Maingot, "Cuba and the Commonwealth Caribbean: Playing the Cuban Card," in ibid., pp. 25, 39.

19. See Valentin Rodriguez Pérez, "Honduras in Reagan's Central American Strategy," *Tricontinental*, no. 106 (1986), pp. 26–35.

20. Tad Szulc writes, in *Fidel*, p. 315, that the CIA intervention in Guatemala "had an enormous impact on Castro."

21. See *Granma*, 12 January 1987. On Guatemala, see the forthcoming studies by Michael Radu, *Revolutionary ideology and Violence in Central America: The Case of Guatemala* and Georges Fauriol and Eva Loser, *Guatemala's Political Puzzle.*

22. Some of this aid went through such front organizations as the OCLAE, which in a celebration of its fifteenth anniversary, "Unidad, solidaridad y lucha antiimperialista," *OCLAE,* no. 8 (1981), p. 11, proudly confirmed that it had "collected and sent material and financial aid" to "repel the Yankee intervention."

23. Dominguez, pp. 175–176, argues that though Cuban involvement was not "the major factor" in the Salvadoran conflict, it was nonetheless "quite extensive" and involved "substantial military support." The most complete study of Cuban and Nicaraguan involvement in El Salvador is John Norton Moore, *The Secret War in Central America* (Frederick, Md.: University Publications of America, 1987), passim. On Nicaraguan support, see Daniel Ortega's comments in Dan Williams, "Arms Shipped to Salvador Rebels, Nicaragua Admits," *Los Angeles Times,* 25 June 1987. For the evidence of a former Salvadoran guerrilla leader, see Javier Rojas U., *Conversaciones con el Comandante Miguel Castellanos* (Santiago, Chile: Editorial Adelante, 1986).

24. Maingot, p. 22.

25. *Ibid.,* pp. 22–23, 38–39.

26. Anthony Maingot, "Grenada and the Caribbean: Mutual Linkages and Influences," in Jiri Valenta and Herbert Ellison, eds., *Grenada and Soviet/Cuban Policy* (Boulder, Colo.: Westview Press, 1986), p. 133.

27. See Juan Mari Bras, *El Independentismo en Puerto Rico* (Santa Domingo, Dominican Republic: Editorial Cepa, 1984), p. 134.

28. See Austin Linsley, "U.S.-Cuban Relations: The Role of Puerto Rico," in Cole Blasier and Carmelo Mesa-Lago, eds., *Cuba in the World* (Pittsburgh, Pa.: University of Pittsburgh Press, 1979), pp. 122–24. For the text of the Non-Aligned statement see *Tricontinental* (September-October 1975), pp. 93–102. No other subject has received so much attention in *Tricontinental* since the Cuba-based Third World journal was founded in 1966.

29. See George Volsky, "Puerto Rico," in *1986 Yearbook on International Communist Affairs* (Stanford, Calif.: Hoover Institution Press, 1985), p. 140.

30. See Juan M. Garcia-Passalacqua, *Puerto Rico: Equality and Freedom At Issue* (New York: Praeger/Hoover Institution, 1984), p. 104; and George Volsky, "Puerto Rico: Colonialism Revisited," *Latin American Research Review,* XXII, No. 2 (1987), pp. 227–34.

31. Jiri Valenta and Virginia Valenta, "Leninism in Grenada," in Valenta and Ellison, p. 5. On the basis of interviews in Grenada, Ashby reports, pp. 83–84, "the overthrow itself was carried out with the aid of a team of black Cuban commandos from the Directorate of Special Operations. . . ."

32. See "Cuba, Nicaragua, Grenada, Together We Shall Win," in Maurice Bishop, *Forward Ever!* (Sydney: Pathfinder Press, 1982), pp. 133, 134 and 137.

33. Liam James notebook, in *Grenada Documents: An Overview and Selection* (Washington: Department of State, 1984), Document 23, p. 1. Although the

airport would have been used for tourism, as Cuban and other bloc leaders said, two features suggested that it was also intended as a refueling point for large numbers of individuals not planning to spend time in Grenada: both the fuel storage tanks and the food service facilities were many times larger than those in comparable international airports. Author interview with U.S. AID director in charge of completing the airport, Point Salines, Grenada, 4 September 1984. On the Americas Department project in the churches, see *Grenada Documents*, Document 2.

34. According to Maingot, Jamaican Marxist Trevor Munroe was the real leader of the movement in mid-1979. See Maingot, "Grenada and the Caribbean," pp. 138–39. Grenada's interest in being a bridge is revealed in a report from the NJM embassy in Moscow, in *Grenada Documents*, Document 29, p. 2.

35. See Ashby, p. 89. The situation clearly "upset the balance in the area," as noted by Francois Moanack, Venezuela's special ambassador at large for the Caribbean, and posed a geostrategic threat in the region; see comments in *El Diario de Caracas*, 11 July 1987, trans. in *Joint Publications Research Service* (15 October 1987), JPRS-LAM-87-068, p. 97.

36. On Cuban relations with Grenada, see chapters in Valenta and Ellison, *Grenada and Soviet/Cuban Policy*, especially Mark Falcoff, "Bishop's Cuba, Castro's Grenada," pp. 67–76; and Ashby, esp. chapter 4. The Cuban position and many international reactions are presented in *Fidel Castro, La Invasion a Granada* (Mexico City: Editorial Katun, 1983). A Soviet perspective is available from the Soviet Academy of Sciences, American Latina, *Granada: Historia, Revolucion, Intervencion de Estados Unidos* (Moscow: Ciencias Sociales Contemporaneas, 1984). Also see wire, "14 Convicted of Murdering Grenada Leader," *Los Angeles Times*, 5 December 1987, and Joseph Treaster, "Since the Invasion, a Grenada in Flux," *New York Times*, 25 October 1987.

37. See Carlos Fonseca Amador interviews and articles in Fonseca, *Bajo la Bandera del Sandinismo* (Managua: Editorial Nueva Nicaragua, 1981, 1985), vol. I, pp. 292, 295, 338, 359; and Borge, p. 107.

38. See Fonseca, *Bajo la Bandera del Sandinismo*, p. 360.

39. See Radio Martí, *Quarterly Situation Report* (July–September 1986), p. II/16, and *OSR* (April–June 1986), p. II/17; the January 1987 poll, by a Costa Rican affiliate of Gallup International, reported in a U.S. Information Agency Research Memorandum, "Central Americans Fear Sandinistas," dated 5 March 1987; for earlier poll see Department of State, *The Challenge to Democracy*, p. 45. For the testimony of the Defense Ministry defector, Major Roger Miranda Bengoechea, see Robert Leiken, "Foes of Contra Aid Are Grasping at Straws," *New York Times*, 28 December 1987. During a trip to Nicaragua in January 1987 I was told repeatedly that if Nicaraguans believed a decisive operation was underway to overthrow the Sandinistas, 90 percent of the Sandinista military would turn on their officers, though such figures can not be verified; business friends who travel frequently in the country and maintain grass-roots contacts have heard the same.

40. See Ortega interview in *Verde Olivo*, Havana, 6 November 1986; Borge, "Carlos, el amanecer," pp. 104–119; and Carlos Fonseca Amador, et al, *Nicaragua: La estrategia de la victoria* (Mexico City: Editorial Nuestro Tiempo, 1980), esp. pp. 58–67; and U.S. Departments of State and Defense, *The Challenge to Democracy in Central America* (Washington, D.C.: U.S. Government Printing Office, 1986).

41. Nicaraguan government sources acknowledge that U.S. aid for the "counter-revolution" was first approved in November 1981, and that private aid began in 1983. See *la Contrarevolución: Desarrollo y Consecuencias. Datos basicos, 1980–85* (Managua: Centro de Comunicacion Internacional, 1985), p. 14. For figures on the size of Central American military establishments see *The Challenge to Democracy*, pp. 19–23. Though the figures vary somewhat, the relative sizes are attested to by the annuals of other research organizations, including the Stockholm International Peace Research Institute, *World Armaments and Disarmament: SIPRI Yearbook 1986* (Oxford: Oxford University Press, 1986), p. 528.

42. López Segrera, p. 52. Major Miranda said that in mid-1987 there were fewer than 500 Cuban military advisers in Nicaragua, Stephen Kinzer, "Soviet is Aiding Nicaragua in Buildup, Defector Says," *New York Times*, 14 December 1987.

43. *New York Times*, 21 March 1985; Defense Intelligence Agency, *Handbook on the Cuban Armed Forces* (Washington: DIA, 1986), p. 8/14; Radio Martí, *Quarterly Situation Report*, April–June 1986, p. II/17; *Christian Science Monitor*, 24 June 1987, *Los Angeles Times*, 21 July 1987; *New York Times*, 20 August 1987; "Soviet Bloc Assistance to Cuba and Nicaragua," U.S. Department of State, October 1987; Maingot, pp. 23–27; Larry Rohter, "Sandinista is Pressing Peace Plan," *New York Times*, 21 March 1985; . . . Doyle McManus, "Soviet Arms for Nicaragua at New High," *Los Angeles Times*, 21 July 1987; Stephen Kinzer, "For Nicaragua, Soviet Frugality Starts to Pinch," 20 August 1987.

44. See Maingot, pp. 23–27.

45. See Georges Fauriol, *Foreign Policy Behavior of Caribbean States* (New York: University Press of America, 1984), pp. 174–79. More acerbically, Thompson is said to have remarked that "to ignore Cuba is sheer stone age stupidity." See Ronald Jones, "Cuba and the English-speaking Caribbean," in Cole Blasier and Carmelo Mesa-Lago, eds., *Cuba in the World* (Pittsburgh, Pa.: University of Pittsburgh Press, 1979), p. 134.

46. See Radio Martí, *Quarterly Situation Report* (October–December 1986), p. II/18.

47. Geyer, *The New Latins* (New York: Doubleday, 1970), p. 266; ellipses in original.

48. See Steve C. Ropp, "Cuba and Panama: Signaling One Way, Going Another," in Levine, *The New Cuban Presence*, p. 62. Ropp suggests other partial parallels in his *Panamanian Politics* (New York: Praeger, 1982), chapter 4, including Peron's Argentina, Barrientos's Bolivia, and Frei's Chile.

49. When I visited Panama in 1972 my suitcase was impounded at the airport because it contained a book with the word "communist" in its title.

50. Interviews with U.S. intelligence officials in Panama, Washington, and San Francisco.

51. There has been a somewhat higher, though very irregular, level of trade with Mexico, and a little with a couple of other countries not included in this chapter.

52. Department of International Economic and Social Affairs, United Nations, *1985 International Trade Statistics Yearbook* (New York, 1987), p. 297.

53. Examples of this mindset abound from Cuba's Sandinista allies, as in the comment Carlos Fonseca made in Havana in 1971 that the United States is "the major threat to humanity" in the world today.

54. Carlos Rangel, "Latin Allies Desert U.S. on Cuba Vote," *The Wall Street Journal*, 27 March 1987.
55. See James LaMoyne's excellent survey of conditions in Nicaragua in "Bitterness and Apathy in Nicaragua," *The New York Times*, 29 December 1987.
56. For a survey of how Cuba's domestic and international conditions have and haven't changed during Castro's first quarter-century, see Robert A. Packhenham, "Capitalist Dependency and Socialist Dependency: The Case of Cuba," in *Journal of InterAmerican Studies* (Spring 1986), pp. 59–92.
57. Dominguez, p. 193.

4

Cuban Foreign Policy toward Latin America

Ernest Evans

Introduction

In examining Cuban foreign policy toward Latin America under the Castro leadership, it is the words of Fidel himself which afford us the best insight into Cuban aims: "We must transform the Andes into the Sierra Maestra of Latin America." "The duty of every revolutionary is to make the revolution." With these phrases, a new era of challenge to the order of Latin America—and an attempt to break the region's "geographic fatalism"—was begun. And, clearly, Havana was to be at the core of continental revolution.

From the outset, these words rang true. Beginning in 1959, and continuing up to the present time, Cuba, albeit utilizing varying tactics and strategy, has sought to export the Cuban revolutionary model throughout the Western Hemisphere. At this juncture the question may be asked: what forces drove Cuban involvement in Latin American revolutionary activity? There were at least three reasons. First, from the outset, the Cuban revolution has not sought to deny its global pretensions. Second, in continuing the phenomenon of "hispanidad," Latin America was viewed as fertile terrain for the duplication of Cuban events. And third, in attempting to fend off regional isolation, the creation of a more congenial regional environment to the Cuban revolution was viewed as a necessity.

In the 30 years since the Cuban revolution, lessons have clearly been learned by the Cuban leadership in its external relations with Latin America. Or, to put it more simply, after a series of initial setbacks, Cuban strategy has clearly been refined and become much more sophisticated.

The 1960s began, quite literally, with a bang. Ché Guevara, the leading ideologue of continental revolution, was afforded "carte blanche" by the Castro regime to test his revolutionary theories outside of the Cuban laboratory. However, given the course of the Cuban revolution, a natural antipathy formed between pro-Soviet Latin American communist parties and the Castro regime. Indeed, the new Cuban leadership viewed the region's orthodox parties as "coat and tie" communists. Thus, with global pretensions intact, Castroite factions within Latin American communist parties were created by Havana.

The divergent views between Castroite and orthodox, pro-Soviet factions related to differences over strategy and the possibility of revolution in Latin America. The former viewed Latin America as ripe for revolution—all that was required was guerrilla "foco" to ignite the embers. The orthodox, pro-Soviet parties saw the situation quite differently, and argued for the path of mass struggle.

The failure of the guerrilla "foco" to produce anything but the death of Guevara in Bolivia, as well as a head-on confrontation with the Soviet Union over Cuban behavior, forced the Cuban regime to reassess its strategy in the latter part of the decade. Thus, the 1970s saw the development of a unified strategy involving both Moscow and Latin America: Cuban idealism and ideology were replaced by the politics of Soviet clientilism and conventional bargaining with Latin American orthodox parties.

Since that time, Cuban strategy has been continuously refined, with major changes in strategy undertaken as regional developments warranted. It is clear that the conditions for other Castroite revolution were not present in Latin America—pragmatism, therefore, has become the core of Cuban strategy. Revolution, where possible, has still been promoted, but diplomatic relations have also been advanced. Indeed, the pariah status that Cuba was relegated to by Latin America has been replaced by a new level of cordiality to Cuba's leaders from numerous regional heads of state.

As a result, the broad outline of Havana's regional efforts can be divided into four principal stages: 1959–68, 1968–78, 1978–82, and 1982 to the present. The remainder of this article will discuss these four stages in further detail.

Stage I: Revolutionary Adventurism, 1959–68

When Castro came to power in 1959, he and his associates, such as Ernesto "Ché" Guevara, believed that Latin America was "ripe for revolution." With the hindsight afforded to us in the 1980s one can see how wrong they were, but in fairness to the Cuban revolutionaries it should be pointed out that they were far from being alone in their belief. Many other Latin American revolutionaries shared their assumption that Latin America was soon to be radically transformed. In its first manifesto, in February 1963, the Venezuelan Armed Forces of National Liberation (FALN) stated: "The situation is ripe and there should not be a moment's delay in bringing together all patriots. . . ."[1] Hugo Blanco, a Peruvian radical who was organizing peasants in the countryside, wrote a letter to friends in 1962 stating: "I am writing to you with the happiness the combattant feels as he sees triumph in the war is near after fighting in a hundred battles."[2] A 1965 communique by the Peruvian Movement of the Revolutionary Left (MIR) states: "The armed MIR calls on all sectors of the people to fight. Victory is ours. The guerrillas are spreading. Armed fighting is seeping [into] the country. Liberation is at hand."[3] In 1964, the Guatemalan's Revolutionary Movement of November 13 (MR–13) issued a declaration which began: "The year 1965 will be of great importance. The Guatemalan Socialist revolution will make an enormous leap forward. The conditions for it exist and are mature."[4]

In the United States, the Kennedy administration was likewise concerned about the spread of revolution in Latin America. In response, the U.S. government began to train Latin American military and police officers in counterinsurgency, introduced a required course on counterinsurgency at the State Department, and expanded the size of the Special Forces (the Green Berets).[5] The Administration also launched the Alliance for Progress, which was designed to undercut the appeals of radical movements in Latin America by promoting peaceful social, economic, and political reforms.

Convinced that Latin America was ripe for revolution, Castro supported a number of revolutionary movements in Latin America during the 1960s.[6] From 1962–64, he supported the efforts of the Venezuelan radical left in its efforts to overthrow the government of Romulo Betancourt. In Peru, he supported the rural guerrilla movements which emerged in the 1962–65 period. In Guatemala, he supported the guerrillas trying to overthrow that country's military dictatorship. And in Colombia, he supported the radical left in its struggle to topple that nation's legitimate government.

Even during this period of seemingly unrestrained revolutionary adventurism, it is interesting to note that there was one country with which Castro did not attempt to meddle—Mexico. The latter was the only member of the Organization of American States (OAS) that did not break diplomatic relations with Cuba in the early 1960s. Castro made no attempt to export revolution to Mexico because he undoubtedly realized he could not fight the whole Western Hemisphere; the Cuban leader realized he would need a few friendly nations in the hemisphere. (As will be seen later in this chapter, Mexican/Cuban relations would not be as strong in the 1970s and 1980s as they were in the 1960s.)

The net result of Castro's attempts in the 1960s to export revolution were a total failure. Not only did revolutions not occur, but in addition, Castro's foreign policy suffered the twin setbacks of regional isolation and increased friction with his chief international protector, the Soviet Union.

The OAS reacted quite firmly to Castro's attempts to export revolution. In 1964, the OAS placed an economic embargo on Cuba and urged all of its members to break diplomatic relations with the island nation. Castro's regime was thus almost totally isolated in the Western Hemisphere. Instead of producing additional revolutionary states with which to ally himself, his policies of trying to export revolution had resulted in the other nations of the Western Hemisphere uniting against him and his government.

Castro's adventurist revolutionary policy had also resulted in considerable friction with the Soviet Union. For a variety of reasons, the Soviet Union was in strong disagreement with Castro's strategy on exporting revolution throughout Latin America. Foremost, the Soviets did not believe Latin America was ripe for revolution. Instead, they felt that given the weakness of most local communist parties, on the one hand, and the clear determination of the United States—the dominant regional power—to prevent revolutionary change, on the other hand, revolutions were most unlikely to transpire in Latin America. However, in light of the Sino/Soviet split, the Soviets were engaged in polemics with the Chinese over the issue of wars of national liberation; thus, the Soviets at times would declare their support of wars of national liberation in Latin America. For example, in 1964 and 1965 *Pravda* ran a number of articles supporting guerrilla warfare in the region.[7] At the 1966 Solidarity Conference of the Peoples of Africa, Asia and Latin America in Havana, the leader of the Soviet delegation, S. R. Rashidov, made a fiery speech in favor of armed revolutionary struggle and declared that the Soviet Union was prepared to assist guerrillas in Venezuela, Peru, Colombia, and Guatemala.[8]

Soviet actions failed, however, to live up to its leadership's rhetoric. The only step the Soviets took to aid guerrillas in this period was a 1965 shipment of $330,000 in cash to the Venezuelan guerrillas. (The shipment was intercepted by the Venezuelan authorities.) Aside from this incident, the Soviets basically continued their policy of supporting the peaceful road to socialism in Latin America.[9]

The Soviets were particularly critical of Castro's so-called "foco" theory of revolution. This theory, developed by Ché Guevara and Regis Debray, held that the method by which to promote revolution was for a small group of armed guerrillas (the "foco") to go into a remote area of a country, gradually build up a base of support, and then, as was the case in Cuba, "come down from the Sierra Maestres" and overthrow the government.[10]

The Soviets were highly critical of the foco theory because it placed no emphasis on an organized, disciplined party as the backbone of the revolutionary movement. As Debray wrote in his book *Revolution in the Revolution?*:

> Under certain conditions, the political and the military are not separate, but form one organic whole, consisting of the people's army, whose nucleus is the guerrilla army. The vanguard party can exist in the form of the guerrilla "foco" itself. The guerrilla force is the party in embryo.
>
> This is the staggering novelty introduced by the Cuban Revolution.[11]

Predating the 1917 Russian revolution, that nation's Communist Party had consistently rejected revolutionary theories which denigrated the role of a revolutionary party. Theories of urban uprisings without a disciplined party structure to carry on the uprising were dismissed as "putschism" or "blanquism" (named after Auguste Blanqui, a French revolutionary who believed that all that was needed to overthrow a government was a few hundred armed men). For similar reasons, Lenin dismissed urban terrorism as an ineffective strategy. It was his belief that urban terrorism distracted desperately needed personnel from the main task of a revolutionary movement—namely, the organization of the working class. Lenin argued that urban terrorism was not in any way connected to more important work of organizing the masses; while he was not opposed to terrorism in principle, he felt that terrorism should be but one instrument of a broad revolutionary strategy.[12]

The Soviet Union was further concerned that the Castro regime had so isolated itself that the survival of the Cuban revolution was in danger. Cognizant of the great distance between Moscow and Havana, the Soviets realized that for Cuba to not have reliable allies in the Western Hemisphere meant that the regime was dangerously vulnerable. While it is true that the United States had pledged not to invade Cuba at the time of the Cuban missile crisis, the Soviet Union was also well aware that changing circumstances (or simply the passage of time) could undo this pledge.

The Soviet Union was equally worried that Castro's attempts to export revolution throughout Latin America would drag them into an unwanted confrontation with the United States. After the Cuban missile crisis, the Soviets were understandably quite concerned about another confrontation with the United States in its own backyard. The Soviets knew that their Third World allies were quite capable of dragging them into confrontations with the United States—witness China's threats to invade Quemoy and Matsu in the 1950s and the Syrian invasion of Jordan in 1970 during Jordan's civil war. They had no desire to be dragged into a confrontation with the United States in the Western Hemisphere where the United States held all the high cards.

Finally, the Soviets felt that Castro was wasting precious resources in his efforts to export revolution in Latin America—resources that could be better used to aid the failing Cuban economy. The Cuban economy performed miserably throughout the 1960s, culminating in the disastrous attempt to produce 10 million tons of sugar by 1970. (Only 8.5 million tons were eventually produced.)[13]

The first phase of Cuban foreign policy came to an end in the late 1960s. Three events influenced Castro's decision to make major changes in his foreign policy toward Latin America.

The death of Ché Guevara

In a final attempt to show that the foco theory of revolution could work Ché Guevara went to Bolivia in 1966; his campaign was a disaster from start to finish. The desperate situation he encountered in Bolivia is graphically shown by the July, August, and September (he was killed in October 1967) summaries from his diary:[14]

July 1967

The most important characteristics are:

1. The total lack of contact (with other groups in the country) continues.

2. The lack of incorporation of the peasants continues to be felt . . .

August 1967

The most important characteristics:

1. We continue without any contacts of any kind and without reasonable hope of establishing them in the near future.

2. We continue without any incorporation on the part of the peasants.

September 1967

The characteristics are the same as those of last month, except that now the army is showing more effectiveness in action, and the mass of the peasants does not help us at all and have become informers.

The death of Ché Guevara served to discredit the foco theory once and for all. Even Castro was forced to accept the idea that Latin America was not ripe for revolution.

Pressure from the Soviet Union

By the late 1960s, the Soviet Union was determined to tighten its controls over Cuba. To this end they slowed down oil deliveries in early 1968.[15] This was a major threat to the Cuban economy, as Cuba had little oil of its own and lacked the foreign exchange necessary to buy oil on the world market. Castro responded by agreeing to certain Soviet demands, including Castro's endorsement of the 1968 Soviet invasion of Czechoslovakia and the improvement of his relations with the rest of Latin America.

The Deterioration of the Cuban Economy

As was noted above, by the late 1960s the Cuban economy was in dismal shape. Castro decided that the Soviets had been right in telling him to concentrate more time and effort on his own economy and less time and effort on spreading revolution in Latin America.[16]

Stage II: Diplomatic Reconciliation, 1968–78

In this second stage of Cuba's foreign relations with Latin America, the Cuban government undertook a number of major policy initiatives. Foremost, it drastically scaled down its support of revolutionary movements. Simultaneously, it sought to expand its diplomatic and economic ties with the established governments of Latin America. And it now closely coordinated its policy toward Latin America with that of the Soviet Union.

The results of these changes in Cuban foreign policy was a profound change in Cuba's relationship with the nations of the Western Hemisphere. On the diplomatic front, a number of Latin American countries moved to reestablish diplomatic relations with Cuba. Not only were such ties reestablished, but Cuba was successful in developing good relations with a number of nations in the hemisphere. In this context, the populist Peruvian military regime that came to power in 1968 established cordial relations with Cuba. Likewise, the Torrijos government in Panama, also a populist military regime, established good relations with Cuba (although, in the case of Torrijos, he exercised restraint in the development of relations with Cuba, in part relating to Panama's efforts to negotiate the Panama Canal Treaties). Michael Manley's socialist government in Jamaica was quite friendly to Castro. In Chile, one of the first acts of the Allende government was to reestablish diplomatic relations with Cuba; Castro later visited Chile at Allende's invitation. In Argentina, the return of Peron in 1973 ushered in a new period of warm relations between Cuba and Argentina.[17] In the case of Brazil, formal diplomatic relations with Cuba were not resumed until 1986 (relations had been broken in 1964 after the overthrow of the Goulart government). However, Brazil/Cuba relations began to thaw a bit after President Ernesto Geisel initiated the policy of "responsible pragmatism" in 1974, whereby Brazil ended its automatic alignment with the United States and sought out nonideological ties with socialist and Third World countries. Brazil also recognized the Popular Movement For the Liberation of Angola (MPLA) government in Angola, and defended the introduction of Cuban troops into Angola on the grounds that South African intervention in Angola was an act of aggression that had to be repelled. Finally, in the late 1970s and early 1980s, a steadily growing stream of Brazilian entertainers and businessmen were invited to visit Cuba.[18]

On the economic front, relations with the rest of Latin America also improved. In 1975, the OAS voted to end its economic embargo against Cuba. A year later, Venezuela agreed to supply Cuba with 20,000 barrels of oil a day in return for the Soviet Union's (the supplier of 95 percent of Cuba's oil requirements) acquisition of some of Venezuela's West European markets. A similar agreement was concluded between Mexico and the Soviet Union in 1978. Mexico agreed to supply oil to Cuba in exchange for Soviet deliveries to Mexico's oil customers in Greece, Turkey, and Eastern Europe.[19]

The increased Cuban willingness to cooperate with the Soviet Union paid off in considerable Soviet economic and military aid. In 1972, Cuba joined the socialist countries' Council for Mutual Economic Assistance (COMECON). Furthermore, the Soviets bought sugar and nickel from, and sold oil to, Cuba at subsidized prices. The Central Intelligence Agency (CIA) estimates that between 1961 and 1980 Cuba received $16.7 billion in economic aid from the Soviet Union.[20] In the same period, the Soviet Union provided $3.8 billion in military aid to Cuba.[21]

Finally, this stage of Cuban foreign policy was marked by coordination rather than conflict with the Soviet Union. The Cubans followed the Soviet line of supporting nationalistic regimes that were hostile to the United States. The Soviet Union was convinced that Latin America was not ripe for revolution; and, consequently, as was noted above, opposed attempts to overthrow governments in Latin America regarded as "putschist." Instead, they urged local communist parties to ally themselves with anti-American nationalists for the purpose of helping the latter come to power. Thus, the Cubans and Soviets cooperated on this policy in nations with nationalistic regimes like Mexico, Peru under the military junta (1968–80), Argentina, Jamaica under Michael Manley, and Panama under General Omar Torrijos.

The Soviets and the Cubans also coordinated their policies on Allende's

Chile.[22] Specifically, both the Cubans and the Soviets were concerned from the first that Allende might try to swing national policies politically leftward too quickly, resulting in his ouster by the military. To prevent such an outcome, they urged Allende to try to maintain a dialogue with the nation's Christian Democrats. It was argued that to totally alienate the Christian Democrats would force the latter into an alliance with the parties of the right.[23] In addition, Castro and the Soviets both cautioned Allende against alienating the United States. Specifically, the Soviets informed him that they could not afford to subsidize him in the same manner that they were subsidizing Cuba, and thus advised Allende to maintain good relations with the United States. In this context, Castro sent Allende a personal letter urging him to maintain good relations with the United States.[24]

To be sure, there was one major difference between the Soviet Union and Cuba with respect to Allende's Chile—and that concerned the MIR. The MIR was a Chilean terrorist organization with close ties to the left wing of Allende's Popular Unity coalition. The Soviets and the Chilean Communist Party were deeply hostile to the MIR. They felt that the MIR's terrorism was quite ineffective in creating revolution in Chile and that its only result would be to increase the dangers of a military coup.[25]

In contrast, Cuba supported the activities of the MIR. The Cuban embassy in Chile operated as a training center for members of the MIR, and the Cubans used their diplomatic pouch privileges to smuggle arms into Chile for transshipment to the MIR.[26]

Stage III: Selective Revolutionary Engagement, 1978–82

In the late 1970s, Cuba's foreign policy toward Latin America entered a new stage. In this stage, the Cubans returned to their earlier policy of supporting revolutionary movements in Latin America. However, Cuban support for revolutionary movements was to become more selective than during the 1960s; while supporting such movements Cuba continued to try to cultivate a number of existing governments in Latin America. Thus, the policy of a near total abandonment of revolutionary movements that had been pursued in the second stage of Cuban policy was reversed in favor of a policy of aiding particular revolutionary movements.

The Nicaraguan revolution had a profound impact on the Cubans (and, as will be noted below, on the Soviets); the latter were impressed with a number of aspects of the Sandinista victory. Foremost, it was recognized that while the so-called peaceful road to socialism had not resulted in any successful revolutions in Latin America (with the 1973 downfall of the Allende government providing a recent painful illustration of the failure of the peaceful road to socialism), the Sandinistas in Nicaragua had succeeded in carrying off a major revolution through armed struggle.

The Cubans were also cognizant of the American role in the Nicaraguan affair and were pleasantly surprised that the United States did not intervene to prevent the Sandinistas from seizing power. They were aware that the Carter Administration, despite its commitment to human rights, did not wish to see Somoza replaced by the Sandinistas. But there was little the United States could do to save Somoza: the OAS almost unanimously voted down a U.S. proposal for a peace-keeping force for Nicaragua. At the same time, U.S. public opinion, still feeling the impact of the Vietnam War, did not support American military intervention to prevent the Sandinistas from coming to power.

The Cubans were also impressed by the development of serious revolutionary movements elsewhere in Latin America. In El Salvador a civil war began in the late 1970s between the government and a coalition of revolutionary groups. In the case of Guatemala, there was a rebirth of activism on the part of several revolutionary movements. In Colombia, a new and quite sophisticated group, the M–19, was started up and directly attacked the nation's government. And in Peru, the government found itself locked in a serious battle with the Maoist guerrillas of *Sendero Luminoso* ("Shining Path").

By the late 1970s, Cuba was no longer the isolated pariah of the late 1960s. In the Caribbean, Cuba had an ally in Michael Manley's Jamaica. In early 1979 a new Cuban ally arose in the Caribbean when the New Jewel Movement seized power in Grenada. And, as noted before, by the late 1970s Cuba had established diplomatic ties and good relations with a number of the nations of Latin America. This partial Cuban reintegration into the region gave the regime a sense of confidence that it could resume support of revolutionary movements without becoming as isolated as had been the case in the late 1960s.

Thus a combination of factors, including the success of the Nicaraguan revolution, the emergence of other serious revolutionary movements in Latin America, and Cuba's new-found acceptance by the nations of the region, all contributed to the decision by the Cuban leadership to once again start supporting revolutionary movements. But perhaps the most important factor in this decision was that, by the late 1970s, the Soviet Union had become more sympathetic toward the use of violence in seizing power in Latin America. In order to fully understand Moscow's new inclination, it is useful to expand upon some earlier points in this article regarding the Soviet Union and revolutionary movements in Latin America.

In retrospect, Soviet hostility to the foco revolutionaries of the 1960s and to the urban terrorists of the 1970s stemmed from four factors.

First, many of these insurgents were considered doctrinally unorthodox. Trotskyism has played a larger role in Latin American politics than in any other region of the world; hence, it is not surprising that many Latin American revolutionary movements have been dogmatically Trotskyist or at least heavily influenced by Trotskyism. For example, many of the members of the revolutionary movements in Peru in the early 1960s were Trotskyists (including Hugo Blanco).[27] Furthermore, one of the major urban guerrilla groups in Argentina, the People's Revolutionary Army (ERP) was created by a group of Argentine Trotskyists.[28]

Second, the revolutionaries were often quite hostile to the local communist parties, which they dismissed as hopelessly "reformist." In light of the fact that most of Latin America's communist parties are Moscow-line parties, the Soviets obviously were distrustful of movements that were hostile to these parties.[29]

Third, the Soviets were skeptical of the guerrillas' chances of success. In this context, Moscow feared that the net result of violence by these guerrillas would be to bring to power staunchly conservative, anti-Communist governments that would repress the local communist party and be hostile to the Soviet Union. Along the same lines, in Uruguay during the early 1970s, the Soviet Union attacked the terrorism of the Tupamaros on the grounds (which ultimately proved to be quite correct) that such terrorism would lead to a military coup.[30] As noted earlier, both the Soviet Union and the Chilean Communist Party opposed, for similar reasons, the terrorism of the MIR in Chile.

Finally, for reasons very different from those of the United States, the Soviets wished to avoid "another Cuba." Specifically, they had no desire to acquire another client state in the Americas that would require the level of economic support that Cuba receives. In other words, while the Soviets would like to have pro-Soviet revolutionary governments in the Western Hemisphere, their enthusiasm for revolutionary governments is constrained by fears of having to provide massive subsidies to the new governments.

With respect to the current generation of revolutionary movements in Central and South America, many of these Soviet concerns have been considerably alleviated. These new revolutionary movements are quite willing to include the local communist parties in their broad opposition coalitions (the communist parties of El Salvador and Guatemala are both active supporters of the revolutionary movements in their countries).[31] Moreover, these revolutionary movements have a number of international backers; hence, in the event of victory, the new government will be able to look to sources aside from the Soviet Union for assistance. For example, Nicaragua has received considerable economic assistance from Brazil, Mexico, and Venezuela.[32] (The Soviet Union has sent a sizable amount of arms to Nicaragua, but has not given much economic aid.)[33] Finally, the Soviets believe these new revolutionary movements have a chance of success. Given their claims to be the world's leading revolutionary power, the Soviets obviously want to be able to claim at least some of the credit for any successful revolution. Moreover, the Soviets are well aware that failure to support a revolutionary movement early enough can aggravate relations with the new government. In the case of Algeria, for example, the Soviet failure to support the insurgents until late in the conflict persuaded the latter to keep a certain distance from the Soviet Union in its foreign policy.[34]

The upshot of these various factors was a major reassessment by Cuba of its foreign policy toward Latin America. The failure of the United States to intervene militarily in Nicaragua appeared to the Cubans to be evidence that, after Vietnam, the United States was neither willing nor able to play the role that it had played historically in Latin America as the center of "counter-revolution." If the United States would not intervene to save Somoza, it was thus reasoned that Cuba had little reason to fear the United States would invade Cuba in retaliation for Cuban support of revolutionary movements. The victory of the Sandinistas in Nicaragua and the emergence of major revolutionary movements in Colombia, El Salvador, Guatemala, and Peru demonstrated that Castro and Ché Guevara may have been correct in the 1960s when they argued that Latin America was "ripe for revolution."[35] The coming to power of Cuban allies in Grenada, Jamaica, and Nicaragua and the widespread regional and international support that the Sandinistas received appeared to suggest that Cuba did not have to fear regional isolation if it supported revolutionary movements. And finally, the changed attitude of the Soviet Union toward revolutionary violence in Latin America meant that Cuba could support revolutionary movements in Latin America without endangering relations with its chief international supporter.

The renewed Cuban support for revolutionary movements that began in the late 1970s was, however, considerably more selective than support given in the 1960s. While Castro may have felt that the chances of revolution had improved in Latin America, neither he nor his Soviet backers wished to lose all of the hard-won improvements in state-to-state relations of the 1970s. Consequently, Castro pursued a broad range of policies toward different types of governments in Latin America.[36]

Cuban Policies toward "Progressive" Governments

Cuba did not support revolutionary movements in Mexico, Panama, or Peru because it considered their governments to be strongly nationalistic and therefore potentially valuable allies.[37] For example, Peru asserted itself against both the International Monetary Fund and U.S. banks with its proposal that its payments on its debt not be allowed to exceed 10 percent of its export earnings, arguing that higher payments would seriously damage the economy.[38] In addition, in each case there were special factors that led Castro not to support revolutionary movements in these countries: Mexico (as was noted earlier) was supplying Cuba with oil; Peru's *Sendero Luminoso* insurgency was Maoist rather than pro-Soviet; and Panama was an area of great sensitivity to the United States because of the Panama Canal.

Cuban Policies toward Key Trading Partners of the Soviet Union and Cuba

Venezuela, like Mexico, supplies oil to Cuba. Argentina has developed close trade relations with the Soviet Union since the cooling of U.S./Soviet relations in the aftermath of the Soviet invasion of Afghanistan.[39] Given the economic importance of such countries to the Soviets and the Cubans, revolutionary movements in these nations have not been supported. In fact, the Soviet/Cuban desire for good relations with Argentina is so strong that both countries remained silent about the savage human rights violations in Argentina during the military's so-called "dirty war" against subversion from 1976 to 1979.[40]

Cuban Policies toward Democratic Regimes with Close Ties to the United States

The Soviets and the Cubans have been training the Revolutionary Movement of the People (MRP), a revolutionary movement in Costa Rica. The Costa Rican government, angered at this support of a domestic revolutionary movement, broke diplomatic relations with Cuba and drastically scaled down the size of the Soviet diplomatic mission in Costa Rica.[41] In the case of Colombia, the Soviets and the Cubans have been providing assistance to the guerrilla group, M–19. The latter has carried out a number of spectacular terrorist acts, including the seizure of a number of diplomats at a party at the Dominican Republic's embassy in Bogotá in February 1980.[42] Soviet and Cuban complicity in this incident is suggested by the fact that diplomats from communist countries left the party en masse before the seizure, leaving the other diplomats to be taken hostage.[43]

Cuban Policies toward Conservative Authoritarian Regimes

After the victory of the Sandinistas in 1979, the Cubans were optimistic regarding the outlook for revolutionary success in several other Central American countries, and were determined to do what they could to move this process forward. In El Salvador, Castro helped to unify the various guerrilla forces into a united revolutionary force. At the same time, the Cubans and Soviets began to supply arms and training to the revolutionaries in El Salvador. The Cubans hoped that the rebels' "final offensive" of January 1981 would result in a rebel victory in El Salvador before the incoming Reagan administration took office.[44]

In Guatemala, the Cubans also helped unify the various guerrilla groups fighting to bring down that nation's government. In addition, they began supplying arms and training to the Guatemalan revolutionaries.[45] In Honduras, the revolutionary movements were not as powerful as in El Salvador or Guatemala; nevertheless, the Cubans have been aiding these revolutionary movements as well.[46]

In 1982 Cuba made yet another reassessment of its foreign policy toward Latin America, reflecting concern for the Reagan administration's policies. As was noted earlier, one of the key assumptions in this third stage of Cuban foreign policy was that the United States, after Vietnam, was neither willing nor able to militarily intervene in the Western Hemisphere. The Reagan administration soon dispelled that assumption. Shortly following his inauguration, Reagan began a major U.S. intervention in Central America. El Salvador was given a large amount of U.S. military aid, and U.S. advisers were dispatched to help the Salvadoran military make proper use of this assistance. El Salvadoran military units were also brought to the United States for training. In addition, a number of U.S. military advisers were sent to Honduras; that country has also received considerable military assistance.

Most alarming of all from the Cuban point of view, the Reagan administration showed itself quite willing to intervene against established revolutionary regimes. Early in the Reagan administration, arms and funding began to be channeled to the so-called "contras" fighting the Sandinista government. Even more dramatically, in October 1983, the Reagan administration invaded Grenada and overthrew the New Jewel Movement government. After the U.S. military involvement in both Grenada and Nicaragua, the Cubans realized they could not afford to overlook the occasional hints by the Reagan administration of military action against Cuba if it continued to support revolutionary movements in Latin America. Thus, beginning in 1982, the Cubans began to scale down (without totally ceasing) their support for revolutionary movements in Latin America.

The Cubans were also disappointed by the failure of other revolutionary movements in Latin America. The Salvadoran rebels' final offensive of January 1981 failed to overthrow the Salvadoran government. Since that time, that civil war has basically been stalemated; while the government is unable to pacify the country, the revolutionaries are likewise unable to defeat the government's forces. In Guatemala, the government carried out a highly successful counterinsurgency campaign from 1982 to 1984. In late 1985, free elections were held and a Christian Democrat was elected president of the country. Thus, while both El Salvador and Guatemala still suffer from insurgent-sponsored violence, the chances of these movements coming to power appears to be much less probable in the mid-1980s than it did in the late 1970s.

From the Cuban perspective, at the time that opportunities for revolutionary change were looking poorer, opportunities for improved state-to-state relations were looking brighter. The American decision to back Great Britain during the 1982 Malvinas/Falklands war resulted in considerable anti-Americanism in Latin America. In contrast, the Cubans and Soviets gained considerable prestige in Latin America for their support of Argentina during the war. In the aftermath, it was clear that the Soviets and Cubans could use this newly acquired prestige to improve state-to-state ties in Latin America. By 1982, while both Cuba and the Soviet Union were increasingly skeptical of the chances of further revolutionary change in Latin America, the opportunities for increased state-to-state relations with the nations of Latin America after the Malvinas/Falklands war were quite appealing to them. In other words, by 1982 the Cubans and Soviets were quite willing to deemphasize support for revolutionary movements whose prospects for success appeared remote—in favor of establishing strong state-to-state relations with the nations of Latin America.

Cuba was also concerned about what appeared to be a renewed danger of regional isolation. It was previously noted that one reason Castro felt capable of resuming support for revolutionary movements in the late 1970s was that he no longer had the sense of regional isolation that he had in the late 1960s. However, by 1982 Cuba was again feeling in danger of being a pariah in the region. Colombia and Costa Rica had both broken diplomatic relations with Cuba because of Cuban support for domestic guerrilla groups. In Jamaica, Michael Manley's government had been defeated by the conservative opposition. In Peru, the new civilian government was less friendly toward Cuba than the military governments of the 1968–80 period had been.[47] And in Panama, Omar Torrijos had been killed in a plane crash in the summer of 1981. Cuba's loss of a number of key state-to-state allies forced Castro to reconsider his support for revolutionary movements in comparison to his efforts to avoid regional isolation. The net result was that support for revolutionary movements, by 1982, had been considerably scaled down.

The Soviet Union agreed with Castro that support of revolutionary movements in Latin America by the communist bloc had to be scaled down. In part, the Soviets were alarmed by the policies of the Reagan administration in Central and South America. The Reagan administration's policies of using both political and military pressure to "roll back" Soviet and Cuban gains in the Western Hemisphere forced the Soviets to confront a new mix of risks and costs in their policies toward Latin America. Whereas under Carter it had seemed that the United States was unable to take any steps to contain the growth of Cuban and Soviet influence in the Western Hemisphere, it quickly became clear under Reagan that the United States was prepared to take forceful action against the spread of such influence throughout Latin America and the Caribbean. In other words, under Carter the risks and costs of Soviet and Cuban expansion in Latin America had seemed quite low. Now, under Reagan, the risks and costs of such expansion were quickly perceived by the Soviets to be much higher.

Particularly alarming to the Soviet Union was the rhetoric early in the Reagan administration about "going to the source" (i.e., Cuba) of the instability in Central America.[48] Such rhetoric forced the Soviets to realize that too much active support for revolutionary movements in Central America could trigger American military action against Cuba.

Soviet support for the Cuban decision to scale back assistance to revolutionary movements was also due to the fact that by 1982 the Soviets had become pessimistic once again about the potential for revolutionary change in Latin America. The Soviets made the same assessment as the Cubans: in essence, it was assumed to be unlikely that there would be any more revolutions in Latin America in the immediate future which might resemble the Nicaraguan case. For example, Soviet pessimism regarding the chances for revolution in Latin America was reflected in the coverage by the Soviet press of the war in El Salvador. In the period from the end of the Nicaraguan revolution in 1979 until the "final offensive" of the El Salvadoran rebels in 1981, there was a good deal of coverage in the Soviet press of El Salvador. Since the failure of the "final offensive," the Soviet press has tended to ignore El Salvador.[49]

Stage IV: Diplomatic and Revolutionary Consolidation, 1982 to the Present

Cuban foreign policy toward Latin America has changed since 1982, but, at the same time, this policy has not reverted to the goals of the 1968 period. Instead, contemporary Cuban foreign policy represents a mix of some of the policies pursued in the 1970s together with some of the policies pursued in the period from 1978 to 1982.

Looking first at Nicaragua—Cuba's closest ally in the hemisphere— Cuba pursues a variety of policies. On the one hand, Castro wants the Nicaraguan revolution to be a social and economic success, in terms of improving the lives of the Nicaraguan people, and has thus been quite generous in supplying Cuban schoolteachers and doctors. Castro is also determined that the Nicaraguan revolution not be overthrown by the U.S.-backed *contras*. To prevent such an occurrence, several thousand security and military advisers have been provided to Nicaragua.[50] Finally, Castro has played the role of "strategic adviser" to the Sandinistas. Drawing on his experiences in Cuba, he has urged the Sandinistas to maintain good relations with as many nations as possible to avoid excessive dependence on the Soviet Union, to keep trying to compromise their differences with the United States, and to "go slow" in building a socialist economy in Nicaragua in order to avoid the massive flight of skilled people that has crippled the Cuban economy since the early 1960s.

At present, Castro has a much less optimistic view of the potential success of revolution in Latin America. This new pessimism stems partly from the failures of revolutionaries in El Salvador and Guatemala, and partly from the renewed willingness of the United States to use political and military measures to counter revolutionary movements. However, Castro views himself as one of the key revolutionary leaders in the contemporary world; in light of this self-perception, it is virtually impossible for him to totally abandon these revolutionary movements in Latin America. So, in spite of the setbacks of recent years, it is unlikely that Castro will completely relinquish his support for regional revolutionary movements. This mix of factors has therefore given rise to the current policy of giving limited aid to a selected number of insurgent groups.

If the chances for revolution do not look bright in most of Latin America, a counterbalancing consideration for Cuba is that the opportunities for improved state-to-state relations appear quite good at present. One important reason for this rather optimistic picture is the recent growth of anti-Americanism in Latin America. The invasion of Grenada, and the backing of the *contras* against Nicaragua, have caused considerable anger in the region. It is important to note that this is not so much due to the fact that the New Jewel Movement government and the Sandinistas are overwhelmingly popular in Latin America as it is to the fact that *any* U.S. military intervention in Latin America creates a great deal of resentment. The resentment raised by these two cases is further amplified by the fact that the United States is perceived as ignoring the views of the region, as expressed through the Contadora process and the OAS.

The regional debt crisis has also contributed to the growth of anti-American sentiment. In the 1970s, virtually all countries in Latin America borrowed heavily from American banks. A portion of this borrowing occurred because the American banks extended loans on easy terms; some of it can also be attributed to the U.S. government's encouragement of the extension of loans to "take up the slack" left by the decline in its economic assistance to Latin America. The upshot of this borrowing was that, by the 1980s, most countries in Latin America were heavily indebted to U.S. banks. At that juncture, the current debt crisis began. Complicating this economic landscape, the collapse of oil prices in the mid-1980s led to the inability of Mexico and Venezuela to pay their large debts. Other Latin American countries were hurt by the fall in world prices for sugar, coffee, tobacco, and cotton; these nations also became unable to pay off their debts.

The result of the debt crisis has been a further rise in anti-Americanism. The countries of Latin America believe that most of the debt will eventually have to be repudiated. By failing to face up to this hard fact, the U.S. banks are instead "putting the economies of Latin America through the wringer" by trying to force payment from countries that cannot pay back their loans. The result, as viewed by the peoples and leaders of Latin America, is that their economies are being bled white by the U.S. banks.

Cuba has sought to capitalize on the anti-Americanism generated by the debt crisis. Castro has called for the formation of a "debtor's cartel" as well as for the repudiation of the debt by the countries of Latin America. To date, Castro's attempts to earn political mileage out of the debt crisis have met with only limited success. This result is in part due to the fact that Cuba itself has a large foreign debt which it clearly has no intention of repudiating. Cuba's unwillingness to repudiate its own debt puts it in a weak position to call on other Latin American countries to repudiate their debt.[51] Furthermore, actions taken by Peru's Alan Garcia have "stolen the Cuban thunder" with his proposal to limit payment on the debt to 10 percent of Peru's export earnings (an initiative that other nations in Latin America may be tempted to try in the near future).

However, there can be no guarantee that the current lack of receptivity to Cuban proposals for repudiation will continue. Since many Latin Americans either now favor repudiation, or will eventually come to favor it if the debt crisis gets worse, Castro's calls for repudiation may in the not-too-distant future find greater acceptance in a Latin America where the redemocratization of a number of key countries has given public opinion new influence and strength. Moreover, while the region's leadership publicly rejects Castro's call for repudiation, privately they are grateful, because they realize that these calls make their own proposals for dealing with the debt crisis seem quite moderate and responsible to the U.S. government and banks.[52]

In the Malvinas/Falklands war, the nations of Latin America were infuriated by the role of the United States, believing that it broke commitments made to Argentina at the onset of the war. Specifically, the United States assumed the role of a mediator between Great Britain and Argentina, with Secretary of State Haig engaging in Kissinger-style "shuttle diplomacy" between London and Buenos Aires. While the region had no quarrel with the American efforts to mediate between Great Britain and Argentina, they were angered by the fact that once the U.S. mediation effort broke down, the United States supported Great Britain. The Latin American countries felt that the United States—by assuming its initial role as a mediator—had, in effect, committed itself to a policy of neutrality in the war. To the countries of the hemisphere, the American decision to back Great Britain once the mediation effort had failed signified that the United States had never been a truly "honest broker" in the confrontation.

On a broader level, this upsurge of anti-Americanism on the part of the leadership and citizens of Latin America promises to lead to some improvements in state-to-state relations for Cuba. The key factor in this anticipated improvement is in the pressure of public opinion. Latin American public opinion that has become increasingly hostile to the United States will be tempted to demonstrate its independence from the United States by improving diplomatic relations with Cuba. In the case of Brazil's decision to renew diplomatic relations with Cuba in 1986, for example, a major factor in favor of this renewal was pressure from public opinion and leading politicians to end the last remnant of Brazil's pre-1974 foreign policy of automatic alignment with the United States.[53] In other words, Brazil and Mexico have finally achieved a "convergence" in their policies toward Cuba. Both countries now favor the policy Mexico has adopted all along—namely, to have good relations with Cuba as a way of demonstrating independence from the United States.

Finally, Cuba continues to coordinate its foreign policy toward Latin America with that of the Soviet Union. The Soviets share Castro's renewed pessimism about the chances for revolutionary change in Latin America, and consequently have also scaled down their support of revolutionary movements in the hemisphere. Like Cuba, the chief Soviet objective in Latin America today is to capitalize on the wave of Anti-Americanism in the region in order to establish better state-to-state relations.

Conclusion

In concluding, how does one evaluate the track record of Cuba in its relations with Latin America? Clearly, there is a mixed scorecard with both significant successes and major setbacks. The policy of indiscriminately supporting revolutionary movements throughout Latin America, as pursued during the first stage of Cuba's foreign policy, seriously endangered the Cuban revolution by leading to the almost complete isolation of Cuba in the Western Hemisphere. That policy also endangered the revolution by causing severe friction with Cuba's chief ally and protector, the Soviet Union. In contrast, the policies pursued since 1968—of seeking to establish good state-to-state relations with a number of nations in Latin America—have resulted not only in Cuba's partial reintegration into the Western Hemisphere, but also in a considerable lessening of tensions with the Soviet Union. Both of these factors have contributed to strengthening the viability of the Cuban revolution over the long term.

In seeking to spread Castroite revolution to Latin America, results have also been quite mixed. The 1960s showed conclusively (most dramatically with the death of Ché Guevara in Bolivia) the difficulty of exporting revolution. The two major ideological revolutions in the hemisphere following Cuba, namely Grenada and Nicaragua, were triggered primarily by indigenous factors rather than early Cuban meddling. But, at the same time, it must be acknowledged that later Cuban assistance not only helped to assure a Sandinista victory, but has likewise played a key role in enabling the Sandinistas to withstand the American effort to overthrow the new regime. In this regard, Nicaragua stands out as a case of Cuban success.

Finally, in terms of economic relations with the region, Cuban efforts have met with little success. The key Cuban export, sugar, finds no available markets in Latin America. Despite its efforts to lessen its dependence on the Soviet Union, Cuba remains entirely dependent on Soviet subsidies to maintain its standard of living. Perhaps the only aspect of economic relations which has generated limited attention has been Havana's attempt to politicize the debt issue. But even here, regional solidarity has not been attained: each Latin American debtor has chosen a go-it-alone strategy in coming to terms with the international financial community.

In concluding, Cuba may have entered the 1960s with the perception that Latin America would provide fertile terrain for the creation of Castro-ite continental revolutions, but, by the late 1980s, the regime has come to appreciate that its policies must be reflective of the political realities of Latin America.

Notes

1. Richard Gott, *Guerrilla Movements in Latin America* (Garden City, N.Y.: Doubleday, 1971), p. 163.
2. Ibid., p. 316.
3. Ibid., p. 369.
4. Ibid., p. 497.
5. For a good discussion of U.S. counterinsurgency policy in the post-World War II period see Douglas S. Blaufard, *The Counter-Insurgency Era: U.S. Doctrine and Performance, 1950 to the Present* (New York: Free Press, 1977).
6. See Gott, *Guerrilla Movements,* for an analysis of these movements of the 1960s.
7. Pedro Ramet and Fernando Lopez-Alves, "Moscow and the Revolutionary Left in Latin America," *Orbis,* Vol. 28, no. 2 (Summer 1984), p. 345.
8. Ibid.
9. Ibid.
10. The foco theory of revolution was put forward by Ché Guevara in his book *Guerrilla Warfare* (New York: Vintage Books, 1961) and by Regis Debray in his book *Revolution in the Revolution? Armed Struggle and Political Struggle in Latin America* (New York: Grove Press, 1967).
11. Debray, p. 106.
12. V. I. Lenin, "Why the Social Democrats Must Declare Determined and Relentless War on the Socialist Revolutionaries" (1902) and "Where to Begin" (1901), in Stefan Possony, ed., *Lenin Reader,* (Chicago: Henry Regnery Company, 1966), pp. 470–72.
13. Cole Blasier, *The Giant's Rival: The USSR and Latin America* (Pittsburgh, Pa.: University of Pittsburgh Press, 1983), p. 104.
14. Ernesto Ché Guevara, *The Diary of Ché Guevara* (New York: Bantam Books, 1968), pp. 150, 164–65, 185–86.
15. Blasier, p. 107.
16. Carmelo Mesa-Lago, *Cuba in the 1970's: Pragmatism and Institutionalization* (Albuquerque: University of New Mexico Press, 1978), pp. 117–18.
17. Leogrande, "Foreign Policy: The Limits of Success," in Jorge Dominguez, ed., *Cuba: Internal and International Affairs* (Beverly Hills, Calif.: Sage Publications, 1982), pp. 171–72.
18. Olga Nazario, "Brazil's Rapprochement With Cuba: The Process and the Prospects," *Journal of Interamerican Studies and World Affairs,* Vol. 28, No. 3 (Fall 1986), pp. 67, 69–70, 72, 81.
19. Garbriel Marcella and Daniel S. Papp, "The Soviet-Cuban Relationship: Symbiotic or Parasitic?" in Robert H. Donaldson, ed., *The Soviet Union in the Third World: Successes and Failures* (Boulder, Colo.: Westview Press, 1981), p. 59.
20. Blasier, p. 100.
21. Ibid.

22. For a good discussion of Soviet/Cuban policy on Allende's Chile see Paul E. Sigmund, "The USSR, Cuba, and the Revolution in Chile," in Donaldson, pp. 26–50.
23. Ibid., pp. 34–35.
24. Ibid., p. 38.
25. Ibid.
26. Ibid., pp. 38–39.
27. Gott, pp. 321–29.
28. Walter Laqueur, *Terrorism* (Boston: Little, Brown and Company, 1977), pp. 203–204.
29. In the Algerian war, a major reason for the Soviet coolness toward the Algerian revolutionaries was that both the French Communist Party (PCF) and the Algerian Communist Party (PCA) had ambivalent attitudes toward the Algerian revolution. The ambivalence of the French Communist Party was due to the fact that the PCF realized that the French working class was to a considerable extent hostile to the Algerian cuase, whereas the ambivalence of the Algerian Communist Party stemmed from the commitment of the PCA to defend the interests of the workers among the French settlers in Algeria. See Alistair Horne, *A Savage War of Peace: Algeria, 1954–1962* (New York: Penguin Books, 1977), p. 405.
30. Roger Hamburg, "The Soviet Union and Latin America," in Roger E. Kanet, ed., *The Soviet Union and the Developing Nations* (Baltimore, Md.: The Johns Hopkins University Press, 1974), pp. 206–208.
31. Daniel Premo, "Guatemala," in Robert Wesson (ed.), *Communism in Central America and the Caribbean* (Stanford, Calif.: Hoover Institution Press, 1982), p. 83; Enrique Baloyra, *El Salvador in Transition* (Chapel Hill: University of North Carolina Press, 1982), pp. 161–62.
32. John A. Booth, *The End and the Beginning: The Nicaraguan Revolution* (Boulder, Colo.: Westview Press, 1982), p. 212.
33. Robert S. Leiken, "Fantasies and Facts: The Soviet Union and Nicaragua," *Current History*, Vol. 83, No. 495 (October 1984), p. 344.
34. Alistair Horne, *A Savage War of Peace: Algeria, 1954–62* (New York: Penguin Books, 1977), p. 559.
35. The Soviet Union rehabilitated Ché Guevara in the early 1980s. Writing in the March 1980 issue of *Latinskaya Amerika,* Boris Koval stated: ". . . the Nicaraguan experience [has] demolished the previous simplistic interpretation of guerrilla action, confirmed the jusice of many of Ché Guevara's strategic principles, and crystallized his idea of creating a powerful popular guerrilla movement."
36. For a detailed discussion of the policies pursued by Cuba concerning revolutionary movements in Latin American countries in the 1980s, see Jiri Valenta and Virginia Valenta, "Soviet Strategies in the Caribbean Basin," in Howard Wiarda, ed., *Rift and Revolution: The Central American Imbroglio* (Washington, D.C.: American Enterprise Institute, 1984), pp. 197–252.
37. Ibid., pp. 197–252.
38. Howard Wiarda, *Latin America at the Crossroads: Debt, Development and the Future* (Boulder, Colo.: Westview Press, 1987), p. 36.
39. Blsier, pp. 55–56.
40. Ibid., pp. 88–89.
41. Valenta and Valenta, pp. 225–27.

42. Ibid., pp. 227–29.
43. Diego Asencio and Nancy Asencio, *Our Man is Inside: Outmaneuvering the Terrorists* (Boston: Little, Brown and Company, 1982), p. 7.
44. Valenta and Valenta, pp. 229–32.
45. Ibid., pp. 232–33.
46. Ibid., p. 234.
47. Blasier, pp. 138–39.
48. In February 1981 the State Department issued a White Paper entitled "Communist Interference in El Salvador." The White Paper argued that the Soviet Union and certain of its allies (including Cuba) have provided military aid to the guerrillas in El Salvador. For the text of the White Paper see *Department of State Bulletin,* March 1981, pp. 1–7.
49. Leiken, p. 317.
50. Harold Sims, "Nicaragua's Relations with the Communist Party States During 1984," *Conflict Quarterly,* Vol. V, No. 4 (Fall 1985), p. 56.
51. Wiarda, pp. 35–36.
52. Ibid., p. 36.
53. Nazario, pp. 71–73.

III
AFRICAN RELATIONS

5

Cuba's African Policy

Juan Benemelis

Introduction

Until Fidel Castro and his revolutionary "banditos" took power in 1959, Cuba was a virtually impotent state lacking a notable foreign policy tradition. Today, however, this island-nation not only wields an unprecedented political and military influence in the Western Hemisphere, but has also attained a power base extending from the Caribbean Basin to Africa and Southeast Asia. It is a remarkable and paradoxical achievement that a territory the size of the state of Virginia—with meager resources, low levels of economic development, and an insufficient pool of highly skilled professionals—has attained such international strength. Nevertheless, Cuba's leader has transformed his country into a significant force with which to be contended in the international system. Unhampered by a restrictive party apparatus or burdensome bureaucratic institutions, Castro has been able to imprint his personal stamp on nearly every Cuban foreign policy action. Thus, Havana's foreign policy appears to be more characteristic of an industrial power than of an underdeveloped Caribbean island.

Immediately following Fulgencio Batista's departure from Cuba on the night of 31 December 1959, Castro's paramount goal was to consolidate his power and ultimately attain absolute control over the entire Cuban political process. Utilizing the charisma which had brought him to Cuba's helm of governance, Castro successfully eliminated any opposition and surrounded himself with leaders who shared his guerrilla experience and, subsequently, his ideology and perceptions. In this context, Castro's position as head of state is of lesser importance; the leader's real support

121

comes from his reputation as a successful revolutionary, remarkably skillful at manipulating large masses of people. As "jefe maximo," Castro guides the nation's new governing elite in their historical mission to establish Cuba as an independent leading global actor and has become their political and moral guru. Thus, Castro's absolute power appears to be one of the most permanent and overriding features of Cuban politics.

Despite the influence of the guerrilla experience on Cuba's new ruling elite, Castro's foreign policy is not constrained by the rigid rules established by the 1959 revolution. Instead, Castro has proved to be quite adept at developing flexible guidelines which measure both the political and economic situation at home as well as the barometer of Cuban/Soviet relations. Simply stated, Castro is fully aware that his domestic political survival and ability to pursue an independent foreign policy path is contingent upon a healthy relationship with the Kremlin. For example, priorities on Cuba's foreign policy agenda were altered according to international developments in the 1960s and 1970s, such as conflicts in the Congo, Vietnam, and the Middle East and the Sino/Soviet split. More importantly, however, Castro quickly learned to assess the international environment for the most opportune moments to advance and retreat in his campaign to establish Cuba as a leading international force. With precise timing, Castro simultaneously sought to convince the world that, first, Cuba was indeed a well-integrated member of the international community, second, "foco" revolutionary warfare was the most propitious manner by which to assume power (and thus pursued relevant policies to convince potential Third World insurgents of this), and finally, he was the author of a "Cuban" socialist model, independent of the Soviet Union.

By the late 1970s, such adept maneuvering had brought Cuban foreign policy to its apex and Castro could point to the following achievements:

- bilateral civilian cooperation with nineteen nations;
- diplomatic relations with over 100 nations;
- expeditionary forces in Angola and Ethiopia;
- over 60,000 soldiers on African soil;
- Cuban subversion in the southern cone of Africa and Central America;
- leadership of the Nonaligned Movement; and
- an active presence in South Yemen, Nicaragua, Grenada, and Mozambique.

Whatever ultimate international goals Castro may envision for Cuba, the fact remains that the nation's foreign policy is rooted in Marxist-Leninist principles. As such, the importance of permanent revolution to reach any goals remains at the heart of Castroite foreign policy. Bearing in mind this ideological dimension, Castro's grand strategy is triangular in practice. First and foremost, the "jefe maximo" seeks to undermine U.S. influence in the Third World. This tactic's rationale is that Castro can only achieve his objectives by placing himself in constant opposition to the United States. Second, Castro seeks to foster the spread of Marxist states around the globe. Completing this triangular strategy, in recognizing the importance of East-West geopolitical rivalry in Cuba's expanding global role, other nations' territories and spheres of influence are treated as tactical theaters in which budding insurgency movements are to be encouraged. Thus, since Castro's international designs are largely based on his need to antagonize U.S. interests, peaceful coexistence is unacceptable to him.

In retrospect, it is ironic that, as a self-proclaimed Marxist, Castro interjects moral and ethical principles into his foreign policy. Nevertheless, Cuba's relations with other states are sporadically contingent upon such ideals. These principles, however, are negotiable—as Cuba's strong relationship with Francoist Spain and its abandonment of the Venezuelan guerrillas in the 1960s illustrate. Consequently, Cuba's bilateral relations and support for guerrilla groups shift in relation to both international conditions and, most significantly, the primary national interests of both Cuba and the Soviet Bloc. Because of this contradictory scenario—principled versus tactical relationships—it is difficult to identify a definitive set of principles governing Cuba's bilateral relations.

While Castro's magnetic personality and dedication to Marxist-Leninist principles are key factors in the understanding of Cuban foreign policy, one must also bear in mind the privileges that Castro's unique situation has afforded him. As leader of a member of the socialist, Latin American, and militant Third World communities, Castro has been able to develop a flexible and multifaceted foreign policy. Such a position has allowed, and will continue to allow, Castro to concurrently wear three different hats on the global stage. First, Castro can portray Cuba as a Soviet Bloc member entangled in the East-West conflict. Second, the leader can present himself as a militant associate of the Nonaligned Movement. And third, the "jefe maximo" can play the underdeveloped nation card—the role of being caught between the East-West industrial poles in North-South disputes. The ability to play any one of these roles when convenient provides Castro with a flexibility few leaders enjoy.

Influential across three continents, Cuba is no longer geographically or politically isolated from the international community. This new international acceptance of the regime reversed the geographic fatalism of the Western Hemisphere—the U.S. can no longer exercise unchallenged authority in its traditional Latin American sphere of influence. Thus, it is likely that Castro's international activism may shatter the geopolitical balance of the region.

The Cuban/Soviet Connection

One of the most perplexing issues in Cuban foreign policy relates to the question of Havana's dependence on Moscow. One school of thought asserts that Cuban foreign policy is clearly independent of the Soviet Union—that it is an autonomous product of the nation's head of state. This notion, however, does not explain the intimate military and intelligence collaboration between Moscow and Havana. Joint action in Ethiopia, Cuban support for the Soviets in Afghanistan, and Cuba's presence in South Yemen all exemplify this teamwork. On the other hand, a second school of thought views Castroite foreign policy as a mere reaction to U.S. aggression. The weakness of this argument is that it fails to explain Castro's unilateral decision to integrate Cuba into the Soviet Bloc or Cuba's commitment to Angola and Ethiopia when it was in the midst of bilateral negotiations with the United States.

A third argument posits that the Soviet Union dictates Cuban foreign policy. However, this position does not explain an array of independent Cuban foreign policy directions which have been developed over the past 25 years. Included in these autonomous actions, for example, are Castro's "foco" guerrilla activity and his call to creditor countries to cancel the financial obligations of debtor nations.

What *is* clear is that Cuba retains very strong ties to the Soviet Bloc; no one doubts the existence of Cuban cooperation with the Soviet Union to meet vital foreign objectives of Cuba and to ensure its economic survival. Instead, the relationship may be characterized as symbiotic, and thus includes a geostrategic commitment on the part of the Soviets and a political-strategic commitment on the part of the Cubans. This coalition has provided Castro with numerous benefits, granting Cuba extraordinary mobility and reducing Havana's vulnerability on the international stage. In this context, Castro, unlike his colleagues in the Soviet Bloc, has been able to devise and pursue a relatively independent foreign policy.

While the alliance with the Soviet Union has provided Cuba with multiple international resources (particularly advantageous in Castro's campaign against the United States) it has had drawbacks as well, namely that Castro has been kept behind a Soviet shield, stifling him in implementing an entirely independent foreign policy. On the other hand, as alluded to earlier, the benefits are clearly numerous. The alliance has permitted the Cuban leader to project his own political vision within the Soviet Union—even to the point where Castro himself has introduced initiatives into the slow-moving Soviet bureaucratic machinery. Castro also had a special arrangement with the Soviets in the latter portion of the 1960s and in the early 1970s: Cuban international activism was to be tailored to the new Soviet strategy of expansionism. In return, the Soviets would provide the Cubans with increasingly sophisticated resources.

While it would be incorrect to label Castro a "Soviet lackey," the Cuban leader has taken actions which have ingratiated him with the Soviet leadership, and ultimately afforded him freer rein in several policy issue areas. As Gillian Gunn points out in her chapter, Castro has utilized Cuba's official position as a nonaligned nation to attempt to forge a "natural alliance" between the Nonaligned Movement and the Soviet Bloc. Combined with active internationalism, these factors have only served to enhance Castro's position and usefulness in the Kremlin's perspective. Thus, in a paradoxical fashion, Castro's cozying up to the Soviets has provided him with an unusual amount of freedom in his pursuit of an independent foreign policy.

One of the most significant bonds between Havana and Moscow is the commitment to spread Marxist-Leninist ideology around the globe. In practice, Africa became a prime target due to the decolonization movement and attendant power vacuums. Since the Soviet action in Africa is subject to domestic constraints and the climate of East-West relations, Castro appeared to take the lead and develop an independent Cuban policy for the continent. But the concept that Castro was an autonomous actor in Africa is deceiving; joint strategy did exist (as will be discussed) which included aid, coordination, and the pursuit of common objectives.[1]

Interpreting Moscow's and Havana's actions as well as collective strategy toward Africa has revealed discrepancies, primarily relating to tactical issues. Likewise, bilateral tensions have arisen over ideological issues, generally relating to the appropriate means by which to assume power. These tactical differences have their roots in the roles the two nations play in the world and their ensuing visions of the role of insurgencies and guerrilla movements. For example, while the Soviet Union has openly stated its opposition to the Eritrean guerrillas demanding autonomy in Ethiopia, the Castro regime has been less outspoken in its opposition.

The motives behind Castro's foreign policy are complex, frequently appearing that the leader has different intentions with each step taken on the international stage. Many times his actions are simply aimed at challenging U.S. influence or serving as military support for the Soviets; however, Castro may also carry out a particular international action to grant a concession to a domestic faction which needs to be appeased. Furthermore, underlying many of his moves is a tireless campaign to obtain a chapter in the international history annals for both Castro and Cuba.

In summary, Castro's principal objectives in his foreign policy can be outlined as follows:

- to preserve his own power as the undisputed Cuban political leader;
- to demonstrate hostility towards the United States, thereby justifying Cuba's military buildup and the regime's disastrous economic performance to the Soviets;
- to assist, directly or indirectly, in spreading the Soviet communist model throughout the globe; and
- to create a political niche for Cuba within the bipolar framework.

Africa constitutes a core part of this international agenda. As such, Castro's goals in Africa are as follows:

- to maintain legitimacy with influential domestic factions and, more broadly, Cuban public opinion;
- to tie down U.S. military resources in the region in order to distract Washington's attention from more strategic areas of the globe;
- to promote Castro's international prestige and influence vis-à-vis an international presence, thereby creating a more favorable environment in which Cuba can operate;
- to mount a Cuban offensive within the Third World, which would reduce Havana's political isolation and increase the cost of military intervention by the United States;
- to obtain greater amounts of Soviet economic, political, and military aid; and
- to support countries and movements which are hostile to the United States.

This chapter will explore these objectives by examining the development of Cuban activities in Africa, which can be narrowed down to three major phases:

1. *1959–62:* This period was characterized by a series of diplomatic and ideological offensives, spiced with the "romantic" export of revolution. In other words, Castro was probing the continent to ascertain which countries might be ripe for revolution. This phase ended with the events of the Sino/Soviet split and the Cuban missile crisis.
2. *1962–70:* During this phase of aggressive guerrilla initiatives, the Soviets implemented their new expansionist policy, Cuba's economy was headed for disaster, and insurgency movements were failing in their attempts to take power.

3. *1970 to the present:* This stage has been characterized by blatant Soviet adventurism and has led to a considerable harmonization of Havana's and Moscow's foreign policies.

Phase I: Castro Plants the Seeds (1959–62)

Castro began to develop an interest in Africa in the early 1960s, as the forces of nationalism and Marxism-Leninism were vying for power throughout the continent. A number of factors combined to polarize forces throughout the region, including population explosions, ethnic tribal conflicts, postcolonial institutional vacuums, and a dearth of technological expertise. Furthermore, the Soviet Bloc-Cuban alliance and Havana's spread of subversion and terrorism, as well as Western indolence to the plight of Africa, only added fuel to this explosive scenario. The continent appeared to be ripe for revolution—and it would not be long before Castro would begin to test the murky African waters.

Cuba's interest in Africa was by no means of a secondary nature; on the contrary, the Cuban leader approached the continent with the fury of an eagle descending on its prey. In fact, in no other region was Castro able to succeed in pursuing such overt policies of violent disruption as he was able to in Morocco, the former Portuguese colonies, Somalia, South Yemen, Ethiopia, Namibia, and Zaire.

Underlying this aggressive thrust into a traditional European sphere of influence was Castro's determination to preserve his power and, more significantly, act on an intense hatred of the United States. Castro transformed this hostility into a convenient mechanism by which his militarism could be justified to the Soviets. Although such militarism has created acute pressure on the Cuban population as well as severe domestic economic strains, Castro was quick to realize that playing up the threat posed by the "colossus of the north" would increase his value to Moscow. However, along with increased levels of economic and military dependency, the international community perceived equally increased levels of political dependency as well. Once again, Cuban militarization created a harsh dichotomy for the Cuban leader.

This first period in Castroite policy toward Africa (1959–62) was marked by high levels of inconsistency, complexity, and instability. It was a time in which the new Cuban leader struggled with two major objectives: to solidify his own power base at home (complicated by rivalries among domestic political factions), and to find logistical support for his foreign policy. His two central themes evolved into: 1) the promotion of subversion and terrorism; and 2) hostility toward the United States. This hatred of the "Yankee imperialist" would become one of the most prominent factors in the formulation of African policy; additional elements which propelled Castro's African campaign included Sino/Soviet rivalry for influence over budding communist movements and Washington's ostracism of Havana.

Following Castro's embarrassing failures at armed insurrection in Latin America (i.e., the Dominican Republic, Panama, and Venezuela), Africa became an increasingly important terrain for cultivation. So, Castro turned his attention to the continent and set out on a series of diplomatic maneuvers and experiments with guerrilla tactical operations. In this context, one of his first moves was to build a consensus for a radical Afro/Asian bloc (in conjunction with North Vietnam, North Korea, Ghana, Guinea, and Mali). These countries were selected in order to create a more militant socialist force—which can be attributed to Castro's unhappiness with the prospects of successful implementation of peaceful coexistence. Concerned that Africans might perceive him as a Soviet puppet, Castro sought to dispel the notion that his country was aligned in any capacity with the Soviet Union; furthermore, preoccupied with Peking's increasing influence on the continent, Castro subsequently launched anti-Chinese campaigns. Finally, the environment in southern Africa was tested by initiating mild attempts to gain a foothold in the "white citadels" of the south.

With "Ché" Guevara (longtime guerrilla compatriot) and Raul Castro (Cuba's Minister of Defense) firmly in charge of guerrilla training camps for Latin American and African militants at home, Castro concentrated on establishing espionage centers throughout the African continent. The first centers were located in Ghana, Guinea, and Mali and were subsequently extended to Egypt, Algeria, Morocco, Tanzania, and the Congo. The purpose of these centers was to pinpoint potential guerrilla campaigns on the continent. Two important openings were shortly discovered: the Algerian struggle against France and the Congolese fight for independence from Belgium. Castro did attempt to convert some of the more moderate states such as Ghana, Guinea, Mali, and Algeria over to the Cuban/Soviet camp, but efforts in this direction fell short of the mark during this early stage. As a counterweight to this failure, however, the Cubans did make some significant military progress in South Yemen, Ethiopia, Angola, and Mozambique—which would later pay off with considerable dividends.

In the interim, the Soviets had their eyes cast in another direction, centering their foreign policy on more limited concerns. The European theater and its campaign to gain worldwide acceptance of the post-World War II division of Europe remained at the top of the Soviet agenda. Other issues of concern to the Kremlin included the political expansion of communist ideology and national communist parties as well as maintaining the levels of its strategic arsenal. With Moscow's attention consumed elsewhere, Castro was able to almost autonomously build a Third World foreign policy without stepping on Soviet toes.

Castro began his Africa campaign by offering material support to the Congolese leader Patrice Lumumba and to the leader of the Algerian National Liberation Front (FLN), Ahmed Ben Bella. From the outset, Cuba sought to rally support for its policies from "progressive" African and Arab regimes which had supported Lumumba and openly defied the European powers during the Congolese episode. At this juncture, the thrust of Castro's campaign centered on hammering out a unified position between the Arabs and the Africans based on common objectives. Such an agreement would clearly be viewed as yielding tremendous benefits to Castro: the isolation to which Cuba was condemned in Latin America was now to be offset by these newly discovered comrades-in-arms.

As decolonization swept across the globe, the Third World began to form diplomatic blocs, and, subsequently, forums in which to discuss the obstacles newly independent countries would face in the future. At the helm of this crusade was Egyptian President Gamal Abdul Nasser, one of the founders of the Nonaligned Movement (NAM). However, Castro's concerns over economic inequality, emphasis on the export of revolution, and strong anti-imperialist rhetoric clashed with the NAM's concentration on diplomacy and peaceful coexistence. The Cuban leader was thus distrustful of the movement, and viewed it as an unreliable interplay and a product of the Cold War which would eventually become an integral part of Western imperialism. Despite a clash with Nasser over Cuban penetration into the Arab world and distrust of other nonaligned allies like Kwame Nkrumah, Jawaharal Nehru, and Modibo Keita, Castro's interests began to merge with the NAM's as North-South issues emerged on the organization's agenda. Since Latin Americans were paying little attention to Africa and the Middle East, Castro would later establish himself as the Latin spokesman at NAM conferences—a mistake his fellow Latin Americans would later regret.

In recognition of the initiatives Ben Bella assumed with France in the early 1960s, Castro initially decided to make Algeria the focus of his African policy. As such, the FLN gained the dubious distinction of becoming the first African liberation movement to receive Cuban aid. More importantly, support for Ben Bella signified a clarification in Cuban policy; it soon became apparent that Castro's strategy was to support armed subversion within newly independent regimes by supporting internal opposition within various political parties, opposition movements, and tribal groups.

On another front, Castro was seeking to diplomatically penetrate the so-called "Casablanca Group"—comprised of Ghana, Guinea, Mali, Egypt, Algeria, Morocco, and Tunisia, and one of several predecessors to the Organization of African Unity. However, Castro was less than successful in infiltrating the group. Friction between Castro and Nasser continued and the Cuban leader was never able to convince the latter to cooperate with him. Further contributing to this diplomatic failure was a dispute between Castro and Sekou Touré over the Guinean president's position of building socialism without a class dictatorship.

Castro's campaign for armed struggle in Africa required increasing levels of Soviet aid. At this point, however, the Soviet leadership was wary of the tribal, political, and national complexities of the postindependence period and chose to exercise caution in its approach to Africa; Castro, on the other hand, chose a riskier course. As Gillian Gunn points out in her chapter, Khrushchev's public handling of the October 1962 missile crisis relegated Cuba's role in the negotiations to a secondary status. Embarrassed by the incident, Castro set out to lessen the diminution of his prestige. The solution was to launch an "independent" foreign policy through the promotion of a worldwide guerrilla warfare campaign.

Castro's determination to demonstrate his independence from the Kremlin after the missile crisis had the temporary effect of diminishing Soviet influence in Cuba. Taking advantage of this temporary loss of Soviet clout in Havana, the Chinese began to move in to fill the vacancy. Despite the existence of a vast pro-Peking faction in Cuba, however, Castro did not switch allegiance to Peking as some observers expected. Instead, Soviet pressure by the mid–1960s forced Castro to detach himself entirely from the Chinese, thus securing Cuba's capitulation to the Soviet Bloc.

Phase II: The Harvest (1962–70)

The second stage of Fidel Castro's Africa policy begins with the aftermath of the missile crisis and ends in 1970, the year marked by the 10 million ton sugar cane harvest failure, that had serious economic repercussions within the country. It is important to bear in mind that several key events outside of Africa shaped the formation of Cuban foreign policy during this period. First, Castro lost his main proponent of "foco" revolutionary warfare when "Ché" Guevara died in the Bolivian jungle in 1967. Second, in the following year, Castro supported the Soviet invasion of Czechoslovakia, thus indicating that Cuba was more willing to accommodate the Kremlin. And third, during the last few years of the 1960s, Soviet attempts to meld Castro's socialist state with Moscow's communist party machinery suggested that the two powers would take joint action in the years to come.

Castro began 1963 with a renewed determination to continue his campaign of support for radical anticolonial movements in Africa. He also expanded his parameters of action by constructing a general plan of subversion against the continent's moderate governments—a constituency which he had basically ignored in the past. On the home front, Castro was firmly entrenched in his role as the undisputed "jefe" and Cuba's internal political groups were adhering blindly to his policies. This last factor, clearly, diminished Moscow's influence in Havana, and the Kremlin had little recourse than to be content with an insecure and mercurial relationship with Fidel Castro.

In October 1963, a dispute which had been incubating since colonial times over a common frontier erupted into a brief war between Algeria and Morocco. The ensuing conflict provided Castro with the first important opportunity for a Cuban military experiment of major importance in Africa. The Cuban leader responded to the dispute by immediately dispatching a mechanized force consisting of a brigade of T-55 tanks and a considerably large field artillery unit to the Sahara. Meanwhile, the Soviets backed Castro's penetration into the Sahara by supporting the Cuban/Egyptian initiative and, subsequently, by providing weapons. Castro's good fortune did not last long, however, as the dispute contributed to the dissolution of the Casablanca Group. The unraveling of the organization proved to be a major blow to Castro's diplomatic offensive on the continent.

While Castro's diplomatic initiative appeared to be faltering, Sekou Touré became the first of several African leaders to expel Soviets from Africa. This, combined with Touré's subsequent tilt toward Peking, quickly soured the Guinean's relations with the Soviets. The final blow to the Cuban/Guinean relationship occurred when Touré, in the midst of the Cuban missile crisis, refused to allow the Soviets to use the Conakry airport for refueling transport planes en route to Cuba.

Because of these losses, it became increasingly clear to Havana that diplomatic efforts would have to be replaced by a more aggressive strategy—as Castro ultimately recognized that his interpretation of the political situation in Africa did not coincide with the perceptions of the continent's leaders. The African leaders did not see their plight in a "capitalist versus socialist" context, but rather viewed it as a tragic dilemma of the industrialized nations, driven by their high consumerism into the exploitation of underdeveloped nations. Castro was convinced that his guerrilla approach would disintegrate these "backward" environments and give rise to class consciousness through ideological shocks.

Ideological differences, however, were not the only obstacles to Castro's penetration of the continent. The Cuban leader became increasingly frustrated when confronted with the different forms of colonization implemented by the culturally divergent British, French, and Portuguese. Furthermore, the lack of development of a concept of nationhood, and various border conflicts and tribal disputes, made it difficult to establish concrete political affiliations with African leaders.

In 1962 and 1963, Cuba began to articulate a definitive and coherent foreign policy of subversion, which publicly emerged through "Ché" Guevara's countless speeches at the United Nations and in Africa throughout 1964. Castro hoped to set in motion an ambitious offensive plan in Africa, led by Guevara. In this context "Ché" would assume responsibility for directing the guerrilla, espionage, and diplomatic operations within a triangle formed by Algeria, Congo-Brazzaville, and Tanzania. Katanga would be especially vital because of its important uranium reserves—a fact which had not escaped either "Ché's" or Castro's attention. This awareness led "Ché" to declare during his 1964–65 tour of the continent that Africa was "one of the most important, if not the most important, battlefield against all forms of exploitation in the world . . .''[2]

Castro found an opening for his offensive through a weak spot in Zanzibar's fragile independence. A radical party (the UMMA), which consisted of 30 Zanzibarans, executed the swiftest coup d'etat to ever take place in Africa. The Cuban embassy, which served as coordinator during the coup, subsequently became the political, military, and civilian advisor to the government of Mohammed Babu and Abeid Karume, and remained so during the brief period of their arrangement.

At this juncture, Castro's ultimate objective was to foment the overthrow of the white governments in Rhodesia and South Africa. Behind this strategy was the hope that the United States would become committed not only in Vietnam, but also in southern Africa, thereby draining the United States of its human and material resources. In June of 1965, "Ché" departed for the Congo, which was to become the nucleus of the guerrilla initiative. The move was entirely overlooked by both the Western powers and the countries affected by the mission. With Washington's attention focused elsewhere—namely, concerned with the invasion of the Dominican Republic, the escalation of the Vietnam conflict, Krushchev's fall from grace, and the coups against Ben Bella and Kwame Nkrumah—little attention was paid to Guevara's relocation. At the same time, the ouster of Bella and Nkrumah worried the Cuban leader as well, as the rear guard of the "next Vietnam" that he hoped to promote was no longer in power.

In the interim, Castro began to implement his strategy by introducing guerrilla forces into Congo-Leopold (Zaire) and establishing two guerrilla sanctuaries in Congo-Brazzaville (Congo) and Tanzania. The Congo was of particular importance because with it under control, it would be easier to deliver lateral blows against Angola, Gabon (vital because of deposits of rare minerals), and Mozambique from Tanzania. Castro then hoped to disrupt and destroy railway and river communications in Rhodesia, thus asphyxiating Africa's "white citadels."

Following up on numerous statements that he would send troops abroad to assist liberation movements, Castro sent 200 well-trained and equipped Cubans to join "Ché" Guevara in Congo-Brazzaville in 1965. This Cuban force was superior even to the command later led by "Ché" in Bolivia in 1967. But the military crusade that the British mercenary "Mike" Hoare unleashed was implacable and almost all the important towns under guerrilla control were recaptured. By March 1966, the situation was bleak for "Ché" and his guerrillas, who were virtually encircled by the mercenaries and the Congolese army. As a result, Osmani Cienfuegos, Emilio Aragones, and Victor Dreke had to rescue the stunned "heroic" guerrilla leader; had "Ché" not immediately abandoned the Congolese battlefield, it is likely that the African jungle—not the Bolivian plateau—would have been his last stand.

The guerrilla debacle in the Congo was followed by additional failures: namely, inability to achieve a unified front of the anticolonial movements of southern Rhodesia, as well as a growing dispute with the top leaders of Front for the Liberation of Mozambique (FRELIMO). Opting for a change in strategy, Castro turned his sights to South America, hoping to form a regional guerrilla command under the direction of "Ché" Guevara. This plan was part of the Cuban leader's broader strategy to create an international umbrella guerrilla organization to ignite revolutionary fervor throughout the Third World; nevertheless, Africa continued to be part of Cuban strategy.

As the prominent Africanist William Durch has aptly stated, ". . . from 1965 on, Cuba devoted a large part of its advisory effort in Africa to the training of popular militias, under the control of ruling parties as counterweights to the regular armed forces. . . ."[3] Thus, the active remnants of the Castro/Guevara operation in the Congo remained in Brazzaville and began instructing militias and organizing Angolan guerrillas. Furthermore, when the Popular Movement For the Liberation of Angola (MPLA) moved its headquarters to Zambia, their Cuban instructors followed them.[4]

Following the January 1966 Tricontinental Conference in Havana and the Congo crises (as previously discussed), Castro shifted his attention to the African Party for the Independence of Guinea Cape Verde (PAIGC) of Guinea-Bissau, where close to 200 Cuban military officers managed the logistics, communications, and other technical functions for the guerrillas. In a separate incident, in June 1966, Cuban military forces departed from their base at Dolissie (Congo-Brazzaville) and joined forces with the

MPLA and the South West Africa People's Movement (SWAPO) to crush a military coup against Congolese President Alphonse Massemba Debat. And at the same time, Castro provided Sekou Touré with Cuban troops to serve as the President's personal presidential guard. These troops were still present when Guinean militias and Portuguese soldiers stormed Conakry in November 1970, and remained at least until 1986.

Soviet involvement in Nigeria's civil war in the mid-1960s provided the DGI (the Cuban intelligence service) with a unique opportunity to observe that country's internal activities from the field. Castro's subsequently improved intelligence capabilities paid off at the end of the decade when the DGI concluded a classified agreement with the Algerian secret service concerning areas on the continent which appeared to be ripe for revolution. Shortly thereafter, and perhaps as a result of the pact, Castro widened his parameters of subversion to include not only the anticolonial movements of Portuguese Africa, but also to Eritrea, Rhodesia, and Cameroon. In particular, Cuban aid was extended for military training, armaments, propaganda, demolition techniques, and communications and secret code apparatuses.

After setbacks in the Congo and Bolivia, Castro decided to exercise greater foresight in his Africa campaigns. In this context, he contacted the leaders of liberation movements ranging from Algiers and Egypt to Tanzania. Osmani Cienfuegos, Secretary General of the Afro-Asian-Latin American People's Solidarity Organization (OSPAAL), was appointed as Castro's representative to Africa. Assisting these new efforts was the fact that the United States was paying little attention to Castro's non–Western Hemisphere activities. Likewise, the Soviet Union exerted little pressure on Castro, provided the Cubans continued to alienate the Chinese in Africa.

In retrospect, Castro's international activism (and his African policy, in particular) did not appear to evoke a reaction from anyone—including the former colonial powers. Military and civilian activities throughout a large part of Africa (including Zambia, Tanzania, Algeria, Benin, Congo-Brazzaville, Guinea, Guinea-Bissau, Madagascar, Mali, Sierra Leone, Libya, and Burundi) were continued. At home, Castro also continued to provide training courses and military aid for various African liberation movements.[5]

In the meantime, Havana also determined that Rhodesia could realistically be penetrated through the vulnerable port of Beira in Mozambique, important for oil and trade flows, and through the mineral exit points of Luanda and Lobito in Angola. The Congo River also represented another potential weak point. This strategy, however, was not implemented because of Castro's disagreements with FRELIMO and the ineffectiveness of both the MPLA and the African National Congress (ANC) of South Africa. Castro therefore contained his exploits, believing the forces of nationalism in the area to be too immature to conduct subversion against South Africa.

Another important stumbling block to Castro's strategy was the fact that Cuba lacked the proper infrastructure of a well-organized communist party such as the Soviet party apparatus. For its part, the Kremlin took a "wait and see" approach toward Cuban involvement in Africa. Clearly the Soviets enjoyed the luxury that they would benefit regardless of which African communist party emerged victorious.

At this juncture, the majority of the Soviet Politburo had opted for the neo-Stalinist orientation of peaceful coexistence. Nevertheless, ideologues and defenders of Third World liberation movements and supporters of a rapprochement with Peking within the Kremlin continued to support Castro's policies. As such, Castro's backers in Moscow further urged a strengthening of the Cuban army by providing assistance and information. It is important, however, to recall that in reality the Soviets never denied support to African national liberation movements; Moscow's strategy viewed both detente and peaceful coexistence as applicable solely to its strategic relationship with the United States and irrelevant to the Third World.

In reviewing the events of the second phase, conditions appeared bleak by the end of the 1960s for the Cubans in Africa, as Havana's policy for the continent was tempered by an unlucky combination of forces. Contributing to this temporary setback were: insufficient Soviet logistical support; the success of a number of pro-Western military coups in sub-Saharan countries; the fall of Kwame Nkrumah, Modibo Keita, and Ben Bella; as discussed earlier, the failed guerrilla campaign in the Congo; and the growth of Chinese political influence in various African nations despite efforts to the contrary.[6]

By the early 1970s, the African landscape once more began to change: interstate conflict was on the rise, and power vacuums were emerging throughout the continent from the hasty flight of the Portuguese. Also, the continuing Sino-Soviet conflict convinced the Kremlin leadership to use African nationalist movements both as a means of expanding the Soviet sphere of influence, as well as to directly confront Peking in the Third World. Following Brezhnev's consolidation of power and the subsequent buildup of the Soviet army, Moscow began to adopt some of Cuba's techniques, utilizing the intelligence and subversion infrastructure that Castro had set up throughout the African continent. At the same time, because of the multiple setbacks Cuba had suffered, Castro had himself become more selective in his African objectives and appeared willing to allow the Soviets to take the initiative. Translated into practice, he there-fore limited himself to providing military collaboration in nations in which Moscow's interests were threatened (such as Vietnam, South Yemen, Somalia, and Syria).

Bilateral relations with Moscow continued to strengthen as Cuba threw its support behind the 1968 Soviet invasion of Czechoslovakia. Shortly thereafter, Castro placed the DGI under KGB supervision, and sent Raul Castro to Moscow in 1970 to personally coordinate the restructuring of the Cuban army.[7] These actions, combined with a general Cuban subservience to the Kremlin's demands, clearly demonstrated that the two countries' interests were merging. No longer was it possible to brush off the overlap-ping of Cuban and Soviet foreign policy in Africa as a mere coincidence. Instead, the international community began to witness an alignment of nearly identical viewpoints and strategies. Within this new framework, Cuba assumed the role of a client-state by providing a proxy army for the hegemonic superpower.[8]

"Protected" by detente in the early 1970s, the USSR began to attempt to increase its influence in the Third World by exacerbating local conflicts.[9] The Cuban army and economy had already been overhauled and suffi-ciently "sovietized" so that Moscow began to reevaluate the role Castro could play in Soviet expansion in Africa. To that end, the Kremlin began a second reshaping of the Cuban army and its command structure and accelerated training and technical modernization programs. The Soviets also proceeded to strengthen Castro's diplomatic missions and intelligence centers in Africa and the Middle East, which now included Egypt, Tanza-nia, Congo-Brazzaville, Guinea, Algeria, and South Yemen. These initia-tives now bring us to the third phase of Cuban policy in Africa, in which Havana's and Moscow's strategies converge to follow an identical path.

Phase III: The Harvest Bears Fruit (1972 to present)

In May 1972, Castro set out on a lengthy tour of Eastern Europe, pledging to the communist leaders that the Soviet economic model would be established in Cuba. This trip was also extended to several African countries, including Algeria, Guinea, Sierra Leone, Congo-Brazzaville, and Tanzania and proved to be fruitful for the Cuban leader. Accompany-ing him on his trip was a corps of Cuban generals—a virtual "war cabinet"—composed of several members who would later return to lead military operations in Africa. Included in the delegation were Arnaldo Ochoa, Raul Menendez Tomassevich, Senen Casas Regueiro, Julio Casas Regueiro, and Rigoberto Garcia Fernandez.

The trip was a success from the start. Castro was able to smooth out his differences with Sekou Touré, through whom military support to the PAIGC in Portuguese Guinea was being channelled. Castro also intensified his nation's presence in Congo-Brazzaville, and reinforced his support for the MPLA in Angola. Castro further began to test the waters of Chinese influence in eastern Africa, particularly regarding Nyerere in Kenya and Mozambique's FRELIMO.

Ethiopia was also included on Castro's travel itinerary. With the help of Yasser Arafat, the Cuban leader drew up guidelines for establishing relations with Syria and Iraq, backing the guerrillas in Oman (through whom he sought direct access to the Persian Gulf), and promoting agitation in the Ethiopian regions of Eritrea and Ogaden. The overriding objective of this multilayered strategy was the complete dismemberment of Ethiopia.

In part, however, South Yemen ultimately became the focus of Castro's efforts. Because of disinformation supplied by the KGB, Castro had mistakenly backed the Front for the Liberation of South Yemen (FLOSY), believing the Front Organization of Fattah Ismail to be pro-Chinese. The South Yemen strategy, which was formulated in conjunction with the Soviets, consisted of placing Castro in a position to act as a counterweight to Chinese influence in the Third World. In particular, Cuba was to act as a buffer against Chinese-supported attacks against Soviet interests in the Third World. With this new African policy in hand, Castro also encountered Libyan leader Mohammar Quadaffi and Zambian president Kenneth Kaunda. Completing the trip, Castro announced support for the Soviet military presence in Somalia.

Upon returning home, Castro proceeded to send military missions to Somalia, Algeria, and Mozambique, similar to the ones already embedded in South Yemen, Syria, and Iraq;[10] a Cuban mission was also sent to train and organize a 500-man militia in Sierra Leone.[11] By the end of the year, the DGI had determined that Equatorial Guinea might also be ripe for revolution. Thus, Castro resumed his previous tactic of training guerrillas and strengthening internal security elements in that country.[12]

With Nasser's sudden death, Castro gained important beachheads in the Middle East for the first time. Despite criticism from the Yemenites, Soviet military "assistance" to North Yemen was continued and a naval base was set up in Berbera, Somalia—thus providing the Soviet/Cuban axis with an important lateral door to the Indian Ocean. Castro further deployed part of a combat division between Somalia and South Yemen, which was reinforced by MIG-21 fighter bombers and defensive missiles. The Cubans were also involved in the 1973 Yom Kippur War. In particular, Israeli sources reported the presence of a Cuban tank brigade in the Golan Heights, which was supported by two brigades.[13]

The first important step in this new joint African campaign was to gain influence in the region south of the Red Sea encompassing Ethiopia, Somalia, and North and South Yemen. The Suez Canal was an equally important target, as the Soviets sought an outlet to the Indian Ocean in order to establish naval bases in both the Atlantic and Indian Oceans. South Yemen was the focus of this operation, and in 1972, a major Cuban military mission comprised of tank, air, and artillery specialists was dispatched. The purpose of the mission was to assemble Soviet military materiel and train the Yemenites in the use of these new arms. In addition to this already considerable Cuban presence, Cuban-flown MIGs were sent to participate in the 1972 skirmish between North and South Yemen.

At this juncture, it became evident that South Yemen was Castro's most important operational center in the region. In the Sixth South Yemen Province, adjacent to Oman, the Cubans established a training center for guerrillas; they further built a transit area for flights from Odessa at Khormaksar base. The Soviets gained an important foothold in the country, as well, in attaining a naval base in the extreme west, with the Port of Aden to accommodate their naval fleet sailing out of Kamchatka. From this point forward, it was clear the southern portion of the Red Sea had fallen under the Soviet/Cuban military umbrella.

With South Yemen under control, Castro turned to Algeria where he stationed a unit of fighter pilots to join Soviet bomber forces and to provide training to Algerian pilots. In fact, the Cubans trained the pilots so well that ". . . Algerian pilots were reportedly sent to man Soviet-built MIGs based in Brazzaville during the conflict. . . ."[14] The Cubans also widened the scope of their guerrilla training program to Rhodesia, and included members of Robert Mugabe's Zimbabwe African National Union (ZANU) and Joshua Nkomo's Zimbabwe African People's Union (ZAPU).

In the following two years a surprising turn of events afforded Castro a golden opportunity to expand his regional strategy. Upheaval in Portugal in 1973–74, and the subsequent fall of Salazar, precipitated the decolonization process of her overseas territories in Africa. The new territories up for grabs encompassed Guinea Bissau, Cape Verde, Sao Tome and Principe, Angola, and Mozambique.

The seeds which Castro had sown in these nations now appeared ready for harvest. Some initial setbacks in these fertile territories, however, had to be overcome. For example, despite the military aid granted by the Cubans to the PAIGC of Guinea, the new leaders of the movement strongly voiced their objection to a large Cuban military presence. As a result, the Soviet objective of obtaining a base on the far eastern shore of the Atlantic did not transpire. In a similar vein, Samora Machel of Mozambique (in practice very cautious in his relations with the Cubans and the Soviets) compromised with the Portuguese in order to obtain his nation's independence, and furthermore made it evident that he wished to maintain his country's independence from other extra-regional powers as well.

Overall, however, the network of support that Castro had provided to the liberation movements in the Portuguese colonies was beginning to bear fruit. The movements were emerging as political agents capable of dealing with the Portuguese and, as noted by Alberto Miguez, "It seems clear today that the Soviets had been playing for such an eventuality with Alvaro Cunhal and the Portuguese Communist Party, the closest aligned to Moscow in Europe."[15]

Angola, however, ultimately proved to be the site where the groundwork laid by Castro in Africa would come together. The three ideologically divergent Angolan independence movements [Agostinho Neto's MPLA, Holden Roberto's National Front for the Liberation of Angola (FNLA), and Jonas Savimbi's National Union for the Total Liberation of Angola (UNITA)] had earlier clashed in an internecine war that promised to be fatal for the Marxist MPLA. The Cubans, however, were not to be discouraged by this temporary setback.

While Castro was sympathetic to the MPLA, his support was hesitant as the organization was involved in an intense struggle between pro-Soviet and pro-Chinese elements. For their part, the Soviets clearly favored the MPLA because of the close ties between Agostinho Neto and the Portuguese Communist Party. A complex scenario rapidly emerged as virtually every African state expressed differing positions on how the conflict should be resolved. Thus, it appeared that the international community had a stake in the Angolan outcome.

Castro's reasons for exercising caution in assisting the MPLA until the mid-1970s were numerous. Not only was the organization the most fragile of the Angolan political and military movements, but it was also plagued by internal factional struggles. The MPLA's membership also consisted of a large number of mixed-blood mulattos and "assimiliados." These two groups were rejected by a large part of the Angolan black population and it is conceivable that Castro did not want to become embroiled in tribal disputes. On the regional level, Holden Roberto and Jonas Savimbi were receiving support from two important African members of the Nonaligned Movement, Sekou Touré and Kenneth Kuanda—and Castro did not wish to alienate either one. In any event, months before establishing his Angolan plan, Castro, in conjunction with the Soviets, began to support the forces of Daniel Chipenda (the former military head of the MPLA who had previously separated his forces from Neto's).

It is apparent that the Soviet/Cuban ability to act in this chaotic environment was facilitated by the revolution in Lisbon and the ensuing decolonization process in Portuguese Africa. However, a strong argument can be constructed to demonstrate that Moscow and Havana were able to proceed because the two powers had already laid the necessary foundations and infrastructure for subversion throughout Angola and the African continent. In this context, the coordinated military and intelligence operations previously established allowed the Soviet/Cuban alliance to capitalize on the upheaval in the country; with regard to Soviet ability to become a major player, Castro's old African policy had afforded the Kremlin the capability to become easily involved. In addition, both powers clearly had much to gain in Africa. Moscow saw potential for tremendous strategic and political advances while Castro, still consumed by personal ambitions, was able to bypass internal pressures in Cuba and obtain significant leverage within and extensive assistance from the Kremlin. The MPLA, of course, had been "prepped" by the Portuguese Communist Party and was a relatively willing recipient of the Soviet/Cuban thrust into Angola.

The plans for Moscow and Havana's Angola mission—which would later become known as "Operacion Carlota"—had been made during Castro's 1972 African tour. Evidence of the operation's implementation began to emerge toward the end of 1974, as the Soviets began to increase their aid to the MPLA. At the same time, Admiral Rosa Coutinho, a member of the Portuguese Communist Party, assumed the colonial governorship of Angola. This event was fortuitous for the Soviets, as Coutinho immediately threw his support behind the MPLA, thus setting up serious obstacles for the other liberation movements.

At this juncture, the governments in Moscow, Havana, Washington, Lisbon, and Pretoria had all escalated their involvement in the area, with each closely monitoring the movements and policies of their adversaries. The Cubans had simultaneously deployed instructors to Angola to assemble Soviet arms, train MPLA recruits, and reorganize the Katanganese forces. Perhaps as a result of this reorganization, 6,000 Katangese soldiers who formed part of the colonial forces were concentrated at the military base of Massangano. Czechoslovak and Cuban military instructors were also sent to this base in December 1974 and January 1975 to assist in the operation.

Rosa Coutinho and his Portuguese subordinates supportive of the MPLA began to pressure the Soviets to further increase Cuba's presence in Angola and to send more armaments. The tactic appeared to be successful, as a Cuban military contingent arrived at the theater of operations at the end of April under the cover of the MPLA.[16] By May/June, the Cubans had widened their operational parameters by establishing military training centers in Henrique de Carvalho, Salazar, Benguela, and Cabinda.[17] Havana planned to yet further increase its involvement as contingency plans were apparently discussed for further Cuban action at a meeting that a Cuban mission held with MPLA President Neto in late June.[18]

On June 9, "Operacion Carlota" commenced when the MPLA unleashed a violent attack against the FNLA in Luanda. T-34 tanks and multiple-reaction weaponry operated by the Cubans were discovered at the site of the attack. A special unit of 50 Cubans also arrived in Congo-Brazzaville to assemble Soviet war materiel which had been brought into the country through the Port of Pointe Noire.

August was to become a key month for Castro's campaign as it marked the beginning of the split between the MPLA and UNITA. At the same time, it became apparent that the Cubans were preparing to take charge in Angola when Raul Diaz Arguelles arrived to take command of both the Cuban troops and the MPLA. Shortly thereafter, the group began to act in a coordinated fashion and opened fire on Jonas Savimbi's airplane, utilizing Cuban-operated antiaircraft batteries which had been stored in Bie. This incident launched the dispute between the MPLA and UNITA, and the conflict deepened when the rivals engaged in a bloody battle at Benguela.[19] The Cubans oversaw this offensive, along with the attack on Novo Redondo and on Savimbi at Quibala. While Havana was less than successful in Benguela (UNITA managed to capture several Cuban soldiers), the FNLA conceded a margin of defeat:

> . . . we can verify Portuguese and Cuban troops in these battles in Luanda, which ended with the temporary defeat of the FNLA forces and resulted in their evacuation from the capital. This was part of the program very carefully prepared with the assistance of the Cuban expeditionary force . . .[20]

One decisive event prompted Castro to intervene more directly in support of the MPLA. In September 1974, the leftist government in Luanda was overthrown. The coup threatened to endanger the support that Agostinho Neto was receiving from the colonial government in Luanda and Lisbon. During this decisive month, the Cubans began to intensify both their activity and presence in Angola by sending reinforcement troops, while the Soviets increased their arms and munitions transfers to the country. Furthermore, Congo-Brazzaville became a clearer participant in the campaign, as evidenced by the September 19 agreement reached between President Marie Ngouabie and Castro in Havana. Through this agreement, the details for a massive military strike using Brazzaville as a base were ironed out.

Havana's involvement in the conflict continued to escalate as Cuban soldiers, tank commanders, and artillery soldiers under the direction of General Arguelles were sighted in Caxito. The Portuguese colonial army received orders from Leonel Cardoso, the High Colonial Commissioner in Angola, to support the planned attack with air and naval forces. The Cubans then launched Soviet EM-21s (122mm) in an attack on Ambriz to paralyze an FNLA offensive, supported by two Zairian battalions. At the end of the month, the Cuban transport vessel "Vietnam Heroica" arrived at Pointe Noire carrying 20 armored cars, 30 trucks, and 120 troops. The cargo was subsequently transferred to Caxito by Portuguese army ships.

The Soviets and Cubans were convinced that the Western powers did not have a rapid deployment force which could counteract their plans militarily. Thus, confident that the West would not be able to react in a timely matter, plans for the invasion remained intact. Clearly the objective was to establish control of very specific areas so that the Soviets could attain a foothold on the Atlantic coastline, bordering on Zaire and Namibia.

One of Cuba's principal objectives was to defeat and liquidate UNITA and the FNLA as military organizations in order to consolidate the MPLA's control of the country, and consequently produce a reaction from Namibia. As anticipated, the West's reaction to the fighting was slow and ambivalent, and it appeared that little would be done to halt the advance of the Cubans. UNITA was quickly sapped of its strength and had to retreat to guerrilla warfare in the jungle. Finally, when the South African column and the FNLA were also sent into tactical retreat, African governments began to expand their recognition of the MPLA government. Several states even provided direct support; for example, as promised in an earlier agreement with Castro, President Ngouabie provided arms and territory for the concentration of Cuban troops. In addition, Sekou Touré made Yemenite airports available for in-transit logistical support of the operation.

In the meantime, the fighting continued. On October 6, Cuban combat troops clashed with South African antitank artillery units in Norton de Matos and serious damage was inflicted on the Cuban units. This was a strong blow to Castro as the troops were part of an elite division under the direct command of both Fidel and Raul Castro. Nonetheless, more Cubans entered the country as a military delegation arrived one week later in Brazzaville to coordinate the assembly of airplanes, tanks, and artillery— of which large quantities were about to arrive from the Soviet Union.

The Soviet Bloc buildup continued through October when two Soviet planes landed in Congo-Brazzaville carrying 1,000 Cuban soldiers and a group of Soviet officials. Simultaneously, several AN-12 and three medium-sized Cuban ships, which would serve as the means of transportation between Brazzaville and Angola, arrived in-country. Furthermore, 500 additional Cuban troops and six tanks landed in Lobito on October 18.

Western intelligence sources estimated that by this point the Soviets had provided Angola with over $400 million worth of military hardware.

Between October 26 and 29, Soviet planes transporting military equipment landed at the Maya-Maya air base in Brazzaville and were subsequently used to transport a contingent of over 1,000 Cubans from Guinea-Bissau to Brazzaville. As an indication that this buildup might be cause for concern, reports began to appear in the Western press criticizing the proximity of Soviet military troops to the theater of operations.

Despite Havana's already considerable presence in the nation, the 4,000 Cuban troops (together with the Katanganese and MPLA recruits) were not enough to prevent the South African mobile assault column from advancing. As William Durch recounts:

> Cuban and South African forces clashed December 9 to 12 between Santa Comba and Quibala, in what has come to be known as the "Battle of Bridge 14". By all accounts, the Cuban forces were severely mauled. At about the same time, UNITA forces, aided by a fresh South African mechanized unit, captured Luso.[21]

In spite of considerable efforts by the FNLA and UNITA, however, the MPLA emerged victorious in 1976. It remains clear that the victory would have been more difficult to obtain had Castro not provided the quantity of support he did to the rebel group. In addition to the MPLA/Cuban relationship, Cuba's victory represented an even more significant turning point in its relations with its Soviet mentor.[22] The days of Castro's solitary campaigns had come to an end as the two acted increasingly in unison.

Of equal importance, armed conflict in Africa (as well as in other areas of the world) provided the Soviet/Cuban alliance with the opportunity to increase its global influence through injections of massive military assistance. Angola was the ideal recipient for such assistance, as the country demonstrated the extent to which Cuba's Revolutionary Armed Forces had become the principal instrument through which Havana's foreign policy objectives could be advanced.[23] Furthermore, Castro gained from the campaign as the Soviets dramatically increased their assistance to Cuba. From 1960 to 1975 the Soviets gave Castro $7 billion; from 1976–79, the amount rose to $9.6 billion.[24] The Angola victory also signified the consolidation of the Soviet presence in Africa. This Marxist penetration into the region provided, in future years, enormous opportunities for action and for maintaining leverage in the South Atlantic.

The surprising victory of the Cuban forces in Angola had a tremendous psychological effect—not only in Africa, but throughout the Third World as well. In this context it appeared as if a new era had dawned in which an already significant military and political force would inevitably seek to expand its influence. Furthermore, the apparent reluctance on the part of the West to contain Marxist-Leninist expansion facilitated the spread of this new challenge.[25] It was not, in fact, until the episode regarding Ethiopia that the West understood it was not facing a crisis-oriented reaction of the Cubans and Soviets, but rather a carefully planned policy of expansionism in Africa. Thus, restraint in the use of military force and the prevailing philosophy of "limited conflicts" would have serious long-term consequences for Western quiescence in the region. In understanding the nature of the threat at such a late date, the West not only found itself in a defensive position vis-à-vis the Cubans and the Soviets, but also found such strategic pillars as the Horn and Southern Africa, sea and land routes, and mineral reservoirs endangered. Furthermore, the damage to the West's political prestige from Castro's advances should not be underestimated.

Since 1975, Havana and Moscow have continued to use Angola as a base for launching their expansionist policies. Some of the activities for which the country has been strategically utilized include armed attempts at destabilizing neighboring countries, serving as a base from which to initiate reconnaissance missions (i.e., the Falklands/Malvinas islands), and acting as a vast training camp for Third World subversive groups.

Ethiopia and the Costs of Intervention

Transiting the continent from Southern Africa to its Horn, in the Ethiopian case, Castro dispatched 30,000 soldiers to rescue the bloody military regime of Mengistu Haile Mariam. At this juncture Cuba received the blessing, patronage, assistance, and encouragement of the Kremlin. Clearly, lessons had been learned in Angola and the Cubans thus embarked on their Ethiopian campaign with more experience and better organization. But, at the same time, although the logistics of the military operation in Ethiopia would be similar to that of Angola, Cuba ultimately paid a heavier price for its involvement in the complex Ethiopian conflict.

As one of the poorest nations in the world, Ethiopia faced threats from two fronts in the early 1970s. On the one hand, the country was involved in a roughly 20-year border dispute with Somalia over the Ogaden territory, which resulted in Ethiopia's eventual invasion of Somalia. Juxtaposed with this contest was the havoc wreaked by several Eritrean separatist movements demanding the independence of their strategic terrain in the northwest province of Ethiopia, bordering on the Red Sea. Castro initially became involved in the imbroglio by arming Somalia and supporting the Eritrean guerrillas. However, a shift of policy in the Kremlin—

prompted by Brezhnev's doctrine of limited sovereignty of socialist states—forced Castro to switch alliances. In this case, the Cuban leader began to aid the Ethiopian government not only in its attempts to quell the Eritrean insurgency, but also in its efforts at fending off Somali aggression. The change, in the course of time, proved to be a wise one; by shifting sides, Castro "traded up" for a larger and more strategically vital power. In addition, this change in allies served to further ingratiate Castro with the Kremlin, as the Soviets subsequently increased their leverage over regional developments.

In related developments, the Ethiopian president paid a secret visit to Cuba in 1976 to discuss the problems he faced with Somalia and the Ogaden region. At that juncture, the two leaders also addressed the continuation of Libyan and Cuban support for the Eritrean guerrillas. As an indication of support for his new Ethiopian ally, Castro agreed to not only mediate in talks with Quadaffi, but also to discuss the Ogaden issue with the Soviet Union and Somalia. At this point, Moscow and Havana were still seeking to clarify their stance on eastern and southern Africa. As such, Castro, Nikloai Podgorny, and Victor Samodurov (a high level KGB official) toured the region and subsequently drew up blueprints of a joint strategy for the area.

Capitalizing on his successful conquest of Angola, Castro set an ambitious agenda for his seven-week-long 1977 African tour. Among Castro's goals were: to convince Quadaffi to increasingly tilt toward Moscow; to serve as a mediator between Ethiopia and Somalia; to test Somalia for reliability; to develop and secure his alliance with Ethiopia; and to soften his differences with Mozambique. Castro was further hoping for the creation of a federated state which would include South Yemen, Somalia, Ethiopia, Eritrea, and Ogaden. For this purpose, he held secret talks in South Yemen with Ethiopia's Mengistu, Somalia's Barre, and the Yemenites. However, no agreement was reached at this meeting.

First, Castro withdrew his military mission from Somalia and gave his approval to the South Yemenites to provide Ethiopia with military supplies should conflict break out. He then continued with his tour and visited Mozambique, Angola, and Congo-Brazzaville. Guinea was the next stop, where the Cuban leader held a meeting with Samora Machel, Agostinho Neto, Pinto de Andrade, Luis Cabral, and Sekou Touré to discuss recent developments in the region. At the head of the list of discussion points were the Ethiopian/Somali conflict and the recent Organization of African Unity (OAU) agreements regarding the presence of Cuban troops in Africa.

In January 1978, Raul Castro paid a visit to Addis Ababa to discuss the new Cuban/Ethiopian relationship, and subsequently journeyed on to Moscow where final plans were made to launch an offensive in the Ogaden.

It was decided at this juncture that Cuba would serve primarily as logistical backup and provide air support in the battle against the Eritrean separatists.[26] In preparation for the offensive, in early 1978, the Soviets airlifted 20,000 Cuban soldiers from Angola to Ethiopia via Mozambique. A Soviet naval unit was also deployed close to the scene, probably to serve as backup support.

By the time the offensive was to begin, the Ethiopian government was well-equipped to fight off the Somali resistance. 30,000 Cuban, 2,000 Soviet, Polish, and Bulgarian troops, and 2,500 Yemenites were complemented by 120 tanks, squadrons of MiG-21s and MiG-23s, and BM-21 artillery batteries. The combined force was effective: at the end of February 1978, the Cuban/Ethiopian formations, directed by a high Soviet command, had succeeded in defeating the Somali resistance. But the victory did not belong to Castro, Cuban intervention in the conflict not only created an opportunity to protect Soviet interests in the region, but also confirmed Ethiopia's integration into the Soviet Bloc.

Among the strategic prizes which the Cubans and Soviets gained from their successful intervention were the vital Ethiopian ports of Massawa and Assad, the Dahlak Archipelago in the Red Sea, and the Asmara airport. In addition, because the Soviet invasion of Afghanistan had shortened logistical distances to the Indian Ocean, Moscow had particularly high stakes in a favorable Ethiopian outcome. Furthermore, as it recognized the seriousness of the invasion, the United States subsequently took the necessary steps to create a Rapid Deployment Force (RDF) in the Persian Gulf as part of the broader Carter Doctrine.

Contrary to his full-scale involvement in the campaign in Somalia, Castro exercised significantly more caution in Addis Ababa's attempts to crush the Eritrean guerrillas. In 1977, Eritrean forces had fought their way into the strategic port of Massawa and were on the brink of victory when they were driven back by the combined effort of the Soviet fleet and Cuban air and Ethiopian ground attacks. Defeat of the separatists, however, continued to allude Addis Ababa. Despite massive Soviet injections of weaponry (approximately $2 billion dollars' worth) and a similarly costly Cuban troop presence, the Ethiopian army (300,000 men strong) did not succeed in ending the country's internal guerrilla wars.

By the late 1970s, the Soviets and Cubans had thus brought a significant portion of Africa under Marxist influence. On the one hand, with the Cubans in control in Angola and Cape Verde, Moscow had gained secured naval implacements in the east Atlantic, thereby linking the Soviet war fleet directly with Cuba and the western portion of the ocean. On the other hand, on the eastern side of the continent, the Soviet Union was able to project considerable naval power in the Indian Ocean due to Cuban control of the Horn of Africa. Of equal importance is the fact that Ethiopia, Somalia, and South Yemen not only form the juncture of black and Arab Africa, but also stand in the southern tip of the Red Sea, the western flank of the Indian Ocean, and are proximate to the Persian Gulf.

The Cubans and Soviets have also ventured into the southern flank of the continent, particularly in central-south Africa. Demonstrating agreement with hard-line strategists in the Kremlin, Castro felt that negotiated solutions to conflicts in the southern cone would be beneficial to the West. In this case, Castro and the Soviets opted for subversion and violence to obtain the victory of pro-Soviet forces in the region. Ultimately, the alliance attained this goal through the training and financing of Joshua Nkomo's ZAPU, Namibia's SWAPO, and the military arm of the ANC in South Africa. With the southern cone already convulsed by apartheid and Namibia's struggle for independence, Soviet expansionism and the presence of Cuban troops only served to complicate an already volatile situation.

In the case of Zimbabwe, Cuban and Soviet initiatives have been met with limited success. In an ongoing battle for influence with Peking on the continent, Castro attempted to pressure ZANU into breaking its ties with China. At the same time, he also tried to encourage Robert Mugabe to accept the leadership of Joshua Nkomo, leader of the pro-Soviet ZAPU. The Cubans, together with the Soviets, even went so far as to train and finance more than 10,000 ZAPU guerrillas.[27] Castro did not gain much ground with these initiatives, however, as even Nkomo ultimately rejected his proposal. Instead, Nkomo chose to reconcile with the provisional government of Bishop Muzorewa,[28] and Castro and many African leaders became convinced that the ZAPU leader's victory was imminent. Mugabe's eventual successful political emergence, however, imposed a temporary setback on Cuban/Soviet designs on the country.

Clearly, a factor which added fuel to this incendiary scenario in southern Africa is the region's tremendous wealth in mineral resources. South Africa, and neighboring states as far north as Zaire, possess a substantial share of the world's known deposits of cobalt, manganese, platinum, palladium, chromite, vanadium, antimony, industrial diamonds, uranium, and tin. In essence, competition for the influence in the southern cone is harsh—as alluded to by its colloquial name: the "Persian Gulf of the mineral world".[29] The resources of this region are essential for the production of submarines, jet engines, frames for advanced aircraft, cars, armor plate, and high-strength stainless steel. In this context, the Soviets perceive the Middle East, Africa, and the Indian Ocean to be declared vital U.S. spheres of interest because of the "imperialist's" fanatic need for other peoples' mineral resources.[30]

The battle for control over Africa's resources also adds an ideological element to Cuba's strategy concerning the continent. Both "Ché" Guevara and Fidel Castro have repeatedly stated that the unraveling of the colonial system, turmoil in the international economic order, and the privatization of vital material resources would provoke widespread discontent and the subsequent collapse of Western economic, political, and military preeminence.

With this ideological element in mind, one should not overlook the core of Castro's southern Africa strategy: mineral-rich South Africa. The ANC had already determined that armed struggle was the most feasible tactic for assuming power. Utilizing the military wing of the ANC (the brainchild of Nelson Mandela and the South African Communist Party (SACP) and funded jointly by the Soviet Bloc and the SACP), Cuba has sought to polarize the white establishment by provoking a subversion/repression cycle.[31] Toward that end, on a tactical level, the communist faction of the ANC played a key role in organizing and arranging for training for young South African guerrillas in Angola following the 1976 Soweto uprising.[32]

In moving from a southern African to a continent-wide strategy, with an aura of confidence from their Angolan and Ethiopian successes, the Cubans continued to maintain a watchful eye on developments in Namibia, the ANC, the Polisario Front, Benin, Ghana, Upper Volta, and Libya. Neither Havana nor Moscow have given up hope on Zaire and anxiously await an evolution in the situation, especially in a post-Mobuto phase. South Africa remains on the agenda, as well. Fueled from neighboring states, the political situation in that nation continues to erode, and the Cubans and Soviets are satisfied that events are moving in a favorable direction.

With regard to the situation in Angola, the continued presence of Cuban troops is due more to Soviet designs on the region and UNITA's undying resistance than to the "threat" posed by South Africa. While Cuban forces have displayed superiority in both tactical offensive and firepower capabilities, they have proved to be significantly weaker in maintaining a strategic defense and have thus experienced difficulty in mobilizing their forces against UNITA. This problem area became even more apparent with Savimbi's recent ability to widen his radius of action; as a result of these weaknesses, the Cubans were forced to assume the principal role in the offensives.

Prior to arriving in Luanda, the Cuban soldiers had been "taught" during their training that they were coming to Angola to "fight" the South Africans.[33] What they did not expect to be confronted with was the unrelenting resistance of the UNITA forces. It has been precisely this unwillingness on the part of the opposition to relinquish in its struggle that has exposed the vulnerability of both the Cubans and the MPLA government. Furthermore, it is evident that Savimbi, aware of the significance of his struggle, will not surrender in his fight against the government.

With regard to the economics of continuing strife, Angola's civil war is costing approximately $1 billion annually. But, in a somewhat paradoxical fashion, the Gulf Oil Corporation together with other investors have eased the financial burden on the Cubans and the Soviets: the oil companies in Angola have provided the MPLA with the financial resources to afford the cost of the Cuban army, East European technicians, and Soviet armaments. Since Angola pays for the Cubans with profits from oil exports to the United States, it has been estimated that this East bloc operation in southern Africa costs Moscow less than maintaining two of its army's 180 divisions.[34]

Finally, in its attempt to bring the continent into the Soviet sphere, Moscow has waged its battle utilizing the Cubans and East Germans as surrogate troops and Angola as the launching pad for guerrilla warfare. This massive Cuban/Soviet military intervention has not only put the region's security into jeopardy, but has also endangered vital Western interests. It is therefore surprising that the West has yet to develop coherent and coordinated countermeasures to address either the conflicts in southern Africa or a broader response to the intrusion of the Soviet/Cuban alliance in the continent's turmoil.

Conclusion

The post-World War II era left a very clear division of power and influence on the European continent. During this period, the Soviets focused most of their attention on the Yalta agreements and the European theater. However, several developments since that time—including the Vietnam War, the Arab/Israeli conflict, the Sino/Soviet split, a renunciation of the Cold War mentality, and significant improvements in Soviet weaponry—have produced a fundamental transformation in Moscow's view of the world. The Kremlin's earlier concerns with promising European political parties were replaced by a new geostrategic global agenda, to be implemented through military force. In this context the newly independent countries of the Third World, characterized by distinct power vacuums, provided alluring targets for the execution of this new strategy.

From this "correlation of forces" joint Cuban/Soviet action in Africa thus cannot be categorized as individual responses to specific crises. Instead, it is evident that Havana's and Moscow's interests in the continent have coincided from the moment the two laid eyes on Africa. While Castro's tactics in the 1960s differed significantly from the Kremlin's, by the 1970s the two were clearly acting in harmony; Cuban cooperation in South Yemen (to bring the southern portion of the Red Sea under the Soviet military umbrella) and Castro's courtship of the pro-Soviet MPLA in Angola (despite initial reservations) reflect examples of a coordinated approach. And, of course, Ethiopia represents the clearest example of the extent to which Castro was willing to place Moscow's concerns and priorities above his own and to act in unison with his mentor.

At the same time, it is important to note that Castro's dramatically successful interventions in the 1970s began to sour and turn to crises in the 1980s. In this context both Moscow and Havana came to appreciate the fact that superior strength did not automatically translate into prolonged victories in the Third World. Overall, the Soviet Bloc failed to understand that the emergence of nationalistic fervor was not synonymous with the desire to become closely aligned with the Marxist powers. As the 1990s approach, it is difficult to predict the future course of Cuban policy toward Africa. Will Castro continue to muddle through and maintain the status quo, or will the leader choose a more radical course by either withdrawing or increasing Cuba's presence? Present Soviet concerns with retrenchment and withdrawal make it improbable that Castro will be permitted to escalate his involvement in Africa. At the same time, Castro's obsession with projecting himself and his country as a powerful global actor virtually assures that his nation's troops will not be withdrawn unless intense pressure is exerted. As a pragmatist, Castro is also aware of the fact that a military withdrawal and return of disgruntled troops to Cuba could provoke a political crisis of unprecedented proportions—a risk at present he appears unwilling to assume.

It thus appears reasonable to assume that the "jefe maximo" will opt for the safest approach—and continue to muddle through in Africa. As his country's undisputed leader, there is no indication Castro would willingly discard what up until now has been a fairly successful foreign policy agenda. On the other hand, Castro will have to come to terms with several critical issues such as succession and domestic economic realities in the near future. These pressing concerns will raise a range of new questions about Cuba's role in the international community and may very likely force this island-nation to reexamine the utility of its present policy toward not only Africa, but, more broadly, the Third World as well.

Notes

1. For further discussion on Cuba's advancement of Soviet objectives in Africa, see Edward Gonzalez, *Cuban Policy Toward Africa: Activities, Motivations and Outcomes,* (unpublished manuscript), p. 2.

2. William J. Durch, *Studies in Comparative Communism,* vol. XI, nos. 1 and 2; Spring/Summer, 1978, p. 46.
3. Durch, p. 48.
4. Durch, p. 49.
5. For a more indepth discussion, see a recent monograph by Alberto Miguez, *Castro's Armies in Africa,* edited by Kenneth August, quoted by permission of the Cuban-American National Foundation, 1985.
6. Miguez, *Castro's Armies.*
7. Brian Crozier, "Soviet Pressure in the Caribbean," *Conflict Studies,* No. 35, May 1973, p. 6.
8. Durch, p. 48.
9. Phillip Abbott Luce, *The New Imperialism: Cuba and the Soviet Union in Africa,* (Washington, D.C., 1979), p. 34, as quoted by John Gerassi, ed., *Venceremos: Speeches and Writings of Ché Guevara,* (Clarion, 1968).
10. Durch, p. 5.
11. Durch, p. 51.
12. Durch, p. 52.
13. Durch, p. 53.
14. Durch, p. 55.
15. Miguez.
16. "F.N.L.A. Bulletin," Speech by Holden Roberto, September 6, 1983.
17. Quoted by Durch, p. 64.
18. Durch, p. 64.
19. U.N.I.T.A., "Daring to Challenge Soviet-Cuban Occupation in Angola," Relatorio p. 3.
20. "F.N.L.A. Bulletin."
21. Durch, p. 68.
22. Peter Vanneman and W. Martin James III, *Soviet Foreign Policy in Southern Africa: Problems and Prospects,* (Pretoria, 1982), p. 20.
23. Gonzalez, p. 8.
24. Gonzalez, p. 22.
25. For more on this subject, see Miguez.
26. Gonzalez, p. 12.
27. Seth Singleton, *CSIS Africa Notes,* April 26, 1983.
28. Vanneman and James, p. 11.
29. W.A.E. Skurnik, "Continuing Problems in Africa's Horn," *Current History: Africa, 1983,* p. 101.
30. Leonid Brezhnev, "Report to the Twenty-Sixth Congress of the Communist Party of the U.S.S.R.," 23 February 1981, *Current Digest of the Soviet Press,* Vol. XXXII, No. 8, p. 10.
31. Subcommittee on Security and Terrorism, "Soviet, East German and Cuban Involvement in Fomenting Terrorism in Southern Africa," United States Senate, November, 1982.
32. Singleton, p. 2.
33. *The Daily Telegraph,* October 25, 1984.
34. Singleton.

6

Cuba and Angola

Gillian Gunn

Introduction

Cuban involvement in Angola is a topic which provokes vigorous, and often emotional, debate. The sudden and dramatic manner in which Cuba intervened, the racial undercurrents stirred by South African association with one set of protagonists, the apparent duplicity of some U.S. government officials in their dealings with the Congress on the Angolan issue at a time when Watergate was still fresh in the public's mind, and the obvious East-West dimensions of the conflict all made, and still make, dispassionate analysis of Cuban actions and motivations extremely difficult.

In this context, discussion of Cuban policy on Angola has become polarized in a manner that facilitates neither the scholar's search for "the truth" nor the policymaker's attempt to define an appropriate U.S. response to Cuban actions. Analyses too frequently deteriorate into stereotypical, ideologically oriented exercises. According to one view, Cuba was the prime culprit in the internationalization of the Angolan conflict, Castro was motivated by economic self-interest and slavish devotion to the Soviet cause, the Cuban presence is currently resented by the Angolan people, and the Angolan government must obey Cuban instructions. In the opposing version, Cuba acted totally independently from Moscow, intervened only in response to U.S. and South African meddling, has been motivated primarily by moral considerations, is welcomed by the Angolan people, and never issues orders to the Angolan government.

This chapter will explore the hypothesis that, as in many other conflicts which provoke intense emotions, the true picture fits neither of the popular

153

stereotypes, but includes elements of both, as well as some factors not considered by either. Specifically, it will propose the following arguments.

- Initial (1961–62) Cuban involvement with the movement that eventually took power in Angola, the Movimento Popular de Libertacao de Angola (MPLA), stemmed partially from a desire to distance itself from Moscow, not from acquiescence to Soviet instructions.
- Most Cuban and Soviet interests in Angola overlap, but in several important episodes the respective national interests have clashed, and will continue to do so intermittently in the future.
- The Cuban, South African, and U.S. decisions to intervene in Angola occurred almost simultaneously, and were in response to suspected but unconfirmed actions by the "other side." Thus Cuba was neither the villain nor the hero in the 1975–76 war.
- The Soviet Union did not instruct Cuba to intervene in 1975, but Castro could not have carried out the action as effectively, or perhaps at all, if the Soviets had vigorously opposed it.
- Cuba has received considerable economic benefits from its Angolan operation in the past, but did not intervene in order to profit economically, and is benefiting far less currently.
- Among the motivations for Cuba's involvement in Angola not addressed in the stereotypical explanations are Cuba's nationalistic pride, Castro's concern for promoting his own and Cuba's international image, and the Cuban leader's personal loyalty to Angola's President Neto.
- The Angolan government is capable of undertaking policy initiatives without consulting the Cubans, and in a manner that is less than entirely respectful of Cuban concerns, though there is no evidence that the MPLA would act directly against Cuban interests.
- Cuba's perception of the advantages of remaining in Angola has not been consistent, and in the early 1980s Havana became ambivalent about maintaining its presence, without actually deciding against it. However, U.S. and South African actions from 1986 to 1988 increased the perceived cost of withdrawal and advantages of remaining. Events in South Africa during this period also caused Cuba to place greater priority on southern Africa than previously, and led Cuban interests to diverge somewhat from those of the MPLA.
- The most important criterion conditioning Cuban responses to MPLA negotiations with the U.S. over Cuban troop withdrawal is the impact such a deal would have upon Cuba's international prestige and influence. A deal which did not damage Cuban prestige would not be vigorously opposed by Havana, whereas an arrangement which left Cuba appearing defeated or "dismissed" would be.

Cuba and the MPLA: The Early Years

The proposal that early Cuban involvement with the MPLA stemmed partly from Cuban unease with its Soviet ties sounds ludicrous on the surface. The MPLA received most of its arms from the Soviet Union and frequently praised the Soviets in international fora. How, then, could Cuban aid for the organization possibly be construed as a gesture of independence from Moscow? The suggestion that Cuban and Soviet interests in Angola diverged also rings false, initially. They both describe themselves as socialist countries, and they both wanted to accelerate the overthrow of Portuguese colonialism and ensure that the government which took power in Angola was well-disposed toward the socialist bloc. Given all these similarities, how could their interests in Angola differ?

Two elements must be examined to explain the paradox: Castro's relations with the Soviet Union and the rest of the international community in the early and mid-1960s when the MPLA and Cuba first struck up their alliance, and the particular nature of MPLA relations with Moscow at that juncture.

When Cuba was first exposed to the MPLA, it was undergoing the process that virtually every revolution has experienced, namely, the desire to "make the world safe for revolution" by aiding similarly inclined governments and movements, and gaining strength through numbers. Many scholars claim that it was this concern which motivated Washington to view favorably the French revolution and challenges to Spanish rule in South America after the U.S.'s victorious independence war against Britain.[1] Cuba displayed this "missionary impulse for revolution" in 1961 and 1962 when it started training troops of the radical government ruling newly independent Ghana,[2] and also when it provided military and medical supplies for Algeria's National Liberation Front, fighting for independence from France, and, following the Front's 1962 victory, established a military mission in Algiers.[3] The MPLA, founded in 1956, had representatives in both the Algerian and Ghanaian capitals, and it was there that Cuban and Angolan radicals were first introduced. At this point, Cuban interest in African revolutions was associated with its desire to establish alliances with similarly inclined powers.

The picture changed dramatically after the October 1962 missile crisis. Castro was outraged by the Soviet Union's decision to negotiate an end to the crisis without consulting him. Relations were also increasingly strained by Castro's rejection of the Soviet economic model and his emphasis on moral incentives. Khrushev's 1964 ouster, his replacement by even more cautious colleagues, and Moscow's pursuit of "peaceful coexistence" with the U.S. despite Washington's growing involvement in Vietnam, all further exacerbated the tensions. In one commentator's words, "They [the Cubans] became increasingly skeptical about the Soviet Union's reliability as allies and sought to create new security options for themselves."[4] Thus, the need to foment revolutions and establish alliances with the governments they produced took on a new urgency. Allies were no longer needed solely against the revolution's conventional enemies, but also as a counterweight to its unreliable friend.

The deterioration of the U.S./Cuban relationship in this period undoubtedly also played a role. The Bay of Pigs incident confirmed Castro's belief that the U.S. would not be easily reconciled to his revolution, and the fact that the MPLA was fighting a close U.S. ally and NATO member (Portugal's Salazar government) was not irrelevant. By helping movements fighting U.S. friends, Cuba could possibly distract some of Washington's energies from anti-Castro endeavors. As Durch has pointed out, "Its [Cuba's] aim was to create 'many Vietnams' on the reasonable supposition that U.S. troops bogged down in several countries at once could combat no single insurgency effectively."[5]

The Soviet attitude toward liberation movements in general, and the MPLA in particular, also must be considered. Throughout the 1960s, the Soviet Union maintained that the Third World was not ripe for revolution, and thus it tended oftentimes to work through moribund communist parties while ignoring or only giving token support to guerrilla movements. With regard to Angola, the Soviets had established contact with the MPLA through the Portuguese Communist Party in the late 1950s. However, the movement's first leader, Agostinho Neto, was a "difficult" man, and while his aims were supported by Moscow, his methods and personality, and especially his refusal to promise the Soviet Union certain privileges in postindependence Angola, irritated the Kremlin. In addition, Moscow was unimpressed when factional problems and difficulty in gaining access to the main infiltration route into Angola slowed MPLA military progress in the early 1960s. The Soviet Union thus became increasingly disillusioned with the movement, curtailing its support in 1963 and 1964.

This was the setting when Cuba/MPLA relations increased from the acquaintance to ally level in 1964. While still a member of the Cuban government, Ché Guevara visited Africa from December 1964 to March 1965[6] to enlist support for a union to combat imperialism, first in Congo-Leopoldville (now Zaire) and subsequently throughout Africa. During his year-long travels, Ché's itinerary took him through Congo-Brazzaville, where the MPLA had its headquarters. Although Neto had little guerrilla action to show him, Guevara nonetheless promised Cuban instructors as well as diplomatic and political support.[7]

The Cuban/MPLA relationship escalated again in 1966. The first MPLA guerrillas were sent to Havana for training, and the MPLA became the exclusive representative of the Angolan nationalists (two other rival movements existed by this time) at the "Tri-Continental Conference" hosted in Havana. Furthermore, the MPLA created a "Cienfuegos Column" named after the Cuban guerrilla leader, and Neto and his top military commander visited Cuba for consultations.

During the takeoff in Cuban/MPLA relations from 1964 to 1968, Moscow became increasingly annoyed with Havana's adventurist policies—which it feared might trigger off difficulties in the U.S./Soviet relationship. The irritation was mutual, and Castro gave Kosygin a cold shoulder in 1967 when the Soviet official visited Havana after a summit meeting in the United States.[8] In a further gesture of defiance, Cuba published and promoted Regis Debray's book *Revolution in the Revolution?* which challenged Moscow's philosophy on revolution in the Third World.[9] Cuban/Soviet disagreements then came to a head in 1968—associated with a number of issues aside from the Cuban/MPLA relationship—as demonstrated by Moscow's delay of the delivery of vital oil supplies to Havana.[10]

The message was not lost on Castro, and Cuban relations with Moscow subsequently took on a new warmth. In August 1968, Castro endorsed the Soviet Union's invasion of Czechoslovakia, and following Cuba's failure to produce a 10 million-ton sugar harvest in 1970, he introduced economic reforms in line with Soviet policy. The rapprochement was finalized in 1972 with Cuba becoming a full-fledged member of the Council for Mutual Economic Assistance (CMEA).

From 1968 to 1972, Cuban and Soviet policy toward the MPLA was also relatively harmonious. Havana continued training operations, but did not become so vigorously involved as to incite U.S. anger. In addition, Castro began to urge its liberation movement allies—as part of the broader Nonaligned Movement (with which the MPLA was affiliated)—to recognize the Soviet Union as a "natural ally" of the Third World.

Cuban/Soviet coordination then fell apart again in 1972 and 1973 as the MPLA was racked by internal conflicts. The movement's commander in the eastern part of the country, Daniel Chipenda, broke away, taking a large number of combatants with him. In addition, Moscow was already displeased by Neto's continued reluctance to pledge facilities in postindependence Angola, his prickly personality, and his lackluster battlefield performance. Apparently believing that Chipenda might be more amenable and militarily successful, Moscow suspended aid to Neto and shifted it to Chipenda.

Neto was furious and believed there was "an American-Soviet agreement that placed Angola within the American sphere of influence and Mozambique within a Soviet sphere of influence".[11] (Mozambican guerrillas were also fighting for independence from Portugal at the time.) In a February 1974 speech at the University of Dar es Salaam, Neto lambasted the Soviet Union, saying "The relations of solidarity have changed. . . ." However, he also noted that "the socialist camp is divided" on this issue, tacitly acknowledging that neither Yugoslavia nor Cuba reduced their support for the Neto group during the Chipenda crisis.[12]

Why did Cuba remain so loyal to Neto during this crisis, while the Soviets flirted with Chipenda? Several explanations are possible. First, as a small, young, and relatively weak country, Cuba was not seeking an additional client to add to an existing network of military bases and other facilities. Thus, Neto's nationalistic stubbornness on the base issue was not a problem for Castro—although it was for Moscow. Second, Cuba was in an idealistic phase in the 1960s, and, to a lesser but still significant extent, in the early 1970s. Therefore the ideological "purity" of an ally was important. So for Cuba, Neto's military reverses were partially counterbalanced by his commitment to shared goals. The Soviet Union was in a more pragmatic phase, and ideological solidarity meant little if an ally was not in a position to take power. Cultural issues and the amount of personal contact between nationalities were also relevant. The Cubans and Angolans shared a common Latin and Third World background, which inevitably helped Havana understand, and have patience with, the complexities of MPLA internal factionalism. Furthermore, Cuba provided training, and personal bonds developed between instructors and students. The Soviet Union, in its role as arms-supplier, had less personal contact with the MPLA, and cultural differences made whatever contact there was less conducive to mutual understanding.

The preceding discussion shows that proposals which appear absurd, initially, actually find considerable support in the historical record. Cuba's decision to increase aid to the MPLA came at a time when Havana was losing faith in the reliability of the Soviet Union and wanted to establish alternative, balancing alliances—and Cuban and Soviet policies on the MPLA did occasionally fall out of alignment. This does not mean that Soviet and Cuban goals were diametrically opposed. Indeed, both nations wished to see a socialist-inclined party sympathetic to the Soviet Bloc assume power. But on a number of important details, their strategies for arriving at that goal diverged.

The 1974–76 War

The claim that Cuba was neither the villain nor the hero in the 1974–76 war, and was not responding to Soviet urging when it intervened, flies in the face of conventional wisdom. It can be argued that somebody intervened first, so if Cuba was not the "bad guy," it must have been the "good guy." And since the result of Cuba's actions favored Soviet interests, is it not logical to assume that Moscow planned the intervention in the first place? Plausible though the above arguments sound, the historical record again suggests they are inaccurate.

Before explaining these claims, however, two important additional actors must be introduced, the Frente Nacional de Libertacao de Angola (FNLA) and the Uniao Nacional para a Independencia Total de Angola (UNITA). Founded in 1962, the former group originally aimed to establish the ancient Kongo kingdom in northeastern Angola as a separate country. Though it soon widened its objectives to include independence for all of Angola, the early regional emphasis ensured it received its main support from the Bakongo tribal group. (This contrasted with the MPLA's Mbundu ethnic base in the area around the capital.) The FNLA had a reputation for antiwhite actions, and its statements revealed a nationalist, rather than socialist, ideological base. In 1962, the CIA began to provide the FNLA with arms and money, but in 1969 the support was reduced, following Portuguese protests, to a $10,000 annual retainer for intelligence.[13] In this context, the FNLA's leader, Holden Roberto, visited Peking in December 1973 and obtained a promise of aid.

The second actor requiring introduction is UNITA. Founded in 1966 by Roberto's former Foreign Minister, Jonas Savimbi, UNITA initially espoused black nationalist or socialist ideals depending upon what potential backer it was addressing—although it later settled into consistently anticommunist rhetoric. Savimbi differed from Roberto by concentrating more on conducting guerrilla war inside Angola than on exile politics. In addition, UNITA drew support from the southern Ovimbundi tribe, in contrast with the FNLA's Bakongo base. Modest Chinese aid to UNITA began in 1970.[14]

These two parties, in addition to the MPLA, fought Portuguese colonialism through the 1960s and early 1970s. However, Roberto's association with the U.S. and China, and Savimbi's friendship with a black, anti-Castro Cuban, as well as his organization's ties to the People's Republic of China, insured that the FNLA and UNITA would not become rivals to the MPLA for Soviet and Cuban support.

With the major actors introduced, the reader is equipped to tackle the confusing events surrounding Angola's independence in November 1975. A detailed chronology of pre- and post-independence developments is provided in Appendix A. Briefly, it shows that following the 25 April 1974 ouster of Caetano by the antiwar, left-leaning "Armed Forces Movement" in Portugal, and the setting of 11 November 1975 as the date for Angolan independence, the three nationalist movements began to vie for power in an increasingly violent struggle. In terms of the situation on the ground, the U.S. awarded military assistance first solely to the FNLA, and later to both the FNLA and UNITA; the Soviet Union and Cuba backed the MPLA; and South Africa backed UNITA. A close reading of the chronology supplied in Appendix A shows that from April 1974 to October 1975 South African, U.S., and Cuban officials were making parallel but fairly independent decisions, responding to their allies' appeals. The results of each secret decision were then seen in the field, in the form of new military equipment and free spending by the aid recipients. Though each side generally could not prove its opponent was making secret decisions, each speculated that the other was preparing to intervene directly and acted accordingly. Thus, nobody really "moved first" and nobody really "responded." Only in October 1975 did the situation become reactive, with each side increasing its involvement in response to known actions by each actor's "enemy." Who started the chain reaction? The chronology supplied in Appendix A suggests everybody: the U.S. and Cuba made their decisions to dramatically increase intervention within days of each other in July 1975—without knowledge of the other's decision—and South Africa made a similar choice the following month, again without full knowledge of its adversary's plans.

Likewise, the chronology shows that Cuba decided independently to intervene with massive troop shipments, and was not responding to Soviet instructions. Henry Kissinger agrees with this account,[15] and the claim is supported by Arkady Shevchenko, a Soviet diplomat who defected to the United States in 1978. Shevchenko indicates that when he asked Deputy Foreign Minister Vasily Kuznetsov in 1976: "How did we persuade the Cubans to provide their contingent?," he was told: "The idea for the large-scale military operation had originated in Havana, not Moscow."[16] And even if the remarks of these two observers with no reason to support Cuban claims are rejected, the Soviet Union's halting of the airlifting of Cuban troops every time the U.S. complained implies Moscow had mixed feelings about the operation.

Castro's decision to formulate Cuba's Angola policy without first fully informing the Soviet Union is in keeping with Fidel's personality. As Tad Szulc has pointed out in describing a political decision Castro took while attending university, "It was in Fidel's nature, as his entire life demonstrates, to accept challenges and take high risks in the name of principle. . . . (I)t was also in his introvert's nature to isolate himself at the start of a crisis and to make the great decisions in solitude."[17]

While it seems fairly clear Castro acted initially on his own, it must also, however, be acknowledged that Cuba could not have "pulled off" the Angolan operation without the Soviet help, at least not on the scale, or at the speed, that it did. If Cuba had to bring all its own heavy arms, it would have threatened its own defense capability, and, more importantly, would have simply run out of equipment. Also, the island-nation simply did not have the logistical ability to transport its troops once the U.S. convinced a number of countries to suspend landing rights for Cuban aircraft en route to Angola. Thus, while Cuba was not operating on Soviet instructions, it could not have executed the operation had the Soviet Union disapproved.

One question, however, remains unanswered. If Cuba did not send troops to Angola on Soviet instructions, and did not have proof of South African invasion plans at the time the troop shipment plans began, why did it intervene? The most important motivation was Castro's forecast—a remarkably astute one as it later turned out—namely, that South Africa and the U.S. would implement their own interventions. Castro acted on a well-informed hunch, and within days was proven correct.

In addition, the weight that must be ascribed to Castro's personality and subsequent decision cannot be overestimated. The Angola situation was an irresistible temptation for someone so anxious to prove himself a major historical figure on the world, and not solely Cuban, stage. Castro's strong personal loyalty to Neto, already exemplified in 1963–64 and 1973–74, was an equally important factor.

The role of culture must also be considered. The Cuban worldview has been intensely nationalistic and "macho" since well before Castro arrived on the scene, and the projection of Cuban force into a conflict on the other side of the world was extremely attractive. The known U.S. affiliation with the MPLA's enemies (even though the extent of its aid to them was not known at the time Cuban intervention plans started) also played on the Cuban culture's anti-Americanism, which similarly dates from the pre-Castro era. And of course, the opportunity to let the Cuban military try out its talents and equipment in an ongoing conflict was also appealing, though it was simply an extra argument in favor of the move, not a determining factor.

Many authors who accept that Cuba did not intervene in Angola on Soviet instructions nonetheless believe Cuba did so in order to gain increased leverage on the Soviets, particularly in regard to economic agreements. They point out that in February and April 1976, Cuba and the Soviet Union: signed five-year bilateral agreements which increased the price subsidy for sugar and nickel; called for a 250% increase in economic and technical assistance; and provided for an indexing of Soviet oil sales to Cuba against the sugar price. Translated into practice, this later meant that Cuba paid a much lower price for Soviet oil than other CMEA countries as the sugar price fell. Furthermore, the agreements gave Cuba better terms for Soviet debt repayment.[18]

However, the fact that Cuba obtained a better economic deal from Moscow after the Angola action does not mean it intervened in order to win those improved terms. Given Soviet ambivalence at the beginning of the operation and its concern about upsetting the United States, Castro could have ended up with a very annoyed Moscow on the other side of the negotiating table. Either due to good judgment or luck, the events turned in Havana's favor, and Cuba did indeed gain enormous leverage with the Soviet Union through the Angola operation. The desire to preserve that leverage undoubtedly helps to explain Cuba's post-1976 willingness to *remain* in Angola, but there is nothing to indicate that it intervened in Angola to *obtain* that leverage.

Similarly, some observers believe Cuba hoped for a non–Soviet oil source in Angola. However, Castro surely realized that Angola would have to sell its oil for hard currency in order to develop, and though he might have hoped that a grateful MPLA would channel some oil to Cuba, he could not have depended on it. In any event, some Angolan oil did reportedly arrive in Cuba, but via a novel route that only brought the Soviet Union advantage. According to Tad Szulc, "(T)he Soviets quietly purchased oil from Gulf on the high seas (through a broker in Curacao) after which the tankers sailed to Cuba. It was much cheaper for the Russians to ship at least some of the oil from Cabinda rather than from the Black Sea."[19]

A less farfetched argument suggests that Havana expected to profit from service contracts with the oil-rich MPLA government once Neto was installed in power. In the mid-1970s, Cuba was indeed discovering that it could reap profits from renting out skilled personel, which its educational system was producing at a brisk rate. The prospect of concluding such service contracts with an MPLA-ruled Angola must have been attractive— but it was certain neither that the MPLA would be amenable to such deals nor what the level of profit would be. The expectation of possible service profits is therefore unlikely to have been sufficiently attractive to justify such a risky action as sending thousands of troops into a foreign war.

It also must be remembered that Cuba paid, or appeared to pay, a price for the intervention: the loss of an opportunity to improve relations with the United States.[20] In early 1975, the State Department had begun quiet conversations with Cuban diplomats at the United Nations to feel out Havana's attitude toward improving relations. In a March 1975 speech, Kissinger indicated there was "no virtue in perpetual antagonism" with Cuba.[21] In May of that year, he approved a policy through which Castro was "informed that the United States was considering lifting sanctions against Cuba selectively and would suspend RB-71 spy plane overflights over the island during preliminary contacts."[22] The U.S. then supported the Organization of American States' (OAS) decision to abolish the collective embargo on economic and political ties with Cuba, and in August, the State Department announced that American firms based in foreign countries would be allowed to do business with the island for the first time in twelve years.[23]

Indeed, Castro himself has characterized this period as the closest the U.S. and Cuba have come to a breakthrough since the revolution.[24] However, while the arrival of thousands of Cuban troops in Angola in late 1975 was not the sole cause of the collapse of this effort (for example, strident Cuban language in the United Nations on Puerto Rican independence also sabotaged the initiative), the Angola decision had a clear cost. In this context, it is probable that the Cuban economy would have benefitted far more from regaining access to the American market—a prospect that appeared possible just before Cuba's intervention in Angola—than it subsequently did from its Angola operation.

In sum, the Cubans did not send combat troops to Angola on Soviet instructions, in response to direct South African or American intervention, or in the hope of receiving economic advantages through increased leverage on the Soviets and/or a profitable trade relationship with the MPLA. Troops were sent because Cuba guessed, but did not know, that South Africa and the U.S. were preparing to become more deeply involved. In addition, Cuba acted because Castro had developed a close personal relationship with Neto, and because the intervention was just the type of grand gesture which appealed to Castro's personality and the Cuban national character.

Cuban Consolidation in Angola: 1976–81

Broadly speaking, in the five years following the MPLA's victory, several phenomena simultaneously developed: Cuba was pulled into a much longer term role in Angola than it originally anticipated; Soviet/Cuban Angola policy differences briefly erupted into overt confrontation; Cuba became increasingly involved in Angola's civilian life (sometimes profitably); and social problems emerged between the Angolan and Cuban populations, though to a lesser extent than many expected.

There is no indication that when Cuba sent its forces to Angola, it expected them to remain for over a decade. Indeed, in early March 1976, Castro and Neto agreed that 200 soldiers would be withdrawn each week, reducing Cuban numbers by 8,000 by the end of the year.[25] Cubans were to prepare Angolan replacements, and on 1 August 1976 an expanded training program was ratified.[26] However, events on the Angolan border with Zaire and inside the MPLA itself then caused a new preoccupation with Neto's security.

During the war, the MPLA had recruited to its ranks Zairean gendarmes, who wanted independence for that nation's mineral-rich Shaba province.[27] In March 1976, the gendarmes invaded Shaba from Angola, and Zaire accused Neto and Castro of aiding the rebels. Cuba denied involvement, and later both U.S. Secretary of State Cyrus Vance and President Carter said there was no evidence of Cuban participation.[28] The Shaba forces were defeated, fled back to Angola, and the Cuban troop withdrawals continued. However, Havana and Luanda began to realize that the possibility of Zairean retaliation could not be lightly dismissed.

While the implications of the Shaba incident were being evaluated, a recently ousted MPLA minister attempted a coup against Neto (possibly with Soviet support) and was defeated by government forces aided by the Cubans. The coup organizer was Nito Alves, Minister of Interior from independence until Neto abolished his post in October 1976. Alves opposed Neto's policy of nonalignment, advocated granting the Soviet Union military base facilities, was antiwhite (and therefore opposed to Neto's multiracialism), called for a swift transition to socialism rather than Neto's gradualist approach,[29] and believed, in the words of a supporter, "the MPLA should be tied to the Soviet Union. . . . in a bond similar to that which unites the Portuguese Communist Party to that [the Soviet] party."[30] Alves was the MPLA representative to the 25th Soviet Communist Party Congress in February 1977[31] and an Alves confidante, Sita Valles, was a frequent guest at the Soviet embassy.[32]

On 21 May 1977, Alves was expelled from the MPLA,[33] and a week later he launched the coup attempt, releasing supporters from prison and taking the Luanda radio station. Neto mobilized loyal armored units from the Presidential Guard and a headquarters force, both of which had Cubans in their midst as the soldiers shared barracks with their Cuban trainers.[34] Loyalist soldiers and Cubans retook the radio station, and a Cuban voice broadcast the announcement that the facility was back under Neto's control.[35] Cuban soldiers then patrolled the streets of Luanda for the following days, as the coup plotters were rounded up. Interestingly, Sita Valles was caught trying to send a message to the Soviet embassy asking for help to flee the country.[36]

Much of the Luanda populace concluded that the Soviet Union had attempted a coup against Neto, and that the Cubans had prevented it. The day after the attempt, the MPLA Politburo indicated the plotters had "a feigned dedication to some friendly country,"[37] and a Mozambican source claims he witnessed Neto tell the Soviet ambassador over the telephone that the MPLA possessed evidence of Moscow's complicity.[38] Initial lukewarm Soviet condemnation of the attempt contrasted with Cuba's response, which included: favorable reporting of Alves's ouster from the MPLA just before the coup; pro-Neto pronouncements immediately after the attempt; and Raul Castro's visit to Luanda on 12 June to emphasize Cuba's support for Neto.[39]

In hopes of salvaging the Neto-Moscow relationship, within a few weeks the MPLA began to downplay allegations of the Soviet connection, but as of June 1986 many Angolans retained their first impression. Indeed, one Angolan said, "Did it never occur to the Americans that one of the reasons we are so reluctant to send the Cuban troops home is that we want them as a balancing force to the Soviets? After all, we all remember 1977."[40]

The Alves attempt showed once again that, as in the 1973–74 period, Cuban and Soviet interests in Angola were not identical. The Soviet Union did not necessarily back Alves as so many Angolans believe, but, as it has elsewhere in the Third World, Moscow certainly did sit on the fence until it saw who won—whereas the Cubans intervened to ensure Neto emerged victorious. In addition, there was not enough time for the Cuban forces to obtain instructions from home on the day of the coup; they must have had standing instructions to back Neto in any unrest. Cuban motivations were the same as in the 1973–74 crisis including: Castro's personal loyalty to Neto; the importance of ideological solidarity; Cuban disinterest in the base facilities Neto refused to grant (to the Soviets); and Cuban cultural empathy with Angolans, which permitted Havana to gauge the local situation more astutely than the Soviets.

The fact that the Alves coup attempt resembled similar scuffles Castro had with the Soviets, specifically the "sectarian" and "microfaction" incidents, also helps explain the vigor with which he lept to Neto's defense. The 1962 "sectarian" challenge began when Castro put an "old-line" communist with Soviet ties, Anibal Escalante, in charge of creating a unified political organization, and then accused him of trying to place the revolution in the hands of orthodox communists.[41] Escalante was purged, and though the Soviets were never outright accused of complicity, Castro pointedly refused to receive Soviet ambassador Kudryatsev for a farewell audience shortly thereafter.[42] The problem reemerged in 1968 when a "microfaction" of old-line communists allegedly tried to convince Moscow to suspend all economic aid to Cuba to force Castro's ouster and put in power a "loyal" communist regime.[43] Thus, the rumors circulating in Luanda prior to the Alves incident that a pro-Moscow faction was being cultivated by the Soviet embassy must have brought bitter memories to Castro's mind, and prompted him to act swiftly and decisively.

Even more important than the Cuban/Soviet conflict which the Alves incident revealed, the coup attempt caused Cuban troop withdrawals to cease. The decision was probably made on 12 June when Raul Castro met with Neto in Luanda. Over the next few months Cuban troop numbers reportedly increased by 20% to about 19,000.[44]

Subsequent events served to reinforce the antiwithdrawal policy: in 1978, UNITA increased its attacks; South African planes bombed 155 miles inside Angola; the Katangan gendarmes (unsuccessfully) reinvaded Shaba from Angola; and Zaire again accused Cuba and Angola of complicity. In 1979, South African airborne commando units bombed roads and railways linking the south and southeast regions of Angola to the Atlantic, the southern city of Lubango was attacked, and the MPLA's army, Forcas Armadas Populares de Libertacao de Angola (FAPLA), began sending Cuban-trained conventional army units south. Furthermore, in 1981 South African troops again invaded Angola.[45]

Once it became clear the Cubans were going to have a longer term presence than anticipated, their task was redefined. The Cubans were given responsibility for the military logistics and infrastructure network, and for defending major towns; local (Angolan) soldiers took the frontline roles against South Africa and UNITA. In 1985, Angolan President Jose Eduardo dos Santos, who took over following Neto's death in 1979, said the Cubans had standing instructions "to intervene in the event that external military onslaughts, particularly by the racist South African army, pass a conventional line" (i.e., the 16th parallel).[46] And in December 1986, he said "The Cuban forces in Angola are not being employed in the struggle against the UNITA bandits. . . ."[47]

The division of labor alluded to above had some advantages for both Havana and Luanda. The Angolans were anxious to avoid accusations of having foreigners fight their battles for them, and the Cubans' rearguard role preserved appearances. In addition, the MPLA did not lack frontline forces, but it did lack technically skilled mechanics, communications engineers, and other support personnel. The Cubans were capable of these tasks, which did not require a frontline presence. Keeping Cubans out of the front line also reduced the likelihood of direct Cuban/South African or Cuban/Zairean confrontations, which both the MPLA and Castro feared could trigger U.S. intervention. And finally, the Cubans' rearguard role reduced Cuban casualties—a distinct advantage for Havana, but an eventual source of Cuban/Angolan friction.

Many Western observers believe that Cuba and Angola also reached an agreement on foreign exchange payments when the Cuban troops switched from a short- to a long-term presence. This issue is extremely difficult to clarify. Payment rates varying from $30 per month per soldier to $50 per day per soldier are rumored. However, in a January 1985 speech President Dos Santos said "Cuba does not receive any material compensation for its exemplary internationalism in the military field in Angola."[48] Also, a Western diplomat who had the opportunity to examine detailed Cuban national accounts in 1983 (which had been prepared in connection with Cuban-European debt negotiations) reported he could identify no foreign exchange payment from Angola, concluding that if such payments were being made, they were quite small.[49]

Inevitably, the Cubans' shift from an expeditionary to a semipermanent presence caused social problems. Cubans established relationships with local women, triggering Angolan resentment. Inconsistent MPLA military training policy, FAPLA recruiting irresponsibility, and occasional FAPLA corruption caused Cuban annoyance. At the same time, perceived superior conditions for Cuban soldiers also exacerbated strains. Since Angola is responsible for providing the Cubans with food, and as war and economic mismanagement reduced agricultural production, the Cubans often ate well while the FAPLA troops received minimal rations. Reports of Cubans loading vehicles, refrigerators, and other large consumer goods in the hold of planes when they returned home also did not help relations. Finally, the Cubans' rearguard role caused problems, as any soldier in the front line envies the secure position of colleagues managing affairs back at base; likewise, if those colleagues are a different nationality, the resentment is inevitably worse. While the above strains were serious, most Western diplomats in Angola claim the tensions in the military field were far less between Angolans and Cubans than they were between Angolans and Soviets.[50]

The final important aspect of Cuban activity in the first few years of Angolan independence was the increase in civilian cooperation. In July 1976, Cuba and Angola concluded agreements covering health, education, engineering, and construction. Over the next eighteen months, about 2,600 Cuban technicians went to Angola. In November 1977, a new series of accords was signed, and a regular transport link between Angola and Cuba for civilian personnel was established.[51] By early 1978, there were 4,000 civilian Cuban personnel in Angola,[52] and by 1980 the number rose to over 6,000.[53]

Cuban civilian services covered a wide range of fields:

- *Health*—A year after independence, fourteen of the sixteen provincial hospitals were almost entirely staffed by Cubans,[54] and by 1981, Angola had approximately 550 Cuban doctors.
- *Education*—In 1976, Cuba offered 500 scholarships to Angolans,[55] and three years later, the number had more than doubled. In the spring of 1978, 732 Cuban teachers went to Angola for one-year programs, and in March 1979, 394 more went for two-year stays.[56]

- *Agriculture*—Cubans took over technical jobs at Angola's four main sugar complexes and began training Angolans in all aspects of production, coffee rehabilitation and likewise received Cuban aid.[57]
- *Fishing*—Contracts were established with the Cuban and Soviet fishing fleets and, although the MPLA was unhappy with the results, when the contracts expired in the early 1980s, the MPLA asked Cuba (along with Sweden) to help build an Angolan fishing fleet.[58]
- *Construction*—Cuba started to build low-cost housing with the "brigade" system immediately after independence, and in November 1979, the Cuban Construction Enterprise agreed to build 50 apartment buildings and three bridges valued at $25 million.[59]

Generally speaking, Cuba's international aid policy is that poor countries receive civilian help free of charge, while those nations with financial resources must pay.[60] With regard to Angola, the economy was visibly disrupted at independence, but its oil revenues were increasing. In this context, although the precise details of the cooperation agreements have never been made public, it seems Cuba classified Angola as midway between the two categories. As such, Angola probably paid for the construction work, and for some agricultural and medical assistance, but did not pay for the education services.

In the civilian field, as in the military, there were strains between Angolan and Cuban personnel. Cubans often applied management techniques inappropriate for Angolan conditions, and were frequently condescending to their Angolan counterparts, while the Angolans complained Cuba too often sent ill-prepared personnel. However, even those Angolans who criticized the Cubans usually compared them favorably to the Russians, the East Germans, and most Western Europeans. The Cubans caught on to the Portuguese language quickly, tolerated infrastructure breakdowns (which they also experienced at home), and had a life-style on the same level with, or only slightly above, that of their local counterparts. Other foreigners, including the Eastern Europeans, enjoyed better living conditions, often in compounds sealed off from the Angolan population by high fences.

By 1981, the basic elements of Cuba's long-term presence in Angola were well defined. As alluded to earlier, the Cubans would: provide military infrastructure and logistics support; stay away from the front-line battle against UNITA; and provide a wide range of services in the civilian sector. Strains between Angolans and Cubans began to appear, but at a controllable level, and Cuba proved itself (in the view of the MPLA) to be a more reliable ally than the Soviet Union.

Why was Cuba willing to take on this longer-term role? The claim that

Cuba received direct Angolan compensation for the military services must be classified as unproven, but there were many other motivations. First, the international political advantages of staying in Angola increased in direct proportion to the level of South African aggression against the MPLA. In this context, Castro could claim he was fighting the international pariah—Pretoria—and thereby enhance his image in the Third World. Conversely, the political cost of leaving the MPLA to its fate increased with the escalation of South African attacks, as Cuba feared it would be viewed as abandoning an ally to the "racists." Furthermore, once the differences over the Alves incident dissipated, Cuba began to enjoy the increased leverage its presence in Angola gave it with the Soviet Union, and staying in for the long term would maintain that leverage. Finally, Cuba was certainly making some profit on its civilian activities, which might suffer if its military role were reduced. Thus, even if direct payments for military services were not offered, the image and indirect economic advantages of a long-term presence were attractive enough to insure a continued Cuban presence.

The Ally Negotiates with the Enemy: 1981–84

In the 1981–84 period, Cuban relations with Angola were strained by the MPLA's decision to undertake independent discussions with the U.S. and South Africa on Cuban troop withdrawal, only keeping Havana intermittently informed. Although withdrawal was never finalized, and it is therefore unknown whether the MPLA would have followed through, events during this period show that, under certain conditions, the MPLA is willing (and able) to put its own interests before those of the Cubans. The latter's reactions to the negotiations also show that despite Cuba's initial enthusiasm for establishing a long-term presence, some disadvantages associated with that role were becoming apparent after eight years in Angola. Furthermore, Cuba became ambivalent about both staying and withdrawing, profoundly aware of the problems associated with both courses of action. The 1981–84 events further demonstrate that the overwhelming Cuban concern was that its international prestige not be damaged.

Reagan's election victory in 1980 changed the MPLA's diplomatic environment with the introduction of "linkage" between Cuban troop withdrawal and the independence of Namibia. American contacts with UNITA in April and November 1981, and South Africa's August 1981 Operation Protea, in which 11,000 soldiers moved into Angola's Cunene province,[61] also increased pressure on Luanda. At first, the MPLA resisted calls for Cuban withdrawal, and in a 4 February 1982 joint communiqué with Havana indicated Cuban forces would leave only when South African threats ceased.

The situation remained fairly stable until 1983, when Cuba waived payments for the services of its civilian personnel, presumably in response to Angola's cash flow problems associated with the increasing cost of the war. This was known to some Luanda-based diplomats at the time, but was only publicly acknowledged in January 1985 when dos Santos stated, ". . . (O)ver a year ago Cuba decided to stop receiving payments for the services rendered by its civilian foreign aid workers in Angola, as a form of aid to the Angolan people."[62] Despite the payment suspension, Cuban civilian personnel rose to near the 10,000 mark, and a new Angolan forestry company was set up with Cuban assistance to exploit timber in the northern Cabinda province.[63] Incidentally, this put a greater number of civilian Cubans with militia training in the vicinity of the crucial Cabinda oil fields.

In December 1983 and January 1984, South Africa launched Operation Askari to expand the area it occupied within Angola. The FAPLA performed relatively well and shot down several South African aircraft.[64] Pretoria's unease over aircraft losses, Washington's desire for a foreign policy victory before the U.S. elections, and MPLA war-weariness culminated in a series of secret meetings, and on 16 February 1984, Angola and South Africa signed the Lusaka Accord. The agreement stipulated that South Africa would withdraw from Angola over four weeks and the FAPLA would reoccupy the vacated territory and bar the South West African People's Organization (SWAPO) from reentering the area. The South African withdrawals began, but slowed amidst mutual accusations of violations, and the process took thirteen months instead of four weeks.

Most Western diplomats believe that Cuba was only informed of the general direction of negotiations in the lead-up to the Lusaka Accord, and was not kept up to date on the details. Cuban concern about rumors that the Accord was just the first phase of a secret Cuban withdrawal agreement between Luanda and Pretoria was possibly the reason for a Cuban/Angolan joint statement on 19 March 1984 restating the terms of the February 1982 declaration.[65]

Despite the slowdown in South African withdrawals and Cuban unease, on 6 and 7 September 1984, the MPLA presented the Americans with a plan for Cuban withdrawal. It proposed that once South Africa met certain conditions (including: withdrawal from Angola, implementation of U.N. Resolution 435 on Namibian independence, attainment of a cease-fire agreement with the SWAPO, suspension of aid to UNITA, and reduction in the number of troops in Namibia to 1,500), Angola would send home 5,000 Cuban troops from southern Angola as a "goodwill gesture." The remaining Cuban troops in the south would not cross the 16th parallel. Withdrawal of Cubans stationed in the northern Cabinda province (where Angola's oil is located) and in "other regions in the north . . . including the . . . capital" would be programmed according to a schedule to be agreed upon by Cuba and Angola. All other Cubans would be withdrawn over a three-year period.[66]

A month later, Angola presented the Americans with a more detailed document. It started with the words: "The People's Republic of Angola and the Republic of Cuba . . . agree to proceed in the following manner,"[67] implying that the MPLA had consulted with the Cubans over the preceding weeks. It stated that as long as the September conditions were met, 20,000 Cubans would be removed from southern Angola over a 36-month period. Cuban units would first be restricted to north of the 16th parallel, and by the end of the 36-month period, would be prohibited from crossing the 13th parallel. Remaining Cubans north of the 13th parallel would be withdrawn later on terms to be agreed upon by Cuba and Angola.[68] Though the text of the proposal, known as the "plataforma," is now public, at the time it was secret.

In early November 1984, articles began to appear in the American press claiming Angola had "given in" on "linkage," and was no longer demanding either an end to South Africa's UNITA aid or implementation of Resolution 435 as a price for Cuban withdrawal. Some Western diplomats believe Castro was offended by the appearance of MPLA capitulation and the consequent damage to Cuban prestige. Likewise, many feel this led the official Cuban Communist Party newspaper *Granma* to report on 19 November the full details of the "plataforma," emphasizing that both cessation of South African UNITA aid and start-up of Resolution 435 implementation were preconditions, and that not all Cubans would be withdrawn.[69]

It is not clear if the Cubans had Angolan authorization to release the information. However, President dos Santos then wrote to the UN Secretary General on 20 November reporting the full details of the negotiations, apparently to clear the air. The Americans were dismayed and felt it would be much more difficult to negotiate once the details were public. In any event, South Africa insisted that all Cubans be withdrawn over a three-month, rather than 36-month, period, and the negotiations stalled.

Diplomats close to the discussions indicate there were some strains between the Angolans and the Cubans during this process. One (non-Angolan) African diplomat said, "The Angolans tell me they have to be careful about what they tell Castro concerning negotiations on Cuban withdrawal because he is so sensitive on the subject."[70] Sources in Luanda also report that the Cubans were uneasy about removing their troops in a phased process, as they feared for the safety of the remaining soldiers. Cuba wanted to either pull out faster, or leave a larger contingent behind once the phased withdrawal was complete. Luanda sources also believe Cuba told Angola that once troops were withdrawn, they would not be sent back.[71]

The above negotiations show that as of 1984, the MPLA did have the ability to undertake independent initiatives concerning Cuban troop withdrawal, and was willing to strain (though not break) relations with Castro in order to improve relations with the U.S. and South Africa. Whether the MPLA was prepared in 1984 to conclude a withdrawal agreement that undermined Cuban interests we will never know, for subsequent actions by other parties stalled the discussions, but as of 1984, Angola was certainly inching in that direction. The events also show that Cuba sought to stage-manage the flow of information on such deals to insure that Cuban prestige was not damaged. And finally, the above events demonstrate that as of 1984, Cuba was willing to reduce its forces in Angola if it could be done in a manner that did not endanger Cuban lives or image, or threaten MPLA security, but that Cuba was not brimming with enthusiasm for such action.

In this vein, Cuba's 1984 ambivalence about withdrawal is understandable. Withdrawal was attractive because, although no official casualty figures were released and the dead were buried in Africa, the cost of the operation in human life was being noticed and sometimes criticized by the Cuban people. Withdrawal would also remove an obstacle in U.S./Cuban relations, and free up troops for operations elsewhere in the world (an increasing concern as Central America became more tense). Even if the Cuban claims of nonpayment for the nation's military services are inaccurate, the 1983 moratorium on civilian service payments made the Angolan operation less profitable than it had been. On the other hand, withdrawal would cut off the Cuban armed forces from further field experience. In addition, as suggested earlier, Cuban influence with the Soviet Union is enhanced by Cuba's Angola operation, since Castro is doing a task the Soviets want done but cannot do themselves; once the former withdrew however, the "tail-wagging-the-dog" effect would be reduced. Finally, Cuban troop presence in Angola made any possible future intervention in other parts of the region easier.

The Negotiations Stall: 1985–mid-1986

In 1985 and the first half of 1986, the MPLA came to believe that the South African and U.S. governments, or at least elements within them, had negotiated in bad faith. This seriously damaged, but did not totally destroy, MPLA discussions on Cuban withdrawal. The deterioration of the internal situation in South Africa and Pretoria's increasingly aggressive attitude toward its neighbors also tipped the balance of Cuban interests in favor of staying in Angola, and caused Havana to outline a new policy for the region. The MPLA at first rhetorically supported the new Cuban approach, despite squabbles with Havana over Luanda's role in the Non-aligned Movement, but then edged back toward it, without totally reembracing its previous and more moderate stance.

The year 1985 seemed to begin on a positive footing. In March, American diplomats tried to reconcile the Angolan and South African withdrawal schedules by putting forward a "synthesis paper" which reduced the timetable for withdrawal of Angola's southern Cuban forces from three years to one.[72] Though neither South Africa nor Angola accepted the proposal, negotiations continued. In April, the diplomatic climate improved when South Africa finally withdrew from Angola, albeit over a year late, and Angola made a gesture to the West by joining the Lome Convention (the vehicle through which European Economic Community aid is channeled to the Third World).[73] (Cuba abstained from the chorus of Soviet Bloc criticisms of the move, which implies Angolan recognition of East Berlin as a part of West Germany.[74])

The tide then turned on 21 May, when a FAPLA patrol surprised a South African commando unit near oil storage tanks in Cabinda province. Its leader subsequently confessed that the unit had planned to blow up the tanks and leave UNITA propaganda at the scene to make it appear Savimbi's group had executed the operation. The MPLA was furious, and though it reaffirmed that the "plataforma" was still valid,[75] the attack ensured Luanda's inflexibility regarding withdrawal of Cuban forces in the north of the country, as the raid illustrated Pretoria's attack capacity in that region.

South Africa then installed a new "transitional government" in Namibia in June, leading Angola to conclude it did not intend to implement Resolution 435. In July, the negotiating climate soured still further when the U.S. Congress repealed the Clark Amendment. The MPLA claimed this was "proof of the complicity there has always been between the U.S. executive and the retrograde racist Pretoria regime," and said Angola had "no alternative but to suspend the contacts it has had with U.S. government envoys. . . ."[76] Nonetheless, quiet discussions through back-door routes continued.[77]

The Cubans maintained a low profile as these blows fell upon the MPLA, quietly pleased that recent events were convincing the MPLA it had been wrong to trust the United States. Cuban/Angolan relations then suffered a new strain in September when the Cubans tried to influence document preparation at the Luanda-based Ministerial Meeting of the Nonaligned Movement (NAM), inserting radical language into the draft declaration at the last moment, leaving the MPLA little time to tone it down.[78] Angolan nationalism was also offended when Cuba took the lead role in calling for Zimbabwe's President Mugabe to chair the next NAM summit. Many MPLA officials, though supporting the Mugabe chairmanship, felt Castro was undertaking initiatives better left to African envoys.[79]

South African actions, however, swiftly ensured that these hiccups in Havana/Luanda relations did not reduce Cuban influence in Angola. In September, Pretoria sent troops into Angola with air cover, allegedly in pursuit of SWAPO Forces—but actually to prevent Savimbi from being overrun by the FAPLA, which had launched a surprisingly effective offensive.[80] The MPLA advance was halted after much loss of life and equipment, and though neither Soviet nor Cuban personnel took a frontline role in the offensive (as claimed in some press reports),[81] the events sharpened MPLA awareness of its reliance on Cuban logistical support and Soviet arms.

The negotiating climate then deteriorated further in the autumn of 1985 as U.S. Congressional calls for aid to UNITA escalated, rumors abounded that parts of the Pentagon and the CIA favored such aid, and legislation limiting U.S. trade with Angola was proposed.[82] On 25 October 1985, dos Santos and Castro met in Havana to discuss the situation,[83] and in November the *Observer* newspaper in London claimed that its Moscow correspondent had been told by a "senior Cuban official" that "Fidel Castro and the Cuban leadership are seeking Soviet approval to declare war on South Africa." The paper reported that "The Cubans believe that the two former Portuguese territories (Angola and Mozambique) are liable to have (their) economies disrupted for years and Namibia has little chance of being allowed anything more than an ersatz independence" until apartheid is overthrown.[84]

The report was denied by Havana, but later events suggest it reflected a real, albeit much less dramatic, change in Cuban policy. In this context, Havana had a new outlook: it stopped assuming Angolan security would improve once Namibia was independent; it concluded that South Africa would continue in its efforts to destabilize the MPLA even after a Namibian settlement; and it decided the real issue was now the overthrow of apartheid.[85] Cuba did not want to "declare war" on South Africa, but it did reevaluate the southern Africa situation.

Cuban and Angolan apprehension grew in January 1986 when Savimbi visited Washington and met President Reagan. The MPLA protested vigorously, but still kept the back door open for discussions with Crocker, hoping to forestall U.S. aid to UNITA. Dos Santos then interjected language similar to the Observer's report into a 23 January speech to the People's Assembly, indicating that "Namibian independence might lessen the current tension, but it no longer constitutes a guarantee of security for Angola."[86]

A week after the Dos Santos speech, the Cuban and Angolan diplomats meeting in Moscow further coordinated positions. Together with the Soviets they declared, ". . . so long as the apartheid regime exists in South Africa it will constitute a serious threat to Angola and other independent states in the Southern Africa horn."[87] They also agreed that in 1986 the FAPLA should focus on Savimbi's operations outside of UNITA's traditional areas, pushing the group back to its southern stronghold, rather than attempting to rout UNITA headquarters again.[88]

The new Cuban policy, foreshadowed in the November *Observer* article and the tripartite communiqué, was clearly declared by Castro in his 7 February closing speech at the Third Congress of the Cuban Communist Party. He announced that withdrawal from Angola depended on both Namibia's independence and the abolition of apartheid, stating, "We are prepared to stay in Angola, ten, twenty, or thirty more years if need be."[89] FAPLA's Chief of Staff Colonel Ndalu echoed Castro's words in his address to the Congress.[90]

Cuba's influence in Angola was then strengthened in February 1986, when America's Assistant Secretary of State for African Affairs Chester Crocker told the U.S. Senate Committee on Foreign Relations, "We intend to be supportive of UNITA in an effective and appropriate manner. . . .,"[91] and in late March when the Pentagon leaked that Savimbi would receive Stinger missiles.[92] Dos Santos responded, "By granting assistance to the UNITA puppet bands . . . the United States has disqualified itself as a mediator, becoming one of the interested parties,"[93] and the MPLA urged the United Nations to take over the mediating role now.[94]

In contrast to previous rhetoric, this time the MPLA seemed to mean it. U.S. diplomats reported that the quiet discussions they had been able to maintain even after the Cabinda raid dried up.[95] Castro made no public remarks at this time, but in late March pledged to increase Cuban aid to the African National Congress (ANC, the guerrilla organization fighting to overthrow the South African government)[96]—fleshing out his policy that peace in the region would be impossible until apartheid was destroyed.

The events from 1985 to mid-1986 lead to the conclusion that it was not Cuban pressure that led Angola to back off from negotiations for Cuban withdrawal. Instead, it was the MPLA's perception of increased aggression from the U.S. and South Africa (in particular the Cabinda incident), the withdrawal of the Clark amendment, and the U.S. decision to aid Savimbi which caused this effect. Cuba might have been pleased by the stalling of the negotiations, but had no control over the events that led to the stalemate. The 1985 to mid-1986 developments also show a Cuban ability to influence MPLA rhetoric, as the "no peace until end of apartheid" refrain seems to have started with the Cubans and then moved to the Angolans.

Why did Cuba adopt a harder line on southern Africa? Part of the reason can clearly be found in the growing violence in South Africa, which led Castro to conclude that Pretoria would lash out at neighbors with increasing frequency, that the MPLA was more threatened than ever, and that Cuban withdrawal from Angola was consequently more risky. But there was also an underlying and unstated change in Cuban interests. Specifically, growing South African external aggression and internal violence made the value of troops located in the region increase dramatically. The Cuban troop presence in Angola provides a convenient launching pad for interventions elsewhere in the region should Cuban services be required, for example, to keep southern Africa's transport routes open. Furthermore, the escalation of the political struggle inside South Africa led Cuba to pledge greater support to the ANC. The ANC has several training bases in Angola, and as long as Cuban military involvement there continues, that country is an ideal location for quiet Cuban/ANC contacts, arms transfers, training, and intelligence exchange.

One final issue which should be addressed is the Soviet position on southern Africa and Angola in 1985–86. American judgments in early 1986 that Angola and southern Africa were low priorities for the Soviets and, thus, that the latter would not respond strongly to South African aggression and U.S. aid to UNITA have, with hindsight, proven inaccurate. Despite the MPLA's decreasing financial capabilities, replacement Soviet arms for those destroyed in the 1985 battles flooded into Angola in 1986. Likewise, high-technology air defense systems were installed in the southern region of the nation. It is thus apparent that defending the MPLA against South Africa and UNITA is important to the Soviet Union's international image. In this case, even under Gorbachev, Moscow has been willing to invest more resources than the intrinsic strategic value of Angola would warrant.

History Repeats Itself: Mid-1986–88

From mid-1986 to the date of writing, Cuban/Angolan relations replayed modified versions of several old patterns, with one new twist. First, the MPLA returned to the negotiating table, causing much Cuban unease, as in the 1981–84 period. Subsequently, in late 1987, as in early 1985, the MPLA's perception of the need to maintain a substantial Cuban troop presence was dramatically heightened by the actions of outside powers. Thus, by early 1988 the MPLA had not abandoned the negotiations, but appeared to be stalling, and was increasing rather than decreasing its reliance upon Cuban troops.

Second, in the 1986–88 period another familiar phenomenon from Angolan history recurred, with yet more divergences between Soviet and Cuban policies on their African ally. While not as dramatic as the 1973–77 Chipenda and Alves incidents, these new discords could have important implications for the future.

The "new twist" was improved Cuban/MPLA coordination on negotiations at the end of the period in question. Both governments seemed to learn from their past mistakes, and while tensions were still highly evident, by late 1987 both were handling the strains in a more diplomatic fashion than previously.

The first signal that the MPLA was ready to return to the negotiating table and distance itself from Castro's hard-line position occurred in September 1986 at the Nonaligned Conference in Harare, Zimbabwe. Dos Santos stated that "if the Government of South Africa renounced violence in the internal and external level and if it ceased the policy of destabilization . . . it would create appropriate conditions for the promotion of a dialogue for negotiated, just and lasting solutions for the problems of southern Africa."[97] Dos Santos thus implied there could be peaceful coexistence with nonviolent apartheid, while Castro stuck to the "no peace until apartheid is abolished" position. Soon after the Harare conference, American officials received messages through third parties that the MPLA was interested in restarting Cuban withdrawal talks. The MPLA apparently realized the U.S. and South Africa were not going to respond to the "silent treatment," and concluded that since a military victory over its opponents was not likely in the near future, little would be lost by returning to the bargaining table.

The MPLA took awhile to follow through, but in March 1987, it finally sent a letter to Washington saying it was "not opposed to renewal of official talks. . . ."[98] The leader of the Organization of African Unity (OAU), Congolese President Sassou Nguesso, then brought Crocker and the MPLA together for their first face-to-face meeting since before U.S. assistance to UNITA began. The move was accompanied by growing rumors that several of the MPLA's African allies were becoming impatient with the slow pace of the talks, and wanted the MPLA to take more initiative. The Soviet Union and Cuba were not informed in advance of the Congolese leader's plans, and both were reportedly displeased by this "discourtesy." The Cuban press mentioned simply that the U.S. and

Angolan governments had met for the first time in fifteen months, and stressed South African cross-border "aggression."[99]

The substance of the 6 April Congo talks was thin, primarily consisting of the U.S. outlining its previous position, and emphasizing exactly what "carrots" it was willing to offer for future MPLA concessions. The U.S. received little response from the MPLA, partly because the Angolan official sent to Congo, Minister of Interior "Kito" Rodrigues, was in the midst of an internal party controversy, and had less authority than previously.

The Cuban attitude toward the negotiations was later affected by the June Radio Martí broadcast of an interview with the Cuban defector Brigadier General Rafael del Piño Diaz. In his statements, he indicated that: the Cuban military suffered a high desertion rate in Angola; more than 10,000 Cubans had died in that nation; morale was very low in the high command of the Cuban forces in Angola; and the policy of burying Cuban soldiers in Angola was intensely resented by the Cuban populace.[100] It would be hard to imagine an event better designed to heighten Cuban desires to promote its prestige and vindicate the Angolan operation. While the U.S. action may not have been calculated to produce this response, in effect it sharply escalated Havana's concern to ensure that any MPLA/U.S. negotiations on Cuban troop withdrawal leave the Cuban image untarnished.

The MPLA, meanwhile, was undergoing its own internal shifts. Most importantly, the "pragmatic" Minister of Interior Kito Rodrigues was removed from the negotiating process, and reprimanded for having travelled to Brazzaville without proper authorization. The controversy concerning his official role meant that several nuances in the American position were not accurately conveyed to the rest of the MPLA leadership. The MPLA was also distracted by internal tensions generated by other matters, including the limits to liberal economic reforms favored by dos Santos, and consequently, various planned meetings with the U.S. were postponed.

In early July, Crocker consulted in London with Soviet Deputy Foreign Minister Anatoly Adamishin under the rubric of periodic U.S./Soviet talks on African affairs.[101] At that time, the Soviet official warned Crocker that the MPLA would not respond positively at the upcoming talks. Crocker, however, was receiving optimistic advise from Portuguese diplomats, and apparently discounted the Soviet warning,[102] setting off for Luanda in mid-July with high expectations.

The MPLA and Crocker entered the conference room in July with differing perceptions of the situation. On the one hand, the MPLA had no answer ready, did not fully understand some assurances the U.S. had offered in Brazzaville, and was meeting with Crocker partly because it did not want to appear churlish by delaying yet again. On the other hand, misled by the Portuguese, Crocker thought the MPLA was ready to announce a Cuban troop withdrawal offer. Thus, at the Luanda meeting Crocker restated the position articulated in April, and the Angolan negotiator (this time, the Foreign Minister) read a prepared statement which offered no changes to the "plataforma," and refused Crocker's request to meet with dos Santos. In addition, many of the U.S. assurances seemed to be news to the MPLA delegation, even though the latter had been stated at Brazzaville.

Not surprisingly, the U.S. and MPLA delegations had sharply differing evaluations of the meeting. A deeply disappointed Crocker remarked on television, "The talks were basically a waste of time. . . ."[103] A senior U.S. administration official then blamed the Cubans and Soviets for blocking the talks, adding, "We sense the Cubans are telling the Angolans it's all or nothing."[104] This American belief was probably reinforced by the fact that Cuban Politburo member Jorge Risquet met with dos Santos three days before Crocker did.[105] In turn, the MPLA responded indignantly; Vice Minister for Foreign Affairs Venancio de Moura remarked, "(W)e do not think it was a waste of time,"[106] and Foreign Minister Afonso Van-Dunem "Mbinda" said, "For the first time we heard some new ideas." These comments were editorialized by ANGOP, which concluded that these new ideas "coincided with some of those put forward by Angola in the course of years of negotiations."[107]

Were Crocker's allegations correct? Did Cuba/Soviet pressure prevent dos Santos from giving an answer on Cuban troop withdrawal? It is certainly plausible. Risquet surely urged dos Santos to be skeptical of U.S. good faith. In addition, the former probably emphasized Cuban concern about the safety of the remaining troop contingent in the north once the southern troops left, which could be interpreted as an "all or nothing" position.

However, the above chronology also suggests another, equally plausible explanation. Internal difficulties, combined with the communication breakdown on the Brazzaville talks they engendered, both distracted MPLA attention from the issue and led the leadership to prepare its answer without a full appreciation of the more accomodating aspects of the U.S. stance. They were also embarrassed at delaying so long, and did not want to irritate Crocker or their African friends who were urging them to negotiate, and therefore agreed to a meeting before they had an answer ready. Indeed, some members of the Crocker delegation came away from Luanda convinced the MPLA would respond positively within the next two months.

Such predictions turned out to be correct. President dos Santos announced at the July Lusaka Southern African Development Coordination Conference (SADCC) meeting, "The Angolan government intends to propose to the concerned parties the general basis of an agreement to achieve a Namibian settlement based on UN Security Council Resolution 435–78 and peace and security in southern Angola," to be signed by the governments of Angola, Cuba, and South Africa, and by SWAPO, under the aegis of the UN Security Council and its five permanent members.[108]

Dos Santos then flew to Havana on 30 July, and on 3 August, he and Castro issued a joint communiqué which indicated that "Cuba and Angola . . . concur on their willingness to be flexible on their common position, based on the principles of the November 1984 platform. . . . Accordingly, the two countries are willing jointly to pursue the negotiations resumed in Luanda in mid-July."[109]

On the following day (4 August), Angola presented the U.S. with a proposal for a General Accord on implementation of UN Resolution 435 and withdrawal of Cuban forces. It accelerated withdrawal of Cubans from the south to two years—one year faster than the plataforma's schedule. However, the proposal also demanded that the Cubans participate directly in the talks, and that four conditions be observed before implementation of withdrawal: 1) "the withdrawal of all South African troops from southern Angola," 2) "the cessation of South Africa's aggression," 3) "respect for Angola's sovereignty and territorial integrity . . . (which means) . . . cessation of all kinds of foreign aid to UNITA, both by South Africa and the United States itself;" and 4) "The implementation of UN Security Council Resolution 435–78 on Namibian independence. . . ." The proposal also maintained that north of the 13th parallel, the presence of Cuban troops was a bilateral issue between Angola and Cuba. Thus, although eventual withdrawal may be accepted in principle, "it could not at this time be the subject of any negotiations whatsoever."[110]

What actually happened in Havana? Outsiders can only guess, but dos Santos, clearly furious at being portrayed as a Cuban-Soviet puppet, wanted to put forward a new offer as soon as possible to disprove this claim, and presumably was informing Castro of his plans. Cuba, believing the MPLA was not always as open as it claimed about the course of the negotiations, in turn seemed to have requested a formal role in the talks, so as to monitor developments and watch for any "prestige-threatening" elements. Inclusion in the U.S./MPLA talks had an added benefit for Castro: it would force the U.S. to sit across the negotiating table from Cuban diplomats as equals.

Dos Santos obviously agreed to the Cuban request. Does this mean he was a Cuban puppet, as UNITA subsequently claimed?[111] One could argue yes, because Cuba did persuade him to include a new element. On the other hand, Cuba was still highly uneasy about the negotiations, and if Castro had possessed veto power over Angola's decisions, he could have simply ordered dos Santos not to make the 4 August offer. The fact that dos Santos did make the offer shows that while Havana could influence the MPLA significantly, it could not prevent Luanda from offering concessions to the U.S. The MPLA's subsequent willingness to continue negotiations—while Crocker resisted Cuban participation—also shows that dos Santos did not intend to make Cuban participation a firm condition for continuing talks.

As the U.S. digested this offer through the month of August, it noticed a new cooperativeness on the part of the Soviet Union. The latter's diplomats privately spoke in favor of a "political solution" to the conflict in Angola and implied they had urged Castro to soften his rhetoric on the withdrawal issue.[112] Similarly, those MPLA officials regarded as most sympathetic to the Castro line had stopped raising objections to Cuban troop withdrawal negotiations after dos Santos's visit to Havana at the end of July.[113] According to Radio Martí, visitors to Havana in mid-1987 came away with the impression that "Castro is prepared to discuss with the U.S. . . . reduction of Cuban troops in Angola."[114]

Crocker then travelled to Luanda for "informal talks" on 8 and 9 September to seek clarification of the 4 August proposal, and was received by dos Santos. Although Jorge Risquet was in Luanda at the time, he was not permitted to attend the talks.[115] Crocker reemphasized to dos Santos the "parameters" of an agreement he thought would be "sellable" to the South Africans. This agreement included the withdrawal of the southern Cuban contingent over one year rather than two, and the provision of a firm date for withdrawal in the north.[116] When the MPLA provided such an offer, Crocker reportedly indicated that the U.S. would convey it to South Africa.

The MPLA met again with Crocker in Belgium in late September;[117] once again Cubans were not present.[118] Castro, meanwhile, told a Zambian official on 11 September that Cuba hoped to withdraw its troops from Angola two years after Namibia's independence.[119] At this juncture, it was unclear if he was referring to the southern group, or all troops in both north and south. The statement did, however, show that Castro was moderating his rhetoric in deference to MPLA concerns.

While Castro did not overtly discourage the negotiations and was moderating his rhetoric, however, he still was uneasy about the talks for two reasons—one old and new. As ever, Havana was determined that Cuban prestige be protected; if this could not be accomplished by inclusion in the U.S./MPLA talks, it would have to be done in some other manner.

In addition, rumors circulating in London and South Africa that the MPLA was considering the removal of ANC facilities from its soil and further restricting SWAPO in return for South African and U.S. concessions on Cuban withdrawal concerned Havana.[120] Cuba had close relations with both movements, and was wary of any reduction of MPLA support for them.

In surveying the negotiating landscape, by September 1987 U.S./MPLA talks on Cuban withdrawal were progressing, albeit slowly, and although Cuba was uneasy, it was taking no actions to sabotage them. However, South African actions in the last four months of 1987 triggered an MPLA reevaluation of negotiations far more effectively than any Cuban pressure possibly could have.

The MPLA had started a gradual advance on UNITA's stronghold of Mavinga back in July, and combined this action with operations to cut UNITA's supply lines further to the east. In mid-September, FAPLA crossed the Lomba river, overran a UNITA logistics depot near Mavinga, was pushed back across the river, and then regrouped and prepared to attack again. At that point, the South African air force launched major strikes against FAPLA, other targets were shelled by South African long-range artillery, and a South African ground force entered the fray.[121]

In early November, UNITA gleefully announced that it had defeated the FAPLA advance, and attributed its success to U.S. Stinger missiles rather than to direct South African assistance.[122] However, domestic South African pressure for an explanation of the relatively large number of white casualties in Angola mounted. Thus, Minister of Defence General Magnus Malan announced the South African Defense Forces (SADF) had "saved" Savimbi, adding that South Africa had been faced with ". . . a clear-cut decision: accept the defeat of Dr. Savimbi or halt Russian aggression."[123] South Africa then revealed that President P.W. Botha and five Cabinet ministers had crossed the Namibian border into southern Angola shortly before the troops went into battle in order to underline their support for the incursion.[124]

South Africa adopted a similarly defiant attitude at the United Nations. On November 25, the UN Security Council unanimously condemned South African actions and called for withdrawal of its troops from Angola by 10 December.[125] In response, South Africa's UN Ambassador counter-proposed that "all foreign forces" be withdrawn by 9 December,[126] and Minister of Foreign Affairs Pik Botha indicated South Africa would keep its troops on "the present battlefield" in Angola until "Cuban and Russian troops and advisors" were withdrawn, or as long as South Africa considered its security threatened.[127] Although South Africa's General Janie Geldenhuys claimed on 5 December that its troops were withdrawing,[128]

Western diplomats and African observers believed only a portion actually departed Angolan soil.[129]

The South African action and rhetoric had three immediate repercussions. First, the enormous FAPLA loss of life (estimated at 1,700 casualties[130]) and equipment intensely focused MPLA attention on its vulnerability to South African action and the need to reinforce its security by all possible means. Thus, in late November, Angola's Vice Minister for External Relations Venancio de Moura stated at the UN that Angola "might have recourse to Article 51 of the UN Charter"[131]—the legal mechanism by which the MPLA justifies the presence of Cuban troops in Angola.

Second, South Africa's action heightened Cuban concerns about the "prestige impact" of negotiations for withdrawal. If South Africa overran Angola following a withdrawal, Cuba's image would be tarnished, and the Cuban loss of life over the preceding years would appear to have been for naught.

Third, and most importantly, the South African actions changed Cuban policy toward MPLA military operations in southern Angola. In the lead until the offensive, Cuba had reportedly differed with both the Soviets and the MPLA about planned tactics; in this context, Havana believed the MPLA relied too much upon heavy, slow-moving equipment.[132] Thus, while the Cubans had continued to perform their back-up logistical role, and some Cubans flew as pilots (two being shot down by UNITA's Stingers), in general, Cuban forces stayed back from the main fighting. Following South African actions, however, the Cuban position shifted. According to Western European diplomats, on 7 November, Angolan President dos Santos met with Castro in Moscow, and the two decided to replace newly recruited Cuban soldiers with experienced men.[133]

In early December, FAPLA Chief of Staff Ndalu told Agencia de Informacao de Mocambique (AIM, the Mozambican news agency), "The Cubans are in Angola with military units whose purpose is to block large-scale South African invasions. . . . We cannot exclude the possibility of combat between the Cuban troops and the South Africans."[134] AIM subsequently reported, ". . . (A) Cuban source (in Luanda) announced that the 50th division of the Cuban Revolutionary Armed Forces was moving towards southern Angola. . . . (Also) General Ochoa Sanchez, who led Cuban troops of the 50th division against South Africa . . . in 1975 and 1976 has returned to Angola."[135] In early January 1988, the Cuban magazine *Bohemia* printed an interview in which Jorge Risquet reported Cuba now had 40,000 troops in Angola[136]—3,000 more than the highest U.S. intelligence estimate. Not surprisingly, a planned December trip to Luanda by Crocker, already postponed from November, was cancelled.

There were signs, however, that the reinforcement of the Cuban presence in Angola did not mean Cuba intended to sabotage MPLA talks with the United States, nor that the MPLA had abandoned the talks. Rather, the reinforcement appeared directly related to MPLA fears that the South African forces remaining in Angola might try to take Cuito Cuanavale, a key southern town from which the MPLA launched its ill-fated 1987 offensive against Mavinga. European diplomats in Luanda also reported in December (well after Cuban troop reinforcement began) that Cuban diplomats were offering to provide necessary details on logistical issues associated with withdrawal, and appeared willing to consider a pullout under certain circumstances.[137] In January, three important events transpired: 1) unconfirmed rumors of Cuban attempts to discuss withdrawal from Angola bilaterally with the U.S. circulated in Washington; 2) dos Santos announced he wished to continue talks with the U.S. on the subject;[138] and 3) the MPLA finally agreed to Crocker's long-delayed trip to Luanda.

Among the issues the MPLA apparently wanted to discuss were firm guarantees concerning possible future South African aggression, cessation of South African and U.S. aid to UNITA, and Namibian independence. For its part, the U.S. appeared prepared to reply that the MPLA must first offer an "acceptable" Cuban troop withdrawal schedule, and only then could other issues be addressed.

A final element affecting Cuban and MPLA behavior in the late 1987–early 1988 time frame which requires exploration is the U.S./Soviet summit, and rumors concerning Angola associated with that meeting. Preceding the summit, Reagan and Gorbachev each indicated they planned to discuss regional conflicts. Concurrently, another rumor surfaced which alleged Gorbachev was ready to consider a "political" solution to Angola which would allow him to reduce expenditures—relating to his "perestroika" policy of cutting military costs. This would also be in line with reports that Gorbachev was "reevaluating" the Soviet relationship with the ANC and quietly urging it to at least consider alternatives to indefinite armed struggle. Many analysts believed these rumors meant Moscow was ready to "dump" the MPLA. However, subsequent events imply that while still ready to play the military "card" if the MPLA's adversaries continued to use military pressure tactics, the Soviets were also considering playing the political "card" should Luanda's adversaries choose a political strategy.[139] Nevertheless, nuances of the Soviet position were not altogether clear to the MPLA and Cuba at the time, and the rumors only added to the anxiety levels of the actors.

Castro already had a rocky relationship with Gorbachev. While Moscow introduced more market forces into the economy with "perestroika," Castro moved back towards Guevara-type moral incentives with the "rectification'' campaign. In addition, the two nations had bickered publicly in a nasty exchange in the Soviet magazine *New Times* in the second half of 1987 over economic matters.[140] Thus, Havana was quite nervous about the summit, and while relieved that the Angola issue was not extensively addressed in that forum, remained concerned about Soviet intentions.

The sequence of events in the 1986–88 period points to five conclusions. First, the MPLA showed itself capable of breaking away from a Cuban position and ''overlooking'' negotiating conditions included to help Havana save face when it suited its interests. This was most clearly illustrated by the mid-1986 decision to restart talks with the U.S. and the 4 August offer on Cuban troop withdrawal. Second, intermittent MPLA intransigence in the 1986–88 period was caused more by internal MPLA tensions and South African actions than by Cuban pressure. Third, it was South African actions, not pressure from Castro, which caused the MPLA to reinforce the Cuban military presence in late 1987. Fourth, on issues ranging from military strategy to the advisability of including Angola in U.S./Soviet talks on arms control and possibilities for a peaceful settlement in Angola, Havana and the Soviet Union still had major differences of opinion.

Fifth, and probably most importantly, the 1986–88 events show that Cuba started to take a far more sophisticated stance than that adopted in 1981–86. In the latter period, it sought to position itself in order to condition the context of, and potentially benefit from, *either* ongoing military confrontation *or* negotiated withdrawal of its troops. Rather than just encouraging the MPLA to make certain decisions, Cuba prepared to turn whatever course the MPLA took to its own advantage, while not giving up on efforts to persuade the MPLA to select the favored option. In line with classic strategic thinking, Cuba was trying to give itself room for ''flexible response,'' leaving several options open.

As the MPLA shifted between hard-line and flexible positions on withdrawal and between military holding operations and offensives, Cuba tried to position itself in the middle of a metaphorical tennis court. As such, it hoped to return any ''ball'' the MPLA, South Africa, the U.S., or the Soviets sent over the ''net.'' Translated into practice, if the MPLA wanted more troops, and if Cuban prestige would suffer should the troops not arrive, the soldiers would be provided. On the other hand, if the MPLA wanted to negotiate withdrawal, Cuba was prepared to uneasily go along. In the latter case, the degree of Cuban reluctance would be most closely related to the level of ''face-saving'' measures for Cuban prestige included in the deal. Secondary considerations would be the amount of damage the deal might do to Cuba's ANC and SWAPO friends and the limits it would place on Cuba's ability to monitor and influence the unfolding drama in South Africa.

Conclusion

Cuban relations with Angola have gone through six phases since Castro's rise to power, each with its own distinct character, but tied to the other phases by the periodic recurrence of common themes. These common threads have included: cycles of convergence-divergence in Cuban and Soviet interests in Angola; a generally greater overlap between MPLA and Cuban interests than between MPLA and Soviet interests, especially in the early years; the value that Cuban culture and Castro's personality placed on national prestige enhancement and maintenance, and the effect of these concerns on the formation of Cuba's Angola policies; Cuban cycles of enthusiasm-ambivalence about its activities in Angola; and the opportunity Angolan involvement has afforded Cuba to exercise indirect leverage over Moscow.

With regard to the six phases of Cuban policy, Phase 1 began with Castro's seizure of power in 1959 and lasted until the coup which ousted the Portuguese colonial regime in 1974. Cuban relations with the MPLA blossomed in this period, from cautious approaches to a full-fledged alliance. Contrary to conventional wisdom, at this early stage, Cuban interest in the MPLA increased in inverse proportion to Cuban compliance with Moscow's wishes. Acrimony between Havana and Moscow from 1962 to 1968 occurred because of differences regarding the 1962 missile crisis, the role of revolutionary guerrilla movements in the Third World, and peaceful coexistence with the United States. Each disagreement with the Soviets strengthened Castro's desire to reach out to ideologically compatible revolutionary movements (such as the MPLA) that could act as a counterweight to the unreliable patron. An intense friendship developed between Neto and Castro; even after Castro mended his fences with Moscow in 1968, Cuba continued to champion Neto's cause when the latter ran into difficulties with the Soviets, as exemplified by the Chipenda incident. Thus, from the very beginning, differences between Cuban and Soviet interests in Angola were evident. For Castro, ideological and Third World solidarity and personal loyalty to Neto were paramount. For the Soviet Union, Neto's ability to gain power, and willingness to subsequently afford the Soviets facilities in Angola were the most important factors. This is confirmed by the fact that when Neto appeared deficient in both respects, Moscow sought out "alternative horses" to back.

Phase 2 ran from the Portuguese coup in April 1974 to the consolidation of MPLA power in independent Angola in early 1976 with Soviet and

Cuban assistance. Again, contrary to the conventional views, Cuba was neither the hero nor the villain in the war. South Africa, Cuba, and the U.S. simultaneously, and to a large extent secretly, increased their involvement in independent, nonreactive decisions from April 1974 to October 1975. In this context, each side speculated the other was preparing to intervene directly, and the various actors responded accordingly; the results of such decisions were seen in the field. Only after October 1975 did the plans of each actor become clear and lead to informed decisions, rather than actions based on hunches. In this period, Cuban and Soviet interests largely overlapped, in contrast to the 1959–74 period. However, the Soviet Union did not instruct Cuba to get involved, and indeed it was Castro that urged Moscow to become more committed to the struggle in Angola. With that in mind, Cuba obviously could not have carried out the Angola operation as speedily or efficiently as it did had the Soviet Union not come to its aid with arms and transportation facilities.

Why was Cuba so anxious to leap to Neto's aid? Castro's personal relationship with Neto, the propensity in Cuban culture toward nationalistic displays of force, and the opportunity to test the Cuban military in the "real world" all played a role. Although Cuba received improved trade terms from the Soviets after the intervention, and made profits in the civilian (but not necessarily in the military) sphere in Angola from 1976 to the early 1980s, economic incentives did not play a significant role in Castro's 1975 decision to intervene.

Phase 3 extended roughly from 1976 to 1981. In this period, Cuba's military involvement in Angola shifted from an expeditionary force to a long-term presence. Planned Cuban withdrawal of combat forces from Angola halted as threats from Zaire and South Africa mounted. The 1977 challenge to Neto's power by the Nito Alves faction—possibly backed by the Soviet Union—and its defeat after active Cuban intervention on Neto's behalf ensured Cuban troops would be asked to remain for the longer term. It further illustrated the tendency for Cuban and Soviet interests in Angola to occasionally diverge. As the Cubans prepared for the long haul in Angola, the rules governing their military activities were agreed upon with the MPLA. The Cubans took on back-up infrastructure and logistics activities, staying away from frontline combat with either UNITA or South Africa. In this phase, Cuban civilian cooperation in Angola also increased dramatically, with large numbers of Cuban doctors, agricultural technicians, teachers, construction engineers, and other specialists arriving. Angolan-Cuban social problems arose in both the military and civilian areas, but to a lesser extent than with some other East and West Bloc nationalities.

Why was Cuba willing to take on the long-term commitments in Angola, which it apparently did not anticipate when the decision to send combat forces was made? Cuba may have been offered financial rewards for its military activities, though the record is still unclear on this issue. But even if military compensation was not offered, other incentives were attractive. Increasing South African attacks on Angola brought Cuba the prestige-enhancing opportunity of presenting itself as a defender of blacks against white racists, an image Castro covets. Conversely, growing South African aggression against the MPLA made the political cost of abandoning Neto greater. In this context, Havana might appear to other Third World leaders to be placing the MPLA at the mercy of the apartheid power. In addition, even if Cuba were not making profits on its military activities in Angola, it certainly made some profits in the civilian sphere. Finally, Cuban long-term involvement in Angola promised to give the island important reverse leverage over the Soviet Union on both political and economic matters—a weapon Havana sorely needed as it sought to get a better deal out of its sometimes reluctant patron.

Phase 4 covered the period roughly from 1981 to 1984. During this phase, Cuban relations with the MPLA were strained by the latter's negotiations with the United States and South Africa on possible Cuban withdrawal from the country. The MPLA informed Havana only intermittently of the course of these discussions, and increasingly placed its own interests ahead of those of the Cubans. In this period, Cuba also became intensely ambivalent about the advantage-disadvantage equation of both staying in Angola and departing. Arguments in favor of staying in Angola included the influence such a presence gave Havana over Moscow, the valuable battlefield experience the presence gave Cuban forces, and the access which the Angola operation gave Cuba to other parts of Africa. Conversely, removal of Cuban troops from Angola would have several impacts, including reducing the numbers of Cuban casualties (a factor causing growing concern at home), removing an obstacle to improved relations with the United States, and possibly even bringing economic benefits. As with the cancellation of payments for Cuban civilian operations in Angola in 1983, the Angola involvement had become far less profitable, and perhaps had even gone into deficit.

Phase 5 ran from early 1985 to mid-1986. It was marked by the collapse of negotiations with the MPLA on the issue of Cuban troop withdrawal following South African attacks on Angolan territory as well as the U.S. decision to aid UNITA. For the first six months of 1986, Cuban and MPLA positions on withdrawal were united in a hard-line stance, shifting from a "no withdrawal until Namibian independence and cessation of South African UNITA support" line to the much stiffer "no withdrawal until apartheid is overthrown" position. In part, Cuba and the MPLA accepted the harder position because of the belief that Pretoria and Washington had adopted an increasingly aggressive posture toward Angola, and therefore Cuban withdrawal would be extremely dangerous both for MPLA survival and for Cuban prestige. Furthermore, the increase in antiapartheid violence within South Africa contributed to the hardening of the Cuban position. Such a setting served to heighten Castro's interest in maintaining a presence in the region from which to possibly launch other, not necessarily military, operations, as well as facilitate quiet contacts with the African National Congress.

Phase 6 ran from mid-1986 to the beginning of 1988 (the date of this writing). It involved a rerun of the now-familiar cycle of MPLA flexibility on Cuban withdrawal, followed by external "aggression," resultant MPLA reluctance to move forward with withdrawal, and in this instance, an actual increase in the Cuban troop presence. As in the previous phases, the Soviet Union and Cuba continued to differ on various Angolan matters, with Moscow now appearing more willing than either the MPLA or Cuba to consider a "political" solution, if it could thereby further other economic and diplomatic interests. As in previous phases, it was primarily actions taken by external powers that hindered Cuban withdrawal talks, not Cuban pressure. And, as in previous times, Cuba's preoccupation in the talks was protection of its prestige—with Castro perhaps willing to even facilitate the talks if this crucial commodity could be protected. Overall, the most important new element in the 1986–88 period was the apparent decision by Cuba to attempt to position itself to derive prestige-enhancing benefits from either ongoing military involvement in, or negotiated withdrawal from, Angola.

The lessons that the preceding description of Cuban policy in Angola hold for scholars and policymakers can be approached on two levels: implications for U.S. policy toward the MPLA and, as well, implications for future Cuban adventures in southern Africa.

With regard to the lessons for U.S. diplomacy with the MPLA, several conclusions can be drawn:

- As the historical record implies, if Cuban policy on Angola is not entirely directed by Moscow, and for short periods can run counter to Soviet interests, then U.S. policymakers presumably cannot just negotiate with the Soviets on Angola, but must take account of, and deal with, the Cuban point of view. While obviously no solution to the Angola situation will have much chance of success if the Soviets oppose it (and therefore Washington/Moscow discussions are essential), any solution which does not respond to Cuba's special interests also risks failure. Cuban behind-the-scenes international connections and direct influence within the

MPLA give it a good chance of sabotaging a deal which does not respect its concerns.

- The history of Cuban involvement in Angola shows that the most consistent and overriding Cuban interest is protection and promotion of its international image. This suggests that U.S./Soviet or U.S./MPLA schemes for obtaining Cuban withdrawal from Angola must either provide a fig leaf for Cuba's image, or be prepared to neutralize the actions Cuba will take to hinder the negotiations.

- The record shows that in certain circumstances the MPLA will put its own interests before those of the Cubans. This suggests that direct bilateral U.S./MPLA contacts are useful, and though Soviet and Cuban concerns must be addressed before a deal can be finalized, U.S./MPLA discussions can structure the diplomatic environment in a manner that limits Soviet/Cuban options.

- The evidence shows that Cuba is currently benefitting far less than previously from its economic involvement in Angola—yet its willingness to remain there is undiminished. This suggests that the U.S. should not expect the deterioration of the MPLA's financial fortunes due to war and the collapse of oil prices to lead to a reduction of Cuban commitment to MPLA defense.

- Historical evidence suggests the main factors strengthening Cuba's willingness to stay in Angola were the deterioration of South African internal stability and the increased South African threats to the region; furthermore, U.S. aid to UNITA reinforced this decision. Thus, U.S. policymakers should expect that the more southern Africa's climate is disrupted, the more interest Cuba will take in it. In turn, this suggests the U.S. should try to stabilize the region—for example by aiding some of South Africa's neighbors—and be prepared for increased Cuban "meddling" should its efforts fail.

The second set of implications concern future Cuban "adventurism" in southern Africa. Although outsiders can only speculate, it seems plausible that Cuba may have drawn the following conclusions from its Angola experience.

- No matter how rich a country may be in natural resources (and therefore how advantageous long-term military and trade partnerships appear), internal instability and unpredictable movements in international commodity prices can render such partnerships direct financial liabilities, rather than assets. These liabilities can be partly offset by the extra bargaining power such unprofitable operations give Cuba in economic negotiations with the Soviets, but cannot be viewed as long-term assets unto themselves.

- Economic and military activities in Africa are very different from such activities in Latin America. The underdeveloped nature of African economies, the complexities of regional ethnic relationships, and the vastness of the terrain suggest unique conditions. Furthermore, the proximity of a relatively well-developed regional superpower (in southern Africa) whose actions are not constrained by the norms of international behavior, imply that military and economic management techniques which work in Latin America have to be carefully adapted to the new conditions—and even then may not work well.

- Once Cuban military involvement in a conflict has been undertaken, it is extremely difficult to remove this actor without damaging its international prestige. Thus, after Cuban troops arrive in a host country, they can become hostages to events controlled by other parties; what is envisaged as a short-term military commitment can turn into an open-ended involvement if prestige is not to be sacrificed.
- Cuban casualties abroad do eventually cause social problems back at home, and though they can be justified for a short-term operation, they are hard to both camouflage and justify over the longer term.
- Military actions in foreign countries can spur unintended conflicts with the Soviet Union when factionalism breaks out in the supported group. Likewise, conflict can be triggered by a reassessment of priorities: namely, the Soviets appear ready to consider placing greater priority on domestic economic matters and/or U.S./Soviet relations, rather than on loyalty to the supported group. Thus, while the potential "up-side" of a military operation is that it can give Havana increased influence on Moscow, the potential "down-side" is that it can create opportunities for Havana/Moscow conflicts, which can erode existing influence.
- A southern African ally will not always put Cuban interests first, and in certain circumstances may threaten to sacrifice that most precious of commodities—Cuban prestige—if by doing so it can more easily fulfill its own needs.
- Cuban civilian personnel have generally been well received in Angola; while there are cultural and racial conflicts with the local populace on occasion, the civilian cooperation has generally enhanced Cuba's image locally.
- Taking, or appearing to take, a stand against South Africa is extremely well received in much of the Third World, and goes a long way toward offsetting criticism of Cuba's support for unpopular Soviet policies.

If Cuba has drawn the above conclusions from its Angola experience—a contention certainly open to debate—then what are the prospects for Cuban intervention elsewhere in southern Africa?

First, it is likely that Cuba will think much more carefully before assuming a deep military involvement in, for example, Mozambique or South Africa. The difficulties associated with military "adventurism" are much more appreciated in Havana than they were in the pre–Angola era, specifically: the problem of surrendering control over crucial prestige-affecting aspects of diplomacy to the host government; the social effects of casualties; the intractable nature of African guerrilla conflicts; and the danger of getting pulled in deeper than originally intended.

However, the Angola lesson has also shown how far "fighting apartheid" can go in enhancing Cuba's prestige in the Third World. With the internal South African situation heating up, with Pretoria increasingly willing to retaliate against neighbors for perceived aid to ANC infiltrators, and with the spotlight of international media attention focused ever more intensely on the apartheid system, the attraction of the "knight in shining armor" role will be hard to resist.

Obviously, the best solution from Cuba's point of view would be to appear to play a "heroic" role, without getting directly involved on a military level. As Cuba cannot offer much financial aid, it must look to other alternatives; in this context, the training of allies in the use of Soviet arms, while staying well back from the front lines of the South Africa conflict, would be one solution.

If this option is pursued, maintenance of a Cuban military presence in Angola takes on new meaning, as it offers a convenient site for Cuban/ANC contacts. Sending civilian "humanitarian" personnel, such as doctors and teachers, to more southern African states, and the offering of Cuban educational scholarships to students from those states, is also relatively risk-free. Facilitating the "armed struggle" in South Africa by providing technicians to help neighboring states rebuild their infrastructures after attack by South Africa would also enhance prestige without bringing the risks associated with massive military involvement. Finally, Cuba's experience in training civilian personnel to act as local militias might be useful for those southern African states which fear attack by South African trained and supported "dissidents." Once again, this could be done without sending an actual combat force to the host country.

The discussion of lessons Cuba may have drawn from its Angola experience, and the way those lessons may affect future Cuban policy in southern Africa, is obviously highly speculative and open to debate. The suggestions are intended more to stimulate the reader's imagination than to be used as concrete predictions. The intended aim in outlining Cuban options, and indeed the goal in documenting Cuban policy in Angola provided in this chapter, is to demonstrate that both the classic conservative and liberal stereotypes fail to explain a wide range of elements in past and present Cuban policy. If this is the case in Angola, it may well be the case in other parts of the world. Thus stereotypical assumptions about Cuban motivations in other regions should be constantly checked against the daily reality of Cuban actions on the ground. If analyses of Cuban policies are not conducted in an atmosphere freed from the constraints of both left- and right-leaning hysteria, Western responses may indeed enhance rather than reduce Cuban influence.

Appendix A
Chronology of Angolan Independence Process

April 25, 1974—A group of captains, major and colonels calling itself the Armed Forces Movement (MFA) overthrows the Portuguese government and exiles its leadership. The MFA is at first ambivalent about African independence and favors a federal system.

June 1974—Radicals committed to immediate independence for the African territories take over the Portuguese government. Chinese instructors for the FNLA arrive in Africa.[141]

July 1974—Soviet aid to the MPLA remains suspended. Small amounts of CIA funds for Holden Roberto are disbursed.[142]

August 1974—An MPLA reconciliation meeting fails. U.S. intelligence reports to Washington that the Soviets are delivering the first consignment of a $6 million shipment of military supplies to African liberation movements through Dar es Salaam. Some of these arms may have ended up with the MPLA, but there is no proof that they did, nor any evidence as to whether Neto or Chipenda was the intended recipient.[143] 450 tons of Chinese arms delivered to the FNLA.[144]

October 1974—MPLA signs a cease-fire agreement with the now radical Portuguese government.

November/December 1974—As Neto's faction of the MPLA receives official recognition from Portugal, the Soviet Union changes its stance (if it had not already done so in August) and begins to send Neto supplies through Congo-Brazzaville.[145] Western observers suspect, but cannot confirm, the new Soviet policy.

January 1975—The MPLA, FNLA, and UNITA sign the Alvor Agreement, which declares all three groups "legitimate" and sets November 11, 1975 as the date for independence. The United States' "40 Committee," a part of the National Security Council, authorizes a covert grant of $300,000 to the FNLA but rejects a proposal to give $100,000 to UNITA.[146]

February 1975—The U.S. decision to aid the FNLA is still secret, but the FNLA's takeover of the Luanda television station and leading daily newspaper alerts observers that it is obtaining funds from somewhere. American diplomats stationed in Luanda receive reports, which they could not confirm at the time, that "Stalins organs" (particularly powerful Soviet multiple rocket launchers) had been sighted in the hands of the MPLA.[147] FNLA hit and run attacks against the MPLA in Luanda begin.

March 1975—The FNLA[148] increases attacks on MPLA installations in Luanda, and in the provinces.[149] Soviet arms supplies to the MPLA increase.[150]

April 1975—FNLA-MPLA fighting escalates with the initiative coming equally from both groups.

May 1975—The MPLA goes on the offensive, forcing the FNLA out of Luanda.[151] Neto meets with Cuban Commander Flavio Bravo in Brazzaville, and asks for light arms and more talks.[152] First Savimbi and then Chipenda go to Namibia for discussions with the South Africans.[153]

June 1975—230 Cuban military advisers begin staffing MPLA training camps. American diplomats suspect, but cannot prove, that Cuban advisers are partly responsible for the increased MPLA military efficiency.[154] South African troops take up positions at the Ruacana Falls on the Cunene River, just inside Angola,[155] with the excuse that they must protect a South African-funded hydroelectric and irrigation scheme.

July 1975—On the 16th Castro secretly asks a left-leaning MFA leader visiting Havana to arrange Portuguese permission for the Cuban military to enter Angola.[156] On the 17th, ignorant of the Cuban/Portuguese discussions,[157] the United States' "40 Committee" authorizes a $32 million program to fund large arms shipments to the FNLA and UNITA, and a covert CIA program involving U.S. military advisors in Zaire. Three days later the FNLA begins an offensive aimed at capturing Luanda before 11 November.[158]

August 1975—The MPLA, unaware of the "40 Committee's" decision, sends an envoy to Moscow to ask for help. He is told Moscow will provide arms, but not troops.[159] A Cuban delegation arrives in Luanda, Neto asks it for more training officers, and by the end of the month 200 more Cuban infantry instructors arrive in Angola.[160] South Africa, ignorant of the Cuban actions, moves northward to occupy the actual Cunene/Ruacana project. South Africa agrees to set up training camps in southern Angola for UNITA and Chipenda's forces.[161]

September 1975—South African instructors arrive at the new UNITA and Chipenda training camps. South African troops move further into Angola in response to an alleged attack by SWAPO (a guerrilla movement fighting for Namibian independence from South Africa).[162] Later in the month,

Cuban ships carrying a modest shipment of (Cuban) heavy arms and a few hundred soldiers begin to arrive at Congolese and Angolan ports.[163]

October 1975—On the 14th, Pretoria mounts a drive (titled "Operation Zulu") for Luanda with Chipenda, UNITA, right-wing Portuguese, and South African forces. A South African officer involved in the operation told this author (in 1985), "We later found out the Cubans were getting involved at about the same time. We didn't know that when the decision was made."[164] The Chinese and U.S.-backed FNLA get within 12 miles of Luanda.[165]

November 1975—On the 4th, an MPLA envoy asks Cuba for a major influx of manpower to help defend Luanda. The Cuban Communist Party Central Committee meets on the 5th, and votes in favor of the request; the Soviet Union is informed by Castro of the decision after the vote. On the 8th, a battalion of Cuban soldiers is airlifted by ancient Cuban planes to hold Luanda until reinforcements can be sent. The MPLA, with help of arriving Cubans, hold Luanda against the FNLA and on November 11 MPLA declares Angola independent. Operation Zulu is still charging northward, and by the 14th, is 500 miles north of the Angola-Namibia border.[166] Additional Cuban troops are dispatched in converted Cuban freighters and fishing ships. Cuba asks the Soviet Union to send heavy arms, which it does, and to help airlift troops, which is also initially carried out, but suspended twice in response to U.S. protests.[167]

December 1975—Cuban troops continue to arrive, the South African commando column stalls at the Queve River 120 miles south of Luanda when it encounters an MPLA unit reinforced with Cuban soldiers and Soviet arms.[168] The extent of U.S. involvement in Angola is made public and the U.S. Senate passes the Clark Amendment halting U.S. aid to UNITA and the FNLA.

January 1976—Seeing the U.S. back out of the conflict, Soviet unease about airlifting Cubans evaporates, and the number of troops in Angola rises to an estimated 12,000.[169] The FNLA is eliminated as a fighting force and UNITA and the South African unit withdraw to Namibia.[170]

February/March 1976—Cuban troops continue to arrive, bringing the total to between 18,000 and 36,000 depending upon the source.[171]

Notes

1. The Stanley Foundation, *U.S. Policy and Radical Regimes: Report of a Vantage Conference 1986* (Iowa: The Stanley Foundation, 1986), p. 8.
2. H. Michael Erisman, *Cuba's International Relations: The Anatomy of a*

Nationalist Foreign Policy (Boulder, Colo. and London: Westview Press, 1985), p. 15.

3. William LeoGrande, *Cuba's Policy in Africa, 1959–1980* (Berkeley: Institute of International Studies, University of California, 1980), p. 9.

4. Erisman, p. 18.

5. William J. Durch, *The Cuban Military in Africa and the Middle East: From Algeria to Angola,* Professional Paper No. 201, Center for Naval Analyses (U.S.), September 1977, pp. 6–7.

6. LeoGrande, p. 91.

7. David and Marina Ottaway, *Afrocommunism* (New York: Holmes and Meier, 1981), p. 101.

8. Erisman, p. 30.

9. Ibid., p. 30.

10. Ibid., p. 35.

11. John Marcum, *The Angolan Revolution Volume II: Exile Politics and Guerrilla Warfare (1962–1976)* (Cambridge, Mass.: M.I.T. Press, 1978), p. 229.

12. Agostinho Neto, "Who is the Enemy?" speech at the University of Dar Es Salaam, 1974.

13. Marcum, p. 17.

14. Ibid., pp. 228–30.

15. LeoGrande, p. 21.

16. Tad Szulc, *Fidel: A Critical Portrait* (New York: William Morrow and Company, 1986), p. 639.

17. Ibid., p. 153.

18. Sergio Roca, "Economic Aspects of Cuban Involvement in Africa," in Carmelo Mesa-Lago and June Belkin (eds.), *Cuba in Africa* (Pittsburgh, Pa.: University of Pittsburgh Press, 1982), pp. 165–67.

19. Szulc, p. 638.

20. The cost may be illusory, as Castro may never have intended to follow through on rapprochement with Washington for fear the resultant decrease in anti-Americanism in Cuban society would undermine his power, but the Angola involvement certainly appeared to wreck a promising opportunity.

21. Szulc, p. 640.

22. Ibid.

23. Ibid., p. 641.

24. Ibid., p. 642.

25. LeoGrande, p. 23.

26. Wolfers and Bergerol, p. 128.

27. Marcum, p. 259.

28. LeoGrande, p. 23.

29. Arthur J. Klinghoffer, *The Angolan War: A Study in Soviet Policy in the Third World* (Boulder, Colo.: Westview Press, 1980), pp. 127–31. Also confidential interviews with Angolans in Luanda, 1985.

30. Wolfers and Bergerol, p. 96, quoting Rui Coelho.

31. Ibid., p. 78.

32. Confidential interviews in Luanda, 1985.

33. Wolfers and Bergerol, p. 86.

34. Confidential interview with MPLA official, Luanda, 1985.

35. Wolfers and Bergerol, p. 93.

36. Ibid., p. 93.

37. *Jornal de Angola,* May 28, 1977.
38. Confidential interview with Mozambican expert on Angola, Maputo, 1986.
39. Klinghoffer, p. 131.
40. Interview with Angolan source, Luanda, 1985.
41. Szulc, p. 570.
42. Ibid., p. 572.
43. Ibid., p. 611.
44. LeoGrande, p. 26.
45. Wolfers and Bergerol, pp. 129–30.
46. Jose Eduardo Dos Santos, interview with *Prisma,* republished by *Agencia Angola Press (ANGOP),* 14 November 1985.
47. Jose Eduardo Dos Santos, quoted in "Angola's Dos Santos says UNITA is Using Zairean Territory," *BBC Summary of World Broadcasts,* 24 December 1986, pp. b5–b8.
48. Jose Eduardo Dos Santos, *Address to the MPLA First National Party Conference,* 14 January 1985.
49. Confidential conversation with Western diplomat, 1987.
50. Interviews with British, French and Italian diplomats in Luanda, 1985 and 1986.
51. LeoGrande, p. 23.
52. Lawrence W. Hendersen, *Angola: Five Centuries of Conflict* (Ithaca, N.Y.: Cornell University Press, 1979), p. 260.
53. Klinghoffer, p. 134.
54. Wolfers and Bergerol, p. 112.
55. Ibid., p. 116.
56. Roca, p. 164.
57. Wolfers and Bergerol, pp. 145–47.
58. Ibid., pp. 145–47.
59. Roca, p. 171.
60. Ibid., pp. 164–65.
61. Marga Holness, "The Struggle Continues," in Phyliss Johnson and David Martin (eds.), *Destructive Engagement* (Harare: Zimbabwe Publishing House, 1986), pp. 95–99.
62. Jose Eduardo Dos Santos, *Address to the MPLA First National Party Conference,* 14 January 1985.
63. Economist Intelligence Unit, *1985 Annual Angola Supplement* (London: The Economist, 1985) pp. 14–15.
64. Holness, p. 102.
65. "Message from the Angolan Head of State to the United Nations Secretary General on the Problems of Southern Africa," *Angola Information Bulletin,* Issue number 97, 26 November 1984, p. 1.
66. Ibid., pp. 2–3.
67. Ibid., p. 3.
68. Ibid., pp. 3–5.
69. *Guardian* (London), 21 November 1984.
70. Interview with Luanda-based diplomat, 1985.
71. Interviews with (non-Angolan) African and European diplomats in Luanda, 1985 and 1986.
72. Interviews with American diplomats, 1985.
73. "Angola to Sign Lome Convention," *ANGOP,* 3 May 1985.

74. Interviews with socialist country and African diplomats in Luanda, 1985.
75. "Special Report on Cabinda," *ANGOP,* 14 June 1986.
76. "Communique of the (Angolan) Ministry of Foreign Affairs," 22 July 1985.
77. Interviews with Angolan and American diplomats, Luanda and Washington, 1985.
78. Interviews of Nonaligned Movement Summit delegates from Indonesia and Singapore, in Harare, 1986.
79. Ibid.
80. Holness, p. 107.
81. Interviews in Washington and Luanda, 1985 and 1986. Cuban and Soviet personnel were often near, but not at, the front line and as frontline action moved rapidly forward and backward in pitched battles, some got caught up in it. But the rules of the game for Cuban involvement in the war did not seem to have changed.
82. Holness, p. 108.
83. "Official Talks between Angola and Cuba," *ANGOP,* 28 October 1985, pp. 2–3.
84. *The Observer* (London), 24 November 1986.
85. Interviews with European diplomats in Luanda, June 1986.
86. "President's Speech," *ANGOP,* 24 January 1986, pp. III–IV.
87. "Tripartite Soviet-Angolan-Cuban Communique," *ANGOP,* 17 February 1986, pp. 15–18.
88. The South African government (incorrectly) believes that there was a conflict between the Angolan and Cuban/Soviet position at this tripartite meeting. It claimed that Moscow and Havana had urged the MPLA to launch another major offensive against UNITA in 1986, while the MPLA wanted to concentrate on UNITA activities that were expanding to the north of the country and protect, above all, the oil installations. Source: Interviews with South African officials, January and February 1986.
89. "Fidel Reaffirms Solidarity with Angola," *ANGOP,* 17 February 1986, p. 9.
90. "Colonel Ndalu's Speech at Cuban Party Congress," *ANGOP,* 17 February 1986, pp. 8–9.
91. Chester Crocker, "The US and Angola," U.S. Department of State, Bureau of Public Affairs, Current Policy no. 796.
92. *The Guardian* (London), 31 March 1986.
93. "President Receives Commonwealth Delegation," *ANGOP,* 7 March 1986, p. 1.
94. Holness, p. 109.
95. Interviews with U.S. diplomats, 1986.
96. *The Guardian* (London), 27 March 1986.
97. Speeches of President Castro and President dos Santos, 8th Nonaligned Summit, Harare, Zimbabwe in September 1986.
98. "Angolan Government Communique on Talks with U.S.A.," *BBC Summary of World Broadcasts,* 17 April 1987.
99. *Cuba—Quarterly Situation Report,* Second Quarter 1987, United States Information Agency, Radio Martí Program, Section II—Foreign Policy, p. 23.
100. "Cuba Is Mired in Angola, Top Defector Says," *New York Times,* 1 July 1987.
101. "Hopes high for Angola peace talks," *The Times* (London) 3 July 1987.
102. Interviews with U.S. officials, August 1987.
103. "U.S.-Angola Talks on Namibia Called 'Waste of Time'," *Washington Post,* 23 July 1987.

104. "Cubans, Soviets Blamed for Stall in Angolan Talks," *Washington Post*, 25 July 1987.
105. *Cuba—Quarterly Situation Report*, Third Quarter 1987, United States Information Agency, Radio Martí Program, Part II—Foreign Policy, pp. 23–24.
106. "Statements by Venancio de Moura on Talks with U.S.," *ANGOP*, 29 July 1987.
107. "Mbinda Denies Crocker's Statements," *ANGOP*, 29 July 1987.
108. "President Dos Santos Proposes Agreement on Namibia," *ANGOP*, 29 July 1987.
109. "Communique Issued after Angolan-Cuban Talks," *ANGOP*, 7 August 1987.
110. "Angolan Commentary on 'Flexibility' of its New Southern Africa Proposal," *BBC Summary of World Broadcasts*, 12 August 1987.
111. UNITA remarked, "Cuba has forced the MPLA not to negotiate with the United States. . . . but insists it ought to be part of the Cuban delegation to the talks." Source: "UNITA Communique says Dos Santos's Cuba visit shows 'dependence'," *BBC Summary of World Broadcasts*, 7 August 1987.
112. Interviews with academics, September and December 1987.
113. Discussion with U.S. diplomat, October 1987.
114. *Cuba—Quarterly Situation Report*, Third Quarter, United States Information Agency, Radio Martí Program, II Foreign Policy 14. See also Wayne Smith, "Why is the US Ignoring Castro's Signals?" *Long Island Newsday*, 4 August 1987, p. 57.
115. "Angola: Dos Santos receives Cuban party official," *BBC Summary of World Broadcasts*, 17 September 1987.
116. Interviews with U.S. officials, 1987.
117. "U.S., Angola discuss Cuban troops pullout," *Washington Times*, 25 September 1987.
118. Interviews with U.S. officials, September 1987.
119. "Angola ready for further talks with USA," *BBC Summary of World Broadcasts*, 14 September 1987.
120. Interview with *Business Day* correspondent Simon Barber, 15 September 1987. See also "Africa: A New Deal on Angola?," *Newsweek*, 28 August 1987.
121. Helmoed-Romer Heitman, "Angola: Crucial Confrontation Ahead," *Jane's Defence Weekly*, 24 October 1987.
122. David Ottaway, "UNITA Rebels Defeat Thrust by Angola," *Washington Post*, 2 November 1987.
123. "South African Defence Minister on Recent Fighting in Angola," *BBC Summary of World Broadcasts*, 13 November, 1987. Savimbi was horrified by the South African claim it had rescued him, and suggested that South Africa was trying to take credit for UNITA's success. See William Claiborne, "South African Military Says Intervention in Angola Staved Off Rebel Defeat," *Washington Post*, 13 November 1987.
124. "Botha Acts to Counter Criticism of South African Role in Angola," *Washington Post*, 15 November 1987; and "Pretoria tries to allay fears over Angolan entanglement," *Guardian* (London), 16 November 1987.
125. "Text of United Nations Resolution 602 on Angola, Unanimously Adopted on 25 November 1987," *ANGOP*, 30 November 1987.
126. "Angola: Mystery of S. A. Attack Deepens," *Southern Africa Report*, 27 November 1987.

127. "SA says troops will remain on the Angola 'battlefield'," *Guardian* (London), 27 November 1987.
128. "South African Force Departing Angola," *Washington Post*, 6 December 1987.
129. Discussions with US and European officials, December 1987, and "Mozambique Agency Director Discusses Military Situation in Southern Angola," *BBC Summary of World Broadcasts*, 21 December 1987.
130. "Cubans on Patrol in South Angola," *New York Times*, 16 December 1987.
131. "For the Record—Escalation of War in Angola," *ANGOP*, 30 November 1987.
132. Interviews with U.S. diplomats. See also "Cuban General and Army Division Return to Angola," *BBC Summary of World Broadcasts*, 9 December 1987.
133. "Cubans on Patrol in South Angola," *New York Times*, 16 December 1987.
134. "South African Force Departing Angola," *Washington Post*, 6 December 1987.
135. "Cuban General and Army Division Return to Angola," *BBC Summary of World Broadcasts*, 9 December 1987.
136. "Cuban Says 40,000 Troops in Angola; Figure Exceeds US Estimates," *Washington Post*, 9 January 1988.
137. Confidential interview, December 1987.
138. "Angola President Asks for Negotiations," *Washington Post*, 10 January 1988.
139. Interview with Soviet expert Helen Desfosses, December 1987.
140. "Soviets, Cubans now washing their dirty linen in public gaze," *Washington Times*, 2 November 1987.
141. Marcum, p. 246.
142. John Stockwell, *In Search of Enemies: A CIA Story* (London: Futura Publications Limited, 1979), p. 67.
143. State Department testimony to Senator Dick Clark, quoted in Marcum, p. 252.
144. Marcum, p. 246.
145. Ibid., p. 253.
146. Marcum, p. 257.
147. Confidential interview with US diplomat, 1986.
148. The claim that it was the FNLA that started the violence is repeated by both Angolan and American observers.
149. Marcum p. 258, and interviews with Lucio Lara (Luanda 1985) and American diplomat (1986).
150. Marcum, p. 259.
151. Confidential interview with U.S. diplomat, 1986.
152. Michael Wolfers, and Jane Bergerol, *Angola in the Front Line* (London: Zed Press, 1983), p. 29.
153. Marcum, p. 268.
154. Confidential interview with US diplomat, 1986.
155. Marcum, p. 268.
156. Marcum, p. 443.
157. Confidential interview with US diplomat, 1986.
158. LeoGrande, p. 17.
159. Marcum, p. 443.
160. Ibid., p. 273.
161. Ibid., p. 269.

162. Ibid.
163. Ibid., p. 273.
164. Confidential interview with a South African official, Pretoria, 1985.
165. Marcum, p. 274.
166. Marcum, p. 269.
167. LeoGrande, p. 22.
168. Marcum, p. 272.
169. Marcum, p. 274.
170. Marcum, p. 277.
171. LeoGrande, p. 19.

IV
RESIDUAL CONCERNS

7

Cuban Foreign Policy
toward Far East and Southeast Asia

William Ratliff

Call me Fidel. Some years ago—after 1959, to be precise, during the bright and ebullient springtime of my career—I first cast a few thoughts across the watery part of the world to East and Southeast Asia. True, most of those lands were poorer than my Cuban Patria and half a planet away, so I wasn't as interested in them as in closer neighbors—in the Americas and Africa—or in governments with the money and power to subsidize my economy and boost my international career. But whenever revolutionary virtue soared up within me, and I felt the compelling need to promote an incontrovertibly moral cause—or when there was an occasional economic or military gain to be had—I looked and still look East. And there in Asia I find what I seek—a senile old Mao Zedong to lambast or the soulmates of revolutionary Vietnam or Korea to extol against the Nazified Yankees and their ilk.[1]

There is no record of Fidel Castro's having spoken publicly on East or Southeast Asian revolutionary issues prior to his victory over Fulgencio Batista in January 1959, even on such events as the Chinese Communist conquest of the mainland and People's Communes or the Vietnamese victory over the French at Dienbienphu. But that changed after Castro moved into the communist sphere after 1959. As the above passage indicates, ideology and polemics, emphasizing "proletarian international-ism," have since that year stood at the heart of Castro's bilateral relations with East and Southeast Asian governments, and especially with the core communist countries of China, Vietnam, and Korea. This has ranged from a decades-long defense of all actions carried out by Ho Chi Minh and his successors in Vietnam, to blasts at the International Olympic Committee for scheduling the 1988 games only in the south of that divided land, bypassing the northern—communist—part of the country. And bilateral relations sometimes have included some trade and personal contacts.

But relations have been on another level as well, namely multilateral, as a component of Soviet global strategy. Castro's roles in Africa and Latin America have been discussed at length for many years, and Cuban involvement has been more important in these regions than in Asia. But Cuba has made greater and lesser contributions to Soviet objectives in Asia, too, ranging from Castro's efforts to tar Uncle Sam with the Vietnam War brush in the 1960s and 1970s, to Cuban support for strengthening the Soviet position in the South Pacific in the 1980s.

This chapter will examine Fidel Castro's interests in, and ties to, East and Southeast Asia since 1959. The focus will be mainly on China—a country which had provided many workers for Cuban agriculture in the nineteenth century—and Vietnam. After considering Korea, the South Pacific, and several other countries, this essay will survey Cuban trade with East and Southeast Asia and conclude with comments on the global significance of Cuba's policies toward the region.

Cuba and the People's Republic of China

Fidel Castro and Mao Zedong

It is one of the ironies of history that although in 1966 Fidel Castro condemned Mao Zedong with a viciousness rarely encountered in modern international relations, the Cuban leader was, in many respects, more like his Chinese counterpart than any other communist chief of state—past or present. Castro once remarked of Mao and his colleagues that prior to their falling out he had been "deeply impressed by their conduct and their high revolutionary morality. . . ."[2] But even before the mid-1960s Castro had turned against the Chinese leadership, as will be later discussed.

The similarities between Castro and Mao—ranging from the creation of personality cults through ideology to specific positions on domestic development and international affairs—undoubtedly came, in part, from somewhat similar experiences as guerrilla leaders seizing power in Third World countries. Beyond this, each was inclined to look at the world through fundamentally anti-Marxist glasses. Judging by their statements and policies, neither leader accepted Marx's conviction that the political and social superstructures of a society flow from the economic substructure, but rather believed that the economic system must and can be changed by the communist party's prior ideological and political transformation of the masses into "new men." These convictions were most clearly manifested in Mao's Cultural Revolution and Castro's Revolutionary Offensive, the

former evidently an important inspiration for the latter.[3] These revolutionary experiments reflected the two leaders' greater attention to subjective
rather than objective conditions, to moral over material incentives, to
guerrilla-oriented Sierra Maestra (and Yenan) mentalities with their fundamental skepticism toward the institutionalization of a revolution.[4] On
political and often strategic matters, during the late 1960s, Castro and Mao
often agreed with each other and disagreed with the Soviet Union, though
neither government drew any attention to this fact. The issues included
the conviction that the basic contradiction of the present age was between
imperialism and the Third World, support for guerrilla warfare in most
underdeveloped countries, and concern that "peaceful coexistence"
would benefit only the imperialists."[5]

On the surface, as Castro presented the case at the time, rice was the
cause of the open conflict between Cuba and the Chinese that erupted in
1966 (the details of which are related below). During this period, the Cuban
leader heaped invective on Mao while the latter responded only indirectly
through nameless bureaucrats and foreign parties. In reality, Castro turned
on the Chinese leader and revolution for other reasons and used a dishonest tale of Chinese skulduggery as a pretext. To some extent, Mao, just
beginning to push the Chinese revolutionary model for Latin America,
may have seemed to be trying to upstage Castro as the guru of the
antiimperialist revolution in the Third World, and even in Latin America.
And for Castro, there is room for only one such guru. In later years, a
Cuban analyst argued a reversed variant of this case, claiming that Cuba
stood directly in the way of the Chinese and the promotion of their
intentions in Latin America; thus, China sought to reduce Cuban influence
by criticizing its "exemplary friendship and solidarity" with the Soviet
Union and undermining its influence among the nonaligned nations.[6]

But the main reason Castro turned like a mad dog on his Chinese soul-
brother was much more practical, one of the most coldly calculated and
consequential decisions of the Maximum Leader's career. By the early
1960s, Castro knew that the Soviet Union and China were heading into a
feud that would surpass even that of Stalin and Trotsky, and that friendship
with both contestants was impossible. Castro further realized if he had to
choose between them, only the Soviet Union was close enough geographically, and powerful enough economically and militarily to help him
achieve his own extraordinarily ambitious personal objectives as self-
appointed nemesis of the "U.S. imperialists."

As early as 1958, while he was still fighting Batista, Castro wrote to
Celia Sanchez about the United States: "When this war is over, a much
wider and bigger war will begin for me; the war that I am going to launch
against them (the United States). I am saying to myself that is my true

destiny."[7] Given this objective and the relative size and geographical proximity of Cuba and the United States, Castro had little choice but to ally himself with the closer and more powerful of the two communist powers. He could see that the Soviet Union alone had both the resources and the national interest to provide the aid he would need, including a defensive shield, in his self-ordained battle against the Yankee giant.[8] Castro made his choice and, in most respects, the decision has paid off handsomely for him.

After Castro had destroyed the Cuban economy in the late 1960s, the Soviet Union forced some rationality and institutionalization on the Cuban Revolution, in exchange for massive aid. But Castro was never satisfied with this approach and beginning in 1984, launched a national campaign against the Soviet approach, while maintaining a close alliance with Moscow. The movement took clear ideological and practical form during 1986, the year of the Third Congress of the Cuban Communist Party, with Castro charging that the Soviet program had brought "many vices and distortions" to the land. Several times during the year, Castro even suggested his positions were enriching the theory of Marxism-Leninism. On 2 December 1986, at the closing session of the Congress, he stated that "economic mechanisms are auxiliary instruments of political and revolutionary work . . . the construction of socialism and of communism is fundamentally a political and revolutionary task." One need not listen very carefully to hear Mao shouting "Right On!" and Marx and Lenin croaking "petty bourgeois infantilism!"[9]

Cuba and China: Bilateral Relations

Chinese ties to Cuban communists—that is, to the pre-Castro communists of the People's Socialist Party (PSP)—date back to 1949 when labor leader Lazaro Pena attended a trade union conference in Beijing. Other Cuban communists who visited China prior to Castro's victory included party leaders Anibal Escalante and Blas Roca. China's active program of cultural diplomacy during the 1950s and early 1960s included the founding of the Institute of Latin American Studies (in 1961), the exchange of scholars for academic and language studies, and the translation of several Cuban literary works into Chinese, among other activities. According to one Chinese literary critic, PSP writer Nicolas Guillen, who himself had visited China before 1959, was one of the Latin American writers best known to Chinese readers.[10]

Many PSP members were impressed by what they thought was going on in China and some—though not the party as a whole—were early supporters of the armed (i.e., the "Chinese") road to power. As early as January

1959, one PSP leader suggested that the party had helped "open the way for the 'Chinese road' " used by the Castroites. In 1959–60, the party officially tried to get Castro to adopt China's relatively moderate example of utilizing a broad united front for early socialist construction.[11]

The relationship between Castro and his government—as distinct from the PSP—and China started off very positively, though the Cuban leader did not acknowledge that he had taken power by the "Chinese road" and he refused to adopt China's united front for building socialism. In large part, Castro's early favorable response to the Chinese probably resulted from their common Third World roots, and China's enthusiasm from 1960 until the mid-1960s for the revolutionary example the Cubans had given Latin America in their struggle against "U.S. imperialism." A joint communiqué issued at the end of Ché Guevara's official visit to the People's Republic of China (PRC) in November 1960 stated that the Chinese side:

> considers that the Cuban people's struggle and victory have provided abundant experience and set an example for all oppressed peoples in the world, particularly the Latin American peoples in their struggles to win and safeguard national independence.[12]

But shortly thereafter, discussions of the armed road to revolution moved beyond the mere "example" stage. With more detailed discussions undertaken vis-à-vis strategy and tactics, and the emerging Sino/Soviet dispute, important differences between the Cuban and Chinese roads emerged. In tandem, intensified conflict between the two countries grew, as will be discussed below.

Economic ties, as well as media and intelligence contacts—through a New China News Agency office in Havana—began in 1959; diplomatic relations were established in 1960. Shortly after Castro marched into Havana, a Chinese journal of literature in translation carried a wide variety of Cuban works, ranging from poems by Jose Martí and selections from Jose Pardo Llada's *Memorias de la Sierra Maestra* to woodcuts of Fidel among the peasants.

In the early 1960s, the Chinese published Castro's two "Declarations of Havana" and Guevara's *Guerrilla Warfare: A Method,* among other works, and the Cuban government reported the importation and publication of several hundred thousand copies of Chinese communist writings for circulation throughout the hemisphere. Between 1959 and 1961, the number of Cubans visiting China jumped from about 25 to more than 175, though the number declined again as the problems of the 1960s emerged.[13]

But shortly thereafter, the emerging Sino/Soviet dispute began to take its toll. For a short time Castro may have tried to remain aloof, but in the early 1960s he stepped firmly into the Soviet camp. The alignment was unmistakable and officially proclaimed at the November 1964 Conference of Latin American Communist Parties in Havana. The first pro-Chinese communist party in Latin America had been founded in 1962 in Brazil, a year before the Chinese call for the establishment throughout the world of what were called true Marxist-Leninist parties. But Castro systematically excluded pro-Chinese individuals and groups from the Havana conference. In addition, the final communiqué took the Soviet line by calling for all communists to unite just as the Chinese were insisting that all true Marxist-Leninists had to denounce Soviet "revisionism" and form separate organizations.[14] From that point on, the Sino/Cuban dispute moved in two mutually reinforcing directions: hostility between the two governments, deriving broadly from the conflict between the Soviet Union and the PRC; and dispute over the strategy of guerrilla warfare—both with repercussions throughout Latin America.

Bilateral relations degenerated rapidly during 1965, though Chinese regard for Guevara, who visited the PRC in February of that year, remained high. On 16 February, the Albanian Communist Party organ, which often expressed Chinese positions on international affairs, warned the Cubans to beware of "falling into the revisionist trap."[15] Castro responded on 13 March, stating that Sino/Soviet polemics were "Byzantine discords and academic charlatanry", and repeated his request of the previous year that the Soviets and Chinese stop the distribution of their tracts in Cuba, itself a fundamentally pro-Soviet stand he later admitted had been aimed primarily at the Chinese.[16]

Relations nose-dived in 1966, first at the January session of the Afro-Asian-Latin American People's Solidarity Conference in Havana, and subsequently when Castro accused China of confusing Marxism-Leninism with fascism, and of criminal economic aggression for cutting back its rice shipments to Cuba. Castro even suggested that Mao was a senile old man who "in spite of having done good things in his life, committed great barbarities at the end of his life."[17]

Maurice Halperin has documented the Sino/Cuban "rice war" that surfaced in early 1966, pointing out four aspects of the crisis. First, Cuba is the only Latin American country with rice as a staple in its diet. Second, Cuba had been almost self-sufficient in rice when Castro assumed power, but the Cuban leader reduced Cuban production by almost 90 percent within six years. Third, for several years, the Chinese made up much of Cuba's self-created shortage by providing rice in increasing amounts, unquestionably hoping the gesture of proletarian internationalism would draw Castro politically closer to China. And fourth, the Chinese cut back their shipments—though substantial trade continued nonetheless (see below)—when Castro refused to respond politically. As Halperin concludes, the Cuban leader lashed out at Mao "to distract the attention of the Cuban people from his own political naivete (which he could not completely conceal) and its disastrous economic and social consequences."[18]

Diplomatic ties at the ambassadorial level were broken in 1966 and were not to be reestablished until the end of 1970. Relations continued to improve through the early 1970s, despite Cuban distaste for China's rapprochement with the United States. Relations nose-dived again in the mid-1970s when Cuba and the Soviet Union supported the Popular Movement for the Liberation of Angola (MPLA) in the Angolan civil war, while China threw its backing to the National Front for the Liberation of Angola (FNLA) and the National Union for the Total Independence of Angola (UNITA). In his Report to the First Congress of the Cuban Communist Party (PCC—Pantido Communista de Cuba) in December 1975, Castro passed over China with the comment: "because of their well-known political positions," Cuban relations with the PRC "are merely state relations."[19]

The death of Mao did not bring a significant improvement in Sino/Cuban relations, principally because that period also brought an intensification of conflict between China and Cuba's much-admired Vietnam. After the Chinese attack on Vietnam in 1978–79, Castro condemned the "mad neofascist faction that rules China." He continued:

> to all appearances, the man who's at the head of this skulduggery, this crime, the number one man responsible seems to be this numbskull (laughter), this puppet, this brazen Deng Xiaoping; they purged him once, he came back, they purged him again, he's back again, and one fine day they'll purge him once again. It could happen. . . . The factions have gone back and forth purging each other for years. . . . one fine day the Chinese people will purge them all once and for all. (applause) Ah, but they're dangerous, infinitely dangerous![20]

On 3 September 1979, in his speech at the opening of the Sixth Summit Conference of Nonaligned Countries meeting in Havana, Castro stacked up his objections to Chinese policy positions:

> What right does China have to teach Vietnam a lesson, invade its territory, destroy its modest wealth, murder thousands of its people? The Chinese ruling clique, which supported Pinochet against Allende, which supported South Africa's aggression against Angola, which supported the Shah, which supported Somoza, which supports and supplies weapons to Sadat, which justifies the Yankee blockade against Cuba and the continued existence of the naval base at Guantanamo, which defends NATO and sides with the United States and the most reactionary forces of Europe and the rest of the world, has neither the prestige nor the moral standing to teach anyone a lesson.

At the Second PCC Congress in December 1980, the Cuban party blasted the "expansionist, hegemonic, Beijing clique's craven, criminal attack" on Vietnam, carried out with "collaboration and support provided by its Yankee imperialist allies." The Second Congress report then condemned the Chinese for supporting the "genocidal regime" in Kampuchea. A Cuban journalist added that as far back as 1965, the Chinese had obstructed the transport of Soviet military supplies to Vietnam; in 1981, he added, they formed an alliance with reactionary powers: the United States, Western Europe, Japan, South Africa, and Israel.[21]

Despite continuing suspicions—not the least of which related to Deng's slight reduction of centralized power in the economic sphere—ties became closer during the mid-1980s. Though differences remained, as Castro pointed out in his address to the Third CCP Congress in February 1986, the Cuban leader had mellowed enough to say "the positive position China has been adopting in recent times regarding important international matters has not failed to produce an impact."[22] By the beginning of 1986, the relationship seemed to be warming rapidly, if judged by the increasing number of Cuban delegations in China, and Chinese visitors to Havana. The main dark cloud was China's policy toward Vietnam, as Castro noted in his speech at the Party Congress in February.

Sino/Cuban Guerrilla Strategies

The second major aspect of the Sino/Cuban dispute related to the proper strategy for revolutionary war in the Third World. China's early support for the Cuban example in Latin America declined after the November 1964 communist party congress in Havana, from which they and their followers had been excluded.

For a couple of years, through their allies the Chinese attributed Cuba's deviation from the true path—and Havana's tilt in the Sino-Soviet dispute—to "the exit from the Cuban political scene of one of its foremost leaders, E. Ché Guevara."[23] Between 1959 and 1967 the Chinese had been much impressed by Guevara. They had published his *Guerrilla Warfare: A Method* in the early 1960s for circulation around the world, in the belief that when the Argentine revolutionary wrote about people's war, people's army, and mass support, he meant the same thing they did. To them, Guevara seemed to stand in contrast to Soviet "do-nothingism" and the simplistic *foco* Castroism which emerged full-blown in 1967. But much to their surprise and dismay, Guevara himself turned up in Bolivia as the very model of the modern impatient "petty bourgeois adventurer."

The mid-1960s had been a harrowing time for Castro, and to some extent, his experiences encouraged him to dive into the extreme "adventurism'' of the late 1960s which upset both the PRC and the Soviet Union, if for different reasons. The United States had made several abortive efforts—by invasion and assassination—to remove him from power. In February 1965, the United States had started bombing Castro's great North Vietnamese ally, and neither the Soviets nor the Chinese had done anything about it. Two months later, the U.S. invaded the Dominican Republic, right next door to Cuba in the Caribbean, set up a government it liked, and got away with it. No doubt Castro wondered if he might be next, and may have wondered if he, too, would get little or no real support from his communist "allies." As these concerns were festering, Ché Guevara returned to Cuba from the Congo.

These experiences fed Castro's and Guevara's natural impatience and helped lay the groundwork for the rise and fall of the most extreme form of *foco* Castroism during 1967. This line, as codified by Regis Debray in *Revolution in the Revolution?* (published in Havana in January 1967), held that a small core of guerrillas, the *foco,* could launch a struggle against almost any government and by its daring actions draw in the public support needed to topple those in power.[24] Castro assembled bands of this sort of revolutionary-oriented groups in Havana during the July–August 1967 period for the first (and last) Latin American Solidarity Organization (OLAS) Conference.[25]

Sometime in 1966, Guevara began seriously planning his campaign to make what his chief Bolivian lieutenant called "another Vietnam out of America, with its center in Bolivia," and by the end of the year was in that pivotal South American land launching his hands-on *foco* failure of the following year. In his famous "Message to the Tricontinental," released a month after his first (and premature) military encounter in Bolivia, Guevara asserted:

> What a luminous, near future would be visible to us if two, three or many Vietnams flourished throughout the world with their share of death and their immense tragedies, their everyday heroism and their repeated blows against imperialism obliging it to disperse its forces under the attack and the increasing hatred of all the peoples of the earth![26]

Guevara was not about to let anyone but himself generate this "Vietnam War" in Bolivia. He not only denied the pro-Soviet Communist Party of Bolivia a leadership role, he refused to let the pro-Chinese PCB-ML even be involved. In his "Necessary Introduction" to the Cuban edition of Guevara's diary, Castro accused the Maoist PCB-ML of betraying Guevara, to which the pro-Chinese party head responded: (1) nowhere in his diary had Guevara accused the Maoist party of doing any such thing; (2)

the PCB-ML had planned an insurrection in Bolivia with Guevara during a visit to Havana in September–October 1964; (3) Castro had "sold out" to the revisionists in the November 1964 Congress of Latin American Communist Parties and evidently persuaded Guevara to go along with him; and (4) from then on, the Maoists knew nothing about Guevara's plans, arrival, or whereabouts in Bolivia. To these four points, Guevara's chief Bolivian aide replied, Zamora was "as opportunistic and false as the other self-proclaimed vanguardists."[27]

To the Chinese, the *foco* was childish—if deadly—nonsense. Their attacks on this extreme form of Castroism came indirectly, usually in two ways. First, they stated and restated their own position:

> that armed struggle can be victorious only if it follows the revolutionary line pointed out by Chairman Mao: relying on the peasants, establishing rural base areas and using the countryside to encircle the cities.[28]

And during 1968 in particular, they published a series of indirect attacks on Castroism by pro-Chinese parties around the world. An unusually colorful one came from the party in Ceylon, which often voiced Beijing's positions in Chinese international publications. True Marxist-Leninists, the Ceylonese party said, reject any form of guerrilla warfare which is

> based fundamentally on romantic and petty-bourgeois ideology which is characterized by negating the necessity for the leadership of the Communist Party and by a lack of faith in the masses. Rather than on the masses, it places it reliance on a band of swashbuckling three musketeer type of bravadoes who are expected to perform miraculous exploits against terrific odds.[29]

Castro responded to such critiques by blasting "theorists of guerrilla warfare . . . who have never and never will fire a shot." He even picked up Mao's description of imperialists as "paper tigers" and called these theorists "paper revolutionaries," a charge he was then also making about Soviet-Bloc, Trotskyist, and most other revolutionaries around the world.[30]

Pro-Chinese organizations in Latin America also published critiques of the Cubans and *foco* Castroism in their own publications. The Bolivian Maoists (cited above) were one such group. Among the others were the Revolutionary Communist Party (PCR) of Chile and the Movement of the Revolutionary Left (MIR) in Uruguay.[31] In an attack on the Chilean Castroites, the PCR tried to deflect the charge that it was merely an appendage of the Chinese:

> People's war is an expression of proletarian ideology just as "focoism" and urban terrorism are the expression of petty-bourgeois ideology. Our differences

with the MIR (the Chilean Castroites) are not, as they claim, those of following or sympathizing with this or that foreign country, but very profound ones corresponding to the different classes which we represent.

Shortly after the Uruguayan National Liberation Movement (MLN) (better known as the Tupamaros), with its strong Castroite tendencies, murdered U.S. citizen Dan Mitrione in the summer of 1970, the Uruguayan Maoists— who called themselves the Movement of the Revolutionary Left (MIR)— slammed the MLN as a "natural expression of the focoist doctrine," which was "a deformation of the Cuban experience." The MIR said the MLN was characterized by adventurism, subjectivity, leftist opportunism, and terrorism and thus was "totally at odds with Marxism." In a typical Maoist critique, the MIR charged that the Tupamaros were mistaken about the role of the people and the party in the revolutionary struggle.[32]

But after 1970, Cuba and China stopped their incessant harping on the need for guerrilla wars throughout the Third World. As their loud advocacy declined, so did their conflict over the proper road to power. Conflicts between Cuba and China—and almost all critiques were by Cuba of China, not vice versa—were centered on international positions taken by the Chinese, as previously noted.

Cuba and the Socialist Republic of Vietnam

Symbolism and Strategy

The primary importance of Vietnam to Castro and his Cuban followers was as a symbol and force in the struggle against "U.S. imperialism." In his 1967 "Message to the Tricontinental," Ché Guevara placed Cuba and Vietnam in this global context with his comment that the Cuban Revolution "has before it a task" of creating "a second or a third Vietnam, or the second and third Vietnam of the world" so that U.S. imperialism would become over-extended and defeated, and the oppressed people of the world set free.[33] Similarly, on 2 January 1967, the beginning of the peak year of *foco* Castroism, Castro declared:

> The battle in Vietnam is being waged for all humanity, and Vietnam, victoriously and heroically standing up to the most powerful and hated imperialists in the world, is also waging a battle for us.

He then proclaimed 1967 "The Year of Heroic Vietnam."

In September 1979, after the United States had been long defeated, Castro summarized what he considered the importance of the Vietnamese experience in his remarks to the Nonaligned Movement:

No other people of recent times has paid such a high price in sacrifice, suffering and death in order to be free. No people has made a greater contribution to the national liberation struggle. No other people has done so much in this period to create a universal anti-imperialist consciousness. . . . The most powerful imperialist country had its claws cut off in Vietnam. Vietnam taught all oppressed nations that no force can defeat a people that is determined to fight for its freedom. The struggle in Vietnam reinforced the respect and unity of all our peoples.[34]

An example of the cross-fertilization of revolutions, according to Cuban leaders, is the inspiration and guidance the Cubans claim to have received from their Vietnamese comrades in incorporating the masses into a national system of self-defense against "U.S. imperialism." Shortly after President Ronald Reagan took office, an invasion scare swept Cuba, and Castro developed the concepts and practice of the "War of All the People" to prepare the nation to resist a possible U.S. attack through both unconventional and conventional methods. In late 1985, the Cubans published a series of articles by Vietnamese General Vo Nguyen Giap which explained how the armed forces could raise the level of mobilization of the masses under the leadership of the party. In his closing speech at the February session of the Third Congress in 1986, Castro pointedly thanked the Vietnamese for the role they had played and continued to play in this Cuban defense program.[35]

On a more elementary level, typical expressions of the Cuban attitude ranged from the Cuban press practice of spelling the name of U.S. President Richard Nixon with a swastika in place of the "x," to assorted expressions of admiration and camaraderie with the Vietnamese people. Examples of the latter included: the presence at the Tricontinental Conference in Havana in January 1966 of a Vietnamese militiawoman who gave Castro a ring she said was made from the wreckage of an American plane she had shot down over North Vietnam;[36] the proclamation of 1967 as the "Year of Heroic Vietnam" in Cuba; the designation of "Solidarity with Vietnam" weeks in the years that followed; the formation of an "Heroic Vietnam" sugarcane-cutting brigade; and the Cuban publication of a monthly illustrated magazine called *Vietnam*, which surveys that country's domestic and international policies. The Vietnamese communists responded in kind, for example in naming a fighting unit of the National Liberation Front in South Vietnam the "Glorious Giron Battalion" in honor of Cuba's 1961 defeat of the invading U.S.-supported "worms" at the Bay of Pigs. A Vietnamese guerrilla hero visiting Havana in 1972 lauded Castro's and Guevara's statements of support—particularly the one on "two, three, many Vietnams"—and proclaimed that the two armed nations, Vietnam and Cuba, stood together as brothers against Yankee aggression. And the Cubans often reported on U.S. servicemen (and others) who protested against U.S. policies.[37]

Cuban and Vietnamese Relations

Ties between the Cuban and Vietnamese governments took many forms over the years. The most dramatic was the sending of Cubans to serve in Vietnam during the war against the United States. In October 1966, after a visit to Hanoi by Raul Castro, Cuba offered "yet another time" to send volunteers "to fight at the side of their Vietnamese brothers against the common enemy, aggressive Yanqui imperialism." The following year, the Cuban Communist Party daily editorialized that the Cuban people were ready to "shed their blood . . . fighting at the side of the Vietnamese for their full liberation." The Cuban Communist Party Politburo did not ratify "the willingness of (Cuba) to send volunteers to fight for the Vietnamese cause when the leaders of that sister nation deem it necessary" until early 1968, clearly demonstrating that Castro—not the Communist Party—made policy on such matters.[38]

Cubans evidently were sent to Vietnam at least as early as the summer of 1967, at which time they reportedly began conducting experiments on U.S. prisoners of war. Jim Stockdale, the highest-ranking U.S. Navy officer held as a prisoner of war (for eight years after his plane was shot down in 1965), wrote in his autobiography:

> Two Cubans were out there (in Vietnam) working over Americans on a carrot-and-stick basis, evidently trying to figure out whether prisoners who had been tortured could ever be made safe bets for good Vietnamese propaganda agents in America if talked into fink releases. In the process these Cubans had driven an American out of his mind. . . .[39]

Other, more traditional contacts were made as well, some of which put the Cubans in particularly good standing with the Vietnamese communists. According to the Vietnamese Workers Party organ Nhan Dan in September 1967:

> Cuba is the first country in the world to accept a permanent mission of the NLFSV (National Liberation Front of South Vietnam), to found a national committee of solidarity with the people of South Vietnam, and to raise the South Vietnam permanent mission in Cuba to the level of an official diplomatic organ. Cuba is also the first country in the world to establish a diplomatic mission and appoint an ambassador to the NLFSV.

In March 1969, Cuba was the first country to open an embassy in South Vietnam—reportedly in a tent—which was recognized by the NLFSV. In

May, Cuba announced its full support for the ten-point program of the NLFSV and in June, became the first government to recognize the Provisional Revolutionary Government of South Vietnam (PRGSV) and raise the diplomatic representation of the NLFSV in Cuba to the status of the embassy of the PRGSV. In 1973, Castro called upon all delegates to the Fourth Conference of Nonaligned Nations in Algiers to recognize the PRGSV and then became the first head of state to visit the "liberated areas" of South Vietnam.[40]

In the years that followed, Vietnam remained the primary focus of Cuba's Asian policy, with numerous delegation exchanges. Prominent among them was the delegation led by Carlos Rafael Rodriguez, representing Cuba at the funeral of Le Duan, general secretary of the Vietnamese Communist Party, in mid-1986.

Other contacts have included exchanges and aid, emphasizing education, health, and construction—although on a lower scale than with some countries in the Americas, Africa, or the Middle East. At least as early as 1969, Cuba was providing hundreds of fellowships to Vietnamese students for technological training. According to some reports, 75 Cuban technological aid personnel were in Vietnam in the late 1970s; these may have been so-called "construction brigades" and individuals performing civilian tasks, who were in fact, civic soldiers. In 1985, the number of civilian personnel was estimated at approximately 300.[41] Undoubtedly the most controversial cooperative effort involving Cuba and Vietnam was the 1980 transfer of arms and ammunition from U.S. military stockpiles captured after the war with Vietnam, through Cuba to the guerrillas in El Salvador. Cuba also serves as a conduit for other forms of aid from other Soviet Bloc countries to the Salvadoran guerrillas.[42]

Cuba and the People's Democratic Republic of Korea

After Vietnam, North Korea was Cuba's closest ally in East and Southeast Asia. To Castro, Korea resembles Vietnam as a developing Asian country which stood up to the military challenge of "U.S. imperialism." But Korea's war was not as long, though longer ago, and the country is still divided, with its fate undecided. Over the decades, the Cuban press published statements by Korean leader Kim Il-Sung calling for the unity of North and South Korea, and blaming continuing separation on the United States. Kim and Castro stand tall in the Soviet Bloc for having established the two foremost communist family dynasties, for both leaders have designated a member of his family to succeed him in power. Cuba and the People's Democratic Republic of Korea (PDRK) established diplomatic relations in 1960. A joint communiqué issued by the two governments on 31 October 1966, at the end of a visit to Korea by Raul Castro and other Cuban leaders, asserted the two sides' "unanimous opinion that the policies adopted by both parties and governments in the current development of the international situation are correct." Both countries took a strong stand against "U.S. imperialism" and against the escalation of the Vietnam War.[43]

In late 1968, the Cuban Communist Party Central Committee had occasion to commend the Koreans for standing up to the challenges of the United States:

> The unshakable, revolutionary position of the people of Korea and their exemplary attitude with respect to the criminal activities of the Yankee spy ship *Pueblo* are an important contribution to the revolutionary cause of the whole world. This has served to demonstrate the enormous value of the firmness and determination of the peoples in the face of imperialist acts of aggression.[44]

For years thereafter, Korea and Cuba formed a front with Vietnam in militant verbal defense of the latter's cause.

After the Vietnam War ended, the Cubans increasingly charged that the United States, South Korea, and Japan had formed a "political-military triangle" that posed an "immense regional threat." As one analyst stated in 1985:

> The policy of the United States and its allies on the Korean peninsula has turned South Korea into the Asian front line in their strategic policy against communism, stability and world peace. By trying to set up an aggressive, NATO-type organization in Northeast Asia, it puts the world on the brink of a new Korean War, with the imminent danger of becoming a worldwide conflagration.[45]

Actual contacts—beyond the exchange of delegations and pronouncement of declarations—surged forward in 1985, in part inspired by the decision to hold the 1988 Olympic Games in South Korea, which both the PDRK and Cuba found unacceptable. Cuba immediately pledged to boycott the games if they were not shared with North Korea, and elevated the issue to one of an honorable stand against imperialism.

Cuba played an active role in the special meeting of ministers from the Nonaligned Movement held in Pyongyang in June 1987, during which Cuban Foreign Minister Isodoro Malmierca met with leaders from Korea and Vietnam, among other countries. Castro sent a personal message—adopted as an official document of the conference—which called for increased cooperation among Third World and "nonaligned" countries, and warned that the Third World foreign debt "cannot be paid." Malmierca followed up by calling on the industrialized countries to reduce military spending because only thus "could enough resources be freed for the cancellation of the foreign debt without affecting creditor banks. . . ." The move, he concluded, would also "strengthen world peace."[46]

There also have been unconfirmed reports that at least 3,000 Korean combat troops and 1,000 military advisers arrived in Angola between 1983 and 1986, a country where Cuba had some 35,000 troops in early 1987. Furthermore, North Korean military advisers reportedly have been training militia and special forces in several other African countries where Cuba is involved, including Zimbabwe and Uganda.[47]

In late 1985, the two countries signed their first scientific and cultural cooperation agreement, and in March 1986, Castro and Korean leader Kim Il Sung signed a 20-year Treaty of Friendship and Cooperation. The treaty pledged "strong support for the struggle of various peoples against imperialism, colonialism, neocolonialism, racism and Zionism," and added that "should the imperialists and their puppets threaten or attack one of the high contracting parties, the other will consider itself to be threatened or attacked and will lend all possible support and assistance." Castro's visit also led to a North Korean credit for Cuba to purchase 100,000 rifles and much ammunition. Castro subsequently remarked on the imperialist-imposed division of the country during his trip to Korea in early 1986 and again in his February 1987 address to the Third Party Congress.[48]

Since 1985, Cuba has pushed the International Olympic Committee (IOC) to schedule the 1988 Olympic Games in North as well as South Korea, but without success. In comments reported in *Granma* on 11 July 1986, he challenged Third World and socialist countries to boycott the games if the IOC did not permit joint hosting of the games, but as of early 1988, when Cuba announced it would not participate, only five other socialist and Third World countries were staying away: besides Cuba, there were North Korea, Nicaragua, Ethiopia, Albania, and the Seychelles Islands.

Cuba and the South Pacific Connection

Since the end of World War II, for most Americans "South Pacific" has meant little more than a Broadway musical featuring nearly forgotten superpower rivalries, Mary Martin, Ezio Pinza, and a happy-talking native whose name is a popular drink of vodka and tomato juice. How curiously appropriate that vodka association has become, for since the Vietnam War superpower rivalry has again become a factor in South Pacific affairs. However, by 1987 the competitor of the United States had become the Soviet Union and its allies, including Cuba, instead of Japan. Since the mid-1970s, the Soviet military presence has expanded rapidly in Southeast Asia—especially through ties to Vietnam—and in the South Pacific. In the latter region, Cuba plays a secondary but significant role, softening up the major islands and promoting radicalism on the smaller islands. These Cuban activities, which began seriously after the Vietnam War, reflect Castro's effort to influence noncommunist countries, and radicals out of power, in pursuit of Soviet Bloc objectives.

Cuban ties to Australia have expanded since Castro hosted the Tenth Congress of the World Federation of Trade Unions (WFTU) in 1982. These ties reportedly played an important part in the integration of Australia's Socialist Workers Party (SWP) into the pro-Soviet camp. The SWP has considerable influence in the nuclear disarmament movement, which peaked during the 1984 elections and has declined since then, and on the forces opposing the American military presence in the South Pacific. This Cuban policy is conducted along with one promoting a "Zone of Peace" in the Indian Ocean.[49] The party has pushed the line the Cubans preached at the WFTU Congress: capitalism is responsible for world hunger, and the United States for world tensions. The SWP runs the Australia-Cuba Friendship Association, the Committee in Solidarity with Central America and the Caribbean, and other such solidarity groups. It also has put Cuban intelligence officials in touch with leftist students, academics, unionists, and public servants, many of whom have done voluntary work in Cuba and Nicaragua since January 1984. On trips to the Caribbean island, these radical Australians have met revolutionary groups from other parts of the world, among them the African National Congress of South Africa and the South-West African People's Organization (SWAPO).[50]

A second important development is the Cuban relationship with the South Pacific island of Vanuatu, formerly the New Hebrides. Cuba sponsored Vanuatu to become the 155th member of the United Nations and has—along with Libya and several other Soviet Bloc countries—sent advisers to the island who have reportedly provided assistance to the radical Kanak Socialist National Liberation Front from nearby New Caledonia. The New Caledonian government even warned that its country could become "another Cuba" in the South Pacific if the Kanaks take over.[51] In late 1986, Vanuatu was considering selling access to Soviet fishing fleets and Soviet aircraft. This development came just as another South Pacific island, Kiribati, sold the Soviet Union fishing rights which may create a commercial dependency and will certainly increase Soviet intelligence opportunities in the South Pacific. The most important of these opportunities is the monitoring of the American SDI-related missile test facility just to the north.[52]

Cuba and Other Asian Countries

Cuba has demonstrated periodic interest in some other countries in East and Southeast Asia; foremost among them are Kampuchea (Cambodia) and Laos. Cuba actively promoted the removal of the Pol Pot government from the United Nations and, in recent years, has given "unconditional support" to the Vietnam-maintained government of Heng Samrin in Kampuchea. In June 1987, Cuba condemned a forthcoming congress which it claimed was convoked by China, with the complicity of Taiwan and the United States, in support of the so-called Coalition Government of Democratic Kampuchea under Pol Pot and his followers.[53] Statements on Laos are less frequent, but considerable attention is given to what Cuba calls the peace-seeking alliance of Vietnam, Kampuchea, and Laos which confronts the aggressive United States and its Association of Southeast Asian Nations (ASEAN, composed of Singapore, Indonesia, Malaysia, Thailand, and the Philippines). Support for the three countries includes not only published statements at "Nonaligned" and other conferences, but also convening their own sessions like the International Seminar in Solidarity with Vietnam, Laos and Kampuchea which was organized by OSPAAAL and held in Havana in November 1981.[54]

Typically, occasional delegations from other East and Southeast Asian countries have visited Cuba, and Cubans have stopped off in their capitals; during his June 1987 attendance at the nuclear disarmament conference in Tokyo, Jose Felipe Carneado met in Japan with delegates from East and Southeast Asia as well as other parts of the world. Limited aid programs have been conducted and in 1986, there were believed to be about 20 Cuban civilian personnel stationed in Kampuchea and 100 in Laos.[55]

Cuban Commercial Relations with Asia

Cuban commercial relations with Asia have been insignificant except with two countries—China and Japan. As the "rice war" with China in 1966 demonstrated, Castro's nationally destructive domestic development policies made the importation of Chinese rice beginning in the 1960s a matter of great importance to the Cuban people and government.[56] By 1962, Cuban rice production had plummeted by about 50 percent from 1958 levels and grain, along with other foods, was being rationed. During that year, Cuba imported 120,000 metric tons of rice from China, considerably relieving the rice ration. This increased the Cuban trade deficit with China; thus, the rice transaction was charged to a $60 million credit China had granted Cuba in 1960, on typically generous terms—payable in fifteen years, without interest. As Cuban rice production continued to decline, imports from China increased to 135,000 metric tons in 1963. In 1964, China raised the figure to 150,000 tons. However, since Cuban production had declined another 81,000 tons Castro still had to buy a lot of rice on the expensive open market.

At the end of 1964, Castro made a personal appeal to the Chinese to increase their shipments by 100,000 tons. The Chinese agreed, undoubtedly for political reasons (as Halperin noted), and sent 250,000 tons in 1965. But, having made no political headway—the Latin American Communist Party conference having been held in the meantime—and having other uses for their rice, the Chinese reduced their shipments to 135,000 in 1966, the amount sent in 1963. Castro exploded, but took the rice.

He has continued doing so until today, with quantities fluctuating above and below the 1966 level. The Chinese cut back on rice shipments and sugar purchases in 1975 because of differences with Cuba over the civil war in Angola. Between 1975 and 1983, imports from China, with few significant shifts, averaged 2.6 percent of Cuba's total imports; exports, with greater fluctuations, averaged 3.7 percent of Cuba's total exports. In value, imports between 1980 and 1983 have ranged from $146 million (1980) to $262 million (1982); exports have ranged from $161 million (1980) to $366 million (1982).[57]

Between 1961, when trade was cut with the United States, and 1981, Japan was one of Cuba's two main trading partners outside the socialist camp—where dealing in hard currencies has always been a major obstacle—though Castro considers the Japanese government a bulwark of the U.S. military force in Asia. Interestingly, it is via the embassy in Tokyo, not Hanoi or Pyongyang, that Cuba runs and monitors its activities and operations throughout East Asia.

In 1962, when Japan first became Cuba's main trading partner among market economies, that nation accounted for 2.8 percent of Cuba's total trade. In 1968, Japan accounted for 4.7 percent of Cuba's trade. Over the next ten years, Japan's percentage rose to as high as 12.4 percent (1974), and averaged 10.4 percent between 1972 and 1975. It was 3.5 percent in 1978, however, and lower thereafter, until 1983, when it had fallen to an all-time low of 1.3 percent.[58]

Trade with Vietnam, according to a Cuban trade official, should be seen in two periods. The first was from 1961 to 1977, during and just after Vietnam's war with the United States, when Cuban exports to Vietnam were, at most, 15,000 tons of sugar annually. Trade rose somewhat in 1978 when Vietnam joined the Soviet Bloc Council on Mutual Economic Assistance and both products and quantities were determined by that international organization. Total trade with Vietnam rose from $8 million in 1980 to $43 million in 1983. In 1986, sugar was still Cuba's main export to

Vietnam, though a number of other products, including textiles, medicines, and paper had by then been added. In 1986, Vietnam reportedly exported more than a dozen products to Cuba, among them rice, ornamental glass, natural rubber, and tires.[59]

Total trade with North Korea increased from $12.7 million in 1980 to $22.7 million in 1983. Total trade with Hong Kong between 1979 and 1983 was $10.5 million; with Australia, $10 million; and with Mongolia, $6.5 million.[60]

Conclusions

There is little evidence that Fidel Castro ever thought once about East or Southeast Asia before taking power in 1959. Even the major events in those regions seem to have passed him by. This is hardly surprising. Prior to 1959, Castro's primary attention had been focused largely on his homeland and the United States, secondarily on other parts of the Western Hemisphere. While it is true that he had read some books from farther afield (including parts of Marx's *Das Kapital* and Hitler's *Mein Kampf*), his active interests were more localized because local was where he was.

But there was another reason for this indifference to Asia, hinted at in Castro's maxim, "Nothing gained, nothing ventured."[61] In the final analysis, Castro always seem to ask, "What is in this relationship for me?" Consciously or otherwise, Castro repeatedly posed this question, and his answers to it have set the direction of his career, from his manipulation of *New York Times* correspondent Herbert Matthews in 1957, through his choice of allies and enemies around the world, including the East and Southeast Asia region for the nearly three decades surveyed in this chapter.[62]

Utilizing personal experiences and natural inclinations as a yardstick for measurement, Castro had a real soul-mate in China's Mao Zedong. If he had chosen his closest allies on these grounds, Castro would have formed an alliance with Mao and focused on Third World revolution in cooperation with the Chinese. For many years he would have worked on behalf of the Vietnamese as well. Given the direction of Sino/Soviet relations after 1959, which were beyond Castro's power to influence, he might have become the Albania of the Americas.

There is a high probability that Castro considered these prospects immediately after taking power. He told K.S. Karol of his early admiration for the "high revolutionary morality" of the Chinese. Many of his own convictions paralleled Mao's, and ties between the Chinese and Ché Guevara were particularly close. But taking this route would have derailed Castro's "true destiny," namely his determination to become an influential international leader at war with the United States. On the other side of the equation, the Chinese tried to pull Castro in their direction, both by promoting the Cuban model for revolution in the Third World, and giving such limited aid and trade as they could. Not the least of this assistance was the rice, which saved the Cuban people from some of the worst consequences of Castro's foolish economic policies of the 1960s, and even subsequently.

But Castro could not help seeing that the Soviet Union and its allies were geographically closer, relatively richer, and more technologically advanced, and that Moscow was the effective international center of hostility toward the United States. Castro correctly calculated that the Soviet Union would pay plenty and put up with a lot from him to get an ally just off the shores of the United States. In one of the most coldly calculated, unprincipled, self-serving, and effective decisions of his career, Castro concluded that he would have much more to gain by siding with the Soviet Union and its allies. And, in typical Castro fashion, he turned on the Chinese in a thoroughly dishonest way, spewing distortions and falsehoods to smear the Chinese, and to some degree, ingratiate himself with the Soviet Union. Thus, given the development of the Sino/Soviet dispute and Castro's stake in Moscow, the direction of Cuban relations with the major communist power of East Asia was set for decades to come.

Castro's main interest in the region became Vietnam, for obvious reasons: Vietnam was a Third World country at war with the First World, and most importantly, with the United States. Furthermore, the Vietnamese leaders never attempted to sell their model of revolution abroad, and thus offered no challenge to Castro's goal of becoming the guru of the Third World Revolution.

The Cuban leader particularly welcomed the Vietnam War and promoted the Vietnamese communist cause for several reasons. Foremost, it galvanized international opposition to the United States, and in time, discredited the U.S. government—at home and abroad—and reduced its ability to influence events beyond its borders. Indeed, the defeat in Vietnam caused the U.S. to withdraw, in some degree, from world affairs and, in particular, from active opposition to revolutionary movements in the Third World. Thus, even without the "two, three, many Vietnams" Guevara and Castro wanted, the one Vietnam relieved some of the pressures on Havana and opened doors to Cuban activities, in varying degrees of cooperation with the Soviet Union, particularly in Africa and the Caribbean Basin. If some of this increased security for revolutionary movements disappeared with the advent of the Reagan administration, even the new American president was, to some degree, tied down by much of the Vietnam legacy.

And beyond the war's impact on the international balance of power—or correlation of forces—Castro used the conflict to elevate his own position as spokesman for the "oppressed world." In the so-called Nonaligned Movement and beyond, Castro promoted Vietnam. The latter was promoted first against the United States, and at the end of the 1970s against China, which the Cuban leader said had become an ally of the United States. In many countries around the world, sympathy for the Vietnamese cause was accompanied by some admiration for Castro. It likewise appeared to some as seemingly selfless revolutionary solidarity.

Any weakening of the United States benefited Castro and his position in the world. But it also strengthened the Soviet Union. By his support for Vietnam and Korea, in particular, Castro has drawn attention to what Cubans refer to as the warmongering ASEAN bloc, and the Tripartite Military Alliance of the United States, Japan, and South Korea. An important campaign serving Soviet Bloc objectives has been the one to turn U.S. allies in Asia into neutrals or active opponents of U.S. policy. This has been reflected in rising opposition to the United States and its nuclear presence in the Indian and Pacific Oceans, manifested in many ways, from shifting political orientations in New Zealand to the June 1987 nuclear disarmament conference in Tokyo.

On a more tangible level, Cuban ties to the countries of East and Southeast Asia have put some Cuban military, intelligence, and civilian experts in positions of some importance in the region's governments. The Cubans themselves have gained from some of the trade—especially, at times, with Japan, and even after the 1966 and subsequent showdowns, with the Chinese.

There can be no escape from the fact that East Asia, Southeast Asia, and the South Pacific have generally been something of an international affairs sideshow for Castro. Policies toward this region have complemented his main, and in most cases more deadly, performances in Africa and Latin America, often in cooperation with the Soviet Union. But these policies have likewise been a complement of some consequence, because they helped elevate Castro to a leadership role in the Third World and beyond. In addition, they helped the Cuban leader repay the Soviet Union for the critical role it has played in making the Maximum Leader what he has been over the decades. And in this sense, above all, he has served the Soviet Union and struck a blow at the hated United States.

Notes

1. Said to be from an unpublished—probably unwritten—autobiography by Fidel Castro, doubtless without abject apologies to Herman Melville.

2. K.S. Karol, *Guerrillas in Power: The Course of the Cuban Revolution* (New York: Hill & Wang, 1970), p. 386. It should be recalled that Karol is grinding a sharp pro-Chinese/anti-Soviet ax in this volume and bitterly lamenting Castro's noisy public denunciations of the Chinese in early 1966.

3. According to Karol, many Castroists in the late 1960s said that their Revolutionary Offensive was "a Cuban version of the Cultural Revolution." *Guerrillas in Power,* p. 441; see also pp. 306 and 549. And Hugh Thomas, a much more objective observer, writes in *The Cuban Revolution* (New York: Harper Torchbooks, 1977), p. 669, that the Cuban Revolutionary Offensive owned much in inspiration to the example of the Cultural Revolution. On the other hand, Castro once told a reporter from the New York Times that "If we did some things like the Chinese Communists . . . it was an accident of history." Herbert Matthews, *Fidel Castro* (New York: Simon and Schuster, 1969), p. 193.

4. In a remarkable example of the pot calling the kettle black, Cuban analysts have actually criticized the Chinese for carrying out "hasty anarchic measures" and for fomenting splits in the revolutionary movement, two of Fidel Castro's own great specialties. See Estrella Rey, "Beijing's Policies in Latin America," *Tricontinental,* No. 82 (1982), pp. 30–42. The Afro-Asian-Latin American People's Solidarity Organization (OSPAAAL), which publishes *Tricontinental,* is not an official Cuban government agency, though from its founding in 1966 it has been completely controlled by the Cubans and its usually bimonthly journal, *Tricontinental,* always emphasizes issues and analyses promoted by the Cuban government. Most of its articles are by Cubans.

5. On these and other parallels, see my "Cuba" in Richard F. Staar (ed.), *1969 Yearbook on International Communist Affairs* (Stanford, Calif.: Hoover Institution Press, 1970), esp. pp. 201–202. See also Carmelo Mesa-Lago, "Present and Future of Revolution," in C. Mesa-Lago (ed.), *Revolutionary Change in Cuba* (Pittsburgh, Penn.: University of Pittsburgh Press, 1971), esp. pp. 510–24. It is not clear what influence Mao's writings on guerrilla warfare may have had on Castro's forces before and during their times in the Sierra Maestra. Regis Debray, in his *Revolution in the Revolution?* (New York: Bantam Books, 1967), p. 20, says the Cubans encountered Mao's *Problems of Strategy in Guerrilla War Against Japan* after they had worked everything out for themselves. Ché Guevara, on the other hand, both acknowledged and denied Chinese influence: see my "A New Old Che Guevara Interview," *Hispanic American Historical Review* (August 1966), pp. 289–90.

6. Rey, p. 35.

7. Quoted in Thomas, p. 278.

8. On Castro's decision to turn to the Soviet Union, see Tad Szulc, *Fidel: A Critical Portrait* (New York: William Morrow and Co., 1986), pp. 463–78, and 510.

9. See *Granma,* weekly English edition, supplement, 14 December 1986, p. 12.

10. Wang Shou-peng, "Latin American Literature Comes to China," *China Reconstructs* (October 1960), p. 14. Also see my "Chinese Communist Cultural Diplomacy Toward Latin America," *Hispanic American Historical Review* (February 1969), pp. 53–79 passim, and Carmelo Mesa-Lago and Shirley Kregar, *Latin American Studies in Asia* (Pittsburgh, Penn.: Center for Latin American Studies, 1983), p. 30.

11. On PSP support for Chinese experiences, see articles by top party leaders in the PSP organ *Hoy* (Havana): Carlos Rafael Rodriguez (24 May 1959), Blas

Roca (6 October 1959) and Anibal Escalante (19 August 1960). See also Theodore Draper, *Castroism: Theory and Practice* (New York: Praeger, 1965), pp. 81–84, and Thomas, pp. 137, and 537.

12. See *Peking Review* (13 December 1960), p. 41. See also Chou En-Lai's comments to Guevara in ibid. (22 November 1960), p. 5; and Mao Zedong's remarks in 1962 to an Argentine visitor, in Bernardo Kordon, *Testigos de China* (Buenos Aires: Carlos Perez, 1968), p. 14.

13. See Ratliff, "Chinese Communist Cultural Diplomacy," pp. 59, and 73; and William Ratliff, "Communist China and Latin America," *Asian Survey* (October 1972), p. 854.

14. The text of the communiqué, in *Cuba Socialista* (February 1965), pp. 140–42, is translated in William Ratliff, *Castroism and Communism in Latin America* (Stanford, Calif.: Hoover Institution Press, 1976), pp. 195–98.

15. See *Zeri i popullit*, Tirana, 16 February 1960.

16. See Ratliff, "Communist China and Latin America," esp. pp. 853–57 and Ratliff, *Castroism and Communism*, pp. 17–25.

17. Castro, "Discurso pronunciado el 13 de Marzo de 1966," in *Política Internacional de la Revolución Cubana* (Havana: Editora Política, 1966), esp. pp. 186–89, and 245–48; see also Ratliff, "Communist China and Latin America," p. 855.

18. Maurice Halperin, *The Taming of Fidel Castro* (Berkeley: University of California Press, 1981), p. 206. For Halperin's detailed analysis of the dispute and its underpinnings, see pp. 195–207.

19. Fidel Castro, *Report of the Central Committee of the Communist Party of Cuba to the First Congress* (Havana: Department of Revolutionary Orientation of the CC of the PCC, 1977), p. 339.

20. Castro speech of 21 February 1979, "Vietnam is Not Alone," *Fidel Castro Speaks* (New York: Pathfinder Press, 1981), pp. 145, and 139.

21. Castro speech of 3 September, in ibid., p. 171; "Resolutions Adopted by the 2nd Congress of the CPC," *Second Congress of the Communist Party of Cuba: Documents and Speeches* (Havana: Political Publishers, 1981), p. 355; and Carlos Iglesias, "The Alliance Against Progress," *Tricontinental*, No. 77 (1981), pp. 46, 48, and 50.

22. Havana Domestic Service, 4 February 1986, in *Foreign Broadcast Information Service*, Latin America, 7 February. Among the frictions was imprisonment for 20 years of a Cuban convicted of espionage on behalf of China; the public prosecutor list accused him of "maintenance of a Maoist, pro-China, anti-Soviet and non-Cuban attitude, detrimental to the international solidarity practiced by Cuba." Quoted in *Amnesty International Report 1986* (London: Amnesty International Publications, 1986), p. 145.

23. Statement by the pro-Chinese Communist Party of Ceylon, in *Peking Review* (25 February 1966), p. 24.

24. Guevara had not argued this line in his famous book *Guerrilla Warfare*, published in 1960 and circulated throughout the Americas. There he wrote that "where a government has come to power through any form of popular consultation, fraudulent or not, and maintains at least an appearance of constitutional legality, it is impossible to bring about a guerrilla outbreak inasmuch as all the possibilities of civic struggle have not been exhausted." See *Che Guevara: Escritos y Discursos* (Havana: Editorial de Ciencias Sociales, 1977), Vol. I, p. 34.

25. For a survey of the conference, see Ratliff, *Castroism and Communism,* pp. 199–208.

26. Guevara's aide was Cuban Communist Party Central Committee member Harry Villegas Tamayo; see entry of 15 November 1966 in "Pombo's Diary," in Daniel James (ed.), *The Complete Bolivian Diaries of Che Guevara and Other Captured Documents* (New York: Stein and Day, 1968), p. 287. For Guevara's "Message," see Rolando Bonachea and Nelson Valdes (eds.), *Che: Selected Works of Ernesto Guevara* (Cambridge, Mass.: MIT Press, 1969), p. 182.

27. See Fidel Castro, "Una Introducción Necesaria," *Ernesto Che Guevara: Escritos y Discursos,* Vol. 3, p. 10, translated in *The Diary of Che Guevara* (New York: Bantam Books, 1968), p. 14; Oscar Zamora M., "Partido Comunista de Bolivia (ML) responde a Fidel Castro," *Causa Marxista-Leninista,* Santiago, Chile. (January–February 1969), p. 36; Inti Peredo, *Mi campaña con el Ché* (Buenos Aires: Edibol, 1971), p. 47.

28. See *Peking Review* (20 October 1967), p. 31.

29. See Ibid. (21 June 1968), p. 14.

30. See *Política Internacional de la Revolución Cubana,* 1971, Vol. I, p. 186.

31. Movement of the Revolutionary Left (MIR) was a popular name for revolutionary organizations in Latin America after 1960. Usually MIRs had a Castroite orientation, as did the MIR in Chile; only in Uruguay was it pro-Chinese.

32. See Partido Comunista Revolucionario de Chile, *Una linea pequeno-burguesa y una linea proletaria* (Santiago, Chile: Espartaco, 1967), pp. 30, and 31; and Movimiento de Izquierda Revolucionaria, *Tupamaros, Conspiración or Revolución? Repuesta de los Marxistas-Leninistas del Uruguay* (Montevideo: Ediciones Voz Obrera, 1970).

33. See *Bonachea and Valdez,* pp. 178–79. Several pages later Guevara mentions the "two, three or many Vietnams" quoted above.

34. Fidel Castro, *Granma,* weekly English edition, 8 January 1967; and Castro, *Fidel Castro Speaks,* pp. 170–71.

35. See *El Oficial,* September, October, and November 1985; and Havana Domestic Service, 7 February 1986. Cuban analysts lauded Ho Chi Minh as an unsurpassed statesman, strategist, politician, and guerrilla who maintained single party leadership and united all patriotic forces for the war of all the people; Luis Arce, "Vietnam: On the Path to Glory," *Tricontinental,* No. 104 (1986), pp. 27–37.

36. Carla Anne Robbins, *The Cuban Threat* (New York: McGraw-Hill, 1983), pp. 31–32.

37. See Nguyen Van Quang, "Only a Hero," *Tricontinental,* Nos. 27–28 (1972), p. 143; and David Dorey, "Soldiers Against the War," Ibid., No. 31 (1972), pp. 78–93.

38. See *Documentos de Política Internacional de la Revolucion Cubana* (Havana: Instituto Cubano del Libro, 1971), p. 43; *Granma,* English, 18 July 1967 and 15 February 1968. Vietnamese guerrilla Nguyen Van Quang pointedly thanked the Cubans for their offer of troops in "Only a Hero," p. 143.

39. Jim and Sybil Stockdale, *In Love and War* (New York: Harper and Row, 1984), p. 348.

40. See my articles on Cuba in Richard Staar (ed.), *Yearbook on International Communist Affairs,* 1968 edition, pp. 149–50; 1970 edition, p. 395; 1971 edition, p. 420; and H. Michael Erisman, *Cuba's International Relations* (Boulder, Colo.: Westview Press, 1985), pp. 64, and 47.

41. See my article in *Yearbook on International Communist Affairs*, 1970 edition, p. 395; Erisman, p. 79; Jorge Dominguez, "The Armed Forces and Foreign Relations," in Cole Blasier and Carmelo Mesa-Lago (eds.), *Cuba in the World* (Pittsburgh, Penn.: University of Pittsburgh Press, 1979), pp. 65–66; and U.S. Defense Intelligence Agency, *Handbook on the Cuban Armed Forces* (Washington: DIA, May 1986) p. 8:19.

42. U.S. Departments of State and Defense, *The Challenge to Democracy in Central America* (Washington, October 1986), pp. 48–49; U.S. Department of State, *Revolution Beyond Our Borders: Sandinista Intervention in Central America* (Washington, September 1985), esp. pp. 119–22. Some 66 percent of 1,600 M-16 rifles captured in El Salvador between 1981 and 1985 can be traced by their serial numbers to the Vietnam War. Documents on the Vietnam connection were published by the U.S. Department of State, *Communist Influence in El Salvador* (Washington, February 1981). This connection was confirmed by an independent observer, William Shawcross, who traveled to Vietnam in 1981 and asked a Vietnamese military official: "Had Vietnam been distributing any of the vast pile of weapons left by Americans? Colonel Bui Tin acknowledged, in effect, that it had. In Salvador? 'It's not fair to say the U.S. can help the junta but we cannot help our friends. We do our best to support revolutionary movements in the world.' " Shawcross, *New York Review of Books* (14 September 1981). For an example of the other aid, see report of "comprehensive donations" from the German Democratic Republic to the Farabundo Martí de Liberación Nacional (FMLN) through Cuba, on East Berlin ADN International Service, 25 May 1987, in *FBIS*, Latin America, 26 May, Q2.

43. See *Documentos de Política Internacional*, III, pp. 30–37.

44. See *Granma*, English edition, 20 October 1968.

45. See Mauro Garcia Triana, "The Aggressive Policy of the U.S. and its Allies on the Korean Peninsula," *Tricontinental*, No. 102 (1985), pp. 53–69.

46. See Castro's message, broadcast on Havana Radio Rebelde Network on 11 June, in *FBIS*, Latin America, 12 June; Malmierca's address, on Havana Television on 11 June, is in *FBIS*, 12 June.

47. Radio Martí, *Cuba: Quarterly Situation Report* (QSR) (January–March 1986), section II, pp. 23–25; and *Cuba: QSR* (July–September 1986), II, p. 27.

48. See *Granma*, English edition, 11 and 12 March 1986.

49. According to Havana's Radio Reloj (16 June 1987), an Australian delegation attended a symposium on nuclear disarmament in Tokyo, sponsored by the Communist Party of Japan, and met with Cuban Communist Party Central Committee member Jose Felipe Carneado. Carneado had addressed the meeting on the need to remove nuclear weapons from the region. Radio Reloj (16 June 1987), in *FBIS*, 18 June. On the Australian situation, see *Washington Post*, 21 June 1987. On the Cuban campaign for a "Zone of Peace" in the Indian Ocean, see Castro's speech to the UN General Assembly on 12 October 1979 and Miguel D'Estefano's "The Indian Ocean: An Angle of the Afro-Asian Problem," *Tricontinental*, No. 73 (1980).

50. See John Whitehall, "Peace in the Pacific," *Freedom at Issue* (September–October 1984), p. 13; *Social Action*, October 1985; Havana Domestic Service, 16 January 1984, in *FBIS*, Latin America, 18 January; and Havana Television, 26 January 1984, in *FBIS*, 27 January. I am grateful to Douglas Payne and Bruce McColm for furnishing some of the materials used in this section.

51. See *Washington Post,* 5 December 1984.
52. William Branigin, "Soviet Military Operations Seen Increasing in the Pacific," *Washington Post,* 1 August 1986; AP wire report, "Soviet Influence Up in South Pacific," *Journal of Commerce,* 5 August, 1986.
53. See, for example, Virgilio Calvo, "Recognition of the People's Republic of Kampuchea," *Tricontinental,* No. 75 (1981); Havana Television, 2 June, in *FBIS,* Latin America, 3 June.
54. On Laos, see Francisco Ramirez, "Laos: Five Years of Encouraging Progress," *Tricontinental,* No. 79 (1982); and on the communist alliance, see Mirta Rodriguez Calderon, "From Asia: Hopes and Concerns," ibid., No. 89 (1983), and Estrella Rey's already cited report to the Havana seminar in ibid., No. 80 (1982).
55. Defense Intelligence Agency (DIA), *Handbook on the Cuban Armed Forces,* p. 8:19.
56. Most of the figures on Cuban rice production and importation come from Halperin, pp. 195–207.
57. United Nations Department of International Economic and Social Affairs, *1983 International Trade Statistics Yearbook,* (New York, 1985) Vol. I, p. 205.
58. See *1983 International Trade Statistics Yearbook,* p. 205, and Carmelo Mesa-Lago, *The Economy of Socialist Cuba* (Albuquerque: University of New Mexico Press, 1981), p. 93.
59. Interview with German Callejas, deputy director of the Cuban Foreign Trade Ministry, Havana International Service, 31 October 1986, in *FBIS,* Latin America, 4 November; and *1983 International Trade Statistics Yearbook,* p. 205.
60. See *1983 International Trade Statistics Yearbook,* p. 205.
61. I have not been able to track down where Castro made this remark; it may even be apocryphal.
62. On the Matthew's affair, see William Ratliff, "The New York Times and the Cuban Revolution," in Ratliff (ed.), *The Selling of Fidel Castro: The Media and the Cuban Revolution* (New Brunswick, N.J.: Transaction Books, 1987), p. 5. For an excellent analysis of Castro's motivations and operational style, see Edward Gonzalez and David Ronfeldt, *Castro, Cuba, and the World* (Santa Monica, Calif.: Rand Corp., 1986).

8

Cuba's Relations with Europe and Canada: Accommodation and Challenges

Scott B. MacDonald

Introduction

The relationship between the nations of Western Europe and Canada and Cuba since Fidel Castro came to power in 1959 has been characterized by elements of both accommodation and challenge. For their part, the European nations have accommodated, in varying degrees, to the Cuban revolution. This has meant maintaining diplomatic and trade relations, occasionally provoking disapproval from the United States. Such policies provided Cuba with a degree of access to the West that would otherwise be lost due to Washington's attempts to contain the spread and acceptance of the Castroite revolution. At the same time, Western European nations, especially those with national interests that collide with those of Cuba, have found the relationship a challenge. The French, in particular, have been willing to meet a Cuban or Cuban-inspired challenge, in either the Caribbean or Africa in the late 1970s and 1980s. While most Western European nations have alternated between accommodation and challenge with Cuba since 1959, Canada's policy has been principally accommodationist. This has been largely the result of the Canadian/American relationship and the northern nation's quest for a separate identity and foreign policy, apart from its larger and more powerful southern neighbor.

This chapter will examine the parameters of Cuba's relationship with Europe (referring to Western Europe) and Canada. At a very fundamental level, the "who gets what and why" in the various relationships will be analyzed. The chapter's emphasis is on country-to-country relations, and many of the conclusions offered are generalizations.[1]

In this context, it is advanced that the Castro regime has long used its ties to Western European nations and Canada to maintain an open door to the West through which Cuba has sought to obtain a package of goods that its major international patron, the Soviet Union, has been either unable or disinclined to supply. This package of goods ranges from access to commercial credits from European and Canadian banks to manufactured goods and, when possible, high-technology products. For Cuba, the motivation is clear-cut: initial stages of relations (1959–68) functioned, in a very limited way, to create a third pole of influence beyond those of the United States and the Soviet Union. Specifically, ties to Canada and France were particularly important as these nations clearly sought to be independent of U.S. policy. However, as Cuba increasingly turned to closer linkages with Moscow in the late 1960s and early 1970s, the relationship between the Caribbean nation and Europe changed. Fidel Castro's endorsement of the 1968 Soviet invasion of Czechoslovakia was especially distasteful to Europeans, and helped place a certain distance between their governments and Havana.

In the mid-1970s, as Cuban troops fought wars in Angola and Ethiopia, advisers were sent to Mozambique, Cape Verde, Guinea, Afghanistan, and South Yemen, and Katagian secessionists sought to cut Shaba province from pro-Western Zaire, the overall European assessment of the Castro regime developed in two dimensions. The first dimension was strictly related to each European nation's global perception. Although rarely stated by European officials, the concept of spheres of influence has considerable continuity in foreign policy matters. While the Western Hemisphere begrudgingly evolved as an American sphere in the twentieth century, and Eastern Europe with little choice as a Russian sphere, Africa was and, to a certain extent, remains a European sphere. Consequently, West Europeans have not found events in Central America and the Caribbean as alarming as the Americans. As Wolf Grabendorff commented: "Many West Europeans who have come to accept the ever-present missiles on the other side of the Iron Curtain as a fact of life find it hard to understand the 'Cuban trauma' that has haunted U.S. policymakers since the Cuban missile crisis and that seems to be of special importance to the Reagan administration."[2] Thus, Western Europe has maintained diplomatic and trade relations with Cuba, even in the face of American opposition.

For France, West Germany, Belgium, Spain, Italy, and Portugal, African nations represent markets for their goods, capital, and expertise. Colonial linkages are maintained through such multinational organizations as the

Commonwealth and the Lomé accords between the European Economic Community (EEC) and the African, Caribbean, and Pacific (ACP) nations. Moreover, financial, technical, and military personnel from France, the United Kingdom, Belgium, and Portugal operate in many former colonies.

Cuban involvement in African affairs—the actual buildup of over 20,000 troops in Angola, 14,000–16,000 troops in Ethiopia, and a sprinkling of advisers throughout the sub-Saharan region—caused some of the European nations to take a different approach to Cuba outside of the Western Hemisphere than when dealing with Cuba in the Western Hemisphere. While trade (defined within the parameters of the U.S. high-technology embargo) has continued, there has been an overall hardening of views vis-à-vis Cuba. Cuban policy objectives of creating a regional environment of friendly regimes collide with a quiet, yet resurgent, European role in Latin America, especially in the Caribbean, where the French, British, and Dutch still have a presence.

The second dimension of European policy, and, to a large degree, the premise of Canadian policy, has been to quietly court Fidel Castro in the hope that if shown the benefits of close relations with the West, ties to Moscow will be gradually loosened. In addition, without the U.S. military "sword of Damocles" hanging over the Cuban head, the Castro regime might ultimately move toward a more open and pluralistic society. At the very least, this policy, favored by such nations as Sweden and Canada, seeks to maintain an opening to the West. At the maximum, it seeks to diminish Soviet ties and create a more democratic Cuba, one that leans toward a third—namely, European—pole of influence. It would appear that this dimension of European policy is usually pursued until accommodation results in a clash of interests, particularly outside of the American sphere of influence. Even within that sphere, a hard line of military policy, as exemplified by the existence of French, Dutch, and British troops in the Caribbean and joint training programs with American forces, is still pursued.

Cuba and Canada

One of the most enduring relations with the West for Cuba has been with Canada. The relationship has encompassed trade, cultural exchanges, state visits between dignitaries of both nations, and lines of credit. It has also been the source of some American/Canadian tension, especially during the Cuban missile crisis. To understand this triangle of Cuba, Canada, and the United States, it is necessary to understand the Canadian perception of international relations, as well as Canada's vision of its place in the Western Hemisphere.

In the twentieth century, particularly since the two World Wars, Canada and the United States changed from "mere neighbors to seemingly inextricably associated trading partners and allies."[3] Force, or the threat of force, was not part of the relationship, though Canadians have found it irritating that American policymakers often forget that they exist. This has generally been an issue during trade legislation.

For Canada, there is another danger in the close relationship with the United States: such close ties have been perceived as a threat to the development of a Canadian national identity apart from the larger and culturally influential southern nation. Additional concerns have been generated by apprehension over control of the Canadian economy relating to American direct foreign investment. Considering these factors, Canada in the mid-twentieth century, especially during the Trudeau periods in the 1970s, has sought equilibrium in the conduct of its foreign affairs. As a leading scholar on Canadian affairs, Charles Doran, has noted:

> Just as Canada thought of herself as a "linchpin" between Britain and America during the World Wars I and II, so Canada seeks today to act as the linchpin between the United States and the Southern Hemisphere. Regardless of the triangle as far as Canada is concerned, however, Canada occupies one corner, the United States, a second, and a third actor (or actors) has always been sought to complete the equilibrium.[4]

The integrationist mentality of the United States has also reinforced the Canadian need to emphasize a separate identity. One of the areas in which this issue of separate identity has been most evident has been in foreign affairs. While the Southern Hemisphere may be the third party of the triangle, Cuba, as a distinctive member of that group, has played a larger role than most, as it has been a nation over which American and Canadian policies sharply diverge.

The parameters of Canada's relationship with Cuba and, for that matter, with the rest of Latin America, are defined by two common themes: 1) the United States is the dominant power in the Western Hemisphere; and 2) in certain government circles and the academic community, Cuba and other Latin American nations have been victims of U.S. imperialism. In turn, Canadians perceive themselves as experiencing similar problems in the preservation of national independence in the face of American dominance.[5]

When Castro came to power in 1959, Canada was one of the major economic powers on the island, largely involved in banking and other forms of commerce. That situation changed, however, when the Royal Bank of Canada and other major banks were nationalized by the new government. While Canada remained a somewhat distant friend, receiving reparations for its assets, American/Cuban relations deteriorated sharply in the 1959–61 period. The divergence between Washington and Ottawa over Cuba was further marked by the latter's disdain for the Bay of Pigs fiasco in 1961, and by Canada's slow response to side with the U.S. during the Cuban missile crisis in 1962. At the time of the missile crisis, Canadian Prime Minister John Diefenbaker, angered by the lack of advance consultation and concerned that a Canadian alert would provoke the Soviets and damage his government's uncertain stand on nuclear weapons, hesitated for three days before agreeing.[6] Canada did, however, agree to prohibit the exportation of items on the controlled goods list, granting only a limited number of low-technology products for sale to Cuba. Since the 1960s, permits have not been issued for military or strategic goods and no American product that has been changed in value, form, or use in Canada can be exported to Cuba.

While Canada joined the high-technology embargo of Cuba, at the same time it refused to join a full U.S.-led economic embargo of Cuba. This refusal was the reason for declining membership in the Inter-American System. The argument advanced was that Canada preferred its freedom to maintain diplomatic and trade relations with Cuba over membership in the Organization of American States (OAS), if the latter meant having to adhere to OAS sanctions against the Caribbean nation. The transparency of Canada's claim to the moral high ground was evident in 1975, when OAS sanctions were dropped and Canada still declined the organization's membership. As has been noted: "Apparently Canada's real reason for remaining aloof from Pan Americanism is its perception of U.S. primacy in the Inter-American System and an aversion to submitting to a further form of U.S. dominance in addition to existing U.S. economic and cultural influence."[7]

Cuban/Canadian relations reached a high point during the administrations of Liberal Prime Minister Pierre Trudeau (1968–79 and 1980–84), as his governments demonstrated more interest in Latin America than any of their predecessors. For Trudeau, American dominance was indeed a concern shared with Castro, and the two nations maintained stable trade relations. At the same time, Trudeau's strong nationalism and his occasional anti-American rhetoric appealed to the Cuban leader. This perception of shared common ground in dealing with the United States provided the fundamental basis for a smooth relationship between Havana and Ottawa and led, at times, to tensions with the United States.

In 1972, the U.S. and Canada clashed over a major trade deal between the Cuban government and a Montreal subsidiary of Studebaker-Worthington, Inc., of Harrison, New Jersey. The company had an offer to sell 25 diesel locomotives to Cuba, legal under Canadian laws, but not permitted under U.S. regulations. The stakes were high for Canada: the sale would earn the Montreal subsidiary $18 million and maintain employment for about 2,000 workers. Considering the positive effects on employment and profit for his nation, Trudeau gave his approval, over American protestations. The Nixon administration regarded this as another indication of the Liberal Canadian's leftist views, while the Canadian perception was best summarized in the *Montreal Gazette:* "How many people lie awake at night worrying about a massive locomotive attack from Cuba?"[8]

Trudeau also benefited from relations with Cuba in 1970. The two governments cooperated when Cuba agreed to provide asylum to the Canadian kidnappers of British Trade Commissioner James Cross in exchange for the life of the victim. The smoothness of Cuban/Canadian ties was further evidenced in bilateral cooperation that held the hijacking of Canadian aircraft to a minimum, in Cuban purchases of Canadian products that helped the northern nation's economy, and in Cuba becoming one of Canada's best customers in Latin America, behind the larger nations of Brazil, Venezuela, and Mexico. Moreover, Cuba has become a popular tourist destination for Canadians seeking a vacation in warmer climates.

For Cuba, the relationship has been exceedingly positive. Although the Cuban trade delegation in Montreal was bombed in Canada in 1972 (possibly conducted by Canadian intelligence to gather information), the Trudeau government was willing to tolerate Cuban military activities in Angola and Ethiopia, while making little fuss over the Cuban presence in Grenada after the New Jewel Movement's March 1979 coup.[9]

Trudeau, in his support of the Third World, and in an effort to bolster Canada's ties to Latin America, visited Cuba in 1976 along with Mexico and Venezuela. As noted by two Canadian scholars, the Liberal leader was ". . . a supporter of left-of-center political and social revolutions in Latin America."[10] Castro, therefore, had at least a modicum of support from one of the more developed nations in the world, and found what some might regard as a weakness in the U.S. policy of containment.

Cuba's trade is clearly dominated by the Soviet Union, and Canada ranks well behind that nation and the Eastern European nations of Bulgaria, Czechoslovakia, and Poland. In 1985, Canada accounted for 4 percent of Cuba's exports and 11.3 percent of its imports, with total trade having a value of $302.5 million. The terms of trade were substantially in favor of Canada: in 1985 Cuba's deficit with Canada was $239 million.[11] This trend has been evident throughout most of the post-1959 period, and it is likely that the difference has largely been made up by Soviet balance of payments assistance. Considering the terms of trade, Canada has been an important market for Cuban sugar, molasses, shrimp, lobster, and tobacco. In turn, Cuba imports Canadian wheat, flour, and corn. In 1984, of all sugar imported into the Canadian market, Cuba accounted for 26 percent, following Australia and just ahead of South Africa.[12]

In recent years, Canada has occasionally found itself on the same side as Cuba regarding Caribbean and Central American affairs, creating yet another area of tension with Washington. The Trudeau administration has disagreed with U.S. policy toward the Sandinista regime in Nicaragua since 1979, as well as its handling of the New Jewel Movement (NJM) regime in Grenada. The Canadian response to the self-destruction of the Grenadian revolution and the subsequent U.S.-led intervention in October 1983 was reflected in the publication *Canada and the World:* "However, does the end justify the means? A free Grenada may be a fine aim, but is invasion justified as a means of getting there?"[13]

Canada had provided economic assistance to the NJM government and did not appear to have any major problems with the Cuban mission there. The self-destruction of the Grenadian revolution and the U.S.-dominated intervention came as rude shocks to the Canadians, especially as the regional governments involved turned to Washington, capital of the Canadian "big brother," and not Ottawa. This occurred, in large part, because of the perceived need for quick and resolute action in Grenada—action which the United States was willing to immediately take—as opposed to the probable Canadian response of seeking to develop negotiations with Bernard Coard, the hard-line Marxist who had killed Bishop. The Canadian view was typified in *Canada and the World:* "Most other Western countries, including Canada, feel that negotiation and moderation would have been better means to arrive at democracy on the island."[14]

Lacking a sphere of influence, Canada has continued to perceive the world in a different fashion than the United States. Thus, an open door to relations with Cuba has been allowed despite ideological differences, particularly in terms of the structure of the two nations' political systems. As has been noted of Canada's relations with Central American states, "Canada does not see conflicts in the area as an East/West issue as much as a North/South issue. . . . It feels all diplomatic actions taken should emphasize pragmatism rather than ideology, although Canada gives top priority to protection of human rights." This likewise provides insight into Canada's approach to Cuba.[15] In Cuban/Canadian relations, each nation has found the linkage to be a means of emphasizing its independence from its larger and possibly threatening neighbor (at least in economic and cultural areas). At the same time, Canada has been able to pursue lucrative trade, heavily in its favor, with a nation in which it need not compete with the United States. Furthermore, the pragmatic element of Canada's Cuban policy has been to ignore, in most cases, human rights violations, illustrating that a demonstration of Canadian independence vis-à-vis the United

States and a profitable trade balance weigh heavier on Ottawa's agenda than the Castro regime's human rights violations.

Cuba and Europe: The Spanish Equation

With regard to the component of trade in bilateral relations, Spain has had the most substantial commercial relationship with Cuba, especially in the 1980s. It should also be stressed that the relationship has developed along other lines: until 1898, Cuba was a Spanish colony.[16] Although Spain's global empire has long since disappeared, there remains an Iberian interest in its former colonies and the Spanish/Cuban relationship has evolved along in its own peculiar fashion. It was the Spanish-American War that broke the link between colony and motherland, but formal ties between the sovereign state of Cuba and Spain were maintained through the Spanish Civil War and the ensuing Franco era. Franco insisted on retaining diplomatic relations with Castro's Cuba, despite obvious ideological differences. For the Spanish fascist general and the revolutionary Cuban *lider maximo,* the relationship benefited national interests. Both nations gained by trade and diplomatic contact in light of their relative isolation in the 1960s: Spain was regarded as a brutish authoritarian regime almost alien to the new postwar democratic Western Europe; and Cuba was perceived as a revolutionary leper, capable of and willing to export radical revolution to the rest of the Americas.

The revitalization of democracy in Spain in the 1970s renewed an interest in Latin America and vice versa. As has been noted: "Spain hopes to act as a broker between Latin American concerns and other EC members over external debt rescheduling, protectionist and preferential EC trade policies, interest rates, and other issues."[17] The renewed interest in Latin America, and for that matter Cuba, came in 1976, the first year of democracy under Prime Minister Suarez (1976–81), who quietly maintained diplomatic relations with the Castro regime already established under Franco. As Spanish democracy was consolidated under Calvo Sotelo's administration (1981–82) and Felipe Gonzales since 1983, Madrid has pursued an active diplomacy, allying itself with "progressive" forces in the Caribbean and Latin America. Support was given to the Contadora Group in its search for a peaceful Central American solution, and Spanish good offices were used in facilitating contacts between Colombian President Belisario Betancur and various guerrilla leaders (some of whom were backed by Cuba) interested in an amnesty.[18] These "services" were also extended to Salvadoran political exiles and guerrillas. In addition, strong relations were established with the newly democratic governments in Argentina and Uruguay.

The three nations in Latin America that have proven the most problematic for Spain have been Cuba, Chile, and Nicaragua; the authoritarian nature of each government has raised serious obstacles to better ties. While Spain under the Socialists has emphasized to the Sandinistas the importance of maintaining and developing political pluralism, it has experienced a strong counter-influence from the forces of the Cuban revolution and Cuba's lack of dissidence. The Spanish example of redemocratization has had little impact in Managua, which has increasingly come to rely upon Cuba and the Soviet Union due to U.S. hostility, the latter nation's support for the *contras*, and the Sandinista's inability to gain the support of the majority of the Nicaraguan people. Indirectly, a Spanish-Cuban rivalry has evolved over the soul of the Sandinista revolution. This indirect competition in Central America, already tilted heavily in favor of the Cubans, has complicated bilateral relations between Havana and Madrid.

The major plank of Cuban/Spanish relations has been trade. In 1985, Cuba became Spain's major Latin America market, overtaking Mexico and Venezuela—a trend further strengthened by a series of economic cooperation agreements signed in Madrid on 3 October 1986.[19] The package, signed by the Cuban Minister-President of the State Committee for Economic Cooperation (CECE), Hector Rodriguez Llompart, and Spanish Commerce Minister Luis de Velasco, included a $62 million credit line for Cuba to purchase Spanish goods, as well as a guarantee by Spain to help the Caribbean nation overcome its shipping bottleneck by building eight freighters.

TABLE 8.1
Cuba's Trade Partners in Europe
(in millions of U.S. dollars)

Nation	Value of Trade
Austria	$ 20.1
Belgium-Luxembourg	31.5
Denmark	11.9
Finland	16.7
France	51.8
West Germany	134.7
Ireland	.7
Italy	104.0
Netherlands	89.6
Norway	2.6
Spain	432.5
Switzerland	36.4
United Kingdom	92.0

Source: Direction of Trade Statistics Yearbook 1986, p. 148

For Spain, strengthened trade relations with Cuba benefited the nation's economy: in 1986, Spain was second only to Japan among the market economies supplying Cuba, and has become the island's main European customer.[20] Spanish imports have largely been coffee and tobacco, while Cuba's imports have been machinery, freighters, vehicles, and entire industrial plants. This has caused some concern in the United States over Cuba's access to certain sensitive technologies. The exports to Cuba, however, benefits those sectors of the Spanish economy confronting the greatest difficulty in competing with other Western nations. Those industries are steel, shipbuilding, and transport, as well as sectors the Iberian nation is seeking to stimulate, such as chemicals and agricultural machinery.

In the late 1980s, Spain and Cuba have developed a relationship which is largely based on trade and a common language. Some of the political closeness that had occurred earlier in the decade, however, was negated by the November 1985 "Madrid incident." In that incident, four Cuban "diplomats" attempted to abduct a defecting Cuban official from a crowded street. A crowd quickly gathered to protect the defector from his would-be abductors, who at one point drew guns. The Spanish response was prompt: asylum was immediately granted to the defector; the four Cuban diplomats involved were expelled; and the Cuban government was denounced for an attempted violation of human rights.

Cuba and Europe: The French Connection

Cuba's relationship with France has been most defined by accommodation and challenge and is anchored in the Caribbean nation's need for credit, goods, and diplomatic contacts. For France, unbroken diplomatic ties to Havana have been in indication of its independence vis-à-vis Washington, and a signal that Paris still has an important global role. Part of such a global role is projected from France's continued holdings in the Caribbean—Martinique, Guadeloupe, and French Guiana. These islands and territories voted in 1946 to be converted into constitutional and political parts of the French nation-state, referred to as Départements d'Outre-Mer, or DOMs.[21] France's continued influence in the Western Hemisphere has thus been guided by these departments.

The French military presence is one of the largest in the Caribbean, with approximately 7,000 soldiers in Martinique, Guadeloupe, and French Guiana.[22] Garrisons are located at Port-du-France, Pointe-à-Pitre, and Cayenne. Along these lines, the French Caribbean departments are fortified military bases which in case of war could be used to quickly project a French armed force. Many of the military plans project the possibility of a conflict in the Caribbean in which action is taken against Cuban and Soviet forces and their proxies.

Under Socialist President François Mitterand (elected in 1981), the French global role became more active and visible. France continues to hold possessions in the South Pacific, the Indian Ocean, the Atlantic, and the Caribbean, as well as having troops, advisers, and educational personnel in several African and Middle Eastern countries. Mitterand was strong in "standing up" to the Soviets, supported the installation of American missiles in Europe, and countered Libyan aggression in Chad. In the Caribbean and Central America, the Socialist government pursued a policy that was largely independent of Washington. In the late 1980s, there was, however, a shift back to the right as the "cohabitation" government of Mitterand and Jacques Chirac moved closer to the U.S. position.

French concerns in the Caribbean have been dominated by the need to secure their enclaves against the radicalism that disrupted many of the newly independent island-states in the Eastern Caribbean. Initially, the Mitterand administration sought to implement a liberal policy vis-à-vis Cuba and the NJM in Grenada. In August 1981, Antoine Blanca, personal assistant to then-Prime Minister Pierre Mauroy and head of the Socialist Party's Latin American section, stated that the new Socialist government would "not tolerate any aggression, whatever form it might assume," against Cuba.[23] At the same time, the French government provided financial assistance for Grenada's controversial Point Salines Airport, recognized the Salvadoran opposition (jointly with Mexico), and repeatedly supported a negotiated settlement in Central America.

The Mitterand administration felt that dialogue (accommodation) was sorely needed in the Caribbean and Central America—regions in which the conservative Reagan administration was following a strong anticommunist policy directly aimed at Cuba, Grenada, and Nicaragua. As the Caribbean Basin polarized between the forces of the political left and right in the early 1980s, Mitterand presented France and, to a lesser extent, the European Economic Community, as an alternative political and economic pole which was democratic and tolerant of ideological plurality.

Although France's accommodationist stance vis-à-vis Cuba gradually moved to a more conflictual mode due to alleged Cuban aid to proindependence groups in the French Antilles and growing Cuban influence in Africa, the Franco/Cuban relationship (unbroken since 1959) has produced certain positive results, especially in terms of the release of Cuban political prisoners. Through the good offices of the French government, and by the personal intervention of individuals such as Jacques Cousteau, a number of political prisoners were freed in the early and mid-1980s. This included the Cuban poet Armando Valladares Perez, who was released into exile in

France in October 1982, after more than 20 years in prison on charges of counterrevolutionary activity. The poet's release had followed a visit to Cuba by Regis Debray, then special adviser to Mitterand and a former comrade-in-arms of Castro. The significance of this was noted by *The Economist:* "The decision to release the Cuban poet, first imprisoned in 1960, was a calculated concession by Castro in recognition of the fact that France's friendship is very important diplomatically to Cuba amidst the overall atmosphere of hostility among Western nations."[24] In 1986, the French were also partially responsible for the release of other prisoners, and in August of that year, Mitterand quietly sought to persuade Castro to allow one of Cuba's most prominent dissidents, Ricardo Bofill, to leave the country.[25]

The French have also benefited from the Cuban relationship through trade, which is encouraged by the Castro government. An example of the infrastructural assistance that Cuba badly needs and France is willing to supply has been in the field of thermal power. In 1983 and 1984, French assistance was acquired for a thermal power plant being constructed in Matanzas by Alsthom-Atlantique. While France benefited in terms of export gains, Cuba received technological aid, required for infrastructural development, that the Soviets have not provided.

While a policy of accommodation—characterized by dialogue and reinforced by trade—has marked Franco/Cuban relations, there have clearly been tensions between the two nations over the decades. Cuba's shipment of weapons and medical supplies to independence forces fighting the French in Algeria in the early 1960s, and its vocal condemnation of French imperialism in international forums on the same issue, came close to breaking relations. Cuban involvement in Africa—in Zaire in the 1960s, and later in Angola and Ethiopia in the 1970s and 1980s—also was a source of friction. As it has been noted: "Cuban deployment of up to 50,000 combatants and civilians in the two countries (Angola and Ethiopia)—the communist world's biggest-ever overseas military venture—transformed the political map of Africa."[26]

This aforementioned development threatened the Giscardian "Holy Alliance" that sought to unite the technology of the EEC with the oil of Arabia and the minerals of Africa. The Metternichian concept of a new geopolitical alliance, originally conceived in the aftermath of the first oil shock (1973–74), has continued to provide a framework for policy action from that period on through the advent of the Mitterand government. Although French and Cuban troops never clashed, their proxies and allies have: the most well-known clash of interests came in the two Katangian secessionist sorties from Angola in the late 1970s, which ultimately resulted in the sending of French and Belgian paratroopers into Shaba

Province, Zaire. The French also supported one of the losing sides in the Angolan civil war, while the Cubans backed the winning Popular Movement for the Liberation of Angola (MPLA).

Africa has thus been an arena of Franco/Cuban competition. However, as France has granted independence to its former colonies and Cuban activities have been primarily focused in the former Portuguese colonies and Ethiopia, there has been a shift to another zone of contention between Paris and Havana: the Caribbean Basin. In that region, the French nation-state, through its DOMs, is a Caribbean nation and thus, in a sense, has Cuba as a neighbor. Though not to be overstated, the Overseas Departments have become a source of tension in the Franco/Cuban relationship, which both nations are careful not to blow out of proportion.

After a number of bombings in Martinique, Guadeloupe, French Guiana, and Paris in 1983, the Direction de la Surveillance du Territoire (DST) suggested that the terrorists were Cuban-trained. This view was supported by Lucette Micheaux-Chevry, then-president of the General Council of Guadeloupe, who stated: "The name of the ARC-Caribbean is sufficient to say it is not just a matter of the French Antilles. Until the present, Cuba has succeeded in exporting just one thing: armed men."[27]

The combination of terrorist attacks and the high probability of Cuban involvement resulted in a return to a more traditional policy, that of "cordon sanitaire." This "protective zone" encompassed the French enclaves and the surrounding island-states of Dominica and St. Lucia. Questions were also quietly raised concerning Cuban involvement in Grenada, particularly the arms buildup and training of other nationals. There was apprehension that the Cubans and Grenadians, in wishing to spread revolution through the region, had targeted Guadeloupe, Martinique, and French Guiana.[28]

Cuban involvement in the French Caribbean, however, is difficult to measure—but should not be overstated. What *is* certain is that Cuba and its revolutionary tradition under Castro of defying the United States has a distinct appeal to the radical Antillean Left which would like to do the same to the French. This is particularly evident in that almost every proindependence group in Martinique and Guadeloupe has a picture of Fidel, Ché, and Trotsky in its offices. The larger and more active left-wing parties, however, go further in their ties to Cuba (attending conferences in Havana), while the smaller groups maintain a degree of distance. The latter's fear of being coopted into a larger movement over which they have little control, and suspicion of the local communists, who have linkages to the pro-Soviet French Communist Party, have made these smaller groups relatively isolated from the political mainstream. In general, for Cuba, the small terrorist parties offer few advantages and, although assistance is provided to a selected few, Havana's support is largely reserved for the larger and better-organized Communist parties.

France has demonstrated its resolve in maintaining its sphere of influence in Africa and the Caribbean, even against Cuba, while at the same time leaving the door open to dialogue. French and Cuban troops have not yet exchanged fire as did American and Cuban troops in Grenada. However, French and Belgian paratroopers did rout Katangian secessionists armed and trained by the Cubans. Zaire and Angola remain somewhat unsettled areas, and it is possible that in the foreseeable future, French and Cuban aspirations could clash head-on, placing accommodation in the background and putting conflict in the forefront. Further Cuban ventures in the Caribbean, especially in Martinique and Guadeloupe, could also shunt aside accommodation benefits such as new credits, lenient debt reschedulings, and badly needed imports for more direct military options. In many respects, Cuba has come to need the French more than the French need the Cubans—something that is apparently carefully weighed in Havana.

Cuba and Europe: The Other Nations

Cuba's involvement with other Western European nations has been much less significant than relations with either France or Spain. For a number of nations, such as Ireland and Luxembourg, Cuba has remained a peripheral issue, registering little trade and not significant enough to exchange ambassadors. Other countries, such as Austria, initially broke relations with the Castro regime but in time renewed ties. The nations of most importance for Cuba after Spain and France in Europe are the United Kingdom and West Germany.

Although West Germany is Cuba's third most important European trade partner, the Caribbean nation, like the rest of Latin America, remains on the periphery of Bonn's foreign policy concerns.[29] West German foreign policy remains primarily concerned with the integration of Europe, the North Atlantic Treaty Organization, and maintaining the demand for future German unification. Most development aid has gone to Asia and Africa as the Germans have felt the need to work alongside France, Belgium, the Netherlands, and the United Kingdom in the discharge of their obligations overseas.

In this scenario, Cuban/German ties have been and remain insignificant. German holdings in Cuba at the time of the revolution were relatively small, largely confined to a supermarket chain which had opened in 1955. As part of the Cold War, Germany also supported the United States during the missile crisis, but was irritated about not being informed of key decisions. In 1963, the Federal Republic broke relations with Cuba when Castro established relations with East Germany. However, relations were later reestablished and West German imports, consisting largely of machinery, have been regarded as important by Cuba. West Germany has also been one of the major Western creditors to Cuba, and ties have developed with the Socialist International (SI) as Willy Brandt visited the island-state on 14 October 1984 in his capacity as president of the SI. The purpose of the visit by the German former head of state was to receive the views of the Cuban leadership on the Central American situation.[30] While West Germany has an interest in the affairs of the region, including Central America and Cuba's odd-man-out role, there remains a reluctance to become more involved beyond symbolic gestures or joint EEC efforts.

Though Britain was one of the major weapon suppliers to the Batista regime in the late 1950s, had investments in the economy (Shell refinery and a number of insurance companies), and had sided with the United States during the Cuban missile crisis, diplomatic relations continued as both sides found it advantageous in terms of trade. Anglo/Cuban relations were particularly strong during the Labour Party governments of the 1970s, as methods were sought to improve trade. As Britain has withdrawn from the Caribbean—granting independence to its various colonies in the 1960s and 1970s—much of its defense responsibilities were passed on to the United States.[31] By the late 1980s, Britain's once extensive empire in the Western Hemisphere was limited to the small possessions of Anguilla, the British Virgin Islands, the Turks and Caicos Islands, and Montserrat, while close to 2,000 troops and four Harrier jump-jets remain in Belize to protect that nation's borders from Guatemala's territorial claims. Areas of possible conflict with Cuba, therefore, have diminished considerably.

The British perception of Cuba has been formed by its relationship with the Commonwealth Caribbean. Britain has clearly become disillusioned with Castro and has opposed, with a minimum of effort and cost, Cuban expansion in the area. Outside of its military presence in Belize, London regards the United States, Venezuela, and Mexico as more effective counterweights to contain any Cuban efforts of destabilization. In this context, the British have been keen to limit direct military involvement, participating in occasional joint maneuvers with the United States.[32] This, in part, explains Britain's reluctance to participate in the Grenada intervention in 1983. Britain's major concerns in the Western Hemisphere have also shifted away from its remaining Caribbean possessions to the Falkland Islands in the South Atlantic, where a sizeable garrison is maintained to secure it from future Argentine attacks.

Cuban/Swiss relations have evolved along a unique track. When the United States and many of its close Latin American allies severed diplomatic ties to Havana in the early 1960s, Switzerland did not follow suit. The Swiss remained in Havana and offered their good offices as middlemen between Cuba and some of those nations which severed diplomatic relations. Among those nations were the United States, Argentina, Brazil, Chile, Colombia, Ecuador, Haiti, Honduras, and Venezuela. Consequently, the Swiss ambassador developed a unique role: the Swiss Embassy worked on issues ranging from thousands of notary documents, to the care of American prisoners in Cuban jails, to the organization of flights of Cuban refugees to the United States.[33]

Despite the renewal of diplomatic relations with Cuba on the part of a number of Latin American countries, the tenor of Cuban/American relations have meant the continuation of the Swiss role. During the Carter administration, a brief period of improved relations between Washington and Havana made it appear that Swiss services had a shortening life span. However, the hardening of American policy toward Cuba in the last years of the Carter administration and during the Reagan years guaranteed the continuation of the Swiss role in Havana. That role has been based on the Swiss global perception that neutral nations can also play an important role in world affairs. Moreover, maintenance of relations with Switzerland has meant access to a limited amount of credits and manufactured goods. At the same time, the Swiss have not harbored any illusions regarding the nature of the Cuban regime. As Beat Amman, a Swiss journalist noted in 1984: "Cuba against the rest of the world. Few friends with only limited means. Spanish tradition, harsh ideology. No future. Hardly a present. But a great past."[34]

Cuba has been open to developing improved trade relations with the West, as reflected by its importation of goods from Britain as well as from Italy, the Netherlands, Sweden, and Switzerland. The significance of these other trade partners was emphasized in 1984 when a consortium composed of Andritz of Austria and the Swiss company, Brown Boveri, won an order from the Cuban government to supply $10 million worth of electrical equipment to a thermal power plant being constructed at Felton.[35] Cubaniquel, the Caribbean nation's ferro-nickel company, also depends on exports to Western European countries, especially Italy and West Germany.

While Cuba has found its foreign policy with Western Europe and Canada to be a mixture of accommodation and challenge often linked to geopolitical concerns regarding a variety of issues, it is in the economic realm where the Cuban government has found the need of outside expertise the most necessary. Despite almost three decades of "revolutionary" government, the Cuban economy remains dependent on the production and exportation of sugar. Moreover, the dramatic and widely proclaimed termination of dependency on the United States was transformed into an equally heavy dependency on the Soviet Union. Cuban/Soviet ties, essential to the survival of the economy, have not always been cordial as the dominance of the larger partner has, at times, been less than subtle. Consequently, improved and increased linkages to the West are perceived by Havana as a means to reduce its heavy dependence on trade with the Council for Mutual Economic Assistance (COMECON), which purchases approximately 85 percent of Cuban trade.[36]

A major complication to the development of this policy line for the Castro regime has been the poor condition of the Cuban economy and its expanding external debt burden. While owing the Soviet Union close to $21 billion at year-end 1985, Cuba has also tapped Western creditors for loans to help facilitate trade and develop infrastructural programs. By August 1986, Cuba's total external debt with the West, excluding the United States, was $3.5 billion, most of which was owed to Canada, France, Japan, and Switzerland.[37]

While Castro has advocated a debt moratorium for Latin America, he has quietly dealt with his Crédit Lyonnais-led steering committee of major commercial creditors, as well as the Paris Club group of creditor nations. The poor performance of the Cuban economy has been amply reflected in its multiple reschedulings (three times since 1982), the most recent of which was negotiated in 1986. In particular, low sugar and oil prices, (Cuba's two major exports), problems with marketing of its other products, economic mismanagement, a lack of production incentives, the costs of maintaining close to 50,000 military personnel overseas, and high military spending have translated into a hard-pressed economy, incapable of sustaining forward momentum, let alone repaying its loans.[38] Added to these factors has been the toughening of the U.S. economic embargo of Cuba in 1985 and 1986. Although Cuba earns most of its hard currency from sales of dollar-denominated commodities, the U.S. embargo has forced it to pay for imports in other currencies, which, in 1986, rose against the dollar. During this period of difficulties in commercial debt repayments, three of the five main suppliers of hard currency imports— Japan, Spain, and West Germany—imposed a clamp-down on trade credit. Only Canada, of the five suppliers, continued to offer limited export credit guarantees.[39]

Castro has also lashed out at Europe for contributing to the problems of the Cuban economy. In particular, the Cuban leader has found the EEC's policy of agricultural subsidies harmful to his nation's major export, sugar. As Castro stated: "The European position is even worse: it subsidizes sugar at very high prices and exports the surplus. It used to import millions of tons of sugar; now it is demanding a quota of 5 million tons on the world market."[40]

Cuba's debt crisis has demonstrated the limitations of both Havana and the Western European nations and Canada. For all the rhetoric and actual improvements, the Cuban economy remains as it was prior to 1959—dependent on both sugar and a major outside political and economic power. In the latter case, the Soviet Union has supplanted the United States. A new twist has been the deployment of Cuban troops overseas—a costly policy in terms of capital and personnel. In this situation, Western Europe and Canada function as a half-open door willing to be a third force, but without the costs incurred.

In July 1986, Sir Geoffrey Howe, the British foreign secretary and then president of the EEC's Council of Ministers, asserted that the Community was indeed a world superpower.[41] In sticking to what has emerged as a "European line," he presented the Community as an equal of the United States and the Soviet Union, and as a bridge in the improvement of relations between East and West. Yet, despite this emerging line of thought and self-image, performance has not matched aspiration. The EEC, as a collective force, has not demonstrated its ability to substantially shape events, even within its traditional spheres of influence, Africa and the Middle East. For a nation such as Cuba, the EEC is not a feasible alternative pole to the U.S. or the Soviet Union. It is also doubtful that the Europeans would have any real interest in maintaining Fidel Castro's communist and military dictatorship at the cost of $4–5 billion annually, as the Soviet Union does. As it stands, Cuba's debt problems with Western creditors, which are relatively small, have been some cause of irritation.

Conclusions

Europe's relations with Cuba have been largely characterized by accommodation and challenge. Depending on the nation examined, a conflictual mode has been undertaken when national interests collide, as with France in Africa and the Caribbean, or with Spain when kidnapping was attempted on the streets of Madrid. As Europe increasingly seeks to emphasize its role as a global "superpower," the Cuban card allows policymakers in Brussels, Paris, Bonn, London, and Madrid to present themselves as a significant third force. This has been done by providing Cuba over $3 billion in loans and by maintaining diplomatic relations. In a similar fashion, Europe has also sought to project its influence into Central America, which could ultimately place it at odds with Cuban aspirations in the region. The Castro regime, in turn, has found its relationship with Europe and Canada crucial in providing a small amount of leverage vis-à-vis the Soviets and Americans. In return for the occasional release of political prisoners, it receives credit, imports of otherwise unavailable items, and hard currency earnings from trade and tourism. This relationship, however, has not forced it to halt its activities overseas, some of which challenge European interests.

Cuban/Canadian relations are likely to continue to be unique. It has been a considerable Cuban achievement to have maintained diplomatic relations with both the immediate neighbors of the United States, Canada and Mexico. Throughout the years of U.S.-imposed isolation, Cuba has swapped diplomats with Canada and Mexico. For Canada and Cuba, a mutual independence vis-à-vis their larger neighbor was emphasized. That relationship was strengthened by the time of Prime Minister Trudeau and Canada's ongoing search for a third member (or members) to balance U.S. dominance in North America.

One of the major and ongoing elements in Cuba's relationships with Europe and Canada has been the debate over "giving Cuba a chance." It has been argued that if Cuba is welcomed back into the Western community of nations and U.S. hostility is terminated (i.e., embargoes and support for anti-Castro forces), Cuba will move toward a more open, pluralistic society along the lines of Yugoslavia. The major stumbling block, it is maintained, has been the United States. Without American pressure, Cuba could move on a more "normal" path of development. For much of the European left, Cuba has been a victim of U.S. aggression and misinformation. According to one prominent Swedish Social Democrat: "Cuba constitutes a factor of moderation (in the region) and, where the Cubans have intervened (as in Africa), the sins of colonial Europe and of the Western powers (had) created the need for external aid."[42]

Although the argument on "giving Cuba a chance" has not ended, it is certain that Castro has no intention of relinquishing power or loosening his control of Cuba. A hesitant European "superpower" with a half-open door, operating in the shadows of the United States and the Soviet Union, is not yet a strong enough pole of influence for Castro to jettison his current patron.

For Europe to make a difference in Cuba's interaction with the world, the EEC would have to provide a constant $4–5 billion annually to Castro to keep the economy afloat, put considerable pressure on the socialist caudillo to make meaningful political reforms (which means intervening in another nation's internal affairs), and "stand up" to both the United States and the Soviet Union. It also means curbing Cuban expansion in Latin America and the Caribbean and, in opposition to Cuban and Soviet goals in those areas, helping to consolidate democratic structures (including democratic parties of the left and the right). The reality of the situation in the late 1980s is that Europe has no inclination to fund the Cuban revolution, nor can it put pressure on Castro to change the structure of his

regime. It is also doubtful that Castro would find such a situation acceptable, considering how Machiavellian he has been in maintaining himself and
his followers in power against all forces throughout the entirety of the
revolution. A European influence in the Cuban revolution is not likely to
change that, although it could promote the development of a Social
Democratic or Eurocommunist faction of the Cuban Communist party.

The Cuban Revolution remains Fidel Castro's revolution, and in the
triangle of U.S./Cuban/European relations, this basic factor almost guarantees a continued status quo: the European superpower door will remain
half-open to the Caribbean nation; Castro will continue to use Europe (and
Canada) for diplomatic leverage, credits, and imports; and relationships
with European capitals (and Ottawa) will be a source of irritation for the
United States.

Notes

1. For party-to-party relations, see Eusebio Mujal-León, "European Socialism
   and the Crisis in Central America", in Howard J. Wiarda (ed.), *Rift and
   Revolution: The Central American Imbroglio* (Washington, D.C.: American
   Enterprise Institute for Public Policy Research, 1984) pp. 253–302.
2. Wolf Grabendorff, "Western European Perceptions of the Central American
   Turmoil," in Richard E. Feiberg (ed.), *Central America: International Dimensions of the Crisis* (New York: Holmes and Meier Publishers, 1982), p. 204.
3. Charles Doran, *The Forgotten Partnership: U.S.-Canada Relations Today*
   (Baltimore, Md.: The Johns Hopkins University Press, 1984), p. 31.
4. Ibid., p. 36.
5. Greme S. Mount and Egelgard E. Mahant, "Review of Recent Literature on
   Canadian-Latin American Relations," *Journal of Interamerican Studies and
   World Affairs,* Vol, 27, No. 2 (Summer 1985), p. 128.
6. For further details, see Barry Brown, "Canada maintains cordial, though wary,
   ties with Cuba," *The Washington Times,* October 1, 1986, p. 7.
7. G. Pope Atkins, *Latin America in the International Political System* (New
   York: The Free Press, 1977), p. 322.
8. Ibid.
9. Ibid.
10. Mount and Mahant, p. 128.
11. International Monetary Fund, *Direction of Trade Statistics Yearbook, 1986*
    (Washington, D.C.: International Monetary Fund, 1986), p. 148.
12. D.L. Aubé, *Canada's Trade in Agricultural Products, 1982, 1983, 1984* (Ot-
    tawa: Ministry of Supply and Services, August 1985), p. 105.
13. "Grenada: Invasion or Rescue?" *Canada and the World,* (December 1983),
    pp. 4–5.
14. Ibid.
15. Jonathan Lemco, "Canadian Foreign Policy Interests in Central America:
    Some Current Issues," *Journal of Interamerican Studies and World Affairs,*
    Vol. 28, No. 2 (Summer 1986), p. 130.
16. See Jules Robert Benjamin, *The United States and Cuba: Hegemony and*

Dependent Development, 1880–1934 (Pittsburgh, Pa.: University of Pittsburgh Press, 1974) and Hugh Thomas, *Cuba: The Pursuit of Freedom* (New York: Harper and Row, 1971).

17. Aaron Segal, "On the road to mutual respect, Spain as a hemispheric broker," *The Times of the Americas,* April 2, 1986, p. 11.
18. Ibid.
19. *Latin American Weekly Report,* 18 October 1986, p. 3.
20. Ibid.
21. For a more detailed discussion of departmentalization, see Albert L. Gastmann, *Historical Dictionary of the French and Netherlands Antilles* (Metuchen, N.J.: The Scarecrow Press, Inc., 1978), pp. 46–48, and Jean Pouquet, *Les Antilles Françaises* (Paris: Presses Universitaires de France, 1976), pp. 32–34.
22. *Le Point,* 19 September 1983, p. 62.
23. *Latin America Regional Report: Caribbean,* 21 August 1981, p. 4.
24. *Quarterly Economic Report of Cuba, Dominican Republic, Haiti, Puerto Rico,* 4th Quarter, 1982, p. 9.
25. *The Washington Post,* 31 August 1986, p. 47, and *The New York Times,* 31 August 1986, p. 9.
26. Arthur Gavshon, *Crisis in Africa: Battlefield of East and West* (New York: Penguin Books, Ltd., 1981), p. 107.
27. *Le Point,* 2 January 1984, p. 31.
28. See Robert F. Lambberg, "Brazil and the Guianas," *Swiss Review of World Affairs,* Vol. XXXV, No. 8 (November 1985), p. 31.
29. As Manfred Mols noted: "In Bonn's current deliberations on a foreign policy for the 1980s, Latin America is only a marginal concern," in his article, "West German Involvement in Latin America," in William Perry and Peter Wehner (eds.), *The Latin American Policies of U.S. Allies* (New York: Praeger Publishers, 1985), p. 1. Also, see Hans-Dietrich Genscher, "Deutsche Ausenpolitik fur die achtziger Jahre," *Europe Archiv,* Vol. 35 (1980), p. 371ff.
30. *Latin America Regional Report: Caribbean,* 2 November 1984, p. 2.
31. As Sir Kenneth Blackburne commented: "Britain was anxious to relieve herself of her burdensome overseas responsibilities . . ." in the author's article, "Changing Patterns of Caribbean International Relations: Britain and the 'British' Caribbean," in Richard Millett and W. Marvin Will (eds.), *The Restless Caribbean: Changing Patterns of International Relations* (New York: Praeger Publishers, 1977), p. 204.
32. George Philip, "British Involvement in Latin America" in Perry and Wehner, p. 33.
33. Werner Imhoof, "Switzerland's Good Services in the Caribbean," *Swiss Review of World Affairs,* Vol. XV, No. 10 (January 1966), p. 19.
34. Beat Amman, "Don Quixote in Cuba," *Swiss Review of World Affairs,* Vol. XXXIV, No. 2 (May 1984), p. 19.
35. The Economist Intelligence Unit, *Quarterly Economic Review of Cuba, Dominican Republic, Haiti, Puerto Rico,* No. 3, 1984, p. 15.
36. Frank Gray, "UK and Cuba sign 250m trade deal," *Financial Times,* 31 January 1986, p. 20.
37. *Reuters News Service,* 6 August 1986.
38. For further information, see *Cuba's Financial Crisis: The Secret Report from the National Bank of Cuba* (Washington, D.C.: The Cuban-American National Foundation, Inc., February 1985).

39. *Reuters News Service,* 6 August 1986.
40. Interview by Jeffery M. Elliot and Marvyn M. Dymally, *Fidel Castro: Nothing Can Stop the Course of History* (New York: Pathfinder Press, 1986), p. 72.
41. Paul Cheeseright, "Howe promotes EEC as third superpower," *Financial Times,* 9 July 1986, p. 2.
42. Mujal-Leon "European Socialism and the Crisis in Central America," in Wiarda, p. 272.

V
FUNCTIONAL POLICY AREAS

9

The Cuban Security Apparatus

Michael J. Mazarr

Introduction

For many years, Cuba has been viewed as the United States' most ardent antagonist in the international community. Because of its limited size and weaponry, it has not posed the overwhelming threat to U.S. security as has the Soviet Union. But Castro's importance is often measured—by him and others—by the degree to which he can disrupt U.S. policies and damage U.S. interests, and he has been far more persistent, ambitious, and (some would say) successful in this than the often cautious men in the Kremlin. Indeed, many of Castro's difficulties with Moscow can be traced to his dissatisfaction with the recurring lack of Soviet support for revolutionary movements in the Third World.

Castro's fervor can perhaps be judged by the numbers of troops he has drafted and sent abroad. Consider the facts: Cuba has a population of roughly 10 million, has a land area comparable to the state of Virginia, is located just 90 miles from the shores (and overwhelming military power) of its chief adversary, and is beset by a permanent economic malaise; yet, Cuba maintains armed forces of some 162,000 active, 150,000 reserve, and over a million and a half paramilitary personnel, about 65,000 of which have until recently been stationed abroad. The Cuban international presence is also advanced by the use of tens of thousands of both quasi-military development support personnel (such as the construction workers the United States encountered in Grenada in 1983) and nonmilitary education, health, and sports envoys.

The enormous efforts required to sustain this international presence have caused severe socioeconomic dislocations within Cuba. A nationwide draft law requires three years of service for all eligible males. Recent estimates suggest that Cuba has suffered at least 10,000 casualties in Angola alone. Economically, Cuba's domestic and international military might absorbs a significant percentage of Cuba's budget and of its most talented technical personnel; the equipment and strategic lift requirements of the armed forces have arguably forced Cuba into a cycle of dependency on the Soviet Union.

How has Cuba been able to mount such a geopolitical presence, while maintaining internal order? Castroist doctrine and Marxist-Leninist ideology explain the motives for Cuba's international efforts, but do not speak to the institutions that have supported Cuba's global stretch. Cuba's leaders may have long held desires to project their power against U.S. interests, but only the existence of a refined military instrument has allowed them to do so.[1]

This chapter, therefore, examines the development, evolution, organization, and future prospects of the Cuban military. It does not offer a detailed sociological portrait of the military's role in Cuban society, although it touches on that subject. It restricts its discussion to the development and employment of Cuban armed forces, largely ignoring cases of military aid or support for terrorism or insurgency that did not involve commitment of troops; the latter topics are covered extensively in other chapters. The chapter does make reference to the Ministry of the Interior (MININT), because it provides paramilitary forces for internal security and because its relationship with the Ministry of the Revolutionary Armed Forces (MINFAR) is so important.

Nevertheless, any analysis of Cuban military and paramilitary organizations that neglected their domestic role would be incomplete. The chapter thus examines how the evolution of the military paralleled the domestic course of the revolution. Indeed, it seems that the notion of "military organization as a basis for communist revolution"[2] has been borne out by the Cuban case. Whether the Cuban polity is truly "militarized" in the full meaning of the term is, however, as we shall see, a controversial point.

The role of the Cuban military has evolved significantly since 1959. It has served as internal and external defender of the revolution, source of civic and economic labor, and most recently as the arm of Cuba's international socialist mission. Cuba's ideological commitment to its international presence leads it to claim a moral mandate for its adventures almost unique in the world, and this role, in turn, is intimately related to the personality and ambitions of Fidel Castro. It is to an analysis of the development of these roles and the military institutions that have supported them that we now turn.

Evolution of the Cuban Military Tradition

One of the principal goals of Castro's regime has been the destruction of the prerevolutionary order and the creation of a new society. Two aspects of Cuba's political culture have remained constant, however: the importance of the military tradition as a bulwark to the nation's political structures, and the involvement of foreign powers in the structure, doctrine, and organization of the Cuban military. Before 1959, those powers used either units of their own militaries or Cuban militia and armed forces to keep order and exercise dominance over many aspects of Cuban life. Since 1959, these tasks have been passed on to Castro's own government.

The history of Cuba's protracted war of independence from Spain, beginning in earnest in 1868 and continuing, with several pauses, through to 1898, is well known and need not be recounted here.[3] After the Spanish-Cuban-American War, American influence, spurred by a recognition of Cuba's strategic significance and institutionalized in the Platt Amendment of 1901, was overriding within Cuba. U.S. administrators in Cuba reconstructed the island's devastated infrastructure of education, health, agriculture, and government, and used those institutions to subtly advance American interests in Cuba. Within this context, the United States became directly responsible for the formation and management of the Cuban military and police forces.

The American occupying forces immediately recognized the need for some form of police units, partly to provide employment for the 30,000-odd ex–Cuban rebels. Through 1898–99, this need drove the gradual formation of small policing groups, which would eventually be known collectively as the Rural Guard. When Cuba was granted independence in 1902, the Guard continued to operate, and was used by middle- and upper-class Cubans and foreigners to protect property. Its services proved so useful that most of its facilities—260 of 288 buildings in 1905, for example—were provided for it by municipalities and companies. By 1906, the Guard comprised about 5,000 men scattered throughout 250 outposts.

Yet the Guard was unable to preserve order. That same year, an opposition challenge to the rule of then-president Tomas Estrada Palma, which required American intervention and the establishment of a U.S. provisional government, exposed the inadequacy of the weak, dispersed Guard and made clear the need for a professional military. The Guard had also become unpopular due to its political activity and support for the existing regime. By 1907, the first military schools were opening in the provinces, and in April 1908 the provisional government created the Permanent Army, at the time merely an infantry brigade. The Guard was not abolished, however, and retained 5,180 men in 380 posts.[4]

The development of a professional military continued apace after 1908. The first military college was established in Havana in 1911, and in 1915 the Rural Guard and army were combined into the Ejercito Nacional or National Army, a title changed in 1933 to Constitutional Army of Cuba. A Coast Guard was formed in 1901, and a navy in 1909; the first proposals for an air corps surfaced in 1915, followed several years later by the first squadrons of the Cuerpo de Aviación, which was divided in 1933 into army and naval air sections.

The Cuban military was not formed solely along American lines—Spanish influence within the military (on doctrine, training, and military traditions) remained strong, and other European nations and Mexico provided supplies to the Cuban military. Cuba's thirty-year war for independence also allowed its nascent armed forces to develop their own organizations and tactics. Nevertheless, American influence was the key variable in the development of the military, and this carried a number of implications. The Cuban military, for example, employed U.S. weapons and, for the most part, drew on American traditions.

The most significant result of U.S. influence, however, was that U.S. backing for the Cuban military called attention to its growing domestic role as guarantor of order, though the use of the military for this purpose would prove counterproductive. The Cuban colonial experience under Spanish rule had already laid the foundations for the real and perceived role of the military in society. Foremost in this regard was the military's function to maintain the ruling political class in power, rather than the more traditional function as guardian of the homeland against external enemies. Over time, it became increasingly apparent to Cubans and foreigners alike that members of the military establishment ignored constitutional practices. As with other parts of the government, the Cuban military became a corrupt institution and was used as a means to personal enrichment or political power—or both. And the military in Cuba was seen as a tool of outside powers, designed and built by them to serve their interests.

The composition of the military exacerbated these institutional flaws. The lower ranks—enlisted men—were filled by members of Cuba's lower classes, who viewed the military as a source of employment and enrichment. Cuba's officer corps consisted of middle- and upper-class men who also treated the military as a means to personal wealth. Thus the armed forces were plagued by both an enlisted-officer cleavage (that would lead to a "revolt of the sergeants" and actual street fighting between officers and enlisted in 1933) and a military-wide attitude of personal aggrandizement that firmly embedded corruption as a way of life within the armed forces.

The development of the armed forces continued during and after World War II. In December 1941, Cuba supported its American ally with a declaration of war against the Axis powers, and a 1942 law required all fit men aged 20–24 to complete four months of military training. After the war, more modern U.S. military equipment arrived, including the first modern aircraft operated by the Cuban air force. The army and naval elements of that service were recombined in 1955 into the Fuerza Aerea Ejercito de Cuba.

The flaws of the military had not been corrected, however, and in the 1950s it remained a corrupt and inept organization. Fidel Castro took advantage of this corruption (his men sometimes purchased weapons from army officers) and the weakness of the military during his rebellion. His small band of rebels did not win a military victory—Batista's armed forces merely collapsed in late 1958 when it became apparent that their sponsor and guardian, the United States, was abandoning Batista. In retrospect, while American concerns for regional stability fueled U.S. involvement in the development of the Cuban military, the growing corruption and domestic role of the armed forces stymied U.S. efforts.

Origins of the Revolutionary Armed Forces

In the aftermath of Fidel Castro's victory over Batista and his triumphal march on Havana, the Batista military was dissolved by Castro and his associates. Within ten days, dozens of Batista's soldiers and police were tried and executed, a process that would continue for months and result in the deaths of hundreds of *batistianos*.[5] Batista's armed forces, which had numbered some 40,000 in 1958, were no more.

Forming the MINFAR

In its place, Castro immediately moved to establish a professional military of the revolution, and placed rebel leaders at the head of as-yet unformed services.[6] Yet Castro faced numerous problems. His Rebel Army numbered only 3,000, and many of them were illiterate. The revolutionary army would have to be formed with units from various—and competing— opposition groups, including Castro's own 26 July Movement, the Revolutionary Directorate (DR), the Cuban Communist Party (Partido Socialista Popular, or PSP, renamed PCC under Castro), and the Organización Autentica (OA). Apart from a few chief lieutenants, Castro could call upon no one with military experience, and even his veterans of the Sierra Maestra were untrained in traditional military science. And his government was faced with the imminent, twin requirement of forestalling a domestic counterrevolution (potentially supported by an external power) or an invasion.

The revolutionary government set out to rectify these organizational deficiencies rapidly, and the institutions it created responded to its two needs—internal and external security. In March 1959, Ché Guevara began forming worker's militias. From August to the end of the year, Castro stamped out opposition to his rule among moderate elements within the nascent military.[7] In October 1959, the framework of the military began to take shape: the Ministry of the Revolutionary Armed Forces (MINFAR) and its arm, the National Revolutionary Militias (which included thousands of rural and urban workers), were created. Raul Castro was appointed to head the MINFAR, with Fidel Castro as commander in chief. The MIN-FAR was seen as a response to external aggression, with the militias (and other paramilitary organizations that would follow) designed to keep internal order, though the roles would overlap.[8] In the early stages of the revolution, the militias were roughly ten times as large as the MINFAR.

The militias were popular, at first. Their blue uniforms became a symbol of the revolution. Carlos Franqui, an intellectual leader of the revolution and editor of its chief paper, *Revolución,* demonstrates the enthusiasm with which even moderates treated these new groups:

> They were volunteers, they were hard workers, and they were somewhere between soldiers and civilians. They represented spontaneity and organization. The militiaman was the third hero of 1959. He was the collective hero, the true "Party of the Revolution." Men, women, young, old, black, mulatto, peasants, students, professional people, intellectuals, middle-class people, the poor. The militia was the new revolution that gave an identity to all, without prejudice. It asked only for volunteers; it gave military training, it provided care for factories, and it endowed all with political and human awareness. It was armed democracy and came to have a million members.[9]

On 28 September 1960, Castro bolstered his domestic forces by creating the Committees for the Defense of the Revolution (CDR). These paramilitary units, of which by 1963 there were over 90,000, monitored daily life in Cuba on a block-by-block level, recording the behavior of virtually every Cuban. Some of its operatives were trained by the KGB and GRU in the Soviet Bloc. Castro himself defined their mission as "a crushing and militant response by the masses to counterrevolutionary terrorism."[10]

By December 1960, Castro, perhaps feeling the pressure of the growing CIA campaign to unseat him, met with representatives of the various opposition groups to Batista which had participated in the revolutionary movement. The meeting produced the Escuelas de Instrucción Revolucionaria (EIR), new schools for revolutionary education with courses ranging from Marxist-Leninist ideology to job training. The Escuelas Basicas de Instrucción Revolucionaria (EBIR) were special EIR for particularly militant followers of the revolution. Some of these schools specialized in military science, and began quickly to produce graduates who took command of units in the mushrooming MINFAR. Importantly, too, by providing a single channel for revolutionary education, the EIR and EBIR began the difficult process of subsuming factional rivalry among various groups of the anti-Batista opposition. Later all were combined into the Organizaciones Revolucionarias Integradas (ORI), by which time Fidel Castro had become firmly entrenched as the commander of the revolution.

Castro quickly sought equipment and training for the MINFAR from his new ally, the Soviet Union. Somewhat late in recognizing Castro's potential value, Moscow did not begin significant aid until February 1960. By September, however, the Cubans were receiving heavy military equipment—82mm mortars and 122mm howitzers, in addition to thousands of small arms. Soviet World War II-vintage tanks, such as the very effective (if aged) T-34, arrived in 1961.[11]

The First Tests

The first test for the MINFAR emerged almost immediately in the Escambray mountains, where a dedicated counterrevolutionary movement deployed some 3,000–5,000 guerrillas. The government's effort became known as the Lucha Contra Bandidos (LCB or "Struggle Against the Bandits") and comprised operations by both CDR and National Revolutionary Militia units, first formed in September 1960 and eventually including over 100,000 people. Castro feared that the United States would use the rebel bands to support an invasion, and thus desperately wanted to crush them as quickly as possible.

Castro called upon his experience as a guerrilla to develop tactics for this war. He took part of his militia and spaced the soldiers 40–50 yards apart in trenches and foxholes to seal off the mountains, and used other units in search and destroy operations within guerrilla areas. The militia were given a mere three weeks of training before combat; up to 6,000 militia were trained at one time. Castro also displayed his famous ability for underhanded dealing, pursuing quiet negotiations essentially to buy off several of the rebel groups.

After some initial setbacks, Castro's troops crushed the guerrillas, who were handicapped by a lack of both equipment and popular support. Also, the guerrillas had no coordinated leadership, no particularly charismatic leaders, and little communication between their small bands of 20 men or more. The rebels were beaten down by 1961, only to reappear in 1962; the last "bandidos" were not eliminated until 1965–66.[12] Most importantly, Castro's nascent armed forces had already shown themselves to be stronger than Batista's had been in 1958.

A much more serious threat emerged in April 1961 when the U.S.-supported Brigade 2506 landed at the Bay of Pigs. Castro deployed roughly 25,000 FAR troops and about 200,000 militia, though only a fraction of those would see combat. As would later become the custom, the army was divided into three regional commands—the east under Raul Castro, the center under Ché Guevara, and the west under Juan Almeida. Fidel himself exercised overall command from a secret post in Havana. He hoped to use the militia to meet the invaders on the beach and only employ the FAR, with its tanks and artillery, as a mobile reserve to crush the invasion once it was underway.

When Brigade 2506 landed, Castro immediately committed the students from two nearby military schools—a cadets' school and the elite Militia Officers' School—along with Militia Battalion 339 and a few T-34 tanks that were on hand. As with the Escambray guerrillas, Castro recognized that time was of the essence—if the beachhead became firmly established it could become a serious threat to his rule; and like the Escambray campaign, at the Bay of Pigs Castro would rush to the front lines and take charge of the battlefield himself. (He knew it well—it was one of his favorite fishing grounds.) The first attack on the beachhead, 500 militia and cadets with small arms, machine guns, and mortars, was repulsed with heavy losses. Without the direct U.S. support that the Kennedy administration had pledged but found impossible to deliver, however, the Brigade was doomed. Eventually, however, as the Brigade ran out of ammunition, food, and water, and as Castro mustered more and more militia and tanks outside the beachhead, the invasion collapsed.[13]

The 1960s: Institutionalization of the MINFAR

If the 1970s are often viewed as the period of the "institutionalization of the Cuban revolution," then the 1960s must be thought of as the time of the "institutionalization of the military." The Cuban military led the development of the revolution during this decade. As Jorge Dominguez pointed out in 1976, "The armed forces were already well along the road to institutionalization in the 1960s; what has occurred in the 1970s is the consolidation of these trends."[14]

In part, the rapid development of the military was a product of the regime's threat perceptions. Castro reacted violently to the Bay of Pigs invasion. He ordered mass arrests—a quarter of a million people were rounded up in three days. Most importantly for our purposes, he thrust Cuba further into the Soviet camp, declaring it a socialist country on the eve of the Bay of Pigs and himself a Marxist-Leninist at the end of 1961. Expanded Soviet military aid soon followed, and, as Carlos Franqui explains, "The long, expert Soviet repressive arm was now joined to the Castroite military body, which meant total repression. . . . Fear, the mortal enemy of our revolution, grew like a weed."[15]

Development of an Institutionalized Armed Forces

In June 1961, Castro again bolstered his domestic paramilitary capabilities by forming the Ministry of the Interior (MININT), comprising the National Revolutionary Police, the Department of Technical Investigations, the Department of State Security, and the International Section and related Liberation Directorate (DL). The latter fell under the General Directorate of Intelligence (DGI), the Cuban counterpart to the Soviet KGB. The DL immediately began training revolutionary cadres to send abroad.[16] MININT also came to deploy military units, the Batallones Fronterizos (Bons, the coastal guards) and the Milicias Serranas (also known as LCBs—Lucha Contra Bandidos, internal forces patrolling Cuba's provinces). These units played an important domestic political role, potentially serving as a bulwark against a coup by the regular army.[17]

For the regular army, the growing Soviet ties meant an increase in training, arming, and influence. In 1961, Castro established the Air and Air Defense Force (DAAFAR) and developed the militia officers' school into a MINFAR officers' school. The highest military rank continued to be *comandante* or major, a symbol of revolutionary egalitarianism.

By 1963, the institutionalization of the military was in full swing. On 26 July of that year, Castro declared his intention to seek mandatory, universal military service. On 26 November 1963, Law 1129 of the revolutionary government required all males between ages sixteen and forty-four to register for military service. The CDRs supported this plan by issuing Servicio Militar Obligatorio (SMO) cards. The Revolutionary Navy (MGR) was founded the same year.[18]

In 1964, however, as the initial draft pool made its way into the increasingly numerous military schools, the popularity of the Cuban military appears to have begun to decline. The post-Bay of Pigs police state atmosphere in Cuba had already placed its people on guard, and many Cubans now expressed resentment of the registering requirements, the draft, the militarization of society, and eventually the risks of war in service of Castro's international adventures. The Cuban people had de-tected a disturbing trend: the increasing organization of Cuban life on a regimented, military model.

As the importance of the military grew, so did the emphasis accorded creation of Communist Party cadres within it. As early as 1961, the government established the Osvaldo Sanchez School for Revolutionary Instruction for political instructors within the military, and in 1963 Raul Castro inaugurated an intensive effort to build up the party in the military. This campaign utilized the mass media, classic Marxist-Leninist texts, the best of the officer recruitment pool, and lessons from political commissars of other communist nations. It was aimed at firmly entrenching the influence within the military of Castro and his followers, as opposed to former members of the PSP or other anti-Batista groups. Top political commissars from the military often moved on to fill important government posts on the civilian side. Military resentment against the graduates of the Sanchez political school, who had little military training, led to a 1963 decision to draw all MINFAR political officers from the military itself. The rebels had come full circle—from undoctrinaire, nonparty (even antiparty) guerrillas to institutionalized Marxist-Leninist party ideologues. In both cases, however, the military instrument was paramount.[19]

Now that the military had been firmly established and brought firmly under Castro's control—and since the MININT had been created as an independent protector of the regime—the role of the militia, the original revolutionary/democratic form of the Cuban military, could be drastically reduced. In keeping with its paranoia regarding domestic security, the government spared no effort in attempting to eliminate possible resources for a counterrevolution, and in 1964 disarmed the militia. The militias were replaced by a more conventional military reserve, the Popular Defense Forces, composed of individuals who, unlike members of the militias, did not keep their own weapons.

The beginnings of dissatisfaction within the military and society, and the regime's obsession with security, led to the November 1965 formation of the Military Units to Aid Production (UMAP) in Camaguey province. The government assigned to these disciplinary units "problem" recruits—among them homosexuals, criminals, the actively religious, and the politi-cally flawed. The purpose of the UMAPs, as Fidel said, was "ideological rehabilitation," and as their name implied they performed labor-intensive support tasks for various military units, including many engaged in civic or economic tasks such as raising crops. The units would also become a dumping ground for uneducated former rebel officers unsuited for the modern army Fidel had begun to build. In practice, UMAP members were treated little better than prisoners, watched by armed guards, enclosed in barbed-wire and masonry jails, fed meager rations, and worked for long hours—in some cases, to death. As the word spread about the abuses of the UMAPs, a public outcry forced Fidel to abolish them in December 1966.[20]

Refinement of the Military Instrument

The institutional framework of the military continued to evolve in the later 1960s. Castro's regime made extensive use of youth groups to promote a martial spirit and to obtain military personnel; the Union of Young Communists (Unión de Jovenes Comunistas or UJC) had been formed in 1962, and a subset of that organization, the Union of Cuban Pioneers (UPC), provided officer recruits to the armed forces and trained children in basic military arts and political doctrines. The UPC enrolled children aged seven to fourteen, and by 1970 boasted a membership of over a million. Later, at the EBIR, such education continued. In 1966, the Camilo Cienfuegos military schools were opened, the first one with 300 students, instructing young Cubans of both sexes aged eleven to seventeen in secondary school subjects and military regimentation.

For higher military education, the Centers for Military Studies (Centros de Estudios Militares or CEM), a group of military academies, was founded in 1966. It took students from the Camilo Cienfuegos schools and from other secondary institutions. The CEM's flagship school was the Instituto Técnico Militar, or ITM. Other institutions established under the aegis of the CEM included the General Maceo Inter-Arms School, which specialized in infantry and communication training; the Maximo Gomez Military School for artillery and armor; and the Advanced School of War, a sort of postgraduate training center for the best military officers. The MGR kept active the prerevolutionary Naval School in Mariel, which produced 1,200 officers between 1959 and 1974; the air force built its Aviation Cadet School in San Antonio. By the early 1970s, these five schools of the CEM were graduating 1,200 to 1,600 officers annually.

The military continued to represent the most efficient portion of the government, and as such was employed in tasks extending far beyond its purely military role. Those tasks—harvesting, building, educating, cane cutting, and so on—were at first apparently welcomed by a military anxious to preserve its importance in the postcounterrevolutionary era. But the military's civic duties would lead to a conflict of roles—"the field officer had to decide whether to give priority to the harvest or to combat preparedness, to social rehabilitation or to shooting practice, when all were mandated by the armed forces ministry."[21]

By the end of the 1960s, then, the Cuban military had evolved into a reasonably efficient fighting force. A plethora of military schools improved the quality of officers and molded a politically unified military. The rough basis for a truly modern military had been established, and developments at the outset of the 1970s, including an increase in Soviet influence, would complete that process.

Nascent Militancy in Cuban Foreign Policy: The 1960s

Against this background of the early development of the Cuban military infrastructure and its relationship to the regime's ideological development, how did Cuba's first attempts at a militant foreign policy fare? In a word, poorly. Other chapters in this volume have examined these episodes in great detail, and in any case the armed forces were not significantly involved in the first two phases of Castro's international revolutionizing— it had not yet become "part of the mission of the armed forces as an institution."[22] Rather, the Cubans who went on such missions theoretically volunteered for their international socialist duty, and most Cuban troops served as advisors, not combatants. Only the broad outlines of involvement, therefore, will be discussed here.

These early years can be broken down into two major phases: 1959 to 1965 and 1966 to 1969. In the first phase, the fledgling Cuban government pursued policies which can best be described as reflecting a revolutionary exuberance. Conveniently coinciding with Soviet leader Khrushchev's activist support for fraternal revolutionary movements in the Third World, these efforts were not the product of a sophisticated strategy. Instead, they involved sending marauding bands of Fidelistas—little more than troublemakers—to create unrest in neighboring countries. Or, in some cases, direct military assistance was provided to fraternal movements within the region. These efforts required little in the way of traditional military forces. Targets on the anointed "hit list" included dictatorships such as the Dominican Republic, Nicaragua, Panama, and Haiti. Castro also acquired an interest in Africa, and established contacts throughout the continent during the 1960s, demonstrating the seriousness of his intent as early as 1963 with the shipment of troops to Algeria. However, as William Durch has noted, there is little evidence that those Cuban troops were directly engaged in combat.[23]

The second phase of Cuban activism (1966–69) proceeded ahead in a much more institutionalized fashion, but met with as little success as the preceding phase. Sponsored by Havana in January 1966, the meeting of the Tricontinental Congress provided the ideological framework for Cuban foreign policy during these years. The two principal contenders at the conference, the Soviet Union and Cuba, advocated divergent tactics: the

Soviets promoted a peaceful road to power via the ballot box and the formation of broad coalitions with other political parties, while Fidel eschewed such means, instead promoting violent revolutionary struggle. Ultimately, however, the Cubans came to dominate the event, with the result that the conference advocated the concept of wars of national liberation and pledged support to fraternal revolutionary movements.[24] As a by-product, in 1967 the Organization of Latin American Solidarity (OLAS) was formed under Castro's leadership to actively promote the concept of continental revolution.

Despite such optimistic beginnings, Cuban efforts at a militant foreign policy in the late 1960s were dealt a series of severe blows. First, the ideological differences between Cuba and the Soviet Union that had emerged at the 1966 conference disrupted Cuban/Soviet relations. Second, despite active Cuban training, financing, and equipping of regional insurgent groups throughout Latin America, none came to power. Their failure can be attributed to the uniqueness of the Cuban revolution. When Fidel and Ché attempted to apply its lessons, through the "foco" theory developed by them and Regis Debray (which called for small revolutionary cores to create revolutionary conditions where none existed before), they failed miserably in Argentina, Colombia, Ecuador, Guatemala, Peru, Venezuela, and Bolivia, where Ché was killed. Third, Cuba's domestic fortunes plummeted as well; the economy was in a shambles, a fact clearly apparent after the failure of the 1970 "10 Million Tons" sugar harvest effort. The question of where the revolution was headed was on everyone's lips in Cuba by the late 1960s.

The answer was provided by Cuba's relationship with its preeminent patron, the Soviet Union. After varied attempts to modify Cuban behavior, including an oil squeeze in 1968, the Soviets managed to bring Havana largely into line with Moscow's policies, a trend confirmed in 1968 with Castro's expressed approval of the Soviet invasion of Czechoslovakia. This subordinance, however, was implemented in a uniquely Cuban manner under Fidel's direction. In essence, the Cuban revolution underwent a process of institutionalization and restructuring of the domestic and foreign policy realms. The military was modified as a part of this process, an issue to which we now turn.

The 1970s: Sovietization of the Armed Forces

During the 1970s, Cuba emerged from its largely regional confines and assumed a truly global rule. This was certainly a product of Fidel's closer ties with the USSR—Soviet arms, economic aid, and military sealift and airlift assets were integral aspects of Cuba's foreign policy. To what degree the Soviet Union controlled, encouraged, or merely assisted Castro's adventures is a matter of dispute, and Jiri Valenta, William Ratliff, and Constantine Menges address this subject in other chapters. What was undisputedly clear in the development of Cuba's armed forces, however, was that its uses abroad were indicators of the military's growing importance as an arm of a revolution with worldwide ambitions. "Between 1970 and 1974," Pamela Falk explains, "the FAR changed significantly, setting the stage for a massive military involvement in Africa."[25] This change is the subject of the present discussion.

Developments within MINFAR and MININT

During the early 1970s, under Soviet tutelage, Castro molded his army into a smaller, more professional fighting force. The basic set of reforms was accomplished in 1973. The bases for military service were (and remain) the August 1973 laws of General Military Service and Social Service. Various nonmilitary youth organizations were combined into the Youth Army of Work (EJT), which continued to draw its personnel from military conscripts (though it generally received the least qualified of them) and to operate under MINFAR; it maintained its own military ranks and education and promotion systems. Many thousands of Cuban military personnel were forced into the reserves or retirement to thin the MIN-FAR's active-duty ranks. Draft policies were altered, in many cases by Soviet edict.

As a result of these and other changes, manpower levels in MINFAR shrank from 300,000 in the early 1960s to 250,000 in 1970 and 100,000 in 1974. In the process, the MINFAR was transformed into a better organized, equipped, and disciplined force, and later growth built upon this stable foundation. The cost of military efficiency was high: the 1974 force, less than half the size of the army of 1970, cost twice as much.

Importantly, these active-duty cuts were made up by the growth of the reserves. "The change from 1970 to 1974 can be attributed almost entirely to a shift of personnel from semiprofessional, full-time military activity to the military reserves," writes Jorge Dominguez, who notes that the result was a shift from the "labor-intensive military" of the early to mid-1960s to a "smaller, capital-intensive, highly professional military with modern inventories."[26] The reserves used six classification categories to outline the service requirements of its members, with obligations ranging from 12 to 90 days a year. During the 1970s and 1980s, it participated extensively in all significant military exercises within Cuba. Men served in it until they reached 50 years of age, women to 40. The units were supervised by municipal and regional military committees.

Simultaneously, many of the civic tasks previously assigned to the military were turned over to strictly reserve or paramilitary organizations, allowing the active-duty MINFAR to concentrate on military professionalism. Soldiers serving in civilian posts were stripped of their military titles, though they could recover them should they be reposted to a military command. However, since the MINFAR still controlled the EJT, its influence over civil matters remained relatively constant, or perhaps even increased; only the combat armed forces themselves had been removed from civic duties.

The selection service for the military was controversial. All Cuban males were required to give some form of national service, but not necessarily in the military. Military service remained unpopular (especially for the enlisted ranks), and many well-qualified, highly educated candidates apparently opted for nonmilitary service. This trend hampered the military's ability to recruit talented people and created a context in which tensions between educated, reasonably content officers and poorly qualified enlisted personnel could arise.

Other reforms were undertaken. In 1973, the government created a new system of military rank, replacing the older, "egalitarian" hierarchy whose primitive and sometimes obscure lines of command were unsuited, as Fidel Castro recognized, to the demands of a modern army. By mid-1975 the military had created three ranks of officer—superior, commissioned, and petty; within these categories were various subranks.[27]

Finally, the Soviet-inspired reorganization plan for Cuba also deeply affected MININT, in particular its General Directory of Investigation (DGI) and the Committees for the Defense of the Revolution (CDRs)—the former in 1971, the latter in 1973. The DGI was coordinated and integrated with the Soviet Union's intelligence apparatus. The responsibilities of the CDRs were upgraded in 1973 to include management of Cuba's rationing system for basic supplies (such as food and clothing) and the delivery of government services. MININT also maintained its set of elite and border patrol combat units.

Tools of the Trade: Military Equipment

During the Sovietization of the armed forces, Soviet military aid continued, but contrary to popular impression did not significantly increase. Soviet deliveries in 1968 and 1974 were almost indistinguishable, both quantitatively and qualitatively. In the early 1970s, Soviet military deliveries averaged 13.2 million metric tons, a figure that would grow significantly (to 37.7 million tons) only when Castro initiated his African adventures. Once the Angolan operation was underway, new Soviet aid worth billions of dollars did arrive. Soviet technical advice also increased; the number of Cubans annually trained in the U.S.S.R. doubled from 400 to 800.

Instruction Manual: Military Doctrine

Though the MINFAR acquired many aspects of Soviet doctrine along with Soviet weapons, it retained uniquely Cuban aspects of waging war. In particular this meant that the Cuban military never discarded the notion of guerrilla war, a Maoist "people's war" in the defense of the country. "Theoretically, the FAR has the capability to atomize into hundreds or thousands of guerrilla columns to oppose an enemy like the United States."[28] Specifically, the MININT's Batallones Serranos operated in the mountains, forests, and fields of Cuba's interior, where they maintained secret supply dumps and cultivated a knowledge of the terrain that would be useful should they be required to conduct guerrilla operations.

In part, these tactics were dictated by a central theme of Cuban military doctrine: the defense of the revolution is a solely Cuban responsibility. Soviet help can be expected, but not counted on. Cuba's military leaders know well that the only credible way to suggest that they alone can defend the island against the United States is with the threat of guerrilla tactics. This was especially true during periods of tension with the U.S.S.R. Thus, Castro concluded in July 1967 (during the period of greatest differences with Moscow) that the Soviet Union was too far away to provide reliable help: "We must learn to accustom ourselves to the idea that we are going to fight alone."[29]

Use of the Tool: Military Operations

By the early 1970s, the Cuban military had become a significant international presence, and would remain so for well over a decade. Its "civic soldiers" helped established socialist governments, defeat insurgencies (though not with the same zeal as the U.S.S.R.—Castro for a time retained his sympathy for national liberation movements, even under socialist systems), aided revolutionary movements, defended socialist states against attacks from other states, and aided friendly countries in attacks on unfriendly ones. These roles were accomplished almost solely by MINFAR, rather than MININT, and MINFAR units provided economic assistance (building schools, roads, airports, and hospitals), gave military training and basic education, helped maintain and operate advanced military equipment, and in some cases engaged in actual combat.

Cuban troops pursuing socialist internationalism were showered across the globe. Thousands of Cubans, including several hundred combat troops, aided the Syrians in the 1973 war, operating tanks and advanced aircraft. Castro gave military and socioeconomic aid to the Polisario rebel group fighting against Morocco, the Algerian rebels and later the revolutionary Algerian government, the Katangian rebels against Zaire, rebels in Guinea-Bissau against the Portugese, Somalia (until 1977) against Ethiopia, South Yemen against the North, and Vietnam and Cambodia against all their adversaries, as well as Guinea, Peru, Tanzania, Jamaica, the Congo, Laos, Sao Tome and Principe, and Equatorial Guinea. These commitments had by the mid-1970s replaced subversion as Castro's primary means of expressing revolutionary solidarity; unlike the subversive efforts of the 1960s, these ventures involved the military as an institution.

This new role became especially manifest in the chief Cuban commitment in the mid-1970s—of course, the commitment to Angola. The specifics of the context, the war, and the Cuban troop presence are detailed in the chapters on relations toward Africa. Most important from the Cuban military's perspective was that it had acquired a new role, a new justification for continued size and strength: international power projection. MINFAR would henceforth serve as the vanguard of a more distinctly military program of aid to fraternal socialist regimes, and its budget shot up to 500 million pesos or more after having dipped far below that level in the late 1960s. It therefore acquired "an institutional stake in the continuation of an activist foreign policy."[30]

The Cuban presence in Angola was one made up about 70 percent by reserves. The active army, slimmed as it had been in the previous years, was simply unable to perform both home defense and power projection missions, and the number of reserves trained doubled from 1974 to 1975.

Several problems for the military emerged in Angola. Employers in Cuba opposed the sudden recall of reservists. Public resentment against the military—against the draft, recall of reserves, and combat service including casualties thousands of miles from home—grew, building on the base of displeasure that had formed earlier. Military service was increasingly resented and feared, so much so that the threat of it was used as a motivational tool. This was a significant change for a country where military service had been viewed as an egalitarian avenue to technical training and prestige. MINFAR attempted to counter these impressions by having military officers speak with localities through CDRs, and though this effort was of questionable value, no evidence emerged of massive opposition to the regime. Finally, the rigors of combat exposed the difficulties of the joint political/military command structure and caused tension between professional military and political officers.

The other major ground force commitment during the 1970s was made to Ethiopia. The 1974 coup of military officers against the pro-Western regime in Ethiopia set in motion a chain of events that saw Cuba and the U.S.S.R. switch allegiance from Somalia to Ethiopia, and support the latter both against Somalia and against Eritrean rebels. Early in 1977, an advance party of Cuban advisers arrived in Ethiopia; through the rest of that year, Cuban and Soviet aid grew significantly. From December 1977 to March 1978, as Ethiopia's conflict with Somalia (which expected American aid that never arrived) heated up, the number of Cuban troops in Ethiopia jumped from 400 to 11–15,000.

Cuban military units operated artillery, tanks, and aircraft. Cuban units spearheaded major Ethiopian attacks, and many reports suggested that advanced Cuban armor and tactical air units had a decisive effect. The Soviet Union increased its military aid to Cuba to compensate for the equipment and personnel that had been sent abroad.

Implications of the Sovietization of the Military

The Soviet-guided modernization of the military carried a number of implications. Most important, it finally provided Castro with a credible capability to defend the island against even a long-anticipated large-scale American attack, as well as against counterrevolutionary movements from within. Internally and externally, the revolution was therefore regarded as basically secure.

Castro and the Soviets had also created an impressive force that could—and would—be projected into areas of mutual Cuban and Soviet concern. Crucially, though, the Soviets would not give Cuba the strategic airlift or sealift forces necessary to ship its army abroad, so Castro remained dependent on the Soviets for force projection.

Some contend, too, that the Soviets have created a pro-Soviet faction within MINFAR and MININT. Certainly, the DGI was subordinated to the KGB. In 1967–68, a pro-Soviet faction within the Cuban Communist Party (PCC) had been uncovered, arguably intended as the seeds of an eventual Soviet-led coup against Castro. There is no reason to believe that the Soviets would not take the opportunity afforded by their extensive training of Cuban officers, and the top posts Soviet-trained Cubans receive, to bolster their influence in Havana.

The growing importance of Soviet training also created rifts among the Cuban officer corps. Graduates of Soviet technical schools, including the Frunze military academy (*frunzistas*), seem to have been granted priority in command and promotion. Those Cuban officers who had attended Cuban technical or military schools, or those who had attended no schools at all (mostly veterans of the Sierra Maestra campaign), enjoyed far less success in the military.

The interlocking of the government, party, and military continued during this period. Between 75 and 90 percent of the population belonged to CDRs; 74 percent of the military were members of the Young Communist League or the Communist Party. However, as recent defectors have testified, such membership was often nominal, obtained because officers recognized it as a pre-requisite for advancement. Perhaps a better representation of civilian/military crossover is the percentage of government officials who were members of the FAR: by mid-1975, 80 percent of the Executive Committee, the top government organ, were FAR, as were 50 percent of the Council of Ministers, 69 percent of the Central Committee, and a majority of the Cuban Communist Party leadership. Even the decline of such figures through the 1970s pointed to increased party/government contacts: as noted, military men shifted to government positions lost their military titles, so technically they did not count in the percentages of FAR men in the government.

The party within the military functioned as an independent organ, and its members were not answerable to nonmilitary party members. The PCC maintained a structure within the MINFAR that paralleled the military's hierarchy but attempted not to compete with it. The basic unit of party organization was the cell, led by a political officer (who was subordinate to the military officer) and carrying out courses of instruction in Marxist-Leninist doctrine, recruiting new members, and maintaining discipline and morale. The PCC did, however, control promotion and transfer within the military, so that by the 1970s it appeared that "membership in the PCC has become a prerequisite to leadership in the FAR."[31]

Finally, the growing Soviet influence, and the arguable "Stalinization" of the Cuban polity, led to charges that Cuba had become "militarized." In part these charges arose out of the military's growing influence in daily Cuban life: the military was one of the more efficient institutions in Cuba, and its role in the 1970 10 Million Ton sugar effort was crucial. Combined with the role of paramilitary organizations such as the CDRs and the MININT security apparatuses, these developments led some to contend that Cuba had become a militarized society.

This is a vexing issue, though an important one in any analysis of the development of the military in Cuba. Some have argued that the military's role was almost accidental. Thus Max Azicri writes that "Cuba did not become a militarized society in the true meaning of the term. It was more a case of fusing civilian and military roles into one and downplaying the importance of the distinction as irrelevant to Cuba's revolutionary needs and circumstances."[32] Azicri's notion is similar to the concept of a Cuban "civic soldier" discussed by Jorge Dominguez and others.[33]

Staunch defenders of the militarization thesis, such as Irving Louis Horowitz, have attacked the civic soldier concept insofar as it implies that military personnel become civilians, and fails to recognize this process as the militarization of a polity. Dominguez replies that the militarization thesis misinterprets what is an essentially unique model of civilian/military relations and which does not therefore conform to traditional models.

In fact it seems that the "militarization" of Cuban society as such is an accomplished fact; even Cuban officials choose to defend rather than deny it. The real question is how one chooses to interpret that fact. Some observers suggest that a military/civilian convergence was necessary for both internal and external military, economic, and political reasons; others view the same phenomenon as a blatant imposition of a military dictatorship possessed of brutal internal security agencies and powerful force projection units; and some political scientists contend that the military's role in society is unique and cannot be compared with truly "militarized" societies.

Whatever the truth, it seems clear that a powerful driving force behind the military's role in Cuban society has been Fidel's experience as a guerrilla and his desire to assume the role of traditional Latin American *caudillo* or military strongman. His biographer, Tad Szulc, points out that:

> Fidel Castro's conditioning as a *guerrillero* is therefore an extremely significant element in understanding and defining his personality today. He cherishes the title of Commander in Chief and the laurel leaves of rank on his military uniform. The total militarization of the Cuban society is a concept stemming from his formative experiences. He learned the very hard way—in urban insurrection, Sierra war, creating from those siege conditions a siege mentality for this hostility-surrounded island where at least one half of the population is trained and organized for defensive combat. He also learned that to survive, he must be absolutely and undeviatingly uncompromising.[34]

By the close of the 1970s, MINFAR had become a critical instrument in the execution of Cuban foreign policy. That foreign policy continued its support for armed revolutionary movements across the globe through military assistance, training, and equipping, a trend born in the early days of the Cuban revolution. By the late 1970s, Cuban foreign policy had come to depend heavily on the use of MINFAR's conventional force capabilities in order to ensure the consolidation of fraternal revolutionary regimes.

The 1980s: Threats and the Development of the MTT

With the election of Ronald Reagan and the tough talk of his first Secretary of State, Alexander Haig, about "going to the source" of

Central American instability, Fidel Castro believed that he was confronted with a renewed American threat. Perhaps in anticipation of a tougher U.S. line in the wake of Angola and Ethiopia, Castro had already called in his May Day 1980 speech for the reformulation of a civilian militia. The flight of over 100,000 Cubans in the Mariel crisis might also have reemphasized the need for better control of an obviously dissatisfied population.[35] The new organization would become the Territorial Militia Troops (MTT), an organization that immediately held great significance within Cuba.

The original purposes of the MTT were threefold: to defend local areas against domestic or foreign attack, to serve as a pool of replacements for the MINFAR, and to aid the MINFAR with construction of defenses, delivery of supplies, and other efforts. The MTT's own tactics were a reemphasis on "people's war" doctrines: its members, women and children included, were trained in hand-to-hand combat, and the MTT promised fierce guerrilla resistance from the whole population.

Once the Reagan administration had assumed power, Castro firmly linked the creation and perpetuation of the MTT to the harsher U.S. anti-Cuban line. "We had to change our views and prepare ourselves for the war of all the people," Castro told the French Communist Party daily *L'Humanité* in 1987. "We did not have arms for everybody at that time. Today, we do. . . . Everything is ready to confront a total blockade, invasion, and occupation of the country. . . . We do not underestimate the danger."[36]

Domestically, the MTT serves various purposes, which have been summarized by Leon Gouré: "A new form of mobilization of the population and reinforcement of the country's garrison state mentality; a strengthening of the party controls and its role in defense matters; and the creation of a counterweight to the Soviet-influenced FAR while enhancing the party's influence within it."[37] As General Rafael Del Pino, who defected in 1987 from Cuba has pointed out, the MTT counters the MINFAR, not by potential force of arms, but by giving the regime a barrier of women and children to place between itself and any military coup. The MTT thus "hinder any action by the military, because the troops will never fire on the people."[38]

The longevity of the MTT, however, is questionable, for three major reasons. First, the continuously deteriorating Cuban economy indicates that the expense of the MTT cannot be borne indefinitely. Second, and related to the first point, is the potential for conflict between the MTT and MINFAR. On an operational level, the MTT was ostensibly formed as an integral part of MINFAR. In practice, however, this has not been the case, since the MTT has created its own defense zones and councils led by Party, not military, officials, and since the MTT has established its own chain of command and officer corps. Third and finally, the original justification for the MTT was that an American invasion was imminent. As acute tensions between the United States and Cuba have continued to decline, however, the specter of an American attack must seem very dim indeed. Over time, calls may arise to eliminate the costly and unnecessary militia.

The other major development of significance to the Cuban military during the Reagan administration was the U.S. operation in Grenada. Cuban involvement in the island began in earnest in 1979 with the overthrow of Eric Gairy's government by Maurice Bishop's New Jewel Movement. In the fall of 1983, Bishop was assassinated by radical, pro-Soviet military officers. On 25 October 1983, citing the plight of stranded American medical students and the threat of a large runway under construction on the island, the Reagan administration intervened.

Within 48 hours, U.S. forces had secured the island. Some 600 Cubans surrendered; 24 were killed in action with American forces, including UJC workers as well as MINFAR regulars. Castro gave returning prisoners of war released by the Americans a hero's welcome, but reports from Cuba made clear that he was extremely dissatisfied with the conduct of the battle. He apparently expected all Cubans to fight to the death. Those high-ranking officers who surrendered subsequently dropped from sight within Cuba, perhaps after court-martials.

The invasion of Grenada held more implications for Cuban foreign policy than for the MINFAR itself. Immediately, Suriname's left-leaning ruler, Colonel Dese Boterse, expelled the Cuban ambassador and 105 Cubans within his country and suspended the Cuban aid he had been receiving; Nicaragua's government moderated its rhetoric about spreading its revolution within Central America. On the other hand, the fact that a few hundred Cuban construction workers and MINFAR personnel had been surprised and defeated by a much larger U.S. force heavily supported by air and naval units says little about the real status or effectiveness of MINFAR. The true test of the armed forces' continued reliability and dedication to the regime must await another day.

The Cuban Military Today

The Cuban military in 1989 remains a powerful, efficient, battle-tested force. Fidel Castro is of course commander in chief of MINFAR, and his brother Raul serves as minister of the armed forces. A Joint General Staff under Raul's direction oversees the operations of the services, each of which in turn has its own staff. The military is divided into three geographical commands: Western (headquartered at Havana), Central (headquartered at Matanzas), and Eastern (headquartered at Santiago de Cuba). The Isle of Youth is an independent military area.

All males aged sixteen to 45 must serve at least three years in MINFAR, MININT, or various social service organizations. Women's participation in MINFAR is voluntary, and they perform support tasks. As before, preference in promotion is granted to members of the Communist Party or UJC. The Camilo Cienfuegos schools continue to train eleven- to seventeen-year-old Cubans in military arts, and graduate 75 percent of the young men who will become officers.

Data on Cuban military spending are somewhat unclear, insofar as the exchange rate of the peso is approximate and the Cuban government can "hide" military expenditures in other programs. Estimates are, however, that Cuban military spending grew from 1.05 billion pesos (with each peso worth about 80 cents) in 1980 to 1.6 billion in 1987, an increase from 8.5 percent of the budget to 11.1 percent. These figures do not include Soviet military aid, of course; of the $6–7 billion worth of aid the Soviets provided in 1986, roughly $1.5 billion was military. In 1984, these figures placed Cuba only 45th in the world in total military expenditure, 37th in military expenditure as a percentage of GNP (roughly 6 percent), and 40th in military expenditure per capita. Cuba ranked much higher (7th) in a key measure of societal militarization—military per 1,000 people.

Organization and Composition

The general organization of MINFAR is summarized in Table 9.1.

The reserves are an integral part of MINFAR today. Reservists fall into one of two categories: "first reservists," who train 45 days annually; and "second reservists," males with no military training or who are unfit for military service. The integration of military and civilian roles is seen in the fact that the salary and disability benefits of reservists on active duty are paid by the reservists' civilian employers, not MINFAR.[39] The military reserves include about 150–160,000 people.

Each service has unique characteristics; the equipment and organization of the army are summarized in Table 9.2. Its units are not all at full strength; like its Soviet counterpart, the Cuban army maintains formations at three categories of readiness: Category 1, or full readiness (the 1st Armored and all four mechanized divisions, along with the infantry division on the Isle of Pines, are at Category 1); Category 2, at 60 percent of full strength with the balance to be made up of reserves (2nd Armored division and one infantry division of each army corps); and Category 3, at 30 percent of full strength (all remaining units). A high degree of secrecy is preserved about units and deployments, so that, for example, even

TABLE 9.1
MINFAR Organization

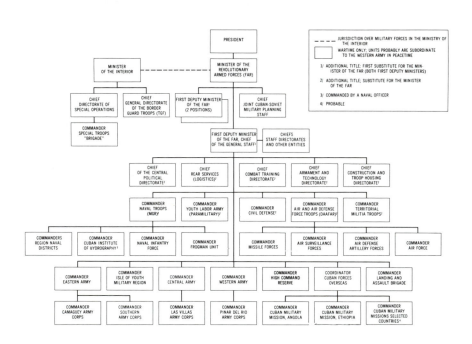

Source: Defense Intelligence Agency, *Handbook on the Cuban Armed Forces* (Washington, D.C.: DIA, 1985), pp. 1–9.

members of divisions theoretically only know it by a three-, four-, or five-digit identification number, not by its actual designation.

Cuban units are very small compared to their Western counterparts. An infantry division only contains 5,900 men; each of its regiments is only 1,010 strong, with two battalions of 349 each. A mechanized division deploys 8,200 men; an armored division contains only 6,200; each armored regiment has only 720 men; each battalion only 110 men and 21 tanks. The army's "Frontier Guard Brigade" performs security around the perimeter of the American naval base at Guantanamo Bay.

TABLE 9.2
The Cuban Army

Forces

Total Manpower: 130–145,000, active and reserve

Units: 3 armies with 4 army corps: 2 armored divisions; 4 mechanized divisions; 11 infantry divisions; 1 artillery division; 1 airborne brigade; 1 frontier brigade (these are a mix of active and reserve forces)

Armored Fighting Vehicles: 300–350 T-62 and 650 T-54/55 battle tanks; 60 PT-76 light tanks; 150 older T-34 tanks; 100 BDRM-1/2 scout cars; 50 BMP combat vehicles; 500 BTR-40, BTR-60, and BTR-152 armored personnel carriers

Artillery: 1,400 total: M-30, A-19 and D-74 122mm guns; M-46 130mm guns; D-1, D-20 and ML-20 152mm guns; SU-100 self-propelled 100mm guns; M-1943 160mm mortars; 122mm, 140mm, 132mm, 200mm and 240mm multiple rocket launchers; 65 Frog 4-7 surface-to-surface missiles

Air Defense: 1,600 total: 14.5mm, 23mm, 30mm, 37mm, 57mm, 85mm, and 100mm guns; SA-2, -3, -6, -7, -9, -13, and -14 surface-to-air missile systems

Anti-Tank Defense: 57mm, 76.2mm, and 85mm guns; Sagger and Snapper anti-tank guided missiles

Commands
(All unit compositions are estimates)

Western Army (HQ Havana): Pinar del Rio and La Habana Mixed Security Regiments, 1st Armored Division and 20th Mechanized Division; and Pinar del Rio army corps, with 11th, 12th, and 24th Infantry Divisions

Central Army (HQ Matanzas): Matanzas, Santa Clara and Cienfuegos Mixed Security Regiments, 40th Mechanized Division; and Las Villas army corps, made up of 42nd, 67th, and 68th Infantry Divisions

Eastern Army (HQ Santiago de Cuba): Santiago, Holguin, and Camaguey Mixed Security Regiments; 2nd Armored Division, 30th and 50th Mechanized Divisions, the Guantanamo Frontier Brigade; the Holguin army corps, made up of the 37th and 38th Infantry Divisions; and the Camaguey army corps, made up of the 55th and 56th Infantry Divisions

Isle of Youth Military Region (HQ Nueva Gerona): 71st Infantry Division

Source: International Institute for Strategic Studies (IISS), *The Military Balance, 1987–88* (London: IISS, 1987); and Adrian English (ed.), *Regional Defence Profile, No. 1: Latin America* (London: Jane's Publishing Co., 1988).

Cuban military and civilian combat and advisory contingents remain stationed abroad in many countries. As of 1988, these included Afghanistan (100 military advisers), Algeria (170 military and civilian advisers), Angola (27,000 military and 8,000 civilians, to be largely withdrawn), the Congo (300 military and 200 civilians), Ethiopia (3,000, mostly military who are being withdrawn), Guinea-Bissau (100 military and 50 civilians), Iraq (2,200, mostly military), Libya (3,000 military and civilians), Malagasy (50 military), Mozambique (750 military and 150 civilians), Nicaragua (500 military and 3,000 civilians), Sao Tome (75 civilian medical personnel), South Yemen (500 military), Tanzania (100 civilians), and Zambia (25 military advisers). The value of the MINFAR in foreign adventures was undoubtedly declining, however, with the accord reached in Angola and other conflicts on the decline.

The Cuban navy remains essentially a coastal defense force; its organization is outlined in Table 9.3. The only significant power projection units it possesses are three aging Soviet Foxtrot submarines. Despite Cuba's status as an island, its small size and the huge expense of naval units have traditionally dictated that the navy remain based on small patrol craft, and it remains so today.

In the 1970s the naval academy at Mariel was moved to Punta Santa Ana west of the capital, and since 1977 it has enjoyed the status of a full university. Naval cadets undergo a four- to five-year course of study, and the school graduates roughly 100 officers annually. Exceptional naval officers can pursue postgraduate study at Cuba's Maximo Gomez school or in the U.S.S.R. The navy also maintains two other independent schools, one at Playa del Solado for naval specialists and one at Cienfuegos for submariners. The Cuban air force maintains some of the most powerful weaponry in the Cuban military. Its relatively modern MiG-21 and MiG-23 aircraft probably represent Cuba's single most dangerous strike force.

In addition to the geographical commands outlined in Table 9.4, the Cuban air force is also broken down into functional commands. The Air Defense Command oversees interceptor and air defense brigades. The Tactical Air Command has control of fighter-bomber squadrons and one squadron each of attack and ASW helicopters. Transport aircraft fall under the Logistical Support Command, and training aircraft under the Training Command.

The Aviation Cadet School at San Julian runs a four- to five-year course of study for prospective air force officers. The Military Technical Institute (ITM) provides advanced training in various specialties, including communications, aerospace engineering, and antiaircraft equipment. All pilots and combat aircrew obtain some training in the Soviet Union, and Soviet advisors are intimately involved in training of air force officers within

TABLE 9.3
The Cuban Navy

Forces
Total Manpower: 12–13,500 (including Marines)
Major Units: 2 Koni-class frigates; 4 submarines, including 3 Foxtrot and one Whiskey for training; 22-23 Osa I and II and Komar missile attack boats; 10-12 Turya and Stenka-class hydrofoil torpedo boats; 4 SO-1 submarine hunters; 26-40 fast patrol craft; 14-15 minesweepers; 2 Polnocny-class landing ships, and 6 smaller T-4 landing craft
Marines: 1 assault battalion of 500-600; various base security units, totalling roughly 500
Other Equipment: BTR-60PB armored personnel carriers; SSC-2b surface-to-surface missiles; and 122mm, 130mm, and 152mm guns for coastal defense

Commands
3 Territorial:
Western (covers coasts of Pinar del Rio and Havana provinces and Isle of Youth; bases: Havana, Mariel)
Central (covers Matanzas, Villa Clara, Cienfuegos, and Sancti Spiritus; bases: Cienfuegos and Varadero)
Eastern (covers Ciego de Avila, Camaguey, Las Tunas, Holguin, Granman, Santiago de Cuba, and Guantanamo; bases: Punta Ballenatos)
4 Operational (deployed to territorial commands as needed):
Submarine command
Fast Attack Craft (Missile) command
Fast Attack Craft (Torpedo) command
Anti-Submarine Warfare command

Cuba as well. MINFAR and MININT also continue to deploy various reserve, militia, and paramilitary organizations. MININT is technically responsible for all internal security, and in this capacity it has at its disposal some 15,000 National Revolutionary Police, 3,500 Border Troops with 20 patrol boats, and 2,000 elite commando parachutists (the latter of which have also been deployed abroad). Under MINFAR (theoretically) falls the MTT, which today consists of 1.2 million members armed with serviceable enough second-generation weapons passed down by MINFAR. The MTT is made up of men over sixteen years old who are exempt from military service, and women who do not join the military (and represent 40 percent of the MTT's strength). It is organized in 200 regiments and 1,000 battalions, a few of which contain heavier weapons such as antiaircraft guns and artillery. The Youth Labor Army contains roughly 100,000 members armed with light infantry weapons who participate mostly in

TABLE 9.4
The Cuban Air Force

Forces

Total Manpower: 18,500 (including air defense forces)

Ground Attack Aircraft (4 squadrons): 15+ MiG-17; 30 MiG-19; 36 MiG-23BN Flogger F

Interceptors (16 squadrons): 30 MiG-21F; 34 MiG-21PFM; 20 MiG-21PFMA; 80-100 MiG-21bis; 15 MiG-23 Flogger E

Transport (4 squadrons): 16 Il-14; 35 An-2; 3 An-24; 22 An-26; 4 Yak-40

Helicopters (8 squadrons): 60 Mi-4; 40 Mi-8 (some armed); 18 Mi-24 Hind D; 4 Mi-14 Haze antisubmarine warfare helicopters

Training: 12-20 MiG-21U; some An-2; 30 Zlin 326; 20-25 Aero L-39; 2 MiG-23U

Air Defense: Over 200 surface-to-air missile launchers, including SA-2, SA-3, SA-6, SA-7, SA-9, and SA-13

Civil Airline: 10 Il-62; 7 Tu-154; 2 Il-76

Commands (estimated)

Western Air Brigade (Bay of Pigs Brigade): 2 interceptor regiments with 6 squadrons of MiG-21s based at San Antonio de los Banos; tactical support regiment, 3 squadrons of MiG-23s based at Guines; an independent fighter squadron with MiG-23s based at San Julian; and two transport squadrons

Central Air Brigade (Battle of Santa Clara Guard Brigade): 2 interceptor regiments with 6 squadrons of MiG-21s at Santa Clara and Sancti Spiritus; tactical support regiment with three squadrons of MiG-17s at Santa Clara; an ASW helicopter squadron with Mi-14s at Cienfuegos; and a transport squadron

Eastern Air Brigade: one interceptor regiment with 3 squadrons of MiG-21s at Camaguey; one tactical support regiment with three squadrons of MiG-19s at Holguin; and one helicopter and one transport squadron at Santiago de Cuba

Air Defense: Divided in Air Zones, each with an antiaircraft missile brigade; one independent air defense brigade for Havana. Each brigade consists of three battalions and three dozen SAM batteries

civic action. Finally, Civil Defense organizations contain another 100,000 individuals who serve as a security militia and disaster relief force.

Modern Character of the Military

The modern Cuban military shares much in common with the modernized force that emerged in the mid-1970s. Many of its primary characteristics—with regard to the war in Angola, relations with the U.S.S.R., and domestic roles and image—have changed little since then.

Reports of Cuban performance in Angola are mixed. Some of the bleakest testimony has come from General Rafael Del Pino, a defector, who has provided a high level of insight into the Cuban security apparatus. As such, he has noted that Cuban officers were often of poor quality and that promotion based on political connections and Soviet training, not quality, had sapped the morale and ability of the officer corps. With regard to the situation in Angola, Cuban units are often thrown into battle without a knowledge of either the terrain, National Union for the Total Independence of Angola (UNITA) tactics, or the customs prevalent within the country. In addition, at that juncture, the remains of Cuban dead had not yet been returned—and soldiers who did return to Cuba with AIDS were confined to a prison called *Los Cocos* where they were left to die. Finally, according to Del Pino, the role of the political officers is resented; furthermore, these officers often run fake missions to obtain combat medals and promotion.[40]

There is much evidence that the Cubans have only strained relations with their Angolan hosts. Recent reports point to mutual disrespect and accusations of cowardice. Different logistical systems apparently mean that Cubans are much better supplied, fed, and clothed than the Angolans, many of whom are reported to see the Cubans as lazy and soft. Such tensions run even to the social level—it has been reported that prostitutes in Luanda will not serve Cuban customers. There have even been reports of Cuban/Angolan exchanges of fire.[41]

Yet the picture is far from totally bleak. Many Cuban units have fought well, a fact to which many South African soldiers will testify. Publicly, Cuba and Angola remain the staunchest of allies. And while Jonas Savimbi's UNITA has not been defeated, neither has it been allowed to topple the government.

Cuban military relations with their Soviet advisers, both in Angola and at home, are, Del Pino says, "indifferent and, at times, antagonistic." Cuban officers often disagree with the Soviets over tactics or training, but Soviet advisers always win out. Technical scholarships in the Soviet Union are not free—they cost Cuba between 100,000 and 200,000 rubles, which are added to Cuba's debt to the U.S.S.R. And officers trained through those scholarships—often unruly children of high Cuban officials, sent not for their qualifications but because of connections—are promoted most quickly, almost regardless of their abilities.

Yet Cuban/Soviet military cooperation is still strong. MINFAR contains some 2,000–3,000 Soviet advisors, the senior officer of which is usually a colonel general who directly advises MINFAR chiefs. Approximately

300,000 Cubans study the Russian language annually. Soviet deployments in and to Cuba include the 2,800-man motorized rifle brigade, visits of reconaissance and antisubmarine aircraft (80 since 1981), the high-technology Soviet listening post at Lourdes which employs 2,100 Soviet specialists, and numerous visits of naval units.[42] Cuban/Soviet relations are, as always, publicly strong, moreover; at the May 1988 celebration in Havana of the 43rd anniversary of the Soviet Union's victory over fascism, Soviet officials decorated many Cuban officers and both sides praised their strong relationship.

Finally, within Cuba itself, the military institution has declined from one of relative efficiency to a corrupt, stagnant bureaucracy that is not respected, especially by the young. Yet the military is still the most honest branch of government, and its quality officers do not trust the regime; "the career officer class in Cuba," Del Pino contends, "does not believe in and has no faith in the leaders of the revolution," and many officers feel "that Cuba is collapsing. The country has been led to a quagmire by the group that holds power in Cuba." This perception is especially strong in young Cuban soldiers, whose loyalty is based only on the fact that they "cannot leave the country." The unpopularity of service has led to new recruitment procedures, utilizing, as was done in the 1970s, neighborhood "counselors" to motivate individuals.

As Del Pino has stated, MINFAR officers distrust MININT officials to the extent that the military:

> see the Ministry of the Interior as a rival, because it really holds the power in Cuba. Socialist legality is a fairy tale. . . . Indeed, it is said, or averred, by the officers of the military that, for instance, a major at the Ministry of the Interior can be compared to a general of the military in terms of privileges, sinecures, manner of living and all the corruption involved. So, really, the Ministry of the Interior is not accepted by the military. Although it is attempted to give the appearance of great unity, it is a myth.[43]

The privileges of MININT extend down to prices of goods: a refrigerator that would cost an average Cuban 1,200 pesos costs the military (which has its own stores) 595—and only 250 for MININT officials.

Despite such tensions, the military/government/party confluence continues. Raul Castro inaugurated in 1987 a renewed campaign to emphasize the rule of the party over, and its role within, the military. Individual services and armies conduct their own party conferences. Cuban officials have stressed the principle of *mando unico* or unified command, under which party and military leaders jointly lead the armed forces, although MINFAR officers who often serve in both capacities technically have the final say on military matters.

Still, the problems of the military are manifest in the fact that tens of thousands of men—56,000 according to Del Pino—had deserted in the early 1980s. A special unit was created within MINFAR, "Prevention" or the "Purple Berets," to catch deserters. A prison called "El Pitirre" had supposedly also been established to abuse selected soldiers who, when released, would relate their horror stories to other recruits, stories that would perhaps deter further desertions.

None of these tactics has worked, however, in part because families and friends often hid deserters—right under the noses of the CDRs, which, according to Del Pino, "gossip and do nothing." Some reports suggest that as many as 30,000 deserters are imprisoned. The unpopularity of military service is reflected in the fact that Cuban parents reportedly urge their children to study so that they might qualify for an academic exemption from MINFAR. Veterans have sometimes had difficulty obtaining jobs when returning from duty. The military has also adopted a policy of "early outs" based on good performance, something which a nation with very popular armed services need not consider. The military also employs a system of rotation of commands to ensure that no officer cultivates a personal following among the soldiers.

The government has attempted to respond to these problems. A December 1984 plenum at the PCC Central Committee meeting, for example, complained that military service was increasingly viewed as a punishment rather than a duty. Official pronouncements constantly stress recruitment and socialist military duty. New rules have eliminated or qualified former exemptions, such as education. In 1987, MINFAR apparently reached an agreement with the State Committee for Labor and Social Security establishing preferences for veterans in the job market. UJC units attempt to inculcate socialist military values, as does the Society of Military-Patriotic Education (SEPMI), which has tried to link the romanticism of Fidel's Sierra Maestra campaign to modern Cuban service.

Cuban military doctrine, stressing a Maoist-type people's war, has remained essentially unchanged. It provided the motivation for the MTT, and has been institutionalized in such tactics as the Turquino Plan, an attempt to make Cuba's mountains into a haven from which guerrillas could harry a U.S. invasion. Newly created "areas of attention" oversee local military readiness. And these plans are tested in a constant series of exercises.

Finally, Fidel Castro has also attempted to use change within the military as an example of the process of rectification. He has called for the creation of a system of party ideologue cadres within the military to encourage socialist morality. Cuban officials refer to "new management principles"—yet most amount to little more than a resort to socialist exhortations. The prospects that such programs will root out any of the corruption or inefficiency that exist within the military are as small as those for a reinvigoration of Cuban society in general.

The Future: A Diminution of Importance?

MINFAR's basic purposes since 1959 have been fourfold. It has been charged with defending the revolution against external attack. It serves, along with MININT, as an internal security force. From time to time it has been pressed into service as a civic and economic support force. And most recently, MINFAR has served to project Cuba's influence across the globe in both military and nonmilitary spheres.

The phases of MINFAR's development have moved from one of these purposes to another, with a good degree of overlap. From 1959 to about 1965, MINFAR was an unprofessional, paramilitary militia primarily concerned with defeating counterrevolutionary forces and U.S. support for them, including a possible U.S. invasion. From 1965 to 1968, once the counterrevolution had been defeated, as tensions with the U.S.S.R. reached an apex, and as the risk of a U.S. invasion was viewed as large, MINFAR developed into a more professional force whose primary mission was external defense; its newfound free time was used to assist economic agencies with domestic production and civic duties. This general role continued, modified by better relations with the U.S.S.R. and the professionalization and Sovietization of the military, until 1974. In 1975, the projection of military and economic power, the seeds of which had been laid some time earlier, began in earnest in Angola and later Ethiopia. The MINFAR thus developed from a primitive rebel militia to a sophisticated internal and external tool of a radical government.

The history of MINFAR, in turn, parallels the history of the revolution itself. Through 1965, Castro's regime was primarily concerned with securing its power in Cuba and warding off U.S. invasions. By the late 1960s, socioeconomic development had also become a high priority. Beginning in the 1960s, Castro pursued socialist internationalism, and once he had resolved his feuds with Moscow, his projection of power began in earnest. The moral commitment to these efforts, and the almost total mobilization of the Cuban polity to support them, seem more than anything to be a product of Castro's own ambitions, mixed with and supported by a healthy dose of long-repressed Cuban nationalism. Some analysts argue that its evolution has transformed it into a tool of Soviet global ambitions, although most recognize that Castro has managed to maintain considerable independence.

These parallel trends point to the fact that MINFAR will have to evolve in the 1990s to meet the needs of a changing revolution and the regime that oversees it. Arguably, all of its former roles have been vitiated. The counterrevolution has been defeated and there is little internal opposition; internal security is, in any case, the official function of MININT. The civic mission has been transferred to civilian agencies and paramilitary off-shoots of the MINFAR which no longer include MINFAR combat units. The risk of U.S. invasion is minimal. And with the withdrawal of troops from Ethiopia, and if or when the Angolan accord is executed, MINFAR's internationalist role may be severely circumscribed. There are some risks in a MINFAR of the 1990s that becomes an organization without a purpose.

Speculating in 1979 on essentially the same problem, Jorge Dominguez noted that Castro's government had always contended that a large military was necessary, even if the immediate risk of war seemed small, "because the imperialists cannot be trusted." Also, the role of the civic soldier in a broader sense justified a large military establishment even in the absence of counterrevolution or war; "a moral claim has been made about the value of the virtues of military training, policies, institutions, and life values in the building of a socialist society." Given these facts, a decline in internationalism might not result in a smaller MINFAR role.[44] Indeed, more recently an emphasis on rectification within the military has pointed to the role of the military as "an effective means of inculcating proper attitudes and dedication."[45]

Another important determinant of the future role of MINFAR will be the status of Cuban/Soviet relations. Fidel Castro's rejection of Mikhail Gorbachev's reforms as inapplicable to the Cuban case, and Castro's public criticisms of the renewed Soviet dissatisfaction with wars of national liberation, have reopened for the first time in a quarter century the prospect of an ideological chasm on the scale of the 1965–68 split. Castro took the occasion of his speech commemorating the 30th anniversary of the revolution in January 1989 to excoriate those who would apply the Soviet model of reform to Cuba. As in 1966, Cuban officials today speak of military independence from the Soviet Union, and have backed their rhetoric with the completion of a small-arms plant in Camaguey that gives Cuba an embryonic ability to produce its own military equipment.[46] Their statements recall one of the central themes of Cuban military doctrine—that the revolution must be capable of defending itself. Should the Soviet/Cuban gap widen, MINFAR's internal and external roles will grow, perhaps irrespective of the degree of threat from the United States.

Yet such a justification might be untenable in the longer term, as the weight of the military's role in society continues to drag down Cuban economic performance and human rights guarantees. In the immediate future, MINFAR's role in a transition post-Fidel seems clear enough: Raul Castro heads the armed forces, and would undoubtedly use them as his chief claim to power (besides his established stature as Fidel's successor). Yet the resentment of the government within the military, the tensions between MINFAR and both MININT and the PCC, and the probable unwillingness of Cubans to accept a purely military dictatorship suggest that such reliance on military force to maintain internal order would not succeed.

A much more likely long-term development, after Fidel and Raul have both passed from the scene, is the transition to a more mellowed form of socialism that would ease internal restraints on enterprise and liberty and pursue closer ties with capitalist states—that is, a tropical *perestroika* and *glasnost* of the sort that Castro has so far rejected. But the risks of reaction to such a move are great; no one fully understands the Party-military-government dynamics at work within Castro's personalized government, and how they will play out after he is gone is a mystery. Should a reformist government emerge, the role of the military—both domestically and internationally—will decline, just as it has in the U.S.S.R. (and Cuba enjoys a further advantage of not having to maintain order in satellite states). Should reactionaries come to power, the imposition of a brutal military dictatorship—perhaps too desperate about its grip on internal power to project any force beyond its shores—seems likely. As before, the status of the Cuban military will therefore parallel the development of the revolution itself.

Notes

1. A useful general history of the Cuban military, to which this essay will make reference, is Rafael Fermoselle, *The Evolution of the Cuban Military: 1492–1986* (Miami, Fla.: Ediciones Universal, 1987).
2. Irving Louis Horowitz, "Military Origins and Outcomes of the Cuban Revolution," in Horowitz, ed., *Cuban Communism* (New Brunswick, N.J.: Transaction Books, 6th Edition, 1987), p. 593.
3. The best history of the war is probably G. J. A. O'Toole, *The Spanish War: An American Epic—1898* (New York: W. W. Norton and Co., 1984). Some classic texts regarding the American motives involved include Walter Mills, *The Martial Spirit: A Study of Our War with Spain* (Boston: Houghton-Mifflin, 1931); Julius Pratt, *Expansionists of 1898: The Acquisitions of Hawaii and the Spanish Islands* (New York: Quadrangle Books, 1936); and Ernest R. May, *American Imperialism: A Speculative Essay* (New York: Atheneum Books, 1968).
4. Louis A. Perez, Jr., "Supervision of a Protectorate: The United States and the Cuban Army, 1898–1908," *Hispanic American Historical Review* 52 (May 1972): 250–71. See also Perez, "The Pursuit of Pacification: Banditry and the

United States' Occupation of Cuba, 1889–1902," *Journal of Latin American Studies* 18 (November 1986), pp. 313–32.

5. As Carlos Franqui, a Cuban writer who had backed Castro but later turned against him, has recognized, however, the domestic consensus for these executions was at the time strong. Franqui, *Family Portrait with Fidel* (New York: Vintage Books, 1984), pp. 17–19.

6. Fermoselle, pp. 265–74; Marta San Martin and Ramon L. Bonachea, "The Military Dimensions of the Cuban Revolution," in Horowitz, ed., *Cuban Communism,* pp. 37–60.

7. These opponents included Major Pedro Diaz Lanz, who fled, Major Huber Matos, who was imprisoned, and Major Camilo Cienfuegos, whose aircraft disappeared in mysterious circumstances in October 1959. Many people believe Castro had Cienfuegos, who like Matos was a moderate, killed; ironically, one branch of Cuba's military education system is named after Cienfuegos.

8. Horowitz, "Military Origins," p. 602; Max Azicri, *Cuba: Politics, Economics, and Society* (London: Pinter Publishers, 1988), p. 197.

9. Franqui, p. 33.

10. Pamela Falk, *Cuban Foreign Policy* (Lexington, Mass.: Lexington Books, 1986), fn. 27, p. 125; on the formation of CDRs see p. 121. See also Defense Intelligence Agency, *Handbook on the Cuban Armed Forces* (Washington, D.C.: Defense Research Reference Series, DIA, may help. (DDB-2680-62-86), p. 1–1.

11. Tad Szulc, *Fidel: A Critical Portrait* (New York: Avon Books, 1986), pp. 584–85.

12. Ibid., pp. 584–86, 636–38.

13. Ibid., pp. 602–13. The militia's role in the invasion is ably chronicled in Peter Wyden, *Bay of Pigs: The Untold Story* (New York: Simon and Schuster, 1979), esp. pp. 222–88.

14. Jorge I. Dominguez, "Institutionalization and Civil-Military Relations in Cuba," *Cuban Studies* 6 (January 1976):47; cf. pp. 39–40.

15. Franqui, pp. 127–28.

16. For an outstanding, detailed account of the DL and other MININT international departments, see Rex A. Hudson, "Castro's Americas Department" (Washington, D.C.: The Cuban-American National Foundation, 1988), esp. pp. 5–10.

17. Martin and Bonachea, p. 49. In this sense they could almost be compared with Hitler's SS armies. More recently, Castro has established another territorial militia, the MTT, that some contend is a further barrier to military coups; see below.

18. Anticommunist desertions from 1959 to 1961 had gutted the prerevolutionary navy, small as it had been; it therefore took little part in the Bay of Pigs operations. Adrian English, *Regional Defence Profile No. 1: Latin America* (London: Jane's Publishing Company, 1988), p. 126.

19. See Horowitz, "Military Origins," p. 593. Azicri sums up the result well: Fidel and Raul's roles at the head of party and military (and, Azicri could have added, the politicization of the FAR) "have maintained the ultimate supremacy of the party (political) over the FAR (military), but *at the expense of a clear distinction between the two." Cuba,* p. 198, emphasis mine.

20. A good account of life in the UMAPs is to be found in Jose Luis Llovio Menendez, *Insider: My Life as a Revolutionary in Cuba* (New York: Bantam

Books, 1988), pp. 143–59ff. This book must be approached with extreme
caution, however; the jury is still out on its accuracy and truthfulness.
21. Dominguez, "Institutionalization," p. 50.
22. Jorge I. Dominguez, "The Cuban Operation in Angola: Costs and Benefits for
the Armed Forces," *Cuban Studies* 8 (January 1978), p. 10.
23. William Durch, "The Cuban Military in Africa and the Middle East," Center
for Naval Analyses, Professional Paper No. 201, September 1977.
24. It should be noted, however, that Fidel appeased the U.S.S.R. by breaking
from the PRC and from Trotskyite parties and by targeting his revolutionary
efforts at governments in Colombia, Guatemala, Peru, and Venezuela—countries "without major diplomatic or trade importance for the Soviets." Hudson,
p. 9.
25. Pamela Falk, *Cuban Foreign Policy: Caribbean Tempest* (Lexington, Mass.:
Lexington Books, 1986), p. 121.
26. Dominguez, "Institutionalization," pp. 44, and 46.
27. Jan Knippers Black et al., *Area Handbook for Latin America* (Washington,
D.C.: Government Printing Office, 1976), pp. 303–304, 467–68.
28. Martin and Bonachea, p. 53.
29. Dominguez, "Armed Forces and Foreign Relations," p. 59.
30. Dominguez, "The Cuban Operation in Angola," p. 11.
31. Black et al., p. 305.
32. Azicri, p. 198.
33. Dominguez, "Institutionalization."
34. Szulc, pp. 11–12.
35. Defense Intelligence Agency (DIA), *Handbook on the Cuban Armed Forces,*
pp. 3–4.
36. U.S. Information Agency, Radio Martí Program, *Quarterly Report on Cuba,*
Second Quarter 1987, 15 September 1987, pp. 11–12.
37. Goure, Leon. "Cuban Military Doctrine and Organization," prepared for
Radio Martí Program, VOA/MR, US Information Agency, Washington, D.C.,
Contract No. 609-7188, 14 Nov. 1986, p. ii. Cuban American National Foundation, *General Del Pino Speaks: An Insight Into Elite Corruption and Military
Dissertion in Castro's Cuba* (Washington, D.C.: Cuban American National
Foundation, 1987).
38. "Gen. Del Pino Speaks," pp. 22–23.
39. For an extremely detailed portrait of the Cuban military today, see the DIA
Handbook.
40. All quotes in this section are from *General Del Pino Speaks.*
41. These reports, and much of the evidence cited below, come from various
editions of the U.S. Information Agency's Radio Martí *Quarterly Reports* on
Cuba. These are a mine of information on modern Cuba, and each report
contains a specific section on the military.
42. David W. Fitz-Simons, "Soviets in Cuba," *Journal of Defense and Diplomacy*
7 (January 1989) pp. 3–5.
43. "Gen. Del Pino Speaks," pp. 464–465.
44. Dominguez, "The Armed Forces and Foreign Relations," pp. 79–80.
45. Radio Martí *Quarterly Situation Report,* Fourth Quarter 1987, 15 April 1988,
p. 21.
46. " 'Stormy' Talks with Gorbachev Delayed," *Caribbean Report,* January 19,
1989, pp. 1–2.

10

Castro: Nearly Thirty Years of Revolutionary Warfare

Constantine Menges

Introduction

In January 1959, Fidel Castro came to power in Cuba heading a coalition of communist guerrillas and genuine democrats, who believed the charismatic guerrilla chief's oft-stated promises that democracy in Cuba was to be established. Television newsreels testify that as late as 1958 Castro was assuring listeners that his political views were that of a democrat in the Jeffersonian mold.

These promises received a sympathetic hearing from numerous media figures and State Department officials in the United States. A *New York Times* reporter met with Castro in February 1957, by which time the rebel leader's initial force of 82 insurgents had been reduced to eighteen. The reporter subsequently described Castro as "the flaming symbol of the opposition to the regime" and predicted that "from the looks of things, General Batista cannot possibly hope to suppress the Castro revolt."[1] By early 1958, "foreign journalists were visiting with such frequency that a sign reading 'Press Club' in English and Spanish was placed on the . . . hut where the foreign visitors were received in insurgent headquarters. . . ."[2] Indeed, Castro's propaganda and deception worked so effectively that in March 1958, the United States decided to suspend arms shipments to the Batista regime. This cutoff marked the beginning of the dictator's denouement, which culminated in his flight and Castro's triumphal entry into Havana on New Year's Day, 1959.

Within months, the long-suffering Cuban people discovered that the old dictatorship had been replaced by another one, but more brutal and repressive. Gradually, the new Cuban ruler eventually froze out, imprisoned, or killed the genuine democrats who had helped him take power. At the same time, Castro moved quickly to establish warm relations with the Soviet Union. Throughout his first two years in power he spurned numerous friendly overtures from the United States—including offers of economic assistance made during Castro's visit to the U.S. in the spring of 1959.

While repressing genuinely democratic groups in Cuba, Castro lost no time in constructing a formidable apparatus for revolutionary aggression against nearby states. Within weeks of taking power he worked to create and sustain Marxist-Leninist insurgencies and terrorist groups in other Latin American countries. He also expanded the Cuban armed forces, which had numbered about 40,000 under Batista—and now number about 280,000 in the regular army and an estimated 500,000 militia. Ultimately, using an ever-wider array of subversive methods, and with alternating intensity against various target governments, Castro's revolutionary warfare has caused immense human suffering, economic deprivation, and political setbacks in many countries friendly to the United States.

Following the visit of a high-level Soviet delegation to Cuba in early 1960, the principal strategic targets of Castro's indirect aggression and subversion have coincided with those of the Soviet Union and its other allies. Soviet premier Nikita Khrushchev publicly proclaimed in 1961 that Moscow intended to help bring pro-Soviet groups to power through "wars of national liberation" on every continent. In 1973, Soviet premier Leonid Brezhnev highlighted two main geopolitical objectives in a speech to communist political leaders: "Our aim is to gain control of the two great treasure houses on which the West depends . . . the energy treasure house of the Persian Gulf and the mineral treasure house of central and southern Africa."[3] During the 1970s, Soviet- and Cuban-supported indirect aggression brought new pro-Soviet regimes to power in a number of states, including: Laos, Cambodia, Vietnam, Angola, Mozambique, Ethiopia, Afghanistan, South Yemen, Grenada, and Nicaragua. Immediately upon taking power, these regimes murdered, cumulatively, several millions of their own peoples and aided Soviet efforts to overthrow neighboring governments. As the late CIA director William Casey put it:

This (subversive aggression) is not a bloodless war. Marxist-Leninist policies and tactics have unleashed the four horses of the Apocalypse—Famine, Pestilence, War, and Death. . . . In the occupied countries—Afghanistan, Cambodia, Ethiopia, Angola, Nicaragua . . . there has occurred a holocaust comparable to that which Nazi Germany inflicted in Europe. . . .[4]

Cuba has faithfully aided the Soviets in this subversive aggression. The following schematic chart (Table 10.1), written in 1980, still illustrates and summarizes how Cuba's subversive aggression reinforces the Soviet pursuit of its principal strategic objectives in Latin America, Africa, and the Persian Gulf.

From time to time, Castro has disagreed with the Soviets on tactics and opportunities for supporting anti-Western violence and revolution—especially during the 1960s. One should recall President Kennedy's explicit statement that the Cuban missile crisis settlement reached with Khrushchev in October 1962 included the understanding that Castro would terminate the "export of subversion."[5] Nevertheless, since 1960 the Soviet Bloc has given economic and military assistance to Cuba amounting, in the 1980s, to 25 percent on average of Cuba's GNP annually (about $3 billion per year). This aid has allowed Castro to finance his increasingly active subversive aggression. Historian Hugh Thomas has observed that

TABLE 10.1
Political-Paramilitary War Against U.S. Interests in Three Strategic Arenas

Target Countries	Destabilization Coalition
Latin America	
Colombia	*Cuba*
Venezuela	Regional communist/guerrilla groups
Central America	U.S.S.R.
Panama	Palestinian terrorists/Libya
Belize	
Mexico[1]	
Middle East	
Israel	U.S.S.R.
Egypt	Pro-Soviet regimes (South Yemen, Syria)
Iran (post-Khomeini)	*Cuba*
Oman	Palestinian guerrillas
North Yemen	Libya
Persian Gulf regimes	
Saudi Arabia[1]	
Africa	
Zaire	U.S.S.R.
Morocco	*Cuba*
Sudan	Libya
Namibia	Pro-Soviet regimes (Ethiopia, Angola, Mozambique)
South Africa[1]	Regional guerrillas/Communist groups (SWAPO)

Source: C. Menges, November 1980
[1]Designates the main strategic target.

not only has Cuba remained economically stagnant and dependent on a sugar monoculture under Castro, but the Soviet Union has claimed an even larger share of Cuba's annual trade that resulted from the close relationship with the United States during the Batista period.[6]

Figure 10.1 documents the massive levels of Soviet weapons shipments to Cuba since 1961. It also suggests a correlation between Soviet purposes and the amount of weaponry delivered. In 1961, the Soviets shipped 250,000 tons of weapons to Cuba, just as they were planning to use the new Castro regime to help tilt the strategic balance in their favor by installing medium-range ballistic missiles on the island. Likewise, Soviet arms deliveries increased in the mid-1960s, as Castro stepped up armed subversion in Latin America. After a brief decline, arms shipments increased once more in the mid-1970s, as Cuban troops helped Soviet-armed revolutionary movements seize power in Angola, Mozambique, and Ethiopia. Finally, annual Soviet weapons deliveries to Cuba increased sharply after the 1979 communist Sandinista success in Nicaragua and the acceleration of communist insurrection in other Central American countries.

Castro's subversive aggression can be divided generally into four phases, with each new set of actions building upon—instead of replacing— those that preceded it in a pattern of ever-expanding operations and methods. From 1959 to 1966, Castro emphasized bilateral support to communist political and guerrilla groups in Latin America and in some African countries. Although it had become clear by 1966 that this revolutionary strategy had failed in Latin America, Castro continued to funnel supplies to the guerrilla groups and increased cooperation with and support to hostile anti-Western groups from other regions, notably southern Africa and the Middle East.

Since 1973, Castro has complemented his political, propaganda, and military support for these movements by sending tens of thousands of Cuban combat troops abroad to help other pro-Soviet movements take or keep power. During the 1980s, this indirect aggression has been continued in a large number of countries throughout the world, through the use of political penetration, armed subversion, and Cuban combat troops.

The First Attacks

In April 1959, only four months after taking power, Castro sent a guerrilla squad to destabilize Panama. The Organization of American States (OAS) investigated the incursion and the guerrillas were captured. This abortive action against Panama marked the beginning of nearly 30 years of Cuban aggression against free nations through both armed and unarmed subversion.

FIGURE 10.1

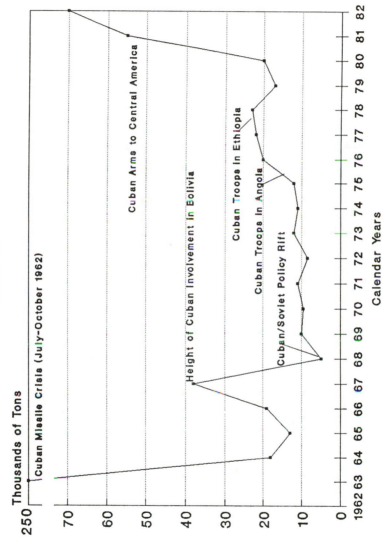

Source: White House Digest, *Soviet-Cuban Threat and Buildup in the Caribbean,* 6 July 1983, p. 4.

Two months later, in June 1959, Castro sent an armed guerrilla group to begin operations in Nicaragua. Dictator Anastasio Somoza's National Guard captured them, and the OAS again condemned Cuba's subversive aggression. In the summer of 1959, Castro began a decade-long guerrilla and terrorist war against the fragile new Social Democratic government of Romulo Betancourt in Venezuela, which only a year before had replaced the military dictatorship of Marcos Perez Jimenez. In 1964, after confirming and condemning this act of aggression, the OAS voted sanctions against Cuba and declared that its armed subversion had constituted illegal aggression. In that same year, the OAS stated:

> The Republic of Venezuela has been the target of a series of actions sponsored and directed by . . . Cuba . . . to overthrow the democratic government of Venezuela through terrorism, sabotage, assault and guerrilla warfare, and . . . (the OAS) resolves to declare that the acts . . . are considered an aggression and an intervention on the part of the government of Cuba in the internal affairs of Venezuela, which affect all member states.

With help from the United States and other democracies, Venezuela's democratic leaders eventually contained and isolated the guerrillas. In the context of the 1980s, only a small number of Marxist-Leninist terrorists (mostly affiliated with rebels in neighboring Colombia) operate against one of Latin America's most successful democracies.

In 1961, Castro armed and trained terrorists who worked to undermine the Manuel Prado government of Peru, as the OAS subsequently confirmed. A left-wing military junta overthrow civilian President Fernando Belaunde Terry in 1968 and ruled until the return of democracy in 1980, when Belaunde resumed the presidency. Since that time, two Marxist-Leninist guerrilla organizations—the Cuba-supported Tupac Amaru Revolutionary Movement and the Maoist Shining Path Movement—have conducted an ever-expanding series of terrorist actions. In this instance, Castro supplies the Tupac Amaru terrorists while simultaneously maintaining apparently friendly relations with the current leftist government of President Alan Garcia.

The year 1961 continued to be an active one for Cuba: Colombia accused Cuba of arming and supporting Marxist-Leninist guerrillas in that country, which had just emerged four years earlier from a decade of brutal civil war. The OAS confirmed the charge and excluded the Castro government from futher participation in the Inter-American System.[7] Although Colombia had managed for 20 years to isolate and contain the various Marxist-Leninist guerrilla organizations, increased support from Cuba and Libya in recent years has allowed the insurgent coalition to build up its strength to about 10,000.[8]

In a 1984 raid on a jungle drug-processing laboratory, Colombian authorities captured the largest amount of narcotics ever seized. Communist guerrillas had provided security for this particular narcotics factory in exchange for payoffs and political support from the traffickers. This and similar captures, along with the indictment in U.S. federal courts of senior Cuban officials for drug activities, illustrate the importance to Cuba and communist guerrilla movements of illegal drug smuggling as a device both to obtain money and to corrupt and undermine target governments.[9]

In 1965, Cuba assisted a subversive campaign to destabilize the Dominican Republic. In response, the OAS dispatched a peacekeeping force of both U.S. and Latin American troops, which restored order. Due to President Lyndon Johnson's decisive action, the Dominican Republic has since evolved into a functioning democracy. In 1984, then-president Jorge Blanco made the first official visit ever to Washington by a Dominican head of state. Since the early 1980s, though, Cuba has incited small communist and other radical left groups in this fledgling democracy to unite and prepare for renewed military action. Many Dominican guerrillas have received military training in Cuba, and more than 800 persons selected by the Dominican Communist Party have "studied" in Soviet Bloc countries.[10]

In January 1966, Castro organized the Tricontinental Conference as a means to promote violent revolution in Africa and Asia as well as Latin America. Participants included representatives of North Korea, North Vietnam, the Palestine Liberation Organization (PLO), and other radical Arab groups. At this conference, Cuba and Latin American Marxist-Leninist terrorist groups began their collaboration with the PLO and radical Arab groups in the training and arming of terrorists. This collaboration has taken most visible expression in the support provided by Libya and the PLO to the Sandinista regime in Nicaragua.[11]

Following the Tricontinental Conference, Cuba increased its support to Marxist-Leninist terrorist groups in Argentina and Uruguay. For several years thereafter, the Uruguayan Tupamaros and the Argentine Montoneros carried out a savage campaign of kidnappings, murders, and bombings in an effort to first polarize and then overthrow those governments. In Argentina, this campaign of terror precipitated a military coup in 1976 against the regime of Eva Peron and led to the subsequent "dirty war" in which an estimated 9,000 Argentines disappeared and were presumably killed. In the 1970s, Uruguay had been called the "Switzerland of Latin America" because of its well-established democracy, high living standards, and extensive social welfare programs. The terrorism launched by the Tupamaros destroyed that nation's democratic and social progress and provoked a takeover by a military junta that ruled Uruguay until the return of democracy in 1985.

In 1967, Castro dispatched Ché Guevara to start a peasant insurgency in Bolivia. After the effort failed and Guevara was killed, both Bolivia and Venezuela asked the OAS to act against this continuing subversion. The OAS once again confirmed the facts of Cuban indirect aggression and increased its sanctions against Castro's regime. Having failed by 1970 to bring even one communist government to power, Castro switched tactics and gradually sought to normalize relations with many Latin American countries while continuing covertly to aid communist and other radical groups.

The Use of Cuban Troops

While the Cuban regime was active in its promotion of subversive activities, Cuban activism reached a new plateau with the introduction of Cuban troops outside of the Western Hemisphere during the 1970s. In addition, this decade also introduced a new level of Soviet/Cuban cooperation in Third World adventures. Let us now examine a few of these instances.

In October 1973, Castro sent Cuban combat troops abroad for the first time as Israel fought to repulse the surprise Yom Kippur attacks by Egypt and other Arab states. Cuban troops and tank units were sent to Syria, where they blended in with Syrian military units and assisted a months-long series of harassment attacks against Israeli forces.

In 1974, the Soviet Union decided to intervene more aggressively in Angola to assure the victory of the pro-Soviet Popular Movement for the Liberation of Angola (MPLA), then competing with two pro-Western guerrilla movements for power once the Portuguese withdrew from their former colonial possessions. In 1975, while the Soviets flew in tens of thousands of tons of weapons—including mobile rocket launchers, armored personnel carriers, and tanks—Castro sent in 20,000 Cuban troops to defeat the pro-Western forces. In early 1976, the U.S. Congress reacted to news reports about U.S. efforts to help the democratic forces resist this Soviet-Cuban indirect aggression by passing the Clark amendment, which prohibited U.S. covert action in Angola (subsequently repealed in 1985).

In 1977, Marxist-Leninist military officers in Ethiopia overthrew Emperor Haile Selassie and established a bloody pro-Soviet dictatorship dependent on Soviet weaponry, about 15,000 Cuban troops, and East German operatives in internal repression. Today, an estimated 70,000 Cuban military and other personnel support communist dictatorships in Angola, Mozambique, and Ethiopia, and they assist Soviet Bloc and

Libyan agents in fomenting insurgencies or coups in a number of African countries currently friendly to the West.[12]

Castro's hostile activities against Israel and other pro-Western Middle Eastern governments began after the Soviet KGB assumed control of Cuba's international subversion apparatus in the late 1960s. By 1968, Castro was trying to involve the PLO in Latin America, and Cuban intelligence and military personnel were working with the PLO in North Africa. The following year, Cuban and PLO personnel began to receive joint military training in the Soviet Union, and in 1972, Castro and PLO leaders agreed at a meeting in Algeria to step up their joint activities. Since then, Castro has participated with the PLO in training West European and Latin American terrorists at camps in communist South Yemen, Libya, and PLO-controlled sections of Lebanon.

The Marxist-Leninist Sandinistas of Nicaragua have received crucial support from Castro ever since he helped to establish the Sandinista Front in 1961. Numerous Sandinista leaders received training in Middle Eastern terrorist camps as well as in the Soviet Bloc. Tomas Borge, a cofounder of the Sandinista Front and currently Sandinista Interior Minister with control over the secret police, received training from the PLO and spent much of the early 1970s working for Castro—frequently in the Middle East, where he used Libyan money and his Palestinian connections to obtain weapons for Central American guerrilla movements.[13]

In February 1978, the PLO and the Sandinistas publicly confirmed their alliance in a joint communiqué, issued in Mexico City, that affirmed their "ties of solidarity" and condemned "the racist state of Israel." In March 1978, the Sandinistas joined the pro-Soviet Democratic Front for the Liberation of Palestine in a "declaration of war" against Israel. In July 1979, immediately after seizing power in Nicaragua, the Sandinistas sent a mission to open official contacts with the PLO. At the present time, Nicaragua is one of the few countries in the world in which the PLO mission (housed in the former Israeli embassy) is officially designated an embassy.

Communist guerrillas in El Salvador also have close links with Palestinian terrorist organizations. They rank Israel as their principal enemy, after the United States. In May 1980, Salvadoran guerrilla leaders met in Lebanon with the assertively pro-Soviet Popular Front for the Liberation of Palestine (PFLP) to arrange for its help with training and weapons. Shafik Handal, the leader of the Salvadoran communist party, is himself of Palestinian descent. In 1981, he travelled to Lebanon to arrange additional cooperation with the Palestinian terrorist groups. In 1982, the PLO publicly boasted that it was fighting together with the Salvadoran guerrillas. There is also evidence that some Salvadoran communist guerrillas have received training in Palestinian camps.[14]

Central America: The Cuban Offensive Since 1978

Beginning with Nicaragua in 1978, the Castro regime sharply increased its armed subversion in all of Central America.[15] After nearly two decades of failure, a new pattern was established with a Cuban strategy having the following components:

- Unite traditionally splintered radical groups behind a commitment to armed struggle with Cuban advice and material assistance;
- Train ideologically committed cadres in urban and rural guerrilla warfare;
- Supply or arrange for the supply of weapons to support the Cuban-trained cadres' efforts to assume power by force;
- Encourage terrorism in the hope of provoking indiscriminate violence and repression and generalized disorder in order to weaken government legitimacy and attract new converts to armed struggle; and
- Use military fronts and radical governments through armed pro-Cuban Marxists.[16]

The 1981 government report, "Cuba's Renewed Support for Violence in Latin America," was only the first in a series which documented Cuban and Soviet activities.[17] The following description summarized the Cuban apparatus, which has become even more dangerous since this was written in 1981:

> . . . Cuban subversion today is backed by an extensive secret intelligence and training apparatus, modern military forces, and a large and sophisticated prop-aganda network. Utilizing agents and contacts nurtured over more than 20 years, the Castro government is providing ideological and military training and material and propaganda support to numerous violent groups, often several in one country.[18]

There were two recent phases in the successful communist seizure of power in Nicaragua. The 1978 attempt has been well summarized:

> In 1977 and early 1978, a high-ranking Americas Department official, Armando Ulises Estrada, made numerous secret trips to facilitate the uprising by working to unify the three major factions of the FSLN. . . . At the same time, Estrada concentrated on building a supply network for channeling arms and other supplies to guerrilla forces. International sympathy for the struggle against Somoza provided a convenient facade for Cuban operations. In preparation for the first FSLN offensive in the fall of 1978, arms were flown from Cuba to Panama, transshipped to Costa Rica on smaller planes, and supplied to Nicara-

guan guerrillas based in northern Costa Rica. To monitor and assist the flow, the Americas Department established a secret operations center in San Jose. By the end of 1978, Cuban advisers were dispatched to northern Costa Rica to train and equip the FSLN forces with arms which began to arrive direct from Cuba. FSLN guerrillas trained in Cuba, however, continued to return to Nicaragua via Panama.[19]

In March 1979, several months after the first Sandinista insurrection attempt failed, Castro called the principal Sandinista leaders to Cuba and supervised the formation of the current nine-man ruling Directorate. Castro pressed upon the *comandantes* the need to promise political democracy and to form a broad alliance with the genuine democrats opposed to the Somoza regime, in order to both increase the chance of victory inside Nicaragua and, equally important, to deceive Western governments and public opinion about the communist nature of the Sandinista Front. Castro urged the three Sandinista factions to unify and, once they did so, markedly increased his covert military and propaganda help.

The Sandinistas followed Castro's advice, forming a broad political front with genuinely democratic opponents of Somoza—all the while keeping military power in Sandinista hands. The Sandinistas further deceived the West by promising to hold free elections "within a few months" of taking power, respect basic human rights and civil liberties, and follow a non-aligned foreign policy. Armed with that commitment, the OAS transferred its diplomatic recognition from Somoza to the Sandinista-led interim government on 23 June 1979. The Sandinista promise formed the basis for what the Carter administration and other Western governments viewed as a workable political solution: Somoza would cede power voluntarily to avoid further battles, but his army would remain substantially intact to be integrated with the Sandinista guerrillas and then function as a peace-keeping force until the agreed-upon elections, to be held "within a few months," resulted in a new and democratic government.

We should keep in mind the terms and results of this so-called political solution to the Nicaraguan problem, since the same approach—power-sharing with communist guerrillas—is being recommended for democratic governments in Central America by a few Western countries and by some domestic opponents of the Reagan administration's Central America policy.

Virtually from the moment the Sandinistas and their initial cadre of 50 Cuban advisors moved into Managua on 19 July 1979, they have continuously violated the key tenets of the OAS settlement:

- *First,* by repressing the genuinely democratic political, trade union, and civic groups within Nicaragua; by adamantly refusing to allow genuinely democratic elections (elections held in November 1984 were a Soviet-style fraud); by systematically persecuting Christian and Jewish religious groups (with especially violent persecution of the English-speaking and Protestant Miskito Indians, thousands of whom have languished in detention camps since December 1981);

- *Second,* by rapidly building up a Soviet Bloc and Cuban presence now totalling about 8,000, of whom an estimated 3,500 to 5,000 are secret police, military, and covert action personnel who have constructed the internal police apparatus and supervised the military buildup and the export of subversion;
- *Third,* by carrying out an immediate and sustained military buildup, despite generous, immediate, and sustained Western economic and diplomatic support, including $118 million from the United States and hundreds of millions in other Western economic aid. Under this buildup the Sandinistas have increased their active duty troop strength from 10,000 to about 80,000 (although Costa Rica has no army and Honduras has only 22,000 in its armed forces), added 30 new military bases, received delivery of $2 billion worth of Soviet Bloc weapons including 110 tanks, 250 armored vehicles, and mobile rocket launchers—weapons never before seen in Central America.[20] This military buildup gives Nicaragua, with one-tenth of Central America's 25 million people, an army more powerful than those of all the other countries combined. This uninterrupted nine-year-long buildup became visible in late 1979 and continued through all of 1980 and 1981—that is, for two and a half years *before* an armed resistance became active, and during the nineteen months *before* the Reagan administration came to office; and
- *Fourth,* by joining with Cuba, the Soviet Bloc, Latin American communist terrorist groups, and the PLO in the armed subversion of El Salvador, Honduras, Costa Rica, and Guatemala. Within weeks of coming to power, the Sandinistas opened training camps in Nicaragua for Salvadoran guerrillas. In 1988, the guerrillas continue to maintain these camps, along with a command and control center, radio communications center, propaganda office, and printing press in Nicaragua.[21] This support has continued into 1988, despite the Sandinistas' obligation under the August 1987 Arias accord to stop aiding guerrilla movements in neighboring countries. President Jose Napoleon Duarte of El Salvador presented new evidence of this support several days before the 15 January 1988 summit meeting of the five Central American presidents.[22]

Democratic and Republican members of the House and Senate intelligence committees accept these facts, as the May 1983 report of the Democratic-led House Intelligence Committee indicates. That report stated that Cuban and Sandinista aid for guerrillas constitutes "a clear picture of active promotion for 'revolution without frontiers' throughout Central America" and that the Salvadoran guerrillas "are well trained, well equipped with modern weapons and supplies and rely on the use of sites in Nicaragua for command and control and for logistical support.''[23]

The bipartisan consensus on the facts about communist indirect aggression in Central America is illustrated by the 17 January 1981 action of the Carter administration in suspending U.S. economic aid to Nicaragua. The Carter administration said its aid ceased because the Sandinistas had provided ''arms, ammunition, training and political and military advice'' to the Salvadoran guerrillas to make possible their ''final offensive,'' begun on 10 January 1981. President Carter ended U.S. economic aid to Nicaragua and resumed U.S. military aid to El Salvador in his last three days in office. As a gesture of goodwill to the Sandinista government, the incoming Reagan administration restored economic aid, with the proviso that Nicaragua stop its indirect aggression against El Salvador. U.S. economic assistance was again stopped in April 1981, as required by Congress, when the Sandinistas continued exporting subversion.

The Sandinistas themselves confirmed their role in subversive activities when they publicly stated after the restoration of democracy in Grenada in 1983 that the Salvadoran guerrillas would have to move their headquarters out of Nicaragua. In 1980 and 1981, before there was an armed resistance opposing the Sandinista regime, Nicaraguan agents and diplomats had been caught in democratic Costa Rica and Honduras supervising bombing and terrorist attacks carried out by Argentine, Colombian, Salvadoran, and other communist terrorists, all of whom maintain headquarters in Nicaragua and Cuba.[24] In essence, the function that Cuba has performed for the Soviet Bloc of providing an intervening layer of deniability for this indirect aggression is now being performed for Cuba by the Sandinistas, who have become, in effect, the Cubans' Cubans!

In late 1979, Castro watched the United States and other regional governments do nothing while the Sandinistas abrogated their OAS commitments to implement real democracy, and while the new radical regime of Maurice Bishop in Grenada moved into the Soviet/Cuban orbit. Castro recognized that the Carter administration was preoccupied by the fall of the Iranian government, by the ensuing hostage crisis, and later by the Soviet invasion of Afghanistan. Thus, he decided to step up the pace of the Salvadoran insurgency. In December 1979, Castro summoned the leaders of the Salvadoran communist party and the five Marxist-Leninist terrorist groups to Havana. Castro demanded unity and promised greatly increased military and financial support.

A unified guerrilla command structure was consequently formed, the Farabundo Martí National Liberation Front (FLMN). At same time, Castro emphasized the need for noncommunist partners in the coalition in order to broaden the base inside El Salvador, deceive Western governments and public opinion during the insurrection, and then have the political connections to obtain substantial Western economic assistance after a communist victory.

Unfortunately, the small social democratic party of El Salvador, with a few hundred members, and some other noncommunists deceived themselves into thinking that they could moderate the communists by entering into coalition with them. The result was a union between a Marxist-Leninist tiger and a noncommunist rabbit. In the ensuing coalition, the noncommunist element has not held real power, but has been very useful in helping the communist element deceive important segments within Western society: some political movements, a few governments, and portions of the media.

It is a standard Soviet Bloc tactic of indirect aggression to invest substantial resources in political action and propaganda within Western nations by using lies and half-truths to discredit target governments, bring about a cutoff of all Western economic and security assistance, and create false hopes about the flexibility or nationalist credentials of communist insurgents. As Castro and the Sandinistas recognized, a coalition with noncommunist partners—no matter how little influence or power they really have—provides the opening to feed the illusions of some Westerners who seem never to learn from the painful, tragic lessons of history. Thus, they delude themselves into thinking that a communist movement is really nationalist; that differences among the communist components and between them and the noncommunist partners will permit negotiated political solutions through forced power-sharing; and that even if a communist regime were to emerge from this process, it would live peacefully with its neighbors if the West remains friendly and provides sufficient economic aid.

The Soviet Bloc and Cuba have sought to spread these illusions through a mutually reinforcing four-level propaganda network: 1) communist government facilities; 2) communist parties in free world countries; 3) known and clandestine communist front groups; and 4) the communist governments' own propaganda facilities in the West. The Salvadoran guerrillas, for example, have about 60 propaganda offices in 30 countries. These offices produce a steady flow of "peace proposals," press releases, films, and video tapes, and they cultivate Western media and opinion leaders, especially those in politics, the churches, and labor unions. This combined propaganda network hopes to mislead the free world regarding the course of events in Central America.

Honduras made a peaceful transition to democracy in 1981. Thus far, its constitutional government has thwarted Cuban and Nicaraguan efforts to mount major terrorist and insurgent operations there. During 1979, 1980, and 1981—before there were any paramilitary democratic resistance forces in Nicaragua—Honduras reported many incursions and cross-border attacks by the Sandinista army. These assaults formed part of a deliberate Cuban/Sandinista effort to intimidate Honduras into permitting its territory to be used as a conduit for weapons and supplies to communist guerrillas in El Salvador and Guatemala. In 1981, the military government ended as democratic elections opened the way to a democratic transition. In April 1983, Castro unified the Honduran communist party and four Marxist-Leninist terrorist groups, just as he had three years earlier in El Salvador. The democratic government of Honduras has worked closely with the United States and its neighbors to contain the Sandinista regime. That effort, along with a modest amount of military aid, has sharply reduced Nicaraguan cross-border incursions.

Guatemala, the most populous Central American country, shares a long open border with Mexico. Castro aided communist guerrillas there in the 1960s, partly in revenge for Guatemala's support of the Bay of Pigs operation in 1961. Although Guatemalan security forces defeated that insurgency, Cuba sharply increased its assistance to Guatemalan guerrilla movements after the Sandinistas took power in Nicaragua in 1979.

Again, following the more assertive methods used in Nicaragua, Castro summoned the Guatemalan guerrilla factions to Havana in 1982, where they formed a united command group, Guatemalan National Revolutionary Unity (URNG). This new guerrilla command later went to Mexico to announce formation of the Guatemalan Committee for Patriotic Unity (CGUP) as the front—including a few noncommunists—to be used to deceive the West. The number of Marxist-Leninist guerrillas increased from about 600 in 1980 to about 2,500 in 1982. Then, guerrilla strength declined again to fewer than 1,000 by 1984 as Guatemalan authorities developed a program to provide peasants with "rifles and beans." The government has armed about 75,000 peasants in self-defense committees and has also provided medical aid, food, and other services. The military government held constituent assembly elections in July 1984 and invited the OAS and other democratic observers. Political parties and trade unions were again able to function. Guatemala returned to democratic government with the presidential election of 1985 and the inauguration of a new president, Vinicio Cerezo Arevalo, in January 1986.

Looking Toward the Future

From 1974 to 1980, this indirect aggression by the Soviet Bloc, Cuba, and other Soviet allies succeeded in ten countries. Since 1981, no additional pro-Soviet regimes have come to power, and democracy has been restored in Grenada.

Since taking office in 1981, the Reagan administration has pursued a prudent policy in Latin America of encouraging democratic institutions, aiding economic improvement, and helping the people to defend themselves against *both* the violent right and the violent left. The people of Latin America accomplished transitions back to democracy in at least ten Latin American and Caribbean countries since 1980. This progress is fragile and could be reversed if this Cuban/Sandinista/Soviet Bloc's subversive aggression continues or increases. And this *could* happen, since Castro has not yet been defeated in Nicaragua.

The evidence found in Grenada—the secret treaties with the Soviet Bloc, the nearly 1,000 Soviet, Cuban, Bulgarian, Libyan, and North Korean personnel (many there to train visiting Caribbean radicals in subversion), the bloated armed forces (from a few hundred to more than 4,000 after the New Jewel Movement coup), and the weapons for 20,000— all demonstrated conclusively that "the Soviets and Cubans were planning to use Grenada as a support base for guerrilla movements throughout the region."[25]

Further, communist activities on and from Grenada were proven to be even more menacing than the Reagan administration had believed and publicly declared. In the same way, it can be stated that this summary of Castro's aggression has only provided a partial insight into the extent of hostile Cuban actions around the world.

Will this continue into the indefinite future? Perhaps, but the good news from the 1980s is that despite the enormous human and material resources Castro has spent on his quest for power and communist victories around the globe, he has not been successful. Moreover, armed resistance movements opposing the brutal pro-Soviet dictatorships which Castro supports—in Afghanistan, Angola, Ethiopia, Mozambique, and Nicaragua— now total some 400,000 combatants. One way the free world could sharply reduce and in time defeat this Cuban/Soviet indirect aggression would be by providing adequate help to assure that these resistance movements, in President Reagan's words, "not only fight and die for freedom, but fight and win freedom."[26]

U.S. aid to freedom fighters, concerted efforts to encourage and assist defection from Cuban armed forces and personnel abroad, factual news to the Cuban people through Radio Martí about what Castro is doing—all of these can contribute to reducing this threat. In 1987, a senior Cuban general defected and eloquently described the military dissension and corruption of the communist elite within Cuba.[27] A coalition of Cuban exiles estimates that about 7,200 of Castro's political prisoners are government officials who tried to defect or were refusing or evading military service.[28] Castro saw vivid evidence of his subjects' discontent when in 1980 he declared that any Cubans who wanted to leave for the United States could do so; subsequently, tens, and then hundreds, of thousands did just that.

Equally important, our government must work consistently to help friendly governments defend themselves, to tell the truth about Castro's aggression, and to persuade free world countries to provide no economic benefits of any kind to Cuba—to totally isolate Castro—until his regime ends its participation in violence which has over the years caused the deaths of tens of thousands in Latin America, Africa, and the Middle East.

Notes

1. United States Government, *Cuba: Castro's Propaganda Apparatus and Foreign Policy,* 1984, p. 1.
2. Ibid., p. 4.
3. United States Senate Select Committee on Secret Military Assistance to Iran and the Nicaraguan Opposition, "Terrorism in Southern Africa. . . . Soviet Support for the Use of Armed Propaganda by National Liberation Organizations," Joel S. Lisker, Associate Counsel, Cumberland Lodge, Windsor, Berkshire, U.K., 4 July 1987, p. 5.
4. Speech by William Casey as published in *The Washington Times,* May 17, 1985.
5. President John F. Kennedy, press conference, 22 November 1962, Presidential Documents, 1962, p. 831.
6. Hugh Thomas, *The Revolution on Balance* (Washington, D.C.: The Cuban-American National Foundation, Inc., 1983).
7. U.S. Department of State, "Cuba's Renewed Support for Violence in Latin America," *Special Report #90,* 14 December 1981 (hereafter cited as "Cuba's Violence").
8. U.S. Department of State, *Libyan Activities in the Western Hemisphere,* August 1986, p. 4.
9. *Castro's and the Narcotics Connection,* Report #8, (Washington, D.C.: The Cuban-American National Foundation, 1983), pp. 25–29.
10. "Cuba's Renewed Support for Violence."
11. David J. Kopilow, *Castro, Israel, and the PLO,* (Washington, D.C.: The Cuban American National Foundation, Inc., 1985); White House Digest, "The PLO in Central America," July 20, 1983.
12. Pamela S. Falk, "Cuba in Africa," *Foreign Affairs,* Summer 1987; summarizes current Cuban activities.
13. Constantine C. Menges, "Central America and its Enemies," *Commentary,* August 1981, p. 36; U.S. Department of State, *The Sandinistas and Middle Eastern Radicals,* August 1985, pp. 7–8.
14. Ibid.
15. Constantine C. Menges, "Central American Revolutions: A New Dimension of

Political Warfare," in *The 1980s: Decade of Confrontation*, National Defense University, 1981.

16. "Cuba's Renewed Support for Violence."
17. U.S. Departments of State and Defense: "Background Paper: Central America," 27 May 1983; "Background Paper: Nicaragua's Military Build-up and Support for Central American Subversion," 18 July 1984; "The Soviet-Cuban Connection in Central America and the Caribbean," March 1985.
18. "Cuba's Renewed Support for Violence."
19. Ibid.
20. U.S. Departments of State and Defense, "The Sandinista Military Build-up: An Update," October 1987.
21. U.S. Department of State, "Revolution Beyond Our Borders: Sandinista Intervention in Central America," Special Report 132, September 1985.
22. *Washington Post*, January 7, 1988.
23. U.S. Departments of State and Defense, "Background Paper: Central America," 27 May 1983.
24. U.S. Department of State, "Revolution Beyond Our Borders" page 7; "Cuba's Renewed Support for Violence," p. 3.
25. U.S. Department of State, "Lessons of Grenada," February 1986.
26. President Reagan's State of the Union Address, January 1986.
27. *General Del Pino Speaks: An Insight into Elite Corruption and Military Dissension in Castro's Cuba*, Report 23, (Washington, D.C.: The Cuban-American National Foundation, Inc., 1987).
28. Junta Patriotica Cubana, Presentation to the OAS, 9 November 1987, p. 8.

11

Cuba's Foreign Economic Relationships

Jorge F. Pérez-López

A small, island economy with a limited natural resource base, Cuba has traditionally depended on foreign trade and capital flows from abroad to increase its national wealth. The high degree of openness of the Cuban economy, and hence the disproportionate importance of the external sector, can be illustrated with a few statistics. In the 1940s and 1950s, for example, the ratio of the value of exports to total goods and services produced by the economy (as measured by the gross national product, GNP) averaged about 31 percent, while that of imports to GNP was nearly 26 percent, so that the ratio of foreign trade turnover (exports plus imports) to GNP during this period was about 57 percent.[1] Moreover, prerevolutionary Cuba had few barriers to incoming foreign investment, and foreign capital was actively sought in many sectors. Foreign capital played a key role in financing the expansion of the sugar industry and national electrical power system, the establishment of telephone service, the construction of railroads, the provision of banking and insurance services, the construction and operation of oil refineries, and the development of the mining industry.

More than 25 years of socialism in Cuba has not changed either the basic openness of the Cuban economy or the need for capital flows from abroad to finance development. The openness of the economy of revolutionary Cuba can be inferred from data in Table 11.1. These data, which relate the value of total exports and imports during 1962–78 to the value of the gross material product (GMP), confirm that the Cuban economy remains eminently open and, in fact, the degree of openness has tended to increase over time.[2] Thus, while in the 1960s and early 1970s trade turnover on average accounted for about 41 percent of GMP, during 1974–78 it rose to an average of 66 percent. Unfortunately, official statistics on GMP are not available after 1978 and therefore it is not possible to update the figures in Table 11.1 for more recent periods; the performance of the economy and of merchandise trade since 1978 suggest that the degree of openness of the economy has not decreased—and probably has increased—in more recent years. In fact, a case can be made that in some respects, Cuba's vulnerability to external sector developments (fluctuations in foreign trade, access to external financing, exchange rates) has been exacerbated by policies of the revolutionary regime which have emphasized sugar specialization and intensive trade relations with socialist countries and virtually prohibited foreign investment in the island.

It is critical for the Cuban economy that its external sector—merchandise and services exports and imports, capital flows—develop in an orderly fashion lest it strangle economic growth. In the words of a Cuban economist, the external sector is the "strategic variable" in the performance of the Cuban economy.[3] Recently, the external sector has been under intense pressure. Radical measures to deal with a severe shortfall in hard currency, including the slashing of imports, were announced in December 1986. As

TABLE 11.1
Foreign Trade as a Percent of Gross Material Product
(percent)

	Exports	Imports	Trade Turnover
1962	14.1	20.5	34.6
1963	14.6	23.2	27.8
1964	17.5	25.0	42.5
1965	16.7	20.9	37.6
1966	14.9	23.2	38.1
1967	17.3	24.4	42.7
1968	14.9	25.2	40.1
1969	16.0	29.2	45.2
1970	24.9	31.2	56.2
1971	17.8	28.7	46.6
1972	12.7	19.7	32.4
1973	17.2	21.8	39.0
1974	30.0	30.0	60.0
1975	33.2	35.0	68.2
1976	30.3	35.8	66.1
1977	31.5	37.1	68.6
1978	33.8	35.1	69.3

Source: Carmelo Mesa-Lago, *The Economy of Socialist Cuba* (Albuquerque: University of New Mexico Press, 1981), p. 79.

President Fidel Castro explained in his Central Report to the Third Congress of the Cuban Communist Party in February 1986,

> The basic problem of the nation's economy in the five-year period 1981–85 was that, although we had an acceptable overall economic growth rate, it was not sufficiently high in the area where it was most needed, that is, in [the growth of] exports of goods and services and in import substitution.[4]

And later, at the closing session of the Third Party Congress in December 1986, he stressed the seriousness of external sector imbalances and their potential impact on economic performance:

> . . . there are some aspects of the economy which face difficult and complex situations. . . . The country is not going to lack, for example, the fuel which is needed; this fuel is guaranteed. It is not going to lack many other things that are also guaranteed by virtue of economic relations with the socialist countries. But we are going to lack convertible currency imports. Yes, [convertible currency imports] are going to be scarce and we do have a complex situation regarding these imports which is going to bring us problems! We are going to face problems such as delays in importing raw materials, inability to import some spare parts or delays in obtaining them, as a result of the severe constraints we face regarding convertible currency balances, constraints which are greater than ever![5]

This chapter will examine the performance of the external sector of the Cuban economy, with emphasis on convertible or hard currency balances. Because systematic data on trade in services are not available, and neither are those on the balance of payments, the analysis focuses on merchandise trade. In particular, this chapter will address three characteristics of the Cuban external sector which have an important bearing on the current hard currency problems faced by Cuba: (1) the persistence, and growing magnitude, of merchandise trade deficits; (2) the chronic shortage of convertible currencies; and (3) the inability to take advantage of foreign direct investment as a source of incoming long-term capital.

Merchandise Trade Deficits

Table 11.2 presents data on the value of Cuban merchandise exports and imports, and on the merchandise trade balance (exports minus imports), for each of the years from 1959–85. It is striking that over the 27-year period, Cuba recorded a positive merchandise trade balance in only two years, 1960 and 1974, and ran up a staggering cumulative merchandise trade deficit of over 12.2 billion pesos.

TABLE 11.2
Cuban Merchandise Trade, 1959–85
(in millions of pesos)

	Exports	Imports	Balance
1959	636.0	674.8	−38.8
1960	608.3	579.9	28.4
1961	626.4	638.7	−12.3
1962	522.3	759.3	−237.0
1963	545.1	867.3	−322.0
1964	714.3	1018.8	−304.5
1965	690.6	866.2	−175.6
1966	597.8	925.5	−327.7
1967	705.0	999.1	−294.1
1968	651.4	1102.3	−450.9
1969	666.7	1221.7	−555.0
1970	1049.5	1311.0	−261.5
1971	861.2	1386.6	−525.4
1972	770.9	1189.8	−418.9
1973	1153.0	1462.6	−309.6
1974	2236.5	2225.9	10.6
1975	2952.2	3113.1	−160.9
1976	2692.3	3179.7	−487.4
1977	2918.4	3461.6	−543.2
1978	3440.1	3573.8	−133.7
1979	3499.2	3687.5	−188.3
1980	3966.7	4627.0	−660.3
1981	4223.8	5114.0	−890.2
1982	4933.2	5530.6	−597.4
1983	5534.9	6222.1	−687.2
1984	5462.1	7207.2	−1745.1
1985	5982.8	7904.5	−1921.7

Sources: 1959–84: *Anuario Estadístico de Cuba 1984*, p. 284. 1985: Banco Nacional de Cuba, *Economic Report* (March 1986), p. 9.

Direction of Trade

During the 1981–85 period, merchandise trade balances with socialist countries and with market economy countries tended to follow the same pattern as overall trade balances: relative improvement in the trade deficit during 1982 and 1983, and worsening in 1984 and 1985. Trade balances with developing countries deteriorated steadily during the 1980s (Table 11.3).

As is evident from Table 11.4, over time Cuban foreign trade has become increasingly concentrated in the socialist countries—for example, the Soviet Union and other members of the Council for Mutual Economic

TABLE 11.3
Cuban Merchandise Trade by Broad Country Groupings
(in millions of pesos)

	1965	1970	1975	1977	1978	1979	1980	1981	1982	1983	1984	1985
Socialist countries												
Exports	537	777	2002	2443	2916	2884	2786	3179	4172	4765	4893	5310
Imports	659	917	1605	2341	2849	3053	3613	4114	4908	5414	6058	6640
Balance	−122	−140	397	102	67	−169	−827	−935	−736	−649	−1135	−1330
Developed market countries												
Exports	107	224	771	336	365	454	553	557	459	470	377	672
Imports	166	370	1299	934	602	578	904	922	556	631	868	1265
Balance	−59	−146	−528	−598	−237	−124	−351	−365	−97	−161	−491	−593
Developing market countries												
Exports	47	48	179	139	159	161	628	488	302	300	192	(1)
Imports	41	24	209	187	123	57	110	78	67	177	281	(1)
Balance	6	24	−30	−48	36	104	518	410	235	123	−89	(1)
Total												
Exports	691	1049	2952	2918	3440	3499	3967	4224	4933	5535	5462	5983
Imports	866	1311	3113	3462	3574	3688	4627	5114	5531	6222	7207	7905
Balance	−175	−262	−161	−544	−134	−189	−660	−890	−598	−687	−1745	−1922

Sources: 1965–81: Anuario Estadístico de Cuba 1982, p. 317.
1982–84: Anuario Estadístico de Cuba 1984, p. 289.
1985: Banco Nacional de Cuba, Economic Report (March 1986), p. 9.
(1) Included in figures for developed market economies.

TABLE 11.4
Distribution of Cuban Merchandise Trade by Broad Country Groupings
(percentages)

	1965	1970	1975	1977	1978	1979	1980	1981	1982	1983	1984	1985
Exports												
Socialist countries	77.7	74.1	67.8	83.7	84.8	82.4	70.2	75.3	84.6	86.1	86.5	86.1
Developed market countries	15.5	21.4	26.1	11.5	10.6	13.0	13.9	13.2	9.3	8.5	9.8	13.9
Developing market countries	6.8	4.5	6.1	4.8	4.6	4.6	15.8	11.6	6.1	5.4	3.7	(1)
Imports												
Socialist countries	76.1	70.0	51.6	67.6	79.7	82.8	78.1	80.4	88.7	87.0	89.6	88.8
Developed market countries	19.2	28.2	41.7	27.0	16.8	15.7	19.5	18.0	10.1	10.1	6.9	11.2
Developing market countries	4.7	1.8	6.7	5.4	3.4	1.5	2.4	1.5	1.2	2.9	3.5	(1)
Trade turnover												
Socialist countries	76.8	71.8	59.5	75.0	82.2	82.6	74.4	78.1	86.8	86.6	84.1	84.0
Developed market countries	17.5	25.2	34.1	19.9	13.8	14.4	17.0	15.8	9.7	9.4	12.0	16.0
Developing market countries	5.7	3.0	6.4	5.1	4.0	3.0	8.6	6.1	3.5	4.0	3.9	(1)

Sources: 1965–81: *Anuario Estadistico de Cuba 1982*, p. 317.

1982–84: *Anuario Estadistico de Cuba 1984*, p. 289.

1985:   Banco Nacional de Cuba, *Economic Report* (March 1986), p. 9.

(1) Included in figures for developed market economies.

Assistance (CMEA) and the People's Republic of China. In mid-February 1960, Cuba and the Soviet Union entered into a trade and payments agreement, as well as a credit agreement.[6] Pursuant to the trade and payments agreement, the Soviet Union committed itself to purchase one million tons of Cuban sugar during each of the years from 1960 to 1964; 80 percent of the value of sugar purchases would be paid with Soviet commodities (e.g., crude oil, fuel oil, chemicals, machinery), and the remaining 20 percent with convertible currencies. The credit agreement granted a line of credit of $100 million to Cuba for the purchase of new factories. Shortly after, other socialist countries followed suit, also establishing commercial and credit ties with Cuba. As relations with the United States deteriorated during the second half of 1960, relations with socialist countries intensified. In 1960 alone, Cuba entered into at least 70 bilateral agreements with socialist countries; no agreements with these countries were recorded in 1959.[7]

The process of shifting trade relations from the United States and the West to the Soviet Union and other socialist countries moved at a very rapid pace during the 1960s. In 1961, Cuba's exports to socialist countries already accounted for 73 percent of the value of all exports, and imports from these countries accounted for 70 percent of the total. In contrast, during 1961, the United States—formerly Cuba's most important trade partner—purchased 4.8 percent of Cuba's exports and supplied 3.7 percent of imports.[8] During the rest of the decade, socialist countries maintained their position as Cuba's primary trade partners. In 1965, for example, socialist countries accounted for 77 percent of Cuba's foreign trade (Table 11.4).

Economic relations between Cuba and the socialist countries during the 1960s were based on a web of bilateral agreements covering merchandise trade, payments, credits, and technical assistance in areas such as agriculture, fishing, geological exploration, manpower development, etc. During the period from 1961 to 1969, Cuba concluded over 400 bilateral agreements with socialist countries, the vast majority of which dealt with aspects of the economic relationship.[9] To coordinate the burgeoning economic and scientific-technical assistance relationship, several government-to-government commissions were established in the 1960s and early 1970s with East Germany (in 1964), Bulgaria and Czechoslovakia (in 1965), Hungary (in 1966), Romania (in 1967), North Korea (in 1968), Poland (in 1969), and the Soviet Union (in 1970).[10]

Cuba's economic relations with the socialist countries deepened in 1972 when Cuba became a member of CMEA, the customs union of the socialist countries.[11] Since then, Cuba has participated actively in the activities of that institution and progressively integrated its economy to those of CMEA members.[12]

In 1980, trade with the socialist countries accounted for 70 percent of Cuba's exports and 78 percent of imports; in 1985, the socialist countries took 86 percent of Cuba's exports and provided 88 percent of imports. Cuba's trade deficits with the socialist countries during 1981–85 averaged 960 million pesos per annum; in 1985, the trade deficit reached an all-time high of 1.3 billion pesos. These deficits would have been considerably higher had the Soviet Union and other CMEA nations not extended special price treatment to Cuban exports and imports.

Since the 1960s, the Soviet Union has purchased Cuban sugar at fixed prices for multiyear periods. As the world market price for sugar fluctuated—sometimes exceeding, but more often falling below the contracted price—the arrangement has tended to favor Cuba. In December 1972, two agreements were reached between Cuba and the Soviet Union which formalized a system of preferential (i.e., higher than world market) pricing for Cuban sugar, and extended it to nickel exports.[13] As the world market price for sugar rose strongly in 1973 and 1974, the contract price for exports to the Soviet Union and other CMEA nations was renegotiated and adjusted upward. Subsequently, Cuba and the Soviet Union agreed to a mechanism whereby sugar export prices are adjusted annually, above a very high floor, in proportion to changes in the prices of a basket of commodities which Cuba imports from the Soviet Union.[14] As a result of this indexing scheme, the price of Cuban sugar exports to the Soviet Union has consistently exceeded the world market price by a considerable margin. Cuba has also negotiated agreements with East Germany, Bulgaria, Czechoslovakia, Hungary, Poland, and Romania which have granted preferential price treatment to Cuban sugar exports.[15]

For example, based on the most recent Cuban official trade statistics, the contract price of sugar exports to the Soviet Union in 1982 was 29.9 centavos/pound, to CMEA members 28.9 centavos/pound, and to capitalist countries 7.7 centavos/pound.[16] Meanwhile, the world market price for sugar in that year was 7.1 centavos/pound.[17] It has been reported that the contract price for Cuban sugar paid by the Soviet Union was 46 centavos/pound in 1983, 44 centavos/pound in 1984, and 45 centavos/pound in 1985.[18]

Although the world market price of oil nearly quadrupled at the end of 1973 following the Arab oil embargo, Cuba was shielded from that increase as a result of trade arrangements with the Soviet Union which had fixed the export price of oil for the five-year period from 1971 to 1975. To be sure, in early 1975 the Soviet Union did increase oil export prices to Cuba (and other CMEA nations) and introduced a formula, based on a multiyear moving average of world prices, to increase oil export prices annually.[19] Nevertheless, since 1973, Cuba has benefitted from the substantial price advantage in Soviet oil relative to what it would have had to pay in the world market. In an environment of rising oil world market prices, the moving average formula smoothed price increases and passed them on to Cuba with a significant time lag. In this context, it appears that the benefit of Soviet oil prices lower than market prices had disappeared by 1985. In fact, in 1985 Cuba may have paid substantially higher prices for Soviet oil than those prevailing in the world market as world oil market prices fell sharply in the closing days of 1985 and the first quarter of 1986 while the Soviet Union continued to use the formula-derived prices in trade with CMEA members.[20]

It has been estimated (Table 11.5) that over the 1961–82 period, the Soviet Union subsidized merchandise trade with Cuba to the tune of nearly $20.5 billion, 68 percent of which related to sugar price subsidies, 29 percent to oil price subsidies, and the remainder to nickel price subsidies.

TABLE 11.5
Estimated Price Subsidies in Cuban-Soviet Trade
(millions of U.S. dollars)

	Sugar	Nickel	Oil	Total
1961–67	632			632
1968	150			150
1969	86			86
1970	150			150
1971	56			56
1972	0			0
1973	97	53		150
1974	0	38	369	407
1975	580	31	290	901
1976	977	18	362	1357
1977	1428	16	328	1772
1978	2435	38	165	2638
1979	2287	15	365	2667
1980	1165	0	1480	2645
1981	1366	122	1657	3145
1982	2580	107	1006	3693
Total 1961–82	13989	438	6022	20449

Sources: 1961–70: Central Intelligence Agency, *Cuba Foreign Trade,* AER 75–69 (July 1975), p. 15.

1971–79: National Foreign Assessment Center, *The Cuban Economy: A Statistical Review,* ER81-10052 (March 1981), p. 39.

1980–82: Central Intelligence Agency, *The Cuban Economy: A Statistical Review,* ALA 84-10052 (June 1984), p. 40.

These calculations, which are based on the difference between the price of these commodities in Cuban-Soviet trade and their world market price, may yield upper-limit subsidy estimates (e.g., because another preferential price, rather the world market price, may be used as the hypothetical price at which Cuba would sell its sugar to the Soviet Union and other purchasers).[21] Nevertheless, they suggest that had Cuba maintained the same import and export patterns during the 1959–85 period, in the absence of these subsidies, its cumulative trade deficit would have been several-fold higher than the 12.2 billion pesos actually incurred.

Although quantitatively small and declining—probably about 12 percent of trade turnover in 1985, compared to 17 percent in 1980 (see Table 11.4)—trade with market economy nations is critical to the Cuban economy. These nations provide Cuba with goods and technology either not available, or available only in limited quantities, from socialist nations. Exports to developed market economies are one of the key sources of hard currency to finance imports from these nations and to service the hard currency debt.

After recording deficits in merchandise trade with developed market economies in 1980 and 1981 on the order of 350 million pesos, in 1982 and 1983, Cuba reduced imports from these countries by about one-third, so that merchandise trade deficits were relatively small: 97 million pesos in 1982 and 161 million pesos in 1983 (Table 11.3). However, in 1984, imports from developed market economies rose by nearly 250 million pesos and exports weakened, resulting in a trade deficit with these nations of 490 million pesos. Preliminary data for 1985 suggest that the situation in 1985 was not significantly better.

In the late 1970s, Cuba began to record sizable merchandise trade surpluses with developing market countries. Merchandise trade surpluses with developing market economies grew rapidly—36 million pesos in 1978, 104 million pesos in 1979, 518 million pesos in 1980—and had a positive impact on the overall trade balance. An important contributor to this favorable development was trade with Africa. In 1979, for example, Cuban exports to Africa amounted to over 69 million pesos, while imports from that continent were only 6 million pesos; in 1980 and 1981, Cuba recorded surpluses in merchandise trade with Africa of nearly 229 million pesos and 256 million pesos, respectively.[22] Arguably, their increase in Cuban exports to Africa and other developing countries is partly associated with Cuba's internationalist policies and the link between Cuban personnel abroad (whether soldiers, medical doctors, or technicians) and merchandise exports from Cuba.[23] In the 1980s, the merchandise trade surplus with developing market economies declined steadily. By 1984, Cuba recorded a trade deficit of 89 million with these nations.

Commodity Composition

Cuba's export and import trade baskets are very similar to those of other oil-importing developing countries in Latin America: heavy concentration on exports of basic commodities (agricultural products and raw materials) and on imports of fuels, semifinished products, and capital goods. Although Cuban foreign trade statistics are distorted by the special trade relationships with the Soviet Union discussed above (high export prices for sugar and nickel exports to the Soviet Union, which tend to overstate these products' share of total exports relative to others, and low price of imports of Soviet oil, which tends to understate the latter's share of total imports relative to other products), it is instructive to examine Cuba's composition of trade based on official data.

An examination of the commodity composition of Cuban exports points to a concentration on primary and intermediate products. In the 1980s, for example, over four-fifths of Cuba's exports were accounted for by food and live animals, primarily sugar (Table 11.6). Exports of beverages (e.g., rum) and tobacco products and of raw materials (primarily nickel) accounted for about one-tenth of the value of exports. Despite efforts to diversify exports and develop new export lines,[24] the Cuban export basket continues to be composed primarily of "traditional" products: sugar, tobacco products, fish and seafood, beverages, citrus fruits, and nickel. In 1984, for example, official statistics report a handful of chemical products, cement, henequen rope, textiles, and flat-rolled steel products as the only significant nontraditional manufactured export goods.[25] In that year, exports of nontraditional exports (chemicals and manufactured products combined) accounted for merely 0.5 percent of the value of total exports. Indeed, it is the continued dependence on traditional exports, characterized by a slow growth in demand and high price volatility, that is primarily responsible for the lack of dynamism of the Cuban export sector and its inability to generate sufficient revenue to finance imports.

Since the mid-1970s, Cuban official statistics have also reported exports of oil and oil products. Initially, these fuel exports consisted of relatively small shipments of naphtha refined from Soviet crude oil. In the 1980s, fuel reexports broadened to include crude oil and other products and their volume skyrocketed: according to data in Table 11.6, fuel reexports accounted for 10.6 and 10.1 percent, respectively, of the total volume of exports in 1983 and 1984. Although Cuba does not publish statistics on the volume of fuel reexports, it has been estimated that they amounted to some 400,000 metric tons (MT) in 1980, 650,000 MT in 1981, 1.1 million MT in 1982, and nearly 2.6 million MT in 1983 and 1984.[26] According to Castro, fuel reexports in 1985 amounted to around 3 million MT.[27]

TABLE 11.6
Distribution of Cuban Merchandise Exports by Major Division of the Standard International Trade Classification (SITC)
(percentages)

SITC		1965	1970	1975	1977	1980	1981	1982	1983	1984
0	Food and live animals	86.6	79.5	92.7	87.8	88.1	84.4	82.5	79.3	80.1
1	Beverages and tobacco	4.8	3.3	2.3	2.8	2.2	1.7	2.6	2.4	1.7
2	Raw materials, inedible, except fuels	7.4	16.7	4.7	6.5	5.0	8.0	6.7	5.6	6.0
3	Fuels	0.0	0.0	0.1	2.3	4.2	4.2	6.9	10.6	10.1
5	Chemicals	0.1	0.1	0.0	0.0	0.0	0.1	0.1	0.2	0.1
6	Manufactured products classified chiefly by material	0.0	0.0	0.0	0.2	0.4	0.4	1.0	0.5	0.4
	Not classified	1.1	0.4	0.2	0.4	0.1	1.2	0.2	1.4	1.6

Source: Anuario Estadístico de Cuba 1984, p. 302.

Imports of machinery and transportation equipment have traditionally dominated Cuba's import basket, accounting for well over one-third of the value of imports and rising to over 40 percent in some years (Table 11.7). In the 1980s, the machinery and transportation equipment import share fell to less than one-third, as that of fuels rose very rapidly. This can be attributed not only to rising domestic consumption and higher prices for oil imports from the Soviet Union (in accordance with the pricing formula), but also to large volumes of imports needed to accommodate reexports. By 1984, fuels had become the most important category of Cuban imports, surpassing machinery and transportation equipment imports. The share of imports accounted for by food products (primarily grains and processed meats) has tended to decline, while that of chemicals (fertilizers and basic chemicals) and other manufactured goods (steel products and textiles) have remained relatively constant.

An examination of the distribution of Cuban imports by end-use categories (Table 11.8) reveals a steady increase in the share of imports accounted for by intermediate goods (semifinished goods, raw materials, spare parts) accompanied by a decline in the share accounted for by both consumer and capital goods. The large and growing participation of intermediate goods in Cuba's import basket is explained by a Cuban economist as follows:

> . . . a large part of Cuba's industrial activities are concentrated in the final stages of the production of consumer goods. This confirms the deep dependence of the domestic consumer goods industry on external supplies.[28]

Under these circumstances, reductions in intermediate goods imports to address trade deficits can have a severe adverse impact on domestic economic activity.

Export Promotion Efforts

In an attempt to close the merchandise trade gap, the Cuban five-year plan for the 1981–85 period set a target for the growth of exports of 7 percent per annum, a higher rate than the projected annual growth rates of imports and of overall growth.[29] To this end, the plan contained a number of directives to enterprises producing exportables to improve quality of products, meet production schedules, etc. Exporting enterprises were also directed to step up marketing efforts abroad, eliminate or reduce shipment delays, etc. To complement the export drive, import substitution was also given a higher profile.

Evidence of the high priority attached to the export promotion effort

TABLE 11.7

Distribution of Cuban Merchandise Imports by Major Division of the Standard International Trade Classification (SITC)
(percentages)

SITC		1970	1975	1977	1980	1981	1982	1983	1984
0	Food and live animals	20.0	19.1	16.5	16.1	15.0	14.7	12.6	11.2
1	Beverages and tobacco	0.2	0.1	0.0	0.3	0.2	0.2	0.2	0.1
2	Raw materials, inedible, except fuels	5.5	5.9	4.0	4.1	4.2	3.3	3.2	3.5
3	Fuels	8.8	10.3	14.4	19.7	22.8	27.1	29.9	30.8
4	Animal and vegetable oils and fats	1.6	1.3	1.4	1.2	1.1	0.9	1.0	1.1
5	Chemicals	9.2	8.0	5.3	6.2	6.1	6.5	6.8	5.9
6	Manufactured products classified chiefly by material	15.7	18.4	13.3	14.7	14.8	13.0	12.3	13.3
7	Machinery and transportation equipment	36.4	31.1	42.3	35.4	33.6	31.0	30.6	30.5
8	Other manufactured products	2.6	5.8	2.8	2.2	2.2	3.3	3.4	3.6

Source: Anuario Estadístico de Cuba 1984, p. 303.

TABLE 11.8
Distribution of Cuban Merchandise Imports by End-Use Categories
(percentages)

	Consumer Goods	Intermediate Goods	Investment Goods	Total
1965	24.6	38.0	37.4	100.0
1970	17.1	59.3	23.6	100.0
1975	13.3	63.1	23.6	100.0
1977	12.9	55.4	31.7	100.0
1980	11.6	61.0	27.4	100.0
1981	13.1	62.6	24.3	100.0
1982	13.8	63.3	22.9	100.0
1983	12.2	65.5	22.3	100.0
1984	10.9	67.1	22.0	100.0

Source: Anuario Estadístico de Cuba 1984, p. 301.

was the decision in early 1981 by the State Committee on Prices (Comite Estatal de Precios) to permit, for the first time, an "economic link" between enterprises which produce exportables and the overseas market for their products. The regulations would permit enterprises producing exportables to control the largest share (70 percent) of the "profit" which results from differences between the domestic price of a product and the price it might command abroad. Enterprises would thus have an incentive to maximize export volumes since the profit they are allowed to retain would be directly related to export volumes.[30] Similarly, in May 1983, the State Committee on Labor and Social Security (Comite Estatal de Trabajo y Seguridad Social) established a national system of wage premiums for workers in enterprises that exceeded their export commitments.[31]

Early import substitution efforts in revolutionary Cuba were directed at manufacturing replacement parts for U.S.-vintage capital stock. In particular, enterprises within the sugar industry developed the capability of manufacturing replacement parts for sugar mills and refineries. Over time, metalworking facilities, manufacturing a broad range of other replacement and spare parts for industrial and transportation equipment, were also established.[32] Import substitution activities have been given a higher profile since early 1982, when the First National Forum on the Recovery and Manufacture of Spare Parts and the First Symposium on Import Substitution were held within a few weeks of each other.[33]

Although Cuba exceeded its targets for export expansion in 1981–85, imports grew much faster than planned. As a result, Cuba experienced a sharp deterioration in its merchandise trade balances, incurring cumulative deficits of 5.8 billion pesos during this period. Cuba's average annual merchandise trade deficit during the 1981–85 period rose by 190 percent compared to the 1976–80 period (the average annual trade deficit was 402.6 million pesos from 1976 to 1980, and 1,168.8 million pesos from 1981 to 1985). In 1982 and 1983, the trade deficit was reduced substantially from the then-record deficit of 890 million pesos recorded in 1981. In 1984, however, the merchandise trade deficit grew by more than 1 billion pesos, from 687 million to 1,745 million. A new record merchandise trade deficit was recorded in 1985: 1,923 million pesos.

The draft economic and social development plan for the 1986–90 period, discussed at the Third Congress of the Cuban Communist Party in February and November–December 1986, singled out export expansion and import substitution as the key objectives for this period.[34] The 1985 plan had already given the highest priority to:

> investments that guarantee a sustained growth of capacities for producing export goods rationally [and for] replacing imports, and whose start up will favorably influence the current account in convertible currency of the country's balance of payments.[35]

Specifically, the 1986–90 plan calls for exports to increase at a rate of at least 5 percent per annum, and for nontraditional exports in hard currency to increase by 1,000 million pesos over the period in relation to 1984 levels; imports and national income are projected to grow at a lower rate than exports.[36]

Although data for 1986 are not available as of this writing, there is evidence that no significant improvement in the balance of payments occurred in that year, and prospects for a turnaround are dim. According to Castro, exports in 1986 were adversely affected by a poor sugar crop, the drop in the world price of oil (which reduced in half the income Cuba obtained from oil reexports), and the change in the value of the dollar.[37] In addition, the performance of import substitution plans in 1986 was disappointing.

In early 1986, a special group was established within the Central Planning Board (Junta Central de Planificacion, JUCEPLAN) to identify areas susceptible to import substitution, particularly from hard currency areas, and to incorporate import substitution proposals into the central planning process; for the 1986 plan, this group identified 240 specific import substitution objectives.[38] The reduction in imports in 1986 as a result of domestic substitution schemes, originally projected at 60.3 million pesos, was revised downward in July 1986 to 50.0 million pesos; by mid-July 1986, a reduction in imports of only 19 million pesos had been attained.[39]

In the closing days of 1986, Castro announced a broad austerity program aimed at reducing hard currency imports (reportedly from 1,200 million pesos in 1986 to 600 million pesos in 1987) and balancing domestic revenues and expenditures. Among the specific measures were: reductions in rations of meat, milk, and kerosene to the general public; reduction of 20 percent in the allocation of gasoline to state administrators; exportation of 10 million square meters of textiles previously earmarked for domestic consumption; elimination of snack service in state offices; modification of the afternoon meal in child care institutions to a snack; and implementation of increased (double) fares for urban transportation and increased prices for electricity and other products sold in the parallel market.[40] It appears that the system, instituted in 1983, of wage premiums for workers in industries that exceed export goals may fall victim to the economic "rectification" campaign which began in Cuba in early 1986, however. At the concluding session of the Third Party Congress, Castro characterized the system of premiums for those industries surpassing export targets as "absurd" and as typical of "methods conceived to give away money by those who forget that what does not exist can not be given away."[41]

Hard Currency Shortages

The bulk of Cuba's trade with socialist countries is conducted through bilateral balancing agreements—tantamount to barter arrangements—in which individual transactions are made, and accounts settled, using either the currency of one of the two trading partners or "transferable rubles," an artificial currency whose sole role is to serve as a unit of account in transactions among socialist countries. Because neither the currencies of the socialist countries nor the transferable ruble can be freely converted into "hard currencies" (e.g., dollars, Swiss francs, deutsche marks) to purchase goods and services in international markets, these nations make efforts to balance trade bilaterally each year. Socialist countries have routinely financed Cuba's trade deficits in soft currency by extending low-interest loans. Further, the Soviet Union, by far the largest creditor, has rolled over these loans twice, first in 1972,[42] and more recently in 1985.[43] The probability that they will be fully repaid is low.

In contrast, trade with developed market economies (and with many developing market economies) is conducted following common commercial practices and using hard currencies. Western governments, financial institutions, or suppliers provide credits to finance exports to Cuba; these interest-bearing credits must be repaid, in hard currencies, according to a predetermined schedule. Because of inconvertibility, Cuba can not apply surpluses in trade with the socialist countries to offset deficits with developed market economies or to service debt with these nations.

In essence, Cuba's foreign accounts are segmented: a soft currency account which covers most of the commercial and financial relations with the socialist nations, and a hard currency account which refers to economic relations with the rest of the world. (A fraction of Cuba's exports to socialist countries earn hard currencies. Arguably, socialist countries are willing to purchase Cuban products for hard currency as a concession to Cuba. Therefore, in what follows, hard currency exports are associated with exports to hard currency areas.) The relative magnitude of these two accounts in recent years can be seen from data in Table 11.9. Over the period 1978–85, Cuba sold on average about 24 percent of its exports for hard currency, while hard-currency imports averaged about 17 percent of total imports. The share of exports to hard currency areas peaked in 1980 and 1981—when world market sugar prices were high—at about 32 percent of the value of exports. Since then, they have declined steadily: 28 percent in 1982, 23 percent in 1983, 20 percent in 1984, and under 20 percent in 1985. The hard currency balance of trade, which recorded substantial surpluses in the 1979–83 period, turned negative in 1984 and 1985. The deterioration in the hard currency balance of trade in 1984 was very significant, as it swung from a surplus of 455 million pesos in 1983 to a deficit of 69 million pesos in 1984.

In the mid- and late 1970s, taking advantage of a relatively strong domestic economic performance, high world market prices for sugar, and the availability of international credit (because of the recycling of so-called "petro-dollars"), Cuba borrowed funds from Western credit institutions and government to finance its development plans. While a portion of these funds were used for infrastructure improvements (e.g., electric power plants), the bulk were used to finance productive investments. Cuba expected that these investments would not be a burden on its hard currency balances as they would either generate additional hard currency exports or reduce hard currency imports (through import substitution) to permit servicing of the debt.

For a host of reasons—the precipitous decline and continued weakness in the world market price of sugar, plagues that affected the sugar and tobacco crops, inclement weather, delays in the completion of projects, product quality problems, inability to penetrate Western markets, overall low production efficiency, rise in international interest rates which increased debt servicing—in 1981 and 1982, Cuba's hard currency balance of payments deteriorated severely. In August 1982, the Banco Nacional de Cuba proposed to its Western creditors (public and private) a renegotiation of the terms of part of its debt. According to a report issued by the Banco Nacional in support of its request,[44] the hard currency debt in August 1982 amounted to $2.9 billion, $1.65 billion of which was due to private sector

TABLE 11.9
Cuban Merchandise Trade Balance in Soft and Hard Currency
(in millions of pesos)

	1978	1979	1980	1981	1982	1983	1984	1985
Soft Currency								
Exports	2776	2759	2683	2881	3551	4248	4366	4800
Imports	2844	3047	2956	4126	4899	5390	6042	6603
Balance	-68	-288	-923	-1245	-1348	-1142	-1676	-1803
Hard Currency								
Exports	664	740	1284	1343	1382	1287	1096	1183
Imports	730	641	1011	988	632	832	1165	1302
Balance	-66	99	273	355	750	455	-69	-119
Total								
Exports	3440	3499	3967	4224	4933	5535	5462	5983
Imports	3574	3688	4627	5114	5531	6222	7207	7905
Balance	-134	-189	-660	-890	-598	-687	-1745	-1922

Sources: 1978–80: Banco Nacional de Cuba, *Memorandum to the Group of Experts on the Rescheduling of the Cuban Debt* (1982).
1981–82: Banco Nacional de Cuba-Comité Estatal de Estadísticas, *Cuba: Informe Económico Trimestral* (December 1982).
1983–85: Banco Nacional de Cuba, *Economic Report* (February 1985 and March 1986).

institutions (banks, suppliers, financial institutions) and the rest to public sources (e.g., insured export credits). The bulk of the debt from private institutions was in the form of short-term loans.

In March 1983, a group of creditor countries (West Germany, Austria, Belgium, Canada, Denmark, Spain, France, Italy, Japan, the Netherlands, England, Sweden, and Switzerland) agreed to reschedule Cuba's principal payments due in 1982 and 1983 over a five-year period, with a grace period of three and one-half years.[45] With regard to debt held by private banks, an agreement rescheduling repayments due in 1982 and 1983 on medium-term debt was reached in April 1983, and on short-term debt in 1984.[46] Cuba was again successful in rescheduling public and private debt repayments due in 1984 and 1985.[47] In 1986, however, faced with a deteriorating balance of payments in hard currency, Cuba was unable to reschedule repayments due that year. In fact, in mid-1986, Cuba suspended debt service payments to Western creditors.[48] At a meeting of the National Assembly in the closing days of 1986, Castro admitted that in 1986, Cuba had not been able to meet its international financial obligations, and intimated that the situation in 1987 would not be significantly better.[49]

To a large extent, Cuba's chronic hard currency deficits may be rooted in factors which are intrinsic to centrally planned economies (CPEs).[50] Holzman has analyzed the hard currency shortages of CPEs in terms of three "illusions" which afflict planners: a "salability" illusion, a "terms of trade" illusion, and a "macro-balance" illusion.[51] Because Cuban planners also appear to be afflicted by these "illusions," it is useful to discuss them in some detail.

Salability illusion. Central planners suffer from a "salability" illusion which usually leads them to overestimate the amount of hard currency exports they will sell in the West each year. Because imports are highly desirable, planners attempt to sell more hard currency goods to the West than is feasible; the more their need for imports, the greater the temptation to place products in developed market economies which are not able to be sold. As *ex ante* export plans are not fulfilled, the *ex ante* balanced trade plan results in *ex post* trade deficits; these deficits require unplanned borrowing or drawing down of reserves.

The tendency on the part of CPE planners to overestimate export sales in the West results from a combination of factors, among them: difficulties in assessing Western demand; the expectation that their goods would be sellable in the West based on their sales experience domestically or to other CPEs; inability of export planners to influence the quality of products or the schedule of production; and the tendency for foreign trade plans to be as chronically "taut" as the national economic plans.

While all CPEs encounter discriminatory tariff treatment of their exports in Western markets (i.e., higher levels of import tariffs than those imposed on goods originating from most other trading partners), Cuban exports face more severe impediments. First, there is an outright ban on exports to its closest and traditional market, the United States, which has been in effect since late 1960. And second, at least through the mid-1960s, Cuba has experienced difficulties in exporting to other Western nations as a result of pressure by the United States on these nations to isolate Cuba economically. After nearly 27 years, the case can be made that the Cuban economy has adapted to the U.S. economic sanctions and has redirected its trade so that the impact of the trade embargo on the economy is no longer significant. Yet, there is little doubt that U.S. policies have had a profound influence on the difficulties which Cuba has faced, and will continue to face in the near term, in increasing exports to Western countries and in diversifying its export basket.

Cuban planners' affliction with the "salability" illusion can be illustrated with an example. In 1973, as sugar world market prices finally recovered after an eight-year spell of extremely low levels, Cuban export revenues surged by almost 50 percent. The sugar bonanza continued and intensified in 1974, when sugar world market prices averaged 30 cents/pound for the year, compared to just under 2 cents/pound five years earlier, and export revenues rose by an additional 94 percent. The very high 1973–74 sugar prices reduced substantially the merchandise trade deficit in 1973 relative to previous years and produced a very small merchandise trade surplus in 1974, the first time the merchandise trade account had been in the black since 1960.

Planners took advantage of the 1973–74 windfall in export revenues, which extended to hard currency earnings, to boost imports. Thus, overall imports in 1974 were 53 percent higher than a year earlier. Significantly, imports from developed market economies increased even faster, with imports from member nations of the Organization for Economic Cooperation and Development (OECD) more than doubling, from $415 million in 1973 to $896 million in 1974 (Table 11.10).

In 1975, as planners were putting the final touches on the 1976–80 plan, sugar world market prices remained at very high levels (the annual average was 20.3 cents/pound). Imbued with the "salability" illusion and anticipating continued strength of sugar prices,[52] the five-year plan 1976–80 contemplated extremely ambitious levels of investment in the productive sphere and the importation of technologically advanced capital goods.[53] Although there is no information on the proportion of capital goods imports to be procured from the West, it can be surmised that it was to be substantial. For example, during the first two years of the plan, OECD exports of capital goods (machinery and transport equipment) to Cuba averaged

TABLE 11.10

Exports to Cuba from Members of the Organization for Economic Cooperation and Development (OECD)[1]

(in millions of U.S. dollars, f.o.b. value)

SITC		1964	1965	1966	1967	1968	1969	1970	1971	1972	1973
	Total	231.3	165.3	212.4	207.1	207.6	280.7	370.7	349.4	276.8	415.4
0	Food and live animals	69.3	52.4	66.6	49.9	51.7	45.8	73.7	73.4	70.3	90.2
1	Beverages and tobacco	2.5	0.6	0.9	0.7	0.3	0.6	0.7	0.2	0.2	0.3
2	Raw materials, inedible, except fuels	7.9	0.8	2.9	2.8	2.3	3.7	2.7	5.4	4.9	5.9
3	Fuels	0.2	0.1	0.0	0.2	0.3	0.6	0.7	0.3	1.7	0.9
4	Animal and vegetable oils and fats	3.3	1.7	2.0	0.0	0.0	0.3	0.9	0.6	0.6	3.0
5	Chemicals	36.4	11.2	28.2	51.0	53.1	57.4	63.9	37.0	41.0	56.5
6	Manufactured products classified chiefly by material	48.4	23.4	17.0	28.8	15.9	37.1	59.4	45.4	46.2	94.5
7	Machinery and transportation equipment	54.4	70.0	90.4	66.6	79.9	128.8	160.4	176.2	101.6	146.3
8	Other manufactured products	8.7	4.9	4.0	6.9	3.9	6.9	8.1	10.2	9.7	17.2
9	Transactions not classified according to kind	0.3	0.0	0.3	0.0	0.0	0.0	0.3	0.8	0.3	0.5

TABLE 11.10 (cont.)

SITC		1974	1975	1976	1977	1978	1979	1980	1981	1982	1983	1984
	Total	895.8	1499.1	1164.2	1163.2	882.1	970.2	1509.3	1350.7	907.9	883.1	1188.8
0	Food and live animals	178.3	233.2	241.7	164.4	201.1	243.2	456.3	399.5	398.4	332.7	285.6
1	Beverages and tobacco	0.6	0.5	0.7	0.4	0.8	1.9	8.8	3.9	3.8	2.0	1.7
2	Raw materials, inedible, except fuels	20.1	22.1	12.5	5.6	6.9	10.6	26.9	32.5	24.5	14.2	23.5
3	Fuels	2.6	6.0	1.2	3.0	3.8	4.0	126.6	41.4	19.2	13.2	31.2
4	Animal and vegetable oils and fats	7.6	8.2	6.0	2.7	2.3	2.6	3.9	3.9	1.9	2.8	3.7
5	Chemicals	119.9	164.7	88.0	84.9	116.9	146.4	184.8	168.8	97.3	144.9	153.3
6	Manufactured products classified chiefly by material	234.8	414.6	220.1	198.1	152.6	158.4	240.8	224.6	100.7	132.4	213.3
7	Machinery and transportation equipment	298.4	586.9	537.0	654.8	347.4	359.5	412.1	427.0	226.4	197.8	398.0
8	Other manufactured products	32.1	57.1	52.9	45.3	46.4	40.1	44.7	46.0	33.3	40.8	68.3
9	Transactions not classified according to kind	1.4	5.8	4.1	4.2	4.1	3.4	4.4	3.3	2.4	2.2	10.3

Source: Organization for Economic Cooperation and Development, *Statistics of Foreign Trade*, Series C, various volumes.

[1]Australia, Austria, Belgium, Canada, Denmark, Finland, France, the Federal Republic of Germany, Greece, Iceland, Ireland, Japan, Luxembourg, the Netherlands, New Zealand, Norway, Portugal, Spain, Sweden, Switzerland, Turkey, the United Kingdom, and the United States. Exports from Yugoslavia, a nonmember who participates in certain OECD activities, are also included.

nearly $600 million per year (Table 11.10), compared to an annual average of $262 million in the period 1971–75 and $180 million per year during 1971–74.

As the bottom fell out of the sugar market (world market prices averaged 11.6 cents/pound in 1976, 8.1 in 1977, 7.8 in 1978 and 9.6 in 1979), Cuba was forced into the unenviable position of slashing imports and turning to Western financial markets for short-term credit to make up for the shortfall in export revenue. In several instances, import orders ready to be shipped to Cuba had to be either postponed or cancelled because of the unavailability of hard currency;[54] according to a Cuban official, 22 investment projects were affected by the shortfall in export revenues.[55] Cuba's hard currency foreign debt, which had been estimated at $960 million in 1975, more than tripled to $2.9 billion by 1979 as Cuba attempted to maintain reasonable levels of hard currency imports by relying on a combination of supplier credits and short-term loans from the Eurocurrency market.[56]

The miscalculation regarding sugar export revenues was again repeated in the 1980s. After hovering for four years at levels around 10 cents/pound, in 1980, the year during which the five-year plan 1981–85 was being finalized, sugar world market prices rose to nearly 29 cents/pound. While planners might have been less apt to factor in very high sugar prices for the next five-year period based on the 1976–79 experience, the high prices undoubtedly influenced their thinking.[57] As before, sugar world market prices receded sharply, dropping to an average of 17.0 cents/pound in 1981 and 8.5 in 1982. The sharp drop in sugar export revenues, coupled with high levels of hard currency imports, put in jeopardy Cuba's ability to service the foreign debt and contributed importantly to the financial crisis of mid-1982 which forced Cuba to seek a renegotiation of its hard currency foreign debt.

Cuban planners' swiftness to increase imports from developed market economies whenever hard currency becomes available is evidence of Cuba's preference for imports from developed market economies and the pent-up demand for such imports.[58] In 1975 and 1980, for example, two years when world market sugar prices were high and therefore hard currency revenues from sugar exports were relatively abundant, the share of Cuban imports procured from developed market economies was very high relative to neighboring years: 41.7 percent in 1975 and 19.5 percent in 1980 (Table 11.4). The strongly positive relationship between Cuban imports from developed market economies and availability of hard currency can be seen from Figure 11.1. In this chart, Cuban imports from OECD countries and world market sugar prices have been plotted against the same time scale. The strong resemblance in movement of the two series for the period 1972–83 is striking: both series show a bimodal distribution,

FIGURE 11.1
World Market Sugar Prices and Cuban Imports from OECD

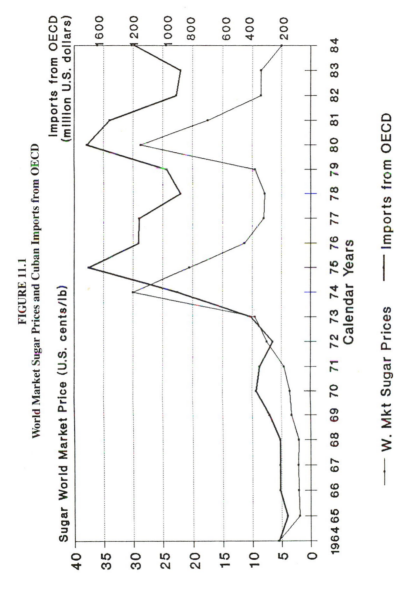

— W. Mkt Sugar Prices   —— Imports from OECD

Sources: World Market Sugar Prices: International Monetary Fund, *International Financial Statistics,* various volumes. Imports from OECD: Table 17.

with peaks in 1974–75 and 1980, and local minimum in 1978. Interestingly, however, while world sugar market prices dropped abruptly during 1975–78, Cuban imports from OECD nations dropped much more moderately, reflecting not only normal delays between orders and deliveries, but also the ability to maintain imports at high levels through credits. The close correlation between the two series evident throughout the 1972–83 period does not hold for 1984. Although world market sugar prices tumbled to their lowest level since 1971, Cuban imports from OECD nations rose by almost 35 percent. This probably occurred because reexports of Soviet oil and oil products for hard currency offset the decline in revenues from sugar exports brought about by the sharp decline in the sugar world market price.

Terms of trade illusion. Market economies experiencing persistent foreign trade deficits such as those which have characterized the Cuban economy might be diagnosed as having an overvalued currency. An overvalued currency tends to make the foreign-currency price of exports relatively high and the foreign-currency price of imports relatively low. This can create a so-called "terms of trade illusion" and can lead to foreign trade imbalances.

It is widely accepted that the official exchange rate of the peso vis-à-vis the U.S. dollar far overstates the purchasing power of the former. However, there are no reliable estimates of the extent of overvaluation. *Pick's Currency Yearbook* reports black market Cuban peso exchange rates, resulting from unauthorized dealings of foreign currency banknotes and/or unlicensed transfers abroad, that suggest very wide differences between official rates and purchasing power (e.g., in 1979, the average black market exchange was 14.17 pesos to the dollar, compared to the official exchange rate of 0.725 pesos to the dollar.) Another source has estimated that in 1976 the official exchange rate overvalued the peso by 34 percent vis-à-vis the U.S. dollar.[59]

While CPEs can not formally devalue their currencies, they could simulate the effect of a devaluation on the export side, and stimulate export revenues, by unilaterally reducing the prices of their exports. It is not clear that this policy would markedly benefit Cuba's balance of payments situation since the demand for Cuba's main exports (sugar and other basic goods) tends to be quite price-inelastic. Under these conditions, reductions in export prices would have little impact on export revenues, and in fact could lead to a worsening of the balance of payments situation and to additional borrowing to finance imports.

It is worth noting that, although Cuba does not have commercial or financial relations with the United States, the recent weakening of the U.S. dollar vis-à-vis other Western currencies has contributed to Cuba's hard currency woes. This comes about because while Cuba's imports from the market economies, as well as its debt with Western nations, are denominated in hard currencies other than the U.S. dollar, the world market price of its key hard currency export earners—sugar and oil—are quoted in U.S. dollars. As other currencies (e.g., the Japanese yen) have appreciated against the U.S. dollar, Cuba has seen a significant increase in the price of imports and in its debt service payments relative to earnings from exports whose prices are quoted in terms of U.S. dollars.[60] According to Castro (presumably in 1986), the devaluation of the dollar translated into higher prices of imports to the tune of $150 million.[61]

Macro-balance illusion.   Full employment and price stability are explicit objectives of capitalist economies and CPEs alike. In capitalist nations, simultaneous achievement of both objectives has proven to be unfeasible. Unemployment can be reduced by increasing aggregate demand, which in turn stimulates output and increases employment. However, as full employment is approached, prices tend to rise. Similarly, efforts to reduce inflation through a reduction in aggregate demand and output tend to add to unemployment. Hence, in capitalist economies, certain levels of unemployment and inflation tend to coexist. Depending on the national priorities, capitalist policymakers at times might pursue policies which emphasize either reduction in unemployment or price stability, but there is broad recognition that there is a trade-off between the two.

In theory, CPEs can simultaneously achieve both full employment and price stability. Full employment of resources, the macroeconomic balance, is achieved through establishment of very high output targets in the plan. Unlike capitalist economies, however, full employment of resources in CPEs does not lead to inflation (i.e., open inflation) since the state controls wages and prices. Foreign trade is also planned and efforts are made to prevent balance of payments difficulties which might arise from unforeseen internal or external disturbances.

In reality, CPEs are notorious for having difficulties in fulfilling economic plans. To a large extent, this is the result of the tendency among CPEs to rely on overfull employment, or taut, planning. This form of planning is characterized by setting output targets for enterprises which are unrealistic in terms of available resources and possible rates of productivity growth. Simultaneous achievement of price stability and the over-ambitious output targets established by taut planning is illusory, however. The overcommitment of resources results in excess demand (by consumers for final products and by enterprises for factor and intermediate goods) and inflationary pressures. Domestic producers and consumers compete for exportables and demand more imports, creating pressures which, if unchecked, lead to a deterioration in the balance of payments.

Notwithstanding statements by the leadership to the contrary,[62] there is little doubt that Cuba engages in taut planning and has experienced many of the negative effects of such policy. Pursuit by the Cuban government of full employment of labor has given rise to chronic shortages of workers in the agricultural sector and to the necessity of relying on volunteer workers and other stop-gap measures to harvest crops. Two independent evaluations of the results of the five-year plan 1976–80 conclude that many of the economic targets—particularly those related to physical output—were underfulfilled, and suggest that there was a tendency for targets to be set too high.[63] A preliminary evaluation of the results of the five-year plan 1981–85 concludes that the same was true during this more recent period.[64] Finally, there is ample evidence that, although open inflation does not exist, excess demand by consumers and producers far outstrips supply, giving rise to many of the economic distortions described above.[65]

The following two examples illustrate the impact of taut planning and excess demand on the Cuban balance of payments. The first gives an indication of the competition between domestic entities and exporters for goods capable of contributing to hard currency export receipts. The second shows the type of situations which arise when export commitments are not met.

As noted earlier, cement is one of Cuba's few success stories in developing new export lines which can contribute to hard currency earnings. In 1977, in the depth of a serious hard currency shortage, Cuba began to export significant quantities of cement for hard currency to a number of developing countries. Thus, in that year, 7.6 percent of cement output was exported; the share of cement production exported in subsequent years hovered around 8–9 percent, but rose to 12.3 percent in 1980.[66] At the same time that cement was being exported, its domestic availability was severely restricted, with the bulk of the cement earmarked for domestic consumption being allocated to non-residential construction. The complaints from consumers, unable to obtain cement to repair homes at the same time that the press ballyhooed the nearly four-fold increase in cement production over the period 1958–78,[67] were so intense that in March 1979 the JUCEPLAN Chief, in an unusually candid interview, admitted that consumer needs for cement were being sacrificed in order to obtain foreign exchange and develop markets for a product whose supply was expected to grow in the future.[68]

Yet another example of the allocation of goods from domestic consumption to exports took place in the textile industry. Consumption of cloth and apparel has been rationed in Cuba since the introduction of the rationing system in 1962. During the period 1977–83, annual production of cloth (primarily cotton and cotton blends) ranged from 140 to 155 million square meters, and some exports (e.g., 4 million pesos in 1983) have been recorded.[69] In July 1983, President Castro inaugurated a very large textile complex in Santiago de Cuba, with production capacity—when fully operational—of 80 million square meters of fabric per annum.[70] Output from this plant was heavily counted upon to increase the availability of cloth and apparel items for consumers.[71] As the hard currency balance of payments situation deteriorated in 1986, President Castro argued that the additional output from this plant should be exported rather than consumed domestically. On 2 December 1986 he said:

> If we have a new plant capable of producing 60 million [sic] square meters of fabric, work must be carried out efficiently in that plant. And it should not be done with the idea that we are going to wear the output of that plant, because we should export it in order to solve other problems. Before we do that, we must guarantee [access to] medicines and food.[72]

Indeed, among the austerity measures announced on 27 December 1986 was the diversion of an additional 10 million square meters of fabric from domestic consumption to exports.[73]

Traditionally one of the world's largest sugar producers and the premier exporter, in 1980 Cuba for the first time in its history was forced to import sugar in order to meet export commitments. The 1979–80 sugar harvest was disastrous for Cuba. At the end of 1979 and into 1980, sugar fields were affected by an epidemic of *roya,* a type of smut or rust which dried up sugar cane and sharply reduced the yield. As a result, sugar output in 1979–80 was approximately 6.5 million tons, a decline of 1.3 million tons over the level reached a year earlier. To make things worse, the poor Cuban sugar harvest coincided with sugar production shortfalls in the Soviet Union, Poland, and Czechoslovakia. Thus, at precisely the time when these CMEA nations required added sugar imports, Cuba was not in a position to deliver. Reportedly, Cuba was able to negotiate reductions in export commitments with CMEA nations of up to 30 percent, but evidently this was not sufficient, and in mid-1980 Cuba purchased sugar from the Dominican Republic and Colombia, presumably for reexport.[74]

A report issued by the Banco Nacional de Cuba in February 1985 indicates that in 1984 and 1985, Cuba again bought sugar in the world market for reexport to the Soviet Union.[75] Presumably, Cuba has turned to the world market because of the inability to meet domestic production and export targets. Considering that the 1986 and 1987 sugar crops have been affected by adverse weather conditions—a drought—it can be anticipated that Cuba will continue to turn to the world market for sugar imports. According to press reports, the Dominican Republic has already indicated interest in selling to Cuba the quantities of sugar that will not be shipped to the United States because of the reduction in U.S. sugar import quotas for 1987.[76]

Capital Flows and Foreign Investment

Current account deficits are not uncommon for developing countries, whose consumption levels tend to be high relative to domestic output. It is also well established that the developing countries tend to have an overabundance of investment opportunities relative to available domestic savings, thus drawing capital resources from abroad. These incoming flows originate from other nations farther along in the development process, which experience an excess of domestic savings relative to investment opportunities. They can take different forms: official grants and/or credits (bilateral or multilateral), private sector loans (from commercial banks or other financial institutions, such as the Eurocurrency market), supplier credits, direct investment, portfolio investment, extraordinary financing (such as compensatory financing from the International Monetary Fund), etc.

In certain regions, such as Latin America and the Far East, foreign direct investment (FDI) has traditionally played a major role as a source of external resources. For example, in the 1960s, FDI provided 30.4 percent of the external financing resources of Latin America. During the first half of the 1970s, FDI's share of the region's incoming external resources fell to 25.3 percent, declined to about 15 percent from 1976 to 1978, and rose to 22.5 percent in 1979–80.[77] It again receded to about 18.5 percent during the 1981–84 period.[78]

The positive contribution that FDI can make to the economic development process is well documented in the literature. A study of the subject by the OECD notes that FDI "provides a unique combination of long-term financing, technology, training, know-how, managerial expertise and marketing experience"[79] which is particularly useful for the industrial development of developing nations. In addition, FDI is increasingly attractive to developing nations because of its potential for having a more favorable impact on the balance of payments than other forms of capital flows.[80]

First, as a recent study of the external sector of the Latin American nations points out,[81] payments of FDI earnings (in the form of repatriated profits) tend to fall in periods of recession and to rise in periods of expansion of international economic activity. As a result, the demand for foreign exchange (for repatriation of profits) accruing to foreign equity investors tends to fall with the decrease in export possibilities of the host country and to increase when the opposite situation occurs. That is, profit remittances tend to be negatively correlated with cycles in the international economy and therefore have a stabilizing effect on the balance of payments of the host nation.

Second, unlike external capital obtained through debt, which demands a fixed outflow of resources (in the form of interest and amortization payments) regardless of the condition of the national economy or the viability of the project for which funds are borrowed, remittances associated with FDI are variable and are tied directly to the commercial success of the investments. There is an incentive for the foreign investor to make ventures commercially viable. The more profitable a foreign equity investment turns out to be, the higher the level of remittances it might send abroad, and the more benefits it is likely to bring to the host economy in terms of job creation, tax revenue, etc.

Third, FDI places the risk associated with an investment on the foreign investor rather than on domestic investors or on the state (if the state guarantees loan repayment). Investments financed through external borrowing must be able to generate a flow of resources capable of at least matching interest and amortization payments on the borrowed funds. Failure of a project to do this results in a drain on the balance of payments over the life of the loan. In projects financed through FDI, however, foreign investors assume the commercial risks. An unsuccessful enterprise results in a loss to the foreign investors but does not create a long-term drain on the balance of payments. Resources flow out of the host nation (in the form of repatriated profits) only when enterprises are successful and able to generate profits.

Faced with very high external debt accumulated over the 1970s, and recognizing the beneficial aspects of FDI, in the 1980s many developing nations have begun to reexamine regulations governing foreign investment in their domestic economies. There is renewed interest among these nations in creating a climate which encourages foreign firms to enter and undertake both manufacturing and resource development activities consistent with development objectives.[82] This is not to say that the concerns of developing nations regarding the proper conduct for foreign investment in their economies have been allayed. Developing countries continue to support the adoption of an international code of conduct for multinational corporations, but it is evident that a more pragmatic attitude toward FDI exists today on the part of the developing countries than existed over the 1960s and 1970s. Centrally planned economies, with the exception of Mongolia and Czechoslovakia, have passed special legislation to regulate foreign investment in their territories;[83] in January 1987, the Soviet Union published guidelines under which joint ventures between domestic and Western firms will be permitted to operate in the Soviet Union.[84]

Because during the first two decades of revolutionary government Cuba did not permit foreign investment to locate in the island, non-concessional capital receipts have been composed overwhelmingly of loans with relatively short maturities and at floating interest rates. According to official figures from the Banco Nacional de Cuba (table 11.11), at the end of 1981, Cuba's foreign debt in convertible currency amounted to 3.17 billion pesos, 1.86 billion pesos of which was due to private sector sources (banks, financial institutions, suppliers) and 1.31 billion pesos to public sources. The bulk of the debt owed to private sources was in the form of loans from banks and financial institutions (1.83 billion pesos), primarily in the form of short-term loans (1.28 billion pesos). In that year, interest payments on the hard currency debt amounted to 338 million pesos, or 10.7 percent on the disbursed amount.[85]

Primarily because of the rescheduling of principal, Cuba's hard currency debt has gradually grown since 1982. In 1985, the most recent year for which such data are available, the hard currency debt was nearly 3.26 billion pesos, 1.69 billion of which was in the form of official loans and 1.57 billion in private loans. Within the category of private capital, short-term loans dropped considerably in importance (42 percent in 1985 compared to 63 percent in 1982 and 64 percent in 1979), although suppliers' credits—whose maturity also tends to be short—rose significantly. Within official capital, there was a shift away from development loans, presumably with long-term maturity, and in favor of guaranteed export credits.[86]

In this context, it is not surprising that in February 1982, the Cuban Council of State approved legislation that for the first time would permit Western investment in the island in the form of joint ventures with domestic enterprises.[87] This "new form of cooperation" responded to several Cuban priorities, among them:

- Maximize overall investment resources by drawing on external sources for partial financing of projects;
- Minimize Cuban hard currency outlays in investment projects, by shifting to the foreign party the burden of providing funds to meet the need to import investment goods from hard currency areas;
- Attract Western capital to develop international tourist facilities, with the expectation that foreign investors would market Cuban tourism internationally;
- Operate more efficiently manufacturing facilities already in place which are underutilized because of lack of imported raw materials or technological problems; and
- Improve the overall hard currency trade balance, by imposing certain

TABLE 11.11
Cuban Hard Currency Debt
(in millions of pesos)

	1979	1980	1981	1982	1983	1984	1985
Total Debt	3267.3	3226.8	3169.6	2668.7	2789.7	2985.8	3258.9
Official	1279.9	1361.5	1308.9	1294.0	1357.5	1592.9	1691.2
Bilateral¹	1279.9	1353.6	1293.7	1275.8	1332.5	1575.7	1672.8
Multilateral	0.0	7.9	15.2	18.2	25.0	17.2	18.4
Private	1985.8	1864.1	1859.8	1374.1	1431.6	1392.7	1567.5
Suppliers	33.2	27.0	33.4	46.8	96.7	228.5	365.6
Financial institutions	1952.6	1837.1	1826.4	1327.3	1334.9	1164.2	1201.9
Medium-term	658.6	562.9	505.3	416.8	495.2	453.6	443.5
Short-term	1269.1	1237.9	1281.9	860.2	789.3	622.9	666.1
Import credit lines	24.9	36.3	39.2	50.3	50.4	87.7	92.3
Other	1.6	1.2	0.9	0.7	0.7	0.2	0.2

Source: Banco Nacional de Cuba, *Economic Report* (March 1986), Annex 6.

¹Includes government-insured export credits.

hard currency export requirements on joint ventures and reserving the right to purchase, for domestic currency, the output of the joint ventures which might substitute for products imported from hard currency areas.[88]

For several reasons—concerns about the security of investments, lack of access to the domestic market, export requirements, unattractive fiscal and financial incentives, potentially onerous management requirements, prohibition on participation by United States investors—the response from Western investors to the new legislation has been very cool. Reportedly, discussions have been held with businessmen from several Western nations,[89] but so far there has been no confirmation that a single joint venture pursuant to the February 1982 law has been established.[90]

Conclusion

Cuba's current economic woes are not unanticipated events. Rather, they are the predictable result of chronic external sector imbalances which have plagued revolutionary Cuba. Throughout over 25 years of revolutionary rule, Cuba has been unable to diversify its export basket and expand overall exports to finance the growing import and investment needs of the nation. Despite preferential treatment from the Soviet Union—and massive price subsidies on exports and imports—Cuba has been unsuccessful in balancing merchandise trade even with that nation. In fact, in recent years trade deficits have mushroomed as Cuba, the premier sugar exporter, has been unable to meet sugar export commitments and has had to turn to other producing countries for additional amounts of sugar.

The current hard currency crisis has its roots in a number of factors which are intrinsic to centrally planned economies, including the inability to attract private investment from abroad to finance development or to turn to international institutions (such as the International Monetary Fund) for relief during periods of severe balance of payments difficulties. Heretofore, Cuba had been able to postpone potential hard currency crisis through a combination of credits from the West, extraordinary aid from the Soviet Union (e.g., permitting Cuba to reexport Soviet oil for hard currency), and a measure of good luck (in the form of high world market sugar prices at some critical times, e.g., in 1980).

At the end of 1986, however, with sugar and oil prices at very low levels, combined with the loss of purchasing power in hard currency areas as a result of the devaluation of the U.S. dollar, the situation borders on the critical. To be sure, slashing hard currency imports by one-half, as has already been proposed by Castro, may contribute to balancing hard currency trade in the short term. However, doing so is bound to have an adverse impact on current and future economic performance and on the living standards and consumption levels of the population.

Notes

1. The data, which refer to the period 1945–58, are from Carmelo Mesa-Lago, *The Economy of Socialist Cuba* (Albuquerque: University of New Mexico Press, 1981), p. 79.
2. The indicators of openness of the economy in prerevolutionary and revolutionary Cuba are not comparable. The national accounts of prerevolutionary Cuba followed the System of National Accounts (SNA) methodology, the system followed by nearly all market economies, in which overall economic activity is measured by GNP. In the early 1960s, Cuba switched to the Material Product System (MPS), a national income accounting methodology more compatible with central planning, used by the Soviet Union and other socialist countries. The macroeconomic activity indicators under the MPS include the global social product (GSP), the gross material product (GMP), and the net material product (NMP). GNP and GMP can be substantially different from each other. See Carmelo Mesa-Lago and Jorge Pérez-López, *A Study of Cuba's Material Product System, Its Conversion to the System of National Accounts, and Estimation of Gross Domestic Product per Capita and Growth Rates* (Washington, D.C.: World Bank, 1985).
3. Julio Diaz Vazquez, "Cuba: integración económica socialista y especialización de producción," *Economia y Desarrollo,* no. 63 (July–August 1981), pp. 137–38. See also idem., "Cuba: industrializacion e integracion economica socialista," *Cuestiones de la Economia Planificada* 5:13 (January–April 1982), p. 143.
4. Central Report by President Fidel Castro to the Third Congress of the Cuban Communist Party, as reproduced in *Bohemia* 78:7 (14 February 1986), p. 58.
5. Speech by President Fidel Castro to the closing session of the Third Congress of the Cuban Communist Party, as reproduced in *Granma* (5 December 1986), supplement p. 6.
6. For a brief description of these two arrangements, as well as of other bilateral agreements concluded by Cuba during this period, see Jorge F. Pérez-López and Rene Pérez-López, *A Calendar of Cuban Bilateral Agreements, 1959–1976* (Pittsburgh, Pa.: University Center for International Studies, University of Pittsburgh, 1980), p. 2.
7. Jorge F. Pérez-López and Rene Pérez-López, *Cuban International Relations: A Bilateral Agreements Perspective,* Latin American Monograph Series, no. 8 (Erie, Pa.: Northwestern Pennsylvania Institute for Latin American Studies, 1979), p. 11.
8. Calculated from data in Cuba, Ministerio de Relaciones Exteriores, *Desarrollo del Comercio Exterior de Cuba* (La Habana, n.d.), p. 19; and 'Planificando el Intercambio," *Panorama Economico Latinoamericano,* vol. 6 (La Habana: Ediciones de Prensa Latina, 1967), p. 257.
9. Calculated from data in Pérez-López and Pérez-López, *Bilateral Agreements Perspective,* loc. cit.
10. Based on information in Pérez-López and Pérez-López, *A Calendar of Cuban Bilateral Agreements.*

11. For a discussion of alternative explanations of Cuba's entry into CMEA see Edward A. Hewett, "Cuba's Membership in the CMEA," in Martin Weinstein, ed., *Revolutionary Cuba in the World Arena* (Philadelphia: Institute for the Study of Human Issues, 1979), pp. 51–76.

12. The Cuban literature on Cuba's participation in CMEA is quite extensive. See, e.g., Roberto Villar, "A proposito de los diez anos de Cuba en el CAME," *Economia y Desarrollo*, no. 68 (May–June 1982), pp. 140–56; Jose Peraza Chapeau, *El CAME y la intergracion economica socialista* (La Habana: Editorial de Ciencias Sociales, 1984); and Julio A. Diaz Vazquez, *Cuba y el CAME* (La Habana: Editorial de Ciencias Sociales, 1985).

13. A description of the two agreements appeared in *Granma* (4 January 1973), p. 2.

14. The arrangement was part of a long-term economic and scientific-technical cooperation agreement for the period 1976–80 signed with the Soviet Union on 14 April 1976. See *Granma* (15 April 1976), p. 8 and Jose Luis Rodriguez Garcia, "La economia cubana entre 1976 y 1980: resultados y perspectivas," *Economia y Desarrollo*, no. 66 (January–February 1982), p. 131. However, there is evidence that the indexing arrangement was in effect prior to 1976. For example, a September 1975 publication of the Banco Nacional de Cuba refers to an arrangement whereby the price of Cuban sugar exports to the Soviet Union had been set at 30 cents/pound, with the possibility of adjusting the price according to the price of imports from the Soviet Union. See Banco Nacional de Cuba, *Development and Prospects of the Cuban Economy* (La Habana, 1975), p. 32.

15. Maria Teresa Valdés, "La evolución de la producción azucarera en Cuba y su papel en las relaciones economicas externas, 1959–1983," *Temas de Economia Mundial*, no. 10 (1984), p. 138.

16. Comite Estatal de Estadisticas, *Anuario Estadístico de Cuba 1984* (La Habana, 1986), p. 374.

17. Based on world market price of $0.0838 per pound from Organization of American States, *International Commodity Quarterly Price Bulletin* (January/March 1986), p. 4, converted to Cuban currency at the official exchange rate of 1 peso = $1.20.

18. Comisión Económica para America Latina y el Caribe (CEPAL), *Estudio Económico de America Latina y el Caribe*, LC/L.390/Add.18 (December 1986), p. 18. It should be noted that although CEPAL claims that its figures originate from Cuban official sources, they differ from those in the *Anuario Estadístico de Cuba 1984* cited above. Further, at odds with the CEPAL information is a statement by Castro that Cuba is receiving "twenty-odd centavos per pound of sugar [from the Soviet Union], when [world market] prices are at 6 and 7 centavos." See *Granma* (1 December 1986), p. 4.

19. See Jorge F. Pérez-López, "Sugar and Petroleum in Cuban-Soviet Terms of Trade," in Cole Blasier and Carmelo Mesa-Lago, eds., *Cuba in the World* (Pittsburgh, Pa.: University of Pittsburgh Press, 1980).

20. Leslie Collitt and David Buchanan, "Oil price plunge hits East Europe," *Financial Times* (19 February 1986), p. 8; Peter Marcos, "Plight in Eastern Europe: 'Political' Oil Supply by Moscow," *Die Press* (Vienna) (18 March 1986), p. 3, in German, as translated in Foreign Broadcast Information Service, *Daily Report—Eastern Europe* 2:53 (19 March 1986), pp. AA2–AA3.

21. See, e.g., Willard W. Radell, "Cuban-Soviet Sugar Trade: How Great Was the Subsidy," *Journal of Developing Areas* 17:3 (April 1983).

22. Calculated from official merchandise trade data in *Anuario Estadístico de Cuba 1983* (La Habana, 1985), pp. 299 and 303.

23. Some of the economic implications of Cuba's internationalist policies have been explored in Sergio Roca, "Economic Aspects of Cuban Involvement in Africa," *Cuban Studies/Estudios Cubanos* 10:2 (July 1980) and Susan Eckstein, "Structural and Ideological Bases of Cuba's Overseas Programs," *Politics and Society* 11:1 (1982). Edith Felipe, "Cuba y la Colaboración Económica con el Mundo Subdesarrollado," *Temas de Economia Mundial*, no. 15 (1985), pp. 96–97 indicates that Cuban construction activities abroad often involve shipping equipment and construction materials from Cuba.

24. See, e.g., "Cuba: Growth of Exports," *Direct from Cuba*, no. 280 (30 April 1982), p. 12. The State Standardization Committee (Comite Estatal de Normalización) has developed a quality rating system for manufactured products, with the highest quality products being identified as potential exports. A list of more than 200 Cuban products and services available for export, together with information on Cuban export enterprises and export promotion representatives overseas, is included in Chamber of Commerce of the Republic of Cuba, *Directory of Cuban Exporters* (La Habana, 1982). A more recent source of information on the export capability of Cuban enterprises is Camara de Comercio de la Republica de Cuba, *Empresas cubanas relacionadas con el comercio exterior* (La Habana, 1984). For information on Cuba's marketing efforts in Western markets see Jo Thomas, "Cuba is Moving to Broaden Trade in Dollars," *The New York Times* (25 June 1981), p. 1.

25. *Anuario Estadístico de Cuba 1984*, p. 308.

26. Jorge F. Pérez-López, "Cuba as an Oil Trader," *Caribbean Review* 15:2 (Spring 1986), p. 28. See also idem., "Cuban Oil Reexports: Significance and Prospects," *The Energy Journal* 8:1 (January 1987).

27. Speech by Castro to the concluding session of the Third Congress of the Cuban Communist Party, *Granma* (5 December 1986), supplement p. 6.

28. Diaz Vazquez, p. 139.

29. *Lineamientos económicos y sociales para el quinquenio 1981–1985* (La Habana: Editora Politica, 1981), p. 169.

30. Ramón González Vergara and Zoila Gonzáles Maicas, "Sistema de estimulo a los fondos exportables en moneda nacional," *Economia y Desarrollo*, no. 75 (July–August 1983).

31. The regulations appear in *Gaceta Oficial* (8 July 1983), pp. 746–51. Earlier regulations on the same topic but restricted to specific enterprises are given in *Gaceta Oficial* (8 May 1983), pp. 360–64.

32. Ramón Pérez Cabrera, "La sustitución de importaciones en Cuba: realidad y perspectivas," *Cuba Socialista*, no. 20 (March–April 1986).

33. For example, see Joaquin Oramas and Fernando Dávalos, "Entregó Fidel diplomas a los autores de las mejores ponencias discutidas en el Forum Nacional sobre Piezas de Repuesto," *Granma* (4 February 1982), pp. 1, and 3; Fernando Dávalos, "Recibidas 213 ponencias para el Simposio Nacional de Sustitución de Importaciones," *Granma* (17 February 1982), p. 2.

34. *Lineamientos económicos y sociales para el quinquenio 1986–1990 (Proyecto)* (La Habana, 1985), pp. 10–11.

35. Banco Nacional de Cuba, *Economic Report* (La Habana, February 1985), p. 10.

36. *Lineamientos económicos y sociales para el quinquenio 1986–1990 (Proyecto)*, p. 43.

37. Speech by Castro to the concluding session of the Third Congress of the Cuban Communist Party, *Granma* (5 December 1986), supplement pp. 5–6.
38. Jose M. Norniella, "Existen posibilidades de sustituir importaciones en cerca de 240 producciones," *Granma* (17 March 1986), p. 1.
39. Fernando Dávalos, "¿Como estan los planes de sustitucion de importaciones?," *Granma* (20 September 1986), p. 2.
40. The 27 measures appear in *Granma* (27 December 1986), p. 1.
41. Interventions by several delegates criticizing the use of export premiums, as well as the statements by Castro, appear in *Granma* (1 December 1986), p. 4.
42. The agreement to roll over the accumulated debt with the Soviet Union until 1986 was part of a package of accords between Cuba and the Soviet Union signed at the end of 1972. Other agreements included in this package, e.g., those establishing above-market prices for exports of sugar and nickel to the Soviet Union, have been discussed above. See *Granma* (4 January 1973), p. 2.
43. Presumably during 1985, Cuba and the Soviet Union rolled over the debt which was to become due in 1986. The terms of the referral, e.g., when the debt will again be payable, has not been made public. Thus, a report of the Banco Nacional de Cuba which made public that the debt had been renegotiated only said: "Cuba's debt service to the Soviet Union, which should start in 1986, shall not affect the balance of payments in the five-year period that will begin that year [the period 1986–90], because these liabilities have been refinanced on favorable terms." Banco Nacional de Cuba, *Economic Report* (February 1985), p. 3.
44. Banco Nacional de Cuba, *Economic Report* (August 1982).
45. Alfredo G. Pierrat, "Suscrito acuerdo para el refinanciamiento de deuda externa cubana," *Granma* (2 March 1983), pp. 1, and 5. See also Jose Luis Rodriguez, "La renegociación de la deuda cubana y la crisis de endeudamiento de America Latina," *Cuba Socialista,* no. 19 (January–February 1986).
46. "Western Banks Agree to Reschedule Payments," AFP news wire, reproduced in Foreign Broadcast Information System, *Daily Report—Latin America* 6:72 (13 April 1983), p. Q1; "Cuba: tasting its own medicine," *The Latin American Times,* no. 48 (1984), p. 29.
47. See, e.g., "Cuba—Debt," *Direct from Cuba,* no. 329 (July 1984); Francisco Forteza, "Redujo Cuba sostenidamente la proporcion del servicio de su deuda externa," *Granma* (20 May 1985), p. 8.
48. "Payment Halt by Cuba Cited," *The New York Times* (29 July 1986), p. D9.
49. *Granma* (22 December 1986), p. 2.
50. The discussion on systemic factors that affect hard currency balances draws heavily on Jorge F. Pérez-Jópez, *The 1982 Cuban Joint Venture Law: Context, Assessment and Prospects* (Coral Gables, Fla.: Institute of Interamerican Studies, University of Miami, 1985), pp. 16–30.
51. Franklyn D. Holzman, "Some Systemic Factors Contributing to the Convertible Currency Shortages of Centrally Planned Economies," *American Economic Review* 69:2 (May 1979); and Holzman, "Systemic Bases of the Unconventional International Trade Practices of Centrally-Planned Economies," *Columbia Journal of World Business* 18:4 (Winter 1983). The discussion of these three "illusions" below relies heavily on these two contributions by Holzman. See also Toma Gudac, "Pricing and Exchange Rates in Planned Economies," *Finance and Development* 21:3 (September 1984).
52. According to then-JUCEPLAN chief Humberto Perez, the 1976–80 plan as-

sumed a sugar world market price of 15 cents/pound, an assumption which "in 1975 could be considered to be conservative since sugar had reached a price of over 40 cents/pound." See Ciro Bianchi Ross, "El quinquenio arroja un saldo positivo," *Cuba Internacional* 12:133 (December 1980), p. 36; and Jose Luis Rodriguez, *Dos Ensayos sobre la Economia Cubana* (La Habana: Editorial de Ciencias Sociales, 1984), p. 117. However, another source suggests that the 15 cents/pound assumption was only for the first two years of the plan; further, the sudden drop in the world market price of sugar in the final months of 1975 led to an adjustment of the plan, with the sugar price assumption changed to 11 cents/pound. See Banco Nacional de Cuba, *Economic Report* (La Habana, August 1982), p. 34. Carmelo Mesa-Lago has reported that a Cuban official told him that three variants of the 1976–80 plan were prepared, corresponding to optimistic, fair, and pessimistic forecasts of the sugar world market price. As it turned out, even the most pessimistic alternative could not approximate the sharp decline in sugar prices which took place in 1976–79. See Carmelo Mesa-Lago, "The Economy: Caution, Frugality and Resilient Ideology," in Jorge I. Dominguez, ed., *Cuba: Internal and International Affairs* (Beverly Hills, Calif.: Sage Publications, 1982), pp. 120–21. Castro has disclosed that Cuban and foreign experts had predicted that during the period 1976–80, the world market price for sugar would not fall below 16–17 centavos/pound. See his confidential address to the National Assembly of 27 December 1979, p. 1.

53. The plan called for a level of investment in 1976–80 at least twice as high as that realized during 1971–75 (7.5 billion pesos); approximately one-fourth of the planned investment would be earmarked for the industrial sector and three-fourths for the productive sphere. See Comite Central del Partido Comunista de Cuba, Departamento de Orientación Revolucionaria, *Proyecto de directivas para el desarrollo economico y social en el quinquenio 1976–80* (La Habana, 1975), p. 40.

54. "In the fall of 1976 . . . [Cuba] . . . began to ask several Western suppliers (Argentina, Japan, Canada, Spain) to postpone deliveries of imports already contracted for and to accept delayed payments of a total sum of over $1 billion." Carmelo Mesa-Lago, "The Economy and International Economic Relations," in Cole Blasier and Carmelo Mesa-Lago, *Cuba in the World* (Pittsburgh, Pa.: University of Pittsburgh Press, 1979), p. 183. According to press reports, in early 1977, Cuba asked Japan to postpone for one year shipments of goods valued at $91 million. See "Cuba's Foreign Currency Almost Gone, Japan Says," *The Wall Street Journal* (21 January 1977), p. 25.

55. Mesa-Lago, "The Economy: Caution, Frugality and Resilient Ideology," loc. cit.

56. Lawrence H. Theriot, "Cuba Faces the Economic Realities of the 1980s," in U.S. Congress, Joint Economic Committee, *East-West Trade: The Prospects to 1985* (Washington, D.C.: U.S. Government Printing Office, 1982). A partial list of the loans made by Western financial institutions to Cuba during this period is given in Ernesto Betancourt and Wilson Dizard III, *Castro and the Bankers: The Mortgaging of a Revolution* (Washington, D.C.: The Cuban-American National Foundation, 1982).

57. Speaking before a convention of the Sugar Workers' Union on 30 October 1980, Castro was once again optimistic on the prospects for sugar world market prices. He recalled that prices at that time were five times higher than in 1977 and "reasonable forecasts" for 1981 and 1982 predicted strong prices in those two years. See *Granma* (1 November 1980), p. 4.

58. It has been observed that the proportion of Cuba's trade conducted with socialist economies has tended to be inversely correlated with world sugar market prices: trade with socialist economies was at its lowest point in 1964 (64 percent) and 1974–75 (59 percent) when world market sugar prices were very high, and at very high points (over 80 percent) in 1966–67 and 1978 when world market sugar prices were very low. Carmelo Mesa-Lago, *The Economy of Socialist Cuba,* pp. 94–95. See also John T. Smith, "Sugar Dependency in Cuba: Capitalism versus Socialism," in Mitchell A. Seligson, ed., *The Gap Between Rich and Poor* (Boulder, Colo.: Westview Press, 1984), p. 369. In 1980, when world market sugar prices were again high, socialist countries accounted for about 74 percent of Cuba's trade; in subsequent years, when world market sugar prices tumbled, this share rose to over 80 percent (Table 11.4).

59. Central Intelligence Agency, *The Cuban Economy: A Statistical Review, 1968–76* (Washington, D.C.: December 1976), p. 1.

60. Banco Nacional de Cuba, *Balance of Payments Highlights for 1986–1987* (La Habana, April 1986), p. 9.

61. *Granma* (27 December 1986), p. 2.

62. E.g., referring to the 1976–80 plan, Castro stated that its modest growth objectives reflected a "realistic assessment" of Cuban economic possibilities. See his central report to the First Congress of the Cuban Communist Party, in *Economia y Desarrollo,* no. 36 (July/August 1976), p. 47.

63. Mesa-Lago, "The Economy: Caution, Frugality and Resilient Ideology"; Sergio Roca, "Economic Policy and Institutional Changes in Socialist Cuba," *Journal of Economic Issues* 17:2 (June 1983).

64. Jorge F. Pérez-López, "Cuban Economy in the 1980s," *Problems of Communism* 35:5 (September–October 1986).

65. An excellent discussion of inflationary pressures in the Cuban economy and their effects appears in Mesa-Lago, *The Economy of Revolutionary Cuba,* pp. 47–50.

66. Calculated from data in *Anuario Estadístico de Cuba 1982,* pp. 166, 336–37.

67. E.g., Marta Jimenez Almira, "Major Achievements of the Construction Materials Industry in 20 Years of Revolution," *Granma Weekly Review* (18 February 1979), p. 7.

68. Interview of JUCEPLAN Chief Humberto Pérez by Marta Harnecker, published as "Lo que el pueblo debe saber sobre la escasez de cemento," *Trabajadores* (6 March 1979), p. 2.

69. *Anuario Estadístico de Cuba 1983,* p. 157.

70. A translation of the radio broadcast of the speech appears in Foreign Broadcast Information Service, *Daily Report—Latin America* 6:147 (29 July 1983), pp. Q1–Q17. See also Manuel Somoza, "Por donde cortar," *Cuba Internacional,* no. 8 (August 1983). In December 1986, Castro indicated that operation of the plant was facing some difficulties, as it was built with a flat roof and water leaks had developed. See *Granma* (22 December 1986), p. 2.

71. Jesus Abascal Lopez, "¿De qué modo la moda?," *Cuba Internacional,* no. 3 (March 1985), p. 34.

72. *Granma* (1 December 1986), p. 7.

73. *Granma* (27 December 1986), p. 1.

74. *El Tiempo* (Bogota, Colombia) (17 July 1980), pp. 1A, 7A, as reported in Foreign Broadcast Information Service, *Daily Report—Latin America* 6:149

(31 July 1980), p. Q1. Interestingly, although the statistics of the International Sugar Organization do record the Cuban imports of sugar (12,391 tons from Colombia and 73,722 from the Dominican Republic), they list them as occurring in 1982 rather than in 1980. See International Sugar Organization, *Sugar Year Book 1982* (London: International Sugar Organization, 1983), p. 55.

75. Banco Nacional de Cuba, *Economic Report* (La Habana, February 1985), p. 35.

76. "Consideran los dominicanos como nuevos posibles mercados a Cuba y otros paises," *Diario las Americas* (18 December 1986).

77. Calculated from data in Ricardo French-Davis, "External Debt and Balance of Payments of Latin America: Recent Trends and Outlook," in Inter-American Development Bank, *Economic and Social Progress in Latin America: 1982 Report* (Washington, D.C.: Inter-American Development Bank, 1982), p. 165.

78. Calculated from data in Inter-American Development Bank, *Economic and Social Progress in Latin America: 1986 Report* (Washington, D.C.: Inter-American Development Bank, 1986), p. 37.

79. Organization for Economic Cooperation and Development, *Investing in Developing Countries: Fifth Edition* (Paris: OECD, 1982), p. 7.

80. The discussion that follows on the differential impact on the balance of payments of investments financed through external borrowing or foreign equity only applies to identical projects. To be sure, regardless of how they are financed, investments have different balance of payments effects depending on the percentage of inputs that are domestically produced versus imported, whether the output is for export, substitutes for imports, or is for domestic consumption, etc. See Frank Valero, Jr., "Foreign Investment and the Balance of Payments: Some Negative Implications for Developing Countries," *Inter-American Economic Affairs* 28:2 (Autumn 1974).

81. *Economic and Social Progress in Latin America: 1982 Report*, p. 58.

82. United Nations, Department of Economic and Social Affairs, *World Economic Survey 1980/81* (New York: United Nations: 1981), pp. 82–85.

83. General descriptions of the foreign investment provisions of Eastern European CMEA nations (Bulgaria, the German Democratic Republic, Hungary, Poland, and Romania) and of Yugoslavia appear in United Nations, *Transnational Corporations in World Development* (New York: United Nations, 1978), pp. 193–201. A foreign investment code was adopted by Vietnam in 1977. See Nayan Chanda, "Vietnam Opens the Door to Investors," *Far Eastern Economic Review* (13 March 1977), pp. 40–42. In 1979, the People's Republic of China enacted legislation permitting joint ventures. See "The Law of the People's Republic of China on Joint Ventures Using Chinese and Foreign Investment," *Beijing Review,* no. 29 (29 July 1979), pp. 24–26. According to press reports, North Korea has adopted a joint venture law; see John Burgess, "N. Korea to Allow Foreign Investment," *The Washington Post* (11 September 1984), p. A20.

84. Gary Lee, "Moscow Woos Westerners for Joint Ventures," *The Washington Post* (28 January 1987), pp. F1, and F5; Bill Keller, "Joint Ventures, Russian Style," *The New York Times* (6 January 1987), pp. D1, and D6. In December 1986, prior to the publication of the guidelines, at least two U.S. firms (Monsanto Co. and Occidental Petroleum Corporation) signed letters of intent regarding joint ventures. See Rose Horowitz, "Monsanto Signs Deal with USSR," *The Journal of Commerce* (10 December 1986), pp. A1, A2 and idem.,

"Occidental Petroleum Plans Soviet Venture," *The Journal of Commerce* (11 December 1986), pp. A1, and A2.

85. CEPAL, *Estudio Economico de America Latina y el Caribe 1985*, p. 26.
86. Ibid., p. 25.
87. The official text of the law appeared in *Gaceta Oficial* (15 February 1982), pp. 11–15.
88. The economic rationale for the law given here is drawn from Jorge F. Pérez-López, "The Economics of Cuban Joint Ventures," *Cuban Studies,* vol. 16 (1986). See also Pérez-López, *The 1982 Cuban Joint Venture Law: Context, Assessment and Prospects* (Miami, Fla.: Graduate School of International Studies, University of Miami, 1985); Sula Fiszman, "Foreign Investment Law: Encouragement Versus Restraint—Mexico, Cuba, and the Caribbean Basin Initiative," *Hastings International and Comparative Law Review* 8:2 (Winter 1985); Jean G. Zorn and Harold Mayerson, "Cuba's Joint Venture Law: New Rules for Foreign Investment," *Columbia Journal of Transnational Law* 12:2 (1983); and Patrick L. Schmidt, "Foreign Investment in Cuba: A Preliminary Analysis," *Law and Policy in International Business* 15:2 (1983).
89. According to press reports, discussions have been held between Cuban officials and potential joint venture partners from England, Brazil, Canada, France, Spain, and Mexico. See Pérez-López, "The Economics of Cuban Joint Ventures," p. 182.
90. Jorge I. Dominguez, *To Make a World Safer for Revolution: Cuban Foreign Policy,* manuscript in progress, Chapter 9 reports that by early 1985, a joint venture with Spanish investors to recycle and export scrap metal had been established. However, another source has indicated that as of mid-1985, not a single joint venture had been registered pursuant to the February 1982 law. See Jeremy Main, "Castro Tightens Cuba's Belt," *Fortune* (16 September 1985), p. 128. Argentine cooperation with Cuba in building tourist hotels on the island appears to be pursuant to credit arrangements rather than joint ventures. See Banco Nacional de Cuba, *Economic Report* (February 1985), p. 1.

12

Cuban and Latin American Economics: Doctrine and Praxis

Jorge A. Sanguinetty

Introduction

In studying macrosocial processes, the social scientist must deal with a methodological trade-off between the level of rigor of his research approach and the comprehensiveness—and even the relevance—of his analysis. On the one hand, the complexity of social phenomena forces us to work with severely constrained sets of information should we decide to follow a positive methodological path in order to support our findings. On the other hand, a more comprehensive treatment of a given topic can be performed on incomplete information or even on speculative or subjective perceptions.

Too frequently methodological rigor is achieved at the expense of omitting important variables from the analysis. In such cases, a strictly positive approach can lead to inaccurate or erroneous implications from a normative standpoint. In general, the researcher prefers neither to take that risk nor to be evaluated by his peers as a sloppy investigator incapable of rigorous or elegant methodological exercises.

The study of the evolution of the Cuban economy during the revolutionary period is a case in point, for several reasons. First, the Cuban regime is particularly secretive, and the availability of data is subject to political criteria. In this regard, the lack of complete information on the balance of payments or labor markets are good illustrations. Second, the type of information that exists, regardless of its availability, does not always conform to the research requirements of the positive tradition which predominates in economic research. For instance, information on price variations in Cuba is virtually nonexistent, preventing any well-grounded study of the economic evolution of the country in real terms.[1] A third reason relates to the information needed for particular analyses. For example, information regarding the rationale behind important economic decisions is virtually impossible to obtain. In a highly centralized economic management system such as Cuba's, macroeconomic phenomena are strongly influenced by the personal views and motivations of the one person who, in spite of the so-called institutionalization of the regime, commands an overwhelming degree of power: Fidel Castro. This was recently shown by his thorough sweep of the market experiments he had personally permitted to develop for some time.

The available information on the Cuban economy allows us to conduct some valuable research exercises with the necessary methodological rigor, to arrive at certain conclusions. This has been demonstrated by such skillful and dedicated researchers as Carmelo Mesa-Lago and Jorge Pérez-López.[2] Nevertheless, many important topics cannot be well investigated without additional data. At this point, however, we must decide how far we can go in trying to understand the Cuban economy with limited information or with information that is based on individual, casual, and, therefore, subjective observations.

My experience as an official on the Central Board of Planning in Cuba until 1966 has allowed me to assess the high level of quality of the research done on the Cuban economy by the above-mentioned investigators and others. Yet, there are topics that deserve treatment even at the risk of being less methdologically rigorous. This chapter will seek to address one of these issue areas, namely, through a discussion of the roots of Cuba's economic thought in the revolutionary period and their relationships with predominant (post-1953) currents of thought in Latin America and the Caribbean.

The central thesis of this paper is that some specific ideological factors (not all necessarily Marxist) explain a great deal of Cuba's economic performance since 1959. Ideological factors have replaced knowledge as a source of political decision making and action—a phenomenon which plays an important role in today's Latin America and the Caribbean and Cuban economic affairs. In addition, these factors could assist in understanding the roots of the economic crisis currently affecting the entire region. In this perspective, we will see that Cuba's economic stagnation is a Marxist version of a deeper crisis that has its origins in a negative perception of the potential of private or decentralized initiatives for development purposes.

In the second section, this essay will examine the evolution of economic thinking after World War II and some of its economic, social, and institutional implications for Latin American, Caribbean, and Cuban development. These implications are more carefully examined in the following section, in considering the role of investment planning as the main engine of economic development. The fourth section focuses on how individuals behave under conditions in which economic freedom is constrained by ideologically inspired economic policies. And the final section will draw together several conclusions.

Public Versus Private Economics

The Economic Doctrines After World War II

Development economics studies after World War II were based on a macroeconomic vision of growth processes. The corresponding literature reflected the Keynesian notion that public policy, or more simply, the government, could affect the level of economic activity by direct interventions. Even though Keynesian policies were based on the stimulation of aggregate demand through government spending, they opened the door for governments to play a more active role on the supply side. Another source of inspiration for development policy designs were the Harrod-Domar type of growth models that so neatly capture the macrovariables that play a critical role in development processes: capital, labor, and technical progress.

At the same time, comparative studies between developed and underdeveloped countries yielded significant differences in terms of output per capita, saving rates, capital per capita, levels of productivity, and levels of education of the labor force, to mention just a few areas. It is important to note that the body of economic development studies produced since World War II was based on the type of data available to support such studies, principally national account statistics. The tradition of observing economic activity through national account statistics with the purpose of predicting the "business cycle" in developed economies also focused on the same type of variables. Keynesian economics established the impact of investment growth—public or private—on the level of output via the multiplier. On the other hand, growth theory models showed the importance of the aggregate stock of capital in the level of aggregate output. Logic dictates that to accelerate economic development, as measured by the levels of aggregate output and output per capita, investment activity had to be accelerated as well. The problem is how to implement such acceleration in investment activity. It was thus necessary to identify specific sectors and projects, and the sources of funds to finance new investments in the presence of insufficient savings.

This approach toward finding solutions to the problems of secular stagnation and poverty was based on a set of functional relationships, in the form of general mathematical equations. The central methodological principle better suits an engineering system than one in which human behavior plays a critical role. This is not to say that the recipes were fundamentally erroneous, for they remain as valid today as they were in the past; the problem is that as recipes they are grossly incomplete. A number of important factors have been omitted—they still are today—because they are considered formally intractable. Institutional, cultural, and other qualitative factors such as the reliability or security of contractual relationships, the necessary mass of entrepreneurial talents and energies, the quality of the labor force, and many others have been mostly taken for granted. Schumpeter's contributions to explaining development processes via the role of the entrepreneur have not been recognized.

The installation of international and bilateral development funding agencies, in addition to the almost universal adoption of the philosophy of the welfare state in the 1950s, laid the groundwork for the growth of the public sector as a *deus ex machina* capable of replicating development miracles. The uncertainties and risks of entrepreneurship became socialized; the individual was to be protected and benefited by centralized entrepreneurship assumed to be potentially better suited to look not only after the acceleration of the economic development, but also after its distributive implications. International organizations, in particular the United Nations Economic Commission for Latin America (ECLA) tacitly fostered these views by developing methods and techniques for the organization of public planning agencies—a process that took place in almost every Latin American and Caribbean country.

In 1959, with the success of the revolutionary forces in Cuba, the transition toward a centrally planned economy was facilitated by these currents of thought. Ironically, another facilitating element was the existence of the National Board of Planning created during the dictatorship of Batista, which served as the institutional basis for the socialist Central Board of Planning. Even before the adoption of a socialist model in Cuba, there was an explicit acceptance of the notion that the state could play a strategic role in the economic development of the country through direct intervention in the economy. Although prerevolutionary Cuba did not experiment with public enterprises, the mechanism and the philosophy were already in place.

Planning and the Individual

The development of planning agencies in less developed as well as in socialist countries has had a number of common denominators. First is the idea that an economy can be managed as an engineering system; a second assumes that only a highly centralized planning system can look after the public good.

With respect to the first idea, we must point out that a frequent instrument in the planning agencies' tool kit is the input-output model. The agencies that never developed one generally employ officials that dream of having their own input-output model one day. In some cases, the dreams reach hallucinatory proportions. In Cuba, for instance, students of economics were trained at one time with input-output matrices that, instead of relying on fixed coefficients, depended on the specification of intricate integral equations to capture the corresponding intersectoral functional relationships. Within this mental context, planning becomes an almost quantitative exercise. The incentives for the worker to increase productivity, the entrepreneur to be more efficient, or the engineer to be more creative are absent; they are considered important only at a rhetorical level. There exists no knowledge as to how to incorporate individual behavior into the plans or their execution in a form consistent with development objectives.

After several years of failure, the planning system drifts toward a monumental bureaucracy—more an obstacle to development than an instrument to promote it. Exceptions have been the Eastern European economies whose relative early successes resulted from the imposition of a highly disciplined management system that served to imitate industrial structures, technologies, and prices from more industrialized countries. It is not coincidental that agricultural planning has generally failed in these countries, perhaps due to the fact that the uncertainties natural to this sector require a more committed attitude from workers and managers. Manufacturing, after all, is more docile to be organized along the engineering lines implicit in planning methodologies. Cuba, on the other hand, has failed in achieving even modest successes in planning. A possible explanation is that Fidel Castro has not been willing to sacrifice his popular appeal—or whatever remains of it—by imposing the type of managerial terror that characterized the Eastern European planning style.

The concept that a planning system can look after the public good better than any other mechanism has not been supported by the experience. In fact, whatever our concept of public good is, it is hard to imagine how it can be achieved or improved without the free participation of its private counterparts. The mass of information necessary to make the relevant decisions is unmanageable, and its size and complexity is usually under-estimated. What results is a management information glut at the central planning level that reduces decision making to either crisis management or a highly primitive style of economic direction. The outcome is that planning systems end up creating barriers to private initiatives that could play a significant role from the supply side. The private good is thus less than it could be with more private participation, and the gains in public good are debatable. For instance, exaggerated protectionist policies or outright prohibition of certain imports have forced the consumer to purchase extremely inferior goods or depend on contraband or black markets. Access to consumer credit is limited or virtually nonexistent, especially financing for housing. Mobility in labor markets is low, impeding a higher level of utilization of human resources and discouraging its development. Workers are not necessarily paid in terms of their marginal productivities, as a result of rigidities in management. In general, the real value of what the consumer buys with the fruits of his effort as a worker is reduced, which diminishes significantly the incentives for increases in labor productivity, a sine qua non condition of economic development.

One of the great paradoxes of planning, at least in its current conception, is that due to the manner in which it is implemented—"to look after the public good"—it ends up constraining, and perhaps reducing it, by neglecting the individual and his/her private welfare. In this regard, Cuba has been particularly effective, but the effects of this planning failure have been softened due to Soviet subsidies. In other Latin American and Caribbean economies, the failure of planning mechanisms have left the corresponding agencies playing a marginal role in their societies from the point of view of effective development efforts, and a not-so-marginal role in impeding the realization of the development potential of private initiatives.

Investment Planning

The Automation of Economic Growth

Cuba's development strategy in the 1960s was based on the assumption that massive allocations of funds in investment projects could generate rates of growth as high as 15 percent per annum in the aggregate level of output.[3] It was also assumed that such rates of growth could be sustained for long periods and would automatically follow the growth in the stock of capital. Many other factors were taken for granted, explicitly or implicitly, particularly the managerial capacity to identify, design, install, and run specific investment projects, and the workers' behavior consistent with the planned targets.

The formula to determine the level of investment activity consisted of increasing the aggregate rate of savings at the expense of the level of personal consumption, thus liberating resources for investments, especially of imported capital goods. As is well known, the investment plans from 1962 through 1964 put a great deal of emphasis on investments in manufacturing, while actually cutting back on sugar sector financing. The project identification process during the initial years was highly improvised. When the first planning exercise started in 1961, covering the 1962–1965 period, a number of projects had to be included in the plan. This was a result of what was literally a shopping spree by Ernesto (Ché) Guevara through several socialist countries in 1960, when he signed agreements for the purchase of a number of complete industrial plants, including a steel mill, without performing one single feasibility study.

In 1964, a major revision in the sectoral composition of investments was implemented. Greater emphasis was placed on the sugar industry and agriculture, and less on heavy industry and manufacturing in general. In 1970, when it became apparent that the plan to produce 10 million tons of sugar had been extremely costly while falling short of the target, new revisions in development policies took place. None of these changes in policies modified the initial assumption that massive investments were a necessary condition for accelerated development. The formula of maximizing investment expenditures remained untouched.

This system of forced aggregate savings—the income of the unaware Cuban worker is implicitly taxed at a rate he does not even know— liberates investment resources in magnitudes that go beyond the administrative capacity for the creation of real capital. This gap was identified by some officials in the Central Board of Planning as early as 1963, as a result of increasing evidence that a large proportion of the investment expenditures was being wasted due to all sorts of inefficiencies.[4] In order to distinguish between the financial capacity to invest, provided by forced savings, and the actual capacity to generate productive investments, the latter was denominated "organic capacity to invest." This concept cannot be measured, and only a close observation of the investment scene—an exercise that can more easily be performed by insiders—allows one to realize that the decision to maximize investment was highly arbitrary and unrealistic.

There are no mysterious ingredients in the "organic capacity to invest." However, their identification has proven to be quite elusive to the eye of bureaucrats that have never been involved in creating, organizing, and successfully developing and managing an enterprise. Some of the most important components are:

- experience in plant design and layout;
- plant building management experience;
- technical qualifications of personnel in charge of installation;
- timely access to supplies with the right specifications;
- availability of specialized construction and installation equipment;
- quality of inventory control and warehousing of materials and equipment; and
- reliability of cost control systems.

This list covers formal items only. Other components are: discipline of the personnel; degree of responsibility in maintaining the equipment and preventing waste; motivation to complete specific tasks on time and with the required quality; the degree of teamwork; precision of the coordination among the different tasks; workers' and managers' disposition to work harder to solve unexpected problems; etc.

It is important to point out that these elements are necessary just for the completion of investment projects. Nothing has been said about the efficiency requirements of individual investment projects after they are operational. For an investment expenditure to become real capital in the productive sense, it must be capable of operating either socially or privately at a certain level of profitability. The value of the resources spent in a given investment project and in the operation of that project after completion must generate a minimum amount of wealth to justify the investment.

Cuba, however, developed its planning system on the incredible assumption that, as the country was going to move quickly toward communism—where, according to the utopian doctrine, money is not necessary—accounting systems and procedures were not important.[5] This was mirrored by the significant decrease in the enrollment and graduation of students of accounting during the second half of 1960. As a direct consequence, the Cuban economic system became increasingly myopic in monitoring efficiency at any level, compounding inefficiencies already built in a rigid price mechanism that reflected neither private social values nor costs. This situation was partially corrected after the 1970 crisis, when the Cuban authorities began to pay more attention to prices, costs, and even some market mechanisms.

In spite of the adjustments, there are many indications which suggest that the efficiency of the investment activity in Cuba has remained precarious. Thorough market studies have been practically nonexistent as prerequisites of investment decisions. Other necessary conditions for efficiency have usually been neglected or underestimated, such as minimum product quality requirements, or personnel qualifications and experience.

These considerations imply that what are reported as investment expenditures in Cuban statistics overestimate the real capital formation in the country by an unknown magnitude. Besides, the effort to invest more than what the Cuban economy could absorb efficiently has resulted in other inefficiencies not captured in the statistics. The latter refers to situations in which, in the presence of new and large investment projects, the Cuban authorities have transferred resources, especially human, from other activities to oversee the installation and operation of new ones.

Moreover, in the rush to maximize new investments, other resources— mainly building materials—have been committed to the detriment of the maintenance of old capacities.[6] This can be observed today in the serious deterioration of housing, water supply, and sewage systems affecting many cities throughout the country. In other words, the investment rush has not only resulted in waste but has also caused disinvestment in many other sectors of the economy. The magnitude of this process is also unknown.[7] The implication is that there is no evidence that net capital formation in Cuba has not been negative throughout the revolutionary period.

There is no readily available information to conduct a rigorous comparison of Cuba's investment performance with public sector investment activity in Latin American and Caribbean countries. Casual observation, however, indicates many points in common between Cuba and many countries of the region. The failure of the Cuban economic system and Latin American and Caribbean public enterprises in achieving minimum levels of efficiency and, consequently, promoting economic development have a common source: the assumption that growth in capital stock is uniquely linked to the growth of output as if they were connected by a mathematical equation or an engineering device. Managerial capabilities and the motivation of workers and managers have been grossly neglected in all cases. There are many indications that the funds made available— either by international or private lending agencies—surpassed the borrowing countries' organic capacity to invest, to the point of making new investments incapable of generating the funds to repay the loans.

Cuba appears to have been less efficient than the rest of the region in investing its resources, possibly because the total lack of private sector activities—with the exception of some small farms—prevents the authorities from having a benchmark for investment or entrepreneurial efficiency. Besides, the existence of a private sector in the Latin American and Caribbean countries, however strangled, tends to guarantee that a certain volume of resources, even from a social point of view, are more efficiently used. This tends to be the case because many private firms would not be able to stay in business without showing some profits.[8] On the other hand, though Latin American and Caribbean countries have a weak tradition in investigative journalism, especially regarding business and economic matters, they have intermittently reflected complaints about inefficiencies in public enterprises, generating certain degrees of pressure to correct them. In spite of the fact that public sector inefficiencies in Latin American and Caribbean countries are well entrenched, it is difficult to believe that such pressures have not had any impact.

In any event, Cuba has not had the same opportunity, as the media are not designed to play such a role. In this manner, Cuba has deprived itself of feedback mechanisms to correct performance in the utilization of its resources, whether through the press, planning control systems, or management information systems at the level of individual enterprises.

Secular Stagnation and the Debt Crisis

Cuba has suffered a chronic crisis in its balance of payments since the beginning of the 1959 revolution. Despite short periods of apparent prosperity, always fueled by high sugar prices in the world markets, it can be stated that the country is in a state of stagnant equilibrium, sustained by heavy Soviet subsidies. The amount of the Cuban external debt, on the other hand, is not precisely known, particularly with the Soviet Union. This situation resulted from the Cuban investment rush and chronic inefficiencies. In this context, Cuba began experimenting in the 1970s with market mechanisms and some private initiatives, in an effort to break its economic inertia. These experiments have been severely curtailed recently since Fidel Castro's perception that such private activities were weakening his political power.

Meanwhile, frustrations relating to poor public sector efficiency in other Latin American and Caribbean countries, combined with—and highlighted by—the debt crisis which took off in 1982, have created a curious convergence with Cuba. In fact, it is difficult to argue against the concept that Latin American and Caribbean development policies since the 1950s, with heavy reliance on public investments and subsequent growth of the public sector, are the main causes of the crisis affecting the region. Now there is a cautious interest in private sector initiatives as a potential force in promoting economic development. In the Cuban case, private sector initiatives are limited to foreign entrepreneurs and subject to strict government controls, a factor that seems to have discouraged investors to the point that no major breakthroughs are reported on this front. Latin American and Caribbean countries, on the other hand, have more freedom from highly structured ideological tenets to allow private initiatives—but they still have public sector structures, legal systems, and policies that do not facilitate private sector development, and a great deal of prejudice against this new approach still prevails.

Despite the ideological and politico-institutional differences between Cuba and the other Latin American and Caribbean countries, they have followed parallel roads. To synthesize, they generally relied on massive investments to promote development beyond their "organic capacities" to invest; their public sector grew significantly and became more a hurdle than an instrument for development; all became immersed in unmanageable external debts, partly as a result of development efforts; and they started looking at private initiatives as a way out of the current stagnation.[9]

Latin American and Caribbean countries and Cuba have paid a high price for the mechanical application of development recipes of the postwar era regarding the role of investments in the development process. Investment activity should have been preceded by the development of an entrepreneurial base. Investments are not only expenditures in physical capital, but much more. As any entrepreneur knows, success in any business requires a great deal of dedicated effort, creativity, and stamina. Aside from the financial requirements of investments, there is also a heavy investment in effort and organization. These factors do not come with physical capital nor can they be purchased; they are inherent to the individuals involved in the investment process. When only the financial component of investments is considered, investments fail to achieve their productive purposes, leaving behind a wake of financial burdens.

The Survival of Individual Preferences in Strangled or Distorted Markets

The Labor Markets

One essential characteristic of Cuban labor economics is that the worker tends to be paid at wage levels that are inconsistent with the supply of goods and services during any given period. This disequilibrium is caused by the official policy of employment maximization regardless of the employment-generating capacity of the economy. It results in artificial generation of employment which is a means to more equitably distribute the structural unemployment of the Cuban economy. The main advantage of such a policy is social, because it allows many individuals that otherwise would be unemployed to earn a level of income to cover minimum expenditures. The main disadvantage is economic, since it limits the incentive to work of the most productive workers as the necessary rationing system does not allow them to realize the corresponding benefits, even if they are paid higher wages. Employment maximization is also motivated by the political need to exert control over the population: the idle worker is a political risk, especially in a country with a long tradition of subversive activities.

Thus, the levels of labor productivity in Cuba are low and stagnant. This creates a vicious cycle with respect to the official desire to produce more to reach a level of equilibrium between supply and demand of consumer goods and services, and rid the economy of the embarrassing rationing system, and the even more embarrassing segmented consumer markets for high government and party officials.

Formally, labor markets do not exist in Cuba; however, market forces and individual preferences always find a way to express themselves. The chronic problem of absenteeism is a case in point. The "overpaid" worker does not have strong incentives to save the portion of his earnings that cannot be spent because of rationing quotas. As most workers are subject to work a fixed number of hours per week—a means to ration leisure time—the incentives to "escape" from work are strong. Throughout the years, the Cuban worker has become increasingly sophisticated in the ways he can move up and down his individual labor supply curve. Aside from being absent from work by feigning illness or having to stand in line for hours to buy some rationed goods, workers also use other excuses to be absent from work a certain amount of time, or to diminish the work load without being absent—a form of underground leisure time.

Since prices of goods and services tend to be fixed by government policy, the combination of absenteeism and disequilibrium in the goods (rationing) and labor markets generate a phenomenon that is the opposite of an inflationary spiral—a production deflationary process. Instead of having a process where too much money goes after too few goods, the rationing has created a process where too much money goes after relatively insufficient leisure time.[10] This process not only reduces the degree of utilization of installed capacities, but it also limits the efficiency of the investment process in Cuba. This fundamental disequilibrium in the Cuban economy results from official illusions and arbitrary conceptions about how to solve the problem of chronically high unemployment, in addition to an extreme commitment to equal opportunities in the job market. In trying to resolve this problem overnight, the Cuban government created a new problem of chronic and pervasive underemployment and stagnation.

The economics of labor markets in Latin American and Caribbean countries are dominated by similar illusions but with entirely different results. The presence of politically strong labor unions, overoptimistic labor codes, and minimum wage standards has aggravated the problem of structural unemployment in those countries where labor legislation is effectively enforced. As labor laws can force an employer to pay a higher wage rate *if* he employs workers—but cannot force him to employ—the relatively higher wages result in a lower level of employment for the economy as a whole. In nations where labor laws are ineffectively enforced, unemployment is not as high as it could be, but a significantly large proportion of the labor force is employed illegally. Yet, even in these countries, the employer avoids creating employment due to the perception that labor costs are uncertain due to instability in labor relations. In other words, even if the employer pays wages below the legal minimum, in a situation where labor conflict is likely in a given firm, if the marginal productivity of labor is sufficiently low, he is never certain when a conflict with the workers could force him to pay salaries beyond their productivity level, or to stop operations during a strike.

Despite the differences between Cuba and Latin American and Caribbean countries regarding their respective systems of labor economics, the net results regarding economic development are similar. In Cuba, development is impeded by the lack of workers' incentives. In Latin America and the Caribbean, the nations' developments are impeded by the lack of incentives for the employer to create jobs. Both effects have their origin in a capricious conception of how labor economics affect the economics of the firm. In Cuba, the reasoning adopts a Marxist language, but, in essence, it carries the same unrealistic message as in other countries. The Latin American and Caribbean tradition of believing that significant economic improvements can be legislated or mandated by executive powers is quite strong and crosses ideological lines.

The Consumer Markets

In Cuba, consumer markets exist despite the fact that they are constrained in two ways. The first relates to the general lack of flexibility in prices; the second is the rationing system that limits the supply of goods to quotas determined by the government. About the only thing that has remained free is the set of preferences of the consumers, whose demand functions determine the supply-demand imbalances in such markets. Nevertheless, those demand functions are not free to find socially satisfactory equilibrium positions due to the constraints. The demand functions themselves, however, are constrained because consumers (workers) are not free to enhance their earnings by becoming entrepreneurs or freely investing in education.[11]

One of the most important forms of adjustment of consumer preferences in these constrained markets consists of the reallocation of time toward less time at work, as discussed in the previous section. Another form consists of the secondary trading of consumer goods between individuals of complementary tastes. For example, consumers that are not coffee drinkers may trade their coffee quota for another product. This secondary trade opens the door for black markets where not only goods primarily traded through the ration system are exchanged, but also goods that are primarily outside the legal market system. This includes goods stolen from government warehouses and stores, agricultural produce that is not subject to mandatory delivery ("acopio") to the government, and a small amount of contraband, usually in the form of imported goods brought by foreigners and relatives of Cubans who live abroad.

The Cuban government has never shown an awareness of the magnitude of the inefficiencies that secondary trading and black markets carry over to the national economy. The time consumers spend searching for trading partners adds up to the time the consumer must spend in long lines to purchase rationed goods. The ingenuity and energy of the Cuban consumer to solve his needs is testimony to what is one of the last bastions of private enterprise still existing in Cuba. The invisible hand is tied, but it seems that there is still some movement in the tips of its fingers!

In periods of severe scarcity, the time needed for the satisfaction of basic consumer needs increases, which tends to decrease the time available for work, thus negatively affecting levels of production, and contributing to more scarcity. How this production deflation spiral is reversed or stopped is not clear. A possible explanation is that the government increases imports of some critical goods or the raw materials to produce them domestically. This could be done by reducing investment expenditures, increasing the level of external indebtedness, or taking advantage of periods of bonanza in sugar prices.

Direct intervention in consumer markets is not exclusive to the Cuban economy. We can observe many forms of intervention in Latin American and Caribbean countries, although none of them involve severe rationing. A typical form of intervention is through control of prices of so-called necessities, generally agricultural products. The net result has generally been the strangulation of the producer who ends up abandoning his land and migrating to the cities.

Government intervention in consumer markets in Cuba, as well as in the Latin American and Caribbean countries, is characterized by the same principle: excessive government control over a politically weak population, justified by a paternalistic philosophy, but essentially exercised as an instrument of power. While it is true that a Marxist mantel is adopted in Cuba, the predominant doctrine of government control allows for more structured forms of intervention. In both cases, however, economic development prospects are negatively affected since production, as well as consumption possibilities, are at odds with consumer preferences or production capabilities.[12]

Nonmonetary Markets

In Cuba, the highly constrained consumer and labor markets have opened the way to certain forms of transactions in which money is not involved—better explained with a typical example. Upward mobility is generally tied to individual allegiance to the government's policies. The most mobile individuals tend to be party members or workers who distinguish themselves in political events. Many positions in the government or in the Cuban Communist Party entitle the holder to privileges that are not accessible to workers in lower echelons. Typical privileges are: access to segmented consumer markets, where there is a wider choice of goods; perks such as cars, foreign travel, better housing, and access to social events such as invitations to diplomatic receptions; and a certain amount of influence through contacts that could help to obtain favors such as better medical services if ever needed, spare parts for the car, and a better job. Many of the corresponding jobs are considered positions of confidence—which invariably means political allegiance. Without excluding the possibility that an individual without political credentials could gain access to some of these positions on the basis of professional or technical merit alone, they are generally reserved for workers that enjoy the confidence of their superiors on political or ideological grounds. Under these circumstances, the "currency" that the worker holds to "buy" access to the most attractive jobs is his loyalty to the government and its leaders, as measured by the level of active participation or vociferous allegiance to government policy.

Even though this type of transaction takes place in any society, its frequency in Cuba appears to be much higher. While many individuals do not sell their loyalties as a matter of principle, many others succumb to the attraction of the perks in an atmosphere dominated by scarcities and little individual freedom.[13] The nature of these transactions, translated into practice, thus determines that they take place in very subtle ways. They are generally not observable, much less measurable. Nevertheless, they exist and form part of Cuban daily life. Their social value, if any, reside in the fact that they tend to alleviate the severity of the lifestyle under socialism. The main disadvantage is that they replace a system of allocation of human resources based on merit with a system based on the histrionic skills of the actors. Ultimately, what suffers is the productive capacity of the Cuban economy due to the concomitant loss of efficiency. At the same time, these practices lead to very subtle forms of corruption that are hard to detect because of the subjective nature of the transactions. But their frequency must have reached significant proportions as the denunciations against "sociolismo" or "buddy socialism" appear repeatedly in Cuban leaders' speeches and in the official press.[14] In the long run, this practice subverts the foundations of socialism and communism and destroys the utopian goal of creating "a new man."

Nonmonetary transactions were not invented in Cuba, as we all know. Their frequency seems to be inversely related to the level of freedom that individuals have in a particular social context. In Latin American and Caribbean countries, these transactions take place very frequently in the public sector, given its characteristic rigidities regarding workers' mobility. They also take place in private sector circles—including labor unions—caused by the lack of flexibility typical of stagnant societies.

Conclusions

As a costly experiment in social and economic reform, the Cuban revolution offers a great wealth of experience. Unfortunately, the Cuban authorities have remained incapable of learning from their own lessons. The current wave of reforms in other socialist countries, including Soviet "glasnost," does not seem to have any impact on the official Cuban mentality. Mentality, on the other hand, becomes an extremely important variable when a society is organized along highly centralized and essentially simplistic—yet formally baroque—lines of command. In this respect, Cuba's economic system resembles more the administration of a tribe or a plantation than that of a modern society. Consequently, Cuba's secular economic stagnation results from the stagnation of the Cuban leaders' mentality, or perhaps, the one single mentality that has been predominant in the country's affairs for more than a quarter of a century: Fidel Castro's. Economic analysis thus seems limited to the symptoms of the illness, not is causes, and psychology appears to be a more relevant discipline to explain the performance of the Cuban revolution.

Two hypotheses can be offered to explain this situation. The first is that the Cuban leaders are ignorant and dogmatic, and cannot understand that the building of a new society is too complex an enterprise to be carried out by a small group of individuals alone, without trusting the abilities of their fellow countrymen, or being able to organize them effectively. However, this line of reasoning is indulgent because it implies a certain degree of sincerity on the part of the Cuban leaders. The second hypothesis is that they are selfish and megalomaniac, unwilling to adopt policies that, based on more individual freedom in a collective search for economic efficiency, could jeopardize their political control.

Wherever the actual explanation lies between these two polar hypotheses, it forces the Cuban leaders, Fidel Castro in particular, to face a crucial historical dilemma: either continue the current development conception and risk going down in history as a monumental political failure, at best—or an internal revolt, at worst—or create the individual incentives through a set of liberal policies and risk the political uncertainties that China currently faces.

Belatedly, the Cuban failure to promote economic prosperity is becoming apparent in Latin American and Caribbean countries. Yet, the Cuban lesson has not been learned in its entirety. Despite the rhetoric about the need to rely on private sector development, most of the old obstacles are still in place: excessive government control; inefficient public enterprises; inadequate legal systems; private sector dependence on government-sponsored protection; and barriers to entry in specific sectors.

Latin American and Caribbean nations are still dominated by uncertain economic policies, currently aggravated by the debt crisis and internal conflicts. However, in their cases, it is not accurate to attribute this situation exclusively to the public sector or government authorities as in the Cuban case; one must also look for responsibilities in other segments of the Latin American and Caribbean societies. It is evident Latin American and Caribbean governments can learn something from the Cuban example, particularly regarding the inefficiencies of public enterprises, the negative impacts of price control mechanisms, and the dangers of an arbitrarily conceived development strategy. The latter is always misunderstood because Latin American and Caribbean policymakers fail to understand that Cuba's problems are not rooted in its Marxist approach alone. These problems also lie in the systematic lack of knowledge about economic concepts and human and institutional behavior—hence the extreme dependance of the countries of the region on becoming absolute importers of doctrine instead of producing their own. In other words, these nations have embarked upon a healthy import substitution initiative.

Aside from the governments of Latin American and Caribbean nations, private sector entrepreneurs, political parties, judicial and legislative powers, and organized labor can learn from the Cuban experience. Latin American and Caribbean countries are plagued by economic constraints that, if not as restrictive as Cuba's, do impose a heavy burden on the development of their economies. Price controls, for example, are not the exclusive conception of governments in Latin America and the Caribbean. They are requested and supported by some circles, to the detriment of the development possibilities of others. A case in point is price ceilings on agricultural products that strangle and finally ruin the farmer. Excessive and permanent protectionism fosters private monopoly powers. Unrealistic labor codes increase the cost of labor and create labor conditions which discourage labor-intensive investments, necessary to generate employment. Legislative actions that are not carefully examined for their economic implications frequently damage the investment climate. Inefficient justice administration reduces the security of contractual relations and property rights, indispensable elements in economic development.

The list is very long. There is no single bottleneck that can be pointed out as the main obstacle to economic development. What was the role of the mentality variable in Cuba, is much more complex in Latin America and the Caribbean.[15] When responsible individuals, public or private, can view the advantages of free markets, as Cuba's leaders fail to see, the creative energies, the desire of personal advancement—or even the freedom to contribute to social development—and the talent and potential of the peoples of the region will be unleashed, and economic prosperity may follow. In this context, the challenge is educational, formal and nonformal, and, therefore, requires long-term implementation. Policymaking in Latin America and the Caribbean, as well as in Cuba, has depended more on ideology than on knowledge. The dependence on ideology must be reduced and instead replaced with knowledge about how an economic system could work. The present inventory of economic knowledge is clearly incomplete, but, if more effectively disseminated, could have great impact. This would appear to be the best manner through which other Cuban disasters could be avoided.

Notes

1. Price variations in Cuba are erroneously believed by many to be of no significance due to the existence of rationed markets. This line of thinking neglects the black consumer market—whose dimension has never been precisely known—and the "market" of intermediate goods reflecting transactions among government enterprises and agencies.
2. I must apologize for not including all the names that deserve credit in this respect.
3. This optimistic projection appeared in the first four-year development plan covering 1962–65. The plan was virtually abandoned at the outset, and the planning exercises were reduced to one-year budgetary designs.
4. In order to dramatize the situation, the report on the execution of the investment plan of 1964—a confidential report addressed to top government officials—included the category "piling up of hardware" (amontonamiento de hierros, in Spanish), with an estimate of 80 million pesos. The total investment in equipment and machinery for that year was of 250 million. This was only a partial measure of the waste in investment projects, easily detected due to its visibility. It mostly covered imported equipment that had been in their original crates for more than a year. Much of this equipment was not protected in

warehouses. The equivalent waste in agricultural and construction projects was never known.

5. This brings to mind a conversation I had in 1960 with a university professor of statistics when he pointed out that as economic planning would develop in Cuba, the need to learn statistics would disappear. Another notion uttered by a professor of economics at the University of Havana in 1963 was that econometric methods were a bourgeois approach to economic science and, therefore, were not necessary in the building of a new society. These extreme views seem to have been abandoned in Cuba, but they reflected the level of thinking that prevailed in Cuba during the early periods of the revolution.

6. The stories about significant quantities of cement getting spoiled at construction sites because of lack of complementary materials such as sand, wood, or steel beams have become part of the planning folklore, and contrast with the enormous difficulties that a common citizen must go through to get some supplies for small repairs in his/her house.

7. The magnitudes seem to be unknown to the Cuban authorities, too.

8. The topic is very complex and cannot be dealt with in its entirety given the scope of this paper. However, we must point out that many private firms in Latin America only exist due to a combination of protectionist practices and monopolistic privileges that keep them alive. The net social contribution of many of those firms could very well be negative.

9. Brazil has been a special case, though not entirely different than other Latin American and Caribbean countries regarding the importance of the public sector. Its size and entrepreneurial energy have combined to develop an economic base where the private sector plays a significant role.

10. When a worker is willing to sacrifice income by working less, he is tacitly "buying" leisure time.

11. We must keep in mind that vocational and higher education in Cuba is also rationed and generally distributed to politically acceptable individuals.

12. Even the urban consumer who apparently benefits in the short run from lower agricultural prices suffers in the long run when domestic production is replaced by more expensive imports (foodstuffs) or simply reduced.

13. The popularity of the Cuban revolutionary leaders may have been greatly overestimated due to this phenomenon. We must take into account that many of the Cuban defectors, during any given time, were former government officials that either had the opportunity to defect—such as officials that had access to foreign travel—or decided to confront the risks involved in their actions after reaching a level of dissatisfaction with the government that could not be concealed.

14. The newly minted word "sociolismo" is a combination of socio (buddy or partner) and socialismo (socialism).

15. Cuba may still have the same problem after the most important one today is solved.

13

Novel Revolutionary Forms:
The Use of Unconventional Diplomacy in Cuba

Paula J. Pettavino

Introduction

Socialism found fertile soil in China. . . . If the coming of a socialist revolution to Cuba was not inevitable, the spread of socialist values, though also not inevitable, is less surprising. Government intervention was already extensive before the revolution and prepared the way for the state that burgeoned after it. Political participation, an essential part of Cuban revolutionary politics, is not new to Cuba either, although it has taken *novel revolutionary forms*. [Emphasis added.][1]

As suggested above, in both the foreign and domestic policies of revolutionary Cuba, such "novel revolutionary forms" are evident. The utilization of unconventional methods of diplomacy has been raised to the level of a fine art in Cuba with phenomenal success. In this context, this chapter will focus on the manner in which Cuban leaders use these forms in enacting their foreign policy.

Broadly defined, unconventional diplomacy encompasses a wide range of methods of disseminating propaganda both within Cuba as well as externally, in the developed and the developing world. These forms include: the astute utilization of media; communications; tourism; health systems; cultural activities; and sporting and athletic events in order to foster a positive image of the nation. Although these methods may be used in such a sophisticated manner that they become heavily politicized (which is clearly the case in Cuba), novel revolutionary forms can still be easily distinguished from the more widely recognized political, military, and economic conventional modes of diplomacy. The latter would include the most obvious examples of exchange of ambassadors and embassies, as well as a military presence. Among the various methods that fall under the heading of unconventional, this chapter will focus at length on the system of physical culture or sports within Cuba. Sport provides a vivid case study of one of the most successful Cuban diplomatic tools. For this reason, it merits an in-depth view. This essay will also discuss, though in lesser detail, the use of the media and tourism to accomplish foreign policy goals.

Cuban Foreign Policy

Cuba is an island country of 44,128 square miles and approximately 10 million people. It almost seems ludicrous to speak of such a small nation— especially one located in the shadow of the United States—as conducting a global foreign policy. Yet, Cuba does indeed have a "big country's foreign policy."[2] In fact, since 1959, Cuba has conducted itself as a leading player in the international arena, yet one without the necessary domestic resources.

Cuban foreign policy as a whole has served clear defensive interests since 1959. These objectives, though specific to the Cuban situation, are not too dissimilar from the initial foreign policy objectives of any new regime. Castro's first priority has been, and continues to be, to insure and enhance his political base within Cuba. His second concern is to assure the security of the regime from hostile outside powers, particularly the United States.

With a realistic eye toward the limitations of the level of economic development in Cuba, Castro has had to seek external economic assistance to insure the continued development of his country, if not its very survival. This straightforward objective, however, has been complicated by Castro's ego and ambition. The dilemma has been how to remain on the receiving end of what now amounts to $8 million a day, or $3 billion a year, in economic assistance from the Soviet Union, and yet still retain more than a façade of autonomy and independence. In large measure, Castro has found the solution to that dilemma in his astute use of unconventional methods of diplomacy.

In 1978, Henry Kissinger remarked that "It is time to overcome the ridiculous myth of the invincible Cubans. Whoever heard of Cubans conducting a global foreign policy?"[3] Although it is true that Cuban foreign policy is certainly not conducted on the same scale as that of a superpower, Castro has been successful at developing a unique brand of foreign policy that undoubtedly qualifies as global.

In the early years of the Castro regime, the focus of Cuban globalism was on legal and extra-legal military aid, assisting fraternal revolutionary movements struggling to seize power, as well as helping established governments friendly to Cuba to defend themselves against aggression.[4] After increasing controversy over such methods (e.g., in Angola and throughout Africa), Cuban foreign policy began to emphasize developmental assistance, which includes economic, technical, and cultural aid. In this manner, Cuba has been at least partially able to distance itself from the Soviet Union and develop an independent, albeit limited, foreign policy.

The driving force behind this policy of globalism is the strong personal ambition of Fidel Castro, for whom Cuba has never been quite big enough. Realizing the limitations imposed by the sheer size of his country and lack of domestic resources, Castro wisely chose to emphasize global aspirations and policies that were less likely to place him in direct conflict with his benefactor.

Since current Cuban leaders have always considered their island to be a part of the Third World, the Nonaligned Movement has provided an ideal vehicle for assuming a credible and attainable international leadership role. In 1961, Castro joined the movement as a charter member—the only one from Latin America. He was able to prove the legitimacy of his leadership aspirations by the selection of Cuba as the site to host the 1979 summit conference. This distinction meant that Castro would then serve as chairman and spokesman for the organization until 1983.

Solidarity with the Third World remains a core element of Cuban globalism. As such, it is to developing nations that the bulk of Cuban economic, technical, and cultural assistance is directed. In turn, Cuba's success in its promotion of unconventional diplomacy is effective in promoting the image of Cuba as a global leader in the developed world. Castro's international success in foreign policy, albeit predominantly in the unconventional realm, has allowed him to increase his maneuverability with Moscow, to come to terms with the United States, and place Cuba as a leading model for the developing world.

Indeed, choosing such methods of diplomacy conveniently fits into Cuba's strong tradition of forceful nationalism. Adopting the ideology of communism has served to enhance Castro's chosen methods of building his image and realizing his ambitions. Based on that ideology, all efforts toward development come under the category of developing the "new man."

The Role of Unconventional Diplomacy

Propaganda is the cornerstone of unconventional diplomacy. In 1954, Fidel Castro wrote to a fellow revolutionary: "Propaganda cannot be abandoned for a single minute, because it is the soul of every struggle. Ours should have its own style and adjust itself to the circumstances."⁵ Based on his actions as "jefe" over the past 25 years, it appears that that statement was still fresh in his mind. Indeed, it was propaganda and image-building that aided Castro in his rise to power. That same philosophy, broadened beyond the traditional scope of the media and communications alone, has helped to secure Cuba a visible role in the global theater. Although heavily politicized, media, the system of sports and competitive athletics, and the burgeoning tourism industry are essential elements of the phenomenally successful propaganda machine the Cuban government operates today.

Fidel Castro: Media-Made

An editorial cartoon in 1959 depicted Fidel Castro as a successful applicant for president of Cuba proclaiming, "I got my job through the *New York Times*."⁶ It can be argued that one of the key figures in helping to bring Fidel Castro to power was Herbert Matthews of the *New York Times*. At Castro's invitation (and orchestration), Matthews visited the revolutionaries in the Sierra Maestra in mid-February 1957. Based on his experience, Matthews wrote three articles in the same month, with the first two published on the front page of the newspaper. Castro's media exposure from the series then helped to insure his role in the revolution.

> Matthews' article on his first visit to the Sierra published on 24 February immediately made Castro an international figure. Since the censorship was by chance lifted in Cuba the very next day, the news that Castro was alive became known quickly in Cuba also. The imprecise overestimate of the size of Castro's forces helped attract urban Cubans to his cause. It was supposed that Castro was winning, that Batista's reports could not any more be relied on, and that his side was therefore the right side to be on; Castro's morale was raised. The morale in Batista's army was further depressed, and afterwards, when the Minister of Defense, Santiago Rey, denied both that Matthews could have penetrated the army's ring round the Sierra and that Castro was alive, the government was made ridiculous, since Matthews next published a photograph that he had taken of himself with Castro.⁷

Thus, even before assuming power, Castro exhibited skill and cunning in manipulating the media to his own ends, and an appreciation of the power that could be wielded with that weapon.

The Revolutionary Government: Media-Made

Over the past 25 years, the media and other methods of unconventional diplomacy have served to secure the status of the revolutionary government of Cuba. In 1958, Castro stated:

The Cuban press has the quite legitimate right to be informed about all matters of national interest, and to disclose them faithfully to the people. . . . It is time we put an end to the unjustifiable limitation that has been imposed on the Cuban press by not permitting even one of its reporters to visit our camp of operations in fifteen months of fighting. . . . Our primary condition for peace is that Cuban journalists be allowed to come to the Sierra Maestra. Peace must be preceded by the truth. The press has the right to report it and the people have the right to know it.[8]

Shortly after taking power, however, Castro was more in agreement with Napoleon who said that "four hostile newspapers are more to be feared than a thousand bayonets." By the end of 1959, a form of censorship was already in place. Newspapers were forced to close their doors because of government intimidation, either in the form of "spontaneous" demonstrations and physical threats or through withdrawal of advertising money. The Cuban people found themselves with two choices: revolution or counterrevolution. Only one path was acceptable to the revolutionary government.[9]

The success of the revolutionary government's efforts at image-building has also served to institutionalize the regime.[10] The mass media, for example, has been instrumental in performing the functions of distribution control and feedback control. In the former, the government maintains the revolutionary process by selectively distributing images and messages that depict the regime as the Fidelistas would like it to be seen. The first decade of the revolution saw mass media used astutely for political mobilization and character formation.

Even casual observers of the Cuban scene have been struck by the extent to which social and political life have been reorganized under Castro in order to provide the Cuban citizen with a carefully controlled view of the world. The carriers of the officially approved images fall rather naturally into the following five categories: (1) mass media; (2) armed forces; (3) mass organizations; (4) special schools and structures; and (5) the Party. These are the institutions being used to forge the new Cuban man and to tell the masses the story of the Revolution.[11]

Castro seemed to realize the importance of the second function of mass media after the setbacks of the early years—in particular, the failure of the *Gran Zafra* in 1970, when the sugar harvest goal was unrealistically set at 10 million tons. Although a surprising 8 million tons was harvested, the effort left the economy in shambles. Castro turned to his most widely known use of the media, the marathon television speech, and blamed the disaster in part on the lack of feedback from his people.

At this juncture, mass media began to perform the function of feedback control. According to one source, at least, "a regular perusal of the Cuban media indicated a consistent attempt to link the masses and the increasingly distant leadership," through the use of regular features such as consumer action-type columns and letters to the editor.[12]

There is some question, however, as to the willingness of the regime to tolerate (much less utilize) public criticism. Although there has not been a Cuban purge on the scale of "Let a Hundred Flowers Bloom" in China, it is unlikely that Heberto Padilla, Armando Valladares, and the more than 100,000 Cubans who left through the port of Mariel in 1980 would agree there is freedom of expression and criticism in Cuba. There is equally clear reason to believe that dissent from the party line is considered counterrevolutionary. In 1959, Castro himself wrote that "capitalism starves people to death, while Communism . . . resolves the economic problem, but suppresses the liberties which are so dear to man."[13] He was partially correct about communism, as his own path has shown.

The role of mass media in Cuba, in spite of shifts to adjust to external circumstances, was established early on in the life of the regime. The philosophy of the revolutionary media was described in 1964:

> . . . the desire of all the revolutionary leaders, beginning with Fidel Castro, is to transform radio and television into educational instruments through which the masses may be both *informed* and *formed*. Each appearance of the leaders of the Revolution is always a lesson in economics, politics, history, and even in specialized techniques, with a profound Marxist-Leninist revolutionary meaning. . . . What is sought . . . is the formation of a new type of intellectual, of socialist man, a conscious actor in the formidable tasks of his time.[14]

Key to the positive image of Castro's Cuba is the negative view of the United States held by the regime. Cuban anti-Americanism did not begain in 1959, but rather has been a recurring theme since the days of Jose Martí. The pervasive influence in Cuba of the North American sugar industry prompted one Havana newspaper to print the following headline in 1922: "Hatred of North Americans will be the Religion of Cubans." The editorial itself said "The day will have to arrive when we will consider it the most sacred duty of our life to walk along the street and eliminate the first American we encounter."[15] Thus, virulent anti-Americanism espoused by Castro does not constitute a break with the past.

The argument can be made that if an enemy such as the United States did not exist, Castro would have had to invent one. In this context, such a perceived threat allows the revolutionary regime to call for tremendous sacrifice from the people, and justifies extraordinary measures of control and, ultimately, repression imposed by the government. Perhaps even more importantly, such image-building permits individuals to feel a part of the revolutionary process. As Richard Fagen has aptly noted, the fight against such a visible and well-known enemy affords in some cases the only level of the ideological struggle in which the majority of the population can participate.[16]

Sports: The Unprecedented Cuban Success

There is no aspect of Cuban life that more clearly epitomizes the emphasis of the leadership on image-building and individual participation than the system of physical culture and competitive athletics. Indeed, the Cuban record in international athletics is the most universally recognized success of the revolution. It is also an area in which Cubans have clearly adopted the system used in the Soviet Union and other communist countries yet, at the same time, have injected substantive differences which make the system truly Cuban.

The revolutionary government knew from its inception that such a powerful image could serve the regime well and, indeed, it has. Developed countries are almost forced to admire Cuban athletic prowess. Developing countries are hopeful that emulation of the Cuban system will give them similar results.[17]

Cuba's surge of athletic strength is a consequence of its conversion to communism. With athletic superiority as a political goal, the Cuban government has imitated the Soviet system of physical culture—modifying it where necessary and expedient. Some of the similarities relate to the organization of the system and the goals of the physical culture program. The Soviet Union discovered the value of sport as a political tool over a period of time, formulating sports policy as a consequence of initial successes. Cuba immediately incorporated this tool into its system and ideology after seeing the positive effect of sport used in the Soviet Union. Thus, the Soviet Union began with victories which led to policy; in contrast, Cuba laid down policy which led to victories.

Cuba approaches the type of system that the Soviet Union is *supposed* to have. The differences are of degree rather than substance. The Cuban system is a clone of the Soviet model, emphasizing central control for the goals of mass participation and development of champions. Yet, the results of the two systems are different. The Soviet athlete appears cold, calculating, machine-like, and ruthless. The Cubans appear warmer, more human, and less regimented. Cuban athletes emerge as more well-rounded individuals than their Soviet counterparts, closer to the ideal ''new communist man.''

The Soviet system is older and more established. Its policies are characterized by science, routine, and no-nonsense regimentation. It produces athletes and personnel who are followers, rewarded for their discipline and obedience. The Cuban system is still emerging, characterized by newness, creativity, and experimentation. Those individuals involved in sports have a greater degree of efficacy and freedom. They are seen and see themselves as innovators, discoverers, and leaders. In addition, they work within a system that is still developing, and is still in an experimental stage.

Overall, Cuba provides the world with a clear example of how a communist system can help a developing country move from backwardness to excellence in a single area. The phenomenal success of the sports system is inspirational to both sides of the ideological spectrum. Yet the cost of developing the sports program has been high. Sacrifices have had to be made in other areas of society. For other nations, especially those with different political systems, such sacrifices would have been impossible.

The name of the athletic system in communist countries itself deserves special attention. The term physical culture reaches much deeper into society than the Western idea of an athletic program. It involves the mind and personality, as well as the body. To the communist, physical culture is a means by which the new man will be developed. It implies belief in the perfectability of human nature. Besides keeping the body fit, physical culture plays an integral role in the political and cultural training of the masses.

Sport is even more important for a country such as Cuba than for the Soviet Union. On economic and military levels, the Soviet Union has proven itself a world power. The positive image of victories are merely boosts for an already secure world status. On the other hand, the positive impact through the universal interest in sport is a major method by which Cuba can prove itself of world caliber.

For politicians, the virtue of sport is readily understandable, it has tremendous worldwide exposure and, at first glance, is apolitical. Ironically, it is precisely for its surface innocence that sport is so well-suited as a political tool. In summation, Cuba's athletic strength is a result of its conversion to communism. The political motivation behind the system of physical culture in Cuba does not dull the justified pride in its effectiveness.

The Background of Sport in Cuba

A billboard in Havana bears the following slogan, attributed to Castro: *No se concibe un joven revolucionario que no sea deportista.* (One cannot conceive of a young revolutionary who is not a sportsman.) Given the results of the Cuban sports system as measured since 1959, it is clear that the Castro regime has strongly acted on this belief. Before the revolution, Cuba, with a population smaller than New York City, was known in sports circles solely for its professional baseball players and boxers, all of whom went to the United States to "make it big." By 1976, Cuba ranked eighth overall in the Montreal Olympics, according to the unofficial points table.[18]

The Cuban sports system should be judged on the basis of what existed before the revolution. The real achievement in sports is not the number of medals won or the world champions produced, though the rate of success in both of these categories is phenomenal. Instead, the real success is that the majority of the Cuban population, without regard to social class, has access to and is strongly encouraged to use sports facilities.

The two most characteristic elements of Cuban sport before 1959 were its classicism and professionalism. In organized amateur sport (which is supposed to be the source of all Olympic athletes), only the privileged classes had the leisure time and the access to private sports clubs—the necessary requirement for practice. For those less privileged, there was baseball and boxing—sports which constituted a possible ticket out of poverty, and into what seemed the charmed life of American professional sports. Sport for the general public was not promoted but gambling was, in the form of horse races, dog races, jai alai, billiards, lotteries, dice, roulette, and slot machines.[19] Cuba constituted a sort of playground for the wealthy North American capitalists.

Cubans are fond of the expression that before the revolution, the nation had athletes but no sports.[20] For those who failed to make it big in professional sports, little opportunity existed.

> Sport . . . what had become of sport? Apart from providing entertainment for the children of rich families in their aristocratic schools and clubs, sport had become a form of business. It had turned into a piece of merchandise, an object of exploitation. . . .[21]

Shabby treatment of Cuban athletes before the revolution was the rule rather than the exception. This was especially true toward track athletes who were frequently poor and black. Interviews with former, prerevolutionary athletes revealed that during the 1948 Olympics in London, only three runners could be sent for lack of financial resources, effectively shutting Cuba out of the 4×100-meter race.[22]

Before 1959, the history of sport in Cuba constituted *un mal rato*.[23] Only 15,000 people participated in sports, with the majority of these in baseball and boxing; the rest were rich students at private schools.[24] Among the latter was Fabio Ruiz, formerly deputy director of INDER and a past member of Cuba's 1948 and 1952 Olympic basketball teams.[25] In the 1900–56 period, Cuba participated in six Olympic Games with a total of 107 athletes, only one of whom was a woman. For over half a century, these 107 athletes won only thirteen medals: six gold, four silver, and three bronze. By way of contrast, in Moscow alone in 1980, Cuba was represented by 237 athletes, including 36 women. They won 20 medals: eight gold, seven silver, and five bronze.[26]

According to Raul Castro, the theoretical basis of the Cuban system of athletics is simple: capitalist sport versus socialist sport.

> Sport, like everything, is a reflection, simply of a country's social system. . . . Sport under socialism is neither restricted nor commercialized. It is mass sport with the participation of the people, of all of the people, of all those who want to participate voluntarily. It is a means.
>
> Under capitalism, sport, like almost everything, was an end, and the end was profit. Sport under a socialist regime is a means, before everything else, for the self-improvement of the citizen, for the betterment of his health, constituting, also, a type of prophylactic measure. At the same time it creates the conditions and makes the citizens capable even to the point of increasing production, defending the country, and [providing] a healthy means of recreation.[27]

It is in the paths chosen to reach the goals of physical culture that Cubans have shown creativity and independence. Unlike the Soviet Union, Cuba had the luxury of choosing from policies which had already been tested and proven successful. They exercised their right to reject those policies which had failed, or more importantly, those which produced results that were not consistent with their aspirations.

According to Jorge Garcia Bango, the former director of Instituto Nacional de Deportes, Educacion, Fisica, y Recreacion (INDER), "Our first reform measure was to open to everyone the private sports clubs that abounded on the island."[28] With this act, the revolutionary government implemented the most oft-repreated and most important objective of the sports program: mass participation. Sport is viewed simply as a right of the people.

The second goal of the system is to seek and produce champions. Castro himself has warned, however, that this goal is second in importance.

> It is very important that we do not be mistaken, that in the search for champions we do not neglect the practice of sports. Everyone should practice sports, not only those in primary schools but also adults and the elderly. The elderly need it even more than the young. The youths sometimes need sports to use their excess energy. Moreover, sports is an instrument of discipline, education, health, and good manners. Sports is an antidote to vices. Youth needs sports. And the elderly need sports not to use excess energy but to adequately conserve

the energy which they still have and their health which is so important for a full life.

You can have the most complete assurance that whatever we spend on sports and physical education we will save in health and we will gain in the well-being and increased longevity of our citizens.[29]

Organization of Sports

INDER is the central governing body for sport entrusted with the responsibility of attaining these "revolutionary" objectives. It is clearly based on the model used by other communist countries. As is clear from its title, National Institute for Sports, Physical Education, and Recreation, INDER is responsible for virtually everything connected with sports: physical education, competitive athletics at all levels, as well as recreation and the use of free time. It is also responsible for national athletes and their training, as well as further field research.

Central INDER offices are located in Sports City *(Ciudad deportiva)*, a huge complex of sports facilities on the outskirts of Havana. Also located there are the Higher School of Physical Education *(Escuela superior de educacion fisica)* or ESEF, also called Comandante Manuel Fajardo; the Institute of Sports Medicine *(Instituto de medicina deportiva)*, all the facilities available to the National Training Center, some of which are available to the public; and the Sports Industry *(Industria deportiva)*, where most of the athletic equipment for the country is manufactured. Directly under the authority of INDER are national coaches and all of the Sports Schools *(Escuelas de iniciacion deportiva escolar)* or EIDEs and, of course, all of the provincial branches of INDER.

A legal vehicle was needed to implent this ambitious plan for mass participation in sport. When Law 939 created INDER in 1961, it also created (in Article 5) the voluntary sports councils *(consejos voluntarios deportivos)* or CVDs. These councils are the backbone of the Cuban sports network. They are the:

> nuclei of citizens who, in every factory, on every farm, in every peasant association, in every cooperative, in every instruction center, in every military unit, in every municipality and every province, that is, wherever the people work, dedicate themselves to sports activities.[30]

There are more than 6,000 CVDs in Cuba today, with over 55,000 individual activists. "Their role is not merely to organize sports activities and programs, it is more essentially to promote and popularize sport."[31] As such, they do everything from organizing team games at factories or community centers to producing posters, writing press reports, or even promoting sports through films and television. Less glamorous, but equally important, is CVD work at the grass roots level, where a massive sports system truly begins. A nationwide publicity campaign for family involvement in sport is conducted, beginning with the children at very early ages.

To the Cubans, children are considered the "most precious treasure of the nation." Castro himself has said there is "nothing more important than a child"; the latter are perceived as the true hope for the development of the new communist man, whether Russian, Cuban, or German. With such a lofty goal in mind, it is too risky to leave any childhood activities to chance. The games children play are still supposed to be fun, but they constitute a means to an end—with that end being a Cuban molded into the new socialist man.[32]

Physical Education

A criticism of the Cuban system is that it has been given a mass nature only as insurance against passing over a potential champion at the lower levels. This argument is not completely valid since there is no hope of a champion emerging from a gymnastics class of the *Federacion de mujeres cubanas* or a baseball game at the psychiatric hospital. On the other hand, the Cubans review all possible recruits with a fine-tooth comb—the physical education system.

Castro has said that "physical education of the people is the basis of sport,"[33] thereby an integral part of the Cuban education system. The system enables the government to have control over an important part of the developmental process of forming the new Cuban man.

> In keeping with the characteristics of its Revolution and the country's particular conditions, Cuba is developing a new type of man that the revolutionary process requires. This process is based on specific morality and idelogy chiefly by active participation of the people in the tasks set by the Revolution. . . .
>
> From the beginning, our education is aimed at the complete formation of man and joins, in a harmonious whole, study, work, defense, sports, art and recreation.[34]

However, in spite of the emphasis on mass participation in sport, the Cubans never lose sight of the secondary goal of developing international champions. In an attempt to find these individual "sports treasures," all school children are tested frequently, either individually or through a well-organized system of competition.

This system of competitive athletics is called *emulacion,* a socialist form of competition and self-improvement, without prizes; instead the reward comes from having succeeded. Begun in 1963 with 3,500 students in eight sports through this system, athletes with the greatest talent and potential become more visible. At present, over 9,000 Cuban children participate in over 22 sports; as a result, many of Cuba's top athletes began their careers in the School Games. According to Gilberto Herrera, coach of the Cuban men's volleyball team that won third place in Montreal, 90 percent of the national team had come from this system.[35] In 1975, Pablo Velez, official of INDER and manager of the Cuban delegation to the Central American and Caribbean Games, referred to the school sports system as the basis for national-level sport, indicating that 95 percent of the top athletes began at that level. In 1980, Huberto Gil, of the programming department of INDER, stated that 60 percent of the Cuban athletes at the Olympic Games in Moscow came from the School Games. He speculated that in the future it would most certainly be 100 percent.[36]

In this system, every person with talent is given the chance to be "discovered," and the opportunity to develop that talent. At every level, beginning with the individual schools, a championship team emerges. At the same time, another team, called *seleccion,* is chosen from the best players from all of the losing teams at that level. For example, if ten teams had competed for the municipal title, a *seleccion* would be chosen from the remaining nine teams. In this manner, two teams actually move on to the championship, representing their particular unit; in this context, there have been times when the "selection" has beaten the champion team. This process is repeated at every level up to the national one.

The talent that emerges is groomed meticulously at the various sports schools throughout the country. Housing first-rate rate sports facilities, these schools record the students' progress and evaluate them often. Although they do get a taste of general physical education, the basic formula is "one child, one sport, year-round." And the Cubans claim to know the one sport in which the child excels by the time he is nine years old.[37]

Despite the perquisites of life in these special schools, such as the individual attention from talented coaches and access to high-quality facilities, entrance to one of these schools does not spell the life of leisure. Students are continually evaluated, not only for their athletic performance but also for the academic level they maintain and their degree of political commitment. This attitude is clearly revealed in the following statement:

> You are not going to be professional athletes; you are not going to make a living at sports . . . you will make it from your *work*. You will also be able to go as far as you wish as citizens and as professionals and technicians.[38]

This attitude is consistent with the treatment accorded champions. Though it is true that Cuban athletes do not receive exorbitant, disproportionate wages that set them apart from the rest of society, they are given special consideration in many ways. A worker who is an athlete will be given time off from his job to train and to compete; his coworkers will take up the slack caused by his absence.

A student athlete, working toward a future profession, is paid, during training and competition, the salary he will make when he begins a job in his chosen field. He is given the extra time necessary to complete his degree—such as six years instead of the usual four—because of required time off. In addition, where food is rationed throughout Cuban society, athletes, from the sports schools on up, receive more and better quality food to adequately sustain them.[39]

The case of Alberto Juantorena Danger, Athlete of the Year in 1976 for winning gold medals in both the 400- and the 800-meter races at the Olympics in Montreal, is instructive. While training for competition and studying postgraduate economics at the University of Havana, he received a "grant" equivalent to the salary he could expect to make as an economist (approximately 320 pesos a month.) In addition, he was given a schedule that allowed for the necessary absences, namely, six years to complete a three-year program. In a typical day, Juantorena was at the University from 8 a.m. till 1 p.m. The rest of the afternoon was spent training.[40]

Today, Juantorena is vice-president of INDER, with an office in *Ciudad deportiva* and six phones on his desk. At 36, he is retired from competitive athletics. He has two children, two cars, a salary of 385 pesos or $292.60 a month. The rent for his four-bedroom apartment is, like all athletes, ten percent of his monthly salary.[41]

To hear the Cubans speak of it, the greatest motivating factor relates to politics. According to a Cuban gymnast who defected, "at least thirty minutes of political indoctrination is mandatory before every training session."[42] It is certainly true that political courses are required study in the sports schools. Judging from comments made by several famous Cuban athletes, it is clear they have been well-coached in how to respond to questions with apparently stock, revolutionary slogans. Yet, perhaps Teofilo Stevenson really does believe his now-famous statement, "What is one million dollars compared to the love of eight million Cubans?"

In order to judge the success or failure of the Cuban sports system, it is necessary to look at a number of indicators. Based on the record Cuban athletes have set in international competition, they have achieved an unprecedented level of success. Another indicator is the type of athlete INDER officials have been seeking to develop and the kind that has actually emerged. According to Raudol Ruiz,

We do not aspire to have athletes like robots, or athletes who represent our country at the cost of their own alienation. We want men and women who represent this nation who can relate to other people educated in the revolutionary process, who are capable of feeling the Revolution as a natural feeling not as something imposed and who are capable of defining the Revolution as a result of their own feelings. Moreover, they must acquire a cultural level which allows them to understand and evaluate what goes on in the world and be able to identify clearly its ideological framework. Further, they must have sufficient sophistication to recognize their own efforts and to value them. They should be able to converse with the trainers, doctors, psychologists, and not be just on the receiving end of orders. Only in this manner can we really obtain the kind of athlete who is revolutionary.[43]

In addition, the Cubans are insistent that neither stars nor heroes develop. An individual athlete is singled out only when his performance has been extraordinary. Photographs printed in *Granma, Bohemia, Juventud Rebelde, LPV,* and *Deporte: Derecho del Pueblo* and other publications are typically of action, not of individuals, and often lack identifying captions. Publishing the technical aspects, such as rules and tips for playing, helps to "demystify" sports and, furthermore, prevents it from being the preserve of naturally talented athletes. Such a philosophy serves to greatly reinforce the Cuban government's commitment to mass participation. Thus the gap is partially closed between ordinary people playing for fun and health and Olympic gold medal winners.[44]

Cuban Athletes in International Competition

Cuba has produced what appears to be an amazing blend of athlete and revolutionary. In the early stages of international competition, perhaps the Cuban representatives could be accused of having taken themselves and their politics too seriously. Press articles and comments from U.S. opponents depicted Cuban sportsmen and women as being "out for blood." The 1971 Pan American Games were fraught with rumors about defections, suicides, fights, and the physical beating of a top sprinter who supposedly tried to defect.

Over the years, however, the Cubans seem to have grown in maturity and sophistication. Indeed, in the recent Pan American Games in Indianapolis, the participating Cuban athletes (the first to compete in the U.S. since 1959) were the *victims* of political discrimination and violence, not the perpetrators. Political tension erupted into violence when anti-Cuban demonstrators ripped Cuban flags, distributed anti-Castro leaflets, and taunted Cuban athletes. Before the Games even began, the American Legion declared it did not wish either to see the Cuban flag or hear the Cuban anthem if the closing ceremonies were to be held in an American

Legion hall. In fact, the Reagan administration balked at letting the Cubans fly directly here from Havana.[45]

Although the Cubans may not have instigated the vilence, the political message delivered through sports comes through loud and clear. When Cuban weightlifters Pablo Lara and Francisco Allegues defeated Roberto Urrutia, former world champion for Cuba who defected in Mexico City and now competes for the United States, Castro declared that the Cubans "have demonstrated that before dignity and principle, all the money of the imperialists is worth nothing."[46] As for the money, the Cubans are planning to spend $27 million as hosts to prepare Havana for the Pan American Games in 1991.[47]

Based on the number of medals alone, the United States prevailed in the recent Pan American Games, earning a record 369 medals, 168 of which were gold. However, Cuba was the real winner, with 175 medals, including 75 gold; a record ten of those first-place awards went to Cuba boxers. In other high-profile events, the U.S. was also shut out of the gold in baseball, Cuba's passion, and in basketball. But Cuba's real success is indicated by its record over the years, as displayed in Table 13.1 below. At the Pan Am Games in Mexico City in 1955, it won only 13 medals—only one a gold. By 1967, however, Cuba's deliberate emphasis on sport and physical education began to pay off and the successes increased.

Baseball: The Cuban Obsession

Baseball in Cuba is more than a pastime; it is an obsession, with baseball diamonds everywhere. The game is played year-round, although top-level play is tied closely to the other important season on the island: sugar. Castro has said that "Baseball helps the harvest; it is tied to the heart of

TABLE 13.1
Cuba's Pan Am Medals

Year	Site	Total	Gold
1951	Buenos Aires	28	9
1955	Mexico City	13	1
1959	Chicago	20	2
1963	Sao Paulo	44	21
1967	Winnipeg	127	11
1971	Cali	254	82

Sources: Ron Pickering, Cuba, p. 150 and Lourdes Casal and Andres Hernandez, "The Role of Cultural and Sports Events," p. 6.

our economy.'' Over half a million Cubans play organized baseball in one form or another. The rest participate as "active" spectators. According to Sanchez, right fielder for the Matanzas team, "After every game, I have nine and a half million people waiting outside the stadium who want to explain to me, for the good of Cuba, what I did wrong."[48]

Since baseball is so closely tied to the Cuban identity, it has been instrumental politically. In 1961, an intelligence analyst in the United States studying aerial photographs taken over Cuba noticed a military camp. The usual soccer field has been marked off and some of the men were playing a game. Upon second thought, the analyst remembered that Cuban military installations always set up baseball diamonds, not soccer fields. With closer examination, the camp turned out to be Russian, set up to help install missiles in Cuba. The rest is history.

The first baseball stadium in Cuba, Palmar de Junco, was inaugurated in Matanzas in 1874. Today, it is a museum to the sport. The first game was played there on 27 December 1874, with Havana defeating the home team, 51-9. Havan's left fielder was Emilio Sabourin, who helped to organize the country's first professional league in 1878. He died in 1897 in the Spanish prison, Castillo del Hacha, during the Cuban war for independence.[49]

Most of Cuba's legendary players migrated to the professional leagues in North America. There were players such as Esteban Enrique Belan, Adolfo Luque, Camilo Pascual, Minnie Minoso, Conrado Marrero, Dagoberto "Campy" Campaneris, Rigoberto "Tito" Fuentes, Tony Oliva, Miguel Gonzales, Tony Perez, Mike Cuellar, Luis Tiant, Tony Taylor, Jose Cardenal, Pedro Ramos, and Cookie Rojas. The most famous of all was Martin Dihigo, who had the misfortune of being a black ballplayer in the 1930s, when it was still a white man's game. His fame was limited to his home island until a special committee on black players recently named him to the Hall of Fame in Cooperstown.

With the onset of the revolution, professional baseball was abolished. Ironically, the game remains the common denominator between Cuba and the United States; indeed, it is not a game shared with the socialist brotherhood. As Don Miguel Cuevas, perhaps the greatest living baseball hero in Cuba, stated, "The Russians have yet to come up with a good left-handed hitter."[50]

Unfortunately, the political situation allows Cuba and the United States to share only the memories of baseball in days gone by. Even today, the most influential American players in Cuba are probably Ted Williams and Mickey Mantle. They were the featured players in the last training films shipped to Cuba before relations were severed. In addition, it is the era of Williams and Mantle that the older Cubans, now coaching younger players, remember, and the one about which they reminisce.

It has been said that "Cuba has two distinct baseball generations: that which remembers and that which does not."[51] Those who have grown up with the revolution can say with conviction that they have no interest in the Major Leagues. There is no reporting on Cuban television, radio, or in the press about U.S. baseball. But for those over 40, it sometimes appears they remember too much; the memories are recalled in infinite detail, made more vivid through 20 years of rehashing with others who also remember.[52]

In postrevolutionary Cuba, if the level of play is *beisbol de maniguas* (bush league), it is easier to depart the stadium early. The fans are not sacrificing their entrance fee, because none exists. In addition, all foul balls are returned. This is but one example of what appears to be a truly cooperative effort—still unknown in the United States.

There are other differences, especially in contrast with the Soviet Union. For example, crowd behavior is impeccable. Though ready at the drop of a bat to show disapproval for a bonehead play, the crowd, players, and officials treat each other with utmost respect. Anger, on all sides, is subdued as much as humanly possible. And this occurs without a policeman in sight.

> Cuba's top hitter, Wilfredo Sanchez, was once called out by a "blind" umpire in Matanzas when he was safe by a yard, leaped high in the air, spun around and made the psychic transformation from complete disbelief and fury to resigned composure before he returned to the earth. He walked off the field without any show of displeasure except that four-foot vertical catapult when he first saw the umpire's thumb. . . .

> Cuban ballparks may be the only ones in the hemisphere that combine rabid partisanship, ferocious noise and umpire baiting with a sense of total personal security.

> The crowd has the right to yell, "we are being robbed" and "we are playing nine against thirteen." But when the ump has heard enough, he calmly raises a hand like a school principal and the sound turns off like a faucet. It is an impressive and somewhat unnerving sight.[53]

Although baseball appears to be the least political of Cuba's sports, the revolution is never far from view; the stadiums themselves are a testimony to it. The fences are unblemished by advertising signs and the foul poles are lighted for night games. The electric scoreboard lists the batting orders and game and player statistics rather than quizzes or cartoons. The games themselves are shorter, seldom over two hours. There are "no ushers, no concessionaires, no hawkers, no panty-hose night, no exploding scoreboards, no inessential public address announcements."[54] Basepaths are swept by "middle-aged groundskeepers in coveralls" rather than by "nubile teenagers in hot pants.'' As for the liquor that is such an integral part of American sports, "baseball is thought to be sufficient inebriation for any Cuban."[55]

The other side to the baseball story is that of the counterrevolutionaries. In 1980, Johnny Carson made the comment that "Bowie Kuhn isn't worried about the baseball players going on strike. He's got 65,000 replacements who just got to Miami ready to step in."[56] Carson was referring to the new wave of refugees who came to Florida from Mariel harbor through the Peruvian embassy.

The "Free Cuban Baseball Team" story smacks of politics: they were all prohibited from playing ball in Cuba because they were anti-Castro. Refugees claim that baseball players are second-rate compared to other athletes because the game cannot be exported for political purposes, as can Olympic sports. Contrary to what INDER officials and most Cuban players state, Cuban boys view the leagues as only a stopping point on their way to the Great Leagues. Although the first goal of these men is to make the majors, the second goal is political revenge.

> Someday, I want to go back to Cuba and play an exhibition tour. I want to show people what a free Cuban can do, given the chance. I want to go back and prove what they wouldn't let me prove before.[57]

These refugees admit the only reason they came to the U.S. was to play baseball. At first, it seemed they would get their chance: within 72 hours of the refugees' arrival, the Cincinnati Reds had two scouts there—until Commissioner Kuhn said the Cubans could not be recruited until their status was established.

The Cuban Sports Industry

At the XII World Amateur Baseball Championships in 1971, Cuba scored two victories. One was on the field itself, where, for the third year in a row, the Cubans became the undisputed world champions in "the game." The second victory was more subtle, but perhaps more important. The Cuban-produced *Batos* baseball was accepted as the official baseball to be used at this prestigious international tournament.[58] The Cubans had, indeed, come a long way.

Following the revolution, a blockade of the island was imposed, making normal trading and importing impossible. This loss was felt strongly by the Cubans and, perhaps, most particularly in the field of sports. Although nations willing to help were quite advanced technologically, or would be in the near future, the problem was that none of them had a tradition of baseball—either in the playing or manufacturing of equipment. Thus, as a country of agriculturalists (with little manufacturing capacity), Cuba had to create a sports industry from scratch.

After several false starts, the Zarabozo brothers were able to produce 850 baseballs. In September 1961, with five machines, they established the Sports Industry *(La industria deportiva)* in the Latin American stadium. The industry began with 40 workers making poor-quality bats and balls. By 1980, in the Havana plant alone, there were almost 1,300 employees making 623 different types of sports articles.[59] The high-quality balls are used in the world championships and the bats are all hand-tooled.

Seventy percent of the sports equipment in Cuba is manufactured in the Havana plant, now located in the Sports City. Another plant is already in operation in Santiago de Cuba, while another is being built in Las Villas. Future plans project the bulk of the equipment being made in Las Villas, equipment which is distributed free to schools, colleges, clubs, wherever there are competitors. The machinery in the plants comes from Spain, Italy, and East Germany. Much of the plastic used comes from Japan, England, and the Soviet Union, while the fabrics come from China, Bulgaria, Italy, Japan, and Czechoslovakia.[60]

An interesting point is that there are two categories of equipment being made: high quality for competition, equal to 10 percent of the output; and mediocre quality, equalling 90 percent for the rest of the population. Once the Las Villas plant is in operation, the Havana plant will produce only the top-quality products. In addition, it seems that the people producing the high-quality equipment and those using it are from different segments of society.[61]

The Cubans are fiercely proud of the sports industry. One reason is because it was built truly from scratch. There existed no prior industry that was merely nationalized. Without assistance from the United States, the Cubans developed it from one machine made of an old jukebox and cash registers turning out not-quite-round balls to an industry producing more than 8 million pesos worth of equipment in 1980.[62]

However, the blockade still makes it difficult for the Cubans to improve their methods of manufacture. They are forced to go to Europe for assistance, and they copy whatever they can. The routine return of foul balls during baseball games is further evidence of the pride and respect Cubans hold for this native industry. Every time they return a foul ball, they help to break the blockade.[63]

Sport: Policy Implications

Cuba has been "accused" of making sport an instrument of politics. Castro does not deny the accusation any more than he could deny being Latin American. He merely clarifies the Cuban position.

Really, it is just the other way around. Politics is an instrument of sports. That is, sport is not a means, but rather an end, like every other human activity, every other activity that has to do with man's well-being, just as education, health, material living conditions, human dignity, feeling and man's spiritual values are all the objectives of politics.[64]

Ostensibly, politics (or the revolution) exists to serve the ends of the people—that is, to serve all human activity. In this context, sport is merely one of these activities.

The successful mass participation in sport has affected three very important political factors: nation-building, political socialization, and political integration. As Alberto Juantorena said, "Americans live in a country; we Cubans are *building* a country."[65] Through sports, Cubans are able to feel personally involved in the process, thereby creating strong feelings of national pride.

Quite naturally, people who believe they have helped to create something identify more closely with it. The goal of mass participation, which Cuba has achieved so successfully, serves to break down class differences and, therefore, leads to increased feelings of cohesiveness.[66] The result is a system or network between government and people, and among the people as a whole, that is mutually supportive.

This supportive system also flows from the people to the talented athletes who emerge from the population. These outstanding sportsmen and women subsequently become powerful role models for society as a whole; it is a responsibility they do not take lightly. Cuban athletes have always recognized the role the population plays in their victories. Stevenson's refusal of a million dollars in a professioonal boxing match to retain the love of his countrymen is the most obvious example. Another is Juantorena's dedication of a gold medal to his compatriots and his gift of the other to Fidel to "share" with them. Winning is merely "complying with their duty" to the revolution.[67] It is a mutually supportive and beneficial cycle: athletes are inspired by the Cuban people to win; the Cuban people are inspired by the athletes and their victories to participate. Thus, both sides gain personal and national pride.

In the realm of foreign policy, sport serves as a very powerful political tool. The value of a victory in the Olympics or any international sporting contest undoubtedly goes beyond the gold medal. It is but a short distance from an individual athlete in his national uniform to the strong symbol of the country he represents.

For this land, whose boundaries are set by the sea, sports has become a kind of Cuban equivalent of 19th century American Manifest Destiny. The Olympics are their Oregon Trail, their Northwest Territory, their visible evidence of national accomplishment and a rallying point for morale.[68]

Perhaps even greater proof of Cuba's success is the existence of depth behind gold-medal winners. Cuba has not taken just one or two especially talented individuals such as Juantorena and "moulded" them into world champions. Instead, behind each champion there are dozens of others—the second- or third-place winners or those who simply make a good showing. With every international contest (and Cuba enters almost all of them), they are growing in experience and ability, moving toward winning gold. This depth is a clear result of Cuba's dedication to the goal of mass participation. Without a solid emphasis on sport at all levels, immature talent would never have the opportunity to develop. This, in turn, is one reason why Cuban athletes are never allowed to think they are indispensable. Behind each one is a host of promising talent, waiting to be given the chance to compete on a national team. In a country the size of Cuba, such depth could only develop from a system dedicated to mass participation.

It has been said that the Cubans "appear to have married their background of American 'know-how' to socialist planning, and have not stifled the Latin exuberance which makes them such exciting and attractive athletes."[69] With time and maturity, and in spite of their ideological proclamations, the Cuban athletes have emerged as warm people with human qualities, much more so than the Soviets or Eastern Europeans. It is hard to imagine a Soviet boxer carrying Rufus Hadley (of the U.S.) back to his corner after Hadley wobbled over to shake hands following his defeat. Furthermore, it takes a certain type of athlete to merit the almost incredibly glowing description accorded Juantorena after he had lost to an American in Los Angeles earlier in 1979. It seems his defeats and graceful acceptance of them have only served to strengthen his image.[70]

At the same time, sports provide a convenient stage for displaying the physical prowess (i.e., superiority) of a country's athletes. The implication is clear: only a superior social system could produce such dazzling champions; also implicit is the inferiority of the loser. The revolutionary government has made good use of its sporting successes. After all, probably more people throughout the world identify Cuba with Alberto Juantorena or Teofilo Stevenson than with Moncada or Granma or even the Bay of Pigs.

To the Cubans, sports success as propaganda is important throughout the world, but nowhere is this more the case than in the rest of Latin America. As Castro said:

I can assure you that one of the things most admired by our Latin American neighbors is our sporting successes. We can say that our athletes are the children of our Revolution and, at the same time, the standard-bearers of that same Revolution.[71]

What gives Cuba more credibility with less-developed countries is that Cuba is still "one of their own," in effect, a neighborhood kid made good. This position is strengthened even further as Cuba moves into a leadership role, able to provide technical assistance to other countries. Thus, Cuba provides a powerful example of the potential of a small country whose resources are rationally deployed under what the Cuban leadership describes as a superior social system.

In 1945, George Orwell only slightly exaggerated when he said "I am always amazed when I heard people saying that sport creates good will between the nations, and that if only the common peoples of the world could meet one another at football or cricket, they would have no inclination to meet on the battlefield. . . . International sporting contests lead to orgies of hatred."[72] The recent Pan American Games were a perfect example of what Orwell called "the lunatic modern habit" of equating success in sports with economic, political, or military supremacy.

In particular, the role of sport in conflict seems to loom larger within the Western Hemisphere, especially North America versus South and Latin America. The feelings of hostility run deep.

> Imperialism has tried to humiliate Latin American countries, has tried to instill a feeling of inferiority in them. Let us say that it is part of the imperialists' ideology to present themselves as superior, and to develop in other peoples an inferiority complex. Sport has been used to that effect.[73]

It is for this reason that the victories over the United States always seem sweeter. When Cuba defeated the U.S. in volleyball in Los Angeles in 1976, Castro called it a "sporting, psychological, patriotic and revolutionary victory."[74] In an incident of more sinister circumstances, after the deaths of the fencing team in the bombing of the Air Cubana flight in Barbados, Juantorena did not mince words.

> This is simply another example of the vile and cowardly nature of the imperialists. It reflects the extent of their impotence. They vent their frustration on the innocent. They can't forgive us for the defeats we have inflicted on them. . . .

> Far from intimidating us, these acts make us identify more closely with the Revolution. We will continue to struggle wherever the Revolution and the Party ask us to go, in sports or on the battlefield.[75]

In fact, the Pan American Games have become the symbol of this rivalry, with most of Latin America rallying behind the Cubans.

It is undeniable that the purpose served by sport in the international arena is invaluable. "International sport is one of the strongest, most direct, cheapest and least dangerous foreign policy weapons a nation can use to set the tone of relations."[76] Cuba makes astute use of this weapon as an unconventional form of diplomacy.

Political Tourism

Yet another avenue of blatant propaganda, principally directed toward those outside of Cuba rather than inside, is political tourism. It is also one of the most transparent means and, in some instances, verges on the pathetic. As in several other communist countries, political tourism in Cuba is an important, tightly run, highly organized, monitored institution. Initially, most tourists visited the island to defend the political situation as much as to see the sights. These visitors already believed that Castro had established a socialist paradise of sorts and, since the Soviet Union had been so disappointing, they wanted to see it firsthand. As a political host, Cuba does not disappoint.

There are several preconditions for the exercise of political hospitality to be successful that apply, in fact, to the other methods of propaganda explored in this chapter.[77] Rulers must be determined to shape the image of their country according to rigid, ideological principles. The material-economic resources of the country must be controlled by the state, to enable the necessary control of the itinerary of political tourists, from the hotels and restaurants to the "exhibits." For example, one hospital or model apartment was kept shining and stocked at all times, so group after group could see the "truth" of the revolution. What may appear to be a random stop at a typical apartment is actually a scene from a carefully staged drama. The same old woman reminisces time and time again, for group after group, about life before and after the revolution, "spontaneously" offering refreshments to the "pilgrims" that the ordinary Cuban would never see. A population aware of the penalty for unauthorized contacts with foreigners also makes the job of security easier.

There are two interpretations to every scene, however. Angela Davis may have perceived that "every able-bodied resident of Havana was rushing to the fields as though to a joyous carnival."[78] The other, more plausible interpretation—especially as the hardships of the revolution dragged on for decades—comes from another black American, who lived in Cuba for three years before leaving, disillusioned, particularly with regard to the regime's racial policies. "No one was forced to do so, but everyone in each office was asked if he was going to participate in this 'patriotic' venture." Refusal clearly indicated mere unfriendliness to the revolution or possibly counterrevolutionary plotting. He could expect to be replaced in his job by someone who would participate.[79]

Yet, in spite of evidence to the contrary—such as severe shortages of common goods 20 years into the revolution and would-be refugees still scrambling to get out—the Cuba of Fidel Castro retains an aura of idealism and hope. Castro himself plays a large role in preserving this positive image, playing the role of consummate revolutionary, in full costume, since the days of the Sierra Maestra. The finely honed methods of unconventional diplomacy have contributed greatly to the preservation of this image.

However, with the passage of time, the appeal of Cuba began to waver among some of the more discerning supporters.

> There is one country we looked upon, for a while, as the very embodiment of socialist hopes—Cuba. It very soon stopped being a land of freedom—homosexuals were persecuted and the least trace of nonconformity in dress made the wearer suspect. . . . In an atmosphere of this kind intellectuals are allowed no freedom of any sort. . . . The "honeymoon of the revolution" that had so enchanted us is over and done with.[80]

It has been noted that the disenchantment was mutual. Castro showed no tolerance for criticism, regardless of its validity.[81]

However, up to the present time, there remain "levels," or types, of political tourists for whom the mystique of the Cuban revolution is preserved. The *Venceremos* Brigade, a pro-Castro group that volunteered manual labor in the early years of the revolution, continues to lead groups of political tourists to Cuba, most of whom were merely confirming their preconceived notions of Cuban society.[82] Church groups also tend to return similarly indoctrinated; the lack of a critical approach on such tours was appalling. "Many . . . who visit Cuba . . . have performed a kind of surgery on their critical faculties and reduced their conversation to a form of baby talk, in which everything is wonderful, including the elevator that does not work and the rows of Soviet tanks on military parade that are 'in the hands of the people.' " Common "political commentary" includes "oh, wow" and "neat."[83] But the politically naive are also fickle. In many instances these simplistic loyalties have been transferred to Nicaragua, still untarnished despite Daniel Ortega's penchant for expensive, designer eyewear and even more expensive modern weapons systems.

Conclusion

In whatever form, Castro's Cuba has proven itself a master at the art of unconventional diplomacy. From tourism to communications, from athletics to the health system, Cuba has used these propaganda tools to distinct advantage for 25 years, in an increasingly sophisticated manner.

These novel revolutionary forms have allowed Cuba to achieve a degree of notoriety, as well as to earn a level of prestige on a global scale that would have been impossible for the island-nation through conventional methods of diplomacy. Although the propaganda function of almost all of these forms is blatantly transparent, one is hard-pressed not to award credit to the Castro regime for taking policy areas that receive little attention in other small countries and turning them into tremendous, visible successes.

These methods have successfully given Cuba and its revolutionary government an aura of idealism and hope. Yet the emphasis that the Castro regime has placed upon these novel revolutionary forms has not been without its realistic and pragmatic advantages. The unconventional methods of diplomacy practiced by Cuba have resulted in the following benefits—either in whole, or in part. However, the following conclusions are not meant to be all-inclusive and will deal only with the three areas covered in this chapter: media, the sports system, and tourism.

Legitimacy and Nation-Building

The success achieved by these policy tools has given Cuba a tremendous degree of legitimacy in the eyes of the outside world that would have been unattainable without them. Predating the triumph of the revolution, Castro's manipulation of the media afforded him the legitimacy to seize power without a prolonged struggle. Furthermore, Cuban successes in sports are more widely known than the political ones. Thanks in part to the media, sport policy has given Cubans and outsiders alike strong symbols of a country successfully struggling to build itself. And, finally, the increasing number of tourists visiting Cuba only underscores the country's legitimate role as a unique and successful political system, to be admired and carefully observed.

Institutionalization and Political Integration

Unconventional diplomacy has clearly served to institutionalize the Castro regime. The media reinforces the role (and, therefore, position of power) of the revolutionary government, both within Cuba and in the international community. Indeed, the system of sports has strengthened and integrated the government perhaps more than any other policy; it actively engages ordinary Cubans with its emphasis on mass participation, and provides the opportunity for political identification with its hero/

athletes. Tourism allows participants to see a thoroughly entrenched government, oftentimes viewed with awe by visitors. Such a reaction on the part of outsiders has a powerful effect on the Cuban population as well.

Given his financial reliance and resultant political dependence on the Soviet Union, these unconventional methods of diplomacy provide Castro with a ticket of limited autonomy. In some cases, these methods actually provide vitally needed hard currency. Unlike, perhaps, steel production or consumer-oriented business, novel forms of diplomacy such as the sports system and political tourism have responded well to long-term planning.

Sports—the most successful method of unconventional diplomacy and the focus of this chapter—literally forces admiration from developed countries and leaves developing countries hopeful that the same might be achieved through emulation. The message rings clear: only a superior social and political system could produce the champions that have emerged from the Cuban model. Moreover, the fact that Cuba is itself a small, developing country makes the message even clearer for other countries in similar positions, especially those in Latin America.

Thus, there can be little doubt that sport, communications, and other unconventional methods of diplomacy are inextricably linked to politics; nor does the existence of this link dull the justified pride in their effectiveness. Hence, the blatant political motivation does not negate the positive results of these novel forms. It is essential, however, that unconventional diplomacy be seen realistically for the propaganda tool that it is, rather than proof that a social paradise has at last been found.

Notes

1. Jorge Dominguez, *Cuba: Order and Revolution* (Cambridge, Mass.: The Belknap Press, 1978), p. 465.
2. Jorge Dominguez, "Cuban Foreign Policy," *Foreign Affairs* 57 (Fall 1978):83.
3. Frieda M. Silvert, "The Cuban Problematic," in Martin Weinstein, ed., *Revolutionary Cuba in the World Arena* (Philadelphia, Pa.: Institute for the Study of Human Issues, 1979), p. 23.
4. Jorge Dominguez, "The Armed Forces and Foreign Relations," in Cole Blasier and Carmelo Mesa-Lago, eds., *Cuba in the World* (Pittsburgh, Pa.: University of Pittsburgh Press, 1979), pp. 65, 78–79.
5. John Spicer Nichols, "Cuban Mass Media: Organization, Control and Functions," *Journalism Monographs*, no. 78 (November 1982), p. 4.
6. William E. Ratliff, "The *New York Times* and the Cuban Revolution," in William E. Ratliff, ed., *The Selling of Fidel Castro: The Media and the Cuban Revolution* (New Brunswick, N.J.: Transaction Books, 1987), p. 2.
7. Hugh Thomas, *Cuba: The Pursuit of Freedom,* (New York: Harper and Row, 1971), p. 920.

8. "Un documento sensacional de Fidel Castro a Pardo Llada," *Bohemia*, 9 March 1958, pp. 76–77. Cited in Carlos Ripoll, "The Press in Cuba, 1952–1960: Autocratic and Totalitarian Censorship," in Ratliff, pp. 93–94.

9. Carlos Ripoll, pp. 99–100.

10. "Institutionalize" is used here in the broad sense of the word. That is, there has been created a "more ordered political process and precise definition of the relationship between the state, its organs, and the individual." The narrow definition of institutionalization has not occurred, however. Individuals have not been subordinated to institutions. Power in the Cuban government remains within the individual leaders, not in the institutions themselves. (See Hugh Thomas, Georges Fauriol, Juan Carlos Weiss, *The Cuban Revolution: 25 Years Later*, CSIS Significant Issues Series, Volume VI, no. 11, pp. 41–42.)

11. Richard R. Fagen, "Mass Mobilization in Cuba: The Symbolism of Struggle," in Rolando E. Bonachea and Nelson P. Valdes, eds., *Cuba in Revolution* (Garden City, N.J.: Anchor Books, 1972), p. 205.

12. Nichols, p. 21.

13. Fidel Castro, *Revolución*, 22 May 1959, cited in C. Ian Lumsden, "The Ideology of the Revolution," in Bonachea and Valdes, pp. 541–42.

14. Jose Antonio Portuondo, "Los intelectuales y las Revolución," *Cuba Socialista*, June 1964, pp. 62–63. Cited in Fagen, pp. 206–07.

15. Quoted in Robert F. Smith, *The United States and Cuba: Business and Diplomacy, 1917–1960* (New York: Bookman Associates, 1960), p. 103. See also Fagen, pp. 212–13.

16. Fagen, p. 221.

17. See Paula J. Pettavino, "The Politics of Sport Under Communism: A Comparative Study of Competitive Athletics in the Soviet Union and Cuba," Ph.D. dissertation, University of Notre Dame, 1982.

18. The Montreal Olympics of 1976 are used intentionally rather than the 1980 Olympics in Moscow and the 1984 Olympics in Los Angeles. The absence of so many traditionally strong contenders due to the boycotts would provide an unrepresentative picture.

19. Fidel Castro, from a speech given to the First Congress of the Communist Party of Cuba, cited in an untitled pamphlet received from the Cuban embassy in Canada.

20. "Sport—Why Cubans Win," interview with Raudol Ruiz, *Cuba Review* 2 (June 1977), p. 10. Ruiz was Vice-President for Latin America of the International Council on Sports and Physical Education for UNESCO and a professor at INDER, the National Institute of Sports, Physical Education and Recreation. Before the revolution, he was a trainer for the Cleveland Indians for part of the year, and for the Cuban Sugar Kings for the remainder of the year.

21. Fidel Castro, quoted in Sonia Castanes, ed., *Fidel Sobre el Deportes* (Havana, 1975) para. 67, 1961 speech. Cited in R. J. Pickering, "Cuba," in James Riordan, ed., *Sport Under Communism: The USSR, Czechoslovakia, the GDR, China and Cuba* (London: C. Hurst and Co., 1978), p. 152.

22. Lourdes Casal and Andres R. Hernandez, "The Role of Cultural and Sports Events in Cuba's Foreign Policy," p. 6. Preliminary draft prepared for the conference on "The Role of Cuba in World Affairs," Center for Latin American Studies, University of Pittsburgh, November 15–17, 1976. See also *Listos Para Vencer*, XIV 732–22 (6 July 1976), pp. 20–23.

23. Arnaldo Ribero Fuxa, Director of Teaching at INDER-Havana, in an interview with the author, 18 August 1980.

24. Jose Luis Salmeron, "Despues de Quince Anos," *Listos Para Vencer*, XIV (17 February 1976), p. 11.

25. "In Cuba, Sport is a Mass Effort," *Chicago Tribune*, (20 March 1977), Section 3, p. 5.

26. *Granma Weekly Review*, XV, 33 (17 August 1980), p. 9.

27. Raul Castro, *Discurso a la Primera Plenaria Provincial de los Consejos Voluntarios Oriente, 1 de octubre de 1961*, (Havana: INDER, 1961), p. 6.

28. Fernando Sandoval, "Cuba Catches Up," *Atlas World Press Review* (May 1976), p. 53. Excerpted from *Veja* of Rio de Janiero.

29. Fidel Castro, Speech at the 6 October 1977 dedication of the Havana City Province's sports school, *Los Martires de Barbados*.

30. Fidel Castro, quoted in Luis Sexto, *Listos Para Vencer* (or *LPV*), XIV (17 February 1976), p. 4.

31. Ibid. See also John Griffiths, "Sport: The People's Right" in John and Peter Griffiths, *Cuba: The Second Decade* (London: Writers and Readers Publishing Cooperative, 1979), p. 249.

32. Doctora Margarita Sanchez Rueda, Professor Lazaro Caballero Ramirez, Professor Santos Guerrero Guiterrez, Professors at ESEF and INDER, *Los 100 juegos del plan de la calle: algunos teorias sobre los juegos* (Havana: Editorial Orbe, 1977).

33. Fidel Castro, *Discurso* (de 19 noviembre 1961), p. 11.

34. *School and Society*, 2318 (Summer 1969), Vol. 97, p. 293.

35. Santiago Cardosa et al., *La Juventud* (Havana: Editorial Genite Nueva, 1978).

36. Pablo Velez, *Areito*, II, 2/3 (septiembre/diciembre 1975), p. 74. See also Huberto Gil, *LPV*, 946 (August 5, 1980), p. 29.

37. "In Cuba, Sport is a Mass Effort," *Chicago Tribune*, 20 March 1977, p. 5. This can change, however. Track star Alberto Juantorena began as a basketball player. Champion boxer Teofilo Stevenson, like so many Cubans, played baseball.

38. Fidel Castro, quoted in Griffiths, p. 254.

39. Diamond, *Cuba Review* 7, 2 (June 1977):8,9; *Atlas World Press Review* (May 1976), p. 53; and Pickering, p. 168; Author's interview with INDER officials; Jack Anderson and Les Whitten, "Castro's Force-Trained Athletes," *Washington Post*, 13 August 1976, p. D15; *Chicago Tribune*, 20 March 1977; Griffiths, p. 259; Max Novich, "Why Cuban Athletes Succeed," *New York Times*, 2 November 1975, V. 2:1.

40. Pickering, pp. 167, and 168; Griffiths, p. 255; Author's personal interview with Alberto Juantorena.

41. "Castro Takes Firm Steps Against Flab," *Washington Post*, 23 April 1987, pp. 1, B9.

42. Anderson, *Washington Post*, 12 August 1976.

43. Ruiz, *Cuba Review*, p. 20.

44. Diamond, *Cuba Review*, p. 8; Griffiths, pp. 257, and 258.

45. "On a Mission from Havana," *The Boston Globe*, 16 August 1987, pp. 46, and 67; "Anti-Castro Faction Demonstrates No Class," *USA Today*, 18 August 1987, p. 3C; "U.S. Swimmers Win All Six Gold Medals," *The Washington Post*, 15 August 1987, p. 1; "Security Heightened After Fight," *New York Times*, 16 August 1987, pp. S1, S5.

46. "On a Mission from Havana," *Boston Globe*, 16 August 1987.

47. "Pan Am Games Have Problems to Solve," *New York Times*, 25 August 1987.

48. Thomas Boswell, "Baseball: The Passion of Cuba," *Washington Post*, 5 April 1978, pp. F1, and F4; Boswell, "Island Aches for Yankee Visit," *Washington Post*, 7 April 1978, pp. E1, and E3.
49. Boswell, *Washington Post*, 5 April 1978; Ron Fimrite, "In Cuba, It's Viva El Grand Old Game," *Sport International* (6 June 1977), pp. 68–80.
50. *La Juventud. Sport International.*
51. Thomas Boswell, *Washington Post*, 6 April 1978, pp. D1, and D7.
52. High-spirited discussions of vintage U.S. baseball, including the Negro leagues and obscure players from the 1930's, were observed by the author during several baseball games in Cuba.
53. Thomas Boswell, *Washington Post*, 5 April 1978.
54. Ibid.
55. *Sports International.*
56. John Feinstein, "Cuban Refugees Ache for Shot at 'American Great Leagues,' " *Washington Post*, 25 May 1980, pp. F1, and F14.
57. Feinstein.
58. *Listos Para Vencer*, XIV (17 February 1976), p. 39.
59. Guillermo de la Cuesta, Director of the Sports Industry, in a personal interview with the author, 28 August 1980.
60. Ibid.
61. Ibid.; Thomas Boswell, *Washington Post*, 9 April 1978.
62. Luis Sexto, "Como se Invento Aquella Maquina," *Listos Para Vencer*, XIV (17 February, 1976).
63. De la Cuesta, interview with the author.
64. "Peking and Havana: Sports as a Political Exercise," *New York Times*, 22 August 1971, 1:3.
65. Boswell, *Washington Post*, 8 April 1978.
66. Barry Stern, "Socialization and Political Integration through Sports and Recreation," *The Physical Educator*, 25 (October 1968), pp. 129, and 130; Casal and Hernandez, p. 1.
67. Juantorena, "Muy contento de haber cumplido con la Revolucion," *Granma*, 30 July 1976, p. 4.
68. Boswell, *Washington Post*, 9 April 1978; David Kanin, "The Role of Sport in International Relations," (unpublished Ph.D. dissertation, Fletcher School of Law and Diplomacy, 1976), pp. 6, 7; Andrew Strenk, "The Thrill of Victory and the Agony of Defeat: Sport and International Politics," *Orbis*, Summer 1978, pp. 453–69.
69. Don Anthony in Riordan, p. 8.
70. Thomas Boswell, "Stevenson Sinks Leatherneck in One," *Washington Post*, 13 July 1979, pp. C1, and C3; Boswell, "Juantorena: Mythic Steed Moon-Bound," *Washington Post*, 9 July 1979, p. D1.
71. Fidel Castro, quoted in Pickering, p. 150.
72. Daniel Golden, "The Playing Field—or Battlefield?" *Boston Globe*, 16 August 1987, p. A22.
73. Fidel Castro, quoted in Pickering, p. 149.
74. Ibid, p. 147.
75. *Granma Weekly Review*, Year II, No. 43 (24 October 1976), p. 6.
76. Strenk, p. 457.
77. Paul Hollander, "Political Tourism in Cuba and Nicaragua," *Society*, Vol. 23 (May/June 1986), pp. 28–37. See also Hollander, *Political Pilgrims: Travels of*

Western Intellectuals to the Soviet Union, China, and Cuba, 1928–1978, (New York: Harper and Row, 1981).

78. Angela Davis, *An Autobiography,* (New York: Random House, 1974), p. 204.

79. Hollander, *Political Pilgrims,* p. 253.

80. Simone de Beauvoir, *All Said and Done,* quoted in Hollander, *Political Pilgrims,* pp. 226–27.

81. Jorge Edwards, *Persona Non Grata,* (New York: 1977), p. 44.

82. The tour—taken by the author in 1980, which allowed access to sports and cultural officials and facilities—was led by a member of the *Venceremos* Brigade. For an accurate, although cynical, account of the trip, see John Krich, "Cuban Cruisin'," in *Express: The East Bay's Free Weekly,* 3 July 1981, Vol. 3, no. 36, pp. 1, 5, and 6.

83. Frances Fitzgerald in Ronald Radosh, "The Cuban Revolution and Western Intellectuals," in Radosh, ed., *The New Cuba: Paradoxes and Potentials* (New York: Morrow, 1976), p. 171. See also Hollander, *Political Pilgrims,* p. 227, and John Krich—Both "neat" and "wow" were the frequent comments overheard by the author from other participants on her political tour.

14

Perceptions of Cuba in the 1980s

Juan M. del Aguila

*Varias y enormes son las monstruosidades que se van
descubriendo cada día, pero
desde el fin de la Inquisición
jamás las tierras ibéricas e iberaoamericanas han conocido una
como la que ud. impone:
la exposision del pensamiento.*

Su régimen, en lo criminal, por lo menos, se equipara a los más sanguinarios gobiernos de la triste historia de nuestras tierras. Excédelos a todos, sin embargo, por un peculiar atropello de la mente. No es suyo el inveto, pues es una ciencia que recibió con el comunismo, y que practica con el mismo arte que sus maestros.
—Fernando Arrabal,
1984, Carta a Fidel Castro

Me pregunto como el dirigente cuban consigue combinar, dentro de una agenda de trabajo, las innumerables tareas de gobierno, la voracidad intelectual por los temas más variados y el pacer de conversar. No recuerdo haber encontrado antes otra persona con inteligencia tan aguda y tanta predisposición para el diálogo personal. (Joelmir) observó bien al comentar conmigo que Fidel engrandece todo, imprime a cualquier asunto, desde la concina hasta la deuda externa del Tercer Mundo, una importancia trascendental.
—Frei Betto,
Fidel y la Religión

405

With little doubt, the Cuban revolution constitutes the most dramatic example of radical political change in Latin America in nearly 30 years in terms of several factors: the scope and breadth of socioeconomic, institutional, and cultural transformation; the pace at which changes took place; and the impact that those changes had on the outside world. Beyond Cuba, the revolution set in motion trends that, to this day, continue to affect how the idea of change is perceived and discussed in Latin America. It introduced into the debate both messianic and utopian notions defining how "the good society" is organized and governed. From the start, the Cuban leadership made it evident that its mission would be the transformation of an entire continent, rather than only changing the character of a dependent "sugar island" where intolerable pressures had built up. As the revolution unfolded, Cuba put Latin America on notice, pronouncing itself the site of unprecedented social experimentation, and its regime attempted to change structures as well as values, norms, and habits of mind.

Such a grandiose project could not be ignored. Perceived as the dawn of a new era in Latin America rather than simply as a national undertaking, the Cuban revolution struck an emotional and psychological chord in those committed to the struggle against capitalism and U.S. influence in the region. The whole process soon acquired ontological properties, and Havana's brand of radicalism reawakened Latin America's search for its own identity. Many felt that Havana was leading history, no longer to be its shamed handmaiden, and took the signs to mean that this time the future would work.

That the revolution took place in Cuba, a fairly advanced society in the late 1950s, was quite striking because the fact that Cuba was directly influenced by secular modernization and "Americanization" made it somewhat unique.[1] From the standpoint of revolutionary theory, drastic change would have been unexpected, given the institutional weakness of the working class, the absence of genuine radical movements, and the growing presence of middle-income sectors. The paradox of revolutionary change amidst socioeconomic and cultural homogeneity confounded many observers, who expected "class contradictions" and historical social antagonisms to be the source of the struggle. In effect, since theory was not a guide, a perception emerged that something novel was unfolding in Cuba, markedly different from what had occurred in czarist Russia or in feudal China, and novelties almost always capture our imagination.

For those that despised the old authoritarian order supported by a foreign capitalist power, the Cuban revolution was fascinating, particularly because its leaders were so young and unconventional, full of élan and magnetism, yet so sure of themselves and of their ability to fashion "a new society." Young and audacious Fidel Castro, the enigmatic "Ché," the voluble Camilo, and a host of goateed guerrillas were perceived as charming rogues, untainted with power or corruption, free from the vices of the "ancien regime." Little was said of their inexperience in actually governing a society, or of what path they really intended to take. These were fresh faces, and they were given the benefit of the doubt at home and abroad. No wonder then, that the Cuban experience caught the imagination of a good part of the secular intelligentsia in Latin America, Europe, and the United States, especially after categorical promises were made for bread and freedom, democracy and justice, nationalism without xenophobia, and genuine sovereignty.

On the other hand, the inescapable contradictions produced by a turbulent process of transformation were seldom analyzed, and original perceptions became fixed in time and space. Intentions mattered, even if performance lacked. The future mattered, and present-day sacrifices were expected. Still, would individual freedom be sacrificed to larger social goals? Was political accountability being forgotten? What did Castro really mean when he spoke of "mass democracy"? Was a nation truly caught up in the kind of euphoria that crushes thought and creates the conditions necessary for the usurpation of power by men on horseback? Reality moved fast, images were being created, but illusions replaced rational thought.

The early perception of Cuba through the eyes of influentials like Jean-Paul Sartre, C. Wright Mills, Waldo Frank, Susan Sontag, and a host of Latin American notables was quite favorable, and the revolution was perceived as the genuine article. Many welcomed Castro's categorical declaration that he was a Marxist-Leninist and the revolution a socialist one. Cuban socialism would be different—it would not exhibit the Stalinist excesses of the Russian case, and, in any event, its virulent anti-Americanism was healthy. The abolition of democratic freedoms, the rising influence of communists in government, cultural affairs, and the economy, and the arbitrary arrests and incarceration of dissenters were perceived as the cost of doing business. One was constantly reminded that a revolution, indeed, was "not a dinner party," and since the goals were pure—nothing short of full human emancipation—the means to reach them were entirely acceptable. The assumption that as long as change was advancing it had to be for the better was rigidly held, because the probability that the revolution could produce a new and more rigorous structure of oppression was seldom contemplated.

Those travelling to Cuba, and interested foreign audiences, found all the elements of great drama. First and foremost, there was the charismatic *caudillo,* an elemental force in his own right whose pronouncements on everything from cattle semen to parapsychology soon filled volumes and made headlines. By now, *este niño malcriado*[2] is a living legend. Second, there was talk of plots and conspiracies hatched by agents of the reactionary colossus to the North bent on destroying "a wonderful social experiment" because it could not tolerate genuine sovereignty being exercised by a former vassal. Third, there were the intense manifestations of class warfare, where good and bad were clearly identifiable, where sitting on the fence was unacceptable, and deepening social divisions necessary "so that the working class, the peasantry and all the people" could trample those who were left behind. Fourth, there was retribution, as the new society was systematically purged of tainted elements from its past and gradually emerged from the ruins as a shining new city on the hill. And finally, there was a most welcome form of absolutism, an all-or-nothing approach that set clear limits between what was permissible and what was unwishable, so that everyone knew the nature of the times. Not unlike the time of the Spanish Civil War and other national cataclysms, battle lines were drawn, and one was either with the revolution or against it; there was no middle ground, and definitions were demanded. In the fateful words of Luis Aguilar: "Va llegando la hora de la unanimidad. La sólida e impenetrable unanimidad totalitaria."[3] On the whole, such voices were few and their warnings were rejected, because history was being made, and one dared not get left behind.

Different audiences saw different things in Cuba as the revolution moved on, partly because it appealed to idealists committed to finding heaven on earth, to intellectuals mesmerized by the prospects of fashioning "The New Man," and to vindictive nationalists who had always longed for a frontal challenge to U.S. power and interests in Latin America. The articles and books written, public pronouncements enunciated, and moralistic positions taken in defense of Cuba shaped public consciousness and allowed the regime to enjoy a free ride with a good part of the international left. Critics were few, Cuban exiles were "worms," and the episodic rantings of the U.S. government were scornfully dismissed. To criticize Cuba was to give aid and comfort "to the enemy," even if the criticism was deserved. The urge to question just whose interests were being served by the creation of a pervasive personalistic dictatorship had to be suppressed, lest one fail to recognize that youthful exuberance and sense of energy that captured the imagination of a continent. Cuba offered vicarious thrills, and the revolution was doing things that would eventually take place in all of Latin America. The revolution's commitment to an independent path caught the eyes of the Frenchman Regis Debray, and he glowingly observed that:

> Overnight Cuba stamped the language, style, and content of revolutionary action with a resounding youthfulness. Because of the demographic situation, this

youthful tone has reverberated throughout the continent. These young people, who have short memories, have no intention of following anyone except those who fight beside them.[4]

In short, Havana called for manning the barricades, and a generation of guerrillas was launched against the empire. Subsequent disputes between orthodox communists, Castroites, and factions that subscribed to little-known revolutionary doctrines did not take the edge off Havana's central message: if you want true liberation, follow the path of armed struggle.[5]

Officials in Washington and in Latin American capitals, as well as in parts of the Third World and most surely in the Kremlin, understood the geopolitical stakes that were part of the "Cuban question," but their perceptions stemmed largely from security considerations. The connection between Cuban socialism and the Cuban government's explicit desire to export its model to parts of Latin America affected Washington's view, and it provided Moscow with an unprecedented opportunity for penetration of the region. Moscow and Latin America's radical left did not always agree on ideology or strategy, but it was the left that turned Havana into its political mecca. One needs to recall that the Tricontinental Conference in 1966 and the Organization of Latin American Solidarity (OLAS) Conference in 1967 pointed the way to "a new International" in the region. Guevara himself, in a message to the Tricontinental, counseled the younger generation to take up arms, and to prepare themselves for a protracted struggle against U.S. imperialism. Said he:

> The great lesson of the invincibility of the guerrilla will take root in the dispossessed masses. The galvanizing of national spirit, preparation for harder tasks, for resisting even more violent repressions. Hatred as an element of struggle; relentless hatred of the enemy that impels us over and beyond the natural limitations of man and transforms us into effective, violent, selective and cold killing machines. Our soldiers must be thus; a people without hatred cannot vanquish a brutal enemy.[6]

The Sorelian quality of Guevara's message supported the views of those who advocated the use of violence as a legitimate instrument of change. Its appeal is not lost on the guerrillas of the 1980s, particularly the ones in El Salvador who are now committed to the destruction of a democratic regime. Guevara's example, and Havana's sustained support for armed insurrection, created the myth of *el guerrillero heroico*, a myth sustained by a torrent of revolutionary novels, films, visuals, and revisionist historiography.

Havana's propaganda shaped perceptions in a particularly useful way, because it portrayed Cuba as a besieged, vulnerable, little nation standing up to imperialist aggression. Effective use of the David versus Goliath image allowed Havana to blame others for its own failures, and to generate sympathies even during periods of widespread domestic repression, persecution, and social confrontation. Groups like the Venceremos Brigade started travelling to Cuba precisely at a time when government crackdowns against dissenters—including religious believers—were frequent, but the Brigade was proud of its role during successive sugar harvests.

The use of coercion became legitimate in many eyes because Cuba could not let its guard down and allow "fifth columnists" to destroy the revolution from within. Since the stated goal of the revolution was to further social justice and bring about conditions in which "The New Man" could thrive, the means to that end were necessary and proper. Politics was war at home and abroad, and survival was the only thing that mattered. From this standpoint, the revolution was perceived as a gigantic effort in behavior modification, a sweeping moral crusade whose ultimate goal was to remake the individual to its core. It was a total question, an all-or-nothing approach creating its own truths, values, morality, and worldview; there was no room for second-guessing. Foreign observers were much impressed with the Cubans' sense of mission, and often compared the righteous militancy of Cuban youths with the alienation of their American counterparts. For example, Joseph A. Kahl wrote movingly that:

> American youthful militants (at least the white ones) have too often lost all belief and become nihilists and destroyers; Cuban youthful militants have the security of conviction and the narrowness that goes with it. They are building utopia, and it completely absorbs their energies. The independent intellectual, the critic of all societies and all beliefs, is a luxury they cannot afford.[7]

Paradoxically, it was precisely the lack of ambiguity that Cuba represented that appealed to those uncomfortable with the contradictions and social conflicts of (mostly) their own pluralist societies, where relativism and not moral certainty shapes political behavior. To those looking for answers, Cuba had them; to those hungering for truth, Cuba provided it; moreover, Cuba had a clear and ringing message: it had life and intensity. How could one fail to be converted?

Perceptions of Cuba in Segments of the Intellectual Community

The role that intellectuals (writers, poets, novelists, social scientists, political theorists) have played in Latin America's political life is legendary, as the lives and work of Andrés Bello, Domingo Sarmiento, José Martí, Rubén Darío, Haya de la Torre, Rómulo Gallegos, Mariátegui, and others demonstrate. Enlightened thinkers for the most part, committed to republicanism and to the cultural emancipation of their peoples—these and other intellectuals at times idealized the types of government and social orders that Latin America has for the most part failed to produce. In our own times, exalted figures like Gabriel García Márquez, Mario Vargas Llosa, Mario Benedetti, Julio Cortázar, Carlos Fuentes, Octavio Paz, and Alejo Carpentier articulate political ideas and often make explicit and controversial political choices. The new generation, much influenced by Marxism and revolutionary theory, as well as by nationalism and diffuse notions of Hispanicism and anti-imperialism, is increasingly divided between those who recognize the value of democratic change and those who still hold a brief for revolutionary politics.

With little doubt, the attitudes and perceptions of leading intellectuals at times influence the views of their peers and the public at large, and perhaps those of government, academia, and media sectors. The positions that intellectuals take regarding this or that regime become either the source of inspiration or hostility, depending on where their followers sit. For instance, García Márquez's friendship with Fidel Castro puts him at odds with others who choose not to admire tyrants, but the novelist has not been modest when it comes to praising the Cuban regime. It is expected that such figures identify "Great Truths," but more often than not, passion and ideological euphoria characterize their internecine polemics and public pronouncements. Many feel honored if at times they are designated as enemies by regimes that they in any case despise, and many a dictator has felt their sardonic wit and wrath.

During its "humanistic phase," the Cuban revolution attracted wide praise from prestigious intellectuals in Europe, the United States, and Latin America. They marvelled at a revolutionary process perceived to be genuinely nationalistic, committed to restructuring the bases of a society thought to be little more than an American colony. Cuba generated cultural and intellectual symbols that stirred the hearts and minds of many Latin American intellectuals, and it soon gained the sympathies of those who had always hoped for the kind of political change that promoted social justice without sacrificing political freedom. For many, this was the gist of the matter, and Cuba's promise lay precisely in the fact that its regime was promoting change without undue levels of coercion, with ideas allowed to flourish. Castro's categorical pronouncement in 1961 set the limit on cultural and artistic expression, but his view that "Inside the Revolution everything, against the Revolution, nothing," was not perceived ominously. Vargas Llosa himself, now on Havana's black list because he has forcefully denounced Cuba's transformation into a totalitarian state, visited the country in 1962 and noted the existence of ideological currents other than Marxism, the absence of official censorship, and the sale of publications prohibited in other communist countries.[8] J. M. Cohen, a British observer, went so far as to write in 1966 that while "communist-Puritanism is of course active in petty persecution of so-called Beats and nonconforming students in the universities and art schools," it was "kept in check by the solid liberalism of the Writer's Union, presided over by the liberal Communist Nicolás Guillén and by the liberals of the Casa de las Américas," whose work he found to be analogous to that of the British Council.[9] Finally, Mario Benedetti, in an assessment of culture published in 1968, concluded that a revolutionary process forces individuals to make moral choices, and that the issue of cultural and individual freedom must be understood in a wider social context. Said Mr. Benedetti:

> . . . a revolution has, in its turn, the right not to put up with (that) kind of contemplative people and even to be unjust toward them. A revolutionary event is no parlor game, but rather dilemma and tearing apart, breaking and impulse, but it is also the only opportunity (and watch out when it is lost!) that a human being has for participating in a collective assumption of dignity.[10]

Through these and many other examples, many intellectuals left no doubt that they did not find Cuba to be a cultural wasteland where *apparatchicki* decided what should or should not be published. Rather, they found a society producing the kind of art, literature, and cinema that can only come from countries that have been "liberated." The purity of the revolutionary process was inspiring, and a refusal to participate, as Benedetti believed, was totally undignified.

Favorable perceptions lasted until the early 1970s, despite the fact that evidence was readily available regarding the repression of dissidents, arbitrary arrests, political imprisonment, persecution of homosexuals and others regarded as "deviants," and political executions. Freedom of the press lacked an existence as well as independent trade unions or any other type of antiregime organizations. Religious life was systematically suppressed—the Catholic Church's presence was negligible, atheism was encouraged, and private religious education abolished. In addition, official interpretations of history were the only ones taught, critical thinking suppressed, acceptance of the dialectics of scientific socialism expected, and literary expression was subject to political inspection. Still, many refused to accept that the promise of a democratic revolution had been cynically and consciously abandoned by the revolutionary elite and its communist allies, and a good number attributed the regime's crackdown on freedom to Washington's hostility. A sectarian but influential minority nonetheless held that freedom was a vacuous bourgeois concept that should righteously be discarded into history's ash heap.

The material improvements brought about by revolutionary change were (and are still to some extent) widely hailed. Many believed that Cuba had eliminated illiteracy, that it had created a full-employment economy, that superior health care systems had been put into place, and that chronic rural-urban imbalances were corrected. This created a perception—sustained by the regime's unceasing propaganda—that Cuba had finally solved some of the most perplexing problems associated with underdevelopment, and that its radical brand of socialism offered equality with abundance. As a consequence of this optimism, Cuba became a model to be studied, discussed, emulated, and, if possible, replicated elsewhere, independent of what local conditions were. All along, pilgrimages to the island continued, famous theorists of development like Gunnar Myrdal expressed admiration for Cuba's achievements, and the critical writings of Rene Dumont and K. S. Karol were hardly appreciated. In the words of Carlos Alberto Montaner: "Cuba wanted to be a paradigm, and it needed spokesmen, 'relaying stations,' echoes, mirror games and other tools which would multiply its voice and image. The intellectuals were good for this."[11]

The climate of opinion shifted in the aftermath of the "Padilla affair," and Havana was roundly condemned for its imprisonment of a writer who had not committed any material crime. Heberto Padilla, well known abroad, was arrested by the secret police for allegedly writing antirevolutionary literature and was eventually forced to recant and "confess" to his wrongdoing. Some compared his confession to similar experiences during the Moscow show trials of the 1930s and took Padilla's arrest as an indication that literature was coming under pervasive state control.[12] Fidel Castro, in a fit of rage, denounced the very intellectuals he had been courting, demanding an explanation of the circumstances under which Padilla was humiliated. A group of intellectuals in turn criticized the police state mentality that prevailed in Cuba and exhorted the regime "to prevent Cuba from falling into dogmatic obscurantism, cultural xenophobia and the repressive system that Stalinism had imposed in socialist countries."[13] Castro promptly rejected the written appeal of Vargas Llosa, Carlos Fuentes, Hans Magnus Enzenberger, Juan Goytisolo, Alberto Moravia, Susan Sontag, Jean-Paul Sartre, Simone de Beauvior, and others, calling them "rats" and "imperialist lackeys." Subsequently, the First National Congress for Education and Culture, held in 1971, attacked those opportunists who "tried to penetrate us with their soft ideas, to impose on us their fashions and gestures, and even to act as judges of the revolution." Leaving no doubt of where it stood, the Congress declared that:

We condemn the deceitful Latin American writers who, after the first few successes achieved with works that still expressed these countries' drama, broke their ties with their countries of origin and took refuge in the capitals of the rotten and decadent societies of Western Europe and the United States, where they became agents of the metropolitan imperialist culture. . . . They will only find in revolutionary countries the contempt that traitors and turncoats deserve.[14]

Not surprisingly, this episode put an abrupt end to the idealization of Cuban socialism among many foreign intellectuals, and it forced them to rethink just what values the system which they had long defended really stood for.

From that point on, debate on Cuba focused on the impact that ideological orthodoxy and "socialist realism" had on arts and literature, and on the nation's cultural stagnation. Padilla himself left Cuba in 1980, as did Reynaldo Arenas and several other writers. Finally, Jorge Edward's publication in 1974 of the novel *Persona Non Grata,* in which he demonstrated how manifestations of independent thought in Cuba were suffocated by the secret police and the cultural commissars, ripped open some lingering taboos and shattered the myth that cultural freedom could thrive under totalitarianism.

The Mariel exodus of 1980 provided fresh evidence of the fact that hundreds of thousands of Cubans were dissatisfied with conditions in the island and were willing to assume major risks in order to leave Cuba. Many of those of the 125,000 who left were young, black, poorly educated, and apolitical, precisely the type of individual for whom the revolution was carried out. These *marielitos* are a good cross-section of the revolutionary generation, and Havana's cynical characterization of them as "scum" did further damage to the image of Cuba as a progressive and humane society. More than any other episode, the Mariel crisis affected how Cuba is perceived in the 1980s, because the scope of the discontent could neither be hidden nor rationalized. Mariel stemmed from an accumulation of grievances rather than from any external cause, and Havana suffered a major public relations defeat.

Young refugees spoke about the lack of a future in Cuba, of the hardships of daily life, of regimentation and ubiquitous politicization, and of a growing sense of anomie and alienation.[15] Socialism meant little or nothing to most of them, and whatever material gains it may have brought them failed to generate lasting political loyalty. Castro's efforts to label the refugees with the most vile slurs—traitors, worms, *vendepatrias*—revealed a contradiction that his propaganda could not resolve: if the refugees were scum, the process of socialization had failed. If they were "good socialist men and women," then why did so many repudiate the society that had nurtured them? In effect, the refugees were unwilling to face what was evidently a very bleak outlook at the beginning of this decade, and the subsequent deterioration of the Cuban economy could well produce still another massive outflow.

The impact of the Mariel exodus on Latin American governments, on opinion makers, on a good many intellectuals, and on political observers of different perspectives was substantial. Havana's efforts to minimize the damage to its "progressive" image, such as calling for massive demonstrations in Cuba against the *marielitos,* suggested that it believed the crisis to be real. With little doubt, Castro blundered when he stated publicly that all who wanted to leave could do so, one of his more glaring miscalculations during the crisis. Mariel forced a reassessment of thinking about Cuba, of just what socialism had achieved—and what it had failed to satisfy—and of the values that shaped life in a highly regimented society. Furthermore, a "calculus of pain" was discovered insofar as individual freedoms and entrepreneurial initiative were severely limited as a consequence of forced revolutionary change. All but the most recalcitrant ideologues and apologists for Cuba could not but ask themselves: What did the sacrifice of a generation accomplish? How could Cuban socialism generate so much disaffection? Why are the values that Cuba stands for being repudiated by hundreds of thousands, perhaps millions, of its people? Is the system itself inhuman, or does the responsibility lie with its agents? Thus, partly as a consequence of Mariel, hardly anyone seriously proposes anymore that the Cuban model be emulated, or that revolutionary socialism produces material satisfaction and spiritual freedom, or that communist one-party rule brings anything but political stagnation and servitude. It may have taken more than two decades for the evident failures of this experiment to affect how Cuba is viewed abroad, but the scales have fallen from many eyes and perceptions are becoming more realistic.

Many intellectuals contribute to the international debate on human rights, which has at times focused on Havana's treatment of dissenters, nonconformists, religious believers, and lately, Marxist critics of the regime like the former university professor Ricardo Bofill. Reports from Amnesty International, the Organization of American States' Commission on Human Rights, and the U.S. State Department's Office of Human Rights have been consistently critical of what is deemed to be a conscious and persistent violation of human rights by the Cuban government.[16] The regime's performance in two areas—treatment of prisoners and conditions throughout the penal system, and continuing persecution, harassment, and arbitrary arrest of dissenters—have been severely criticized. The Cuban Committee for Human Rights, established by Bofill and others in 1980, points out that political executions go on, that the legal system does not offer material relief to known dissenters of "scientific socialism," and that Cuba has not allowed inspection by outside observers of its dreaded penal institutions. Fresh evidence of mistreatment is given by Bofill himself, who has to seek asylum in the French embassy in Havana because he is constantly harassed by the authorities. In letters to *The Miami Herald,* Bofill includes the following account:

> Hace unos meses se encontraba en le hospital de la cárcel del Combinado del Este el profesor José Antonio Penabaz, preso político por motivos de conciencia y combatiente por los derechos civiles. Le rompieron el cráneo a culatazos, por cuya causa sufre graves dolencias. El gobierno lo acusa de "propaganda enemiga." Falso. Es un opositor pacífico a la barbarie. Nada más.[17]

At one point, Cuba had the highest ratio of political prisoners to population in the world, and there is reason to believe that several thousand political prisoners are still serving time. In the early 1980s, the Law of Dangerousness *(la ley de peligrosidad)* allowed the authorities to add up to four years to a prisoner's sentence after it had been completed, as a form of preventive detention. It has been used in a number of cases.

Finally, recent arrivals from Cuba provide more credible evidence of the regime's brutality towards a defenseless prison population, and of its willingness to exchange prisoners for episodic recognition. Ramón Pedro Grau Alsina, a nephew of former president Ramón Grau San Martín, was jailed in 1965 for conspiring to kill Fidel Castro, but, along with 64 others, is now a free man. Said Grau upon his arrival in Miami: "Whenever they hit you, when they treat you wrong, when they don't give you food and you are starving, you go on because you have faith. That's why I survived."[18] Similar accounts were provided by several others, many of whom had also served lengthy prison terms. The prisoner's release stems from the regime's desire to improve its image abroad and better its relations with the U.S. Catholic Church. As will be later discussed, the Church was instrumental in obtaining these prisoners' release, and it had engaged the regime in other delicate negotiations.

Much of this evidence reaches the outside world, through personal testimonies, information smuggled out of prisons in Cuba, statements from defectors and former prisoners, and occasional diplomatic *démarches.* Efforts by the regime, particularly in Europe and Latin America, to combat the devastating impact on its image of this kind of information have, for the most part, failed, and the truth about the horrors of life in the Cuban gulag is increasingly accepted. This has also contributed to a further deterioration of Cuba's image, even in some "progressive circles," and to qualitative changes in how Cuba is perceived.

Since 1979, three very different events have contributed to changing the context in which Cuba is viewed abroad. The release in October 1979 of Major Huber Matos, one of Cuba's most famous political prisoners, and the dissemination of his testimony about his 20 years in prison, rekindled interest in the continuing plight of his brethren, and led to thoughtful analysis of the Cuban political system. Matos visited the White House and was received by President Carter; he has traveled to several Latin American countries and spoken of the cruelties inflicted on Cuban political prisoners and is now working as part of a movement for a free and democratic Cuba. His personal testimony, and corroborating accounts from other prisonmates regarding the brutal treatment that Matos at times received, helped to destroy the myth that Cuban socialism was "benevolent."

Films like *Improper Conduct*, widely shown in the United States and Europe, bring out the ostracism and hostility directed at homosexuals and other "social deviants" by an intolerant and repressive culture. The film provoked the ire of Cuba's cultural *apparat* at the Instituto Cinematográfico, but their counteroffensive only suggested that the film sends an effective message. In fact, *Improper Conduct* savages the state's efforts to define what is proper and improper behavior. It brings out deeply rooted homophobic attitudes in Castro and other members of the inner circle, and it documents efforts to stamp out all but the most innocuous forms of artistic, literary, and cinematographic expression. Cuba is portrayed as a cultural wasteland, where censorship is effective but costly, and where open challenges to communist orthodoxy continue to exact official retribution. With sound techniques, the film exposes the regime's paranoia, its fear of ideas and debate, its suppression of independent or "revisionist" trends, and its systematic war against criticism and free thought. In short, the message is that, if anything, the Stalinist practices condemned by foreign intellectuals in the early 1970s have been institutionalized, that all artistic activity must follow Marxist-Leninist orientations, and that a vast cultural bureaucracy is in charge of officially defining reality. Most of the reviews that I have read are quite favorable, and even *The Village Voice* conceded that the film's portrayals raised troubling questions regarding the narrow limits of cultural expression imposed by the Cuban regime.

Finally, the publication of Armando Valladares' prison memories, *Against All Hope* (1986), is bound to have a devastating effect against the views of those intellectuals who, when it comes to Cuba, still "see nothing and approve of everything." It was Valladares' misfortune to serve time in several of Cuba's most infamous penal institutions (Isla de Pinos, Boniato, et al.), and his chilling tale is indeed comparable to Solzhenitsyn's *Gulag Archipelago*. He was subjected to all forms of injury and degradation, served time in solitary confinement and isolation, was beaten on many occasions, and saw fellow prisoners being bayoneted and shot. All of this was done for the explicit purpose of breaking his (and others') will, and to let them know that "The Revolution" was not to be trifled with. In the end, Valladares is thankful for the campaign launched on his behalf by Amnesty International and the Swedish PEN club, and of efforts by prestigious figures like Ernesto Sábato, Vargas Llosa, Eugene Ionesco, Bernard Henri Levy, and Jeane Kirkpatrick. He is quite critical of the double standard that some European social democrats use to judge Castro's dictatorship, still seen as less of an evil than right-wing regimes. Now living in Madrid, Valladares is a strong voice against Cuban totalitarianism, and he is in a position to influence how Cuba is perceived.

Valladares' book is important because it finally lays to rest the pernicious belief that Cuba was building a humane society, one where individual dignity was valued and protected. Reviewers accepted Valladares' indictment of the Cuban regime, and David Rieff wrote in *The New Republic* that, once upon a time, "Cuba certainly didn't seem like East Germany with palm trees. It was a dream—and dreams die hard." Rieff believes that the book "will endure as one of the finest and most moving accounts written in our time of anyone's imprisonment . . . the definitive account of Fidel Castro's particular improvisations in dystopia." But the review's real value lies in Rieff's admonition: "What remains to be seen is whether those of us who gave the Cuban revolution its limitless moral overdraft are willing to accept the shame and discomfiture [the book] should by all rights provoke."

A similar account was written by Ronald Radosh in *The New York Times Book Review* ("Surviving Castro's Tortures"), and Paul Grey wrote in *Time* magazine that the book is "the most detailed and irrefutable description yet published of the suffering engendered in Cuba by communism and Fidel Castro." Grey concludes that *Against All Hope* may not convince Castro's "most determined apologists. . . . But what has altered is the climate in which such defenses will now be heard."[19] In short, serious critics in prestigious publications have clearly seen Valladares' central theme, namely that Cuban communism, in its totality, is antithetical to cherished notions of human freedom, dignity, and self-worth. In the future, discussion and analysis of this gripping indictment of totalitarianism in Cuba will affect many in the scholarly community, in the secular intelligentsia, and in clear-minded intellectual circles.

To recapitulate, a critical body of evidence furnished by Cuban exiles and emigrés, respected writers and artists, scholarly observers, and U.S. government sources has helped to balance the debate on Cuba and given it a much more critical and probing edge. Havana's propaganda machine is effective and extensive, and the regime makes good use of what Paul Hollander calls "the techniques of hospitality" during visits to Cuba by a dwindling number of political pilgrims.[20] Yet time and credible information have turned the lie on the regime, and its image has been tarnished for good. It is the judgment here that qualitative changes in the way Cuba is perceived by serious-minded intellectuals are under way, and that the "hard left" is losing its grip, except perhaps in surrealistic enclaves in some institutions of higher education.

Perceptions of Cuba in the International Community

With a few exceptions, the perception that most states have of Cuba, particularly in the Third World, is favorable. To put it differently, there is a great deal in the Cuban experience that many developing states admire and identify with, particularly with Cuba's ability to defy the United States. President Castro has many friends in the Third World and is held in high esteem by several heads of state and other leaders in the Non-aligned Movement (NAM). Cuba's leadership in the movement is appreciated, and it has yet to be adversely affected by Cuba's special relationship with the Soviet Union. Given the anti-Western tone of NAM, this is not surprising.

The period during which Cuba was ostracized and largely isolated in Latin America has passed, and a number of Latin American nations (Ecuador, Argentina, Brazil, Colombia, Uruguay, and Bolivia) do business with Cuba once again. It would not have been so if Cuba was still perceived as a threat, viewed with suspicion, or if the domestic political costs outweighed by a considerable margin the potential gains that may come from restoring ties to Cuba. Cuban expansionism has receded, except in Central America, and there is some evidence to suggest that Castroism is seen as something of the past, if not a spent force.

Latin America is much better prepared to deal with Cuba in the 1980s than was the case earlier, because the appeal of revolutionary violence is waning, and because the evident failures of the Cuban system weaken Castro's hand. A case can be made that the greater need to restore contacts with key Latin American governments is demonstrably on the side of Cuba, and in fact Havana is making strong initiatives in that direction.[21] The process of reengaging Cuba with the rest of Latin America stems from the belief that significant payoffs will come from a normalization in relations, and Havana's role of a suitor makes it more convenient for Latin America to reciprocate. Cuba needs to take advantage of an emerging structure of incentives offered to it by Latin America, and its conduct intends to create the perception that it is becoming "a good citizen."

It is probable that Latin America finds Cuba's propensity for strategic intrusions to be curbed in the 1980s, except in the vulnerable Central American region. Realistically, Argentina, Brazil, Venezuela, Peru, and even Colombia have little to fear from Cuba, and they perceive Havana to be in a phase of retrenchment. Castro's attempt to build a united front in Latin America around the issue of debt repudiation has failed, weakening his standing on the continent and suggesting that in the end, the emperor has no clothes. Cuba's failure to come to the rescue of its Grenadian client in 1983 showed Havana to be something of an unreliable ally, and had a sobering effect on the regional left. Cuba's position in Nicaragua is not comfortable, and is subject to increasing pressure from Washington; it could well find itself in a very compromising strategic dilemma.[22] In sum, the geopolitical balance in Central America has shifted against Cuba and its allies, and the political balance throughout Latin America favors democratic forces. Structural conditions thus effectively limit Cuba's ability to foster mischief, even if its long-term ambitions remain constant.

The facts about Cuba's overwhelming dependence on the communist bloc are understood in Latin America, and Cuba's failure to repudiate its own massive debt with capitalist countries while calling for Latin America to repudiate its obligations do little for its credibility.[23] Cuba owes over $3.5 billion to Western banks and financial institutions, and it has had to reschedule some of its obligations several times. Cuba's debt to communist countries is more than $11 billion, and there is little likelihood that it will ever be paid. Cuba's trade with the capitalist world has declined from 26 percent of its external trade in 1980 to less than 15 percent in 1986, largely because Cuba has great difficulty in obtaining hard currency. Falling oil prices in 1985–86 have adversely affected Cuba's ability to resell some of the oil supplied to it by the Soviets, and revenues from this source are down substantially. Indeed, as an analysis of a secret report submitted by Cuba's National Bank (BNC) to its creditors makes perfectly clear: "Twenty-seven years after the revolution, Cuba's economic difficulties continue to grow, with no solution in sight. The systematic failure to take off economically is generating tensions with the Soviets, who have become hostage to Fidel Castro's combination of economic incompetence and his ambitions to play a major role in the world arena."[24] Cuba's insertion into a new structure of dependence in the communist world can hardly give rise to favorable perceptions of its economic performance, and in fact, detracts from its attacks on the problems of capitalist economies.

Among radical and moderate Arab states, and in parts of central and sub-Saharan Africa, Cuba is perceived as an antiimperialist fighter and valuable political ally, as well as a nation contributing experience and human capital to the struggle against underdevelopment. Cuba's relations with Zambia, Zimbabwe, Tanzania, and of course, Angola, are close, and black Africa welcomes Havana's militant stand against South Africa and apartheid. Cuba supports the ANC's call for armed struggle against Pretoria, and helps to train fighters in camps based in Angola.[25] Its calls for the independence of Namibia dovetail with the demands of several "frontline" states, all of whom identify South Africa as a detested regional pariah.

Governments in the region view apartheid and South Africa's economic might as a greater threat to their interests than Cuban/Soviet collaboration in Angola and elsewhere, so it may be perceived as a necessary deterrent against massive retaliation by South Africa. Nationalistic regimes of the "African-socialist" or Marxist type, burdened with the legacy of anticolonialism and anti-Westernism that dominates their foreign policy, fail to view Havana's intrusions into Africa realistically, and underestimate the dangers of Moscow's penetration through Havana. In effect, as long as Havana gives material support to black liberation movements like SWAPO and the ANC, and protects the Angolan regime, leaders like Mugabe of Zimbabwe and Machel of Mozambique will not raise their voices against Cuba. For example, President Castro's speech at the Eighth Summit of NAM held in Zimbabwe was welcomed by most African leaders, and Castro once more linked the presence of Cuban troops in Angola to the existence of apartheid in South Africa. He said:

> The presence of Cuban troops in Angola is based on principles, and is not motivated by matters having to do with Cuba's national interest or prestige. When apartheid ceases, when the fascist and racist regime in south Africa no longer exists, no country would feel threatened. Namibia would be immediately independent, not a single Cuban soldier would be needed, and one could proceed immediately in the total withdrawal of Cuban troops in Angola.[26]

If there is some apprehension in the region regarding what is ultimately a substantial foreign military presence in an African state, it has yet to become a salient geopolitical issue. One sees no evidence that the region feels that presence to be a new form of colonialism, or that it may lead to the permanent "satellization" of Angola. It is not unreasonable to conclude that nationalistic African states welcome the extensive Cuban/Soviet presence in their midst, and use it as a bargaining chip with which to leverage the West's support for South Africa. Mired in economic difficulties, and facing various forms of armed internal resistance, the last thing these states need is to ride the Cuban/Soviet tiger by the tail, or to feel confident about their ability to jump off in the future.

Perceptions are directly affected by ideology, and Cuba avoids paying the price for supporting some of the most brutal and repressive regimes in Africa largely because *tercermundistra* rhetoric obscures the sheer cruelty with which some of Cuba's African allies treat their peoples. Such is the case with Ethiopia, where the documented inhumanity of Mengistu Haile's detestable regime fails to make Havana cringe, or move it to disassociate itself from what the Dergue really is—a thuggish clique. Castro has praised Mengistu as "one of the most able" leaders in the developing world, and Mengistu was welcomed with open arms in Havana in late 1985, precisely at a time when hundreds of thousands were starving in Ethiopia. Cuba still has some 5,000 troops in Ethiopia, but the perception remains that Cuban troops are needed in order to deter against a potential attack from Somalia, rather than the fact that Cuban forces are there to serve Soviet interests in the Horn. Some reports suggested that Cubans helped to suppress the rebellion against a pro-Soviet faction in South Yemen earlier this year, and that the Soviets welcome the troops' role as a regional fire brigade.[27]

In any event, the stability of Mengistu's regime is dependent on the presence of Cuban forces in Ethiopia, particularly because his war against rebels in the Tigre and Eritrea provinces shows no signs of ending. Havana cannot clean up Mengistu's image, nor its own Machiavellian designs. In short, as William Ratliff points out: "Castro would like the world to forget some of what has happened in the Horn because events there tarnish the carefully cultivated image of Castro as a selfless revolutionary who supports the rights of all suppressed peoples seeking liberation from oppressive—and particularly 'colonial'—governments. The Horn experience disfigures that carefully crafted image."[28]

The perception of Cuba among European states is not antagonistic, and is partly sustained by the uncritical posture toward it adopted by a large part of the social democratic left. Cuba is viewed as a victim of U.S. hostility, and its system appeals to European socialists. Spain, France, Italy, Great Britain, and the Scandinavian countries maintain broad ties with Cuba, as does the Vatican. European communist parties are sympathetic to Havana, and their leaders, such as George Marchais and others, occasionally visit the island. In Spain itself, the left is quite favorable to Cuba, and President Castro is said to be a friend of Premier González and of the Secretary General of the Spanish communist party, Mr. Iglesias. Mr. Castro has not yet paid an official visit to Spain, but he made a brief stop in Madrid in 1984 upon his return from Yuri Andropov's funeral in Moscow. On the other hand, Mr. Castro has criticized Spain for its entry into NATO, something which he views as a historic betrayal. At times, Mr. Castro speaks as someone who believes in the black legend, and has singled out Spanish colonialism as the root of many of Latin America's ills.[29]

Official delegations as well as private groups visit the island regularly, as do representatives of the Socialist International. Particularly favorable to Havana are the views of prominent individuals like Willy Brandt, and of the late Olof Palme, both of whom consider(ed) President Castro to be a world-class statesman. Large numbers of tourists come to Cuba from Europe, and there is every reason to believe that they enjoy themselves thoroughly. *Granma* takes pride in reporting that many tourists are deeply impressed with the "excellent" services provided, and with the friendly character of the people. It is evident that what the regime considers to be aspects of "a decadent and bourgeois culture" elsewhere serve as tourist attractions in revolutionary Cuba, because tourists in particular are interested in the night life. Nelson Fernández, an official of the Cuban Tourist Agency, admits that "in Cuba we offer to the visitor beautiful beaches, night spots *(centros nocturnos)* and cabarets like Tropicana, which is in high demand."[30] With their Panglossian snapshots, Europeans and Canadians return to the northern latitudes in very high spirits.

On the other hand, a book published by a former French communist, Pierre Golendorff, *7 Años en Cuba, 38 Meses en las Prisiones de Fidel Castro* (1977), took issue with the romantic view of Cuban socialism prevalent in Europe, and provided hard evidence of why many Europeans were not getting the full picture. In the introduction, Golendorff wrote that:

> Este libro está escrito contra el engaño que el régimen ha creado en torno al dogma. ¿Cúal es? Es muy simple: poseedor de la verdad científica y absoluta, el partido comunista debe ostentar el poder absoluto y científico. A partir de este dogma y para protegerlo, para ponerlo fuera de alcance, suprimir las incoherencias que resultan del choque con la realidad, se forma un halo engañoso cuyo guardián es el aparato y la represión su arma. Durante siete años, he visto funcionar de cerca este mecanismo.

A large number of dissident Cuban intellectuals either reside in Spain or visit the country frequently, and the Cuban embassy in Madrid is often irritated at their public criticisms of Cuba. For instance, the Fourth Congress of Dissident Cuban Intellectuals held in Madrid in May 1986 featured Carlos Alberto Montaner, Armando Valladares, and others, and it attracted Havana's attention. In this instance, the embassy invited several writers and artists from Cuba for events which it promoted, suggesting that Havana has deployed something of a cultural offensive in Europe and particularly in Spain, designed to counteract what is perceives is the "black image of Cuba" portrayed in *Improper Conduct* and in a number of emigré publications. Spain's return to democracy permits debate on Cuba to take place freely and without fear of repression, but as a matter of prudence and statecraft, the socialist government is not expected to mount a crusade against Havana. The opposition, particularly that led by Mr. Fraga, remains quite critical of Cuba and Castro.

With the possible exception of London and Bonn, Europe does not perceive Cuba to pose a strategic threat to the United States in Central America—and a good many European officials still hold that the U.S. should not take Cuban expansionism in the region too seriously. On this matter, perceptions take on distinctly partisan nuances. Christian Democrats are inclined to view Cuban penetration of Central America with greater geopolitical realism than their Social Democratic opponents. For example, Alois Mertes, an influential official in West German's Foreign Office during Christian Democratic governments, writes that one of the reasons interest about Central America has been revived in Western Europe is because of "Soviet and Cuban attempts to exploit the situation in the region in order to promote the long-term expansion of Soviet-controlled communist parties, and by Moscow and Havana's use of military intimidation to achieve that end." On the other hand, the former Spanish foriegn minister, Fernando Morán, known to articulate views representative of the socialist party's left wing, holds that Cuban policies in the region stem from Cuba's isolation, because "not having normal relations with the countries of the area may well have made Cuba's influence as a revolutionary power greater than it would have been if Cuba had economic interests to defend."[31]

Some Europeans have trouble accepting the fact that Cuba is a bona fide member of the communist bloc, that it is closely aligned with the Soviet Union, and that the Cuban leadership is comfortable with that status. As one finds a perception in parts of Latin America that Cuba is besieged by the United States and is forced to stand on a permanent war alert because of the U.S. threat, so is the thinking among some in Europe. This view fails to take account of how mobilization and militarization are key features of Cuban communism, and of the reasons why the regime must have a convenient scapegoat like the United States. It appears that perceptions of U.S. policy in Latin America have a bearing on how Cuba is seen in Europe, so the source of this view may well be Washington's conduct and not Havana's. If one believes that Washington is being unreasonable, perhaps aggressive, in the region, one may then view Cuba's conduct as rational or defensive, without taking stock of Havana's actual conduct or past record. This leads to the view that Havana is a victim or a target of U.S. hostility, not an aggressive state in its own right.

The belief that Cuban nationalism is potent and that it may well be the decisive factor in explaining Cuban behavior shapes a view of Cuba that is only partially correct. Revolutionaries, particularly before they gain power, portray themselves as genuine nationalists rather than as communists, in order to confuse their adversaries and hide their long-term goals. At one time, revolutionary leaders like Castro, Ho Chi Minh, Mao Tse-tung, and the Sandinistas were thought of as committed nationalists, rather than either as Marxist-Leninists or disciplined communists. But nationalism and Marxism-Leninism blend well in practice, and in the case of Cuba, infuse its foreign policy with a sense of arrogance and "small power chauvinism" not found in that of conventional states. Furthermore, nationalism has neither been a deterrent against the partial Sovietization of Cuban society, nor has it led to a genuine reassessment of Cuba's growing economic dependence and massive indebtedness with the Soviet Bloc. When Castro speaks of the Soviet Union or to the Soviet leadership, he sounds more like an obedient client than a fiery nationalist, because he has nothing but praise for Moscow.

Nationalistic fervor has made it easier to rewrite history and blame U.S. neocolonial influences for Cuba's stunted development, as if socialism had in fact "developed" the country. Nationalism has failed to stimulate an inquiry into the sources of Cuba's nationhood, partly because its strength has been to create a siege mentality. In short, nationalism has been manipulated by the regime to suit its immediate domestic and foreign policy goals, and in order to sweep its more glaring failures under the rug. Once the source of genuine aspirations for self-determination and viable nationhood, nationalism has turned into a reactionary force placed at the disposal of revolutionary mandarins.

Anti-Americanism also contributes indirectly to Europe's largely favorable perception of Cuba. Cuba is perceived to be the strongest expression of anti-Americanism in Latin America, and its defiance of the United States is taken as evidence of its will and self-confidence. Many on the left who would normally not sympathize with Napoleon-like dictators like Castro admire his stiff backbone and his ability to rile Washington. At the source of this admiration lies Castro's own leadership style, and the sheer force of his personality, but there is also the fact that for many, Castro and Cuba provide vicarious thrills. Indeed, as Edward Gonzalez notes:

> The many sides of Castro's personality have enabled him to attract many different types of followers. He is a man of action, endowed with impressive physical stature, courage and audacity; he is also a leader with superior intelligence, singular determination and strategic vision. The faithful thus include not only revolutionary activists, but also intellectuals and idealists of moderate as well as radical persuasions.[32]

Admiration for Castro is thus a source of favorable perceptions about Cuba, and he is perceived to be at his best when hurling bolts against the despised Yankees.

The sources of anti-Americanism in Europe and elsewhere are multiple, but, as Paul Hollander suggested in his book *Political Pilgrims* (1981), profound alienation and disenchantment with one's own society leads some individuals to idealize other societies, particularly those that pay lip service to abstract notions of social egalitarianism. This applies to intellectuals as well as policymakers, and to members of influential elites (journalists, academics, church leaders) in Western pluralist societies. If postindustrial democracy in the West is perceived as chaotic, materialistic, and invariably dehumanizing, and if the United States in particular is seen as an agent of exploitation and destruction abroad, societies that define themselves to be the very antithesis of "the American way of life" are judged to be superior. Such may be the case with Cuba, where an organic reaction against "the consumer society" and the highly moralistic pursuit of social radicalism are precisely the elements that fascinate many western observers. For instance, campaigns in Cuba about the "New Man" created not just a perception that human nature could be changed through coercive state action, but a *fixation* with the ideal that selflessness could be induced in the new generations and egoistic behavior eliminated. Similar efforts had failed in other revolutionary-utopian societies like the Soviet Union and China, but it was believed that Cuba could really succeed in this area.

Evidence demonstrating that the episodic campaigns to flesh out the "New Man" have been colossal failures, and that profit-oriented and materialist attitudes are part of the new political culture, should lead to the conclusion that the ideal has yet to be realized, and that the process of changing behavior has been quite costly. But to some extent, Cuba is still living off the utopian intentions that are now buried in its most radical past and repressive memories. The powerful millenary myths that they spawned still appeal to deep-seated emotional attachments. As Hollander himself concludes: "Many myths and illusions about Cuba continue to find receptive audiences among those estranged from and hostile to American society. Cuban political hospitality has been successful in confirming and solidifying the beliefs of those who were susceptible to its messages in the first place."[33]

In conclusion, Western European governments maintain normal relations with Cuba, but perceive it in somewhat different terms depending on which party is ruling, or which wing of a particular party is dominant. Moderates and conservatives perceive Cuba to be a focal point of East-West tensions, whereas liberals and socialists view it as a nation struggling to defend itself in the face of a permanent threat. A similar structure of perceptions characterizes how Cuba fits into the thinking of key elites in Europe (and in the U.S. to a lesser degree), but as more evidence becomes available about "the underside of Cuban socialism," favorable perceptions may be revised. Cuba values political and conventional tourism, and it exploits a willingness to believe found in many visitors. Mariel and the activities of dissidents and emigrés are shaping a much harsher image of what Cuban society is really like.

Perceptions of Cuba's Relationship with the Soviet Union

Perceptions about Cuba's relationship with the Soviet Union are contradictory. On the one hand, there are those who believe Cuba's client status to be quite different from, for example, Poland's, because Castro's unruly temperament and Cuba's brand of communism prevent its total Sovietization and subordination. It is thought that nationalism is stronger than ideology, and that Cuba's assertion of its own interests may at times not dovetail with Soviet goals.[34] Those in this camp use Cuba's role in Angola as an example of its assertiveness, and maintain that while joint campaigns in Africa by Cuba and the Soviet Union serve the interests of both, Cuba actually took the lead in Angola and persuaded Moscow to come along. There may be other cases, such as Grenada, where Cuba was much closer to the Bishop regime than Moscow, and the latter failed to make a major investment in the New Jewel Movement. This perception is very strong in the academic community, and has some advocates in U.S. government circles. And, yet, its proponents often overestimate Havana's autonomy, and fail to point out that in the 1980s, nowhere does Havana contravene Moscow.

A second, but not nearly as dominant, group perceives Havana as Moscow's satellite, doing the latter's bidding abroad and accepting Soviet-style communism at home. Many conservatives hold this view, including persons in the foreign policy community and the media. They argue that the asymmetry in power between Havana and its superpower sponsor is such that it would be ridiculous to think that Moscow could not have its way if it really wanted. In March 1985, President Reagan said in response to a question on a possible change of leadership in Cuba that "all of us dream of a Cuba that will one day recognize that it should be once again a member of the American States in the Western Hemisphere and not a satellite of the Soviet Union." Those who hold this view point to Cuba's overwhelming dependence on the Soviet Union, and maintain that it places severe limitations on Cuba and oblige it to defer to Moscow's designs. Some scholars believe that this is a very superficial way to look at Cuba's relationship with the Soviet Union, but recognize that it may be convenient for policymakers to do so.

Still others, including myself, perceive Cuba to be neither a Soviet proxy nor a largely independent actor that can afford to deviate substantially from the Soviet line. Edward Gonzalez uses the notion of Cuba as a "paladin" to reflect its crusading spirit and championing of revolutionary causes that Moscow can also support. David Ronfeldt has called Cuba a "superclient," suggesting that it has some leverage over the Soviets, and that they, in turn, afford Cuba a preferred status among their Third World partners. I am comfortable with either notion, and believe Cuba to have behaved as a "senior partner" of the Soviet Union in several ventures in the Third World. And yet these perceptions were framed at a time when Cuban internationalism was peaking in the late 1970s, and may need to be revised now that its activism is meeting resistance and Cuba has suffered a major defeat in Grenada. There is some reason to believe that the new Soviet leaders do not subscribe to Castro's militant internationalism, and may yet place clear limits on how far out in front Havana can get. In sum, it would be a mistake to perceive Cuba as a passive actor, or as one that has curbed its inclination for adventurism. Castro's *modus operandi* features strategic opportunism with tactical pragmatism, and his regime knows how to take advantage of those who underestimate its will and capabilities.[35]

To sum up, perceptions of Cuba in this area are situational and issue-oriented, and subject to nuances in the global correlation of forces. Perceptions reduce complex phenomena to simple categories and can mislead policymakers who are unaware of the dangers of "psychologic,"—the tendency to see what one wishes to see and respond to situations or crises in line with subjective wishes. This has major policy implications because if one thinks of Havana as little more than Moscow's agent, one is likely to pursue policies that seek to affect Cuban behavior through intermediaries, rather than focusing on Cuba itself.

In practical terms, Cuba's relationship with the Soviet Union invariably constrains its freedom of action, and is in some ways similar to Israel's relationship with the United States. Cuba's right to self-defense is recognized, and the Soviet role in that is seen as legitimate. Given its perception of the U.S. threat, Cuba has a legitimate right to enter into strategic and military relationships that would raise the cost of "imperialist aggression." A mutually convenient understanding between Cuba and the Soviet Union on defense serves that need, even if it falls short of an alliance. In fact, the Soviet Union refrains from explicitly gurantecing Cuba's security, and President Castro believes that in the crunch, Cuba may have to fight alone and depend on itself rather than on Moscow. Contingencies would clearly vary according to circumstances, but it is hard to imagine that the Soviet Union would sit idly by if a major military move is mounted against Cuba—or that Cuba's adversaries could fail to gauge what the probable Soviet response would be under such circumstances.

On the other hand, Cuba has created the perception that it is the bravery and capability of its armed forces, and the "moral courage" of its people, that ultimately deter foreign aggression, rather than any Machiavellian *entente* with Moscow. Not being a member of the Warsaw Pact adds some credibility to Cuban claims, particularly in NAM and with others in the Third World who might be forced to rethink their sympathetic views of Cuba if it entered into a formal military alliance. This situation is highly advantageous for Cuba, because it reinforces the image that it is responsible for its own protection and does not owe its sovereignty to anyone else. It also adds a touch of charm to Castro's harangues against the U.S., and probably brings a measure of admiration from weak nations that insist on viewing themselves as victims of Western powers.

In the 1980s, Cuba's expanding military capabilities are not always perceived to stem from calculated strategic decisions, but as logical responses to aggressive moves by its principal enemy. In other words, there is a tendency to see them as defensive, rather than as adding leverage to its foreign policy. By the skillful use of language, propaganda and disinformation, Cuba manages to be seen not as a major offensive military power, but as a state that must always be on guard because as President Castro reminds us, "imperialism never sleeps." Secretary of State Alexander Haig's remarks in 1981 about "going to the source" in order to stop Cuban meddling in Central America bolstered Havana's claims that it was rapidly acquiring Soviet weapons because U.S. threats could quickly materialize. In such a climate, the perception that Cuba was a target gained wide acceptance, and it actually helped Cuba to strengthen itself militarily without having to pay much of a political price.

It is not the first time that a nation's military buildup is perceived to be legitimate—and not necessarily a threat to the interests of rival powers. The expansion of Germany's military capabilities in the 1930s was thought by many to be logical and justifiable, because of historical threats to Germany and due to the alleged harshness of the Versailles Treaty. Likewise, the Soviet buildup of the 1970s, during a period of spasmodic accommodation between East and West, was seen by many in the West not as a long-term strategic threat, but as a rational improvement in the Soviets' military force posture. Finally, many hold that the unprecedented military expansion under way in Nicaragua, which has brought sophisticated Soviet "flying tanks" into Central America, is intended solely for defensive purposes. Nicaragua's buildup is thus not seen as something that upsets the military balance in Central America, or intimidates Nicaragua's neighbors, largely because the Sandinista regime is not believed to have expansionist aims. In each of these cases, the perception of what is the true nature of arms buildups eventually changed, and led to justifiable alarm in the particular region. Countermeasures were then taken to cope with the new reality, but that, in turn, fed fears on the part of the state that initiated the buildup. Still, time is crucial, and by the time perceptions catch up with empirical changes, the situation is clearly more dangerous. This raises the costs of confronting the state that threatens the balance, and forces a change in tactics and strategy.

Aggressive and expansionist states like Cuba (or Nicaragua) routinely claim that their weapons pose no threat to anyone, and Castro has often said that no government in Latin America has anything to fear from Cuban arms. That can mean a number of different things, because it is a fact that all of Cuba's weapons are acquired gratis from Soviet Bloc countries, and Cuba is a transfer point for weapons (of different manufacture) going to several Latin America guerrilla movements. The real paradox lies in the fact that despite massive evidence of Cuba's aggressive behavior, and of its known links to guerrilla groups in several countries, Havana's claims of noninterference in others' affairs are often believed and ultimately accepted. Self-deception on the part of Havana's adversaries may account for why a most powerful state is perceived as a peaceful one, and a denial of reality may be preferable to having to face unpleasant facts squarely.

Serious scholars and regional experts recognize that with the exception of the United States, Cuba is the most powerful state in the Caribbean Basin, and its aggregate military capabilities are judged to be formidable. In addition, Cuban troops are engaged in combat in Angola, provide support to the Marxist-Leninist regime in Ethiopia, and have been deployed in other parts of Africa and the Middle East. Cuban pilots have been reported to be in combat zones in Nicaragua, where experienced generals like Arnaldo Ochoa and Néstor López are in charge of the Cuban military mission in that country, which has some 2,000 Cuban military advisors. Abundant evidence from various sources makes it perfectly clear that Cuban penetration of Nicaragua is deep and broad, reaching into educational, social, and probably religious institutions. Cuba has provided several hundred million dollars in economic and technical assistance to Nicaragua since 1979, and it has transferred technology and equipment intended to improve Nicaragua's sugar industry. Thousands of technical advisors are stationed in Nicaragua, as well as teachers, construction workers, doctors, and health-care personnel.[36] In short, Cuban influence is felt across the spectrum in Nicaragua, but one gets the impression that key Latin American governments perceive that influence to be benign.

And yet, what would the perception be if, for instance, Mexico were to have 10,000 military and civilian advisors in Guatemala stationed in critical technical, intelligence-related, and consultative roles? More than likely, many would be alarmed, characterize such a massive foreign presence as destabilizing, and insist that the Mexicans leave. Such a presence could reasonably be seen as an effort on Mexico's part to extend its influence over an area in which it has definite geopolitical interest, and it could certainly shift the balance in the region. The case is strictly hypothetical, but not unprecedented if one assumes that ambitious states are looking for targets of opportunity, and attempt to capitalize on vulnerabilities that may emerge in their region. The question then arises: why is the Cuban presence in Nicaragua for the most part not perceived as a clear-cut attempt by Cuba to stake out a permanent presence in Central America? Or to put it differently, why has it blended into the landscape, and become an acceptable type of penetration?

To begin with, Cuban involvement in Nicaragua has been incremental, that is, it has been growing over time rather than coming all at once. This avoids raising the noise level without giving up the element of surprise. By moving in an evolutionary fashion, and staking out positions on a piece-meal basis, Cuba is perceived as contributing to the Sandinista regime's stability rather than to its domination. The massive Cuban penetration is no longer deniable, but it has created a new status quo and forced a reassessment in Washington and in Latin America of what is its ultimate objective. It is multifaceted in character, making it advisable for Cuba to highlight its "humanitarian" contributions to Nicaragua, and dismiss arguments that show its alliance with Nicaragua to be a serious threat to regional stability. Thus, the method used by Cuba—incrementalism—and its insistence that others have nothing to fear from its expression of internationalist solidarity towards Nicaragua sustain the perception that all is well, and that Cuba is acting prudently and responsibly.

Second, antagonizing Castro on the grounds that his intrusions in Central America make it more difficult for Cuba to ease itself back into the hemispheric mainstream is not good politics, if the objective is to rebuild ties between Cuba and Latin America. In fact, Cuba has had it both ways: it *is* resuming normal relations with key countries; *and* it has not retreated an inch from its commitments to the Sandinistas. Latin America's refusal to link a definite Cuban pullout from Nicaragua to a resumption in relations with Cuba gives Castro tremendous leverage, allowing him to set the terms on which bargaining and negotiations may proceed. In the final analysis, Latin American governments are in no position to force a Cuban pullout; Castro correctly perceives them as disunited and embroiled in domestic difficulties, and he is willing to string out the process. Cuban intransigence is seldom criticized by Latin American governments, and it is probable that maintaining a hard line wins Cuba much admiration and respect.

Though difficult to detect, it is probable that some influential factions in key Latin American governments may well perceive the Cuban role in Nicaragua as necessary, in order to balance what many think is deepening U.S. involvement in the region. The much-abused and violated norm of nonintervention applies for the most part to U.S. intervention, but Cuba has not entirely escaped criticism for its own intrusions. Still, fears of U.S. intervention are ingrained in the minds of policymakers, and often override other considerations; such fears may nurture the view that Cuban involvement is a counterweight to U.S. pressures. If this were so, then Cuban inroads would not be seen as threats, but as a shield against further U.S. encroachments. In sum, Cuba may not be perceived as a dangerous intruder, but as an armed sentry whose presence must be tolerated even if it is accepted that no one else but Castro would decide on how long the sentry will stay.

The perception of Cuba's role in Nicaragua and of its larger revolutionary mission is also affected by domestic political considerations. Despite the evident economic failures of Cuban socialism, of its repressive character, and of the growing and undeniable ties between the Cuban regime and international terrorism, a government would pay a heavy political and emotional price if it took on Cuba directly. In leftist sectors in the universities, media, political parties, some trade unions, cultural and educational institutions, and most perplexing, in sectors of the Catholic and Protestant churches, there is unabashed admiration for Cuba. Influential communist parties throughout Latin America have patched up their quarrels with Havana, and would surely mobilize their resources on its behalf if its purity were ever questioned. Organized, often militant, blatantly ideological and well-schooled in agitation and confrontation, these sectors create domestic pressures that governments—especially democratic ones—cannot disregard. This is particularly the case in Mexico, increasingly so in Peru, less of a factor in Venezuela and Costa Rica, but evident in Panama, Colombia, and the Dominican Republic. Cuba has effective allies in Latin America, whom it skillfully courts and on whom it can always grant its revolutionary blessing. A good word from Castro is the modern equivalent of a papal bull, because when Fidel speaks *ex cathedra,* his acolytes listen. To take on Cuba is to incur the everlasting wrath of these elements, and to have to cope with the reflexive charge that such a government is an imperialist stooge. Moderate and centrist governments are particularly vulnerable, even if they have all the more reason to perceive the Cuban threat realistically. In the highly charged regional environment, fervor, not reason, is the decisive factor.

Finally, to perceive socialist Cuba as an aggressive state may be a contradiction which many cannot resolve. Expansionism abroad, loyalty to Marxism-Leninism, militarization at home, and a very questionable return to economic radicalism characterize Cuban communism in the 1980s, but many choose to believe that the Cuban leadership runs a conventional shop. Its geopolitical ambitions are seldom well understood, and neither is Castro's penchant for turning vulnerabilities in other systems into opportunities for political extortion. When it comes to judging Cuba's behavior, the communists' version of "peaceful coexistence" is the criterion upon which judgments are made, rather than on the regime's past record of warfare. And since communist states, by their own admission no less, are peace-loving and committed to international harmony, it is wrong-headed to view them with suspicion and wariness.

To the degree that language has been abused and socialism equated with "revolution" and "liberation," one can only be perplexed at the fact that a state embroiled in conflict on three continents is still perceived by many to be peaceful, or committed to objectives that further world order. A chauvinistic state like Cuba, whose leaders are imbued with absolute truths and manfully demonstrate an aura of invincibility, is not to be trifled with, because when they speak of engaging in a permanent war against imperialism, that is exactly what they mean and intend to carry out. Permanent war through overt and covert aggression is their game, carried out in the name of either socialism or world revolution, and always enjoying the intensity of the battle. In Montaner's felicitous phrase: "El olor de la guerra los vuelve locos."

To recapitulate, Cuba's intrusions into Central America would just as soon not be perceived as real threats by Latin American governments because to do so would affect delicate external and internal political balances. The idealized criteria by which Cuba's behavior is judged (those used by her supporters) sustain the myth that her conduct is just like that of any other state seeking influence beyond its borders. Preoccupied with festering social and economic problems and fully conscious of Havana's ability to engage in political extortion by stirring up trouble in other nations through its ties to guerrilla groups and terrorist organizations (Colombia's M-19 is a prime example), governments in Latin America refuse to make the tough choices that are necessary to confront the Cuban threat. Consequently, the danger of Cuban penetration (particularly in Central America) is rationalized and by now accepted, so the costs of doing away with it do not have to be incurred.

Perceptions of Cuba in the Churches

It is increasingly evident that some churches and religious orders have consciously rejected the idea that the fundamental purposes of religion are to improve the spiritual life of believers, and to prepare the faithful for the afterlife. Religious activism has entered into the secular world in full force, not so much to preach how one can be saved, but in order to transform the world. The focus of religious activity is rapidly shifting from the individual soul to the social realm, and its more extreme doctrines stand on the assumption that salvation can come during, not after, life. A strong missionary sense characterizes the pronouncements of some religious groups in the United States as well as in Latin America, and Caesar's domain is constantly scrutinized with religious fervor. The belief in the perfectibility of man through social engineering motivates the work of some religious institutions, and it is thought that improving life's material conditions leads to greater spiritual fulfillment.

Definitions of the "good society" are articulated with Christian ideals in mind, not in order to preserve the Augustinian distinction between the City of God and the City of Man, but in order to identify the political, social, and economic structures which create the "good society." The language of a good many Catholic and Protestant spokesmen in Latin America suggests that for them, the good society is the socialist society, and some churchmen have gone so far as to suggest that communism is that which most closely resembles the Kingdom of God on earth. This has a direct bearing on how Cuban society is perceived, because Christain radicals are favorably impressed with the material achievements of the Cuban revolution, and some of the more confused among them (like the Nicaraguan priest Ernesto Cardenal) insist that in Cuba, the Kingdom is at hand. Not surprisingly, the Brazilian Frei Betto, wholly in tune with some of the more turgid teachings of Liberation theology, affirmed during his interview with President Castro that: "desde el punto de vista evangélico, la sociedad ella misma, inconcientemente, aquello que nosotros, hombres de fé, llamamos los proyectos de Dios en la historia."[37] For Frei Betto and like-minded churchmen, there is a God of the poor, and one of the rich, rather than a diety without "class preferences."

Socialism, with its redemptive promises, levelling effect, and belief in the perfectibility of man, has a strong appeal for Christian radicals, and for some Catholics disaffected with the traditional Church and often unhappy with the glaring inequalities produced by capitalism. Democratic capitalism in particular has had a bad odor to Latin American Catholics for a long time, and its standing has not improved with the emergence of influential sectors identified with Liberation Theology. Cuban socialism is favorably perceived by the more liberal wings of the Catholic and Protestant churches, partly because it is believed that some of the material achievements of that system fulfill Christian promises that the naked be clothed, the hungry fed, and the sick healed. Capitalist and democratic societies like Costa Rica and others have fulfilled the same mission without the suppression of basic freedoms (including freedom of religion), but what Cuba has done is somehow thought to be spectacular. There is good reason to believe that Havana's claims in the health and education fields are suspect, and that in fact its performance in those and other areas is well behind that of capitalist societies, but these facts have yet to make a dent in the minds of committed religious cretins.[38]

Religious groups from the U.S. and Latin America visit Cuba frequently, and make contacts that often lead to the participation of Christians in religion seminars and workshops in Cuba. The Reverend Jesse Jackson visited a Methodist congregation during his visit to Cuba in 1984, and was photographed smiling and radiant in a group that included that new convert to the faith, President Castro.[39] Castro himself has met with some Cuban Catholic bishops, and several meetings have been held between government officials and members of the hierarchy. In February 1986, an Ecclesiastical Encounter took place in Havana to which the Vatican sent Cardinal Pironio, and during which the difficult situation of the Cuban Catholic Church was discussed. Mother Teresa visited Cuba in 1986 also, and has been given permission to do some social work. Finally, the publication of Frei Betto's long-winded interviews with Castro in *Fidel y la Religión* (1985) is affecting the religious climate in Cuba, and slowly reducing the hostility between Church and State.

The Cuban government no longer perceives the Catholic Church in particular to be an "agent of reaction and privilege," and Rome now believes that the more relaxed climate in Cuba may produce new opportunities for the Church. The regime appears to be willing to consider some of the Church's demands, particularly those that call for greater tolerance of religious practices, and the ending of discrimination against Catholics. The Church has blessed some of the social gains achieved under socialism, and is willing to participate in the struggle against alienation, family disintegration, delinquency, and anomie, all of which are starting to alarm the authorities. The process of accommodation is unfolding with few results evident as yet, but it is clear that Havana, Rome, and the Cuban Church are joined in a dialogue. There is some reason to believe that some in the communist party's bureaucracy and elsewhere are resisting even these minor changes, so it is not inconceivable tht the process may be stopped. Lastly, the Vatican has yet to respond formally to President Castro's invitation to the Pope, but it is engaged in the political aspects of the Pope's probable visit to Cuba. The Pope himself is seriously interested in reenergizing the Cuban Church.[40]

To conclude, some Christian radicals believe that socialism creates the conditions for man's material and spiritual fulfillment, but the evidence from Cuba suggests that the quality of life leaves a lot to be desired, and that spiritual fulfillment is difficult under a system officially committed to atheism. The notion that communism would even remotely resemble the Kingdom of God on earth is such a monstrous fantasy that those who articulate such views are little more than charlatans. The Catholic Church and the Cuban regime are mending fences, but the fact that a dialogue is under way does not necessarily mean that basic principles are being compromised on either side, or that there is no residual hostility. Church and State represent antithetical value systems, and each in their own epistemology advances an absolute interpretation of the Truth, but the Cuban regime knows that it pays a high political price abroad for its suppression of religious freedom. The perception of each side is that the time may be ripe for proceeding along a path of mutual convenience, but it would be ludicrous to believe that Fidel Castro or John Paul II are undergoing substantive conversions regarding the nature of either communism or Catholicism.

Notes

1. See Hugh S. Thomas, Georges A. Fauriol and Juan Carlos Weiss, *La Revolución Cubana, 25 Años Después* (Madrid: Editorial Playor, 1985); Juan M. del Aquila, *Cuba: Dilemmas of a Revolution* (Boulder, Colo.: Westview Press, 1984); Carlos Alberto Montaner, *Secret Report on the Cuban Revolution* (New Brunswick, N.J.: Transaction Books, 1981).
2. In a fascinating portrayal of Castro, Edward Gonzalez argues that Castro, the "artful dissembler, has been many men to many people, including former associates who thought they knew him well. He has shown a masterful ability to dissemble and beguile, both in public and in private. He used deceit to mask true intentions, conceal weakness, exaggerate strengths, disarm opponents, and otherwise gain political advantage." Edward Gonzalez and David Ronfeldt, *Castro, Cuba and the World* (Santa Monica, Calif.: Rand Corp. number R-3420, 1986), p. 44.
3. Luis E. Aguilar, *Cuba, conciencia y revolución* (Miami, Fla.: Ediciones Universal, 1972), pp. 127–28.
4. Régis Debray, "Latin America: Some Problems of Revolutionary Strategy," in *Latin American Radicalism,* Irving L. Horowitz et al. eds., (New York: Vintage Books, 1969), p. 513.
5. William E. Ratliff, *Castroism and Communism in Latin America, 1959–1976* (Washington, D.C.: American Enterprise Institute, 1976).
6. Ché Guevara, "Message to the Tricontinental," in *Latin American Radicalism,* p. 113.

7. Joseph A. Kahl, "The Moral Economy of a Revolutionary Society," in Irving L. Horowitz, ed., *Cuban Communism* (New Brunswick, N.J.: Transaction Books, 1970), p. 113.

8. Mario Vargas Llosa, "Crónica de la Revolución," in *Contra Viento y Marea, 1962–1982* (Barcelona: Seix Barral, 1983), pp. 30–35.

9. J. M. Cohen, *Writers in the New Cuba* (Middlesex, U.K.: Penguin Books, 1967), p. 10.

10. Mario Benedetti, "Present Status of Cuban Culture," in Rolando E. Bonachea and Nelson P. Valdés, eds., *Cuba in Revolution,* (Garden City, N.Y.: Anchor Books, 1972), p. 526.

11. Montaner, p. 115.

12. The episode is discussed in Lourdes Casal, "Literature and Society," in Carmelo Mesa-Lago, ed., *Revolutionary Change in Cuba* (Pittsburgh, Pa.: University of Pittsburgh Press, 1971), pp. 447-69.

13. "Carta a Fidel Castro," in Vargas Llosa pp. 166–68. See also Vladimir Tismaneanu, "Revolutionary Myth and Political Unreason," Review Essay *Orbis* 28, 2 (Summer 1984: 389–400. For a more recent critique of Castro and the revolution coming from the literary world, see Fernando Arrabal, *Carta a Fidel Castro* (Madrid: Editorial Playor, 1983).

14. Montaner, pp. 119-25. The entire statement is found here.

15. Robert L. Bach, Jennifer B. Bach, and Timothy Triplett, "The Flotilla Entrants: Latest and Most Controversial," *Cuban Studies* 11, 2: 12, 1 (July 1981–January 1982): pp. 29–48. See also Gastón Fernández, "Comment—The Flotilla Entrants: Are They different," in same issue, pp. 49–54.

16. Inter-American Commission on Human Rights, OAS, *Sixth Report on the Situation of Political Prisoners in Cuba* (1979) and *The Situation of Human Rights in Cuba, Seventh Report* (1983). (Washington, D.C.: n. p.).

17. Ricardo Bofill, "Crímenes desconocidos de Castro," *The Miami Herald,* September 1986, p. 12; "La lucha por los derechos humanos en Cuba," *The Miami Herald,* September 1986; "Bofill denuncia la situación de Gustavo Arcos," *The Miami Herald,* September 1986.

18. "Joy, tears greet 111 Cubans," *The Miami Herald,* 16 September 1986, p. 1A; "Refugees Warily Embrace Freedom," *The New York Times,* 16 September 1986, p. 7; "69 Ex-Prisoners From Cuba Fly to Life in U.S.," *The New York Times,* 16 September 1986, pp. 1, and 7.

19. For Rieff, see "El Gulag," *The New Republic,* 28 July 1986, pp. 36–40; Paul Gray, "Shades of the Prison House," *Time,* 30 June 1986, p. 79.

20. Paul Hollander, *Political Pilgrims* (New York: Harper and Row, 1981). The two critical aspects of these techniques focus on "the personal treatment of the visitor, his comfort and welfare, and the measures taken to make him feel important, appreciated, well-linked." The second aspect is "the selective presentation of reality, which accounts for the highly organized and planned aspect of the tours." See pp. 16–21.

21. "Castro, Once Isolated, Forms New Bonds in South America," *The New York Times* 19 March 1985, p. 1, and 8; Juan M. del Aguila, "Political Developments in Cuba," *Current History* 85, 507 (January 1986): pp. 12–15, and 36–38.

22. Edward Gonzalez, "The Cuban and Soviet Challenge in the Caribbean Basin," *Orbis* 29 (Spring 1985): pp. 73–94.

23. "Three-sided package of bad news for Cubans as Castro turns 60," *Caribbean Report,* 28 August 1986, p. 1; "Cuba reestructura deuda," *El Miami Herald,* 20 Septiembre 1985, p. 7.

24. *Cuba's Financial Crisis: The Secret Report from the National Bank of Cuba,* no. 12 (Washington, D.C.: The Cuban-American National Foundation, Inc., 1985).
25. Mark A. Uhlig, "Inside the African National Congress," *The New York Times Magazine,* 12 October 1986, pp. 86–87.
26. *Granma Resumen Semanal,* 14 Septiembre 1986, p. 9.
27. David E. Albright, "East-West Tensions in Africa," in Marshall Shulman, ed., *East-West Tensions in the Third World,* (New York: W. W. Norton and Company, 1986), pp. 116–57.,
28. William E. Ratliff, "Follow the Leader in the Horn, The Soviet-Cuban presence in East Africa" (Washington, D.C.: The Cuban-American National Foundation Inc., 1986), number 17, p. 1.
29. See Juan M. del Aguila, "España y el Conflicto entre Cuba y Estados Unidos," in *Realidades y Posibilidades de las Relaciones entre España y América en los Ochenta* (Madrid: Instituto de Cooperación Iberoamericana, 1986), pp. 7–16; "El viaje de González a Cuba está 'políticamente lejano,' " *El País,* 6 octubre 1986, p. 12; "Spain and Latin America," *The Economist,* 11–17 October 1986, pp. 55–56.
30. "Llega a La Habana crucero con 784 turistas europeos," *Granma Resumen Semanal,* 31 agosto 1986, p. 3.
31. Alois Mertes, "Europe's Role in Central America: A West German Christian Democratic View," pp. 106–36 and Fernando Morán, "Europe's Role in Central America: A Spanish Socialist's View," both in Andrew J. Pierre, ed., *Third World Instability, Central America as a European-American Issue,* (New York: Council on Foreign Relations, 1985), pp. 6–44.
32. Gonzalez and Ronfeldt, p. 34.
33. Paul Hollander, "Political Hospitality and Tourism: Cuba and Nicaragua," (Washington, D.C.: The Cuban-American National Foundation Inc., 1986), no. 19, p. 21.
34. This is one of the basic themes of E. Michael Erisman, *Cuba's International Relations: The Anatomy of a Nationalistic Foreign Policy* (Boulder, Colo.: Westview Press, 1985); see also Wayne S. Smith, "U.S.-Cuba Relations: Twenty-Five Years of Hostility," in Sandor Halebsky and John M. Kirk, eds., *Twenty-Five Years of Revolution, Cuba 1959–1984* (Westport: Greenwood Press, 1985), pp. 333–51.
35. Gonzalez and Ronfeldt, p. 55–58. The basic premise of strategic opportunism is seeing "the need to seize the historical moment and exploit it to its fullest to gain maximum strategic advantage." Tactical pragmatism in contrast means that "short-term tactical adjustments must be made to survive, regroup and attain strategic objectives over the longer term."
36. Juan M. del Aguila, "Cuba and the Soviet Union: Fishing in Troubled Waters," in Brian Macdonald, ed., *Canada, the Caribbean and Central America* (Toronto: The Canadian Institute of Strategic Studies, 1985), pp. 20–34; "The Challenge to Democracy in Central America," (Washington, D.C.: U.S. Department of State, U.S. Department of Defense, 1986).
37. *Fidel y la Religión, conversaciones con el Sacerdote Dominico Frei Betto* (A transcript of conversations between Fidel Castro and Frei Betto) (Santo Domingo: Editora Alfa y Omega, 1985), p. 261.
38. Nicholas Eberstadt, "Did Fidel Fudge the Figures?," *Caribbean Review* 15, 2 (Spring 1986): pp. 5–7, and 37; Sergio Díaz-Briquets, "How To Figure Out

Cuba, Development, Ideology and Mortality,'' *Caribbean Review* 15, 2 (Spring 1986): pp. 8-11, and 39.

39. *Granma Resumen Semanal,* 8 Julio 1984, p. 3. In a speech at the University of Havana, the Rev. Jackson left no doubt as to what kinds of societies he most admires. Among other things, he said: ''Water cannot wash away the blood of the martyrs, because their blood is stronger than water; water makes grass and flowers grow; blood makes the sons and daughters of liberation grow. It does not matter how difficult the days are, or how dark the nights, there is always some place that shines: in Angola, Mozambique, Nicaragua, El Salvador, Harlem, Havana, there is always a more brilliant side.'' *Granma Resumen Semanal,* p. 4.

40. ''Bishops defend dialogue with Castro,'' *Caribbean Report,* 13 June 1986, p. 5; ''Nuevo documento del Vaticano en torno a doctrina social,'' *Granma,* 4 Abril 1986, p. 5; Araceli M. Cantero, ''Piden más testimonio cristiano en Cuba,'' *La Voz,* 23 mayo 1986, pp. 1, and 6.

Contributors

JUAN BENEMELIS is a former Cuban diplomat and author of *Castro: Subversao e Terrorismo en Africa*.

JUAN M. DEL AGUILA is associate professor of political science and director of the Emory Center for International Studies, Emory University as well as author, *Cuba: The Dilemmas of a Revolution*.

ERNEST EVANS is professor of political science, Christendom College.

GILLIAN GUNN is senior associate, Carnegie Endowment for International Peace, and author "Angola and Cuba," *CSIS Africa Notes*.

SCOTT B. MACDONALD is employed in the office of the Comptroller of the Currency and is coeditor, *The Caribbean after Grenada*.

MICHAEL J. MAZARR is with the Department of Political-Military Studies, Center for Strategic and International Studies (CSIS) and is author, *Semper Fidel, America and Cuba, 1776-1988*.

CONSTANTINE MENGES is resident fellow, the American Enterprise Institute, former National Security Council (Latin America) director, and author, *Inside the National Security Council*.

JORGE F. PÉREZ-LÓPEZ is director, Division of Foreign Economic Research, U.S. Department of Labor, and author of *Measuring Cuban Economic Performance*.

PAULA J. PETTAVINO is associated with the Analytic Sciences Corporation and is author, *Politics of Sports under Communism*.

WILLIAM RATLIFF is senior research fellow, the Hoover Institution, and editor, *The Selling of Fidel Castro*.

JORGE SANGUINETTY is president, Development Technologies, Inc.

JAMIE SUCHLICKI is director, Institute of Interamerican Studies, University of Miami, and author, *Historical Dictionary of Cuba* and *Cuba, from Columbus to Castro.*

JIRI VALENTA is professor of political science and director of Soviet, East European, and Strategic Studies, Graduate School of International Studies, University of Miami, and coeditor of *Grenada and Soviet/Cuban Policy: Internal Crisis and U.S./OECS Intervention.*

Index